FOURTH EDITION

Music Listening Today

Charles Hoffer

University of Florida

SCHIRMER
CENGAGE Learning™

Australia • Brazil • Japan • Korea • Mexico • Singapore • Spain • United Kingdom • United States

SCHIRMER
CENGAGE Learning™

Music Listening Today, **Fourth Edition**
Charles Hoffer

Publisher: Clark Baxter

Senior Development Editors: Sue Gleason,
Margaret Lannaman

Assistant Editor: Nell Pepper

Editorial Assistant: Ashley Bargende

Senior Media Editor: Wendy Constantine

Marketing Manager: Mark Haynes

Marketing Assistant: Josh Hendrick

Marketing Communications Manager: Heather
Baxley

Content Project Manager: Georgia Young

Associate Art Director: Faith Brosnany

Print Buyer: Rebecca Cross

Permissions Editor: Dean Dauphinais

Production Service: Graphic World Inc.

Text Designer: Ellen Pettengell

Photo Researcher: Jaime Jankowski

Copy Editor: Graphic World Inc.

Autographer: Ernie Mansfield

Cover Image: Steve Dunwell/Index Stock

Compositor: Graphic World Inc.

For product information and technology assistance, contact us at
Cengage Learning Academic Resource Center, 1-800-423-0563

For permission to use material from this text or product,
submit all requests online at **www.cengage.com/permissions**
Further permissions questions can be emailed to
permissionrequest@cengage.com

Library of Congress Control Number: 2009920958

ISBN-13: 978-0-495-57191-9

ISBN-10: 0-495-57191-1

Schirmer Cengage Learning
25 Thomson Place
Boston, MA 02210
USA

Cengage Learning products are represented in Canada by Nelson Education, Ltd.

For your course and learning solutions, visit **www.cengage.com**

Purchase any of our products at your local college store or at our preferred online store **www.ichapters.com**

Printed in Canada
1 2 3 4 5 13 12 11 10 09

To Mimi

Brief Contents

Contents

Preface

A new edition of a book offers an author the opportunity to keep what seemed effective in the previous edition and to add new works and other features to make it even better. The outstanding success of the third edition of *Music Listening Today* indicates that much of it should be retained. But there is always room for improvement.

The fourth edition:

1. *Provides a solid grounding in Western concert music through a careful selection of exemplary works.* Several new works have been added:
   - Britten: *The Young Person's Guide to the Orchestra*
   - Copland: "Hoe-Down" from *Rodeo*
   - Countess of Dia: "A chantar"
   - Machaut: Motet "Quant en moi"
   - Mendelssohn: *Elijah* (excerpt)
   - Puccini: Rodolfo's and Mimi's arias from *La Bohème*
   - Webern: Five Pieces for Orchestra, Op. 10, III

2. *Provides much help in listening to music more perceptively.* In addition to a number of specific suggestions for improving listening skill, *Music Listening Today* contains ninety-one Listening Guides, each one keyed to a recording on the six CDs. At appropriate places these guides provide brief descriptive sentences about the music, translations, and short music examples. Both cumulative and the track-by-track times that computers and CD players show automatically are provided. The headings of Listening Guides also give the date of the work, as well as reminders about such aspects as genre, form, and medium.

   In addition, each work has a downloadable Active Listening Guide that presents a graphic of the musical work on a computer monitor as the music is played. It can also be shown in class situations in conjunction with a computer and LCD projector. The graphic contains an arrow that moves from left to right in perfect continuous synchronization with the music, as well as appropriate information, translations, and music examples. The arrow may be dragged to any point on the line to listen to a specific feature. When using this program, it is impossible to get lost while listening to a work!

   Each Active Listening Guide also includes a biographical sketch, glossary, links through an "Internet Library" to selected websites, and an interactive "Listening Quiz" containing between five and nine questions for every work on the six CDs. These quizzes help greatly in hearing specific aspects of a musical work. They are not intended for grading purposes and may be repeated as often as desired.

3. *Presents information in a clear, concise, and interesting way.* The fourth edition begins with a work that has been heard in television commercials and other places, Copland's "Hoe-Down" from *Rodeo*. Helpful tips and interesting information appear in the margins. The enrichment boxes have been retained, as has a biographical sketch for each composer whose music is included in a Listening Guide. The use of

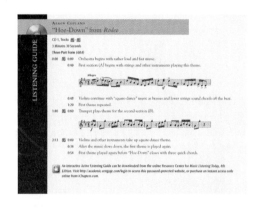

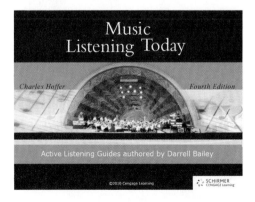

difficult musical terminology has been limited, and key points are highlighted by bullets, numbers, or headings.

New to the fourth edition is a section at the conclusion of each chapter that lists the main points of the chapter and offers a few general listening suggestions for the works included in it. The illustrated timelines and "Features of" charts, which review key features of each part's style, have been retained.

In short, *Music Listening Today* is very user-friendly.

4. *Includes representative examples from cultures and societies around the world and in the United States.* Two chapters are devoted to American popular music, and another chapter presents stage and film music. Four chapters focus on folk/ethnic music, with examples from North and South America, Africa, the Middle East, and Asia.

5. *Contains a passcode to the Resource Center that has been created to enhance the content of the book.* Most valuable are the Active Listening Guides mentioned earlier. In addition, the Resource Center features interactive demonstrations of the elements of music—meters, scales, chords, and so on. Also included is a video demonstrating orchestral instruments, which is followed by a complete performance of Britten's *Young Person's Guide to the Orchestra.* A series of short illustrated lectures is also available. The "Hear It Now" lectures deal with aspects of music that are difficult to describe verbally. The four "Connecting the Dots" lectures help in distinguishing among works in different styles and genres.

6. *Contains all these features in a reasonably sized package.* There is little reason to present more works and information than can be covered in a one-semester course. Therefore, *Music Listening Today* contains about 400 pages and presents its information in forty-three easily digestible chapters.

ANCILLARY MATERIALS

Music Listening Today suits the needs of traditional classroom situations as well as nontraditional online instruction. The basic package consists of the book, two CDs containing a representative sample of its repertoire, and a passcode to the Resource Center. Two other items are available: a *Study Guide* and a four-CD album.

For Students

CDS KEYED TO DOWNLOADABLE ACTIVE LISTENING GUIDES When the two CDs included with the book are combined with the four-CD set, every work presented in a Listening Guide becomes available, keyed to one of the downloadable Active Listening Guides described earlier. All the CDs were prepared by Sony BMG Music Entertainment. The Active Listening Guides were built on the work of Dr. Darrell Bailey (School of Informatics, Indiana University–Indianapolis).

STUDY GUIDE The *Study Guide,* coauthored with Dr. Mary Ray Hoffer (Santa Fe College), includes the following features:

- Reviews in outline form of the main points of each chapter
- Reviews of terms, including some in crossword puzzle format
- Sample test questions
- Suggestions for attending concerts and writing concert reports
- Removable flashcards on thick paper for learning musical terms
- A "Listener's Score" of the first movement of Mozart's Symphony No. 40

COMPANION WEBSITE The website for the fourth edition of *Music Listening Today,* at www.cengage.com/music/hoffer/musiclisteningtoday4e, features the downloadable program for four of the Active Listening Guides that appear early in the book, chapter-by-chapter tutorial quizzes, flashcards, crossword puzzles, and the bank of sound examples needed for the listening questions in the Test Bank.

For Instructors

Resources available to instructors include:

- a Test Bank containing more than 600 questions (about 450 information and 150 listening) that are grouped by chapter to make it easier to create the desired number of examinations
- a PowerPoint lecture for each chapter
- an extensive instructor's manual
- chapter outlines

POWERLECTURE PowerLecture is an instructor's CD-ROM that includes the Instructor's Manual, PowerLecture with ExamView® computerized testing, and Microsoft Power-Point slides with lecture outlines and images that can be used as offered, or customized by importing personal lecture slides or other material. ExamView allows you to create, deliver, and customize tests and study guides (both print and online) in minutes with its easy-to-use assessment and tutorial system. It offers both a Quick Test Wizard and an Online Test Wizard that guide you step by step through the process of creating tests, while its "what you see is what you get" capability allows you to see the test you are creating on the screen exactly as it will print or display online. You can build tests of up to 250 questions using up to twelve question types. Using ExamView's complete word-processing capabilities, you can enter an unlimited number of new questions or edit existing questions.

ACKNOWLEDGMENTS

I wish to thank the following professors for their reviews and suggestions offered for the fourth edition:

Lincoln Ballard, University of Washington, Seattle

Noel Benkman, Chabot College

Mark Bergman, George Mason University

Valerie Calhoun, Gordon College

Wei Tsun Chang, Tennessee Tech University

Laura Feo-Fernández, University of Memphis

Geoffrey Friedley, Idaho State University

Jesse Guessford, George Mason University

Richard Mark Heidel, University of Wisconsin, Eau Claire

Heather Hunnicut, Georgetown College

Dorothy Keyser, University of North Dakota

Francis Massinon, Austin Peay State University

Dwight Monical, Purdue University

Jo Ann Schwader, Northwest Arkansas Community College

Jane L. Viemeister, Bridgewater State College

Thanks also to the many persons in editorial, production, and marketing who contributed to this fourth edition: Clark Baxter, Sue Gleason, Margaret Lannaman, Nell

Pepper, Ashley Bargende, Georgia Brown, Wendy Constantine, Mark Haynes, Josh Hendrick, and Heather Baxley.

Many thanks also to Darrell Bailey, who is responsible for the original program for the downloadable Active Listening Guides.

I especially want to thank my wife, Mimi, for her loving patience during the many hours I spent in front of the computer. In addition to coauthoring the *Study Guide*, as an experienced instructor of music appreciation courses she was able to offer many valuable suggestions and was very helpful reading the manuscript and giving encouragement.

Charles Hoffer

PART I

The
Nature
of Music

Inspirestock Inc./Alamy

Music Listening *and* You

Imagine a world without music—no songs to sing, no recordings to listen to, no music to dance to, no soundtracks with music for films, no music at worship services or football games. What a depressing thought! The world would certainly be a bleaker and more dreary place. No wonder that music has existed in every civilization throughout history and can be found everywhere in the world, even in the remotest places!

Why would the world be a less desirable place? The answer is clear: Music contributes to the quality of life. Music is not the only thing that makes our lives more than physical existence, of course, but it plays an important role in enriching human expression and feeling.

Do people need music? Not in the sense that they need to eat, sleep, and be healthy. But they do require it in terms of the quality of their lives. Human beings need music, beauty, gentleness, sensitivity to others, and all the civilizing elements that create a meaningful life. Music contributes to *living*, in contrast to just *existing physically*.

What does music have to do with adding quality to our lives? Perhaps the American patriot and second president of the United States, John Adams, summarized best the value of the arts in a letter he wrote to his wife, Abigail, in 1780 during the hard times of the Revolutionary War:

> *I must study politics and war, that my sons may have liberty to study mathematics and philosophy, geography, natural history and naval architecture, navigation, commerce, and agriculture, in order to give their children a right to study painting, poetry, music, architecture, statuary, tapestry, and porcelain.*

DIFFERENT TYPES OF MUSIC

Although music can be found throughout the world, it varies tremendously from one culture to another, as you will discover in Part VIII of this book. Not only does it differ from place to place, it also differs greatly in its uses and characteristics within the same culture and society. For this reason, we need to consider also the types and uses of music. Music is used to express feelings while singing or dancing; heighten the drama of a motion picture; provide a "sonic background" while studying, working, or driving a car; and much more. And some of the time, people just listen carefully to music for the intellectual and psychological satisfactions it provides.

Are some uses of music better than others? Not really. Some music is better for unifying a crowd at a football game, but other music is better for expressing love. Some music is more rewarding to listen to in a contemplative way, while other music is very suitable for dancing. People find or create music that is effective for a particular activity, and what they create differs very much according to its purpose.

"CLASSICAL" MUSIC: MUSIC FOR LISTENING

Music created for the intellectual and psychological satisfactions it provides is referred to as *art music* or *concert music*, or by most people as *"classical" music*. (The term *classical music*, however, refers to a particular type of concert music that is presented

IMAGINE THE WORLD WITHOUT MUSIC.

The hammer and the screwdriver are both useful tools, but they are different from each other. It's like that with types of music.

in Part IV.) It is usually the kind composed for performance in concert halls and opera houses. It is music with exceptional qualities that people find psychologically rewarding. In fact, the word *art* describes objects that are created with outstanding skill and devotion. Often the word *fine* is coupled with *art* to distinguish between objects that can be made by most people and those that demand exceptional skill, effort, and talent.

Crafts such as needlepoint and basket weaving are often referred to as "folk arts."

ORDINARY MUSIC AND EXTRAORDINARY MUSIC

It's true. Concert music is heard far less often and in far fewer places than the various types of popular music we encounter every day. Virtually no performer or composer of concert music makes the millions of dollars that some popular musicians do from the sales of their recordings and tickets to performances, and they are given nowhere near the public attention by the media and general public. Few people play it on their radios or listening devices, encounter it at parties or other social occasions, or attend concerts at which it is performed. So why is concert music the main (although not the exclusive) fare in music appreciation courses and college music schools? And why is it considered culturally so important?

It comes down to the difference between things that are *ordinary* and things that are *extraordinary*. Most of what we encounter in life is ordinary — the clothes we wear to class, the food we eat, the work we do, the pictures we see in advertisements and magazines, and the music we hear. Usually we don't give a lot of thought to ordinary things, because they *are* — ordinary. They are not bad or worthless; they are just easily forgotten or overlooked. If someone asks you what you had for dinner two days ago, you would probably need to think a bit to remember it, if indeed you could recall it at all. But suppose you had a dinner at an especially good restaurant and were served something exceptionally delicious, then that experience would be easy to remember. That's why almost all everyday music is "Here today, gone tomorrow," but a lot of concert music is "Here today, here tomorrow."

Fortunately, we don't need to eat extraordinary food at every meal (although that is an attractive thought). Nor do we need to listen only to music of extraordinary quality. But there are times when such experiences are truly enjoyable and psychologically meaningful. And as a part of a college education, it is proper and right that you gain at least a basic level of listening skill and knowledge so that you can understand and value musical works of extraordinary quality. It would be unfortunate to acquire a college education and be culturally illiterate about music and the arts.

Because most works of concert music contain more substance in terms of what happens in them, they often require some instruction to be understood and appreciated. They also require a degree of skill in hearing what is happening with the sounds. Both information and listening skill need to be present. The good news is that the efforts at gaining knowledge and listening skill are well worthwhile in terms of your enjoyment of music that is more than ordinary.

Even watching a football or baseball game is dull if you don't understand the game.

"I KNOW WHAT I LIKE"

Everyone likes at least one kind of music. Usually, it's the type of music they are familiar with — and it's often the only kind they listen to. The saying *I know what I like* is true. But so is the phrase *I like what I know*. It is not surprising that people feel more comfortable and competent with the music they know. The problem with stopping at this comfort level, however, is that it usually confines you to only a tiny bit of the rich world of music.

Consider this analogy: Suppose you had the chance to advise a person from a foreign country about what to see on a tour of the United States. You might suggest seeing the part of the country where you live, and that would be fine. But is that all a visitor should experience of the United States? What about its other great cities and natural wonders? The analogy with music seems clear. There is a vast and varied world of music out there. Why confine yourself to just one small portion of it and miss out on other kinds of music that could enrich your life? The more people know about music, especially concert music, the more quality they add to their lives.

LEARNING TO LISTEN

You deal with acquiring information in every course you take in college. But music is probably the only course that requires listening skill, because hearing what happens to the sounds is the very essence of music. For this reason, it is vital to know what to do to improve your ability to perceive musical sounds. The following are suggestions for doing that.

Realize that hearing sounds and listening to them are not the same thing. Most people use the word *listen* in a very casual way. When musicians talk about listening, however, they mean an activity requiring concentration. There is a vitally important and fundamental point here: *Listening to music is much more than just being aware of its sounds.* Unless you really grasp the basic difference between hearing and listening, chances are that you will hear music only superficially, and as a result, will find limited meaning and satisfaction from listening to it. Unless you have a rather strong background in music, listening perceptively is going to require some effort. It doesn't happen automatically.

Adopt the habit of listening for the features of the particular musical work. Don't just let the sounds wash over you. Don't stop with just being aware that some music is playing. Don't daydream or think about other things or visualize scenes while listening to concert music.

Instead, as you listen, decide something about:

- The nature of melodies and themes
- The texture of the music
- The nature of the rhythm and its patterns
- The changes in dynamic levels
- The more important tone qualities
- The forms and other musical techniques

At first, this will probably not be easy to do. But over time, you will get better at noticing and describing these aspects of music. Try to determine these six points, even if you're not sure your answers are correct. The effort will help you to listen better.

Develop different modes of listening. At least three different modes are available, and each has its place when listening to music. One mode involves listening for the sensuous qualities in a musical work, for the physical effects in produces. The chills that run down a listener's back when an orchestra or choral group reaches a climactic point in a musical work is an example of music's sensual power.

A second mode of listening centers on the expressive power of music. A musical work may give an impression of sadness, for example, but it does not describe what has caused that feeling. The emotional responses produced by music are general, not specific. The fact that music does not express definite meanings is one of its virtues. Words are too conventional and inflexible to allow for full expression. Music can be, and often is, a direct route to one's deepest feelings.

A third mode of listening is sometimes termed "sheerly musical." It consists of listening for what happens in the music, what notes are being played or sung, at what speed, in what combinations with other notes, on what instruments, with what degree of loudness, and so on. It is also the mode in which you become aware of the skill and imagination that musicians bring to creating interesting combinations of sounds. This

Remind yourself often of this crucial fact as you progress through the course.

Fantasizing may be enjoyable, but it takes your attention away from the music.

All of these musical terms are explained in the following three chapters.

Adopting the habit of listening for specific features applies to all kinds of music from all parts of the world.

Sensuous means "of or appealing to the senses."

Listening perceptively is an active experience. It requires that listeners mentally participate in the process.

mode usually requires some education to achieve, something this course and book and its ancillaries seek to provide.

The three modes of listening are not mutually exclusive, of course. People frequently switch back and forth among them as they listen. They can sense the rich warmth of a particular chord, respond to the romantic power of a flowing melody, and also understand that the music follows a certain form.

Develop different expectations about different types of music. Everyday life teaches us not to listen carefully. People learn to ignore the sounds of traffic, clocks ticking, and air conditioners turning on and off. People learn to "tune out" music too. They must, because music is heard nearly everywhere—in airports, supermarkets, dentists' offices, and while driving the car. Music accompanies almost every activity from cleaning house to jogging. People would become mentally exhausted if they listened intently to all the music they hear each day.

What's more, most people don't listen carefully to the popular music they hear. Instead, they get most of what it has to offer by "absorbing" it, much as they absorb the impression of the pattern in wallpaper. It's *not* a question of which kind of music is better! *Popular music and concert music simply have different uses, and therefore they have different listening requirements.* You should use a casual style of listening for most of the music you hear every day. But you should also learn to listen in a contemplative, thoughtful way to concert music.

And what are the differences in listening to classical and popular music?

- Most concert music is not played as loudly as popular music. To a novice listener, concert music may seem pretty pale when heard at its much more restrained level of sound.

- Most popular music consists of short pieces that last only a couple of minutes. The time span of many concert works is *much* longer. To someone not used to it, listening to concert music may seem like watching a video of a basketball game in slow motion.

- Popular music rarely contains any development of themes or the other more complicated musical practices found in concert music. It is simpler and requires little or no effort to understand.

- With the exception of stage productions, concert music is presented without theatrics, flashing lights, or gyrating performers.

Improve your memory for music. Remembering is absolutely essential for understanding music. At any particular moment, only one millisecond of a piece of music can be heard. What was sounded before that millisecond exists only in your memory. What will be heard in future moments can only be a guess based on what was heard previously.

It's not like that with what you see. An entire painting or piece of sculpture can be seen in a second or two. If memory were made an essential part of looking at a painting, it might be something like this: An unfamiliar picture is covered except for one thin vertical opening. You can see the picture only as that opening moves across the painting from one side to the other. Your comprehension of the picture would result from: (1) your memory of what you've seen, (2) the tiny portion you could see at the millisecond, and (3) your guess about what would be revealed in succeeding moments.

The careful analysis of an artwork requires more time, of course.

Would this be a difficult way to see a picture? Definitely! But that is the way music is perceived, and that is why memory is so important in listening to music. To pursue our analogy further, the more times you see the opening drawn across the picture, the better you would recall its images and the more accurate your comprehension of the whole. That is why listening to a musical work several times, especially a complex one, is necessary for understanding it.

Not only is hearing the same work several times a good way to remember it better, it also helps in acquiring positive feelings for the work.

Become more sensitive to musical sounds. Each sound in a musical work evokes some response, *if it is noticed.* A changed rhythm, a note in a chord, or the instrument playing a melody affects a listener's response. A sensitivity to what is heard in music is nearly as important as remembering it.

You can't respond to something you don't hear.

Frances Roberts/Alamy

ArenaPal/Topham/The Image Works

MOST POPULAR MUSIC is heard in situations that focus on activities other than music. The opposite is true for concert music.

Listening to music with no feeling must be something like watching a soccer game in which the goals have been removed. Likewise, listening to music with no feeling has little point. The psychological involvement is missing, and only a sterile, intellectual experience remains.

How can you become more responsive to musical sounds? It seems simple, but just *trying* to be more sensitive to what you hear is a good first step. Open yourself up to the qualities of music. You can play a short section of a work, say, five seconds. Then, ask yourself, *What response did I have to that portion of the music?*

Use the Active Listening Guides and the ancillary CDs to help you develop skill in listening. The *Music Listening Today, 4th Edition,* Resource Center provides demonstrations of many aspects of music. The Active Listening Guides provide a visual overview of each work. They provide a graphic representation of the pattern of a work, an arrow that moves in perfect synchronization with the music, and short bits of text and some examples of music notation. To hear a section again, you can drag the arrow to any point in the music or click on one of the umbrellas. Several other features are contained on the Active Listening Guides, including a glossary and an Internet library containing connections to relevant websites. There is a practice listening quiz for each work to help you practice listening for specific aspects in the music. These quizzes allow you to repeat a question or the entire quiz as often as you wish.

The Listening Guides in this book have several features. The elapsed times from the beginning of the work are listed in the left-hand column. The timings in the next column to the right are from the preceding track point. These times apply only to the ancillary CDs for this book. You don't need to follow the times while listening. But because they offer an idea of how much time will pass between features of the work, the timings can be helpful.

To the right of each track time is a brief description of a feature of the music. These descriptions may refer to the form of the music, instruments playing, quality of the rhythm, or other noticeable elements in the music. The notation for the main themes is sometimes provided as a visual representation of what is being sounded. It is not expected that you be able to read music, but the suggestions offered in the enrichment boxes in Chapters 2 and 3 will help you understand notation better.

The cumulative times in the left-hand column appear on the screen when using the downloadable Active Listening Guides. When the recordings are played on CD players, the times revert to 0:00 with each new track.

A different recording of the same work will not have exactly the same timings but will be approximately the same.

LISTENING AND STUDYING

You have a good idea of how to study for most courses: Read a book and take notes in class, then organize the information in your mind and, if all goes well, remember it. It's somewhat different in a music course because there is an important additional element: listening to music.

When beginning to study/listen to an unfamiliar work, you should:

1. Listen to it while following the arrow, pop-up text, and music examples using the Active Listening Guide on your computer. If you have trouble hearing something described on the monitor, drag the arrow back to that place and listen to that portion again—and again, if necessary. It's also a good idea to go through the listening practice questions for that work.

2. After you feel comfortable in following a work using the CD, listen to it following the Listening Guide in the textbook. When you are able to notice the features as they are pointed out, then you are ready to move to the next step. If you have trouble following the music, you should either go back to the Active Listening Guide or try listening again with the Listening Guide in the book.

3. When you are reasonably successful in following the music with the Listening Guide, listen to the work without any visual aids or cues. This is the way one normally listens to music, of course. See if you can hear the aspects of the music that have been presented in the Active Listening Guide and in the printed Listening Guide.

These practice questions could easily be the types of listening questions included on examinations.

"CONNECTING THE DOTS"

Being able to listen to a musical work perceptively is essential, but something more is needed: Remembering in a general way what you heard and placing it in the right context. It might be thought of as "connecting the dots," because it involves relating what you hear with information about the piece of music. One without the other will limit what you will get out of the course to something like half of what's really there.

You should also be able to recognize broad, general styles of music according to historical periods, as well as know the types of music. The reasons for learning styles are presented in Chapter 10. Some of the differences among them can be described verbally, and such descriptions will help you focus attention on what to listen for. But words can never adequately describe a style. You will need to listen carefully to the works presented in the book enough times that you can recognize a style because it "just sounds like it." A symphony by Mozart simply sounds very different from a symphony by Brahms, even though both are being played by a symphony orchestra. Knowing if the work is for a solo piano or a jazz band or is from an opera or a chamber music work also helps much in perceiving pieces of music.

The ability to remember how music in a particular style and type sounds means that you should try to remember in a general way how each work covered in class and the book sounds. It is *not* enough to remember it for a week or two, and then forget it once it has been covered on an examination.

To help you keep the different types and styles of music in mind, each enhanced CD contains a Listening Summary of all the works contained on that particular CD.

GETTING STARTED WITH COPLAND'S "HOE-DOWN" FROM *RODEO*

Talking and reading about music is useful to a point, but then the time comes to listen to a musical work. "Hoe-Down" is one section of a collection of music for symphony orchestra that the composer, Aaron Copland, extracted from music he wrote for a ballet, *Rodeo*. The music is very American with its energetic square-dance qualities. In fact, it has been used as background music for a number of television commercials.

The music can be divided into three sections, with the opening section returning after contrasting music is heard. The Listening Guide is simple in that it covers only the main parts of "Hoe-Down" and uses as few musical terms as possible. Two short examples of music notation are included to help give the idea of what the theme is like at a particular point.

LISTENING GUIDE

AARON COPLAND
"Hoe-Down" from *Rodeo*

CD 1, Tracks 1 – 3

3 Minutes 30 Seconds

Three-Part Form (*ABA*)

0:00	1 0:00	Orchestra begins with rather loud and fast music.
	0:40	First section (A) begins with strings and other instruments playing this theme.

	0:48	Violins continue with "square-dance" music as brasses and lower strings sound chords off the beat.
	1:20	First theme repeated.
1:40	2 0:00	Trumpet plays theme for the second section (B).

2:13	3 0:00	Violins and other instruments take up square-dance theme.
	0:34	After the music slows down, the first theme is played again.
	0:54	First theme played again before "Hoe-Down" closes with three quick chords.

 An interactive Active Listening Guide can be downloaded from the online Resource Center for *Music Listening Today, 4th Edition*. Visit http://academic.cengage.com/login to access this password-protected website, or purchase an instant access code online from iChapters.com.

Aaron Copland

CBS/Landov Media

Aaron Copland (1900–1990) was born in Brooklyn, New York, the son of Russian-Jewish immigrants. His family had little money, and he took his first music lessons from an older sister. He studied books and scores at the New York Public Library. After graduating from high school, he studied piano and harmony in New York.

In 1921, Copland went to the American School of Music at Fontainebleau in France. The teacher there was a remarkable woman named Nadia Boulanger. Copland became the first of a long list of young American composers to study with her.

Copland became interested in jazz in the late 1920s, and several of his compositions contain elements of jazz. In the early 1930s, his music tended to be more abstract. He began to be concerned, however, about the gap between concert audiences and contemporary compositions. Copland wrote, "It made no sense to ignore them and to continue writing as if they did not exist. I felt that it was worth the effort to see if I couldn't say what I had to say in the simplest possible terms."

His efforts at greater simplicity were successful, and he was able to retain the interest and respect of trained musicians while at the same time pleasing the general concert-going public. Many of his best-known works are excellent examples of music with an American quality. In addition to his music, he lectured at many universities and wrote several very readable books about music.

BEST-KNOWN WORKS

orchestra:
- A Lincoln Portrait
- El salón Mexico

ballet:
- Billy the Kid
- Rodeo
- Appalachian Spring

film scores:
- Of Mice and Men
- The Red Pony
- Our Town

In "Hoe-Down," Copland took a folk music style and created an artistic piece of music, something more than ordinary square dance music. Did you notice the use he made of a short pattern of notes? It appears several times at the beginning of the work, and it also appears at the beginning of the first theme. Did you also notice places where the music slows down and becomes quieter, only for the more vigorous music to start up again? It is such things that make it more interesting to listen to than just simple square dance music.

MAIN POINTS OF THIS CHAPTER

1. Music contributes much to the quality of life.
2. Music exists for many different purposes, each of which encourages a particular style of music.
3. People tend to like the type of music they know, and usually it is the only kind they listen to.
4. "Classical" or concert/art music is an extraordinary type of music created for the mental and emotional satisfaction it provides. Most people need some guidance to perceive the qualities in concert music.
5. Learning to listen to music perceptively is an essential part of a music appreciation course.
6. It is important to connect the dots between information about a musical work and what is heard in that work.

FEATURES TO LISTEN FOR

1. The vigorous, energetic character of Copland's "Hoe-Down" from *Rodeo*.
2. The "square-dance fiddle" pattern of continuous, rapidly moving notes played by the violins at several places during the work.
3. The contrasting middle section of the work, in which the trumpet solo contains short breaks.

2 Rhythm

Music is a time art. Paintings and pieces of sculpture occupy space, but the "canvas" of music is time. Because all music occupies time, all of it has rhythm, even when it's not a toe-tapping rhythm that makes it easy to mark the time. The term for the orderly flow of music through time is **rhythm.** It is a comprehensive word that includes beat, meter, and tempo.

The word *rhythm* comes from a Greek word meaning "flow."

BEAT: THE MUSIC'S PULSE

The **beat** is the regular pulse found in most music. It is what people tap as they listen, and it is most easily heard in marches and dance music when it is marked by the drum sound. Although the beat can be felt most of the time in a musical work, it is not always sounded clearly.

Throughout a piece of music, a drum doesn't need to tap the beat, although it often does in dance music and marches.

Furthermore, not all music has a beat, although most of the music we hear in the United States today does. It is central to most of the music of the Western world. In fact, our sense of meter depends on the presence of beats.

Usually, beats are heard and felt in a steady, even succession. If they are erratic, the effect is something like listening to a person who says a few words very rapidly, and then some more words very slowly, and then some words moderately fast, and so on. It is tiring and irritating to listen to someone talk with such changes of speed. The speed with which beats occur in music can change within a piece of music, but usually the changes are gradual and occur by design of the composer and performer.

Resource Center
See an interactive demo of beat in the *Music Listening Today, 4th Edition,* Resource Center.

METER: THE PATTERNS OF BEATS

The human mind has the tendency to seek out patterns in what is heard and seen. It is easier to remember a telephone number such as 555-1212 than 555-2719 because 1212 has a pattern.

When people hear groups of beats, even though the beats may be exactly as strong as one another, their minds tend to group them into twos, threes, or fours; only occasionally are groups larger than four. Instead of beat-beat-beat-beat-beat-beat and so on, the mind tends to perceive **beat**-beat-beat **beat**-beat-beat or **beat**-beat **beat**-beat **beat**-beat. The grouping of the beats (*not* the notes) into patterns is called **meter.**

Whether the meter is perceived in twos or threes depends on the nature of the music.

Meter is very evident in group cheers and rap music. Here is an example of a cheer (the *1* represents the more strongly stressed beat or the **downbeat**):

Resource Center
Sense the metrical pattern of music in the *Music Listening Today, 4th Edition,* Resource Center.

1   2   *1*   2   *1*   2   *1* 2
Two bits, **four** bits, **six** bits, a **dol**lar,

1 2   *1* 2   *1* 2   *1* 2
All for **Den**ver, **stand** up and **hol**ler!

Here is an example of meter in a poem, "The Raven," by Edgar Allan Poe:

   | ∪ | ∪ | ∪ | ∪
Once upon a **mid**night **drear**y,

   | ∪ | ∪ | ∪ | ∪
As I **pon**dered **weak** and **wear**y,

The familiar song "Jingle Bells" has an easily felt two-beat meter. The beats are marked with short vertical lines.

Horizontal beams are often used in place of flags when two or more notes occur in the same beat. Beams help the eye group notes when reading music notation.

Jin - gle bells,   jin - gle bells,   jin - gle all the way.

The Notation of Rhythm

Music existed long before a system for writing it down was devised. In fact, even today most folk music and jazz are rarely written down. In other words, the sounds used in music and the notation of those sounds are two quite different matters. Hearing the rhythm and other elements of music is clearly the more important and valuable of the two. Knowing about the notation of rhythm, however, usually helps in learning and understanding music better.

Although the applications of the system of notating rhythm can be quite complex, the basic system is rather simple: It consists of various combinations of note heads, stems, and flags.

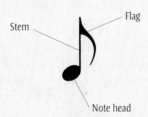

Stem — Flag

Note head

As the combinations progress from an empty oval to a solid head with a stem and flag(s), each note is sounded one-half the length of time that the previous note sounds.

A *whole note* ○ *usually receives four beats.*
A *half note* ♩ *usually receives two beats.*
A *quarter note* ♩ *usually receives one beat.*
An *eighth note* ♪ *usually receives half a beat.*
A *sixteenth note* ♬ *usually receives a quarter beat.*

And the opposite is also true: As the notes change from solid heads, stems, and flags toward empty ovals, the length of the note played doubles. Therefore, all other things being equal, a passage of music that contains notes with many filled-in heads and flags is going to move quickly.

The notation of silences, called *rests,* uses different symbols:

A *whole rest* ▬ *hangs down from the fourth line of the staff.*
A *half rest* ▬ *is placed on top of the third line of the staff.*
A *quarter rest* 𝄽 *has a distinctive shape.*
An *eighth rest* 𝄾 *resembles a fancy number 7.*
A *sixteenth rest* 𝄿 *looks like an eighth rest but with one more flag.*

As can be seen from looking at the different note lengths, the system for notating rhythm is built on a 2:1 ratio, with note lengths being either one-half or double the length of the other. The 2:1 ratio is even carried over into the use of the dots that are sometimes placed to the right of a note. The dot to the right of a note tells a performer to increase the length of the note by one-half. So a note that is two beats long becomes three beats when a dot is added. Dotted notes are used extensively when the beat is divided into threes instead of twos.

The note with a solid head and a stem ♩ (a quarter note) is most frequently used to represent the beat, although any note can be used for that purpose. For example, the following three lines of notes sound exactly alike when performed, even though they look different from one another. The reason they sound the same is the different numbers at the beginning of each line. This vertical combination is the meter signature or time signature.

The top number of a meter signature usually indicates the number of beats in the measure, and the bottom number usually indicates the type of note that should receive one beat. In the first example above, the eighth note (♪) receives the beat; in the middle example, it is the quarter note (♩); and in the last example, it is the half note (♩). The notation of silences follows the same ratios.

Beats normally follow a metrical pattern. If they don't, the music has not been arranged correctly. For example, the punctuation of the sentence *Every piece of. Music can be enjoyed, for its sounds. And rhythm.* tends to obscure its meaning.

The meter of a piece of music is indicated in notation in two ways. One is by a **meter signature** or **time signature.** Usually, they are placed at the beginning of a work or section. In some contemporary works, however, the meter changes every few measures, so meter signatures are sometimes found within the work.

The other way in which music notation indicates the pattern of beats is by vertical lines that enclose the beats in the pattern. These units of rhythm are called **measures.**

Measures are also called bars, possibly because their vertical lines look something like bars on a window.

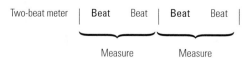

Music students learn that the first beat of a measure is normally performed more strongly than the other beats in the measure. That is why it is the first beat.

Syncopation

Resource Center
Learn syncopation firsthand in the Music Listening Today, 4th Edition, Resource Center.

Sometimes the emphasis, called **accent,** is deliberately placed off the beat. **Syncopation** happens either by adding the emphasis where it is not expected or by removing the emphasis from where it is expected. Here is an example of syncopation from the song "Dixie."

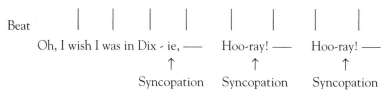

In the example, the *ie* of *Dixie* and the *ray* of *Hooray* occur halfway through beats instead of on the beat. The syncopation could be removed from the melody and the accent would fall normally, but the song would lose much of its character.

TEMPO: THE SPEED OF BEATS

Tempo means "time" in Italian.

Another important aspect of rhythm is **tempo,** which is the speed of the beats. The tempo of a piece of music can be indicated in two ways. One is by a metronome marking such as $\downarrow$ = 84. A metronome is a clocklike device (either windup or electronic) that indicates the beat with audible ticks and/or a flashing light. Metronomes can be set to provide exactly the desired number of beats per minute. With a few exceptions, most tempos in music range between one and three beats per second.

Resource Center
Experiment with different tempos in the Music Listening Today, 4th Edition, Resource Center.

The other way of indicating tempo is through the use of words, which are usually in Italian. These verbal descriptors are general, such as *very fast, moderate,* and *slow.* Because the terms are general, the tempo of a work marked *Allegro* will differ somewhat from one performer or conductor to the next. The words indicating tempo not only provide guidance for performers, they also appear in concert programs and liner notes to identify the large, independent sections, or *movements,* of instrumental works.

The following are the more common terms for tempo.

Largo	Very slow, broad
Adagio	Slow, leisurely
Grave	Very slow, heavy
Andante	"Walking," moderate
Moderato	Moderate

Allegro	Moderately fast, moving briskly
Allegro molto	Much allegro, very brisk
Vivace	Lively
Presto	Very fast
Prestissimo	As fast as possible

Other words are often attached to the indication of tempo. These usually describe the style of the music, not the tempo. Examples of additional words include *con fuoco* (with fire or force), *sostenuto* (sustained), and *con brio* (brusque). Sometimes modifiers such as *meno* (less) and *piu* (more) are added. Two Italian terms affecting tempo that have close parallels in English are *ritardando* (retard, or slow down) and *accelerando* (accelerate, or speed up).

Notes and beats are not the same thing. Although a tempo may be slow, many notes can be played during the beat, giving the impression of much motion. On the other hand, the tempo may be fast but if the duration of the notes is long, the sense of movement is reduced. Of course, all things being equal, more notes are heard when the tempo is fast than when it is slow.

Rhythm in Bizet's *Farandole*

Georges Bizet ("Bee-*zay*") composed twenty-seven pieces of music to go with the play *L'Arlésienne* (*The Woman of Arles*) by Alphonse Daudet. Later, his friend Ernest Guiraud arranged the music into two suites. *Farandole* is from Suite No. 2.

For the main melody, Bizet chose an old song called "Marche de Turenne" from the Provence region of France. The tune is still sung at Christmastime in English under the title "The March of the Kings."

In the world of concert music, it's customary to pronounce names and terms in the language of the particular country. Therefore, the French composer Bizet is pronounced "Bee-*zay*."

Some marches have been written for processions or coronations, and they are slower. Marches at football games are usually played at a much faster tempo than military marches.

Georges Bizet

Georges Bizet (1838–1875) first learned music from his parents and was admitted to the Paris Conservatory at about the age of ten. By age seventeen he had composed Symphony in C, which was not performed until 1935. He was awarded the Prix de Rome and began composing music mostly for the theater and opera. For a variety of reasons, much of his music was not well received, and he earned his living arranging music and giving piano lessons.

After serving in the national guard in the Franco-Prussian War in 1870, Bizet was commissioned to write incidental music for Daudet's play *L'Arlésienne* (*The Woman of Arles*). The play was not successful, but fortunately Bizet's music survived.

Most of Bizet's fame is the result of his opera *Carmen*. Its plot is built around the gradual decline of Don José, a simple honest soldier, caused by his infatuation with Carmen, a Spanish gypsy girl who worked in a cigarette factory. The music is filled with one colorful and beautiful work after another. At first it was not well received and was condemned for its "obscene" text. Apparently, the patrons of the Opera Comique, which was something of a family theater, did not enjoy watching Don José's life being ruined by the amoral Carmen.

Today Carmen is perhaps the best-known and best-loved opera in the world.

Bizet had poured enormous effort into *Carmen* and was worn out by months of rehearsal and tension. His sensitive nature was simply unable to tolerate its initial cool reception. He died three months after its premiere.

Mary Evans Picture Library/Alamy

BEST-KNOWN WORKS
orchestra:
• Symphony in C
• L'Arlésienne, *Suites 1 and 2*

opera:
• Carmen

A meter signature of ¢ represents "Common Time," or 4/4.

Bizet's *Farandole* has both a marchlike and a dancelike theme. Notice that the march and the dance have different meters, as you can see from meter signatures of the music notation in the musical examples. As you listen, try counting the march **1-2-3 1-2-3** instead of **1-2 1-2.** You will quickly sense that the music is in two-beat meter, because the three-beat pattern just doesn't seem to fit.

LISTENING GUIDE

GEORGES BIZET
Farandole from *L'Arlésienne,* Suite No. 2 (1872)

March tempo   4-beat meter   Orchestra

CD 1 Tracks 4 – 6

3 minutes 7 seconds

0:00   4   0:00   Orchestra plays first theme at a march tempo in strong four-beat meter. The first three notes of the theme occur on the beat.

0:33   5   0:00   Tempo becomes faster as second theme enters. The first beat of each measure is emphasized. Music grows in intensity.

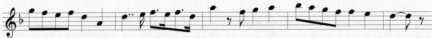

0:43   Strings play second theme. Tempo remains fast.

0:54   Strings play first theme at a fast tempo.

1:05   Woodwinds play second theme.

1:11   Tempo remains fast, and four-beat meter returns as strings play opening theme.

1:22   Woodwinds take up second theme.

2:18   6   0:00   Orchestra combines both first and second themes. Marchlike rhythm of the music continues.

0:50   *Farandole* concludes in a flurry of sound.

An interactive Active Listening Guide can be downloaded from the online Resource Center for *Music Listening Today, 4th Edition.* Visit http://academic.cengage.com/login to access this password-protected website, or purchase an instant access code online from iChapters.com.

POLYRHYTHM

African music has a well-deserved reputation for its exciting rhythms. "Mitamba Yala-gala Kumchuzi" is a good example. It comes from the Zaramo tribe of the coastal region near Dar es Salaam in Tanzania in East Africa.

What makes the rhythm of this music exciting is the appearance of several rhythms at the same time, what is referred to as **polyrhythm.** When you hear "Mitamba Yalagala

Louise Gubb/The Image Works

AFRICAN DRUM ENSEMBLE

LISTENING GUIDE

AFRICAN MUSIC

"Mitamba Yalagala Kumchuzi"

Polyrhythm   Drums, rattles, vocal

CD 3 Track **1**

1 minute 33 seconds

1:33 **1** 0:00   One drummer begins playing two sounds, high and low. Other drummers soon enter. Several different rhythmic patterns are heard at the same time. Rattles enter.

         0:44   A singer begins and is answered by other singers. The rhythmic patterns continue in drums and rattles.

         1:00   Lead singer exchanges portions of the music with other singers in a call-and-response pattern.

         1:33   Although the music continues, often for an hour or more, the recording fades.

An interactive Active Listening Guide can be downloaded from the online Resource Center for *Music Listening Today, 4th Edition.* Visit http://academic.cengage.com/login to access this password-protected website, or purchase an instant access code online from iChapters.com.

Kumchuzi" for the first time, it may seem like one of the drummers is lost and coming in at the wrong time. Not so. Instead, he is playing a different pattern. As the music progresses, other performers join in with their own particular patterns. Although you might expect rhythmic confusion because of the different patterns occurring at the same time, the effect is exhilarating.

Rhythm is not the only interesting feature of "Mitamba Yalagala Kumchuzi." The recording was made with five goblet drums, four cylindrical drums, and tines rattles. Each of the two types of drums has its own distinctive quality of sound, and these different qualities add to the music. The **call-and-response** pattern between the vocal soloist and the group also contributes to the African quality of the music.

MAIN POINTS OF THIS CHAPTER

1. Rhythm is the flow of music through time.
2. The beat is the steady pulse found in almost all music in Western civilization.
3. Sensing the beat is largely a physical sensation, not an intellectual one.
4. Meter refers to the pattern with which certain beats are emphasized.
5. Tempo is the speed of the beats, *not* the notes.
6. The notation of rhythm is based on a 2:1 ratio of notes and rests.
7. Syncopation exists when the emphasis occurs where it is not expected or is omitted where it is expected.
8. Polyrhythms are created when two or more rhythmic patterns occur at the same time.

FEATURES TO LISTEN FOR

1. The steady nature of the beat or pulse in Bizet's *Farandole*. Notice that they tend to follow a strong/weak pattern.
2. The faster tempo of the second melody.
3. "Mitamba Yalagala Kumchuzi" contains several rhythm patterns at the same time. Select one of the instruments, perhaps the low drum, and follow it while listening to the example. Select another instrument and follow it as you listen again to the example on CD 6.

Melody *and* Harmony

It is obvious that most music contains sounds that are higher or lower than others. These differences in high and low sound are the second important element of music.

PITCH: THE HIGH AND LOW OF SOUNDS

As used in music, the word **pitch** refers to the highness or lowness of a sound. It is the result of the number of vibrations made by the sound-making instrument — the human vocal cords, the reed of the clarinet, the string of the violin, and so on. The greater the number of vibrations, the higher is the sound. For example, a sound-producing medium vibrating 440 times per second produces the standard pitch for the note A above middle C. Orchestras tune to this pitch; bands tune to B-flat, which is 456 vibrations per second.

Pitches by themselves are not music. To be useful in music, pitches must meet one of three conditions:

- Be a part of a series of pitches that forms a logical unit of music — melody
- Be a part of two or more logical series of pitches sounded in contrast with each other — counterpoint
- Be a part of several pitches sounded at the same time — harmony

In many cultures pitch is described in terms of large/small or masculine/feminine.

Resource Center
Play different pitches in the *Music Listening Today, 4th Edition,* Resource Center.

MELODY: PITCHES IN A COHESIVE SERIES

The first of these conditions — a series of pitches that forms a cohesive entity — is referred to as **melody.** The important words here are *cohesive* and *entity.* The pitches must seem to belong together and be a unit — an entity. Not just any sequence of pitches will do.

What causes some melodies to be memorable and emotionally moving and others to seem forgettable and senseless? No one really knows, although from time to time scholars attempt to provide general melodic guidelines. For example, a series made up of the same pitch sounded again and again has little chance of being a melody that anyone will want to sing or listen to; it lacks musical interest and variety. On the other hand, a melody in which the pitches seem to have little relationship to each other won't work either; it lacks a sense of unity. A good melody seems to achieve a balance between unity and variety.

Melodies are what people generally remember in music. The melody is what they whistle, sing, and focus their attention on when listening to music. No doubt you can probably recall the opening melody of Bizet's *Farandole.* Some melodies over the centuries have acquired names of their own. In many Protestant churches, the Doxology is sung to a melody named "Old Hundredth." The names of the melodies of hymns are sometimes given in the hymnals just under the title.

Two other terms are sometimes used as synonyms for *melody.* The word *tune* is a less formal term, the implication being that a tune is less serious and complex than a melody or theme. A **theme** identifies an instrumental melody that plays an important role in a musical work. A theme is of interest both for its musical qualities and for what the composer does with it during the course of the piece. In some cases, quite average themes have become the basis for great musical works. A prime example of this is the famous four-note theme in Beethoven's *Symphony No. 5,* which is presented in Part IV.

Many melodies are known by their words, such as "Take Me Out to the Ball Game" and "Anchors Away!" Some melodies have two or more different sets of words. What we know in the United States as "My country 'tis of thee" ("America") is the national anthem of Great Britain, where its first words are "God save our glorious Queen."

Middle C

The representation of pitch in music notation is partly graphic. The horizontal lines and the spaces between them provide a visual image of the distance from one pitch to another. Both lines and spaces are used to represent pitches.

The five lines and their spaces make up the staff. The higher a note is placed on the staff, the higher it sounds. The clef (French for "key" and meaning the key to the staff) sets the general level of pitch for the five lines. For example, in the treble clef, which is indicated by the symbol 𝄞, the inside curl goes

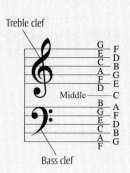

around the line for G above middle C. In the bass clef indicated by 𝄢, the two dots straddle the line for F below middle C. The relationship between the two clefs can be seen when they are combined, as shown here.

Only the first seven letters of the alphabet are used in music. The notes can be modified by a sharp (♯), raising the pitch one half-step, or a flat (♭), lowering the pitch one half-step. Knowing the names of notes is not essential to appreciating music.

Much as words are read on the page, notes placed one after another in a row are to be performed sequentially. Notes that are aligned vertically on the page are sounded at the same time as a cluster or group, called a *chord*. Chords, too, are read from left to right across the page.

Therefore notation gives you a visual representation of what the music sounds like. It can help you sense and remember what you hear.

Features of Melodies

The topic of how composers work with themes in music is covered in Part IV.

We can better understand melodies by considering their various dimensions and features.

LENGTH Some melodies are short and concise; others stretch out over many measures. The themes in "Hoe-Down" are clear and to the point, but in contrast, the melody for Joachin Rodrigo's *Concierto de Aranjuez*, discussed in Chapter 4, seems more flowing.

RANGE Some melodies stay within a narrow range of pitches. Others spread out over a wide pitch distance.

The word *leap* may seem to be an exaggeration for any note that is not adjacent, but it is the appropriate term.

STEPS AND LEAPS Some melodies, such as the beginning of "Row, Row, Row Your Boat," move by small steps from one note to the next. Other melodies leap to a note a distance away. As we all know from the occasional strain of singing "The Star-Spangled Banner," it opens with several leaps that carry it over a considerable range:

CONTOUR Each melody has its own outline, or contour, just as each city has it own skyline. In fact, melody is often referred to as the "line" or "melodic line." Here is the contour for the first several measures of "The Star-Spangled Banner":

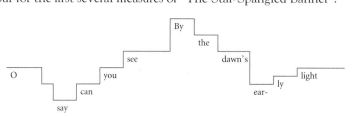

And here is the contour of "America":

DECORATIVE NOTES In some melodies each note seems solid and unadorned. The Shaker hymn melody is a prime example of a straightforward, undecorated melody. "Simple Gifts" is an American Shaker song from around 1840. Notice that the melody moves in a steplike progression complemented by infrequent leaps.

We will hear the opposite in decoration in the melody for Rodrigo's *Concierto*, which has many ornamented notes.

ARRANGED BY AARON COPLAND
"Simple Gifts" (1950)

Strings, piano, vocal

CD 1 Tracks 7 – 8

1 minute 40 seconds

0.00   7   0:00   Short introduction played by strings; then the singer begins:

'Tis the gift to be simple, 'tis the gift to be free,
'Tis the gift to come down where you ought to be.

The melody for the next two lines is very similar to that of the first two:

And when we find ourselves in the place just right,
'Twill be in the valley of love and delight.

0:32   8   0:00   Contrasting section begins:

When true simplicity is gained.
To bow and to bend we shan't be ashamed.

0:09   The melody of the second two lines returns, but with new words and a few small changes:

To turn, turn will be our delight,
'Til by turning, turning we come round right.

0:26   Music and words of the opening four lines are repeated exactly.

0:56   Strings play a short concluding section.

1:02   "Simple Gifts" ends with a cadence.

 An interactive Active Listening Guide can be downloaded from the online Resource Center for *Music Listening Today, 4th Edition*. Visit http://academic.cengage.com/login to access this password-protected website, or purchase an instant access code online from iChapters.com.

The Shakers were a religious sect that earned their name from the "shaking" they experienced when they felt the spirit of God. They lived a simple, celibate life and developed a number of communities in New England and Kentucky. They are known today for the simple, elegant furniture they designed.

LISTENING GUIDE

A **SHAKER KITCHEN** Notice that everything is hung neatly in place from pegs in the upper molding.

Courtesy of Charles Hoffer

What Affects the Impression of a Melody?

Just about everything affects the impression a listener gains of melody.

ACCOMPANYING MUSIC The accompanying music is like a stage setting in that it contributes to the overall effect of a play. Aaron Copland's arrangement of the American Shaker song "Simple Gifts" demonstrates the skillful creation of accompanying music to enhance the melody. He makes the setting clear and simple, which is in keeping with the simple character of the song and its text.

TONE QUALITIES AND INSTRUMENTS A melody played on a flute gives listeners one impression, whereas the same melody played on a guitar gives another. Some melodies seem more suited for certain instruments than for others; a very decorative melody sounds fine on a violin or flute but would sound cumbersome played by a trombone. Copland used the melody for "Simple Gifts" in his ballet *Appalachian Spring,* which is presented in Part VII. In that music the melody is altered to suit the attributes of the different instruments that play it.

RHYTHM The rhythmic properties of a melody can make a big difference. Imagine singing "Jingle Bells" very slowly. A merry winter song would sound like a funeral dirge. In other cases, average melodies are sometimes successful because of their distinctive rhythmic qualities.

PHRASES You can't exactly see phrases in music as you can in written text, which is punctuated with commas and periods. **Phrases** are there in the logical groupings of notes, which vary in length as much as phrases in language do. For example, in the song "America" the words and notes for "My country 'tis of thee" form a short phrase that is coupled to the next short phrase, "sweet land of liberty," leading to the phrase "of thee I sing" to form a logical musical entity.

STYLE OF PERFORMANCE If you sing a melody such as "America" in short, detached notes instead of in a flowing, singing style, it will seem to be a different song, one you almost certainly will not like as well.

QUALITY OF PERFORMANCE The same piece played by two performers, one who is exceptionally able and another who is mediocre, can leave listeners with very different impressions of the music. Outstanding performers can make what are considered average pieces sound fresh and vital, and less able performers can make exceptional works sound pedestrian.

COUNTERPOINT: MELODIES SOUNDED TOGETHER

Melodies can be combined in one of two ways. One is as a *round*. You have known about rounds since you were in elementary school. In a round exactly the same music is sung, but each line starts at a specified time interval. For example, one group of singers sings, "Are you sleeping? Are you sleeping?" and then the second group follows, singing the same melody and words while the first group continues on with "Brother John, Brother John." The process continues with additional groups joining in until the round is sung a given number of times and the last group concludes singing alone.

When one group or instrumental part periodically follows another exactly, it is called **imitation.** When the imitation continues for an entire song or section of music, it is called *strict imitation*, as in a round. The term *round* implies a short song. A **canon** is a somewhat longer and more complex piece than a round in strict imitation.

The second way to combine melodies is to design two different and distinctive lines of music to be performed at the same time. The term for this is **counterpoint.** A composer may add a line of counterpoint to an existing melody, or he or she may compose two fresh lines. Usually, the two lines have somewhat different characters; that is part of the reason why counterpoint is interesting to listen to. One line of melody is likely to be more solid and have longer note values than the other.

The word *counterpoint* comes from the time when notes were called "points." The adjectival form of the word is *contrapuntal.*

Canon means "by the rule." When spelled with one *n,* the word has nothing to do with the artillery weapon.

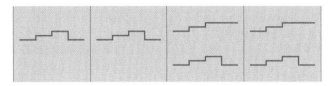

Round

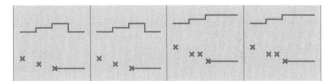

Counterpoint

HARMONY: PITCHES SOUNDED TOGETHER

If melody is the horizontal line in music with its sounds occurring one after another, **harmony** is the vertical line with sounds occurring at the same time. To illustrate this concept, let's return to "The Star-Spangled Banner." Here are the first seven notes in its melody:

Aligned vertically, these same notes form the B-flat major chord, which is the tonic chord in the key of B-flat.

The preceding sentence contains a number of points about harmony that need to be explained.

KEY OR TONAL CENTER Both melodies and harmonies usually have a **tonal center** and are in a **key.** The music tends to move away from and then back to this center. The musical example of "The Star-Spangled Banner" is in B-flat. Like most music we know, our national anthem ends and centers around its tonal center. If "The Star-Spangled Banner" were to end on any note other than B-flat, it would sound incomplete—as if someone had made a mistake.

Some melodies end on the third or fifth note of the scale, but "The Star-Spangled Banner" is not one of them.

MODULATION Can the tonal center or key change during a musical work? To use the musical term for changing key, can the music *modulate*? Definitely! Not only *can* it change key, but in works longer than a song, it usually *does*. **Modulations** help make the music sound fresher. If the music goes on too long in the same key, it can become tiring. Most of the music you hear modulates every so often, but usually people aren't aware that the key has changed.

SCALES A **scale** is a series of pitches that goes upward or downward according to a prescribed pattern. Most scales contain seven different pitches, but a five-note scale is often found in Asian music and some folk music. Few melodies contain a complete scale one note after another, but generally scales are the underlying "skeleton" of melodies and harmonies. The scale for "The Star-Spangled Banner" is B-flat C D E-flat F G A B-flat. Although an alteration or two can occur in a song (and there is one in "The Star-Spangled Banner"), most of the notes come from that scale.

"Joy to the World" is one exception to this statement. Its first eight notes are a descending scale.

CHORDS A **chord** is three or more pitches sounded together. Usually, the notes of chords follow an every-other, checkerboard pattern. For example, the chord for the tonal center in B-flat is B-flat D F, which are the first, third, and fifth notes in that scale. This chord is called the **tonic chord** and is indicated with the Roman numeral I. A chord can be built on each step of a scale, but the I, IV (subdominant), and V (dominant) chords are used more often than the other chords.

The earlier reference to notes forming the tonic chord on B-flat should be clearer now.

OCTAVES You may have noticed that the B-flat scale mentioned earlier began and ended on B-flat. The second B-flat is an **interval** (the distance between two pitches) of an octave higher than the lower B-flat. An **octave** is eight notes higher or lower than another note with the same name. Each octave has double (if it is higher) or half (if it is lower) the number of vibrations of the other. When sounded, octaves blend very well with one another.

The note A above middle C vibrates 440 times per second. With each octave higher, the A on the piano vibrates at 880, 1,760, and 3,250. With each descent, the A vibrates at 220, 110, 55, and 27½ — the lowest note on the piano.

The limits of human hearing range from about 20 to 20,000 vibrations per second.

MAJOR/MINOR Two patterns of scales, **major** and **minor,** are traditional in the music of Western civilization. The main difference between the scales is in the third step, which is one half-step lower in the minor scale. The chords based on these scales are also affected by this difference. To listeners, major and minor sound different from one another, but one is by no means better or more pleasing than the other. *Farandole* by Bizet, discussed in the Listening Guide in Chapter 2, has a marchlike theme in minor and a dancelike theme in major. It offers you a chance to listen to their particular qualities.

Resource Center
Hear differences between major and minor, consonance and dissonance in the *Music Listening Today, 4th Edition,* Resource Center.

CONSONANCE/DISSONANCE **Consonance** implies agreement and equilibrium. **Dissonance** implies the opposite—tension and disequilibrium. If you push your hand down on a keyboard, depressing all the keys under your hand, you will get a very dissonant sound. If you press down every other white key, a rather consonant chord will be sounded. There are no clear standards, however, as to what is consonant or dissonant. These two terms are subjective and relative. Therefore, it is more accurate to think in terms of degrees of consonance or dissonance.

HARMONIC PROGRESSIONS AND CADENCES Because music moves through time, so do chords. They have a logic and a sequence, just as notes do in a melody. If you start on C on a keyboard, play the white keys up to B, and then stop without playing the C an octave above where you started, you will be left with an incomplete feeling—somewhat like someone saying to you, "I have a great idea! Why don't we . . . [silence]."

A progression of chords can give listeners the feeling of either conclusion or incompleteness. Certain patterns of two chords have become traditional for "punctuating" music. These patterns are called **cadences.** Usually, they appear at the ends of phrases and they give a sense that the music is going to come to a musical comma or period.

The word *cadence* is also used to describe the pattern played by the drum in a marching band, but this usage is, of course, quite different from the chord patterns discussed here.

Texture and the Ways Pitches Are Used

Resource Center
Hear cadences in the *Music Listening Today, 4th Edition,* Resource Center.

In music, the word **texture** refers to the basic approaches in the use of pitches. It does not refer to the smoothness or roughness of a melody. The three terms describing texture are monophonic, homophonic, and polyphonic.

The word for a melody alone, with no other accompanying sounds, is **monophonic.**

The term for a melody with accompaniment is **homophonic.**

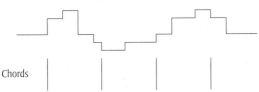

Chords

Bizet's *Farandole* contains portions in each of these three textures.

The presence of two or more lines with melodic character creates a **polyphonic** texture.

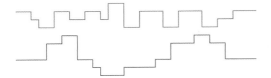

Resource Center
Experience the different textures in the *Music Listening Today, 4th Edition,* Resource Center.

GEORGES BIZET
Farandole from *L'Arlésienne,* Suite No. 2 (1872)

March tempo, 4-beat meter   Orchestra

CD 1 Tracks 4 – 6

3 minutes 7 seconds

0:00 4 0:00 Orchestra plays marchlike opening theme (A) in a minor key with simple accompaniment.

Allegro deciso

ff

0:16 Strings play A theme in imitation. The texture is polyphonic.

0:33 5 0:00 High woodwinds play a faster, lighter theme (B) in a major key with accompaniment. Music slowly grows in intensity.

ppp poco a poco crescendo

0:43 Strings play B theme in major with a homophonic texture.

0:54 Strings play A theme at a lively tempo. Music returns to minor, and the texture is monophonic.

1:05 Woodwinds play B theme as texture becomes homophonic.

1:11 Strings play A theme in minor. The texture is monophonic but changes to homophonic when lower strings add accompaniment.

1:22 Woodwinds take up B theme in major as texture remains homophonic.

2:18 6 0:00 Orchestra plays both A and B themes at a loud dynamic level. The texture is polyphonic, and music remains in a major key.

0:49 Music concludes with several short chords.

An interactive Active Listening Guide can be downloaded from the online Resource Center for *Music Listening Today, 4th Edition.* Visit http://academic.cengage.com/login to access this password-protected website, or purchase an instant access code online from iChapters.com.

LISTENING GUIDE

Homophonic and polyphonic textures are relative, and they are sometimes used at different places in the same work. Often composers include musically interesting patterns in an accompanying part, but these parts lack enough melodic character to be considered another line of music. Occasionally, works that are basically polyphonic include portions containing mostly chords, and vice versa.

Bizet's *Farandole*, explored in the context of rhythm in Chapter 2, also contains many of the musical elements discussed in this chapter: texture, counterpoint, and major and minor scales.

MAIN POINTS OF THIS CHAPTER

1. Sound is created by molecules vibrating and colliding with one another in the air. The more rapid the vibrations, the higher the pitch of the sound, while the opposite is true for lower-pitched sounds.

2. The first seven letters of the alphabet are used to designate pitches. These letter names are repeated for each octave. Each note in an octave is either half (making it lower) or twice (making it higher) the number of vibrations of the note with the same name in the adjacent octave.

3. Pitch levels are depicted in notation on a graph-like staff. Higher notes use the treble clef (𝄞) and lower notes use the bass clef (𝄢), with a half-step higher indicated by a sharp (♯) and a half-step lower indicated by a flat (♭).

4. A melody is a series of consecutive pitches that form a logical entity. Most melodies can be divided into shorter groups of notes called phrases. A listener's impression of a melody is very much affected by other factors in the music such as the accompanying music and instruments or voices performing it.

5. Harmony is the simultaneous sounding of pitches, usually in chords containing three or more notes. Chords vary from sounding pleasing (consonant) to tense (dissonant). Most chords are built in an every-other note pattern such as C-E-G.

6. The music in almost all songs and instrumental works centers around one particular note. Changes of this center (key), called modulations, occur rather often. The music almost always returns to the same tonal center (tonic), however.

7. Scales are the tonal framework around which music is created. Three types of scales predominate in the music of Western civilization: major, minor, and the five-note pentatonic scale. Music using the major scale tends to have a brighter quality than music in minor. Music using the pentatonic scale often has a folk-like or Asian quality.

8. Texture in music refers to the basic arrangement of the lines of melody and harmony. Homophonic texture with its melody-plus-accompaniment character is most familiar to us today. Polyphonic texture, which is two or more different melodic lines occurring at the same time, was especially prominent in music several hundred years ago, however. Monophonic texture consists of only one line of music performed alone.

9. Two types of polyphony or counterpoint exist in music. One occurs when a melodic line is imitated in follow-the-leader fashion several beats later, which happens in a round or canon. The other exists when two different lines with melodic character occur at the same time.

FEATURES TO LISTEN FOR

1. How Copland's arrangement of "Simple Gifts" complements the nature of the song and its text by being so clear and uncluttered.

2. The three-part pattern of "Simple Gifts": First, the music for "'Tis a gift . . ." is sung, then the contrasting "When true simplicity . . .", and then "'Tis a gift . . ." returns.

3. The contrasting character of the two melodies in Bizet's *Farandole*. The first is march-like, whereas the second is light and sprightly.

4. The three textures present in *Farandole*. The first melody opens in homophonic texture, which is followed by the same melody in polyphonic texture as the instruments play it in imitation. Monophonic texture is heard briefly at 0:54 in track 5 and one other short place a little later.

4 Dynamics, Timbre, *and* Organization

Loudness and tone quality have an important impact on how music sounds. Whatever the relative importance of the four basic elements of music (pitch, rhythm, dynamics, and timbre), they amount to little unless they are brought together in an organized way.

DYNAMICS: THE LOUD AND SOFT OF MUSIC

Resource Center
Play with dynamics in the *Music Listening Today, 4th Edition*, Resource Center.

The difference between 100 and 120 decibels may not seem all that much until you consider that the decibel scale is logarithmic; that is, 110 decibels is ten times louder than 100, and 120 decibels is 100 times louder than a subway train.

Every sound has some degree of loudness, or else it could not be heard. The amount of loudness can range from barely audible to earsplitting, although concert music rarely reaches that level of loudness. The term for the levels of loudness in music is **dynamics.** Sometimes the word *volume* is used for dynamics, but technically speaking it is not the correct term.

Loudness can be measured precisely in terms of *decibels*. A food processor reaches a level of 85 decibels, and a New York subway train produces about 100 decibels, which requires shouting over its noise to carry on a conversation. At 120 decibels, rock concerts reach levels louder than those of a jackhammer or a chainsaw.

Dynamic levels in music are indicated only in a general way through the use of terms or symbols representing those terms. The following table lists the commonly used Italian terms and symbols for dynamics.

Term	Symbol	Meaning	Pronunciation
fortissimo	**ff**	very loud	"for-*tis*-si-moh"
forte	**f**	loud	"*for*-tay"
mezzo forte	**mf**	moderately loud	"*met*-zo *for*-tay"
mezzo piano	**mp**	moderately soft	"*met*-zo pee-*ah*-noh"
piano	**p**	soft	"pee-*ah*-noh"
pianissimo	**pp**	very soft	"pee-ah-*nis*-si-moh"

An increase in dynamic level is indicated by the word **crescendo** ("cre-*shen*-doe"), abbreviated **cresc.,** and shown by the sign $\diagup$. The opposite of crescendo is **decrescendo** ("*day*-cre-shen-doe"), which is abbreviated **decresc.** and indicated by the sign $\diagdown$.

Not all changes in dynamics are gradual. Some notes are marked to be accented (>) or suddenly emphasized (*Sfz*). Some changes in dynamic level are to be made suddenly and are indicated by the Italian word *subito*.

Listening to loud music or sounds for several hours causes a temporary partial hearing loss. Doing so often over a period of years can cause a noticeable permanent hearing loss.

Most musical works contain changes in dynamic levels. Such changes are easily heard in virtually every work presented in this book.

TIMBRE: COLOR IN MUSIC

Resource Center
Hear the instruments' different timbres in the *Music Listening Today, 4th Edition*, Resource Center.

The fourth basic element of sound to be presented in this book is its tone quality, its color, which is known as **timbre** ("*tam*-ber"). Timbre in music is as important as color in a picture.

Every musical instrument and every voice have their own particular tone or timbre. If a trombone, clarinet, violin, guitar, flute, and the human voice sound middle C, as all of them can, each will produce it with a different quality. Furthermore, if two or more of them produce the same pitch at the same time, yet another timbre will result.

E. J. Flynn/AP Photo

PAT BENATAR is the national spokesperson for "It's Hip to H.E.A.R." a national initiative whose aim is educating baby boomers about the importance of hearing health. Benatar, shown here wearing ear protectors, says that she knows "firsthand the risks of hearing loss and how it affects your quality of life. Many of my friends have suffered permanent hearing damage, and my husband Neil and I both take proactive steps to protect our hearing health. Unfortunately, many of my peers are in denial."

Why do people and instruments have their own characteristic tone quality? The reason is a bit complicated but worth examining. Almost all musical sounds have pitch (A, D-sharp, G, and so on). But in addition to their fundamental pitch, they also produce small bits and pieces of other pitches, called *partials*, that make up the overtone series for that particular pitch. It's somewhat like getting the accessories (shirt, vest, shoes, cufflinks) that go with a rented tuxedo. The number and the strength of these various partials are what create the timbre of a sound; they make a clarinet sound like a clarinet and a guitar sound like a guitar.

A pitch can be divided in half either by touching the string at half its length or by dividing the air column in half on a wind instrument by opening a key or changing lip tension. Such a division produces a pitch one octave higher than the fundamental. Divide the string or air column into thirds, and a pitch one octave and five notes higher is heard. Divide it into four parts, and a pitch two octaves higher is sounded. The pattern of pitches produced by dividing a string or other sound-producing mechanism into equal parts is called the **overtone series.**

The overtone series is also called the **harmonic series.**

The pattern of the overtone series is exactly the same for every pitch on every instrument. Here are the first seven overtones for the note C:

The importance of the overtone series is described more fully in Chapter 5.

Fundamental

1 2 3 4 5 6 7

Because the timbre of a sound is determined by the number and strength of the partials, the tone quality of instruments can be reproduced on a tone synthesizer. High-quality synthesizers can come surprisingly close to imitating the authentic timbre of an instrument. They cannot produce foolproof imitations, however, because the sounds they produce are too consistent, too perfect.

Because of the subtleties of sound produced by some instruments, technicians make actual recordings (called *samples*) of an instrument's sounds and enter them into a computer for use in electronically produced music.

The timbre of a pitch played or sung by a human being is not the same from beginning to end. The beginning of a sound may have a distinct hard quality that quickly blends into its basic timbre, which often changes slightly as it is being sustained. In fact, many singers, especially in popular music, make wide changes in timbre as they sing a pitch. These changes usually make the music more interesting and expressive.

Composers and arrangers are very conscious of the different timbres of instruments and voices. They know, for example, that the low notes of the flute are mellow, whereas its high notes are more shrill. They also know that adding French horns to a melody played by cellos will give strength and richness to the sound. The possibilities for combinations of timbres are limitless.

Courses in orchestration and arranging are required in university degree programs for composers.

ORGANIZATION: ORGANIZED SOUNDS = MUSIC

Seeing one dot alone has little meaning. But three dots arranged like this

        . .
         .

describe a triangle and have more meaning than just three dots.

Everyone who has taken a psychology course knows this basic principle of Gestalt-cognitive psychology: The whole is greater than the sum of its parts. This principle certainly applies to music. Composers work with a virtually infinite universe of possible combinations of rhythm, pitch, dynamic level, and timbre. But music, which is often defined as *organized sounds occurring in a specified span of time*, is more than just its accumulated total of notes and rhythms and timbres. Something more—and better—is created when they are combined and organized by a skillful composer or improviser. The whole truly becomes greater than the sum of its parts.

Consider again the song "Simple Gifts." It reveals a strong sense of organization. It has a three-part symmetrical pattern, and its phrases have a logical forward motion followed by points of repose. Its chords fit the notes of the melody, and their simple character adds to the thought the song is expressing. The rhythms used in "Simple Gifts" fit the words and are organized into patterns. And, best of all, the musical elements combine into a musically satisfying entity.

The definition of music as organized sound has two implications. One is that any organized group of sounds occurring in a span of time meets the criteria for music. You may or may not enjoy hearing a particular group of sounds, but as long as they are organized, they fulfill the definition of music.

Ignoring what is taking place in a musical work is a little like watching a football game with no understanding of the action while you sit around waiting for the final score.

The other implication is that listeners will understand music better if they can consider how sounds are organized. Why? Because the organization of sounds is the very stuff of music. Listening to music carefully and thoughtfully requires listening for what happens in the music, which in turn means listening for how the elements are manipulated by the composer and performer.

Form: Planning in Music

Over the centuries a number of general plans for organizing music have evolved. These general plans are called **forms.**

Forms were named after they were developed and used often.

Forms developed out of the trials and errors of hundreds of composers over hundreds of years. Musicians discovered, for example, that a three-part pattern with the first and third parts almost the same provides a satisfying logic in a musical work. Someone tried it, and other composers and listeners liked it.

Composing a form is not, however, like filling out a job application in which certain specific information must be supplied. They are not molds waiting for composers to fill with notes. Instead, forms in music are usually constructed around one or more of three broad, general considerations: repetition, variation, and contrast.

REPETITION Because music exists in time, the repeating of ideas in music is probably much more important than in the other fine arts. "Simple Gifts," for example, has a three-part form, with the middle part concluding with music similar to the last two lines of the first part. The first melody, the *a* section of the song, begins, "'Tis a gift to be simple . . ."; the contrasting melody, the *b* section, follows, "When true simplicity is gained . . ."; and the *a* section is repeated by the singer, "'Tis a gift to be simple . . ."

Alphabet letters are used to designate the parts of a work. When the parts are short, the letters are in lowercase. Therefore, the form of "Simple Gifts" is *a b a'*, or what is termed *ternary form*. The prime (') sign is used to indicate that the material is slightly different from its identifying letter. When longer sections of music are repeated, uppercase letters are used.

VARIATION A second broad approach to form is through varying the musical material—to repeat the same basic material but with changes.

CONTRAST A third broad approach is by contrast. In "Simple Gifts" the *b* portion of the song has a different melody and words. The contrasting sections in longer works may have a different melody as well as different tempos, keys, dynamic levels, and instruments. Even when a work does not repeat material, it usually contains contrasting sections unless it is quite short.

Because there are many different musical forms, they cannot successfully be discussed in just one chapter. Forms will be presented and discussed at the appropriate places throughout the book.

Basically, one of three things happens in music: The music you hear can (1) be the same, (2) be somewhat different, or (3) be completely different from what has been sounded.

Genre and Movements

Form in music is largely the result of the pattern in which themes are heard. A **genre** is different. It refers to the type of music—symphony, jazz, chamber music, oratorio, and so on. Think of the word as a synonym for "type of music."

Many instrumental works are divided into large, independent sections called **movements.** In a sense, they are stand-alone pieces that have been grouped together by the composer to constitute a larger work. Usually, the movements in a multimovement work have a contrasting character in terms of tempo and other musical qualities. Some of the time they are also loosely related by key. These individual movements often follow a particular form.

Genre is a French word that is pronounced with a soft *g*.

RODRIGO'S *CONCIERTO DE ARANJUEZ*

An important genre in concert music is the **concerto.** The essential element of a concerto is contrast between a soloist or small group and the remainder of the orchestra. In the case of Rodrigo's *Concierto de Aranjuez,* the solo instrument is a guitar. Many concertos also provide a chance for the soloist to show off his or her technical skill, which Rodrigo's *Concierto* certainly does.

Concerto is pronounced "con-*chair*-toe."

Joaquin Rodrigo

Wedding photo, Victoria and Joaquin Rodrigo 1933, Victoria and Joaquin Rodrigo Foundation

Joaquin Rodrigo (1901–1999) was born in Sagunto, Spain. By the age of three, he was blind. His music studies began at an early age, and they later took him to France, where he studied with the composer Paul Dukas. After his marriage in 1933, Rodrigo returned to Spain, but civil war broke out there in 1936 and lasted three years. During this time he lived in Paris and Germany. He then returned to Spain, and in 1940 his *Concierto de Aranjuez* received a highly successful premiere. He was hailed as Spain's greatest postwar composer. Although he received many honors and continued to compose, none of his works achieved the recognition comparable to that accorded his *Concierto de Aranjuez.*

Events in Rodrigo's personal life are reported to have influenced the second movement. He and his wife, Vickie, lost their first child during childbirth, and it was uncertain whether Vickie would survive. The movement's stormy cadenza is said to express his anger at God, but he finally accepts God's will and is at peace at the end of the movement.

Rodrigo's style did not change over his long life. It is Spanish in character, although he seldom included folk melodies in his music. It also revealed the French influence of his teacher, Paul Dukas. In form, harmony, melody, and rhythms, his music is quite formal and conservative. The dissonances and driving rhythms of other twentieth-century composers seemed not to have affected him. At various times, his music is passionate, colorful, and filled with charm.

BEST-KNOWN WORKS

guitar and orchestra:
- Concierto de Aranjuez
- Fantasia para un gentilhombre

Concierto de Aranjuez, Second Movement (1939)

Adagio (slow tempo), 4-beat meter   Guitar, English horn, strings, woodwinds   GENRE: Concerto

CD 1 Tracks 9 – 12

10 minutes

0.00	9	0:00	The guitar begins softly strumming four chords.
		0:07	The English horn plays the main theme. It begins with a short, three-note motive ♪♪♩ followed by a melody with a tender, mournful quality.

		0:41	The guitar repeats the theme with decorative notes.
		1:14	The English horn plays the theme five notes higher.
		1:48	The guitar repeats the theme in a more decorated version.
		2:25	The cellos play a contrasting figure, followed by violins and English horn.
		2:49	The guitar and woodwinds exchange portions of the theme.
3:56	10	0:00	The guitar plays a version of the theme on its low strings. The music grows more stern.
		1:02	The oboe plays a fragment of the theme, answered each time by the guitar.
		1:37	The flutes and woodwinds play rapidly repeated notes.
5:56	11	0:00	The guitar softly begins a cadenza. The theme is embedded in the repeated notes.

		0:39	The three-note motive is played four times, each time one octave lower.
		1:12	The basic pattern of four notes ascending, then four notes descending, begins. The music slowly becomes more intense and passionate.

		1:53	The cadenza climaxes as the orchestra enters with a loud, short chord, followed by the guitar's rapidly repeated chords.
7:57	12	0:00	The orchestra plays the main theme passionately, but then ends quietly with the flute, oboe, and guitar.
		1:03	The guitar returns, quietly playing a portion of the theme, with two lines that seem to answer each other.
		1:44	The movement seems to fade into space as it closes with the guitar and violins playing high, ethereal notes.

 An interactive Active Listening Guide can be downloaded from the online Resource Center for *Music Listening Today*, 4th Edition. Visit http://academic.cengage.com/login to access this password-protected website, or purchase an instant access code online from iChapters.com.

Only the second of the *Concierto*'s three movements is presented here. Usually, second movements are melodious and have a slow tempo, and Rodrigo follows that tradition. Musical works can be examined in terms of how their melodies, rhythms, and timbres are organized. The second movement of *Concierto de Aranjuez* seems especially well suited for such analysis.

The first and third movements of Rodrigo's *Concierto* have much faster tempos and a more playful quality.

MELODY The basic outline of the melody—its "musical skeleton"—consists of a long note, and then the melody moves up two notes before returning to the original long note. Next, the melody ascends for four notes and then works its way down note by note to four notes below where it began. Up to this point, all the melodic movement has been to adjacent notes.

But there is much more than its melodic skeleton. Rodrigo also adds many quick-moving, decorative notes. These notes are especially noticeable when the guitar takes its turn playing the melody. Then three quick, accented notes begin the melody (♪♪♩), something often found in Spanish music. This short melodic figure is heard frequently throughout the music and contributes to the unity of the movement. Such brief figures are called **motives** when they act as a unifying element in a musical work.

The word *motive* has nothing to do with the reasons why the composer wrote the music.

TIMBRE Much of the second movement of the *Concierto* has a tender, melancholy quality, due in large part to the tone qualities of the English horn and the guitar.

HARMONY The quiet, uncomplicated accompaniment adds to the tenderness of the music while allowing the melody to be clearly heard.

RHYTHM The rhythm is slow and steady with four beats to the measure. Because this movement features the melody, its rhythm is not as noticeable as it is in many works, including the other movements of the *Concierto de Aranjuez*.

Aranjuez is pronounced "A-*rahn*-hou-ayz." It is the name of the former summer palace of Spanish kings.

FORM AND ORGANIZATION The movement opens with the melody played by the English horn; then the guitar enters playing a more elaborate version of the melody. The melody returns two more times between contrasting sections and a long cadenza for the guitar. But that's not all. Rodrigo has the music build ever so gradually to a rather lengthy section for the guitar alone. This section also begins quietly but then slowly increases to a truly passionate level of intensity as the orchestra again takes up the theme with its three-note motive. The music just seems to float away as the movement ends.

The section for guitar alone is called the **cadenza.** Cadenzas allow the soloist to play paraphrases of the themes in a free-sounding and often technically stunning style. Cadenzas are almost always featured in one or more movements of solo concertos.

Everything about the second movement of *Concierto de Aranjuez* works. All the elements are organized into a musically satisfying entity. The whole really is greater than the sum of its parts.

MAIN POINTS OF THIS CHAPTER

1. The term for the degree of loudness in music is dynamics. They are indicated in a general way by the terms "forte" for loud (abbreviated *f*) and "piano" for soft (abbreviated *p*). These basic terms are often modified; e.g., "fortissimo" or *ff* for "very loud."

2. Gradual changes in dynamic level are indicated by the word "cresc." for "crescendo" (get louder) or "decresc." for "decrescendo" (get softer). The symbol for crescendo is ◁———, and the opposite is used for decrescendo.

3. Timbre refers to the tone quality of an instrument or voice. It is determined by the number and strength of the partials sounding in the overtone series. That series is the pattern of pitches that results when a string or column of air is divided in half or at other fractional points.

4. Music is organized sounds occurring in a specific span of time. Often portions of music are organized according to forms or patterns of music. These forms make use of three general aspects of music:
   - repetition—generally repeating the same musical ideas
   - variation—the same basic musical ideas are repeated but varied
   - contrast—entirely different musical ideas are presented

5. Letters in italics are used to designate forms. The larger sections of a work are indicated by capital letters, whereas short sections of a work are indicated in lower case letters.

6. A concerto features contrast between a small group and a larger group or a soloist and a larger group. Concertos often contain a section where the soloist plays alone a free-sounding, often technically impressive section based loosely on one or more of the themes of the music. This section is called a cadenza.

FEATURES TO LISTEN FOR

1. The way the melody becomes increasingly more decorated and intense with each of its four appearances at the beginning of the second movement of Rodrigo's *Concierto de Aranjuez*.

2. The important unifying role the three-note motive plays, and how often it is heard in the second movement.

3. The free-sounding nature of the cadenza in this movement of the *Concierto de Aranjuez*, and how it builds to a high point of intensity as the orchestra enters at the conclusion of the cadenza.

4. The overall melancholy quality of the music, beginning with the haunting timbre of the English horn and the "lonesome" quality of much of the guitar part.

Orchestral Instruments

5

Sounds are produced when something causes the molecules in the air to rapidly collide and bounce off one another something like balls on a billiard table. What a musical instrument does is control and shape the vibrations in a particular way. In doing this, instruments provide the element of tone color in music.

Most musical instruments can be examined for their capabilities in doing four things:

1. Producing their characteristic sound
2. Modifying their basic timbre
3. Playing different pitches
4. Starting and stopping their sounds

The instruments used in the symphony orchestra can be grouped into families according to the way they produce sound.

Resource Center
Learn more about the instruments of the orchestra in the *Music Listening Today, 4th Edition,* Resource Center.

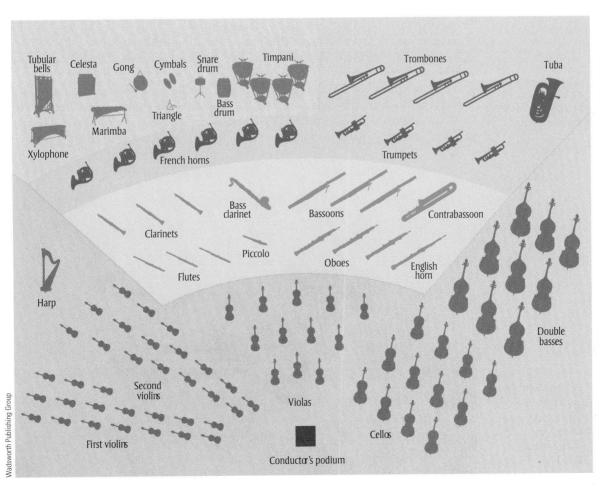

Wadsworth Publishing Group

THE INSTRUMENTS OF THE SYMPHONY ORCHESTRA are grouped into four families according to the way they produce sound: strings, woodwinds, brasses, and percussion. This illustration shows a typical seating plan, although exact number and placement of the instruments can vary.

STRING INSTRUMENTS

The guitar is a string instrument, but it is rarely used in symphony orchestras. It is described in the next chapter.

The difference among the four main string instruments in the orchestra is mostly one of size. The *violin* is the smallest and has the highest pitch. It is held under the chin when played. There is no difference between the instruments used for the first and second violin sections. Only the music written for them differs.

The *viola* ("vee-*oh*-lah") is somewhat larger than the violin but is still played under the chin. Its general range is five notes lower than that of the violin.

The cello ("*chel*-low," officially known as the *violoncello*) rests on the floor when played and is supported between the player's knees. It is one octave lower than the viola.

The *double bass* has several other names: *bass viol*, *contrabass*, and *string bass*. Players of the instrument stand or can sit on a high stool when playing. With its sloping shoulders, the shape of its body is slightly different from that of the other string instruments, and its strings are tuned four notes apart.

The *harp* is quite different from the other string instruments. It's a large instrument that sits on the floor with many strings that are strummed or plucked. Its strings are modified to play different pitches through the use of a pedal mechanism.

Sometimes professional string players can be seen tapping the bow against the instrument as a form of applause. Often they are faking it when they do so, because they don't want to hit a $4,000 bow against a $50,000 instrument—a typical price for a fine string instrument.

The strings are the backbone of the symphonic orchestra, with their number equaling that of all the rest of the instruments put together. By far the largest number are violins (about twenty-four to thirty), with at least twelve violas, twelve cellos, and eight basses.

Sound Production

String instruments produce sounds by vibrating strings. This is done in two ways: by drawing a bow across the string; or by plucking the string with the finger.

Pitchers in baseball often apply rosin to their fingers for better control of the ball.

The bow was originally slightly arched like the bow used in archery. But over the years, its curve was reduced and then curved slightly inward toward the hair, which allowed for more flexibility in the types of bowing. The hair on a bow is from the tail of a horse. If you look at it through a microscope, you will see hundreds of tiny depressions in it. The uneven surfaces of the hair catch on the string, causing it to vibrate. Usually, players of string instruments apply rosin to the hair to help it catch the string better.

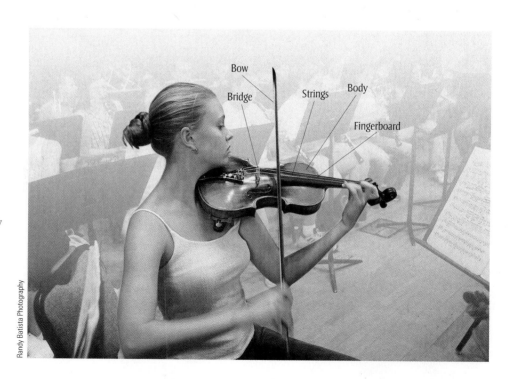

Bow
Bridge
Strings
Body
Fingerboard

Randy Batista Photography

THE VIOLIN The horsehair bow drawn across the strings sets them vibrating. The vibrations are conducted through the bridge and amplified by the instrument's hollow body. The position of the player's fingers pressing down on the strings on the fingerboard determines the pitches that are played.

A string vibrating by itself doesn't produce much of a sound. The vibrations need to be amplified, which is the purpose of the body of the instrument. The strings are held off the body by a wooden bridge. The vibrations of the strings are conducted through the bridge to the largely hollow body of the instrument.

Modifying Basic Timbre

The timbre of string instruments can be affected in several ways. One is to rock the left hand back and forth in small, rapid motions. This creates a **vibrato** ("vih-*brah*-toe"), which adds warmth to the tone quality by causing small alterations of pitch. All advanced string players use vibrato when playing.

Another way of affecting the timbre of a string instrument is to place a **mute** over the bridge. This small wood or plastic device softens the sound and makes it more mellow.

The timbre of string instruments is also affected by the way the bow is drawn across the string. More pressure on the bow makes the tone more harsh. Several different styles of bowing are used, each of which affects the tone and expressive qualities of the sounds.

Regulating Pitch

Different pitches are achieved on a string instrument (1) by the particular string being played, (2) by the length of string allowed to vibrate, which is regulated by the player, and (3) occasionally by the way the string is fingered. All orchestral string instruments (except the harp) have four strings. The strings each have a different thickness, are made of different materials, and are tuned five notes apart (except for double basses) by tightening or loosening the pegs at the end of the instrument.

Some professional-quality double basses have five strings.

THE CELLO Notice the rapid rocking of the left hand to create the small variations in pitch known as *vibrato*.

THE DOUBLE BASS The fingerboard is glued to the neck of the instrument but does not touch the hollow body.

As can be seen in the photos, the neck extends from the instrument, and a fingerboard is glued on top of it. The player depresses a string firmly against the fingerboard to shorten the string and thereby makes the pitch higher.

String instruments can also play *harmonics*, which are the notes in the overtone series above the basic pitch. The player can touch the string lightly at various points to create a *natural harmonic* or use a combination of depressed first finger and lightly touching with the little finger to produce an *artificial harmonic*. Both types of harmonics have a high, ethereal sound.

It is possible to sound two or three notes at the same time on string instruments. These combinations of notes are called *double stops* or *triple stops*.

Starting and Stopping Sounds

The motion of the bow across the string usually determines how long a sound is produced. String players learn several different styles of bowing. Some styles have abrupt, clear-cut beginnings and endings of the sounds, but others are very smooth with less distinct beginnings and endings. Sounds that are made by plucking with the first finger of the right hand, called **pizzicato,** are short and cannot be sustained. Occasionally, the left hand will pluck an open string in flashy solo works.

WOODWIND INSTRUMENTS

The *flute* used to have a wooden body, but since about 1900 silver–nickel bodies have been universally favored because of their more brilliant sound. The flute generally plays notes higher than those of the reed instruments. It has a smaller cousin, the *piccolo*, which sounds one octave higher.

The *oboe* is made of grenadella wood that has been carefully treated to prevent cracking. The oboe has a distinctive plaintive quality. The *English horn* is neither English nor a horn. It is basically a large oboe with a bulb-shaped bell. It sounds five notes lower than the oboe.

The *clarinet* has a wide range, but its timbre differs quite a bit from its low notes (very mellow) to its high notes (quite shrill). Clarinets are made from the same wood as oboes. They come in several sizes, including the bass clarinet, which looks like a wooden saxophone.

The *bassoon* has a distinctive appearance, which, with its reddish brown or black finish, looks somewhat like a long bedpost. Like the clarinet, it has a wide range, but it is more than an octave lower in pitch. The *contrabassoon* sounds another octave lower than the bassoon, going almost to the lowest note on the piano.

Saxophones have a metal body and a distinctive J shape, except for the soprano saxophone, which has a straight body like that of a clarinet. Saxophones use a single reed clamped on a mouthpiece and come in a variety of sizes.

A symphony orchestra has two flutes and a piccolo, two oboes and an English horn, two clarinets and a bass clarinet, and two bassoons and a contrabassoon. Saxophones are not regular members of the symphony orchestra.

Sound Production

With the exception of the flute, the woodwinds produce sound through vibrating reeds. The reeds are cut from cane that looks like bamboo. In the case of the clarinet, a single reed is clamped on a mouthpiece. The oboe and bassoon play double reeds, with two reeds being wired together facing each other.

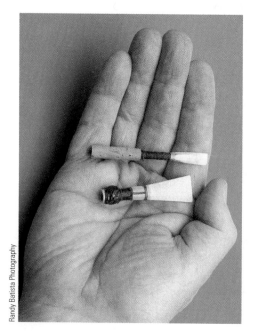

DOUBLE REEDS An oboe reed (top) and a bassoon reed.

The flute produces sound by the "stopped pipe" principle. It is possible to blow across the top of a bottle or jug and produce a sound. The sound is created by the collision of the air going down into the bottle meeting the air coming back out.

Modifying Basic Timbre

All the woodwinds except the clarinet can be played with a vibrato, especially the flute. Only in jazz is a vibrato used on the clarinet.

Advanced oboists and bassoonists make their own reeds, which is something of an art. The cutting and shaping of the double reed has a noticeable effect on the timbre of the instrument.

No mutes are used on woodwind instruments.

Regulating Pitch

All woodwind instruments regulate pitch by shortening or lengthening the column of air inside the instrument. This is done by *key* mechanisms that open or close holes. Some of the fingerings are quite complicated, however. The closer an open hole is toward the end of the instrument in the player's mouth, the higher the pitch will be—usually.

The qualification is included in the preceding sentence because all the woodwinds can move into a new and higher level of pitch by either overblowing at the octave (as on the flute) or opening a key that causes the instrument to overblow (as on the oboe, clarinet, and bassoon).

Starting and Stopping Sounds

Sounds are usually started when air is allowed to go through the instrument as the player's tongue is pulled off the reed, or away from the upper teeth in the case of the flute. Flute players can also use an action called *double tonguing* to articulate notes very quickly. Flutists can also achieve an effect called *flutter tonguing*.

THE FLUTE To generate various pitches, woodwind-instrument players use complex key mechanisms to open and close holes that regulate the length of a column of vibrating air.

BASSOONS AND CLARINETS

BRASS INSTRUMENTS

The *trumpet* is the highest-pitched brass instrument. It has three piston valves that change the length of tubing. The *cornet* is similar to a trumpet except that its tubing is more like a cone; the trumpet's tubing is more cylindrical. The configuration of the tubing affects the timbre of the instruments, with the trumpet having a more brilliant quality and the cornet a more mellow timbre.

The *French horn* contains more than sixteen feet of tubing that is coiled so that it can be handled more conveniently. It has three or four rotary valves, which are operated by the player's left hand. Rotary valves turn to open up different lengths of tubing instead of moving up and down as piston valves do. Most of the time, players insert their right hand into the bell of the instrument to modify the timbre.

FRENCH HORNS Most high-quality French horns are actually double horns, which makes it easier to play the right notes. A valve regulated by the thumb controls which part of the horn is used.

The most unusual feature of the French horn isn't visible. All the other brass instruments utilize the overtone series starting one octave above the fundamental pitch. The French horn uses the overtone series starting two octaves above the fundamental pitch. This means that the notes with the same fingering are closer together and that much precision is needed to produce the desired pitches. The French horn has a rather wide range, however.

The *trombone* is the only orchestral instrument today that uses a slide to regulate the length of its tubing. It sounds one octave lower than the trumpet. The *bass trombone* is somewhat larger than the more common tenor trombone, and it can play several notes lower.

The *tuba* is the largest and lowest in pitch of the brass instruments. Its role is similar to that of the double bass in the string section in playing the important bass line. The tuba seldom gets to play solos. Like the double bass, however, when played well it has a pleasing quality.

A symphony orchestra usually has three trumpets, four French horns, two trombones and a bass trombone, and one tuba.

Sound Production

A brass player's lip membranes can vibrate a thousand or more times each second.

All brass instruments produce sound by the membranes of the player's lips vibrating into a cup-shaped mouthpiece. The buzzing sound is then amplified through a metal tube with a flared bell at the end. For ease of handling, the metal tubing on brass instruments is curled once or twice.

BRASS MOUTHPIECES

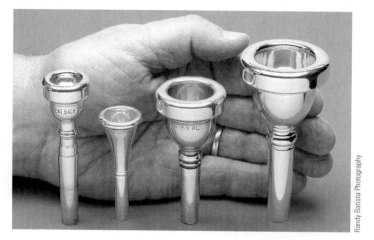

Trumpet   French horn   Trombone   Tuba

Modifying Sound

All brass instruments occasionally use mutes that are placed in the bell of the instrument to alter the timbres. They come in a variety of shapes and materials, including one resembling a rubber sink plunger and another called a "wah-wah mute." A vibrato can be used when playing brass instruments, especially in solo passages.

Regulating Pitch

The pitches on brass instruments are controlled in two ways. One is by subtle changes in the lips, which produce the different pitches of the overtone series. This phenomenon is best explained by considering the bugle. A bugle has no mechanism for changing pitch. All its different pitches are the result of changes in the tension of the bugler's lips. Only the sounds of the overtone series can be produced, however—the ones heard in bugle calls. All brass instruments can play the "bugle" pitches.

In addition, all brass instruments in an orchestra have either a valve or a slide mechanism that allows the player to change the length of tubing. That means that a new overtone series is made available when the length of the tubing is changed. The various combinations of valves and slide positions therefore make it possible for the player of a brass instrument to sound any pitch within the range of the instrument.

Randy Batista Photography

TROMBONES AND TUBA Brass-instrument players can vary pitch by subtle changes in their lips and by mechanical adjustment of the length of the tubing through which vibrating air passes.

It is rather difficult to play the fundamental pitch on a brass instrument, and its quality is not all that satisfying to listen to.

Starting and Stopping Sounds

Brass-instrument players start and stop sounds with their tongue, with the sound beginning as the tongue is pulled back from behind their upper teeth, opening the air stream. They can tongue very rapidly by *double* or *triple tonguing*.

PERCUSSION INSTRUMENTS

Percussion instruments can be divided into those that play pitches and those that don't. The *glockenspiel, xylophone, marimba,* and *vibraphone* are all percussion instruments that have metal or wooden bars arranged like the piano keyboard. They are played with sticks. The glockenspiel has metal bars that produce high tinkling sounds. The xylophone has wooden bars and produces dry, brittle sounds. The marimba is like a xylophone except for hollow tubes hanging below each bar that allow the sound to resonate after the bar has been struck. The vibraphone also has tubes, but in addition has an electrically driven device that adds vibrato to the sounds.

Timpani are two or more kettledrums of different sizes tuned to different pitches. Five are used in symphony orchestras today, and three are a minimum for works composed after 1800. The player positions the timpani around him or her in a semicircular arrangement. The sticks used in playing the timpani have round, padded heads. Professional players have several pairs of sticks of differing firmness to fit the needs of the music.

The *celesta* looks like a small piano, but it is more like a glockenspiel that is operated from a keyboard. *Chimes* sound different pitches. The player strikes the top of the metal tube with a wooden hammer.

The *snare drum* is the most prominent percussion instrument that does not sound a definite pitch. It is constructed around two hollow rings that are 5 or more inches apart. The rings have calfskin or plastic stretched over them. The bottom surface has several strands of wire, called *snares*, that rattle against it. The snares give the drum its characteristic crisp sound. The snare drum is played with a pair of wooden sticks.

Chris Stock/Lebrecht Music and Arts

XYLOPHONE

The singular of *timpani* is *timpanum*.

The piano is described in Chapter 6.

TIMPANI AND BASS DRUM

CYMBALS

The *bass drum* is the largest percussion instrument, sometimes having a diameter of four feet or more. It is placed on its side and hit with a single beater with a round, padded head.

The *cymbals* are large metal disks that are struck against each other with glancing blows. A single cymbal can also be suspended and struck with a stick or a wire brush.

The *triangle* is made of metal and is shaped like a triangle. It is struck with a metal beater while suspended. The *tambourine* has a single calf-skin head stretched over a wooden or metal hoop. The rim hoop contains small metal disks that rattle when moved. The player shakes the tambourine or hits it against the heel of the other hand to produce sounds.

Percussion players get to play a number of unusual instruments. For instance, they play something called a *whip*, which is actually two flat pieces of wood that are slapped together. Occasionally, they even get to sound whistles and car horns.

Fortunately for the orchestra's budget, percussionists play more than one instrument, but not at the same time. Orchestras have four regular percussion players and hire extras when needed.

Sound Production

Percussion instruments make sounds when struck or shaken. None of them can sustain sound, something that all string (except the harp), woodwind, and brass instruments can do. Some percussion instruments are hit together, others are struck with a stick or a beater, and a few are operated from a keyboard.

Modifying Sound

Sticks and beaters are made from different materials and in different sizes, and each has an effect on the sound produced. Sometimes wire brushes are used, and sometimes beaters with round, padded heads are required. Drumsticks come in a variety of sizes. The manner in which percussion instruments are struck or rattled varies and thus can alter the sound produced.

SNARE DRUM

TRIANGLE

Benjamin Britten

Benjamin Britten (1913–1976) was born in the seacoast town of Lowestoft, England, the son of a dental surgeon and a musical mother. He began putting patterns on paper before he was five, and by the age of six or seven, the notes became associated with what he had in mind. By the age of fourteen, he had composed a number of works for piano and voice. He was given a scholarship to the Royal College of Music, and by the age of twenty-one was earning his living largely as a composer.

He immigrated to the United States in 1939, but returned to England in 1942. He toured America again several times, usually giving performances with his lifelong companion, tenor Peter Pears.

Britten wrote for every medium and for varied levels of musical difficulty. He once said of composing: "It is the easiest thing in the world to write a piece virtually or wholly impossible to perform—but—that is not what I prefer to do. I prefer to study the conditions of the performance and shape my music to them."

BEST KNOWN WORKS

opera:
- Peter Grimes
- Albert Herring
- Billy Budd

orchestra and voice:
- War Requiem
- Serenade for Tenor, Horn, and Strings

choral:
- A Ceremony of Carols

Regulating Pitch

Many percussion instruments do not sound definite pitches. But there are a number of percussion instruments that do. One group has wooden or metal bars arranged in the manner of a piano keyboard. The large kettledrums (timpani) regulate pitch with a foot mechanism or handles at the edge of the drumhead that change the tension in the drumhead.

Starting and Stopping Sounds

Because percussion instruments do not sustain sounds, there is little problem with stopping sounds. An exception involves the ring of cymbals, chimes, and the timpani. Sometimes percussion players must dampen the sound of these instruments immediately after playing them to keep them from ringing too long and intruding on the music that follows.

LISTENING FOR INSTRUMENTS

Being able to identify the timbres of various instruments as you listen helps you understand and enjoy music more. You can learn to do this better by noticing the sounds of instruments as they are pointed out in the Listening Guides, in the CDs and downloadable Active Listening Guides, and in *The Young Person's Guide to the Orchestra* tutorials in the Resource Center.

The most sophisticated work created to demonstrate orchestral instruments is *The Young Person's Guide to the Orchestra* by Benjamin Britten. It presents the instruments first by families, then a variation for each instrument, which is followed by a short fugue. The instruments play the melody of the fugue in the same order in which they played their variation on the theme. The work closes with the opening theme in long notes and the fugue melody sounding simultaneously.

Benjamin Britten

The Young Person's Guide to the Orchestra

Variations and Fugue on a Theme by Purcell, Op. 34

CD 3 Tracks 1–6

17 minutes 27 seconds

Theme

1 0:00 Orchestra plays the theme at a loud dynamic level in a minor key.

0:42 Woodwinds play the theme in a major key.

1:11 Brasses play the theme.

1:42 Strings play the theme.

2:07 Percussion, especially the timpani, play the theme.

2:26 Entire orchestra plays the theme.

Variations

3:00 2 0:00 Variation 1. Flute and piccolo play high, fast notes.

0:28 Variation 2. Oboes sound a plaintive, melancholy melody.

1:33 Variation 3. Clarinets play rapidly moving notes.

2:15 Variation 4. Bassoons play a humorous melody.

6:11 3 0:00 Variation 5. Violins play a dancelike variation with rhythmic accompaniment.

0:45 Variation 6. Violas play a slow melody with a wide range.

1:35 Variation 7. Cellos play a rich, flowing variation.

2:32 Variation 8. Double basses play a variation with three-note patterns that ascend one pitch level each phrase and then descend one pitch level each phrase.

9:40 4 0:00 Variation 9. Harp plays the theme in an upside down version.

0:52 Variation 10. French horns play variation built around chords.

1:34 Variation 11. Trumpets feature marchlike figures.

2:07 Variation 12. Trombones and tuba play a heavy, majestic variation.

3:11 Variation 13. Percussion instruments play a variation that starts with the timpani, followed by the bass drum and cymbals, tambourine, triangle, snare drum, Chinese wood blocks, xylophone, castanets, gong, and the whip.

Fugue

14:42 5 0:00 Piccolo presents the main melody of the fugue.

The main theme is played by the instruments in this order:

0:05 Flute

	0:14	Oboes
	0:18	Clarinets
	0:29	Bassoons
	0:38	First violins
	0:40	Second violins
	0:46	Violas
	0:51	Cellos
	0:56	Double basses
	1:07	Harp
	1:18	French horns
	1:24	Trumpets
	1:31	Trombones and tuba
	1:37	Percussion
16:29 **6**	0:00	Both themes are combined: Brasses play the slower opening theme while upper strings and woodwinds continue with the fugue.
	0:31	Percussion enters loudly.
	0:50	The work ends with a long, full-sounding chord.

 An interactive Active Listening Guide can be downloaded from the online Resource Center for *Music Listening Today, 4th Edition.* Visit http://academic.cengage.com/login to access this password-protected website, or purchase an instant access code online from iChapters.com.

For nearly 200 years, the symphony orchestra has been the most important ensemble in instrumental concert music. The instruments that comprise it have a special place in listening to symphonic music. They provide the palette of musical sounds for both composers and listeners.

MAIN POINTS OF THIS CHAPTER

1. The instruments in a symphony orchestra are traditionally divided into four groups: strings, woodwinds, brasses, and percussion. Each of these families of instruments differs in how sounds are produced, basic timbres are modified, different pitches are created, and sounds are started and stopped.

2. Violins, violas, cellos, and double basses produce sound when a bow is drawn across their strings or a string is plucked (pizzicato). Harps can only be plucked. String players rapidly rock their left hand back and forth (vibrato) to add warmth to the sound. String players can also attach a mute to their instrument to produce a more subdued timbre.

3. Pitches on string instruments are determined by where a player places a finger on one of the strings. It is also possible to play on more than one string at a time. Sounds are started and stopped by the action of the bow. Several different styles of bowing can be used.

4. Flutes, clarinets, oboes, and bassoons constitute the woodwind family. All were originally made of wood, but because of their more brilliant sound, metal flutes replaced their wooden predecessors. Oboes and bassoons produce sound through the use of two cane reeds wired together, whereas clarinets use a single cane reed on a mouthpiece. Flutes employ a stopped-pipe principle in which air entering a pipe collides with air moving out to produce sound.

5. A vibrato can be used on all woodwinds except the clarinet, which uses it only in jazz style. Different pitches are produced by opening and closing holes and/or depressing and releasing keys. Sounds on woodwind instruments are started and stopped by the action of the player's tongue.

6. Members of the brass family include trumpets, French horns, trombones, and tubas. All are made of metal. Sounds are produced on them by a buzzing action of the player's lip membranes against a mouthpiece. All produce the pitches of the overtone series. By changing the length of the tubing, by opening and closing valves, or by moving the slide on the trombone, all pitches within the range of the instrument are available.

7. Percussion instruments all produce sound by being shaken or struck, usually by sticks or beaters. Some percussion instruments produce definite pitches. This group includes xylophones, chimes, and timpani. Others sound no definite pitch and include snare and bass drums, cymbals, and castanets.

FEATURES TO LISTEN FOR

1. The tonal qualities of each of the four families of instruments as they play the theme in the opening section of Britten's *The Young Person's Guide to the Orchestra*.

2. The timbre of each of the instruments as it plays its variation. Notice that the starting pitch in each phrase of the variation for double bass ascends one pitch each time for the first half of the variation, and then descends by one step each time for the second half. Notice also that the timpani sounds the opening notes of the theme.

3. The playful character of the fugue theme, and how each instrument enters one after another playing it. Notice also that each instrument plays the fugue theme in the same order it did for its variation earlier in the work.

4. The wonderful musical effect achieved when the stately theme returns in long notes near the end of the work as elements of the fugue theme continue.

Other Musical Instruments

6

The instruments of the symphony orchestra are often discussed together because they make up a rather standardized musical organization. But these instruments represent only one segment of the instruments used to make music throughout the world. This chapter examines the other important types of instruments.

THE VOICE

It may seem odd to talk about the **voice** as an instrument, although singers often refer to a person's voice as his or her "instrument." But it can be examined using the same categories that were used for orchestral instruments. The reason we don't usually think of the voice as an instrument is that we are born with it. We learn to use it for talking and to some extent for informal singing without any special instruction, something that is usually needed to play most instruments competently.

Sound Production

The voice produces sound through the vibration of the vocal cords in the larynx, or what is commonly called the voice box. Air and enough tension in the cords are required before these cords can produce sound.

The correct use of breath helps in both speaking and singing, as well as in preserving the voice.

Having enough air for breathing and enough for singing for an audience without the aid of amplification are two quite different matters. Because singing involves sustaining vowel sounds, good singing requires much control over the air. The muscular floor below the lungs, called the diaphragm, must provide a sufficient amount of breath support. The vocal cords must also be tightened; otherwise, no sound can be sustained.

The lungs are not muscles, hence the importance of the diaphragm.

Modifying Basic Timbre

The timbre of vocal sounds is determined by the shape of the oral and nasal cavities inside the head, as well as the cheeks and tongue formation. Each vowel has its particular formation, which is altered by the placement of the throat and tongue and the shape of the mouth and lips. An infinite number of shadings of timbre are possible.

Regulating Pitch

The pitch of a vocal sound is determined by the amount of tension in the vocal cords in relation to their length and thickness. The shorter the cords and the tighter they are stretched, the higher the pitch.

The difference between men's and women's voices is caused largely by the length of the cords. A man's vocal cords are normally about twice the length of a woman's, and they are also thicker. A larger larynx is required for the male's cords, which explains the more prominent Adam's apple.

Starting and Stopping Sounds

Vocal sounds are controlled by the action of the diaphragm in pushing air through the larynx. Sounds can also be choked off in the throat, but that doesn't sound very attractive, so it is usually avoided in singing.

Types of Voices

These voice parts are often abbreviated as *SATB*.

Voices in choral singing are traditionally divided into four classifications. The higher, lighter women's voice is called **soprano.** The darker, lower women's voice is called **alto.** In the case of men, the higher voice is called **tenor,** and the lower, deeper voice is called **bass** (pronounced "base"). Solo voices are classified using these four basic terms, plus additional modifiers such as *mezzo, dramatic,* and *lyric.* Most of the terms for classifying solo voices are not as well standardized as the four main classifications.

The voice is an instrument in one other way. Training is normally required to achieve the maximum power, beauty, range, and expression. It is, of course, possible to sing simple songs without any formal training. For almost all persons, however, lessons are needed to sing more difficult pieces or to have much power without the aid of a microphone.

It's the same with clothes. College students don't go to class wearing a swimsuit or a tuxedo. Yet both items of apparel are appropriate in other situations.

What people consider singing differs tremendously from popular to concert music and from one part of the world to another. Some singing styles are gentle and smooth, and some are raucous and almost shouted. The style of singing that is typical for one type of music can be very out of place in another style. Because good singing depends very much on the particular type of music, no singing style is inherently superior to another; the styles are just different.

RUTTER'S "OPEN THOU MINE EYES"

Several recordings on the CDs for this book have boys singing the treble parts, including the works by Josquin and Palestrina and Handel's "Hallelujah Chorus."

The choral music tradition in English churches has long been held in high regard among musicians. This tradition is marked by a very polished, refined quality with pitches perfectly in tune. One reason for its beautiful quality is the use of boys with unchanged voices on the soprano and alto parts. When boys are between the ages of about ten to thirteen, their voices have a special brilliance and clarity that disappears once their voices change. The use of boys' voices is developed in England in choir schools in which the students study music extensively as well as their other academic subjects.

John Rutter is one of many excellent composers whose works are largely associated with the English/Anglican choral tradition. Over the years he has written or arranged a number of religious choral works. "Open Thou Mine Eyes" is based on a poem by Lancelot Andrewes (1555–1626) and was commissioned by the Texas Choral Directors Association in 1980. It is a beautiful, simple work, one that many choirs are able to sing well and one that listeners can easily enjoy.

John Rutter

PressNet/Topham/The Image Works

BEST-KNOWN WORKS

choral
- *Gloria*
- *Requiem*
- *Magnificat*
- *Psalmfest*
- *Mass for Children.*

John Rutter (b. 1945) was born in London and attended the Highgate School. He went on to study music at Clare College, Cambridge University. While there, he published his first compositions and conducted for recordings. Although he has written a wide range of music, he is known mainly for his choral works, including four *Carols for Choir* anthologies with Sir David Willcocks.

From 1975 to 1979, he was director of music at Clare College. He gave up that position to devote more time to composing and to form the Cambridge Singers, a professional chamber choir that primarily makes recordings. He has conducted or lectured at many universities and concert halls throughout the English-speaking world. He has been honored by Westminster Choir College in the United States and by the Archbishop of Canterbury in England.

JOHN RUTTER
"Open Thou Mine Eyes" (1980)

GENRE: Church anthem   Unaccompanied voices

CD 1 Tracks 13 – 14

2 minutes 37 seconds

Form: *a a b a a*

0:00   13   0:00   Sopranos sing opening verse.

> *Open thou mine eyes and I shall see;*
> *Incline my heart and I shall desire;*
> *Order my steps and I shall walk*
> *In the way of thy commandments.*

        0:29   Altos enter, and sopranos divide into two parts; repeat first verse.

0:58   14   0:00   Tenors and basses sing contrasting section.

> *O Lord God, be thou to me a God*
> *And beside thee let there be none else,*
> *No other, nought else with thee.*

        0:18   Upper and lower voices combine as *a* melody returns.

> *Vouchsafe to me to worship thee and serve thee,*
> *According to thy commandments,*
> *In truth of spirit,*
> *In reverence of body,*
> *In blessing of lips,*
> *In private and in public.*

        0:57   Opening words and melody sung by sopranos as other voice parts hum accompaniment.

        1:40   Music closes quietly with moving notes in alto and tenor parts.

An interactive Active Listening Guide can be downloaded from the online Resource Center for *Music Listening Today, 4th Edition.* Visit http://academic.cengage.com/login to access this password-protected website, or purchase an instant access code online from iChapters.com.

WIND BAND INSTRUMENTS

The sound of a wind band can be heard on the CD set in Sousa's "The Stars and Stripes Forever."

Wind bands vary in size from thirty to more than a hundred players. The wide range in the size of a wind, or *concert*, band indicates that its instrumentation is not as well standardized as that of the symphony orchestra. The larger groups usually produce a more massive sound, and the smaller groups achieve greater clarity. The larger bands also use more players on many of the parts.

As the name indicates, wind bands are composed almost entirely of brasses and woodwinds plus percussion. Some bands include one double bass but no other string instruments.

Wind bands include a number of instruments not usually found in a symphony orchestra. Additional brass instruments include cornets and euphoniums or baritone horns, which sound one octave lower than a trumpet. Because tubas are difficult to carry while marching, an instrument with the same range and similar timbre was developed in the band of John Philip Sousa. The appropriately named sousaphone is coiled over the player's shoulder and has a large flared bell that faces straight forward.

David M. Grossman/The Image Works

SCHOOL BANDS are common in the United States, in some provinces of Canada, and more recently, in some schools in Japan and Australia.

Wind bands also include saxophones of different sizes: alto, tenor, and baritone. Many times alto and bass clarinets are used in wind bands, and sometimes the low-pitched contrabass clarinet as well.

The wind band is largely an American institution. Bands are seldom found in schools and colleges in the rest of the world. Most bands in other countries are associated with the military. Even in the United States, the most musically recognized professional bands are the armed services bands in Washington, D.C.

TRADITIONAL KEYBOARD INSTRUMENTS

Harpsichord

The *harpsichord* looks something like a grand piano but it operates quite differently. Often it has two keyboards, called *manuals*, plus knobs that affect the couplings of strings to the keys. Sometimes the pattern of black and white keys is exactly the opposite of what it is on the piano.

The sound of the harpsichord is more delicate and lighter than that of the piano. Probably for this reason, it fell out of favor with composers after about 1750 because they preferred the more powerful sounds of the piano. It has, however, enjoyed a revival of interest in the twentieth century.

Piano

The *piano* is a historically younger instrument than the harpsichord, being first constructed in Italy about 1709. Behind or underneath the strings, depending on the type of piano, is the *soundboard,* which amplifies the vibrations of the strings. Throughout its history, the piano has had a differing number of keys. Today that number is standardized at eighty-eight, although keyboards on most electronic pianos usually have fewer keys.

There are two types of pianos, the upright and the grand. The *grand* piano is long and flat, ranging from five and one-half to nine feet in length. With its longer strings and

Harpsichord, by Shudi and Broadwood, English, 1770/Fenton House, Hampstead, London, UK/ The Bridgeman Art Library International

THE HARPSICHORD can be heard on the CD set containing *Brandenburg Concerto* No. 5 by J. S. Bach.

PhotoDisc, Inc.

THE PIANO is included on the CD set with works by Chopin, Liszt, Rachmaninoff, and Debussy.

larger soundboard, the sound of the grand piano is superior to that of the upright piano. Concert music is therefore always performed publicly on a grand piano. The *upright* piano is the type usually seen in homes because of its lower cost and smaller size.

Grand pianos usually have three pedals. One pedal holds the dampers off the strings so that they can ring freely. Another pedal holds the dampers off only certain strings, usually those in the lower half of the keyboard. The third pedal moves the entire mechanism so that the hammers do not strike all the strings for each pitch and thus creates a softer sound. On an upright piano, this pedal moves the hammers closer to the strings, which makes it easier to play the sounds more softly.

Pipe Organ

Although it has a keyboard—usually two or more—the *pipe organ* is a quite different instrument from the harpsichord and piano. Instead of strings, the pipe organ has pipes—hundreds and hundreds of them—into which air is pumped. A piano has a set of strings that produces a uniform timbre. The pipe organ has many sets, or *ranks*, of pipes, each with a large complement of pitches and each with a different timbre. In fact, a large pipe organ can have as many as seventy ranks of pipes; medium-sized organs have forty or so. A rank of pipes is activated when a knob is pulled, and combinations of knobs can be set up in advance to be activated with the hand or foot. The number of combinations of timbres in a high-quality organ is enormous.

A pipe organ has several keyboards or manuals; generally, these keyboards have sixty-one keys. The different manuals make it easier for the organist to change back and forth between ranks of pipes.

A special feature of a pipe organ is the *pedalboard*, which is played with the feet. The pedalboard looks like a series of blond and black wooden slats that have been arranged in the pattern of the keyboard. It sounds many of the low pitches on the organ. Good organists can execute remarkably difficult passages with their feet on the pedalboard. The feet also control pedals for changing dynamic level that look like accelerators on an automobile.

The high cost of professional-quality grand pianos and pipe organs has encouraged the adoption of electronic versions of both instruments. Although electronic organs can sound quite good, they are also expensive, so cheaper, and therefore less authentic, instruments are often heard.

Sound Production

Keyboard instruments produce sounds in one of three ways: (1) In the case of the piano, a hammer of firmly packed felt strikes a string. (2) In the case of the harpsichord, a plectrum or quill plucks a string. (3) In the case of a pipe organ, air is released into a pipe.

THE PIPE ORGAN has been called "the king of instruments." It can be heard on CD 1 in J. S. Bach's *Toccata and Fugue in D Minor.*

Today, air is pushed through the organ by an electric blower. Until the nineteenth century or so, the air had to be pumped through by an assistant.

Modifying Basic Timbre

It is not possible to make obvious changes in the timbre of the piano or harpsichord. Subtle differences are possible, especially on the piano, by the use of the pedals and the manner in which the keys are depressed. The pipe organ contains many timbres, which are activated by pulling various knobs.

Regulating Pitch

The particular pitches sounded on a piano or harpsichord depend on the keys that are depressed. Unless coupled by some mechanical means, which is possible on larger harpsichords, only the pitch of the depressed key is sounded. The pitch of the strings on the harpsichord and piano depends on how tightly they are stretched. The tension, and therefore the pitch, of a string is regulated by the person tuning the instrument. The tuner twists the tuning pins with a wrench until the correct pitch is achieved.

Keyboard instruments also differ from those found in bands and orchestras in that they can easily sound more than one pitch at a time. Therefore, a keyboard instrument can play both a melody and its accompanying part simultaneously. For this reason, keyboard instruments are basically solo instruments; only occasionally are they played in ensembles consisting of only keyboard instruments.

Many piano duets have been composed, but most of them are for amateurs.

Starting and Stopping Sounds

Sounds on keyboard instruments start when a key is depressed. On the piano and harpsichord, the sounds soon fade or decay; they cannot be sustained, as they can on a pipe organ. Normally, they end as soon as the damper returns to the string. This action can be delayed by holding down the key, or, more commonly, holding down a pedal that keeps all the dampers from returning to the strings. Through the skillful use of the pedal, pianists can affect the impression of the music.

Changing Dynamic Level

The harpsichord does not allow the player to alter the dynamic level by the amount of finger pressure; in other words, hitting a key harder does not make it sound louder. The only way to change the dynamic level on a harpsichord is to couple the two keyboards so that the sound is doubled an octave higher on the second keyboard. It's different for the pianist. The piano can be played very softly or very loudly, depending on how forcefully the keys are pressed. A person playing the pipe organ can increase or decrease the number of pipes sounding and can also raise or lower a foot pedal to change dynamic level.

The piano's name comes from its capability for making dynamic changes. It was originally called *pianoforte.*

POPULAR INSTRUMENTS

Guitar

Versions of the *guitar* have existed for hundreds of years in different parts of the world, but it probably originated in the Near East. Actually, the acoustic (nonelectric) guitar of today is not all that different from its ancestors. Some of the older versions had four strings instead of the six used today, and guitars have been constructed in many different sizes.

All guitars produce sounds from the strumming or plucking of the strings by the player. The vibrations of the strings are then resonated by the hollow body of the instrument. The neck of the instrument, where the players place their fingers, has metal

It is easy to strum a few chords in G major on the guitar. It is not at all easy to play complicated music on it, however. Rodrigo's *Concierto de Aranjuez,* for example, is a very difficult piece to play correctly.

strips running across it. These strips, called *frets*, help players find the right place on the fingerboard.

The guitar has two relatives. One is the *banjo*, which has a plastic or parchment head stretched over a hoop and no back. The head gives the banjo a brilliant sound. The other is the *ukulele*, a small four-string guitar.

Accordion

The *accordion* is basically a small organ that the player holds between his or her arms. Air is pushed through the instrument by the in-and-out motion of the player pumping air through the bellows. The sounds are produced by small metal reeds, one for each pitch. The short keyboard is used for playing the notes of the melody, and the chords are sounded by pushing the buttons. One button sounds an entire chord. Expensive accordions can produce several somewhat different timbres.

ELECTRONIC INSTRUMENTS

Electronic instruments are divided into two groups. One group consists of instruments that electronically alter and amplify the sounds of the player. The *electric guitar* is the most prominent of this type of electronic instrument. Unlike the traditional acoustic guitar, the body of the electric guitar is not hollow, even though it is shaped somewhat like a guitar. Instead, it holds the strings and various control knobs, as well as a lever for adding vibrato to the tones. Players still place their fingers on the fingerboard as with the conventional guitar, but there the similarity ends.

The sounds of drums are often altered in popular music by electronic means. As with the electric guitar, electronic drums can produce wider differences in dynamic levels and alter the timbre to some degree.

The other group of electronic equipment is used in creating music. This group includes synthesizers, computers, and tape and disc players. The sky's the limit with such equipment today. Any type of sound and rhythm can be produced. And performances of

Pictoral Press Ltd/Alamy

BLUES ARTIST B. B. KING plays an electric guitar he calls Lucille.

TODAY'S DIGITAL SYNTHESIZERS are compact, sophisticated systems that can produce realistic sounds.

ICP-UK/Alamy

the music are always flawless! There are no performers in the traditional sense who can affect the musical results—a fact that has both good and bad points.

In the 1950s, electronic music was largely confined to the manipulation of magnetic tape. Composers could alter the speed of the tape, splice in other sounds, record different music on two tracks for performance together, and so on.

A generation later, technology had moved from analog to digital processing and production. In *analog* music, sounds are recorded in a continuous, uninterrupted form. Dynamic levels, for example, are changed by increasing or decreasing the power.

In *digital* recording, discrete, noncontinuous bits of information, usually in the form of numbers, are produced, sorted, or analyzed. How is this possible? Computers can process these bits of data at an incredible rate of speed. It is the same principle used in motion picture film. The reel of film contains thousands of individual pictures. When they are projected at the rate of twenty-four per second (*much* slower than a computer!), the eye perceives the individual pictures to be a continuous flow.

The complaint about electronically produced music is that it has a certain manufactured quality about it. To overcome this problem, synthesizers can now store recorded samples of the actual complex sounds of instruments and then have them available anytime the composer wants them. The use of recorded samples is, appropriately, called *sampling*. For example, the sound of a snare drum is complex, with its abrupt beginning and ring in the drum after a tap. Technology can come close to imitating it but does not really capture all the nuances of the tap on a drum or the sounds of other instruments. The inclusion of traditional instrumental sounds on the hard drive helps make the electronic music sound more musical.

MAIN POINTS OF THIS CHAPTER

1. The human voice is an important "instrument" in music. It produces sound as air causes the vocal cords in the larynx to vibrate. The control of the air flow is very important in singing.

2. The pitch of vocal sounds is regulated by the length and tension of the vocal cords. Women have shorter vocal cords; therefore, they produce a higher pitch than men, whose vocal cords are about twice as long. Women in choral groups usually sing the soprano (higher) part or the alto (lower) part. Men in choral groups usually sing the tenor (higher) part or the bass (lower) part.

3. Styles of singing vary enormously in America and around the world according to the type and style of the music.

4. Wind bands usually contain no string instruments. Instead, they often include saxophones, baritone horns, cornets, and a different type of tuba called a sousaphone.

5. Harpsichords, pianos, and pipe organs are instruments that control their pitches from a keyboard. They produce sounds in different ways, however. Harpsichords create sounds when strings are plucked by a mechanism, whereas pianos produce sounds when hard felt hammers strike strings. Pipe organs create sound when air is blown through pipes. Both pianos and pipe organs can vary their dynamic levels, but harpsichords cannot. Pipe organists can produce a wide array of timbres, and they also have pedalboards that organists play with their feet.

6. Guitars and accordions are two of the most popular instruments that are not electronic. Electric guitars are shaped like other guitars, but they are actually electronic instruments. Many versions of electronic keyboards also have achieved wide popularity.

7. Electronic music is created by synthesizers working in conjunction with computers. Early versions of electronic music were created by manipulating tape. Today electronic music is created using digital recording technology.

FEATURES TO LISTEN FOR

1. The beauty of the polished, pure quality of the boys' unchanged voices singing the opening part of Rutter's "Open Thou Mine Eyes." Also listen for the clear, impeccable singing of the entire choral group, which consists of men and boys.

2. Notice that "Open Thou Mine Eyes" begins in monophonic texture. The texture becomes homophonic at 0:29 in the work.

3. Listen for the return of the opening melody after a period of contrasting music.

Concert Attendance Tips

Students in music appreciation courses usually attend concerts as a part of the course work. Here are a few tips about attending concerts.

Types of Concerts

Recitals are usually for two to five performers in a medium-sized room or hall. They usually last about one hour or so.

Song recitals involve one singer with piano accompaniment in a medium-sized room or hall. Songs are quite often in a foreign language.

Large ensemble concerts are for large groups such as bands, orchestras, and choral groups. Because many performers are involved, they are held in large concert halls or auditoriums. They are usually longer than recitals.

(continued)

Operas are dramas in which all the words are sung. In addition, they include scenery, costumes, and actions, and the singers are accompanied by an orchestra. Many operas are in foreign languages, but simultaneous translations are sometimes run on a screen above the stage. Many operas last for two or more hours. They are performed in concert halls or opera houses.

Popular music concerts can be held most any place, ranging from small auditoriums to stadiums and other outdoor venues. Almost all the music at these concerts is miked, and the performances are very casual, often with a little audience participation.

Audience Conduct

The main purpose of attending any concert is to listen carefully and attentively to the music being performed. Therefore, there should be no distractions such as:

- talking or whispering
- shuffling programs or other objects
- eating or drinking

Applause at instrumental concerts is appropriate at the end of every work, but only after the final movement of a multi-movement work. Applause is expected after sizable solos or duets in operas and musicals and after solos at concerts of popular music. Sometimes at the conclusion of an outstanding concert, the audience will give the performers a standing ovation. If you aren't sure about what to do, wait to see what the rest of audience does before starting to applaud or stand.

Often a performing group will perform an extra piece or two in response to the applause of the audience. Such pieces, called *encores,* are short and attractive. They are announced verbally.

Performance Customs

Soloists often memorize their music so that they are not distracted with turning pages and will have a more direct rapport with the audience. Accompanists in recitals do not memorize their music and may have someone turn pages for them. Performers in stage productions must, of course, memorize their music as well as their movements on stage. Because of the number and character of the parts in chamber and orchestral music, such music is rarely memorized. Conductors sometimes conduct without the music in front of them. This does not mean they have memorized every part. Rather, they know the work in a general way, which is adequate for conducting it in a performance.

Orchestra and band concerts tend to follow certain customs. Because the conductor is the leader of the ensemble, he or she is treated with special respect. The conductor is the last to enter the stage and the first to leave when a lengthy work is completed. The audience applauds when the conductor enters. After a work is completed, the conductor often recognizes the efforts of the musicians by shaking hands with the first-chair violinist, in the case of a symphony orchestra. This player sits at the front of the violin section and is referred to as the concertmaster or concertmistress.

Soloists are special guests, so they are treated with even more deference than the conductor. They precede the conductor on and off the stage and receive applause on their own.

The concertmaster follows another tradition by being the last player to enter before the conductor. He or she points to the various sections of the orchestra, and they play a long tone to tune their instruments to the standard pitch of A440. The random sounds made by the musicians prior to that time are just their informal warming up.

Professional orchestras and bands have no systematic procedure for coming on stage. Some choral groups, however, enter row by row.

Orchestral players wear black suits or dresses. Singers in choral groups wear robes or black suits and dresses, except when performing "lighter," more popular music.

The Printed Program

People attending a recital or concert are usually given a program listing the music that will be performed. Rarely are the musical works announced from the stage, except in the case of popular music. The program sometimes contains many advertisements, which give people who arrive early something to read and provide income for the performing group.

On one side of the page, usually the left, the program lists the titles of the compositions. On the opposite side it lists the names of the composers or arrangers. Titles in foreign languages are often not translated. Each movement of a multi-movement instrumental work is usually listed by its tempo (traditionally in Italian) and is indented and placed below the title.

Programs for song recitals list each song by title and composer. Opera programs look more like a program booklet for a play, listing acts and scenes, as well as a synopsis of the story. Programs sometimes contain notes and narrative material interspersed among the ads. These remarks may be helpful, but sometimes they are written in a complex style using language that nonmusicians find difficult to understand.

Dress Up for Concerts?

The idea of people attending concerts wearing fancy clothes has long since passed. Usually it is enough to wear nice, clean clothes. Shorts, tank tops, flip flops, and such should be avoided. Dress for evening concerts is usually more formal than for an event that takes place during the daytime. Dress for popular music concerts can be very informal.

Preparation for a Concert

In one sense, you don't need to prepare for a concert. All you need do is attend, listen attentively, and enjoy it. But you will find it more satisfying if you know what works will be performed. Then you can check in your textbook to see if the work might be described in it, or at least the composer of the work discussed. A little knowledge beforehand will help you better understand what you will hear. It will also help you in writing a report of the concert, in case that should be needed.

Don't let concerns about inadequate musical knowledge prevent you from attending and enjoying concerts or recitals. The enjoyment is not the same as going to a sports event or a theme park. It's different. Attending a concert is more subtle, more thoughtful, more lasting, more refined. Going to a performance can be an enriching experience in your life, and it can provide you with something that can't be achieved in any other way.

PART II

Early, Medieval, and Renaissance Music

	1000 BC	1 AD	500
Historical Events	● Early Hellenic civilization (1100 BC)	Roman Empire (c. 500 BC–476)	Charlemagne (747–814)
	● Greek city-states (800 BC–476)	● Birth of Jesus (1 AD)	Feudalism (9th–14th centuries)
	Golden Age of Athens (5th cent. BC)	Separation of Eastern ● and Western Empires (476)	● Rome falls (476)
Visual Arts		● Parthenon built in Athens (top right) (447–432 BC)	
		Myron, *Discus Thrower* (c. 450 BC)	
		Colosseum built in Rome (70–80)	
Literature and Theater	● Homer, *Iliad and Odyssey* (c. 750 BC)		
	Dionysian festivals (c. 200 BC)		
	Sophocles, *Oedipus Rex* (c. 429 BC)		
		Cicero (106–43 BC), Virgil (70–19 BC), Plutarch (46–120)	
Philosophy and Science	Socrates (469–399 BC), Plato (c. 427–347 BC)		Boethius (c. 480–525)
	Aristotle (384–322 BC)		
Music	Pythagoras discovers acoustical ratios (555 BC)		Pope Gregory codifies liturgy and chant (c. 600) ●
	Plato advocates music for all citizens (c. 360 BC)		

Mary Evans Picture Library/The Image Works

Robert Harding Picture Library Ltd/Alamy

The Bridgeman Art Library

| 00 | 1450 | 1500 | 1550 | 1600 |

Papal schism (1378–1417)

Copernicus (1473–1543)

Council of Trent (1545–1563)

rusades (1096–1270)

niversities founded 088)

"Black Death" (mid 1300s)

Exploration of New World (early 15th cent.–early 17th cent.)

Spanish Armada defeated (1588)

Magna Carta signed (1215)

Gutenberg invents movable type (1439)

Luther initiates Reformation (1517)

Great cathedrals constructed

Ghiberti (1378–1455)

Dürer etchings (1496–1514)

Leonardo, *Mona Lisa* (1503–1506)

St. Peter's built in Rome (1506–1626)

Giotto, *Madonna . . .* (c. 1305–1310)

Van Eyck, *Arnolfini Marriage* (1434)

Michelangelo, *David* (near right) (1501–1504)

Donatello (c. 1386–1466)

Botticelli, *Adoration of the Magi* (1475)

Brueghel, *Landscape with Fall of Icarus* (c. 1555)

Titian, *St. John, the Baptist* (c. 1540)

Dante, *The Divine Comedy* (1308–1321)

Rabelais (1494?–1553)

Ariosto, *Orlando Furioso* (1591)

Marlowe, *Essays* (1586–1593)

Boccaccio, *Decameron* (c. 1350–1353)

Spenser (1552–1599)

Chaucer, *The Canterbury Tales* (1387–1400)

Shakespeare, *Romeo and Juliet* (1595)

belard (1079–1142)

Erasmus, *In Praise of Folly* (1511)

Thomas Aquinas, *Summa Theologica* (1225–1274)

Machiavelli, *The Prince* (1513)

More, *Utopia*

Luther, *Ninety-five Theses* (1517)

Hildegard, *Ordo virtutum* (left) (c. 1130)

Bass voice part introduced
Josquin, *Pange lingua Mass* (1515)

Organum develops (c. 1000)

First music book published (1501)

Motets begin at Notre Dame (c. 1250)

Palestrina, "Sicut cervus" (c. 1577)

Weelkes, "As Vesta . . ." (1590)

7 Early Western Music

There has always been music. Every civilization throughout recorded history and every tribe, even in the remotest parts of the world, had and still has some form of music. We know this because pictures from the various times and places show people singing or playing instruments, and writers have described music and music making. Often, musical traditions have been passed from one generation to another for as long as anyone can determine.

But there is a problem: No one really knows what this music sounded like until the advent of the phonograph and sound recording, which wasn't available until about a hundred or so years ago. Music notation didn't develop to anywhere near its present state until the fifteenth century, and it has been used mostly for concert and church music, which is part of the reason it receives the greater share of attention in music courses. It's difficult to devote much attention to music that no one is really sure how it sounds.

ANCIENT GREEK AND ROMAN TIMES

"Western civilization" is a broad concept consisting of the culture that developed in ancient Greece and then spread throughout Europe and eventually to North and South America. It includes political and religious beliefs, laws, customs, and arts. Traditionally, the contrasts with the Eastern civilizations of the Middle East and Asia were considerable, although they are rapidly being diminished today.

From about 800 BC to the fall of the Roman Empire in AD 476, Western civilization was dominated by various city-states around the Mediterranean Sea. The first were the cities of Greece, especially Athens. Then came the Roman Empire, which dominated most of the known world from the Middle East to England. Although both Greece and Rome were replaced, they left their imprint in architecture, literature, and ways of thinking. In fact, about fifteen hundred years in the future these civilizations would be considered by educated persons as a high point to be greatly admired and copied.

Greek civilization reached its acme in Athens in the fifth century BC. It produced astounding accomplishments for its time. Its architecture can be seen in countless buildings even today. Great works of sculpture were created. Philosophy flourished with Socrates, Plato, and Aristotle, who also is often credited with starting scientific thinking. Great poets such as Homer and dramatists such as Sophocles were active. The ancient Athenians were far ahead of their contemporaries in their type of government, which had the citizens meet and vote in civic matters. Greek religious beliefs revolved around a pantheon of gods and goddesses.

The Greeks, especially those living in Athens during the Golden Age of Pericles, valued music very much. The philosopher Plato (c. 427–347 BC) considered music an essential part of the education of all citizens. One reason for his advocacy of music was his belief that music influenced moral character. The idea that music could influence human behavior largely disappeared with ancient Greek civilization, but remnants of it in various guises are still with us today.

About 555 BC, Pythagoras found that the vibrations of certain intervals—the distances from one pitch to another—can be represented in mathematical ratios. As was characteristic of the Greeks at the time, he ascribed philosophical qualities to the ratios, calling those with simple ratios such as 2:1 and 3:2 "perfect." The ancient Greeks also developed several musical instruments. One of these was the harplike lyre, which is often seen as a musical emblem today.

The term *Western music* does not refer to music in the western part of the United States!

The word *democracy* comes from the Greek word *demos,* meaning "people."

Unfortunately, the development of good character cannot be achieved that easily!

Pythagoras is well known for his contributions to geometry and the theorem named for him.

Robert Harding Picture Library Ltd/Alamy

THE PARTHENON The Greeks
built this celebrated temple
for the goddess Athena in the
fifth century BC. It defines
the classical style still seen in
architecture today.

Music was found in many Greek dramas, too. The chorus did not sing, however; instead, it chanted in a singsong style. Poets such as Homer sang their epic tales in singsong fashion, perhaps accompanied by a simple harplike instrument.

The Roman Republic followed, and the Romans simply took over much of what the earlier Greeks had done. They even adopted and expanded on their religious beliefs but renamed the gods. The Romans were militarily strong. They managed an empire that stretched for a thousand or more miles around the Mediterranean Sea. Holding such a huge empire together was quite an accomplishment when there was no communication faster than a man on a horse. But the character and quality of the Roman Empire deteriorated over the centuries, and it collapsed more than it fell to the invading Vandals and Visigoths from the north.

The Romans had music, too. Probably most of it was taken over from the Greeks. The Romans emphasized military music more than the Greeks did.

Zeus, king of the gods, became
Jupiter; and Athena, goddess of the
arts, became Minerva.

Scala/Art Resource, Inc.

THE MIDDLE AGES

With the fall of the Roman Empire in AD 476, Western civilization slipped into what some historians call the "Dark Ages." For more than five hundred years following the fall of Rome, life in the Middle Ages centered around the manor and the monasteries. A system of feudalism bound peasants to the land and to the lord of the manor. People did not place a great emphasis on life, because they thought that either Jesus would come again and bring a new era or they would soon have a better life after they died. It is hard for us living in America today to understand the hold that otherworldly concerns had on many people during that time, but the impact of this attitude was profound. It is difficult for us to imagine how different and arduous life was for people in the Middle Ages. In short, for most people it was grim.

MUSIC AND THE ARTS during the Middle
Ages were devoted to the worship of God.
Books were handlettered and decorated by
monks, as shown in this capital C for *Cantate
Domino* ("Sing to the Lord").

Monasteries dotted the countryside throughout Europe and England. These monasteries preserved the writings and culture of the ancient world. But there was little interest in the civilizations of the Greeks and Romans, which were considered pagan and to be avoided.

MUSIC IN THE MIDDLE AGES

Christianity had no standard musical practices for its first three centuries. It adopted some aspects of Judaism, including daily prayer hours and the reciting of psalms between the leader and congregation. As the Church expanded throughout Asia Minor into Europe, it adopted other musical practices.

Slowly, the Church at Rome became predominant, and the bishop of Rome became the pope. In an effort to bring order to worship practices, about the sixth century Pope Gregory I directed that the Church's worship and music be codified. Although Gregory I was not a musician himself, the music that resulted is known as Gregorian chant. The Church now had a **liturgy**—a body of rites prescribed for worship. The most important and frequent service is the **Mass,** which is described in the enrichment box, "The Mass and Its Music."

The Mass and Its Music

The Mass is central in the Roman Catholic Church. It is a ceremony that reaffirms in a symbolic way the connection between the believers and Jesus Christ through the reenactment of the Last Supper (Eucharist, or Holy Communion) with the sharing of bread and wine and the miracle of that event.

Michael Newman/PhotoEdit

The term *Mass* comes from the Latin phrase that ends the service: "Ite missa est." The Mass may be spoken or sung, but in the United States today it is largely spoken.

The Mass contains several parts. Some portions vary according to the particular day in the Church year. These parts are called the **Proper,** because they are proper for a certain day in the Church calendar. Some parts are repeated in each Mass; these are called the **Ordinary,** because they are ordinarily included. The sections of the Ordinary are as follows.

Kyrie This is a short prayer using Greek words instead of the usual Latin. The text means, "Lord, have mercy on us; Christ, have mercy on us."

Gloria This section offers praise to God in Latin with the words, "Glory to God on high."

Credo This rather long statement of belief in Latin ("We believe in one God, . . .") is recited or sung in a reciting style.

Sanctus This follows the consecration of the elements when the priest raises the bread and wine for everyone to see. The Sanctus begins with the words, "Holy, holy, holy."

Agnus Dei This section is based on the Latin words that mean "Lamb of God, who takes away the sins of the world, have mercy on us and grant us peace."

Because the Ordinary appears in all Masses, it has been selected by many composers over the centuries as the text for musical works. Ludwig van Beethoven, Wolfgang Amadeus Mozart, and Franz Joseph Haydn—and Igor Stravinsky in the twentieth century—have composed "concert" Masses not intended for use in worship services. Giovanni Pierluigi da Palestrina and other composers of the sixteenth century composed shorter Masses for worship purposes.

A **Requiem** is a Mass for the dead. It omits the Gloria and Credo but adds a section called **Dies irae** ("Day of wrath"), referring to the day of final judgment.

Until Vatican Council II (1964–1967), the Roman Catholic Church specified the content and words for every service, which are in Latin. Since then, more freedom has been permitted, however, and vernacular (non-Latin) languages are now used. Unfortunately, most chants and music for Masses lose their impact when translated, so much of the inspiring traditional music is no longer heard today.

Gregorian Chant

Gregorian chant is very different from the music you usually hear today. Its features include:

- Nonmetrical rhythm: Although there are groups of notes, you will have no inclination to tap your foot as you hear it.
- Monophonic texture: There is no harmony.
- Smooth contour: Its notes generally move by step to the next note.
- *Modal* scales: The melodies generally do not follow the familiar major or minor scale patterns.
- A reverent and restrained mood: No attempt is made to reach out and grab the listener.
- The texts are in Church Latin, not English.
- The texts are sung only by monks and priests.

Gregorian chant is not concert music. Its goal is to contribute to worship. This it does for persons who understand its attributes.

The music example on these pages is the "Dies irae" from the funeral or Requiem Mass. It is probably the best-known line of chant, especially its first several notes, because of its use to represent death or evil by many composers in the nineteenth century. The music is shown in two versions. One is the traditional four-line staff and square notes of the Roman Catholic Church in medieval times. The other shows the pitches of the chant on a five-line staff.

The fact that the early Church included singing in its worship is recorded in Matthew 26:30, Mark 14:26, and other, nonbiblical writings.

Gregorian chant is also known as **plainsong** or **plainchant**.

In 1994 a recording of chant by the monks at the monastery of Santo Domingo de Silos in Spain became the fastest-selling classical CD in history. It sold more than two million copies and reached number five on the U.S. pop charts. The monks used the royalties to help the needy in Third World countries and for badly needed repairs to the twelfth-century monastery.

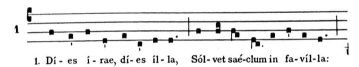

1. Dí - es í - rae, dí - es íl - la, Sól - vet saé-clum in fa - víl-la:

Gregorian musical notation of the Middle Ages

ANONYMOUS
"Dies irae" (opening) (c. 600)

GENRE: Gregorian chant   Unaccompanied vocal

CD 1 Track 15

1 minute 2 seconds

Form: *a a b b*

		Latin	English
0:00 15	0:00	Dies irae, dies illa Solvet saeclum in favilla, Teste David sum Sibylla.	Day of wrath, that day the world will dissolve into ashes, as witness David and the Sibyl.
	0:14	Quantus tremor est futurus, Quando Judex est venturus, Cuncta stricte discussurus!	What trembling there will be when the Judge shall come; all shall thoroughly be shattered!
	0:28	Tuba mirum spargens sonum Per sepulchra regionem, Coget omnesante thronum.	The wondrous trumpet, spreading its sound to the tombs of all regions, will gather all before the throne.
	0:45	Mors stupebit et natura, Cum resurget creatura Judicanti responsura.	Death will be stupefied, also nature, when all creation arises again to answer to the Judge.
	1:02	Recording fades as "Dies irae" continues.	

 An interactive Active Listening Guide can be downloaded from the online Resource Center for *Music Listening Today, 4th Edition*.

The same phrase in modern music notation

Hildegard's *Ordo virtutum*

The Virtues are Knowledge of God, Humility, Discipline, Compassion, Mercy, Victory, Discretion, Patience, Charity, Obedience, Faith, Hope, Chastity, Innocence, World Rejection, and Heavenly Love.

The devil does not get to sing. Instead, he talks.

Most of the creators of Gregorian chant are anonymous. Humility was a virtue in the Middle Ages, especially among the religious men and women. One composer of chant who is known was a remarkable woman named Hildegard of Bingen.

Hildegard's *Ordo virtutum* (*Play of the Virtues*) is a morality play, probably written for the dedication of a convent church. In the play, a soul gives in to the temptations of the devil. The soul is saved through the intervention of the sixteen virtues.

The work contains about eighty chantlike melodies. All the parts were sung by nuns, except the role of the devil, which was played by a priest. Little except the vocal music has survived from most of these medieval plays. Performances today require some creativity in terms of the instruments and staging used.

LISTENING GUIDE

HILDEGARD OF BINGEN
Ordo virtutum, excerpt from Scene 4 (c. 1150)

GENRE: Morality play   Unaccompanied vocal

CD 3 Tracks 7 – 8

3 minutes 42 seconds

	Latin	English
		Devil
0:00 7 0:00	Que es, aut unde venis? Tu amplexata es me, et ego foras eduxi te. Sed nunc inreversione tua confundis me— ego autem pugna mea deician te!	Who are you, where do you come from? You were in my embrace, I led you out. Yet now you are going back, defying me— But I shall fight you and defeat you!
		Penitent Soul
0:22	Ego omnes vias meas malas esse cognovi, et ideo fugi a te. Modo autem, o illusor, pugno contra te. Ine tu, o regina Humilitas, tua medicamine adiuva me!	I realize that all my ways were wicked, so I fled from you. But now, you fraud, I'll fight you face to face. Come, Queen Humility, with your medicine give me aid!
		Humility (to Victory)
1:30	O Victoria, que istum in celo superasti, · curre cum militibus tuis et omnes ligate. Diabolum hunc!	O Victory, you who once bested this in the heavens. run now, with all your military manner, and all of you, tie up this fiend!
		Victory (to the Virtues)
2:01 8 0:00	O fortissimi et gloriosissimi milites, venite, et adiuvate me istum fallacem vincere.	Most brave and glorious warriors, come, and help me to eliminate this false one.
		The Virtues
0:31	O dulcissima bellatrix, in torrente fonte torrentqui absorbuit lupum rapacem— o gloriosa coronata, nos libenter militamus tecum contra illusorem hunc.	O sweetest warrior, in the scorching that swallowed up the rapacious wolf— o glorious crowned one, how freely we will fight at your side against the faker.
		Humility (to the Virtues)
1:10	Ligate ergo istum, o Virtutes preclare!	Tie him up then, you shining virtues!

1:27	O regina nostra, tibi parebimus, et precepta tua in omnibus adimplebimus.	O our queen, we obey you, and we will follow your orders completely.
1:48	Excerpt concludes.	

 An interactive Active Listening Guide can be downloaded from the online Resource Center for *Music Listening Today, 4th Edition.*

Hildegard of Bingen

Mary Evans Picture Library/The Image Works

Hildegard of Bingen (1098–1179) was a powerful abbess; she was also a theologian, naturalist, healer, poet, and musician, and she wrote extensively in these fields. She considered herself an instrument through which God spoke in visions. She was born the tenth child of a noble German family. At the age of eight, she was given to a group of nuns and raised in a Benedictine monastery. During her adult life, she led religious communities for women, first at Disibodenberg and later at Rupertsberg near present-day Bingen. Hildegard used her prominent position with the Church to improve both her own position and that of the women in her charge.

Giving a son or daughter to the Church was a common practice at that time.

MAIN POINTS OF THIS CHAPTER

1. Western civilization and its music developed over 2,500 years ago in the city-states around the Mediterranean, especially Athens. Pythagoras found that the vibrations for certain musical intervals have simple ratios such as 2:1 and 3:2.

2. The only music preserved in written form from ancient times is Gregorian chant. It was the basis for the Mass in the Christian Church. Many of the practices of the early Church such as daily prayer hours grew out of Judaism.

3. Certain Gregorian chants are designated for particular days in the Church calendar, and these chants are called the Proper of the Mass. The Ordinary of the Mass is sung or said at nearly all Masses. It consists of five parts: Kyrie, Gloria, Credo, Sanctus, and Agnus Dei. The text of the Ordinary is what many composers have set to music.

4. The Requiem is the funeral Mass. It includes the "Dies irae" chant, which means "Day of Wrath," referring to the final judgment.

5. The music of Gregorian chant is monophonic, sung unaccompanied in Latin by monks and priests, and has no metrical rhythm. It is intended for worship, not for concert performances.

6. A number of morality plays with music were created to educate listeners about the Christian faith. The music for these plays is similar to Gregorian chant in character.

FEATURES TO LISTEN FOR

1. The reverent, restrained nature of the generally stepwise melodies heard in Gregorian chant.

2. The character of the music sung without accompaniment or metrical rhythm. Notice also that the music is not built around the major and minor keys familiar to us today.

3. The freer style of Gregorian chant found in morality plays. It is sung by both men and women and may be accompanied by an instrument.

Medieval Music

Change came very slowly in the Middle Ages. The Holy Roman Empire ruled over much of central Europe, but Europe was actually a loose confederation of many small states. People lived mostly in small rural communities, often called manors. Communication and travel were difficult and slow, accomplished on foot or on horseback. So what was true in one place could be unheard of only fifty miles away.

MEDIEVAL TIMES

Although very gradual, changes did take place in society and in music. There were several catalysts toward a more enlightened outlook: increased contacts with the Byzantine civilization to the east, better economic conditions and trade, and the influence of education in the monasteries.

The period from about 1100 to 1450 has come to be known as the medieval, or sometimes the Gothic, period. These centuries were marked by continued progress away from the otherworldly outlook that was so strong during the preceding thousand years. The major intellectual movement of the time was Scholasticism, a highly organized and systematic philosophy culminating in the *Summa Theologica* (*Summary of Theology*) by Saint Thomas Aquinas (1225–1274).

The medieval period rejected the absolute power of kings, a rejection that encouraged the signing of the Magna Carta in England in 1215.

Another feature of the medieval period was chivalry, which glorified women and idealized kindness and refined manners. There was an emphasis on the community—the guild, the Church, or the feudal manor; individualism was not encouraged. Many works of art and music were created by artists who did not attach their names to their creations and whose identities are not known.

The medieval period saw the founding of universities. It was also the time when many of the great cathedrals were built. Literary accomplishments were achieved in this period with the poems of the troubadours, the romantic legends of a Celtic chieftain named Arthur, and *The Divine Comedy* by Dante Alighieri.

Giotto's *Madonna and Child* (page 66) has a planned, posed look. This work from the fourteenth century was originally part of a polyptych, or series, of paintings. Several points are worth noting about this painting.

First, it was part of a *polyptych*, which contains the same stem word as *polyphony*, a feature of medieval and Renaissance music. Second, it has a flat, two-dimensional look; only a little shading was used to outline the figures. Third, the outline of the *Madonna and Child* is in a three-quarter position and creates an elegant Gothic shape broken only by the almost geometric figure. Fourth, the hands and faces are not very lifelike. The Madonna's hand looks as though it could be attached to a mannequin. Fifth, the painting is not very realistic: The Child has a mature face and body for an infant; he is also far too big to be held with one arm. Sixth, the gold background shows the influence of Byzantine or eastern European art. But whatever its limitations, it is nevertheless a compelling work of art.

POLYPHONY

Gregorian chant was monophonic, with only a single line of melody. How did music move beyond that to polyphony? Probably at first the Church musicians simply added a second line of music that moved in strict parallel motion with the original line,

The use of the word *Gothic* to designate a particular artistic or musical style has little to do with its use in describing a mystery or horror story.

Chivalry probably existed more as an ideal in literary works than in real life.

MADONNA AND CHILD by Giotto di Bondone. This early Renaissance painting still contains elements of the Gothic style in its shape and two-dimensional look, but it also foretells intellectual qualities found in the music of Josquin and Palestrina.

Kress Collection, Washington, D.C./The Bridgeman Art Library

A **drone** is a steady, continuous sound.

somewhat as the two front wheels on a car move exactly parallel to each other. Scholars suspect that initially such parallel lines, called *organum*, were sung without actually being written down. Some of the monks and priests probably tried singing the same line of chant at different pitch levels. Examples of organum began to appear in notation about AD 1000, and at first the added line matched the original chant note for note. But organum in strict parallel motion is not polyphony.

Gradually, the second part of organum began to show more independence, which marks the beginning of polyphony. Sometimes it would move for a note or two in the opposite direction. Over the years, the second line became even more independent by having several notes to the one note in the original line.

As the idea of polyphony developed, the notes of original Gregorian chant were made longer, sometimes to the point of sounding almost like a drone. The long-note values of the chant became so extended that the chant melody was hardly recognizable, which did not seem to bother the creators of this music. Perhaps they justified this practice because they knew that the music was still based on chant. And the second part, with its several moving notes, certainly did give the music a richer and more interesting quality than that of the original monophonic chant. Shortly before AD 1200 organum became even more interesting when musicians added two lines above the original line of chant. Eventually, a few works included four lines to be sung simultaneously.

This more complex organum was developed at the Cathedral of Notre Dame in Paris by two composers whose names are known: Léonin (active from about 1150 to 1201) and his successor, Pérotin (c. 1160–1236).

Notre Dame means "Our Lady" in Latin and refers to the Virgin Mary.

PÉROTIN'S "ALLELUIA, DIFFUSA EST GRATIA"

Many pieces of music were created to express adoration for the Virgin Mary. In this work, the chant is presented in the usual monophonic texture of Gregorian chant.

The complete work is longer than can be presented here. The "Alleluia" section comes back twice in the complete work. The word "Alleluia" is sung with several notes for each syllable, which was probably intended to give the sense of spiritual joy. It consists of four phrases. The first, having the most notes, is repeated the first time it's heard. The second phrase reaches the highest pitch level, and the fourth is calmer and has a narrower range.

The organum opens with quite long notes before the upper parts begin singing several notes on each syllable of the word "Diffusa" and the words that follow. The lowest line, called the *cantus firmus*, sounds the notes of the chant in long-note values. It became the structure around which the notes of the moving parts are constructed.

By the thirteenth century, another feature had been added to organum: somewhat regular rhythmic patterns. Composers grouped notes into six long-and-short note patterns that are roughly equivalent to the metrical patterns used in analyzing metrical patterns in poetry. For example, ♩♪ is trochaic meter, whereas ♪♩ is iambic meter, and so on. These patterns (called **rhythmic modes**) helped to keep the polyphonic lines of music together, as well as add variety to the music. Notice that the "Alleluia" part of Pérotin's organum is sung without a metrical pattern, whereas the word "Diffusa" begins a section with a somewhat steady rhythmic pattern.

The music notation did not contain bar lines. The patterns were indicated by brackets called *ligatures*.

PÉROTIN
"Alleluia, Diffusa est gratia" (c. 1190)

GENRE: Organum   Unaccompanied vocal

CD 3 Tracks 10 – 12

4 minutes 40 seconds

				Latin	English
0:00	10	0:00	Chant	Alleluia, Alleluia —	Hallelujah
0:37	11	0:00	Organum	Diffusa, est gratia in labiis tuis; *proterea benedixit te deus*	Grace has been poured upon your lips; therefore, God has blessed you
2:37	12	0:00		in aeternum.	eternally.
		1:03	Chant	Alleluia, Alleluia	Hallelujah, Hallelujah

 An interactive Active Listening Guide can be downloaded from the online Resource Center for *Music Listening Today, 4th Edition.*

Léonin and Pérotin had at least three things in common. One is that we know very little about them. Second, much of what we do know comes from one source, Anonymous IV, who was a student from England at the University of Paris with a particular interest in music. Third, they were tremendously important composers at the Cathedral of Notre Dame in Paris.

Not only are we unsure of when they were born and died, but even their names had varied forms. Léonin was also know as Leoninus, Magister Leoninus, Magister Leonius, and Leo. The word *magister* is a title indicating that he had earned a master's degree. He was also a priest, poet, and high-ranking official in the cathedral. He was active there from about 1150 until 1201.

Humility was a virtue during medieval times, as was mentioned in the discussion of Hildegard's Ordo virtutum. Artists and musicians believed that their efforts were for the glory of God. Personal recognition was not considered proper or important. Thus, we know little about them as individuals.

His book of organum, *Magnum liber organi*, contains about one hundred pieces of two-part organum. He composed this music to make the worship services on special days such as Christmas and Easter more outstanding. This music also provides evidence that sometimes the notes were organized into units of twos or threes—the rhythmic modes mentioned in conjunction with the presentation of Pérotin's "Alleluia." Although these were not measures as

Matthew Richardson/Alamy

GARGOYLE on Notre Dame Cathedral in Paris

we know them today, this was an important first step in organizing rhythm.

Pérotin (c. 1160–c. 1236) was also known as Perrotinus, Perotinus Magnus, and Magister Perotinus. He was probably Léonin's successor at Notre Dame. Anonymous IV names seven compositions by him, but undoubtedly there were many more. Whereas Léonin composed for only two voices, Pérotin wrote for three or four voices, something that had almost never been done before. To keep that many parts together required the further development of rhythm. Although the chant-based tenor part usually retains its long notes, the upper two or three parts follow strict rhythmic patterns. His works tend to be more sectional, with shorter complementary units. The tenor also moves in strict rhythm in some of these short sections.

Léonin, Pérotin, and their colleagues created a huge body of music, probably more than one thousand pieces, which later historians have labeled the "Notre Dame School." The University of Paris attracted many students, who learned not only theology but also the music sung in the cathedral. They then spread its features throughout France and the rest of Europe.

These intervals are the same ones Pythagoras considered to be consonant, and they are the most prominent ones in the overtone series.

In these early versions of polyphony, pitches an octave apart and four and five notes apart were considered to be consonant. The interval of a third, which has been the basis for most harmony for the past several hundred years, was regarded as dissonant. That interval was, however, found in the secular music of the time, especially in England. It would be nearly 350 years after Léonin before chords containing thirds would be considered consonant enough to appear in the important final chord of a musical work.

THE MOTET

Polyphony also found its way into secular music in the form of the *motet*. Actually, the motet was a combination of Gregorian chant and secular music that was sung in the courts, not churches. Its religious component was the use of phrases from Gregorian chant as one of its lines of melody as the *cantus firmus*.

The secular element in the motet was its use of texts, often about love, that were in vernacular languages, usually French. In contrast to the *cantus firmus*, these voice parts were quite rhythmic and not based on Gregorian chant. The structure consisted of the *cantus firmus* and two or more lines sounding at the same time.

The lines above the *cantus firmus* included many sophisticated composing techniques. For example, twice as many notes might be used in one of the added voice parts as in another part. A musical phrase might be split up so that one part would sing a couple of notes and then the other part would take up the next couple of notes, only to return to the first voice part and back to the other part in order to complete a melodic phrase. This device was called a *hocket*. Another compositional technique was the use of identical rhythms with different melodies, which is called *isorhythm*. Such complexities are difficult to hear in the music; actually, they can usually be observed only in the written notation. It was a highly intellectual approach to composing music.

The best-known composer of isorhythmic motets in the fourteenth century was Guillaume de Machaut (Ma-show, c. 1300–1377). His motet "Quant en moi" is typical of the genre. The *cantus firmus* is sung in long note values. Each of the two voice parts sings a different poem. Machaut composed different music for each stanza of the poem. He also used several hockets, and the first voice part has twice the number of notes that the second voice part has. The motet also contains some short abrupt starts and stops.

GUILLAUME DE MACHAUT
Motet: "Quant en moi"

CD 3 Track 13

2 minutes 16 seconds

The two singers begin together, and they sing the words for their stanzas at the same time. The examples of hocket are indented and positioned in the same order in which they are sung.

13 **0:00** **Stanza 1: Voice 1**

Quant en moi vint premierement	When I was first visited by
Amours, si tres doucettement	Love, he so very sweetly
Me vost mon cuer enamourer	Captured my heart;
Que d'un regart me fist present,	A glance at what he gave me as a gift,
Et tres amoureus sentiment	And along with loving feelings
Me donna avuec doulz penser,	He presented me with this thought:

Verse 1

Es - poir   d'av - ior

Doubt - er   cel - er

Espoir	*d'avoir*	To hope	to have
Merci sans refuser		Grace, and no rejections	
Mais onques en tout mon vivant		But never in my entire life	
Hardement ne me vost donner.		Was confidence a gift he meant for me.	

Voice 2

Amour et biauté parfaite.	Thanks to love and ultimate beauty.

Doubter	*celer*	Fearing	acting
Me font parfaitement.		Are what consume me completely.	

0:32 **Stanza 2: Voice 1**

E si me fait en desirant	And if, in my passion,
Penser si amoureusement	He makes me think so amorously
Que, par force de desirer,	Thanks, to desire
Ma joie convient en tourment	My joy turns into torment—
Muer, se je n'ay hardement.	Must turn, since I am not confident.
Last et je n'en puis recouvrer,	Alas! I cannot save myself—

Verse 2

Qu'a - mours   se - cours

De vous   cuer doulz

Qu'amours	*secours*	For Love	no help
Ne me vuer nul prester,		Will lend me—	
Qui en ses las si durement		Love, who holds me so tightly	
Me tient que n'en puis eschaper.		In his grasp that I cannot escape.	

Voice 2

Et vrais desire, qui m'a a fait	And true desire, that has made me

De vous	*cuer doulz*	Love you	dear heart
Amer sans finement.		For ever and ever.	

1:03 **Stanza 3**

1:38 **Stanza 4**

An interactive Active Listening Guide can be downloaded from the online Resource Center for *Music Listening Today, 4th Edition.*

Guillaume de Machaut (1300–1377), poet and musician, writing "Les Nouveaus Dis Amoureus." 14th century miniature. Ms Fr. 22546, Fol. 74./Bibliotheque Nationale, Paris, France/Snark/Art Resource, NY

Guillame de Machaut

Machaut was born about 1300 near Rheims, France. For twenty years he served as secretary to the count of Luxemburg and then King John of Bohemia; he also became a priest. After King John was killed in battle, Machaut, whose services were in much demand by then, worked for various aristocrats and rulers. He was released from priestly duties by Pope Benedict II in 1346.

He survived the plague that swept through Europe in the middle of the four-teenth century and lived the remainder of his life in Rheims, composing music and writing more than four hundred poems. He may have composed the first complete setting of the Ordinary of the Mass. His influence was extensive in the many forms of sacred and secular music he com-posed. His death in 1377 was recognized in elegies by several composers.

SECULAR MUSIC

Much of the secular vocal music was performed by wandering musician-entertainers who traveled from place to place singing songs, reciting poems, and even exhibiting trained animals. Later, troubadours dominated secular vocal music in France. They were noble-men who were poets and composers, but usually not performers; they hired minstrels to sing their songs. About 4,000 poems and 1,600 melodies have been preserved. They were for solo voice and may have been accompanied by a mandola, or similar instrument, shown in the *Goddess of Music* painting (page 71) from a medieval manuscript.

Almost all marriages at the time were arranged by the families. Brides were usually in their middle teens.

Provence is in southern France.

Most troubadours were men, but a few were women, with trobairitz used to designate females. One of these was Beatrix de Dia. What little is known about her is that she became Countess of Dia as the wife of the Count of Poitiers. She was also a lover of a troubadour gentleman, Raimbaut d'Orange. She composed a number of poems and songs in Occitan (Provençal), of which only a few have survived.

The text of "A chantar" ("I must sing") tells of a frustrated love, which was a popular topic of troubadour poems. For that reason, Beatrix de Dia may not have been express-ing her own personal feelings in this song. The music is strophic, with its five stanzas of the poem. The basic pitches, the ones that Beatrix composed, are freely decorated by the singer on the recording on the ancillary CD. Troubadours in the twelfth century often exercised liberties in performing their songs. "A chantar" has no metrical rhythm, with the basic pitches of the melody being about equal in length. The recording presents the initial lines of "A chantar."

BEATRIX DE DIA

"A chantar" (excerpt)

CD 3 Track 9

Total time: 1:17

9	0:00	Vielle (a medieval bowed string instrument) plays introduction.
	0:25	The singer begins:

A chantar m'er de so q'ieu no voldria,
Tant me raneur de lui cui sui amia.

I must sing, whether I want to or not,
I feel such pain from him whose friend I am,

0:52   [Melody repeated]

Car eu l'am mais que nuilla ren que sia;
Vas lui nom val merces ni cortesia,

For I love him more than anyone,
But neither grace nor courtesy has any effect on him,

1:17   [Recording ends]

 An interactive Active Listening Guide can be downloaded from the online Resource Center for *Music Listening Today,* 4th Edition.

LISTENING GUIDE

THE GODDESS MUSIC, seated at center, plays a portable organ accompanied by (clockwise from top center) the "pig snout" psaltery, a mandola, clappers, long trumpets, kettledrums tied around the waist, bagpipe and shawm (both reed instruments), a tambourine-like jingle drum, and a vielle (viol).

The tradition of the troubadours was soon adopted in northern France, where they were called trouvères. The tradition then spread to Germany, where they were known as minnesingers. Later troubadour music influenced Church music and other forms of secular music.

The **estampie** was a twelfth-century dance in triple meter and a clear, fast tempo. Only a single line of music was written down, and no instruments were specified. Performers at that time, as well as those today who perform this music, are free to decide which instruments to use for both the melody and the accompanying parts, including a drone, which is heard in the ancillary CD.

MUSIC IN THE REST OF EUROPE

While the medieval motet was reaching its acme with the compositions of Guillaume de Machaut ("Mah-*show*"), interest was waning in this style of music. Medieval motets were developed mainly in France. Composers in other parts of Europe evidently didn't care much for the style or were not advanced enough to attempt composing in it. A blind Italian musician named Francesco Landini ("Lahn-*dee*-nee," 1325–1397) and an English composer named John Dunstable (c. 1385–1453) were writing music that was simpler and easier to listen to. Both men and their successors often used the same text for all parts, which made it possible for the words to be sung about the same time so that they could be understood by listeners.

The windows of the choir section of the Cathedral at Reims.

JTB Photo Communications, Inc./Alamy

ANONYMOUS

Estampie (twelfth century)

GENRE: Dance music   Instruments

CD 3 Track 14

1 minute 14 seconds

Form: *a a a′ a*

0:00 14 0:00	A simple flute and violinlike instrument play a lively melody as a drone part is plucked by a string instrument.
	0:15	Melody repeated.
	0:47	Varied version of the melody.
	1:00	Opening melody returns somewhat varied.
	1:14	The estampie concludes.

An interactive Active Listening Guide can be downloaded from the online Resource Center for *Music Listening Today, 4th Edition.*

These composers also avoided harsh dissonances. A significant contribution of Dunstable and other English composers was the use of simultaneous pitches three and six notes apart. These intervals gave the music a richer sound than the fourths and fifths of Léonin and Pérotin.

The interval of a sixth is the inversion of a third; for example, C up to A is the inversion of A up to C. The musical effect of both is similar.

MAIN POINTS OF THIS CHAPTER

1. The medieval period was the time of Scholasticism and the construction of many of the great cathedrals. It also featured chivalry, guilds, and the founding of universities. Many works of music and art were created anonymously.

2. Polyphony developed in the Cathedral of Notre Dame in Paris. Composers added a third and fourth line to music in organum, which consisted of parallel lines of melody a fourth or fifth apart. Polyphonic religious works were based on phrases from Gregorian chant.

3. Rhythmic modes, similar to those found in poetry, were used to keep the different lines together.

4. The motet was built over a phrase of Gregorian chant, which was sung in Latin in long notes. Two or more different lines of music were added with words in vernacular languages on secular topics. Complicated rhythmic and melodic schemes were worked into the music. Motets were performed in the courts, not churches.

5. Secular music also existed in instrumental dance music and the songs of the troubadours. These were solo songs based on romantic poems.

FEATURES TO LISTEN FOR

1. The smooth flowing quality of the melody on the word "Alleluia" in "Alleluia, Diffusa est gratia."

2. The use of the rhythmic modes in the upper parts at 0:37 when the word "Diffusa" is introduced, as well as throughout "Quant en moy."

3. The contrast between very slow-moving *cantus firmus* based on Gregorian chant and the more rhythmic voice parts moving above it in both "Diffusa" and "Quant en moy."

4. The smooth character of the melody in "A chantar" and the decorative notes added by the singer.

5. The simple, lively quality of "Estampie." Notice also the timbre of the instruments used in the medieval period.

9 Renaissance Music

The word *Renaissance* means "rebirth" in French. Historically, it referred to a revival of interest in the philosophy and arts of ancient Greece and Rome, although there was much more to it than just the admiration of an earlier civilization. Because music had no ancient models to resurrect, for music the term *Renaissance* refers only to the style that predominated from about 1450 to 1600.

THE RENAISSANCE OUTLOOK

The intense interest of Renaissance artists and scholars in the earlier Greek and Roman civilizations led to a curious mixture of Greek and Christian belief. Michelangelo expressed this union of the pagan and Christian by decorating the ceiling of the Sistine Chapel in the Vatican in Rome with alternating figures of prophets (Christian) and sibyls (pagan). Erasmus, the great philosopher, regarded the ancient Athenian Socrates as a pre-Christian saint.

Hedonism is the belief in the importance of pleasure, especially physical pleasure, for its own sake.

Naturalism is the belief that what is natural is right.

Certain intellectual viewpoints emerged during the Renaissance that are still common in Western civilization today. Among them are optimism, worldliness, hedonism, naturalism, and individualism. But the most important of these is *humanism*, which is an emphasis on the human and natural as opposed to the otherworldly or divine. For example, pride, which was considered a sin in the Middle Ages, was elevated to a virtue.

The humanistic view can be seen by comparing the two treatments of the human body shown on these pages. One is a sculpture from the great medieval cathedral at Chartres in France. This figure has a spiritual, otherworldly quality; the head and eyes seem serene, and the position of the body is erect and formal. The proportions of the body are exaggerated to make the figure appear longer; the feet seem to dangle as though they were merely attached to the robes. As with most artworks of the medieval period, the artist is unknown.

Michelangelo's *David*, on the other hand, looks like a magnificent Greek god. Standing about 13½ feet high, the sculpture suggests confidence and an admiration of the human body. David looks natural, almost casual, and free.

With increasing interest in the value of life on earth, there was a corresponding interest in the fine arts. Art was valued for its own sake, not just as a means of religious devotion. The result of this new interest in the arts was a long list of outstanding sculptors and painters: Botticelli, Leonardo, Michelangelo, Dürer, Raphael, Titian, Brueghel, and Tintoretto, to name but a few.

Sandro Botticelli's *Adoration of the Magi* (page 75) depicts the three wise men or kings paying homage to the infant Jesus. It reveals the fondness of artists of the time for order and balance. A group of figures at the left of the painting is balanced by a group on the right, with the Madonna and Child in the center. The painting has a "staged" look. The converging lines of the Greek and Roman ruins add linear perspective to the painting and indicate a renewed interest in these ancient civilizations. Botticelli gives many of his figures brightly colored clothing. In addition, the sky is bright and clear.

Not only were works of art being enjoyed in a new climate of acceptance, but improving economic conditions meant that money was available to hire artists and musicians. The Church sought rich adornment for its buildings, which was one of the practices that led to the Reformation started by Martin Luther in 1517.

MEDIEVAL AND RENAISSANCE INTERPRETATIONS OF THE HUMAN FORM illustrate the advent of humanism, a philosophy that asserts the dignity and worth of humankind and emphasizes secular rather than spiritual concerns.

THE ADORATION OF THE MAGI by Botticelli presents the logical, planned qualities also found in Renaissance music.

Paris Manuscript B, fol. 83v: Page of text and sketches for a flying machine, 1488–90 (pen and ink on paper), Vinci, Leonardo da (1452–1519)/Bibliothèque de l'Institut de France, Paris, France, Giraudon/The Bridgeman Art Library International

A Sketch from Leonardo's Notebooks As can be seen here, Leonardo wrote so that the words read from right to left with the letters reversed. His writing is most easily read using a mirror.

An event that affected education, commerce, and religion was Johann Gutenberg's invention of printing from movable type. His invention made possible the wide dissemination of music, beginning with the appearance of the first printed music books in 1501.

The spirit of the time was one of optimism and discovery. The voyages of Columbus, Cabot, Balboa, and Magellan took place during the Renaissance. Copernicus was announcing his discoveries about the universe. Rabelais, Machiavelli, Boccaccio, Montaigne, More, Bacon, and Erasmus were exploring new ideas in literature and philosophy.

Perhaps the Renaissance is best epitomized by Leonardo da Vinci (1452–1519). It seems there was little that this genius did not do extremely well: design weapons and other devices, recite stories, paint, depict human anatomy, plan cities, make maps, and analyze proportions and things mathematical. He was interested in everything and left seven thousand pages of notebooks!

FEATURES AND TYPES OF RENAISSANCE MUSIC

Musically, the Renaissance started in the Netherlands. The composers there had reached a level of achievement that was the envy of Europe. Many were eventually lured away from their homeland to better-paying jobs in Spain, Bohemia, Austria, Germany, and especially the cities of northern Italy.

The style and techniques of the Netherlanders became internationally known and imitated. Many composers became so cosmopolitan that they thought of themselves as musicians first and citizens of a particular country second.

One composer who shaped the period known as the High Renaissance was Josquin Des Prez. Like composers before him, Josquin used the device of *imitation,* in which one line of melody appears in another part a measure or two later, somewhat like a round. But instead of having all parts singing continuously, as composers before him did, he had each voice enter one after another. This emphasized the imitation and made the words sung by each entering part easier to hear.

Josquin Des Prez

World History Archive/Alamy

Best-Known Works

choral:
- Missa Ave Maria Stella
- Missa de Beata Virgine

The most esteemed composer of the middle Renaissance was **Josquin Des Prez** (*"Jzhoss*-can deh *Pray"*), who lived from about 1440 to 1521. Born in Flanders (now part of Belgium), Josquin was a choir singer in Milan, a musician in the service of the Sforza family, a member of the Papal Choir, a choirmaster, and finally a musician in the service of Louis XII of France. His composing skill was much admired by his contemporaries, including Martin Luther. Josquin composed what and when he wanted, not what his patron wanted, and he was known for his chansons and motets. He also demanded a salary much higher than that of most of his contemporaries, which could explain why he changed jobs rather often. He was also very particular about his music and would become angry if singers tried to make any changes in it.

A **chanson** *was a French polyphonic song of the Renaissance.*

THE RENAISSANCE MASS

It was the custom among composers during the Renaissance to compose music for the Ordinary of the Mass using a phrase from a chant as a cantus firmus. The Mass usually acquired the name of the phrase or chant. For example, Josquin wrote eighteen different settings of the Mass. His *Pange lingua Mass* has many melodies from a Gregorian hymn called "Pange lingua." A portion of both the hymn and the Kyrie section of Josquin's Mass is shown here:

JOSQUIN DES PREZ

Kyrie from *Pange lingua Mass* (c. 1500)

GENRE: Mass, "Kyrie"   BASIS: Gregorian chant   SATB choral

CD 3 Tracks [15] – [17]

3 minutes 15 seconds

0:00 [15] 0:00   Tenors enter singing "Kyrie eleison."

0:03   Basses enter singing "Kyrie eleison" in imitation.

0:12   Sopranos enter singing "Kyrie eleison" in imitation.

0:20   Altos enter singing "Kyrie eleison" in imitation.

0:24   Basses enter again, followed by tenors and then sopranos.

0:50 [16] 0:00   Basses sing "Christe eleison." Altos soon follow.

0:17   Tenors sing "Christe." Sopranos soon follow.

2:16 [17] 0:00   Sopranos sing "Kyrie eleison," but the melody differs from the first Kyrie. Altos, tenors, and basses follow.

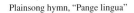

1:02   After an extended cadence, the Kyrie concludes.

 An interactive Active Listening Guide can be downloaded from the online Resource Center for *Music Listening Today, 4th Edition.*

SINGING ANGELS, from the *Cantoria*, or singers' pulpit, by the Renaissance sculptor Luca della Robbia.

The Kyrie has three sections based on the text, and each section contains several points of imitation.

More than any previous composer, Josquin was aware of a consistent organization of harmonies. Closely related to more-sophisticated harmony was the development of the bass line. Before Josquin, composers started adding melodies to chant; they placed the chant around middle C and put the additional melodies above it. But this did not provide a convincing sense of chord movement. Therefore, around the year 1450, composers began to add another line *below* the chant to give the music a more solid foundation. Even today this arrangement of voice parts remains the standard for a choral group containing men's and women's voices. At the time, the sections were called *superius, altus, tenor,* and *bassus;* today they are called soprano, alto, tenor, and bass.

The most esteemed composer of the late Renaissance was Giovanni Pierluigi da Palestrina. Historical circumstances encouraged him to be a conservative reformer, musically speaking. The Council of Trent was held intermittently between 1545 and 1563. The Church felt threatened by the Protestant Reformation, so the council met to respond to that situation and to acknowledge the need for some reform within the Church.

One aspect that was under attack was its music, which over the centuries had strayed far from the ideals of Gregorian chant. Complaints were voiced about the use of secular tunes, the complicated polyphony that made the words nearly impossible to understand, the use of noisy instruments, and the irreverence of the singers. The council directed that the music be purged of "barbarism, obscurities, contrarieties, and superfluities" so that "the House of God might rightly be called a house of prayer." To his credit, Palestrina achieved a return to the purity and reverence of earlier music without discarding the highly developed style of his predecessors.

THE RENAISSANCE MOTET

The Renaissance motet is very different from the medieval motet. The **Renaissance motet** is a unified piece with all voices singing the same Latin text. It borrows some phrases from chant, and it conveys the desired spirit of reverence. Above all, the Renaissance motet is serious, restrained, and designed for inclusion in the worship service.

GIOVANNI PIERLUIGI DA PALESTRINA

"Sicut cervus," Part I (c. 1577)

GENRE: Motet   SATB choral

CD 1 Tracks 16 – 18

3 minutes 32 seconds

0:00   16   0:00   Tenors sing "Sicut cervus."

Sic - ut cer - vus de - si - de - rat ad fon - tes

   0:07   Altos follow with "Sicut cervus" five notes higher.

   0:12   Sopranos sing "Sicut cervus" one octave higher than tenors sang the phrase.

   0:19   Basses sing "Sicut cervus" on the same pitch on which the tenors started.

1.18   17   0:00   Basses sing "ita desiderat." Tenors, sopranos, and altos follow in imitation.

i - ta de - - - si

2:10   18   0:00   Sopranos sing "anima mea ad te Deus." Altos, tenors, and basses follow in imitation.

a - ni - ma me - a

   1:11   After the voice parts have sung "ad te Deus," Part I of the motet concludes.

An interactive Active Listening Guide can be downloaded from the online
Resource Center for *Music Listening Today, 4th Edition.*

Palestrina's "Sicut cervus"

Palestrina's works have a pure, celestial quality. His "Sicut cervus," included on the ancillary CD, is a good example of the Renaissance motet:

- The text is in ecclesiastical (church) Latin. It is a portion of Psalm 42, with Part I using only the first two lines. In the Revised Standard Version it reads:

  As a hart longs for flowing streams,
  So longs my soul for Thee, O God.
  My soul thirsts for God, for the living God.
  When shall I come and behold the face of God?
  My tears have been my food day and night,
  While men say to me continually, "Where is your God"

  The word *hart* means a male red deer, a stag.

- The music is polyphonic. All the lines are given equal attention, and each has melodic character.

- Each voice usually enters in imitation of another when new text is introduced.

- The music does not have a strong feeling of chord progression.

- "Sicut cervus" does not have a strong meter or beat. Although it moves along steadily, it certainly is not toe-tapping music. Today's versions of the music have bar lines, but these have been added by modern editors so singers can more easily keep their place. The bar lines do not imply a metrical pattern.

- Motets today are almost always sung without accompaniment. During the Renaissance, however, the voices were sometimes doubled by a few instruments. But the

The Bridgeman Art Library

BEST-KNOWN WORKS

choral:
- *Pope Marcellus Mass*
- *Sicut cervus*

Palestrina (c. 1526–1594) was born in the small town of Palestrina outside Rome, which provided him with the name by which he is known today. He began his career as chorister at Santa Maria Maggiore in 1537 in Rome. He returned to his native town in 1544 as organist and choirmaster, where he married and had two sons.

In 1550 the bishop of Palestrina was elected pope, assuming the name Julius III. A year and a half later, he summoned Palestrina back to Rome to become choirmaster of the Cappella Giulia in the Vatican. Soon he was to publish his first book of Masses.

Pope Julius III died and was succeeded by Pope Paul IV, who was determined to reform what he considered the excesses in Church music. In 1555 Palestrina was dismissed from his job because he was married. He was soon appointed choirmaster at the Church of Saint John Lateran in Rome, where he stayed for five years. He then returned to Santa Maria Maggiore and published his first book of motets. In 1571 he returned to Cappella Giulia, but misfortune struck when his two eldest sons and wife died of various diseases.

Palestrina married again and entered the fur business, and he proved to be a highly successful businessman. His more than adequate funds allowed him to publish about sixteen collections of music. He died in 1594, leaving a wealth of beautiful and finely crafted music and the distinction of creating the finest church music of his time.

The term *a cappella* literally means "for the chapel."

Women were not permitted by the Church to celebrate the Mass or to sing in choirs.

ideal was a purity of sound, which implies no accompaniment or, in musical terms, **a cappella.**

- A small group of singers is the authentic performance medium for Renaissance motets. Probably no more than three singers were originally assigned to each part. Boys, or men singing in falsetto, sang the high voice parts.
- The lines of melody are very singable. The range for any one voice part does not exceed an octave, except for the bass. Furthermore, the lines do not move far from one pitch to the next. The melodies are quite smooth and conjunct.
- The form of a motet is usually based on the structure of the text, which in this case is a psalm, so each verse has its own polyphonic setting.
- The music has a restrained quality. Bombast and showmanship were considered not in keeping with the attitude of reverence and awe that should prevail in worship.
- The melodic lines are woven together with great skill and beauty. That is the main reason Palestrina's music is so highly esteemed and still sung today.

THE MADRIGAL

The Renaissance also had a distinctly worldly side, as was noted earlier. Many types of secular music were composed and performed, and some of this music contained features of the musical style of a particular country. The most significant type of secular music at this time was the madrigal.

Madrigals are both similar to and different from motets. They are similar in that they were written for a small group of singers. They also have some imitative entrances of new phrases of text, contain singable vocal lines, and are generally more polyphonic than homophonic. But there are some important differences.

There were also a few *madrigali spirituali,* which were nonliturgical songs on religious topics.

- Madrigals are in vernacular languages, and their texts often deal with sentimental and sometimes erotic love.

- They tend to have stronger and more regular rhythm, and most of them are composed to be performed at a faster tempo.
- Madrigals were sung at courtly social gatherings and meetings of learned and artistic societies, so they were not the popular or folk music of the day. They were very popular, however, among the aristocratic, educated class, and an enormous number of them were composed. In England madrigal singing—with its implied requirement of music reading—was expected of educated persons.
- They often contain **text painting,** or **word painting,** in which the music attempts to depict the words being sung.

Because madrigals were written for secular situations, they were not limited by religious traditions. They therefore contained more innovative musical ideas, such as word painting. This practice is especially evident in the madrigal "As Vesta Was from Latmos Hill Descending."

The madrigal was originally an Italian development associated with such composers as Cipriano de Rore and Luca Marenzio. By the mid-1500s madrigals had spread to other countries. Interest in madrigals reached England late in that century. English madrigals are especially enjoyable to listeners today for three reasons:

- Their texts are in English, so no translation is necessary for English-speaking people.
- English composers had a knack for making the lines of music tuneful and singable.
- The English had the delightful trait of not taking themselves too seriously. No matter how sad a song may be, the listener senses a detached quality.

Weelkes's "As Vesta Was from Latmos Hill Descending"

Thomas Weelkes was one of England's finest composers of madrigals. "As Vesta Was from Latmos Hill Descending" is from an anthology of madrigals, *The Triumphs of Oriana.* It was composed in honor of Queen Elizabeth I, who was often called "Oriana." This madrigal is written for six voice parts instead of the usual four. Vesta is the Roman goddess of the hearth and home, and Diana is the goddess of the hunt, chastity, and the moon. The text tells about Vesta coming down a hill with her attendants, who are referred to as "Diana's darlings." At the same time, Oriana, the "maiden queen," climbs the hill with her shepherd attendants. Vesta's attendants leave her and hurry down to join Oriana.

Weelkes's madrigal makes much use of word painting. For example, the words *ascending* and *descending* are each set with scales that move in the direction implied by the words.

Notice the use of characters from Roman mythology.

Queen Elizabeth never married and was often referred to as the "maiden" or "virgin" queen.

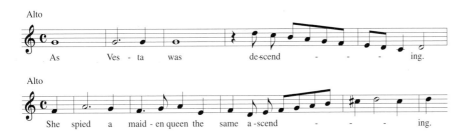

When the text tells about Vesta's attendants leaving her to run down the hill, Weelkes has the appropriate number of singers singing—two, then three, and then one. Later in the piece, the word *long* is the longest note in that portion of the madrigal.

THOMAS WEELKES

"As Vesta Was from Latmos Hill Descending" (1590)

GENRE: Madrigal 6-Part vocal

CD 1 Tracks **19** – **20**

3 minutes 7 seconds

0.00	**19**	0:00	As Vesta was from Latmos hill descending,	*Descending scales*
		0:12	she spied a maiden queen the same ascending,	*Ascending scales*
		0:33	attended on by all the shepherds swain,	
		0:49	to whom Diana's darlings came running down amain.	*Rapid descending notes*
1:12	**20**	0:00	First two by two, then three by three together,	*Two voices, three voices, then all voices*
		0:09	leaving their goddess all alone, hasten thither,	*One voice*
		0:22	and mingling with the shepherd of her train	
		0:29	with mirthful tunes her presence entertain.	*Short, happy phrase in imitation*
		0:43	Then sang the shepherds and nymphs of Diana,	*Flowing melody*
		0:54	Long live fair Oriana!	*Long notes in the bass part*
		1:55	Madrigal concludes with sustained notes.	

The word *swain* in the text refers to male admirers.

 An interactive Active Listening Guide can be downloaded from the online Resource Center for *Music Listening Today, 4th Edition.*

Weelkes also fits the words and rhythm of the music together in a way that would be natural if they were spoken. Often the rhythmic setting of the words contributes to their expressiveness.

Thomas Weelkes

Lebrecht/TL/The Image Works

Thomas Weelkes (c. 1576–1623) was one of several excellent composers of choral music who flourished at the end of the sixteenth century and the early part of the seventeenth. His contemporaries included William Byrd (1543–1623), John Dowland (1562–1626), Thomas Morley (c. 1557–1603), Thomas Tallis (c. 1501–1585), and John Wilbye (1574–1638). Although madrigals were slow in coming to England, interest in them seemed to explode once they finally arrived.

Weelkes was organist first at Winchester College, but spent most of his career in Chichester. There he married the daughter of a wealthy merchant, and they had three children. His most musi-

cally productive years were the early ones in Chichester. As the years went by, he became more negligent in his church music duties and drank heavily. He was reported to the bishop as being "noted and famed for a common drunkard and notorious swearer and blasphemer." By 1617 he was fired from his job and apparently was employed only sporadically after that.

Whatever Weelkes's personal foibles, he composed some of the finest church music and madrigals during that period of English history. Typical of most of his contemporary composers, he wrote madrigals that were lighter and more experimental than his church music.

RENAISSANCE INSTRUMENTAL MUSIC

Composers during the Renaissance devoted almost all their efforts to vocal music. Instruments did often accompany the singing of secular music, especially a lute or harpsichord. Instrumentalists simplified the written parts by reducing the polyphony to chords. The lute was the most popular instrument of the Renaissance. As can be seen in the painting, it has a pear-shaped body, frets, and several strings. Its pegbox is slanted back sharply away from the body. It is played by plucking, and intricate music can be performed on it.

Frets are metal strips placed across the fingerboard to help the player in accurate finger placement.

Instruments were used extensively for dance music. One of the most popular dances of the time was the *pavane* ("pa-vahn"), a solemn dance in two beats to the measure with the dancers moving in a formal way. The pavane was often paired with the *galliard*, which had three beats to the measure. These and other dances are made up of clearly identifiable sections that produced forms such *A A B B* and *A A B B C C*.

A Girl with a Lute, Bartolomeo Veneto, ca. 1520, inv. P2652/Isabella Stewart Gardner Museum, Boston

A GIRL WITH A LUTE, an oil painting on wood by Bartolomeo Veneto. The lute reached its peak of popularity during this time, both as a solo instrument and as accompaniment to singing.

MAIN POINTS OF THIS CHAPTER

1. The word "renaissance" means "rebirth" and is the name given to the period that lasted from about 1450 to 1600, when there was a revival of interest in the culture of the ancient Greeks and Romans. It was also the age of explorers and the introduction of the printing press.

2. The bass voice part became an important addition to choral music.

3. The Renaissance motet was very different from its medieval predecessor. It had a sacred text sung in Latin with all parts singing the same text. New phrases of text were often introduced in imitation. Its mood was reverent and restrained, with no strong feeling of meter. Boys usually sang the soprano and alto parts.

4. Madrigals were the most popular genre of secular vocal music. They were similar to motets in that they were usually sung without accompaniment by a small group of singers. But madrigals have secular texts in a vernacular language, were performed at social gatherings, often contained text painting, and generally are more lively.

5. Instrumental music during the Renaissance featured the lute. Most instrumental music was created as dance music.

FEATURES TO LISTEN FOR

1. The imitation of the first several notes when a change of text is introduced in Josquin's "Kyrie" and Palestrina's "Sicut cervus."

2. The restrained, even quality of the melodic lines in the motets and their lack of a clear sense of metrical rhythm.

3. The skill of Josquin and Palestrina in weaving their melodic lines into a beautiful tapestry of sound.

4. The word painting in Weelkes's "As Vesta Was from Latmos Hill Descending," words such as "descending," "all alone," and "mirthful tunes."

5. The charming quality of most madrigals, including Weelkes's "As Vesta . . ."

PART III

Baroque Music

	1600	1650
Historical Events	First settlements in America (1607)	
	King James version of Bible (1611)	
	Thirty Years' War (1618–1648)	
		Harvard founded (1636)
		Louis XIV reigns in France (1643–1715)
Visual Arts	Poussin (1594–1665)	
		Bernini colonnades at St. Peter's (above, right) (1656–1667)
		Rubens, *Abraham and Melchizedek* (c. 1625)
		Rembrandt, *Descent from the Cross* (1634)
Literature and Theater	Cervantes, *Don Quixote* (1605, 1615)	
Philosophy and Science	Grotius (1583–1645)	
	Galileo publishes on astronomy (1610–1635)	Spinoza (1632–1677)
	Descartes (1596–1650)	
		Locke (1632–1704)
Music	First operas (1607)	Monteverdi, late madrigals and operas (1638–1651)
		Lully at French court (1652–1687)
		Arcangelo Corelli (1653–1713)

The British Library/HIP/The Image Works

1700   **1750**

Ottomans seize Vienna

Salem witchcraft trials (1692)

Boucher (1703–1770)

Gainsborough (1727–1788)

Fragonard (1732–1806)

Watteau (1684–1721)

Milton, *Paradise Lost* (1667, 1674)

Defoe, *Robinson Crusoe* (1719)

Swift, *Gulliver's Travels* (1735)   Fielding, *Tom Jones* (1749)

Newton's laws of physics

Voltaire (1694–1778)

Hume

George Frideric Handel, painting by A. Herrmann. German-English composer, 1685–1759/Lebrecht/The Image Works

Purcell, *Dido and Aeneas* (1689)   Handel, *Messiah* (1741)

Fugues (c. 1700)   Vivaldi, *The Four Seasons* (1723)

◀ J. S. Bach (left) and   ▲ Handel (above), instrumental and choral works
   (1685–1750)   (1685–1759)

10 *The* Baroque Period

Even before 1600, the approximate beginning of the Baroque period, a new style had been emerging. The Renaissance ideals of restraint and balance began to fade. The change could be seen in the growing emotion displayed in the later works of Michelangelo, and it could be heard in Giovanni Gabrieli's massive works for instruments and two choruses. The initial reaction to the new style can be seen in the word *baroque* itself, which was probably derived from a Portuguese word meaning "irregularly shaped pearl."

Sometimes baroque means extravagant, grotesque, and in bad taste, which is perhaps a carryover from its original meaning. In discussions of music, however, **Baroque** refers only to the style that prevailed from about 1600 to 1750. And that style was certainly not grotesque or in bad taste.

STYLES IN MUSIC

What do we mean by a musical style? Simply that the elements in a particular style are generally treated in a similar way. In some styles, for example, there is little sense of meter, in other styles it is very pronounced, and in yet others the metrical patterns are often irregular. The same is true of melodies, size and nature of performing groups, texture, type of harmony, and so on. Many of these similarities can be partly described in words. But a clear understanding of the characteristics of a style can come only from listening for them.

When a large amount of music over a long span of time has used musical elements in a similar way, it has been grouped by scholars and given a name—Renaissance, Baroque, and others. These names are usually designated quite a few years *after* the years in which a style was dominant. No one got up on the morning of January 1, 1600, and thought, "Well, the Baroque period has finally arrived."

Why do writers and scholars designate periods in music and history? Just as it helps to divide a book into units and chapters, it helps to divide the thousands of years of human history into periods. The idea of style periods permits us to organize topics according to similarities and to talk, think about, and remember them more easily.

An understanding of styles in music also clues us in on what to listen for, as well as what not to expect. For instance, you don't encounter an accompanied solo singer in music written before 1600. So, when you hear such a work, you will know that it's not in Renaissance style. Being able to recognize the differences between styles from listening is an excellent indicator of how well you are connecting what you hear with what you know.

Some of the time a style is recognized "just because it sounds like it."

People have always thought of themselves as modern and up to date, which, of course, at the time they were.

What you hear in a piece of music and what you know about it reinforce each other.

CHARACTERISTICS OF BAROQUE STYLE

It is difficult to summarize in a few paragraphs a period of 150 years in which major changes took place and contrasting forces were at work. Three general characteristics, however, mark the Baroque style: grandiose dimensions, love of drama, and religious intensity.

Grandiose Dimensions

The artists and musicians of the Baroque period were fond of the large and grandiose. In music this characteristic is evident in the prominent place given the pipe organ—the largest and most powerful instrument of the time. In architecture the love of grandeur can be seen in Gian Lorenzo Bernini's monumental colonnades encompassing the vast piazza in front of Saint Peter's Basilica in Rome. The huge columns reach out before Saint Peter's like giant arms seeking to draw everyone into the building. Four rows of columns run parallel to one another. But when standing in the center of the piazza, viewers can see only a single row of columns, because the other three rows are perfectly blocked out. The colonnade is made up of 284 different columns, and statues of 140 saints are placed on top of the columns.

Love of Drama

Baroque artists and musicians were fond of drama. Three major dramatic forms were developed in music: opera, oratorio, and cantata. Drama can also be seen in the twisted lines and struggling subjects in artworks. Both size and twisting motion are evident in the ceiling paintings and many other Baroque works of art.

Religious Intensity

The years of the Baroque period were a time of strong religious feelings—and conflicts. The Protestant churches established themselves generally in northern Europe and on the British Isles. Protestant worship was devout, plain, and deadly serious. John Milton's *Paradise Lost* and John Bunyan's *Pilgrim's Progress* were two monumental writings containing the Protestant viewpoint.

The Catholic faith was generally found in southern Europe. The Catholic Counter-Reformation developed in response to the Protestant Reformation and a sense that the Catholic Church was in need of reform. The times were marked by a series of tragic religious wars between Protestants and Catholics. A positive by-product of this religious intensity, however, was the creation of some outstanding art.

Bill Ross/Corbis Premium RF/Alamy

Bernini's Piazza San Pietro is larger than the length of two football fields and took eleven years to complete.

BAROQUE ART

Baroque artworks are very different from those of the Renaissance. Consider Peter Paul Rubens's *The Meeting of Abraham and Melchizedek*, which was painted about 1625 (page 88). Originally designed for a tapestry, this work is the opposite of the calm, posed quality of Giotto's *Madonna and Child*. A similar change can be observed in Baroque music, with its development of opera and oratorio. The painting looks as though a movie director had shouted "Action!" to the figures; even the horse on the left side of the picture appears to have responded to the command. The bodies of the figures are often twisted to add to the dramatic effect. Abraham and Melchizedek lean actively toward each other. The men on each side are set in a tight design of profiles and frontal poses. Their bodies look natural and robust. The edges of the painting show a luxurious carpet piled

Rubens, Peter Paul (1577–1640) Abraham and Melchisedek. Oil on canvas, 204 × 250 cm./ Musee des Beaux-Arts, Caen, France/Erich Lessing/Art Resource, NY

THE MEETING OF ABRAHAM AND MELCHIZEDEK by Peter Paul Rubens. The painting is filled with the sense of drama that Baroque musicians and artists created in their works.

up on a ledge, and the scene is anchored by the columns on the right and clamped into place by the servants in the foreground.

Rembrandt van Rijn's *Descent from the Cross* shows another side of Baroque painting. It features the dramatic treatment of light on the faces of people, much like a spotlight in a stage production centers attention on a particular character. The light focuses on two parts of the painting. One is the body of Jesus and the face of the man helping lower his body. The other, weaker spotlight is on the woman, presumably Mary, on the right-hand side. The light in this painting seems to be coming from the candle shielded by a man's hand, which gives the scene an eerie pall. To increase the spotlight effect, Rembrandt painted an almost black background.

Another Baroque characteristic of Rembrandt's painting is the twisted, almost cork-screw design. Notice that Jesus's body is turned, as are most of the other figures in the painting; none is facing straight ahead or sideways. And the cross is not in the center of the painting, as it would have been if this were a Renaissance work. As if the spotlighting and twisted figures were not enough, you can also see the tenderness and grief in the faces of the people. It's a very dramatic painting.

The Baroque love of size and grandeur is evident in the ceiling painting *Apotheosis of Saint Ignatius* by Andrea Pozzo, which adorns the San Ignazio (St. Ignatius) Church in Rome (page 90). The work is a fresco; that is, it was painted right into the ceiling plaster while it was still fresh. It is one of a number of ceiling paintings completed during the Baroque period, the most famous of which are Michelangelo's frescoes for the Sistine Chapel in the Vatican in Rome. It seems that Baroque artists (and/or their patrons) thought that bigger was better. Works of music became much longer and involved more performers, and artwork became larger, both in concept and in actual size. This fresco tries to exceed its physical limits by creating the illusion that the viewer is gazing into heaven. The scene depicts saints, angels, and sinners all overwhelmed by what they see.

BAROQUE INTELLECTUAL ACTIVITY

Although it was marked by religious fervor, the Baroque period was also a time of important advances in science.

- Sir Isaac Newton developed the theory of gravity.
- Johannes Kepler and Galileo Galilei developed Copernicus's theories about the movements of the planets.
- William Gilbert introduced the word *electricity* into the language.
- Robert Boyle helped develop chemistry into a science.
- Robert Hooke first described the cellular structure of plants.
- William Harvey described the circulation of blood in the human body.
- Gottfried Wilhelm von Leibniz with Newton developed infinitesimal calculus.
- René Descartes founded analytical geometry.

EARLY BAROQUE MUSIC

No musical style is ever fully uniform, and this is especially true of the Baroque. Some scholars have divided the period into three subperiods: early, middle, and mature. Music in the early years of the Baroque was more experimental; the style usually associated with this period developed during the middle and mature years.

The transition from the Renaissance to the Baroque style resulted in some powerful music by a number of composers. An important group worked in Venice, which was a major cultural center throughout the sixteenth and into the seventeenth century. Venice's musical activity centered around the Basilica of Saint Mark. The position of organist-choirmaster there was the most sought after in all of Italy. Over the years the distinguished musicians who held that post composed more and more for two choruses placed with the two organs on each side of the church. And not only were there singers and pipe organs; there were also trombones, cornets, and viols.

The result was a powerful and exciting stereophonic sound with one group of performers answering the other. This technique was known as *polychoral* or *antiphonal singing*. Giovanni Gabrieli (1555–1612) brought antiphonal music to a peak in the early years of the seventeenth century. He was also the first composer to specify particular instruments for a part and the first to indicate dynamics in music notation.

DESCENT FROM THE CROSS by Rembrandt van Rijn. The painting adds to the sense of drama by spotlighting the faces of the figures in the scene, similar to the way that singers and actors are spotlighted on a stage.

René Descartes is also remembered for his "I think, therefore I am" philosophy.

Viols are string instruments that look something like those of today; but viols have frets, flatter and less curving bodies, and more strings.

MUSIC IN THE BAROQUE

During the Baroque period, Europe consisted of many small principalities and states. As expensive cars and designer clothing are today, music and art became status symbols among the nobility and wealthy merchants. Composers often worked under a patronage system in which they composed music exclusively for their employer. George Frideric

There were three hundred principalities in what is present-day Germany.

Pozzo, Andrea (1642–1709) Apotheosis of St. Ignatius. 1691. Ceiling fresco/S. Ignazio, Rome, Italy/Scala/Art Resource, NY

Apotheosis of St. Ignatius by Andrea Pozzo. The pipe organ was the most powerful instrument during the Baroque, and the ceiling painting was the most massive type of painting.

In was not uncommon in Handel's day for a king or queen to be from another country. Royal blood was considered more important than nationality. A monarch from another country would be appointed when the previous ruler had no heir apparent or because there was political turmoil. King George I began England's rule by the House of Hanover, which still rules today.

The Duke of Weimar had his court musician, J. S. Bach, jailed for a month because he refused to leave his job. (Bach could be quite stubborn.)

Handel (1685–1759), for example, was employed by the elector of Hanover in Germany (where his name was Händel) and was on leave for a second time in England when the elector was crowned King George I of England.

The patronage system had its good and bad points. It could provide a composer steady employment, but the position also demanded that he please his employer or he would need to find another job. And the job often involved teaching singers, rehearsing instrumentalists, and even quelling squabbles among the musicians, as well as writing music "on demand."

Being a musician was often a family tradition. For example, the Bach family tree contains about sixty outstanding musicians, including thirty-eight composers. Education beyond the elementary school level was limited to those who were rich or born into noble families. Learning to be a composer consisted of copying music when young and later studying as an apprentice with a master composer. A few musicians studied an instrument or voice at one of the newly emerging conservatories, but rarely was composition taught there during the Baroque.

There was no established body of music such as we have today. Almost all music was expected to be, and was, new. For this reason, many Baroque composers wrote huge amounts of music. Georg Phillip Telemann (1685–1767), for example, composed more than three thousand pieces, and many other Baroque composers produced prodigious amounts of music. How did they do it?

1. They must have worked very hard.

The system is called *figured bass.*

2. They used a shorthand system in which they did not have to write in every note in a chord.

3. They used some of their own themes (and once in a while a theme by another composer) in more than one of their works.

4. They had young boys (future musicians) copy a lot of the parts for the instrumentalists and singers.

5. They didn't fuss over details, often because they were going to perform a work themselves. They never dreamed (at least as far as anyone can determine) that people hundreds of years later would be performing and listening to their music! They probably thought of themselves as skilled craftsmen, not artists who were creating music that future generations would understand and appreciate.

PERFORMANCE OF BAROQUE MUSIC

There were no professional orchestras during the Baroque. The only orchestras were associated with courts and employed part-time performers. The orchestras were also small (about twenty players), and there was no need for a conductor. Usually the keyboard player would simply nod his head to indicate when the music was to begin. Public performances were rare; usually they were held in churches or palaces. Opera companies were a different matter. A number of cities in Italy had them. Performances took place in opera houses and were attended by the public.

At one time in the seventeenth century, Venice, which had at the time a population of 125,000, supported six opera houses.

The quality of playing on most orchestral instruments was probably not at all impressive compared to the quality of performers today. Most players held other jobs, often not associated with music, and the development of playing skills was limited. Many of the instruments were not fully developed. Some organists and harpsichord players were outstanding performers, however. It was different in the case of singers. Some of them were reputed to possess sensational ability.

Woodwinds had few keys, and brasses had no valves with which to produce pitches not in their basic overtone series.

Improvisation was an important feature in Baroque music. An organist was expected to be able to improvise intricate and complex music. During their lifetimes Bach, Handel, and several other Baroque composers were known as much for their ability to improvise as for their compositions. Singers and instrumentalists frequently added ornaments to a melody, so what is seen in the notation of Baroque music was sometimes only a skeleton of what was actually performed.

Handel continued to give organ concerts in which he improvised even after he became blind.

CHARACTERISTICS OF BAROQUE MUSIC

The differences between the Renaissance music of composers such as Josquin and Palestrina and the Baroque music of J. S. Bach, Handel, and Vivaldi are immense.

Homophony

From the monophonic texture of Gregorian chant, music moved to simple organum and then to highly polyphonic music of medieval times and the Renaissance. Polyphonic music can be beautiful and interesting, but it does have drawbacks. When several different voice parts are singing at the same time, the words tend to be obscured by other voice parts. It's somewhat like trying to listen to two or more different conversations at the same time. What's more, because they need to fit with other lines of music, it's difficult for the lines in polyphonic music to be expressive of the words.

Although there are moments in Renaissance music in which all the voice parts move together, these places are not truly homophonic in the sense that one melody predominates and the other parts are supportive of it. Near the beginning of the Baroque period, several composers in and around Florence, Italy, decided to have a singer sing one line and make that line of music expressive of the text being sung, while the other parts became just accompaniment. In this way, the music could be much freer and more dramatic, a characteristic of Baroque music. Homophony developed from these efforts, and over the years it was to become as important as polyphony.

The type of homophony consisting of a solo line with instrumental accompaniment that flourished in the early seventeenth century is often called *monody*.

The transition from the polyphony of the Renaissance to the homophony of the Baroque can be seen in the books of madrigals by Claudio Monteverdi (1567–1643).

Between 1587 and 1603, he published four books of polyphonic madrigals in Renaissance style. In 1605, however, he published a book of homophonic pieces, some of which have accompaniments. By the eighth book in 1638, Monteverdi's music also contained works for small vocal and string ensembles.

Recitative

The early efforts to have one expressive line of melody were almost entirely in a singsong style called **recitative** ("*reh*-si-tah-*teev*"). During some early recitatives, singers went so far as to grimace, act, and imitate inflections of crying and gasping. Whatever the merits of such attempts at artistic expression, they did open up a new dimension in vocal music. The single melody could have a wider range, more movement by half steps, and more rhythmic freedom than a line in a traditional Renaissance motet.

Because the main objective of recitatives was to express the text, composers did not attempt to write memorable melodies for them. They would save such melodies for other pieces of music. They seldom repeated words in recitatives because they wanted to cover the text in as direct and expressive a way as possible.

Metrical Rhythm

Renaissance music usually has a sense of even flow. It does not, however, provide a sense of metrical pattern. That was to change in Baroque music. Regular metrical patterns became the norm. In fact, Baroque music seemed to be subject to what was sometimes referred to as "the tyranny of the bar line." And bar lines began to appear in music notation during this time. Because of its regular beat, and because most Baroque orchestras and choral groups were small, musical works were performed without a conductor.

There is one exception to the strict metrical quality of Baroque rhythm: recitatives. Although the notation of recitatives contains bar lines, musicians understood then, and still understand today, that the music is to be performed very flexibly. The accompanying orchestra or keyboard player follows whatever changes singers make in the flow of the music.

Major/Minor Keys

Actually, the mode from B to B was rarely used. Try playing it on a keyboard instrument, and you will hear why.

Prior to the Baroque period, musicians had used scale patterns called **modes**. The modes followed the pattern of whole and half steps beginning and ending on each of the white keys on the piano—C to C, D to D, and so on. Two of those patterns were retained in Baroque music: the one from C to C, which is major, and the one from A to A, which is minor. The other five patterns were almost never used again until the twentieth century, although they continued prominently in folk music.

Tonal Center

Tonality and cadences are discussed in Chapter 3.

The Baroque period saw the establishment of music with a **tonal center,** or **key center,** and the systematic use of harmony. Prior to that time, composers concentrated on fitting the lines of music together well. Now composers began to think much more about how the progression of chords affected the music. They based their use of chords around the "magnetic pull" of the tonal center.

Modulation

Music with no modulations is like a room with beige carpeting, beige draperies, beige walls and ceiling, and beige furniture.

Having established a key center, Baroque composers then devised ways of changing it during a recitative or other musical work. Today, listeners are so used to hearing music modulate that they are not aware of how monotonous music would sound without it. Changes of key center, or **modulations,** make music more interesting.

Doctrine of Affections

The distinctive treatment of the words in recitatives and other vocal music illustrates the belief of Baroque composers in projecting the ideas of the text in the music. Called the **doctrine of affections** or **doctrine of affects,** this belief is often evident in Baroque music. Because the type of music associated with particular moods or ideas is often not known by listeners today, this doctrine is largely of historical interest; however, the concept of music expressing the text certainly is not. The doctrine of affections is also reflected in the consistent mood that is maintained throughout an entire section of a work.

As used in the doctrine of affections, the word *affections* refers to all feelings, not just love.

HANDEL'S "THE VOICE OF HIM THAT CRIETH IN THE WILDERNESS" FROM *MESSIAH*

The recitative "The Voice of Him That Crieth in the Wilderness" contains all the features of Baroque music discussed thus far, except metrical rhythm. It is for a tenor and appears early in Handel's oratorio *Messiah*, which is presented in the next chapter. It is typical for the following reasons:

The "voice in the wilderness" refers to John, the Baptist.

- It is very expressive of the text. Notice the treatment of the word *crieth* in the first phrase, the word *straight* in the third phrase, and the word *highway* in the fourth phrase. Listen to how the singer brings out these words.

- It features a single melodic line with accompaniment; it is clearly homophonic in texture. Almost all the musical interest is in the melodic line; the accompanying part is limited to a few chords.

- Its melody is not very distinctive. The more memorable melodies are found elsewhere in Baroque music.

- The singer sings the rhythm freely, even though it has bar lines and a meter signature.

- It begins with a tonal center, E major.

- It modulates and concludes with a different tonal center, A major, which is firmly established with a V-I cadence in the final two chords of the accompaniment.

- It demonstrates the doctrine of affections by the emphasis it places on words such as *crieth* and *highway*.

GEORGE FRIDERIC HANDEL
"The Voice of Him That Crieth in the Wilderness" from *Messiah* (1741)

GENRE: Recitative, oratorio   Tenor and orchestra

CD 1 Track **21**

27 seconds

0:00	**21**	0:00	Accompanied by a few chords, the tenor sings:
			The voice of him that crieth in the wilderness,
			Prepare ye the way of the Lord,
		0:15	*Make straight in the desert*
			A highway for our God.
		0:27	Recitative ends with simple V-1 cadence.

 An interactive Active Listening Guide can be downloaded from the online Resource Center for *Music Listening Today, 4th Edition.*

FEATURES OF BAROQUE INSTRUMENTAL MUSIC

Tuning

A significant breakthrough was made during the Baroque period in how instruments were tuned, a problem that had plagued musicians since the time of Pythagoras around 555 BC. Pythagoras's discovery of certain basic intervals did not solve the problem of precisely where the intervening notes should be placed. The situation was made much more difficult by a caprice of nature. Theoretically, if you play a series of intervals of a fifth, ascending or descending from a given note, the thirteenth note should duplicate the original pitch. But if the Pythagorean ratio for the fifth is used, and if the fifths are computed upward, the thirteenth note is noticeably higher than it should be!

This phenomenon is known as the *Pythagorean comma*.

This pitch problem did not bother singers or string players, because they could easily make slight pitch adjustments to account for it. But it was quite different for keyboard instruments, which have fixed pitches. To get perfect tuning in some keys, people who tuned keyboard instruments had to sacrifice the pitch accuracy in others. Keys with several sharps or flats were therefore usually avoided, because keys with few sharps or flats were normally favored in the tuning process. These tuning complications meant that the only modulations likely on keyboard instruments were those to nearly related keys.

Bach's two-volume (forty-eight–piece) work known as the *Well-Tempered Clavier* is a musical landmark.

The problem was resolved through a compromise: Make all the intervals slightly off so that the distance between all half steps is equal. The term for this tuning practice is **equal temperament,** and it is the system of tuning still used today. To promote better systems of tuning and to help develop a player's technique for playing in all keys, a few composers, including Bach, wrote a series of pieces in all twenty-four major and minor keys.

Terraced Dynamics

A gradual increase or decrease in dynamic levels was not common in Baroque music. Renaissance composers placed no dynamic markings in their music at all, and Baroque composers wrote very few. Often composers rehearsed and performed their own music, so extensive markings were not necessary. The few indications that are present, however, call for abrupt changes of dynamic level. A *forte*, or loud level, changed suddenly to a *piano*, or soft level, and vice versa. These abrupt changes are called **terraced dynamics.** They were probably made in this way because Baroque artists and musicians were interested in dramatic contrasts. Also, the keyboard instruments of the time could not make gradual changes. The organ and harpsichord could change dynamic levels only by coupling manuals, adding pedals, or pulling out stops.

Continuo

The harmonies in Baroque music became so well standardized that musicians devised a shorthand system called **figured bass** to notate chords. The composer provided a bass line that contained cues in the form of numbers and an occasional sharp, flat, or natural to indicate the parts between the highest and lowest notes. Keyboard players were expected to read these symbols while performing the music, a process called **realization.**

The highest and lowest parts became the two important lines, with the melody being the most important. The bass part provided a foundation to the music. Because it sounded nearly all the time, it came to be known as the **basso continuo** (continuous bass), which for convenience is usually shortened to **continuo.** A cello, gamba, or bassoon usually played the continuo line along with the keyboard player.

MAIN POINTS OF THIS CHAPTER

1. The Baroque style had three predominate characteristics:
   - Grandiose size and concept—The pipe organ, the mightiest instrument of the time, reached the acme of its development.
   - Religious fervor—The result was the creation of some great works of art but also a series of tragic wars.
   - Drama—Three major genres of musical drama developed during that time: oratorio, cantata, and opera.

2. Many Baroque composers worked under a system of patronage in which they were employed exclusively for one person or institution, often a church. Several of them were outstanding performers in addition to being excellent composers. They were also very good at improvising music at the keyboard.

3. Homophony developed during this time, especially in vocal music. The accompanying parts are based on the system of major and minor chords that still prevails in music today. A tonal center was established for a work, but temporary modulations to different keys became common.

4. Rhythm was marked by regular metrical patterns of strong and weak beats.

5. Recitatives were developed to allow the music to express more effectively the words being sung by the singer. Even though the music notation contains bar lines, recitatives are sung with very flexible rhythm. Usually they are rather short and do not repeat words. Their accompaniments are simple, with occasional places in which they enhance the words being sung.

6. The Doctrine of Affections (or Affects) was the belief in the emotional or affective qualities of music. It is present in vocal music by sometimes linking a melodic pattern to the particular words being sung. Sections of both vocal and instrumental works maintained the same quality from beginning to end.

7. Equal temperament was developed for tuning keyboard instruments. It solved an acoustical caprice of nature by making all intervals slightly less than perfect. When implemented, it allowed for the use of a greater variety of tonal centers. The system is still used in almost all music performed in Western civilization today.

8. During the Baroque period harpsichords and pipe organs could not make gradual changes in dynamic levels. Therefore, these changes tended to be abrupt, or what is termed terraced dynamics.

9. The accompanying bass line in much Baroque music usually has a continuous, steady quality. In fact, it was called basso continuo, or, more commonly, continuo. Keyboard players in the continuo part utilized a system of musical shorthand called figured bass that consisted of numbers indicating changes from the expected harmony.

FEATURES TO LISTEN FOR

1. The dramatic ways in which the words of the recitative "The Voice of Him" from Handel's *Messiah* are emphasized and expressed.

2. The uncluttered nature of its accompaniment that concludes with a solid V-I (dominant-tonic) cadence.

3. The flexible rhythm that allows the singer to emphasize certain words.

11 Oratorio *and* Cantata

Opera is presented in Chapter 12.

Three dramatic genres of music were developed during the Baroque period: oratorio, cantata, and opera. This chapter concentrates on the oratorio and the cantata.

ORATORIO

Because of the cost of hiring an orchestra, oratorios are usually performed with an organ.

An **oratorio** is a lengthy musical work for voices and orchestra. Oratorios consist of many arias, recitatives, and choruses, plus a few sections for the accompanying orchestra. When oratorios first appeared on the musical scene early in the Baroque, they were more like operas on religious topics, complete with scenery, costumes, and actions. Long before the end of the Baroque, however, the stage elements had been discarded, but the idea of drama remained. Soloists still represented specific characters, the text related a story, and the music exploited the dramatic situation.

The Old Testament, with its dramatic stories, is an especially rich source for oratorio texts.

Although oratorios are on religious topics, they are not intended for use in worship services. They are too long and require too many performers. Instead, they were created for performance in concert halls or special occasions in churches.

Handel's *Messiah*

Nearly three hours are required to perform all the music in *Messiah*. Today, conductors usually select which sections they wish to perform.

Word of the new work spread before the premiere. Because only seven hundred people could be squeezed into the hall—even though they stood because the hall had no seats—advertisements requested that ladies avoid wearing dresses with hoops and men come without swords.

Probably the most famous oratorio of all time is *Messiah* by George Frideric Handel. It consists of fifty-three sections: nineteen choruses, sixteen arias, sixteen recitatives, and two sections for orchestra alone. It is typical in terms of its length and distribution of sections. It is not so typical, however, in that its text is taken entirely from the Bible. Although based on biblical stories, oratorios normally were not confined to scripture. *Messiah* also lacks a role for a narrator, usually a tenor, who relates the story. It is primarily a contemplation on Christian belief in three parts: the prophecy and Christ's birth, his suffering and death, and the Resurrection and Redemption.

Messiah is also atypical in terms of its success with audiences over the more than 265 years since it was written, as well as its many translations into other languages and a multitude of recordings.

ARIA

In addition to recitative, a second type of music for one singer with accompaniment that developed during the Baroque was the **aria** ("*ar*-ee-ah"). Arias are very different from recitatives in a number of ways.

1. Arias are much longer than recitatives. For example, "Ev'ry Valley Shall Be Exalted" from Handel's *Messiah* is eight times as long as the recitative "The Voice of Him."
2. The accompanying orchestra has a much larger and more important role in the aria. The accompaniments usually have some musically interesting passages, which they often perform without the soloist. The orchestra may also reiterate a figure that the soloist has sung, or it may play musical material of its own.
3. In arias the soloists frequently sing rapidly moving notes or perform long phrases on one word or syllable, a feature that is prominent in "Ev'ry Valley Shall Be Exalted."

96

4. Although most arias are much longer than recitatives, often their texts are shorter. Arias are usually longer because they often repeat words and phrases, as well as contain passages for the accompanying instruments.

5. The texts of arias dwell on a single idea. Sometimes they are like sung soliloquies that offer reactions to situations. They seldom advance the story by describing an event. The mood of "Ev'ry Valley Shall Be Exalted" is filled with a sense of anticipation.

6. Arias often have a formal pattern, and sections of them are generally repeated. "Ev'ry Valley Shall Be Exalted" follows a binary *A B A B* form.

7. Arias follow the strict metrical rhythm and steady beat found in most Baroque music. Except for unmetered recitatives, Baroque rhythm is very straightforward. Changes of tempo in arias and other works are permitted only near the ends of sections in a long work.

8. Composers intended arias to stand on their own musical merits to a much greater extent than recitatives, which often serve mainly to advance the story or to be a bridge between sections. For this reason, they gave arias more memorable melodic and vocal qualities.

"Ev'ry Valley Shall Be Exalted" from *Messiah*

The upbeat mood of "Ev'ry Valley" allowed Handel to write music that shows off the singer's vocal prowess through long series (called **runs** by musicians) of sixteenth notes on the word "exalted":

These runs are examples of the Baroque practice of *virtuoso singing*. A **virtuoso** is someone who has outstanding skill in performing.

Much attention was given to soloists in the Baroque period. Vocalists competed with one another for the favor of audiences by adding flashy runs and ornaments to the music. This custom grew until the music became merely a framework for soloists to build on as they wished. Some astonishing singing skill was the result, but the quality of the music often suffered. Although the situation had been somewhat moderated by Handel's time, the virtuoso style was still very much alive, and audiences expected to hear some vocal displays.

In "Ev'ry Valley" the runs do more than show off the skill of the singer. Handel integrates them into the overall musical fabric so that they enhance the effect of the music and emphasize the message of the words.

The text of "Ev'ry Valley" says basically that things are going to be turned upside down when the Messiah comes. The valleys will be raised up—they will be exalted. By having the soloist sing long runs on "exalted," Handel emphasizes that thought.

Virtuoso passages in Baroque vocal music are sometimes baffling to people who are not familiar with them. At first glance, it is difficult to understand why one syllable or word is stretched out over forty or more notes. "Exalted" could be sung with just three notes, of course. In everyday practical terms, it seems pointless to use forty notes to sing one syllable or word. But the music would not have nearly so much impact and interest. It is impressive to hear a skilled singer execute long runs and to hear them fit so well into the music.

The word *virtuoso* is not restricted to music. It can also describe performances by very skilled athletes, dancers, and others.

Handel follows the doctrine of affections in the aria as well as the chorus. The words "The crooked straight" are set to pitches that rock back and forth one step apart, except the word "straight," which is a steady long note. The word "mountain" is high, and the word "low" is low. The word "plain" is set in a sequence of smooth planes.

LISTENING GUIDE

GEORGE FRIDERIC HANDEL

"Ev'ry Valley Shall Be Exalted" from *Messiah* (1741)

GENRE: Aria, oratorio   Tenor and orchestra

CD 1 Tracks [22] – [23]

3 minutes 40 seconds

Form: *A B A B*

0:00 [22]	0:00	The orchestra plays a *ritornello* (refrain).
	0:22	The tenor soloist sings "Ev'ry valley shall be exalted" (A).

Ev -'ry val - ley,   ev -'ry val - ley ——— shall be ex-alt - ed,

	0:35	First long run on "exalted."
	0:50	Second long run on "exalted."
	0:58	Aria continues "and ev'ry mountain and hill made low."
1:04 [23]	0:00	B portion begins with "the crooked straight" and continues with "and the rough places plain."
	0:42	A returns with some changes.
	1:24	B returns with some changes.
	1:54	Tempo slows, and some decorative notes are added.
	2:12	The orchestra repeats the ritornello.
	2:36	"Ev'ry Valley" concludes with a solid ending.

An interactive Active Listening Guide can be downloaded from the online Resource Center for *Music Listening Today, 4th Edition.*

What is it about the arias from Handel's *Messiah* that motivates people to listen to them hundreds of years after they were written? They feature several exceptional qualities:

- They demonstrate the expressive impact when words and music are combined so skillfully. When a sensitive recitative or a tender aria is sung well, the music has much expressive power.

- They exhibit the virtuoso techniques of a good singer. Hearing a virtuoso singer executing the difficult or showy passages of an aria is similar to watching a champion figure skater flawlessly execute a difficult routine.

- They contain the qualities of Baroque music that help it "wear well" with listeners.

Handel established a standard for the oratorio in England and America, a standard that has lasted.

George Frideric Handel (1685–1759) was a German by birth, the son of a well-to-do barber-surgeon in the city of Halle in Saxony, who never wanted his son to pursue music as a career. Young George showed much talent in composing and playing the harpsichord and organ. His father's early death removed the obstacle to pursuing a career in music. After a year of college, he went to Hamburg, where he got a job playing in an orchestra.

Handel soon moved to Italy, which was the center for music at that time. He studied composition and cultivated friendships with music patrons. At the age of twenty-five, he returned to Germany as music director of the Electoral Court at Hanover. In two years he managed to take two leaves of absence to go to London, where his operas (in Italian) were very successful. He was in London when the elector of Hanover was proclaimed King George I of England.

Handel stayed in London for the remainder of his life. For eight years he held an important position as director of the Royal Academy of Music, which was founded to present Italian opera. The job was not an easy one. The musicians were temperamental and engaged in much infighting, and the situation was not helped by Handel's stubborn and overbearing personality.

One hair-pulling and shouting fight between singers took place at a performance when Princess Caroline (for whom North and South Carolina were named) was in the audience.

In time, another type of musical theater became fashionable with English audiences. Called *beggar's opera*, it was more like a play with politically satirical songs inserted. Handel refused to abandon his Italian operas, however. After nine more years of writing and losing money in that endeavor, his health broke, and he was heavily in debt. He went abroad to recover.

And recover he did. After a few more futile tries at reviving Italian opera, he turned to oratorios. Within a few years, he was again at the top of the English musical world. He wrote more than twenty-six oratorios, but none is heard as often today as *Messiah*. Handel composed this monumental work in 1741 in a little more than three weeks! He worked at it almost constantly and paid little attention to the meals servants left at his door. Its first performance was a benefit concert in Dublin, Ireland. It was a tremendous success, although later performances in London were received more coolly.

In 1759 Handel collapsed after conducting a performance of *Messiah*. He died eight days later and was interred with state honors in Westminster Abbey.

BEST-KNOWN WORKS

oratorios:
- *Messiah*
- *Israel in Egypt*
- *Samson*
- *Saul*

opera:
- *Acis and Galatea*
- *Giulio Cesare (Julius Caesar)*
- *Semele*
- *Hercules*

instrumental suites:
- *Water Music*
- *Fireworks Music*

CHORUS

The word **chorus** has two meanings in music. One is a group that sings choral music. The other meaning refers to the choral sections of a large choral work such as an oratorio or opera. So a chorus sings a chorus.

Choruses can vary a lot in size. They can have as few as sixteen singers, although that is unusual, or they can have several hundred singers, but that also is unusual. More typical is that they contain approximately an equal number of men and women, unless they are specifically limited to men or women. The choruses that sang Handel's *Messiah* during his lifetime were definitely on the small side; only eighteen singers made up the chorus at its premiere performance.

This is logical, albeit a bit confusing.

A hundred years later at a festival honoring Handel, a chorus of four thousand and an orchestra of five hundred performed his music!

The following are characteristics of choruses in Baroque choral works:

- They are somewhat lengthy and often repeat words.
- The rhythm is strictly adhered to, unlike what happens in recitatives.
- The accompanying part plays an important role.
- The music for choruses normally requires more than average singing skill. In fact, some of them are quite challenging and contain virtuoso-like passages.
- They are often contrapuntal. The various sections often enter in imitation.

"Hallelujah Chorus" from *Messiah*

The "Hallelujah Chorus" is familiar to most people and is traditionally performed at Christmas. In fact, at the first performance of *Messiah* in London, King George II was so impressed when he heard "Hallelujah Chorus" that he stood up. In those days, when the king stood, everyone stood. King George's spontaneous action started a tradition that is still honored today.

As you listen to this chorus, notice how skillfully Handel has placed the words in terms of their rhythmic emphasis. The word *Hallelujah* is written as one would say it when really pleased. In phrases such as "and He shall reign forever and ever," the important words in the phrase land on the important beats and parts of the beats in the rhythm pattern. The important words in the phrase are *He, reign,* and *ev-* of *forever,* because it is the emphasized syllable in that word. It would be much more difficult to sing the phrase, "*and* he *shall* reign *for*-ev-*er*," and it would sound awkward and unmusical.

To realize how important the placement of emphasis in words is, try saying "Hallelujah" in different ways: "*HAL*-le-*lu*-jah," "Ha-*le*-lu-*JAH*," and so on.

LISTENING GUIDE

GEORGE FRIDERIC HANDEL
"Hallelujah Chorus" from *Messiah* (1741)

GENRE: Chorus, oratorio   Chorus and orchestra

CD 1 Tracks 24 – 26

3 minutes 37 seconds

0:00	24	0:00	Orchestra plays a short introduction.
		0:07	Chorus sings "Hallelujah" five times, then five more times at a different pitch level.
		0:24	Chorus sings "for the Lord God Omnipotent reigneth," followed by four "Hallelujahs."

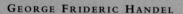

for   the   Lord   God   Om - ni - po - tent   reign - eth.

		0:35	Altos, tenors, and basses repeat "for the Lord God . . . ," followed by four "Hallelujahs."
		0:46	Sopranos sing "for the Lord God . . . ," with chorus singing "Hallelujah" in counterpoint.
		0:53	Tenors and basses sing "for the Lord God . . ." while sopranos and altos sing contrasting "Hallelujahs."
		1:02	Altos and tenors sing "for the Lord God . . ." while sopranos and basses sing contrapuntal "Hallelujahs."
1:12	25	0:00	Chorus sings together "The kingdom of this world is become the Kingdom of our Lord and of His Christ."
1:30	26	0:00	Basses begin new melodic phrase and text, "and He shall reign forever and ever," followed in imitation by tenors, altos, and sopranos.

and   He   shall   reign   for - ev - er   and   ev - er.

0:22	Sopranos and altos sing alternately "King of Kings" and "Lord of Lords" while basses and tenors sing "forever and ever, Hallelujah." Same pattern repeated four times, each time at a higher pitch level.
1:03	Basses begin "and He shall reign . . ." as other sections sing contrasting material.
1:14	Tenors sing "King of Kings" and "Lord of Lords" while other sections respond with "forever and ever" and "Hallelujah."
1:23	Chorus sings together, with basses singing "and He shall reign . . . ," followed by "King of Kings."
2:07	"Hallelujah Chorus" ends after four "Hallelujahs" and one long final "Hallelujah."

 An interactive Active Listening Guide can be downloaded from the online Resource Center for *Music Listening Today, 4th Edition.*

Handel did a lot of things right in "Hallelujah Chorus" in addition to matching words and music so well. In the first part, he contrasts quick "Hallelujahs" with the steady, solid-sounding "For the Lord God Omnipotent reigneth." He uses text painting when he has the first four notes of that phrase ascend by step up to the word "God." In the middle section, the words "The Kingdom of the world" are sung softly at a low pitch level. Then they become much louder and higher as the words progress: "is become of the Kingdom of our Lord . . ." At one point in the third section, he builds on the words "King of Kings, and Lord of Lords" by repeating them several times in succession, each time at a higher level of pitch. Finally, the trumpets enter to bolster the dramatic impact of the music at that point. Especially important is the sense of power and grandeur that this chorus conveys.

Handel's success in matching words and music is especially interesting because he never learned to speak English well after emigrating from Germany in his late twenties.

CHORALE

The chorale was a product of early Protestant belief and practice in the sixteenth century, when Martin Luther's break from the Roman Catholic Church became final. Luther and some of his colleagues set about providing music suitable for worship in the newly developed services. They wanted the members of the congregation to be participants in the service, not just observers.

One way to involve them was to have them sing. But what should they sing? Chant was associated too strongly with the rejected Roman Catholic Church. Also, its style and subtleties are difficult for untrained singers to perform properly. The answer was to create a new body of religious music that had strong, simple melodies. So from German religious songs, from adaptations of chant and secular tunes, and from the pen of Luther himself and others came the **chorale,** which is basically a German Lutheran hymn.

Luther believed not only that worshipers should sing but also that their music should encourage the proper religious attitude. So one purpose of the chorale was to proclaim beliefs and contribute to the spirit of worship. The Protestant attitudes of that time are clearly expressed in "A Mighty Fortress Is Our God." Here is a translation of one verse:

It is very likely that Luther himself composed the words and music for "A Mighty Fortress Is Our God."

> *Though devils all the world should fill,*
> *All eager to devour us;*
> *We tremble not, we fear no ill,*
> *They shall not overpower us.*

As his metaphor for God, Luther chose the German word *Burg*, a medieval stone fortress, a symbol of austere strength. The chorale reflects the serious religious outlook of the early Protestants. Each note in its melody stands like a block of stone in a fortress.

Musically, a chorale-hymn is very different from Gregorian chant:

A chorale is presented as part of Bach's cantata later in this chapter.

- A hymn has a regular rhythm.
- It is in German or other vernacular language.
- It has several verses of words for the same melody.
- It can be accompanied by organ or other instrument.

On first hearing, a chorale, like Gregorian chant, may seem uninteresting. It's true; both lack novelty and flashiness. But religious music seeks to express what the faithful believe to be the ultimate and eternal. Theological beliefs and the music need to be congruent, with one reflecting the other. Furthermore, both the chorale and the chant provide devout worshipers with a sense of communion with believers who have gone before, as well as suggest the timeless nature of their beliefs.

CANTATA

Because of their strong, simple qualities, chorale melodies are well suited for use as themes for other musical works. These melodies are often found in cantatas. Originally, the word **cantata** meant any sizable work, sacred or secular, that was sung. By the time of Johann Sebastian Bach (1685–1750), the cantata had become a short oratorio, with an instrumental accompaniment, arias, recitatives, and choruses. A cantata is much shorter than an oratorio, and it is written to be performed in a worship service. A cantata typically has between five and eight sections and incorporates a chorale melody into some of its sections. It often ends with the chorale on which it is based.

Several types of organ works that use chorale melodies are discussed in Chapter 13.

There was plenty of time in the worship service at Bach's church in Leipzig, Germany, for a twenty-minute cantata. The main service began at 7 AM and could last until noon! There were also three other short services on Sunday, as well as daily services and special religious celebrations. Altogether, Leipzig's Lutheran churches required fifty-eight cantatas each year, as well as other types of music for special occasions. Bach composed about one cantata per month during most of his career in Leipzig.

About two hundred of the three hundred cantatas Bach composed have been preserved.

Bach's Cantata No. 140

One of Bach's best-known cantatas is *Wachet auf, ruft uns die Stimme* (*Wake Up, Call the Voices*), Cantata No. 140. It was written for the Sunday before Advent, which is four Sundays before Christmas. The text, based on Matthew 25:1–13, tells the parable of the five wise and five foolish maidens. The cantata had this message for the congregation: Be prepared and vigilant, because you never know when you will be called to be with God.

Bach did not number his cantatas. Editors did that years after they were composed.

Life expectancy was much shorter in the eighteenth century.

Cantata No. 140 is divided into seven sections. The chorale melody appears in the first, fourth, and seventh sections. The first section is the longest and most complex. It is a chorus that features the driving, uneven rhythm of dotted-eighths and sixteenths played against a contrasting part. The chorale melody appears in long notes in the soprano part. As these notes are sung, the alto, tenor, and bass parts sing contrasting musical lines. This chorus illustrates the interest of Baroque composers in the doctrine of affections, which can be seen in many Baroque vocal works. For example, in Bach's cantata the words *wach' auf* (wake up), *wohl auf* (cheer up), and *steht auf* (get up or arise) are sung to notes that move from lower to higher pitches.

The second section of Cantata No. 140 is a recitative for tenor. It sets forth the image of Christ as the Heavenly Bridegroom and tells about his coming.

The third section is a duet between an anxious soul (sung by the soprano soloist) and Jesus (sung by the bass soloist). This section also features a florid violin solo.

Many cantatas use the analogy of Christ as the groom and the Church as his bride.

The fourth section appears on page 104. A gentle melody is played by the strings while the tenor section in unison sings the chorale melody.

The fifth section is a recitative for bass in which Jesus tenderly greets the bride.

The sixth section is a duet between the soprano (the soul) and the bass (Jesus).

The seventh and final section of Cantata No. 140 is a harmonization of the chorale melody in which the worshipers praise God and rejoice. It was customary for the congregation to join in singing the final chorale. The chorales were familiar to the congregation and were sung in their native language. The chorale melody appears in the soprano (top part in the treble clef). Bach did not compose the melody. He added the alto, tenor, and bass parts to complete the harmony.

The idea of chorale singing by the congregation was also influenced by the educational level of the worshipers. Many people in the Baroque period could not read or write, so pictures, statues, and music in churches were intended to be educational as well as beautiful. A text for a chorale was selected for reasons of instruction as well as worship.

JOHANN SEBASTIAN BACH

Chorale (Section 7) from Cantata No. 140 (melody c. 1600; harmonized 1731)

GENRE: Chorale, cantata Chorus and orchestra

CD 3 Track 18

1 minute 23 seconds

0:00 18 0:00 Gloria sei dir gesungen
mit Menschen und englischen Zungen,
mit Harfen und mit Zimbeln schon.

Glory now be sung to praise Thee
with tongues of all mankind and angels,
with harps and cymbals sounding forth.

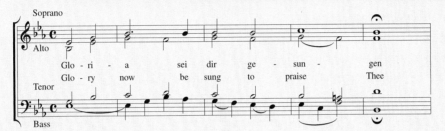

0:24 Von zwölf Perlen sind die Pforten
an deiner Stadt; wir sind Konsorten
der Engel hoch um deinen Thron.

Of twelve pearls are built the portals of
thy fair city, we have joined hosts of
angels high around thy throne.

0:47 Kein Aug' hat je gespürt,
kein Ohr hat je gehört
solche Freude.
Dess sind wir froh,
Io, io!
ewig in dulci jublio.

No eye hath ever seen,
no ear hath ever heard
such wondrous joy.
Thus we rejoice,
io, io!
for evermore in sweetest praise.

1:23 Chorale concludes.

An interactive Active Listening Guide can be downloaded from the online Resource Center for *Music Listening Today, 4th Edition.*

LISTENING GUIDE

OTHER TYPES OF BAROQUE VOCAL MUSIC

lssohn, an important
the nineteenth century,
ible for this performance.
sed in Chapter 23.

The cantata is only one of several types of vocal music composed for Protestant worship services in the Baroque period. Another type is the **passion,** which is like an oratorio except that its subject is the suffering of Christ on the cross. Bach's *St. Matthew Passion* was rediscovered and performed seventy-nine years after his death, and that performance renewed interest in other music by Bach. Like the cantatas, the *St. Matthew Passion* gives a prominent place to a chorale, "O Sacred Head Now Wounded."

There is also a Baroque motet. It is an unaccompanied, religious, and polyphonic work. In the Baroque, however, the music had a strong sense of metrical rhythm and systematic harmony. It was also written in a vernacular language.

JOHANN SEBASTIAN BACH

"Zion Hears the Watchmen" (Section 4) from Cantata No. 140 (1731)

GENRE: Cantata   Tenor section and orchestra

CD 1 Tracks 27 – 28

4 minutes 15 seconds

0:00   27   0:00   Upper strings play a flowing melody above a steady bass:

Violins, Violas

0:43   Tenors sing the first three phrases of the chorale in unison:

Zion hört die Wächter singen,	Zion hears the watchmen calling,
das Herz thut ihr vor Freuden springen,	her heart within her leaps for gladness,
sie wachet, und steht eilend auf,	she wakes and stands to hasten forth,

1:11   The flowing melody is repeated by upper strings.

1:52   The first three phrases of the chorale are repeated, but with different words:

Ihr Freund kommt vom Himmel prächtig,	Her friend comes from Heaven in splendor,
Von Gnaden stark, von Wahrheit mächtig,	In mercy strong, in truth almighty,
Ihr Licht wird hell, ihr Stern geht auf.	Her light grows bright, her star appears.

2:22   The flowing melody is repeated by upper strings.

2:47   28   0:00   The fourth, fifth, and sixth phrases of the chorale are sung:

Nun komm, du werthe Kron',	Now come, thou precious crown,
Herr Jesu, Gottes Sohn,	Lord Jesus, God's Son,
Hosianna!	Hosanna!

0:23   The flowing melody continues, but in minor.

0:41   The seventh and eighth phrases of the chorale are sung.

Wir folgen all' zum Freudensaal,	We follow all to the festive hall,
und halten mit das Abendmahl.	and share in our Lord's Supper there.

1:28   The section of the cantata concludes with upper strings playing the flowing melody.

 An interactive Active Listening Guide can be downloaded from the online Resource Center for *Music Listening Today, 4th Edition.*

MAIN POINTS OF THIS CHAPTER

1. An oratorio is a lengthy work for soloists, chorus, and orchestra. Its many sections are divided into recitatives, arias, and choruses, with an occasional work for orchestra alone. Although their stories are dramatic, often drawn from the Old Testament, oratorios are performed without scenery, costumes, or actions. They are concert works that were not intended for performance during worship services.

2. Arias are sizable vocal solos accompanied by an orchestra. They are much more melodic than recitatives and repeat lines of text. Often their texts are reflective; they do not necessarily advance the story. They usually follow a form, with A B A being the most common one. They are in major and minor keys and have a clear metrical rhythm.

3. Arias often contain virtuoso passages that show off the singer's ability. These passages of rapidly moving notes add to the musical impact of an aria.

4. A chorus is sung by a chorus. It has many of the features found in an aria, but of course is sung by a group of singers. It is also different in that it often contains imitation among the voice parts.

5. A chorale is a Lutheran hymn. It features a strong, simple melody that was created to be sung by the congregation. These melodies were used many times as themes in other Baroque works such as cantatas and organ music.

6. In one sense, a cantata is a short oratorio. It is different in that it uses a chorale melody in some of its parts. Cantatas were composed to be performed during worship services, and they usually contain a religious message.

FEATURES TO LISTEN FOR

1. The affect of the long runs on the word "exalted" in "Every Valley Shall Be Exalted" from Handel's *Messiah*.

2. The examples of text or word painting in both "Every Valley Shall Be Exalted" and the "Hallelujah Chorus."

3. The combination of the solid chorale melody sung by the tenors and the flowing melody played by the strings in Part IV of Bach's Cantata No. 140.

4. The sturdy, solid nature of the chorale melody used in Bach's Cantata No. 140.

5. The cadences at the conclusion of each phrase of the harmonized version (Part VII) of the chorale in Bach's Cantata No. 140. Not all of them provide a feeling of conclusion.

6. The imitation in the "Hallelujah Chorus" that begins with the basses singing "And He shall reign forever and ever," which is followed by the tenors, then the altos, and finally the sopranos.

12 Opera *in the* Baroque

Drama was one of the main features of Baroque style. The carefully planned figures in Renaissance paintings were replaced with twisting lines and energetic poses, and restrained polyphonic motets and madrigals gave way to recitatives and arias that projected emotion and feelings. The goals of artists and composers had changed—dramatically.

Opera was one result of the desire to make music more expressive. It was founded as an attempt to re-create the dramas of ancient Greece. Around 1600 a group of noblemen in Florence, Italy, believed that a single line of melody with simple accompaniment would be much more expressive of the words. The result was the development of recitative. In fact, the earliest operas consisted almost entirely of recitatives.

One of the group of noblemen was Vincenzio Galilei, father of the famous astronomer Galileo Galilei.

But do audiences enjoy listening to a couple of hours of nothing but one recitative after another? Soon composers began to realize that the answer to that question was no. Something more was needed. By the time the first opera house opened in Venice in 1637, the artistic goal of a musical version of ancient Greek drama had been largely forgotten. The stories became burdened by the addition of irrelevant incidents, spectacular scenes, and incongruous comedy episodes. But other changes were more constructive. Arias, duets, and ensembles evolved, and the accompanying orchestra took on more importance.

As opera spread throughout Europe, its dramatic elements were largely absent. The singers reigned supreme. In their desire to hold the attention of the audience, soloists added all sorts of embellishments to a melody to show off their singing prowess.

Although opera was a child of the Baroque, the operas of that period are not often performed today in opera houses in Europe or America. The reason is not that the Baroque operas lack musical merit but that opera companies can produce only a limited number of operas, and subsequent operas have found greater favor with audiences. Nevertheless, the operas of a few Baroque composers stand out, especially those of Claudio Monteverdi and Henry Purcell, which are presented later in this chapter.

THE ELEMENTS OF OPERA

Each element in the amalgam that is opera makes a particular contribution, and each merits further discussion, beginning with singers and their voice ranges and types.

Voices and Roles

In Western civilization there seems to be an association in people's minds between age and the pitch level of the voice: the older a person is, the lower the voice.

Opera has acquired a number of traditions regarding the types of voices and characters portrayed. The heroine is almost always a soprano. In most operas, she is young and beautiful, so a high, lighter voice is appropriate. Often the heroine's part calls for virtuoso singing. Some female parts are written for lower or heavier voices such as mezzo-soprano or contralto. These roles often portray older women, servants, rivals, or villainesses.

The leading male role is often for a tenor. He is young and frequently sings duets with the leading soprano, often doubling her pitches one octave lower. This puts his notes near the top of the male voice range and gives the singing more intensity. Other male parts may be sung by a baritone, a voice that is lower and heavier than the tenor. The bass, which is the lowest and heaviest male voice, is often used to portray villains, older men, or authority figures such as kings.

The vocal and dramatic demands for singing operatic roles are great. Almost all roles require extensive training in the use of the voice to achieve the necessary breath con-

B. Rafferty/Lebrecht/The Image Works

SINGERS PERFORM IN *THE CORONATION OF POPPEA*
Nigel Robson and Marie Angel perform in an Opera Factory production of *The Coronation of Poppea*.

trol, endurance, wide pitch range, richness of tone quality, control of dynamic levels, and technical know-how, not to mention the ability to project the singing over an orchestra all the way to the last row of the balcony. Not only do opera singers sing, but they must also be actors in a drama. They must make their efforts sound and look convincing.

Operas are usually sung without amplification.

Ensembles

Most operas have parts for small ensembles and choruses. **Ensembles** frequently consist of several characters singing different words and music expressing their particular feelings, creating a kind of musical and emotional counterpoint.

Operatic choruses usually appear in scenes with many people—a wedding, a coronation, a crowded tavern. To a degree, the chorus participates in the stage action, but usually from behind the soloists. Often the words the chorus sings are a commentary on the situation.

The Orchestra

The orchestra is placed largely out of sight in a pit in front of the stage. Although unseen, it has an important role in opera. Not only does the orchestra accompany the singers, it also sets moods, enhances the actions onstage, and performs overtures and preludes while the curtain is closed. The orchestral music written for operas by some nineteenth-century composers is so complete that today portions of it are frequently performed as concert works without any singing at all.

The Libretto

The script or text of an opera is called the **libretto.** The composer of the music usually does not write the libretto for the opera. Instead, a librettist generally creates a version of a play, historical event, or story. Often the libretto is set in poetic form, especially the portions that are likely places for arias or choruses. Once the libretto has been written, the composer takes over and sets the words to music.

Libretto means "little book" in Italian.

Staging

Visual elements are an integral part of opera. The quality of acting, costumes, scenic design, lighting, and dancing makes a great difference in the success of an opera. The lighting and stage effects that can be achieved in a first-rate opera house are truly amazing and at times dazzling. For example, if a character is to be demolished in smoke and fire, this can be done in quite a convincing and dramatic way.

The need for set designers, costumers, electricians, and stagehands in addition to singers, orchestral musicians, and sometimes dancers is one of opera's greatest obstacles: It is a very expensive art form. A large opera can require the services of several hundred highly skilled technicians and musicians, and this need is usually reflected in the high ticket prices and the chronic financial problems of opera companies. A lack of funds also discourages touring by opera companies and presentations of new operas. One positive development in making opera more available and less expensive is the projection of performances on large screens in theaters and auditoriums. Not only do these performances cost operagoers a fraction of live performances, they also provide close up shots of the singers and actions on stage. The sound is sometimes clearer than a live performance, depending on one's seat, of course. They do lack the sense of presence that live performances provide, but they are an excellent next-best choice. The fact that opera is still active and vital in American musical life, in spite of its high costs and lack of familiarity to much of the population, is eloquent testimony to its musical and dramatic value.

OPERATIC CONVENTIONS

All forms of theater have conventions and customs that audiences accept. For example, in films an orchestra is heard in the background, adding to the suspense as an actor is about to be attacked in a dark, deserted house. What's an orchestra doing there? No one wonders about that, because viewers are accustomed to the convention of background music. Nor is anyone bothered when a scene changes in a few seconds to one that supposedly occurs hours or even years later, or that the stage in a theater is like a room with one wall removed so that the audience can see what's going on.

The reason people are not bothered by these conventions is simple: They are used to them. On the other hand, most people are not familiar with operatic customs, and so such customs often hinder their enjoyment.

What are the more obvious conventions associated with opera? One is the replacement of speaking with singing. In everyday life a phrase such as "Robert will be here at three o'clock" is spoken. Furthermore, sometimes rather robust singing takes place when logically it does not make a lot of sense—such as when a character is dying or very sick.

Not only are all the words sung, but they are sung in a highly trained style, which is another operatic convention. Most operas have a "bigger than life" quality about them, and that is one of their attractive features. The style of singing, therefore, needs to be bigger than life. It must have enough power to be heard over an orchestra in a large hall, and it should have a quality that moves listeners emotionally. Folk singers can sing their ballads in a simple, unaffected style because they usually perform in a small room accompanied by a guitar, and even then their singing is often amplified.

Another convention concerns the words. Even when sung in English, they are not easily understood. The problem is increased by the large number of operas in foreign languages. These operas can be translated and sung in English, but should they be? Although translations are not easy, involving correct numbers of syllables, natural accents, shades of meaning, and rhyme schemes, the answer is probably yes, at least for people who are not familiar with opera. When operas are sung in languages other than English, listeners need to follow a translation or observe the words projected in English, if available.

A fourth convention involves the element of time. In addition to the usual flexibility in the treatment of time in films and dramas, operas have to deal with the impact of sing-

Smoke and fire finish off Don Giovanni in Mozart's opera.

The technicians and stagehands often are paid more than the dancers or members of the chorus.

Neither singing style is more musical than the other because each is appropriate for a particular type of music and setting.

It is almost impossible to translate the lines of an opera without losing some of the original meaning.

The increased impact of music on words can be demonstrated by reading the words of an aria or a chorus aloud and then hearing those same words as they have been set to music by a great composer.

The most influential composer of the early Baroque period was **Claudio Monteverdi** (1567–1643). He was born in Cremona, Italy, which was famous for its violin makers, and his early musical training included learning to play the violin. His father was a chemist/physician who wanted his son to have a good education in music. Monteverdi was first employed as a court musician at Mantova and later was appointed to be in charge of the music there. He left when the duke failed to pay him some of the wages due him. At the age of forty-five, he was awarded the coveted position as music master at Saint Mark's in Venice.

Monteverdi began writing madrigals in the Renaissance, but slowly his madrigals began to change. Instrumental parts were added, and they became more homophonic in texture. In a real sense, he bridged the Renaissance and Baroque periods and helped bring about major changes in music.

Although his position in Venice was to produce music for the Church, he never stopped composing operas. *L'Orfeo* (*Orpheus*), written in 1607, was his first successful opera and one of the most important in the development of Western music. *L'incoronazione di Poppea* (*The Coronation of Poppea*), composed in 1642, was his last. He was very effective in injecting emotional qualities into his music. He was also probably the first composer to ask the violinists for effects such as *tremolo* (rapidly moving the bow back and forth on the string) and vibrato to add warmth to the tone quality.

Portrait of Claudio Monteverdi (1567–1643) (oil on canvas), Fetti or Feti, Domenico (1589–1624)/Galleria dell'Accademia, Venice, Italy/The Bridgeman Art Library

Best-Known Works

opera:
- *Combattimento di Tancredi et Clorinda*
- *L'incoronazione di Poppea*
- *L'Orfeo*

ing on the amount of time available. If the words "Robert will be here at three o'clock" are spoken, they don't require much time. If those words were set to a nice melody, however, they would take much more time. The difference would be some pleasant music, but an interruption of the story. If the words were to be sung in about the same amount of time as when spoken, they would not be of much musical interest. Operagoers accept the distortions of time caused by the addition of the music because of the heightened overall musical and dramatic impact.

Enjoying Opera

When the conventions of opera are accepted, most people find that they enjoy attending an opera. This is true for several reasons:

- The music is often stunning and beautiful. Operas offer listeners a rich source of flowing melodies, impressive tonal effects, and sensuous harmonies. In addition, there is a great deal of outstanding singing.

- The combined expressiveness of words and music is a pleasure to hear. Opera sets up situations in which the combination of the two can have even greater emotional impact than music apart from the dramatic situation. While the singing of the text may slow down the action on stage, it adds much to the overall drama. Some operatic I-love-yous, for example, can cause chills to run up one's spine.

- Opera appeals to both the ears and the eyes. Looking at an opera without hearing the music is an incomplete experience, just as it would be when listening to the music without seeing what takes place onstage.

- Opera lets people see and hear experiences that are beyond ordinary life. For some rather deep-seated psychological reasons, people enjoy stories, films, television shows, and the like that take them temporarily out of their own everyday existence. In soap operas, for example, the actors undergo traumatic experiences with a frequency and an intensity that (fortunately) far exceed what most people encounter in their lives. Good opera is good theater.

Soap operas were given that name because originally they were often sponsored by soap companies, and also because the characters' lives are much more crisis-ridden than those of ordinary people.

MONTEVERDI'S *CORONATION OF POPPEA*

Actually, he did not fiddle. Instead, he probably played a lyrelike instrument and sang. He thought of himself as a great singer. Before he committed suicide, he is reported to have said, "What an artist the world is losing in me!"

Poppea's success was short lived. She was murdered, possibly by Nero himself, after only a few years as empress.

Is Poppea able to work her charms on Nero? Check out the Listening Guide.

Monteverdi was the most important composer of the early Baroque, and especially of opera. His last opera was *The Coronation of Poppea*. The story is based very loosely on the Roman emperor Nero, who reigned from AD 54 to 68 and who is remembered throughout history for fiddling while Rome burned. He was a weak, vain man who pursued many women. Poppea knew how to play up to Nero's passions, and by careful scheming she was able to dispose of his wife so that Nero would marry her and make her empress.

The plot of Monteverdi's opera is characterized by much intrigue among the characters. Poppea is spared from an assassin by the intervention of the god Cupid, and she achieves her goal of becoming empress of the Roman Empire.

Many characteristics of recitative can be heard in a portion of Monteverdi's *Coronation of Poppea*. In the excerpt presented here, dawn has just broken, and the scheming Poppea, having enticed Nero to spend the night with her, tries to delay his departure as long as possible and make him promise to return. Several times she sings the word "Tornerai?" ("Won't you return?") in a seductive way. Notice how the singers' lines follow the natural rise and fall and changes of speed and inflection as the words would if spoken. The recitative style is broken only by a short solo in which Nero sings passionately that he cannot live without her.

LISTENING GUIDE

CLAUDIO MONTEVERDI

Recitative from *The Coronation of Poppea*, Act I, Scene 1 (1642)

GENRE: Recitative duet, opera   Soprano, tenor, and orchestra

CD 3 Track 19

2 minutes 41 seconds

0:00 19 0:00	POPPEA: Tornerai?	Won't you return?
	NERO: Se ben io vò	I leave you only
	Pur teco io stò, pur teco stò . . .	to be with you all the more . . .
	POPPEA: Tornerai?	Won't you return?
	NERO: Il cor dalle tue stella	My heart can never be torn away
	Mai mai non se divelle . . .	from your beautiful eyes . . .
	POPPEA: Tornerai?	Won't you return?
0:33	NERO: Io non posso da te, non posso da te	I can never really live away from you
	da te viver disgiunto	
	Se non si smembra la unità del punto . . .	no more than a soul can be severed from itself . . .

(Line repeated)

1:04	POPPEA: Tornerai?	Won't you return?
	NERO: Tornerò.	I will return.
	POPPEA: Quando?	When?
	NERO: Ben tosto.	Very soon.
	POPPEA: Ben tosto, me'l prometti?	Very soon, you promise?
	NERO: Te'l giuro.	I swear it.
1:17	POPPEA: E me l'osserverai?	And you will keep your promise?
	NERO: E s'a te no verrò, tu a me verrai!	If I do not come, you'll come to me!

(Two lines repeated)

	POPPEA: Addio . . .	Good-bye . . .
	NERO: Addio . . .	Good-bye . . .
	POPPEA: . . . Nerone, Nerone, addio . . .	. . . Nero, Nero, good-bye . . .
	NERO: . . . Poppea, Poppea, addio . . .	. . . Poppea, Poppea, good-bye . . .
	POPPEA: Addio, Nerone, addio!	Good-bye, Nero, good-bye!
	NERO: Addio, Poppea, addio!	Good-bye, Poppea, good-bye!
2:37	Scene 1 closes.	

An interactive Active Listening Guide can be downloaded from the online Resource Center for *Music Listening Today, 4th Edition.*

PURCELL'S *DIDO AND AENEAS*

Dido and Aeneas was written for a private girls' school in Chelsea outside London. Aeneas, the hero of Troy, is fleeing from his conquered homeland. He sets sail to found the city of Rome but is blown off course onto the shores of Carthage, where Dido is the widowed queen. They meet and fall in love, but soon the gods order Aeneas to continue on to found Rome. Feeling very alone and betrayed, Dido expresses her feelings in the tender and beautiful aria "When I am laid in earth," which is often called "Dido's Lament." Dido and her servant, Belinda, are alone onstage, and only Dido sings. The ostinato is a distinctive feature of this aria.

The term **ostinato** comes from the Italian word for stubborn, and indeed ostinatos are persistently repeated musical phrases. Dido sings her moving melody over the ostinato, and the combination gives the aria the qualities of both unity and variety.

Notice that Dido's phrases are incomplete, as though she were consumed in her thoughts. The exclamation "ah" is sung four times in the aria on a major chord but is followed by a minor chord, as if it cannot shake the shadow of death. Six times she asks to be remembered. She dies as the orchestra plays its closing appearances of the ground bass.

The story of Dido and Aeneas comes from Virgil's *Aeneid*, one of the masterpieces of classical literature.

HENRY PURCELL
"Dido's Lament" from *Dido and Aeneas* (1689)

GENRE: Recitative and aria, opera   Soprano and orchestra

CD 3 Tracks 20 – 21

4 minutes 30 seconds

0:00 **20** 0:00		Music opens with a short recitative accompanied by lute and low strings. Dido sings, "Thy hand, Belinda! Darkness shades me; on thy bosom let me rest. More I would—but Death invades me: Death is now a welcome guest."
0:47 **21** 0:00		Lute plays the basso ostinato (ground bass).
	0:14	Strings join ground bass. Dido sings, "When I am laid in earth, may my wrongs create no trouble in thy breast. Remember me, but ah! forget my fate."

0:34	Ground bass appears seven more times as words of aria are sung.
2:58	Instruments play final two appearances of ground bass.
3:43	Aria concludes quietly.

 An interactive Active Listening Guide can be downloaded from the online Resource Center for *Music Listening Today, 4th Edition.*

Portrait of Henry Purcell (1659–95) (engraving) by English School, (17th century) Bibliotheque Nationale, Paris, France/Giraudon

BEST-KNOWN WORKS

opera and stage works:
- *Dido and Aeneas*
- *The Fairy Queen*

Henry Purcell (c. 1659–1695) was born and lived in England. Despite his short life, he composed an enormous amount of excellent music. Trained as a choirboy, he began composing when he was eight. His voice changed early, so he worked as an assistant in caring for the king's keyboard and wind instruments. He was later appointed organist at Westminster Abbey and composed much music. He probably died of pneumonia. Purcell was buried in Westminster Abbey in recognition of his great contributions to English music.

Purcell was especially adept at writing music for the stage. Although *Dido and Aeneas* was his only true opera, he composed a number of works that combined spoken words with music, as well as music for royal occasions, including the funeral of Queen Mary the year before he died.

MAIN POINTS OF THIS CHAPTER

1. Opera was founded at the beginning of the Baroque period by a group of noblemen in Florence, Italy, who wanted to recapture the drama believed to have existed in ancient Greece. The first operas consisted almost entirely of recitatives.

2. As is true of oratorios and cantatas, operas consist of recitatives, arias, and choruses accompanied by an orchestra. They differ in that they are performed with costumes, actions, and scenery.

3. Operas are much more enjoyable if certain conventions are accepted:
   - All the words are sung.
   - The style of singing is powerful and dramatic.
   - Often an opera is not in English.
   - The progress of the story often almost stops while an aria or chorus is sung. At other times, significant events happen very quickly.

4. Good opera is good theater. Therefore, it must be both seen and heard to realize its full impact. It has a "bigger than life" quality about it.

5. The text of an opera is called the libretto. It is prepared before the composer sets the words to music. Most composers did not write the librettos for their operas.

6. Several traditions exist regarding the types of voices and the roles they sing. Sopranos and tenors often get the lead roles, while altos and basses sing the roles of older persons, villains, or authority figures such as a king.

7. An ostinato is a short phrase of music that is repeated again and again. When it's in the bass part, as it is in "Dido's Lament," it is referred to as a basso ostinato.

FEATURES TO LISTEN FOR

1. Listen to the recitative "The Voice of Him" covered in Chapter 10 with the recitative in Monteverdi's *Coronation of Poppea*. Notice in which ways they are similar, and in which ways they are different. Consider features such as tempo, length, language, character of melodic line, number of singers, accompaniment, and others.

2. Notice how many times Poppea seductively sings "Tormerai" ("Won't you return?") in *Coronation of Poppea*.

3. "Every Valley Shall Be Exalted" in Handel's *Messiah* and "Dido's Lament" in Purcell's *Dido and Aeneas* are both arias. Notice the features that make arias. Also notice the many ways in which they are different. Consider features such as tempo, length, character of melodic line, accompaniment, major or minor key, role of the orchestra, and others.

13 Baroque Instrumental Music: Suite *and* Sonata

Some important differences existed between instrumental and vocal music during the Baroque period. That fact alone makes the Baroque different from earlier periods. Until the Baroque, a piece of music was not composed specifically for a particular instrument, with the exception of works for lute or keyboard instruments. In fact, many works could be performed by instruments or voices or both.

The eventual distinction between vocal and instrumental styles was probably inevitable. Instruments and voices do not produce music in the same ways; certain types of music are more suitable for the voice, and others lend themselves better to instruments. For example, a violin or flute can easily produce sounds that are higher than the upper limits of the human voice. Performers on most instruments can also play notes with a speed and clarity that is impossible for a singer to achieve.

In general, Baroque instrumental music tended to be more contrapuntal than homophonic, but the opposite tended to be true for vocal music. There is a logical explanation for this. In vocal music, composers tried to project a message; recitatives and arias were developed as a means of giving expression to the ideas contained in the text. Instrumental music was, of course, not affected by a text.

The human voice has an expressive capability that cannot be achieved on an instrument.

BAROQUE INSTRUMENTS

Two keyboard instruments were important in the Baroque period: the organ and the harpsichord (described in Chapter 6). The organ had existed in a rudimentary form for fifteen hundred years, but it reached its height of development during the Baroque. In fact, some organs built today attempt to replicate those of the eighteenth century. During the late nineteenth and early twentieth centuries, several ranks of pipes were added to organs, especially those built for use in theaters, to imitate the sound of trombones and other instruments. But these synthesized sounds were seldom musically satisfying.

The harpsichord was frequently played during the Renaissance, and it became even more important in the Baroque. When the Baroque period ended, the harpsichord receded in significance, and it was not heard from much until the twentieth century. There was then a revival of interest in the harpsichord, and new ones are being constructed.

Several orchestral instruments are featured prominently in Baroque music. One is the "whistle" flute, or *recorder*, which is played straight forward from the player's mouth, rather than sideways as flutes are today. This flute was made of wood and had a lighter, less brilliant tone quality.

Peter Usbeck/Alamy

THE ORGAN AND CHOIR LOFT of St. Thomas Church in Leipzig, Germany, where J. S. Bach served for many years.

The trumpet, too, was given important roles during that period. It had no valves, so pitches had to be controlled entirely by the player's lips. Many Baroque trumpets were smaller and had narrower bores, which made it easier for players to reach the high notes found in some Baroque compositions.

The violin also played a major role in the Baroque period. It looked a little different from the violins of today. The fingerboard was shorter because the players did not play very high notes. The bow curved slightly away from the hair, with a shape somewhat resembling an archer's bow, from which it got its name. The tension on the bow hair was looser, too, and the strings of the instrument were set on a flatter plane, making it easier for violinists to play more than one string at a time. Gut strings were used instead of the metal strings generally in use today.

Gut strings are really made from dried and treated animal intestines.

PACHELBEL'S CANON IN D

Pachelbel's Canon in D is an unusual work. To begin with, although it was composed around 1680, it was largely forgotten until the latter half of the twentieth century. Suddenly, it seemed to have been "found" by many musicians and has enjoyed enormous popularity since, at least in terms of concert music. More than two hundred versions of

It has served as background music for commercials ranging from GE lightbulbs to Taster's Choice coffee, and in the Academy Award–winning film *Ordinary People* as well as *Father of the Bride.* It was also played at Princess Diana's funeral.

LISTENING GUIDE

JOHANN PACHELBEL
Canon in D (c. 1680)

GENRE: Canon   String orchestra and continuo

CD 3 Tracks 22 – 24

3 minutes 54 seconds

0:00	22	0:00	Continuo part sounds alone.

	0:09	First violin plays one note to the beat. Second violin follows eight beats later, and third violin eight beats later than the second.
	0:26	First violin plays two notes to the beat. Then it plays:
	0:43	—four notes to the beat
	1:00	—one and two notes to the beat in higher range
1:16	23	0:00	—part with many notes at the speed of eight to the beat
	0:16	—one short note on the beat, and then off the beat
	0:32	—four notes to the beat that alternate between higher and lower pitch levels
	0:47	—four repeated notes on many beats
2:19	24	0:00	—line with two fast notes in each beat
	0:15	—long notes
	0:30	—a contrasting melody
	0:47	—long notes, some starting in the middle of the beat
	1:04	—notes that move one octave to another
	1:35	Canon concludes.

 An interactive Active Listening Guide can be downloaded from the online Resource Center for *Music Listening Today*, 4th Edition.

Johann Pachelbel

Johann Pachelbel (1653–1706) was born and died in Nuremberg, Germany. He was a church organist and teacher, counting among his pupils J. S. Bach's teacher. He held several positions as organist and choir director, including one in Stuttgart from which he had to flee because of the French invasion. His longest position was in his native Nuremberg. He composed a great deal of religious choral music and works for organ, which were much admired by J. S. Bach. It's ironic that today he is remembered mostly for just one work, Canon in D.

BEST-KNOWN WORKS

organ:
- Fugues on the *Magnificat*

Purcell also used a ground bass in "Dido's Lament," which was presented in Chapter 12.

it have been recorded, including a few in rock style, and it has found its way into many television commercials and several motion pictures.

Canon in D is unusual in that it combines two different approaches to composition. It is built on a ground bass of eight notes, all of equal length, with every other note a fourth apart. In addition, melodic variations are played over the ground bass twenty-seven times. They appear in three instrumental parts, one following the other eight beats apart in strict imitation—thus the name *canon*.

Originally for three violins and continuo, today it is usually played by a string orchestra and continuo.

THE SUITE

A contemporary composer might do the same thing by taking a popular dance of a generation or more ago and writing similar music with more-interesting harmonies while retaining the essential rhythm and style of the original.

The word **suite** ("sweet") as used in music is a series or set of musical works that belong together. During the Baroque period, a suite referred to a collection of dances that were intended for performance as a group. Suites were usually written for keyboard instruments.

The dances included in the suites of Handel and other composers of the time were *stylized;* that is, they were "dressed up" to make them interesting pieces for listening. Composers wrote their own music for them, but the meter, tempo, and other characteristics were derived from various types of dances that had previously been in fashion.

View of the Thames River and London with St. Paul's Cathedral by Canaletto (1697–1768). The barges are much more elegant than what we think of as barges today.

Handel's "Hornpipe" from *Water Music Suite*

Typically, stylized dances are charming, enjoyable short works. Not all suites were written for keyboard instruments. Handel and others composed collections of stylized dance music for wind and string groups as well. Handel's *Water Music*, HWV 348–350, consists of an overture and about twenty dances. It was written in 1717 for an excursion by King George I as he and his large party floated down the River Thames on barges. The king reportedly liked it so much that he had it played three times. It was performed on a total of fifty instruments of different types.

A hornpipe is an energetic, jaunty dance in three beats to the measure. It is in binary form, and the theme is repeated by different groups of instruments.

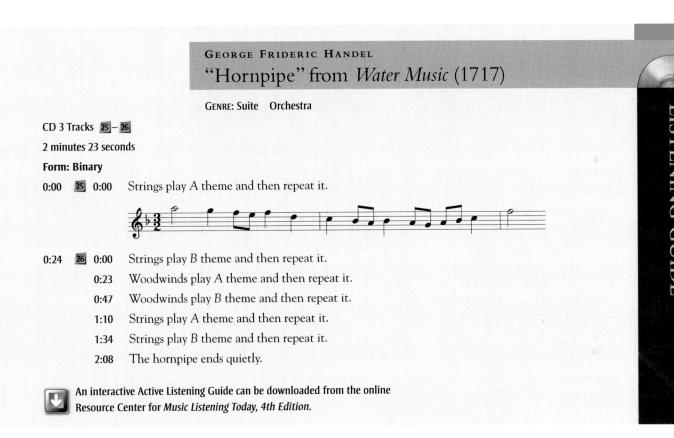

GEORGE FRIDERIC HANDEL

"Hornpipe" from *Water Music* (1717)

GENRE: Suite   Orchestra

LISTENING GUIDE

CD 3 Tracks 25 – 26

2 minutes 23 seconds

Form: Binary

0:00   25   0:00   Strings play A theme and then repeat it.

0:24   26   0:00   Strings play B theme and then repeat it.

0:23   Woodwinds play A theme and then repeat it.

0:47   Woodwinds play B theme and then repeat it.

1:10   Strings play A theme and then repeat it.

1:34   Strings play B theme and then repeat it.

2:08   The hornpipe ends quietly.

An interactive Active Listening Guide can be downloaded from the online Resource Center for *Music Listening Today, 4th Edition.*

THE SONATA

The word **sonata** is used often in music. It first appeared in the Baroque period, and it simply referred to an instrumental work for one or a few instruments. At that time there were two types of sonatas—one was the church sonata (*sonata da chiesa*); and the other, the chamber sonata (*sonata da camera*). The former was more serious and included some thoughtful music and quite a bit of imitation among the melodic lines. The chamber sonata consisted largely of stylized dance music and was lighter in character.

Probably the most prominent type of sonata during the middle of the Baroque was the *trio sonata*. Actually, the designation is not accurate, because it includes two violins and one lower instrument (gamba or cello) plus the continuo, which was usually played by a keyboard instrument.

Almost all sonatas were divided into *movements*, a term introduced in Chapter 2. Four movements were typical, and they were often arranged so that their tempos contrasted with one another.

Numbers are rarely used for works
of vocal music because they can be
identified by the words in their texts.

Corelli's Trio Sonata

The Trio Sonata in F, Op. 3, No. 1, is one of the twelve sonatas published together as "Op. 1." The abbreviation *Op.* is from the Latin word *opus*, meaning "work," and is used to identify individual instrumental works. Generally, the numbers indicate the order in which a composer wrote his or her music, but opus numbers were not employed consistently until early in the nineteenth century. Sometimes publishers attached opus numbers to works composed before then. In some instances, scholars have cataloged the works of composers such as Bach, Schubert, and Mozart, in which cases the name or initials of the cataloger appear along with a catalog number.

Corelli's trio sonata has four movements; the second and third are presented here. The first movement of this church sonata is typically a slow, solemn movement marked *Grave*. The cello sounds a steady stream of low notes while the two violins play higher notes for the first half of the movement.

When used in conjunction with music, the word *grave* is pronounced "grah-vay."

LISTENING GUIDE

ARCANGELO CORELLI

Trio Sonata in F, Op. 3, No. 1, Second Movement (1681)

GENRE: Trio sonata   Allegro   Violins, cello, and continuo

CD 3 Track 27

1 minute 18 seconds

0:00   27   0:00   First violin enters, second violin follows, and then cello.

0:17   Free counterpoint follows.

0:44   Opening theme appears twice as rapidly moving notes are played.

1:05   Opening theme played one more time before movement concludes.

An interactive Active Listening Guide can be downloaded from the online Resource Center for *Music Listening Today, 4th Edition.*

Arcangelo Corelli

Arcangelo Corelli (1653–1713) [oil on canvas], Italian School, (18th century)/Museo di Strumenti del Conservatorio, Naples, Italy/The Bridgeman Art Library

Arcangelo Corelli (1653–1713) lived at a time when the violin was replacing the viol. He was one of the first great violinists, teachers, and composers, and he promoted the technical and tonal capabilities of the violin. He spent most of his life in Rome in the service of Cardinal Ottoboni, whose concerts he directed. His "Christmas" concerto was completed shortly before he died. Unlike many composers, he died having amassed a large fortune. In return, he left the world a fortune in string music.

BEST-KNOWN WORKS
- Violin Sonatas (12)
- Concerti Grossi (12)

The second movement has a fast tempo and contains much imitation among the three instruments. After each instrument enters in imitation, it continues with free contrapuntal material. The opening theme appears four more times in the movement, including a shortened version near the end of the movement.

The third movement has a waltzlike character with its three rapid beats in each measure. Several times Corelli presents a melody consisting of two phrases each four measures long, and then repeats it accompanied by decorative notes played by the violins. Some of the time, he has the two violins playing the same music in imitative lines that almost sound entangled with each other. The two parts can be heard clearly in a live performance where the performers are several feet apart, but the parts are more difficult to hear in a recording when the sounds are coming from loudspeakers.

The fourth movement is similar to the second. It has a rather fast tempo and contains much imitation.

LISTENING GUIDE

ARCANGELO CORELLI

Trio Sonata in F, Op. 3, No. 1, Third Movement (1681)

GENRE: Trio sonata   Vivace   Violins, cello, and continuo

CD 3 Track 28

2 minutes 30 seconds

0:00	28	0:00	A section played, then repeated with decorative notes.
		0:19	A theme continues, ending with echolike phrase.
		0:34	A section repeated, ending with echolike phrase.
		1:03	B section contains changes of key.
		1:52	B section repeated, leading to quiet ending.

 An interactive Active Listening Guide can be downloaded from the online Resource Center for *Music Listening Today, 4th Edition.*

OTHER BAROQUE COMPOSERS

GIOVANNI GABRIELI (1557–1612) studied music with his uncle Andrea in Venice; later he probably studied with Orlando di Lasso in Munich. In 1585 he succeeded his uncle as organist at Saint Mark's, a position that he held until his death twenty-seven years later. Until about 1600, his compositions were in the Renaissance style. His later compositions were in the new Baroque style. Although an organist and master at writing choral music, he is remembered more today for his use of instruments, especially brasses. They included trombones (which were puny instruments compared with the modern versions) and cornetto. His *Sonata pian'e forte* is recognized as probably the first work to specify dynamic levels.

JEAN-BAPTISTE LULLY Though Italian by birth, Jean-Baptiste Lully (1632–1687) made his way into the court of French kings by wit and luck. He changed his name from the Italian *Lulli* to the French version by which he has been known throughout history. Lully was a supreme entertainer in what was the most sumptuous court in Europe. There he staged dance spectaculars and other performances. He developed the *French overture.* It had a slow introduction with many dotted rhythms, a fast middle section with imitation of a short melody, and usually a third section in a slow tempo like the first.

The *cornetto* was a wooden instrument that bears little resemblance to the present-day cornet.

The story of Lully's death is probably true. To keep the performers together, he would mark the beat by pounding a stick on the floor. One day he hit his toe, which later became infected. He died from the infection.

GEORG PHILLIP TELEMANN One of the best-known composers of the first half of the eighteenth century, Georg Phillip Telemann (1685–1767) spent most of his life near Hamburg, Germany. He left a huge amount of music—forty operas, forty-four passions, twelve Lutheran services, and more than three thousand works of other types! He was adept at composing instrumental music, especially for the flute.

MAIN POINTS OF THIS CHAPTER

1. The important keyboard instruments during the Baroque period were the harpsichord and pipe organ, which reached their acme during that time. Flutes were often like recorders that were played straight in front of the mouth, rather than the transverse position used today. Many trumpets, which had no valve mechanisms, were smaller than today's versions; this allowed them to play high pitches more easily. Violins used gut strings, had a flatter bridge, and were played with a more curved bow. These differences from today's violins made them easier to play on more than one string at a time.

2. Ostinato and ground bass were used in some instrumental works. Pachelbel's Canon in D uses both of these techniques.

3. Suites consisting of stylized dance music were popular. They were composed for harpsichord or small instrumental ensembles.

4. Sonatas were first composed in the Baroque period. The church sonata (*sonata da chiesa*) was more serious, whereas the chamber sonata (*sonata de camera*) consisted of stylized versions of dance music.

5. The trio sonata was a feature of Baroque instrumental music. It actually required four players: two violins, one cello, and a continuo part played on the harpsichord or other bass instrument. The short movements of the trio sonata were arranged in contrasting tempos and often contained imitation among the parts.

6. Because instrumental works do not have words, they are usually given generic titles such as sonata or suite. In addition, they are frequently identified further by opus number.

FEATURES TO LISTEN FOR

1. Listen for how Pachelbel builds interest in the first 1:30 of Canon in D. After the slow, steady notes played by the low strings, the three violins enter one after another eight beats apart. At first, they play one note to the beat, then two notes to the beat, then four notes to the beat, and finally eight notes to the beat as they follow one after the other in strict imitation.

2. Notice the similarities and differences between the two halves of "Hornpipe" from Handel's *Water Music Suite*. Check to see if any changes are made in the music between when the strings play the melody and when the woodwinds play it.

3. Notice the style of bowing used by the violins for Corelli's *Trio Sonata in F*. It calls for quick strokes in a back-and-forth movement of the bow that is characteristic of Baroque string music.

4. Notice that both the A and B themes in the third movement of Corelli's *Trio Sonata* end quietly. Also notice that when the A theme is repeated, it is decorated somewhat.

Baroque Instrumental Music: Concerto *and* Fugue

14

In a sense, the concerto grosso, the solo concerto, and the fugue represent the more mature instrumental works composed during the Baroque. They were generally written in the eighteenth century by composers whose music is performed frequently today. The examples of concerto grosso and fugue represent a high point for their particular type of music, and some of the solo concertos of that time are still staples of concert music today.

THE CONCERTO GROSSO

A favorite musical effect during the Baroque period was the contrast between groups of instruments, or what is called **concerted style.** There are two types of **concerto grosso.** One featured the contrast between different types of instruments, such as woodwinds and strings. The other, more common, type presented contrast between a few instruments and the orchestra. The contrast between groups is more than just a case of taking turns in answering each other, especially in the later concerto grossi. They are more subtle and complex than that, but the basic idea of contrast is present. The idea of contrast also carried over to the movements of the concertos. Typically, they consisted of three movements: fast–slow–fast.

The word *grosso* means "grand," not "ugly" or "disgusting."

There is little difference in the difficulty of the music that the small group and the larger group (called the *tutti*) perform. No attempt was made to have one group show off, as is true in later concertos. The small group remains seated and often plays along in unison with the *tutti*. Usually, concerti grossi are composed for strings, with a harpsichord filling in the harmonies. A few wind instruments are sometimes included in the small group.

Players in the small group were generally the first-chair players in their respective sections.

The fact that the same or similar instruments play the same music sometimes makes it difficult to distinguish which group is playing at a particular moment. Orchestras during the Baroque period were small, so the larger group really wasn't large by today's standards. Also, three or four good string players can produce a quite vigorous sound. Recordings tend to make the groups less distinguishable by taking away most of the physical distance of live performances.

The most common form of the movements in a concerto grosso is **ritornello form.** It presents a pattern in which the main theme alternates with a contrasting section, with modifications as the movement progresses.

Bach's Brandenburg Concerto No. 5

The margrave of Brandenburg was one of the more important rulers in what is Germany today. In 1717 Bach was court composer at Cöthen and had a chance to perform for the margrave, who was visiting there. The margrave was so impressed that he asked Bach to write some music for his orchestra. In 1721 Bach sent him six concertos, complete with dedication to "His Highness," that contrasted a variety of small instrumental groups with the orchestra. Later they became known as the Brandenburg Concertos.

Bach may have hoped that his gift of six concertos with a glowing dedication would lead to a job offer from the margrave. None ever came.

Whether the margrave ever responded to Bach's gift is not known. In fact, the concertos were placed in the margrave's library and were never performed by the musicians at his court. They were probably performed by Bach during his tenure at Cöthen, and perhaps while he was in Leipzig.

121

The Brandenburg Concerto No. 5 calls for a flute, violin, and harpsichord contrasted with a string orchestra and continuo. (Actually, the harpsichord has a dual role. It is part of the small group, but it also contributes to the continuo part as part of the *tutti*.) The harpsichord had seldom been given such importance in the concerto grossi of earlier composers. Bach may have given it a prominent place in this concerto because the prince at Cöthen had just purchased a new harpsichord, and Bach was an outstanding keyboard player. The concerto contains much counterpoint throughout and musical "conversations" among the three instruments and between them and the orchestra.

The first movement is the longest and contains a stunning harpsichord cadenza. It is in major and is marked *Allegro*. The second movement is in minor and has a slow tempo.

The third movement is in major and has a happy, dancelike character that moves rapidly with many notes played by the harpsichordist. Its short main theme is imitated and exchanged among the solo instruments alone and then repeated while accompanied by the orchestra. After many exchanges of melodic figures, the music takes a smoother character, often containing three notes on each beat. Fragments of the main theme appear periodically during this part of the movement. Toward the end, the opening music of the movement returns.

LISTENING GUIDE

JOHANN SEBASTIAN BACH

Brandenburg Concerto No. 5, Third Movement (1717–1721)

GENRE: Concerto grosso   Flute, violin, harpsichord, and string orchestra

CD 3 Tracks 29 – 31

5 minutes 10 seconds

Form: Ritornello

0:00   29   0:00   Violin opens with short theme, followed by flute, and then harpsichord.

        0:27   Orchestra joins in.

1:16   30   0:00   Music becomes smoother; fragment of theme heard occasionally.

        0:44   Fragments of theme return.

        1:15   Harpsichord solo, followed by exchanges with orchestra.

3:46   31   0:00   Return of opening music.

        0:27   Orchestra joins in.

 An interactive Active Listening Guide can be downloaded from the online Resource Center for *Music Listening Today, 4th Edition.*

Antonio Vivaldi

Civico Museo Bibliografico Musicale, Bologna, Italy/The Bridgeman Art Library

Antonio Vivaldi (c. 1675–1741) is much admired by musicians today, but not so well known to the general public. He was born in Venice, Italy, the son of a violinist. As a young man, he was ordained a priest, but his was not the typical life of a cleric. He concertized throughout Europe, wrote and produced almost fifty operas, made a good deal of money, and lived with a French soprano for many years.

From 1703 to 1740 he taught at the Ospedale della Pietà in Venice. It was an orphanage for about four hundred young women, probably most of them illegitimate. According to accounts written at the time, each Sunday the girls offered public performances of an exceptionally high quality. His lifestyle got him in trouble with Church authorities, however, and he was forbidden to continue his music-making activities in areas controlled by the pope. The ban drastically reduced his income and seemed to drain

him of his creative juices. He died in Vienna, poor and virtually unknown.

———♦———

Appropriately, the Weather Channel sometimes uses a recording of The Four Seasons.

Vivaldi was a prolific composer who wrote an enormous amount of music of practically every kind. He wrote many works for the girls at the school to play or sing, including concertos for violin (about three hundred of them!), flute, bassoon, guitar, mandolin, and piccolo—more than 450 in all. His music was much admired during his lifetime but had fallen from favor by the time he died. It has enjoyed a rebirth of interest in the past fifty years. For example, more than 150 recordings have been made of *The Four Seasons* alone.

BEST-KNOWN WORKS

concertos:
- Concerto for Two Violins, Strings and Continuo (*L'Estro armonica*)
- Concertos for Violin, Strings and Continuo (*The Four Seasons*)

choral:
- *Gloria*

Vivaldi's Concerto "Spring" from *The Four Seasons*

Antonio Vivaldi's "Spring" from Concerto for Violin and String Orchestra, Op. 8, No. 1, is from a collection of four concertos often called *The Four Seasons*. Each concerto contains elements of a concerto grosso but is more of a solo concerto in that the principal violinist is given a virtuoso part to play. The four concertos each have three movements arranged in a fast–slow–fast order of tempos.

The title of the work comes from the fact that Vivaldi associated each concerto with a different season of the year by its title and by the insertion of lines of poetry in the orchestral score. Such nonmusical associations were not typical of instrumental works during the Baroque period, although they are encountered occasionally. Instrumental works associated by the composer with nonmusical ideas are known as **program music** and were very popular during the nineteenth century.

The Listening Guide is for only the first movement of "Spring."

THE FUGUE

Because a pipe organ can produce a wide variety of tone colors with tremendous power and range, Baroque composers began to write music specifically for it. In the process they developed several forms of organ compositions. The **fugue** ("fewg") is the most important of these forms.

The fugue, as is true of most musical forms, did not appear fully developed. It evolved from less complex types of keyboard music. The fugue and its predecessors have one thing in common: They are contrapuntal, with the lines of music often imitating one another.

The word *fugue* comes from the Italian word *fuga*, meaning "flight."

ANTONIO VIVALDI

"Spring" from *The Four Seasons,* First Movement (1725)

GENRE: Solo concerto   Solo violin and orchestra

CD 1 Tracks 29 – 33

3 minutes 35 seconds

0:00   29   0:00   Entire string orchestra plays the main theme (ritornello) and then repeats it softly. The words in the score can be translated "Spring with all its happiness is here."

0:16   Orchestra plays second half of ritornello theme and then repeats it.

0:33   30   0:00   Solo violin plays chirping, birdlike sounds: "And the birds welcome it with happy songs." Orchestra repeats second half of ritornello.

1:18   31   0:00   Orchestra plays short, flowing, rapidly moving notes: "And the brooks, touched by the breezes, flow with sweet murmurings."

        0:25   Second half of ritornello is repeated.

1:52   32   0:00   Music changes to minor. Orchestra plays rustling, nervous sounds (tremolos), and violins zip up notes of the scale: "Dark clouds fill the sky announced by lightning and thunder."

        0:28   Orchestra plays second part of ritornello again but in minor.

2:28   33   0:00   Solo violin plays birdlike sounds: "But when everything is quiet, the birds begin to sing again their enchanting song."

        0:17   Orchestra plays first part of ritornello in major, and then solo violin enters.

        0:43   Orchestra again plays second part of ritornello and then repeats it softly.

        1:08   "Spring" concludes.

 An interactive Active Listening Guide can be downloaded from the online Resource Center for *Music Listening Today, 4th Edition.*

What makes fugues interesting to listen to? At least three things:

- Fugues are built around one main theme, which helps give the work a strong sense of unity. This theme is featured alone at the beginning and then repeated often during the work.
- Contrasting lines of counterpoint give the work variety and make it more interesting. These lines fit together with the theme and with one another.
- The entire work is crafted so that it evolves in a wonderfully logical manner. The musical process of a fugue is somewhat like a complicated mathematical formula working itself out to a beautifully correct conclusion.

Fugues have their own vocabulary. The various lines are called **voices,** even though they are actually played on an instrument, not sung. The main theme is called the **subject,** and the contrasting theme is called the **countersubject.** The opening section that presents the subject in each voice is termed the **exposition;** the remainder of the fugue is known as the **development.** Sections of the fugue following the exposition in which the subject does not appear are called **episodes.**

The pattern of a typical four-voice fugue is shown in the following diagram:

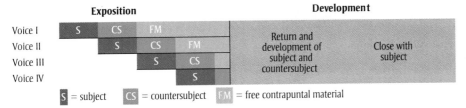

S = subject   CS = countersubject   FM = free contrapuntal material

This fugue has four voices, which is the usual number, but it could have had two, three, or five. The order in which the voices enter is a matter of choice for the composer. Each fugue is structured somewhat differently.

Bach's Toccata and Fugue in D Minor

Toccata and Fugue in D Minor by Bach presents a fugue surrounded by a **toccata,** which is a free-sounding virtuoso work, usually for keyboard. Both the fugue and the toccata offer the organist plenty of chances to show off the tremendous tonal possibilities of the instrument, as well as virtuoso skill as a performer. The third and concluding section of this work is another toccata that Bach labels *recitativo.* The word refers to the free and expressive style of singing described in Chapter 10. It is a work filled with drama.

Three features of Baroque instrumental music are prominent in this fugue. One is the use of **sequence.** A sequence is a pattern of notes repeated several times in succession, but each time at a different pitch level. Sequences are a staple of Baroque music, and Toccata and Fugue in D Minor contains many of them.

Second is the use of repeated notes in a theme. The subject of the fugue contains a lot of notes, which gives the music more energy. But only half of the notes form the basis of the subject. The circled notes in the music example change; the others do not.

For this reason, you should focus on the notes that change as you listen to the subject of this fugue.

The third feature is a bit more complicated. Composers, especially in the Baroque period, created a pattern of tension and release by holding a consonant note from one chord over into the next chord, where it was dissonant, and then resolving that note to a consonant note in the new chord—suspension. Suspensions are more frequent in cadences near the conclusion of phrases. At the end of the entire Toccata and Fugue, it may sound as if Bach is simply holding a long chord. But listen carefully as notes in the middle of the chords change and finally resolve. The interplay of consonance and dissonance makes for some very interesting and challenging listening.

OTHER KEYBOARD FORMS

The fugue was not the only musical form composed for keyboard instruments during the Baroque period. Two forms based on the chorale are chorale variations and chorale prelude. In *chorale variations,* a chorale melody is repeated several times in succession but with changes each time. The *chorale prelude* is usually a contrapuntal piece for organ built on a chorale melody.

A third type of keyboard music, one that is especially suited to the organ, is the **passacaglia** ("pah-sah-*cahl*-ya"). It begins with a statement of the theme in the bass. In a passacaglia, this melody is repeated over and over in its original form, but variations are added in other voices each time. The melody usually remains in the bass throughout. Continuous repetition combined with continuous variation provides both unity and variety in the music. One of Bach's greatest organ works is his Passacaglia in C Minor.

The **prelude** was another common work for keyboard instruments. In the Baroque period, this title simply meant a short piece of instrumental music.

Resource Center
See "Hear It Now: Features of Bach's Fugue," in the *Music Listening Today, 4th Edition,* Resource Center.

Resource Center
See "Hear It Now: Suspensions," in the *Music Listening Today, 4th Edition,* Resource Center.

The pedals are ideal for maintaining the rather slow-moving melody, leaving the player's hands free to play the faster, higher-pitched lines.

Composers from Purcell to Bach to Elton John (in his song "Sorry Seems to Be the Hardest Word") have composed music using persistently repeated bass lines.

Toccata and Fugue in D Minor, BWV 565 (before 1708)

Genre: Fugue with toccata and recitative   Pipe organ

CD 1 Tracks 34 – 37

8 minutes 49 seconds

Toccata

| 0:00 | 34 | 0:00 | Dramatic opening with full organ sound. |

Motive is played three times, each time one octave lower. Leads to a massive, long chord.

		0:28	Three series of fast notes lead to another massive chord.
		0:57	Three passages with many fast notes, changes of pitch level, and rhapsodic flourishes.
		1:12	Four passages of rapidly moving triplets are followed by four descending chords.
		1:53	Toccata concludes with large chords and low notes in pedal.

Fugue: *Exposition*

| 2:12 | 35 | 0:00 | Subject enters alone. |

		0:05	Second voice enters with subject four notes higher. First voice continues with countersubject.
		0:23	Third voice enters in high notes.
		0:28	Section of free counterpoint with much sequence.
		0:55	Fourth voice enters with subject at a low pitch level.
		0:59	Exposition of the fugue concludes as all voices continue in free counterpoint with much sequence.

Development

3:19	36	0:00	Development begins with subject and countersubject followed by descending scale patterns.
		0:12	Sequence of melodic figures in statement–answer pattern. Many changes of timbre.
		0:34	Subject and countersubject sound in high notes followed by more sequence in statement–answer patterns.
		1:16	Subject enters in pedals along with a high trilled note and countersubject.
		1:24	Subject sounds in a middle voice, with a trilled note and countersubject in the pedal part.
		1:34	Subject sounds again as pedal holds long note (pedal point).
		2:18	Subject enters alone in pedals.
		2:33	Pedal persistently sounds the same note on every other beat against sequence in higher notes.
		2:47	Subject is sounded in pedal part.
		2:59	Final entrance of subject with countersubject as the pedal part holds a long note.
		3:08	Fugue concludes with a cadence that gives the feeling that the music is not ending.

Recitativo

6:29	37	0:00	Opens with many short phrases of four fast notes that lead to three loud, very slow chords.
		0:16	Brief pedal solo leads to an "incomplete" cadence.
		0:28	Fast, four-note phrases alternate with slow chords.
		0:56	Three times one note is held into the following chord (suspension), creating a brief dissonance before resolving.
		1:09	Work concludes with a long, powerful minor chord.

 An interactive Active Listening Guide can be downloaded from the online Resource Center for *Music Listening Today, 4th Edition.*

The name **Johann Sebastian Bach** (1685–1750) seems to appear in nearly every discussion of Baroque music. And well it should! He ranks as one of the musical giants of all time.

Bach lived an uneventful life, not very different from that of many gifted musicians of his time. The most notable feature about him was his lineage. Over a period of about six generations, from 1580 to 1845, more than sixty Bachs were musicians of some repute, and at least thirty-eight of them attained eminence as musicians. Included among the latter were Johann Christoph (1642–1703), who was a cousin of Johann Sebastian's father, and several of J. S. Bach's own sons: Wilhelm Friedemann (1710–1784), Carl Philipp Emanuel (1714–1788), Johann Christoph Friedrich (1732–1795), and Johann Christian (1735–1782).

Bach's music is catalogued by the initals BWV, which stand for Bach Werke Verzeichnis—itself an abbreviation of a longer title.

J. S. Bach was born in Eisenach, Germany, the son of a town musician. When he was ten, his father died. Johann's musical training was taken over by his elder brother, Johann Christoph, who was an organist. During his early career, Bach was known more as an organist than as a composer. After two brief positions as organist, Bach was appointed to his first important post as court organist and musician to the duke of Weimar. He stayed nine years, during which he concentrated on organ, as both a composer and a performer.

When the duke failed to advance him, Bach accepted a position at Cöthen. The prince there wanted music for instrumental groups, so the versatile Bach turned to composing for instruments other than organ. During this time he wrote the Brandenburg Concertos. After the sudden death of his wife, Maria Barbara, he married Anna Magdalena and immortalized her by writing a book of keyboard music for her. Piano students today often play pieces from this book.

The third and final portion of Bach's life began with his appointment in 1723 as organist-teacher at Saint Thomas Church in Leipzig. The position called for him to compose, teach the boys in the choir school, and prepare the music for worship services. Ironically, Bach was not the first choice for the position. In spite of the annoyances of the position and tragedy in his personal life (six of his eight children born in Leipzig died), Bach continued his vast stream of great music. Later in life he suffered a stroke and became blind. In 1750 he died, with his true stature still unknown.

His contract also required him to walk with the boys at funerals, not to leave town without permission, and to "chastise them with moderation" if the boys disobeyed. His salary was low, and he had to pay for a substitute in case he couldn't perform a duty.

Except for a few brief journeys in Germany, Bach knew little of the world beyond where he lived and worked. He created no new musical forms and instituted no new compositional techniques. His music was seldom heard outside Leipzig during his lifetime, and even there it was probably not performed well.

Why, then, is Bach so dominating a figure in music? The answer is that he wrote with such skill and effectiveness. Especially remarkable was his ability to write counterpoint. Words are inadequate to describe his genius. Perhaps the late Dag Hammarskjöld, secretary general of the United Nations, expressed it best. In speaking of Bach and Vivaldi, he said, "Both have a beautiful way of creating order in the brain."

BEST-KNOWN WORKS

choral:
- *St. Matthew Passion*
- *Christmas Oratorio*
- *Mass in B Minor*
- *Magnificat*
- Cantatas Nos. 4, 84, and 140

keyboard:
- French Suites (6)
- English Suites (6)
- *The Well-Tempered Clavier*
- *Goldberg Variations*

orchestra:
- Brandenburg Concertos (6)
- Suites for Orchestra (4)

Features of Baroque Music

Melodies	Expressive "reciting style" (recitative) in vocal music
	Quite a few virtuoso passages in vocal and instrumental music
	Many instrumental melodies have a continuous, "spinning out" quality
Rhythm	Strongly metrical with regular patterns of beats (except in recitatives)
Textures	Polyphonic (contrapuntal) and homophonic
Harmony	Tonal in major and minor; tonal center can modulate
	Continuo (basso continuo) part in many works
Dynamic levels	Loud and soft; terraced dynamics in instrumental music
Performance media	Accompanied vocal solos and choral pieces
	Harpsichord and pipe organ
	Small instrumental ensembles
Forms	*A B* (binary)
	A B A (ternary)
	Ritornello
	Fugue
Genres	Oratorio, Cantata
	Recitative
	Aria
	Chorus
	Chorale
	Opera
	Suite
	Sonata, trio sonata
	Concerto grosso
	Solo concerto
	Fugue
	Short organ works

MAIN POINTS OF THIS CHAPTER

1. The Baroque concerto grosso is based on the idea of contrast, usually between a small instrumental group and the orchestra. The players in the small group do not stand or play music that is more showy than what is played by the orchestra.

2. Typically, the three movements of a concerto are arranged in a fast–slow–fast tempo order. Ritornello form, with its recurring theme and contrasting sections, is used for many movements.

3. Program music is instrumental music that is associated by the composer with a non-musical idea or situation. An early example is Vivaldi's *The Four Seasons*.

4. A fugue is an instrumental work, often for organ, that is based on a recurring theme and contrasting theme. They appear between sections of free contrapuntal music. Often a fugue has four lines or voices. The opening section of a fugue is called the exposition, and the remainder is termed the development.

5. Sequence is a music technique encountered frequently in Baroque music. It occurs when a pattern of notes is repeated several times in succession, each time at a different pitch level.

6. Other types of keyboard music composed during the Baroque period include toccata, chorale variations, prelude, and passacaglia.

FEATURES TO LISTEN FOR

1. The imitation among the flute, violin, and harpsichord in the early portion of the third movement of Bach's Brandenburg Concerto No. 5.

2. Notice how Vivaldi changes the character of the music to represent spring, birds, a flowing brook, and a thunderstorm.

3. Listen to how Bach achieves a sense of drama in the opening portion of his Toccata and Fugue in D Minor. Notice how he builds a monumental chord and then has the chords resolve to the home key.

4. Listen for the notes that change, not the repeated ones, in the subject of the fugue at Track 35.

5. Observe how in both the Toccata and Recitativo Bach contrasts passages with rapidly moving notes with sections consisting of solid, mighty chords.

6. Listen for the variety of timbres that are available on a pipe organ.

PART IV

Classical Music

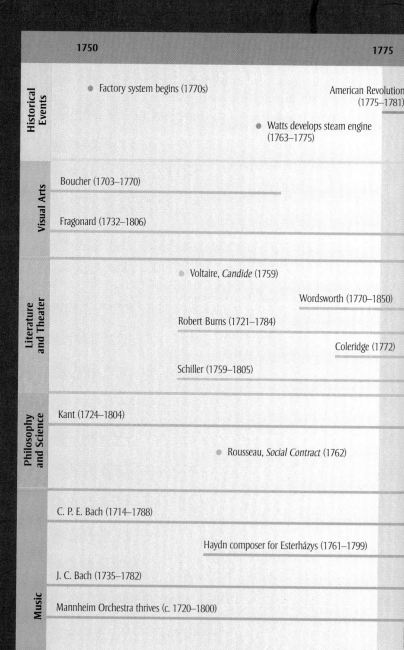

	1750	1775
Historical Events	● Factory system begins (1770s) ● Watts develops steam engine (1763–1775)	American Revolution (1775–1781)
Visual Arts	Boucher (1703–1770) Fragonard (1732–1806)	
Literature and Theater	● Voltaire, *Candide* (1759) Robert Burns (1721–1784) Schiller (1759–1805)	Wordsworth (1770–1850) Coleridge (1772)
Philosophy and Science	Kant (1724–1804) ● Rousseau, *Social Contract* (1762)	
Music	C. P. E. Bach (1714–1788) J. C. Bach (1735–1782) Mannheim Orchestra thrives (c. 1720–1800)	Haydn composer for Esterházys (1761–1799)

Steve Vidler/eStock Photo

1800   **1820**

French Revolution (1789–1799)   Louisiana Purchase (1803)   Napoleon defeated (1815)

David, *Death of Socrates* (1787)   Goya, *The Third of May* (1814)

Goethe, *Faust*   Scott, Ivanhoe (1819)
(1808, 1832)

Portrait of Leopold Mozart (1719–87)
and his Children, Wolfgang Amadeus
(1756–91) and Maria Anna (1751–1829)
(1780–81 (oil on canvas), Austrian School,
(18th century)/Mozart Museum, Salzburg,
Austria/The Bridgeman Art Library

Jenner, smallpox vaccine (1796)

The Art Archive/Beethoven House Bonn/
Alfredo Dagli Orti/Picture Desk

▲ Mozart symphonies and operas (above) (1770–1791)

▶ Beethoven symphonies (right) (1799–1824)

Schubert songs (1823–1828)

15 Classicism *and* Classical Music

When most people use the word *classic* to describe something, they mean that it has an enduring quality of excellence. *The Wizard of Oz* is a classic motion picture, and *Moby Dick* is a classic novel, to give two examples. That use of the word is close to the original Latin *classicus*, meaning "something of highest quality."

When most people use *classical* with regard to music, they mean concert or art music, music that is not popular or folk. On the other hand, when musicians use the word *Classical* (written with a capital C), they are talking about the musical style that prevailed from about 1750 to around 1820.

CULTURAL SETTING

Although the approximate dates of the **Classical period** give it a life span of only about seventy years, it produced much wonderful and enjoyable music. Instrumental music developed and equaled or exceeded vocal music in importance. The symphony, solo concerto, and chamber music and musical forms associated with them were developed. Opera also continued to flourish.

The center of music moved from the cities of Italy to Vienna, the capital of the Austrian Empire. Four master composers lived there—Mozart and Haydn during the Classical period and then Beethoven and Schubert, whose music bridged into the nineteenth-century style.

During the eighteenth century, there was a widespread interest among the educated population in intellectual accomplishments in the philosophy, science, and arts of the ancient Greeks. Therefore, these years are often referred to as the Age of Enlightenment or the Age of Reason. This interest can be seen in the publication of Denis Diderot's *Encylopédie* in France and the *Encyclopœdia Britannica* in England. These books sought to break away from the religious restrictions of the past and promote reason and scientific thinking.

Four Leaders

Four persons are especially representative of the spirit of the time. One was Frenchman François Marie Arouet (1694–1778), who called himself Voltaire. His writings spoke out for justice and challenged the government and religion of France at that time, even to the point where he spent a year in prison for his beliefs. But he had his weak and inconsistent side too. He was shrewd at business and lived comfortably, and some of his writings were published anonymously. Later when questioned about them, he continued to deny having written them. But in the end, his influence toward an enlightened outlook was enormous.

The Swiss-French Jean-Jacques Rousseau (1712–1778), like Voltaire, sought to reform the moral climate and governmental policies. In his writings he strongly urged a less dogmatic, formal system of government. He believed that people were naturally good and that they had been corrupted by civilization, education, and governments. Rousseau was a skilled musician who advocated a new system of music notation. He composed music and wrote comedies. His music was simple and folklike in comparison to the highly decorated style of the other French composers of the time.

A third person representative of the spirit of the Age of Enlightenment was the American Benjamin Franklin (1706–1790). In spite of his rather unkempt appearance,

Haydn, Mozart, Beethoven, and Schubert are often referred to as the "Viennese Classicists."

The word *encyclopœdia* (the traditional English spelling) is from two Greek words meaning "general education." The ligature œ also reveals the word's Greek heritage.

This was the time of the House of Bourbon, and its kings were very repressive and self-indulgent.

Elements of Rousseau's beliefs are still very much alive in the United States today.

The glass *armonica*, as Franklin called it, was a rank of glasses set perpendicular to the player like a series of grindstones. The player used a pedal to spin the glasses as his or her wetted fingers rubbed the rims of the glasses, causing eerie, ethereal sounds.

132

he was a brilliant and well-read man who published books and magazines, promoted education, was pivotal in bringing about the Constitution of the United States, contributed much to the understanding of electricity, invented the Franklin stove and bifocal glasses, and developed a musical instrument called the "glass armonica."

Thomas Jefferson (1743–1826), the fourth representative of the outlook of the period, was not only author of the Declaration of Independence and third president of the United States but was also an outstanding scholar and architect. His ideas can be seen in his home (which he named Monticello) at Charlottesville, Virginia; the University of Virginia (which he founded); and the Library of Congress (which he also founded—his books served as the nucleus of its original holdings). He was also a competent violinist and singer. The music stand he used for string quartet playing is on display today at Monticello.

SUPREME COURT BUILDING

Architecture

Admiration for the ancient Greeks and Romans can also be seen in architecture and art. Greek pillars and symmetrical, balanced designs are found in many public and private buildings in America today. The front of the U.S. Supreme Court Building in Washington, D.C., is very much in the Greek tradition. Note the sensible proportions of the triangle above the pillars; it is neither too tall nor too low from the baseline to the peak. Notice also the symmetry of the columns to each side of the center of the roof.

Philosophy

The philosophical approach of eighteenth-century thinkers was founded on three basic propositions:

1. Reason and logic are the way to truth. Emotions are false and misleading.
2. The universe is governed by permanent laws that people cannot alter. What is true is true throughout the world and for all time. It is universal and eternal.
3. Therefore, the intellect should control people's activities, including art and music.

These philosophical ideas began with Socrates and Plato in ancient Athens, but they were refined and applied to many areas of culture and scholarship by thinkers in the eighteenth century. One of the many areas affected by the Classical outlook was music, which is explored later in this chapter.

TOWARD CLASSICISM: THE ROCOCO STYLE

A forerunner of sorts of the more typical Classical style in the arts was the **Rococo** or **galant style,** which was popular mainly in France during the first half of the eighteenth century. Coming from the French word *rocaille*, meaning "shellwork," the Rococo style marked the acme of the highly decorative, almost frivolous French style of the Court of Versailles. It can be seen in the paintings of François Boucher (1703–1770), Antonie Watteau (1684–1721), and Jean Honoré Fragonard (1732–1806).

Two Rococo composers who merit mention are François Couperin (1688–1733) and Jean-Philippe Rameau (1683–1764). The happy tunes and almost frilly quality in Rameau's music seem perfectly suited for the powder-and-wig world of the Court of

As used in this sense, *galant* is much closer in meaning to *elegant* than to *gallant*. It is pronounced "gah-*lahnt*."

Much of Rameau's and Couperin's music is for a French version of the harpsichord called the *clavecin*.

THE DEATH OF SOCRATES, by Jacques-Louis David. This painting shows the formal properties of balance and restraint that are found in much of the music of Mozart and Haydn.

David, Jacques Louis (1748–1825) The Death of Socrates. 1787. Oil on canvas, 51 × 77 1/4 in. Catharine Lorillard Wolfe Collection, Wolfe Fund, 1931/The Metropolitan Musuem of Art, New York, NY, U.S.A./Image copyright © The Metropolitan Musuem of Art/Art Resource, NY

Versailles at the time of Louis XIV. Rameau is also important in music history for a book he wrote on harmony. In it he outlined principles of chord structure and progressions that prevailed for hundreds of years.

CLASSICAL ART

The Death of Socrates by Jacques-Louis David depicts the great philosopher of ancient Greece just about to drink the poisonous cup of hemlock. His students grieve while he remains composed and upright. In spite of the anguish of the scene, the figures seem almost frozen or posed. There is a detached quality about the picture. The admiration of the culture of ancient Greece and Rome can be seen in its symmetrical, balanced design. Groups of men are placed on each side of Socrates, who is the focus of attention. The colors are somewhat muted, in keeping with the overall nature of the scene. The arches of the building add a linear perspective to the painting.

Boucher's *Venus and Cupid* (page 135) is a good example of Rococo art, which was strongly associated with the court of the French kings at Versailles. Boucher was trained as a decorator by his father, who designed embroideries. That influence can be seen in the exquisite lightness and decorative qualities of his paintings. The aristocracy of the time demanded a type of art and music that was pretty and decorative, even if it was superficial. A wide range of colors was used. Often the subjects of Rococo art were mythological or allegorical. The protagonist almost always appears as a young, elegant, and sensually abandoned woman. Cupids, nymphs, and doves are found in many paintings, which are frequently set in beautiful gardens or forests.

CHARACTERISTICS OF CLASSICAL MUSIC

The overall impression of Classical music is that it is light, airy, elegant, and well thought out. It is music in which reason prevails over feelings. Composers thought more about creating beautiful and interesting works of music than pouring out their personal feelings in their music.

VENUS AND CUPID, by François Boucher. The Rococo subperiod favored decorative works of art and music, including melodies with many ornaments.

Much music of the time was written under a patronage arrangement. The patronage system during the Classical period, therefore, produced a quite homogeneous style of music. For example, although there are subtle differences between the music of Haydn and Mozart, their works tend to sound quite similar. In fact, using themes of other composers was an accepted practice at the time. The original composer of the theme considered its appropriation by another composer a compliment, not a case of plagiarism. One theme called the "Mannheim rocket," for example, was used by Mozart, Beethoven, and many other composers.

People in the Classical period, including composers, seemed to attribute little mystery to the act of creating music, an attitude that would change radically in the nineteenth century. For example, Mozart prepared a booklet with which anyone with a pair of dice could "compose" a piece of music. The booklet contained a short work for two violins, flute, and bass with each measure numbered. A chart indicated which measure of the work should be used for each of the eleven numbers that could appear on the dice. Whatever one's luck with the dice, a pleasant piece of music was certain. The style of Classical music could be systematized to that extent.

The "rocket" is discussed further in Chapter 21.

Mozart's booklet went through six or seven editions. It was published in London under the title *Mozart's Musical Game, fitted in an elegant box, showing by an Easy System how to compose an unlimited number of Waltzes, Rondos, Hornpipes, and Reels.*

FEATURES TO LISTEN FOR IN CLASSICAL MUSIC

Melody

For the most part, the themes are pleasant and tuneful. Most of them can be sung, if put in the right range. These melodies are made up of short phrases of two and four measures in length. And the phrases often are arranged in a statement–answer pattern. They form a musical equivalent of "How do you do?" and "Very well, thank you." Such paired patterns are balanced and symmetrical, and they contribute to the clear, logical quality of the music.

Homophony

The music of the Classical period was usually homophonic—melody plus accompaniment. There is some counterpoint in Classical music, but it is more the exception than the rule.

Harmony

Classical composers used essentially the same system of harmony as Baroque composers, but they made two important changes: (1) They abandoned the continuo part and the filling in of chords from figured bass, and (2) they changed chords less frequently. Sometimes Classical composers would keep the same chord for a measure or two before making a change, and then they might change chords several times in a rather short span of time. Classical harmony has the role of providing a backdrop for the melodies and does not draw attention to itself.

Rhythm

Classical music follows regular metrical patterns with few fluctuations in steadiness of the beat, except for recitatives in operas and oratorios. But it lacks the persistent quality of the rhythm of many Baroque works. Part of the reason for this difference is the result of abandoning the continuo and its steady stream of notes.

Dynamic Levels

The gradual **crescendo** and **decrescendo** developed during the Classical period. These gradual changes in dynamic level were considered quite dramatic at the time. They were an important contribution of that period to the development of music.

Performance

The orchestras of the Classical period grew somewhat but did not reach the size of the symphony orchestras of today. When orchestras today perform a symphony by Haydn or Mozart, they often reduce the size of the string section by about one-fourth. Orchestras during the Classical period used only pairs of woodwinds and brasses. No trombones or tubas were included, and the percussion section usually consisted of the timpani player.

Orchestra players were part-time musicians who also held other jobs, so the level of performance was probably not high by today's standards.

Public concerts began during this time in the sense that performances were not always closed to all except invited guests in a palace. Public concerts were available in a few large cities such as Paris, London, and Leipzig, and they were within the financial means of the prosperous merchant class.

> There were no permanent orchestras in the Classical period.

Forms

An important feature of Classical music is the development and refinement of various forms of instrumental music. Such music is referred to as **absolute music.** The rational outlook of the time encouraged the creation of music that was well ordered and planned, as well as in good taste. Writing music (especially instrumental music with its lack of a story and text) that spans more than a few minutes generally requires some means of organization, some plan. Classical composers continued to use the sectional forms of the Baroque period, but they also developed and expanded sonata, rondo, and theme-and-variation forms. These forms contributed to the creation of symphonies, concertos, and chamber works.

> Absolute music has no association with any object, idea, or event outside itself. It is the opposite of *program music,* which is presented in conjunction with Vivaldi's *The Four Seasons.*

MAIN POINTS OF THIS CHAPTER

1. The Classical period lasted from approximately 1750 to1820, and its artistic center was Vienna. Four persons stand out as representing those years: Voltaire, Jean-Jacques Rousseau, Benjamin Franklin, and Thomas Jefferson.

2. Because of its interest in intellectual endeavors, the Classical period is sometimes referred to as the Age of Reason or the Age of Enlightenment. It admired the logic and rational thinking of the ancient Greeks. During those years intellectuals believed that certain laws of nature and humanity were universal and eternal.

3. The Rococo style predated the Classical period. It existed largely in France, and its decorative and ornate works of art and music reflected the outlook of the aristocracy.

4. Many composers of that time worked under a patronage arrangement in which they composed exclusively for one person such as a count, duke, or king.

5. The Classical style differs from the Baroque style in several ways:

   • Its melodies often consist of short, tuneful figures.

   • Homophonic texture clearly predominates.

   • The continuo part has been abandoned.

   • Gradual changes in dynamic levels are present.

   • The chords that accompany a melody change less frequently.

   • Several important forms of instrumental music are developed.

16 Sonata Form

The most important form developed during the Classical period was **sonata form**, which is also called *first movement form* or *sonata–allegro form*. It became the expected form for the first movements of symphonies, concertos, and chamber music works in the last part of the eighteenth century and, with modifications, in the nineteenth century as well. And it is still used in compositions today. Sonata form was also found in other movements of multimovement works. Although the same word is used, *sonata form* and a *sonata* are different. One is a form, but a sonata is a genre of instrumental music.

DEVELOPMENT IN MUSICAL WORKS

As the word is used in music, *development* does not mean "building up" or "finishing," but rather "working with."

Sonata form is more than just a plan or schema, however. It features a fundamental idea in concert music: *the development of themes*. True, sonata form contains themes, which are of interest, but what a composer does with the themes makes the music even more interesting and enjoyable to listen to. The themes are at best only half of what music in sonata form has to offer. The other half is the way the themes are developed.

Several years ago people in a small town in Ohio realized that zucchini grew abundantly in their gardens and farms. In fact, the conditions one summer were so good that they could never use all of it, and a lot of zucchini would rot unused on the vine. What to do? They decided to hold a "Zucchini Festival," complete with crafts, dancing, music, and, of course, zucchini. Sure enough, it was chopped, sliced, and ground up and incorporated in all sorts of vegetable dishes, made into preserves and pickles, and blended in bread and muffins. Even the arts were included, as many fine pieces of zucchini sculpture were carved.

It's a bit like that with the development of themes in sonata form. Composers take a theme and work with it in all sorts of ways. The themes — or at least parts of them — are still there, but they have been given a variety of treatments.

MOZART'S SYMPHONY NO. 40, K. 550

The *K.* by the title comes from the name of a person — Ludwig Köchel — who catalogued Mozart's music.

As the biographical sketch on the next page points out, Mozart was perhaps the greatest musical genius of all time. He wrote a huge amount of music, much of which is still performed today. His Symphony No. 40 was composed in 1788. Why he composed it and two other symphonies that year is not known. It is unlikely that he ever heard them performed.

The score calls for the typical orchestra of the time: violins, violas, cellos (doubled by string basses in performance), a flute, two oboes, two bassoons, and two French horns. Later, Mozart revised the score to include two clarinets.

The first movement is in sonata form, which is explored in depth here. It has three other movements. The second has a slow tempo and features beautifully crafted melodies. The third is a stylized minuet. The fourth provides a lively conclusion to the symphony. Not typical of symphonies of the Classical period is the fact that three of its four movements use sonata form.

Wolfgang Amadeus Mozart ("Mo-tzart," 1756–1791) is certainly one of the greatest musical geniuses of all time. He was born in Salzburg, Austria, where his father was a recognized violinist and composer in the court of the archbishop. The elder Mozart was quick to realize that his son was a musical prodigy, and he set out to have him bring the family extra income. By the age of five, young Mozart composed his first pieces; at the age of six, he and his sister, who was four years older, toured Europe. By the age of thirteen, he had composed concertos, symphonies, sonatas, religious music, and an opera. At fourteen, he was knighted by the pope.

Mozart had a phenomenal memory for music and the ability to work out entire pieces in his head. When he committed the music in his mind to paper, he said that it rarely differed from what he had imagined. He was an excellent pianist and a competent violinist.

His great talent did not bring him financial success, however. He never had a steady appointment as a composer to a patron. He tried to work for the prince-archbishop at Salzburg, but the archbishop was a difficult man to please. Mozart did not get along with him, so he was dismissed.

At the age of twenty-five, he moved to Vienna, where he spent the last ten years of his life. There he married but had trouble supporting himself and his wife.

———◆———

The motion picture Amadeus *contained many inaccuracies about Mozart's life and death. The probability that he was poisoned by his competitor Antonio Salieri was one such inaccuracy.*

———◆———

As he put it, his existence consisted of "hovering between hope and anxiety." He managed by teaching, giving concerts, composing, and borrowing from friends. During some of those years, he was able to earn a reasonable income, but he was overly generous and not good at managing money.

At the age of thirty-five, Mozart died, probably of complications from rheumatic fever. He was buried on a cold, rainy December day in a common grave, which was customary in those days.

During his short life, he was able to compose more than six hundred works, including many sizable compositions such as symphonies, concertos, and operas. He never assigned opus numbers to his music, but some were added by publishers. All his works were later cataloged by a Viennese botanist and amateur musician named Ludwig Köchel.

Portrait of Leopold Mozart (1719–87) and his Children, Wolfgang Amadeus (1756–91) and Maria Anna (1751–1829) 1780–81 (oil on canvas), Austrian School, (18th century)/Mozart Museum, Salzburg, Austria/The Bridgeman Art Library

BEST-KNOWN WORKS

chamber music:
- Clarinet Quintet
- String Quartet No. 17

choral:
- Requiem

orchestra:
- *Eine kleine Nachtmusik*
- Symphonies Nos. 39, 40, and 41 ("Jupiter")
- Clarinet Concerto
- French Horn Concerto No. 3
- Piano Concertos Nos. 20, 21, 24, and 26
- Violin Concertos Nos. 3, 4, and 5

opera:
- *Don Giovanni*
- *The Magic Flute*
- *The Marriage of Figaro*

THE PLAN OF SONATA FORM

Sonata form itself is divided into three large sections: exposition, development, and recapitulation. Each section has a number of characteristics and features.

Exposition

In the **exposition** of sonata form, the composer presents or exposes the themes for the movement. The first theme is heard immediately:

Resource Center
See "Hear It Now: Melodies in the Classical Style," in the *Music Listening Today, 4th Edition,* Resource Center.

Several features can be pointed out about these eight measures:

- The theme is divided into two equal halves, with the second being nearly identical to the first, but one note lower. Each half is further divided in half, with the first portion sounding like a melodic statement and the second like its musical answer.

- The theme is actually simpler than it seems. The same rhythmic pattern appears on each of the four pitches. The quarter notes (♩) suggest chords: D D D B-flat (G minor) and C E-flat C (C minor) in the first four measures and so on. To this uncomplicated basic structure Mozart adds some musical spice—a little dissonance. The eighth notes marked with an **X** in the example are not in the harmony of the chord. Because they are short and do not occur on the beat, the effect is not harsh. Instead, it is more like a quick nudge.

It's somewhat like saying words several times for emphasis.

- The repeated three-note figure that leans upward creates a sense of forward movement, a necessary quality in concert music.

Composers in the Classical period did not let their personal feelings show through in their music.

- The theme is in a minor key, which is unusual among Mozart's symphonies. The minor mode adds its own particular mood to the music. Many composers in the nineteenth century used the minor mode to suggest gloomy music, but not Mozart. His use of minor in this symphony adds only a tinge of color; never does the music become sticky or sentimental.

- In a sense, the theme is a collection of several melodic fragments. It is not a sweeping, arching series of pitches but instead contains neat and concise phrases that are clearly delineated from each other. This quality makes it easier to develop.

After a few closing chords, the theme starts to repeat. But this time, halfway through, the music shifts to some solid-sounding chords and rapidly moving scales. A transition has begun. Transitions may or may not have much musical character of their own. They can (1) help the music modulate smoothly, (2) make a gradual change to a new theme, and (3) provide new musical ideas. This transition does all three of these things. Two chords followed by a rest mark the end of the transition. Such clear-cut points marking out the form are typical of music in the Classical period.

The second theme is divided between the violins and the woodwinds:

It differs from the first theme in several ways:

- It has longer note values.
- It has no frequently repeated rhythm pattern.
- It contains few skips up or down to other notes.
- It is more difficult to remember than the first because of its chromatic movement.

Chromatic movement is movement by half steps. Usually it can be seen in the added sharps and flats.

- It is in a different key from the first theme, which is true of the themes in the exposition. If a movement begins in a minor key, the second theme is generally in the relative major key. If the movement is in major, the second theme often is in the major key five notes higher.

Following the second theme, another transition appears. Fragments of the first theme are interspersed in it. At this point in sonata form, composers have some options. They can introduce a third theme (sometimes called the *closing theme*), they may write an extended transition, or they may borrow a fragment from one of the themes, which is what Mozart did here.

The transition concludes with a *codetta*, which is a short concluding section. Sometimes codettas have a brief melody of their own.

So far, only the first of the three sections that sonata form comprises has been presented. The exposition can be depicted:

Exposition

First theme	Transition	Second theme	Transition	Codetta
In tonic key		*In dominant key or relative major*		

Classical composers usually indicated that the entire exposition was to be repeated. In performances today the repeat sign is sometimes ignored, and the music moves directly into the next section.

Development

Logically, the **development** section is where much of the development of themes described earlier in this chapter takes place. What does Mozart do in the development section of the first movement of Symphony No. 40? Essentially, he treats the first theme in three ways:

1. The first half of the first theme is played three times, each time in a different key.
2. Counterpoint is introduced. While the lower strings play the first theme in a different key, the violins begin a countermelody of rapidly moving notes:

When the lower strings finish the first half of the first theme, they take up the countermelody while the violins play the theme. A similar exchange occurs two more times, each time one note lower than its preceding phrase.

3. The first theme is fragmented even further. The first few notes are tossed back and forth among the flute, clarinet, and violins. The music modulates often, but this section is quiet compared with the busy, vigorous exchanges between low and high strings that preceded it. Soon the answer in the woodwinds is shortened again to include only its first three notes. Several times the melodic figure is inverted, so it ascends in pitch rather than descends:

Fragments of the first theme appear in *all but the first two measures* of the development section. Fragments of the theme also appear in the transition leading from the development into the next main section of sonata form.

In this particular development, Mozart works with only the first theme. He breaks it apart, modulates frequently, adds countermelodies, and inverts it. Such treatments of the theme are typical of development sections in sonata form. He could have done other things as well. He could have developed the second theme, or he could have introduced a new theme. He might have altered the rhythm, written different chords for it, or combined two themes in a contrapuntal manner. The means of development are endless.

WOLFGANG AMADEUS MOZART
Symphony No. 40, First Movement (1788)

GENRE: Symphony Allegro molto (fast tempo) Symphony orchestra

CD 1 Tracks 38 – 42

8 minutes 10 seconds

Form: Sonata

Exposition

0:00 38 0:00 First theme begins in violins and is repeated. (Repeats at 1:10)

0:33 Transition containing short motive and many scalewise notes. (Repeats at 1:43)

0:51 39 0:00 Violins and woodwinds play second theme. (Repeats at 2:02)

0:11 Woodwinds and violins repeat second theme; then transition begins. (Repeats at 2:12)

0:56 Codetta begins with fast notes by violins. (Repeats at 2:48)

1:09 Codetta concludes with a solid chord. (Repeats at 3:10)

Development

4:02 40 0:00 Development section begins with two short chords and notes by woodwinds.

0:05 First theme appears three times in sequence, each time one note lower.

0:18 Upper and lower strings alternate portion of first theme and rapidly moving notes.

0:46 Motive from first theme alternates between violins and flute.

Recapitulation

5:22 41 0:00 First theme returns played by violins in the tonic key and is repeated.

0:33 Transition begins but is longer and more complex than in the exposition.

1:15 Woodwinds and strings play second theme.

1:26 Second theme repeated; then transition begins.

1:58 Clarinet and bassoon exchange the motive from the first theme.

7:38 42 0:00 Coda begins with fast scalewise passages.

0:11 Strings and woodwinds play motive from first theme several times.

0:32 Movement closes with three solid chords.

 An interactive Active Listening Guide can be downloaded from the online
Resource Center for *Music Listening Today, 4th Edition*.

Recapitulation

The term for the third section of sonata form is **recapitulation**. The first five letters of the word *recapitulation* form the word *recap*. And, sure enough, Mozart comes back to the first theme. It is played by the same instruments and with the same accompanying music. This literal repetition doesn't last long, however. Changes are introduced gradually as the bassoon adds a few notes in contrast.

More changes occur as the music moves into the transition heading toward the second theme. The transition is longer than it was in the exposition. In fact, for a short time it sounds almost as if another development section has begun. While the second violins play rapidly moving notes, the short fragment heard just briefly in the exposition is exchanged between the first violins and the low strings:

The word *recapitulation* literally means "return to the top."

There is another difference. The second theme is not in a new key; it stays in the tonic. If the second theme were in a different key, the composer would have to have the music modulate quickly back to the tonic before the movement ends and sound convincing about it. That is not an easy thing to do. Following the second theme, the transition uses music similar to what was played at the comparable place in the exposition.

The movement ends with a *coda*. The coda is like the codetta, except that it is longer so that it can provide a convincing conclusion to the entire movement. In this coda, Mozart again uses a fragment from the first theme. Dominant (V_7) and tonic (I) chords alternate in typical Classical style to give the movement a solid ending.

Coda means "tail" *in Italian.*

No two movements in sonata form are exactly alike; each is unique. In general, however, sonata form can be diagrammed as shown here.

A simplified line score of the first movement of Mozart's Symphony No. 40 is included in the *Study Guide* that is ancillary to this book.

Sonata Form

Exposition

Introduction (optional)	First theme	Transition	Second theme	Transition	Codetta
	In tonic key		*In dominant key or relative major*		

Development

Working over of musical ideas; sometimes new melodies introduced

Recapitulation

First theme	Transition	Second theme	Transition	Codetta
		In tonic key		

OTHER ASPECTS OF SONATA FORM

The key of the music was important in the Classical period. The key is usually provided along with the title of the work: Symphony No. 40 in G Minor by Mozart. Sometimes a work is referred to by its key, for example, Mozart's G Minor Symphony. Today, however, the key of a work is not particularly important to listeners. Music of the nineteenth century modulated so often and so far from the tonic that the impact of key change has been greatly reduced. And music in the twentieth century continued this trend, even to the point where some music has no key center at all.

You need to keep in mind that *everything* in a movement matters. It is not that the themes are the really good stuff and the transitions are just filler around them. As in doing a puzzle, every piece of it is needed for the complete picture.

Many movements in sonata form have introductions, although Mozart's Symphony No. 40 does not. They are usually in a slow tempo and seldom have much musical relationship with the rest of the movement in terms of their themes.

MAIN POINTS OF THIS CHAPTER

1. The most important form developed during the Classical period was sonata form. It consists of three large sections: exposition, development, and recapitulation. A coda usually concludes a movement in sonata form.

2. The exposition consists of the first theme, a transition to a second theme, and a transition leading to a codetta.

3. In the development section composers could work with fragments of either or both themes, change keys often, invert a motive from a theme, add counterpoint or different chords with the theme, or any combination of these possibilities.

4. The recapitulation returns to the music of the exposition, but usually with small changes as the music progresses. Its key does not change for the second theme. It concludes with a coda.

5. Mozart was one of the greatest musical geniuses of all time. In his short life he composed 626 pieces of music, many of them sizable works such as symphonies, concertos, operas, and chamber and choral works.

FEATURES TO LISTEN FOR

1. Notice the logic and symmetry of the first theme of the first movement of Mozart's Symphony No. 40.

2. Listen to the first theme and then to the second theme of the first movement. Notice the ways in which they differ from each other.

3. Notice how the final chords in the codetta and coda alternate between the dominant (V) and tonic (I) chords.

4. Notice how Mozart comes close to announcing when the second theme will begin by having a clear final cadence just ahead of it followed by a rest.

The Concerto

Neil Simon, the highly successful playwright, has written two plays consisting of three short plays that take place in the same location. But each play has characters and stories not found in the other plays. The location of *Plaza Suite* is New York's Plaza Hotel; *California Suite* utilizes a hotel setting in California. The only connection among the acts of each play is the suite of rooms.

It is somewhat like that with the multimovement works composed during the Classical period. Instead of a single location, however, Classical composers related the movements only in terms of tempos and keys. They planned for contrast among the movements in terms of forms, melodic character, amount of development, tempo, and so on. In this chapter we look at how composers during the Classical period achieved contrast among movements in the solo concerto.

THE SOLO CONCERTO

The word *concerto* is not a new one to you. First it appeared in Rodrigo's *Concierto de Aranjuez* for guitar and orchestra in Chapter 4. Then it appeared in Chapter 14 in Vivaldi's *Four Seasons* and Bach's Brandenburg Concerto No. 5, which pitted a solo part or a part for a small group against a larger group. The difference between these two types of concertos does not involve only the size of the group contrasted with the orchestra. In the solo concerto, the solo part is more showy than the orchestra part.

The concerto grosso of the Baroque period with its continuo part and contrast in size of groups went out of fashion in the Classical period and was replaced by the solo concerto. Since that time, the word *concerto* refers only to a solo concerto.

The advent of the solo concerto also parallels to some degree the beginning of public concerts, for which the composer organized and managed most of the administrative details. Audiences were then, as today, attracted by the opportunity to hear an outstanding performer. The small group was not the best means of presenting the talents of virtuoso performers; it is difficult to write music that really shows off two or more performers.

Mozart and Haydn composed many concertos and brought the solo concerto to a new level of musical sophistication. It is through their works that the solo concerto of the Classical period is examined here.

Most concertos are for the piano or violin, which are the most frequently featured instruments in concertos. Both Haydn and Mozart also composed concertos for less typical instruments such as clarinet, trumpet, bassoon, and French horn. These works are of such high quality that they are performed often today.

In the nineteenth century, Johannes Brahms composed a double concerto for violin and cello, and Beethoven a triple concerto, but such works are rare.

The concertos for these instruments are amazing in terms of overcoming or working around the technical limitations of wind instruments at the time.

MOZART'S VIOLIN CONCERTO NO. 5, K. 219

Mozart must have liked, or thought his listeners would like, solo concertos, because he certainly wrote a lot of them: about twenty-seven for piano, seven for violin, four for French horn, two for flute, and one each for bassoon, clarinet, and oboe. In addition, he composed a number of concertos for two violins and other combinations of instruments.

ncipal instrument,
s the piano.

Mozart composed his Violin Concerto No. 5 when he was nineteen years old. He probably composed it for himself to play as first violinist of the orchestra at Salzburg. In any case, its first movement serves as the exemplar here for the initial movements of almost all concertos of that time.

WOLFGANG AMADEUS MOZART

Violin Concerto No. 5, First Movement (1775)

GENRE: Concerto   Allegro aperto (rather fast)   Violin and orchestra

CD 3 Tracks 32 – 37

9 minutes 43 seconds

Form: Sonata

Exposition 1

0:00   32   0:00   Strings play first theme, which is built around a major chord.

0:35   Strings play contrasting second theme.

1:02   Orchestra plays codetta.

1:18   33   0:00   Solo violin enters playing a calm interlude.

Exposition 2

2:17   34   0:00   Second exposition begins. Orchestra plays first theme while solo violin plays a countermelody above it.

0:28   Soloist and orchestra play a transition.

1:10   Soloist plays second theme.

2:13   Orchestra plays codetta.

Development

4:41   35   0:00   Soloist and orchestra exchange themes as music modulates several times.

Recapitulation

5:32   36   0:00   Soloist plays the return of first theme.

0:20   Orchestra and soloist play transition.

1:19   Soloist and orchestra play second theme.

8:06   37   0:00   Soloist plays cadenza.

1:20   Orchestra begins coda.

1:36   Movement concludes quietly and quickly.

An interactive Active Listening Guide can be downloaded from the online Resource Center for *Music Listening Today, 4th Edition.*

Three features characterize the first movements of Classical concertos.

Double Exposition Although the movement is in sonata form, a second or **double exposition** is incorporated in the form. The first exposition is played by the orchestra; the second by the orchestra and the soloist. Because the second exposition usually includes music that shows off the soloist's prowess on the instrument, it tends to be longer than the first exposition.

Cadenza The movement usually specifies a cadenza just before the coda. The difference between the cadenza in Classical concertos and the cadenza in Rodrigo's *Concierto de Aranjuez* is that Rodrigo wrote out every note for the performer to play. In the Classical period, composers just wrote the word *cadenza* or its abbreviation *Cad.* at the appropriate place in the music. The performer was expected to make up a technically impressive paraphrase of the themes in the movement.

Whether soloists actually did so onstage is open to question. Improvisation was a far more common practice during the Baroque and Classical periods than it is today. Performers at that time probably worked at being good improvisers, but one wonders about doing so before an audience without prior preparation. For this reason, concerto programs today will sometimes indicate who wrote the cadenza for a particular Classical concerto, and the cadenzas will differ depending on the preferences of the soloist.

At some of his performances, Mozart would accept themes handed to him by members of the audience and make up music based on them.

Length Movements written in sonata form tend to be longer than the movements in the typical concerto grosso. Not only does it take more time to perform the various parts of the sonata form, but more time is also needed to show off the soloist's abilities.

No two movements in sonata form are exactly alike. And Mozart adds a few unique features to the first movement of his Violin Concerto No. 5. The orchestra plays the usual two themes in its exposition.

• When the soloist enters, an expressive interlude is inserted before the soloist and orchestra take up the first theme together.

• When the first theme does appear in the second exposition, the solo violin plays a brilliant countermelody above the theme in the orchestra.

• The development section is not particularly complex. The attention in this work is on melodies and the soloist's playing abilities; it is not on the development of themes.

THE SECOND MOVEMENT OF CONCERTOS

The second movement of almost all concertos composed in the Classical period features beautiful melodies and a slow tempo. This practice has continued into the nineteenth and twentieth centuries. As you will recall, the second movement of Rodrigo's *Concierto de Aranjuez* has these qualities, so in that regard it can be an exemplar for the second movement of most concertos, even those composed two centuries earlier.

RONDO FORM

Most third movements of concertos are written in rondo form. The basic idea of a **rondo** is the return of the same themes several times after other themes have been interjected among its various appearances. A rondo can be represented *A B A C A D A* and so on. Theoretically, there is no limit to the number of sections possible in a rondo, but five is the minimum number of sections. The pattern does not need to alternate as indicated by the foregoing example. They can be juggled *A B A C A B A*, or *A B A C D A*, or the shorter *A B A C A*, and so on, so long as the principle of the return of the A theme is followed.

The themes used in rondos tend to be shorter, less complicated, and happier than those in the first or second movements. Because the sections of a rondo are not usually

The word *rondo* comes from the French *rondeau*, meaning "to come around again."

long, composers do not have much room in which to develop themes or complex musical ideas. Movements in rondo form seem especially suited to the final movements of concertos and symphonies because they leave the listeners in an upbeat mood. The principle of the rondo is found in the final movement of most multimovement works composed during the Classical period and many such works since then.

HAYDN'S TRUMPET CONCERTO

h are clearly superior,
s on the trumpet about

Haydn composed his Trumpet Concerto in E-flat in 1796 for a keyed (not a valve) trumpet. Keys were added to the sides of the instrument somewhat like keys on a clarinet or saxophone. The work was written for the trumpet virtuoso of the time, Anton Weidinger.

FRANZ JOSEPH HAYDN
Concerto for Trumpet in E-flat, Third Movement (1796)

GENRE: Concerto   Allegro (lively)   Trumpet and orchestra
CD 1 Tracks 43 – 45
4 minutes 7 seconds
Form: Rondo

0:00 43	0:00	Violins play main theme (A) softly and rather fast.

0:21 44	0:00	Violins play first contrasting theme (B).

	0:15	Solo trumpet enters playing A theme.
	0:44	Trumpet and violins alternate playing B theme in a new key.

1:23 45	0:00	Violins and trumpet play second contrasting theme (C) in minor.

0:22	Trumpet plays A theme.
0:31	Trumpet and orchestra play short development of A theme as music changes key several times.
1:08	Trumpet plays a repeat of A theme.
1:23	Trumpet and violins play B theme.
1:54	Trumpet plays first portion of A theme.
2:03	Violins and trumpet play part of C theme.
2:30	Coda begins as trumpet plays part of A theme softly.
2:46	Rondo closes with a crescendo and a full-sounding chord.

 An interactive Active Listening Guide can be downloaded from the online Resource Center for *Music Listening Today,* **4th Edition.**

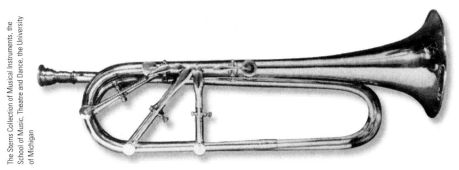

THE KEYED TRUMPET

He must have been quite a performer, because Haydn did not hesitate to write difficult passages for him to play.

What makes Haydn's Trumpet Concerto exciting to listen to?

* The trumpet has a brilliant, full sound.
* The music has a truly happy quality to it, with its bubbling personality.

Franz Joseph Haydn

Franz Joseph Haydn (1732–1809) was born the same year as George Washington, in eastern Austria. An uncle with whom Haydn went to live at the age of six gave him his first instruction in music. At eight he became a choirboy at the Cathedral of Saint Stephen in Vienna. When his voice changed, he was dismissed. For the next few years, he managed to exist doing odd jobs and teaching, as well as studying music theory. At the age of twenty-nine, he was taken into the service of Prince Paul Anton Esterházy, head of one of the richest and most powerful noble families in Hungary.

The next year Nicholas Esterházy succeeded his brother Paul. Nicholas was a connoisseur of music. Most of the time, the Esterházys lived at a country estate that rivaled the French court at Versailles. On the estate were two concert halls and two theaters, one for opera and one for marionette plays. Prince Nicholas was also an amateur performer on a string instrument called a baryton that looks something like a cello.

As was typical of the time, Haydn not only composed but also conducted the performances, trained the musicians, and kept the instruments in repair. Fortunately, he had twenty-five good instrumentalists and a dozen or so fine singers. His contract was typical in that it required him "to produce at once any composition called for" and to smooth out all difficulties among the musicians. He was expected to present himself twice daily to await orders.

For the most part, Haydn's experience with the Esterházy family represented the patronage system at its best.

After Haydn had been with the Esterházys for thirty years, Prince Nicholas died. Haydn subsequently made two visits to London in the 1790s. For each trip he composed six symphonies. After the London visits, he returned to work for a while for Nicholas Esterházy II, who was not as interested in music as his father had been. He gradually retired from composing and died in 1809, the same year Abraham Lincoln was born.

Haydn is sometimes referred to as the "father" of the symphony, the string quartet, the modern orchestra, and instrumental music in general. Although such claims are exaggerated, they give an indication of his importance. What Haydn actually did was work out a better balance for the new forms. For example, he developed the finale of the symphony. Before him, the fourth movement had been no more than a light little section.

BEST-KNOWN WORKS

chamber music:
* String Quartets (6) Op. 76
* Piano Trios Nos. 27, 28, and 29

concertos:
* Concerto No. 1 for Cello
* Concerto for Trumpet

choral:
* *The Creation*
* *Lord Nelson Mass*
* *The Seasons*

orchestra:
* Symphony Nos. 92 ("Oxford"), 94 ("Surprise"), 100 ("Military"), 101 ("Clock"), and 104 ("London")

ESTERHÁZY PALACE, the "Hungarian Versailles," where Haydn was court musician for thirty years

Vittorian Rastel/Corbis

- Rondo form gives listeners the expectation that the main theme will return. When it does, they have the satisfied feeling of being right.
- Rondo form contains both something old and something new. The main theme appears a number of times with new material interspersed.

Often the contrasting sections in a rondo do not have memorable themes. Also, occasionally the composer works the material into a short development section, as Haydn does in this concerto. The movement concludes with a coda that contains two brief statements of the main theme.

MAIN POINTS OF THIS CHAPTER

1. The solo concerto for soloist and orchestra replaced the concerto grosso of the Baroque period as the main type of concerto. The solo part became more technically difficult and showy than the orchestra part, and soloists were placed in front of the orchestra.

2. The first movements of most concertos are in sonata form that consists of an exposition for the orchestra alone followed by a second exposition for the soloist accompanied by the orchestra.

3. At least one of the three movements of a concerto usually includes a cadenza. During that time, the cadenzas were not written by the composers. Instead, they merely indicated where a cadenza should occur, and the soloist was expected to improvise it.

4. At least five sections are required for rondo form: the main theme with two contrasting themes inserted between its appearances to give the movement an *ABACA* form. The A theme is in the same key, and the contrasting sections are usually in different keys. Many rondos contain more than five sections.

5. Rondos usually have a bright, happy quality, and are often the final movement of instrumental works in the Classical period.

FEATURES TO LISTEN FOR

1. Notice that the first theme of the first movement of Mozart's Violin Concerto No. 5 consists almost entirely of the notes of the tonic (I) and dominant (V) chords.

2. When the first theme is played in the second exposition (CD 3 Track 34), notice that the music the violinist plays is a very decorated version of the first theme, which is being played by the violins in the orchestra.

3. Listen to the cadenza (CD 3 Track 37) in the first movement of Mozart's Violin Concerto No. 5. Notice that the fragments of the themes and figures heard earlier in the movement pop in and out of it.

4. Notice how short the themes are in the third movement of Haydn's Trumpet Concerto. Its rondo form consists of many short sections that last for only a little more than four minutes.

18 Classical Opera

A span of about 185 years passed between the first Baroque operas and Mozart's highly successful operas. In some ways, the genre had changed somewhat during that time, but in other ways it was similar. It was still the great amalgamation of the arts that brought together vocal and instrumental music, theater, and sometimes dance. And the music still consisted of accompanied recitatives, arias, and choruses that are clearly distinguishable from one another.

THE DEVELOPMENT OF OPERA

But changes had taken place. Although operas began around 1600 consisting largely of dramatic singing in recitative style, that soon became much less important than arias displaying virtuoso singing. The combination of music and drama had grown so out of balance that near the end of the Baroque, the composer Christoph Willibald Gluck (1714–1787) felt compelled to lead a reform movement. Gluck had composed many operas himself, so he knew the genre well. He tried to bring back its dramatic integrity by making the music serve the text. Everything in opera, including ballet, was to be an integral part of the drama. Gluck composed several operas that demonstrated his reforms.

In the decades following the opening of the first opera house in Venice, opera divided into two rather distinct styles. **Opera seria** had a serious nature and was closer to the original dramatic intent of the first operas. **Opera buffa** ("boo-fah") was a light style that was often comic.

"The War of the Buffoons" between those who favored opera buffa and those who favored the more serious court opera occurred about the middle of the eighteenth century in Paris. The word *buffoon* is derived from *buffa*.

MOZART'S OPERAS

Mozart's operas differed from Baroque operas in several ways. For one thing, his more successful ones were not based on historical or mythological characters such as those in Purcell's *Dido and Aeneas* (mythological) or Monteverdi's *Coronation of Poppea* (historical). In short, they were much more human. They were often about the nobility, who sometimes came off looking less than noble.

Another difference was that Mozart composed in both the seria and buffa types. His biggest successes were of the buffa type, which were in German, his native language. His seria operas were in Italian, a language that Mozart knew quite well because of his visits to Italy. Opera audiences in Vienna at the time were used to hearing operas in Italian and were fond of that style.

The play on which Mozart's *The Marriage of Figaro* is based has a servant outwitting a count. The play was forbidden in Vienna. The libretto was made less offensive and was acceptable because it was sung, not spoken.

Mozart's operas also differed from Baroque operas because he was such a gifted composer. His arias are usually of exceptional musical quality, so much so that many of them are often sung at performances apart from the opera. Several of the orchestral overtures to his operas enjoy similar status.

MOZART'S *DON GIOVANNI*

Don Giovanni (Don Juan) is a legendary Spanish nobleman whose appetite for women attracted many composers and playwrights before Mozart. Don Juan's exploits seemed to provide a source for artistic ideas. Mozart received a commission for the opera from an opera company in Prague, largely because of the huge success a year earlier of his opera *The Marriage of Figaro*. The libretto for both operas was written by the Italian Lorenzo da Ponte, the most recognized librettist of his day. *Don Giovanni* was warmly received in Prague but was less successful in Vienna. Apparently, the Viennese did not take to what seemed to them the opera's heavier qualities.

For the most part, *Don Giovanni* is opera seria. It contains some humorous moments, but its outlook is serious. Because of the opera's length, the discussion here is limited mainly to the last portion. The plot is intricate, so the opera should be listened to with the aid of an English translation of the libretto.

Don Giovanni opens with a typical overture. The stage action starts as Don Giovanni begins his adventures with Ottavio's fiancée, Donna Anna. She refuses his advances, and her father, the Commendatore (the Commandant), is killed by Don Giovanni in a duel while defending his daughter's virginity. At an engagement party, Don Giovanni attempts to seduce Zerlina, the bride of the peasant Masetto.

Later, Don Giovanni plays a cruel trick on Donna Elvira, whom he had seduced long ago and then deserted, and pursues other sexual adventures and pleasures. During one of his escapades, he takes refuge in a cemetery, where he discovers the statue of the Commandant and mockingly invites it to dinner. The statue nods its head to accept the invitation.

The final scene is set in the banquet hall in Don Giovanni's palace. The light, bouncy music lets the audience know immediately that the Don isn't worried. In fact, he seems to have forgotten all about the graveyard and the statue. He commands his private orchestra to play some dinner music. A wind ensemble plays a song from a popular opera of the day:

Leporello serves the table and looks hungrily at the food. "What a greedy appetite," he complains as he watches Don Giovanni down one mouthful after another.

A second piece is heard from the wind ensemble:

Leporello pours the Don some wine and, thinking that he won't be seen, stuffs some food in his mouth. As the third number begins—"Non più andrai" from Mozart's own *Marriage of Figaro*—Leporello helps himself to more food.

The Don, realizing that Leporello's mouth is full, asks him to whistle along with the music from *Figaro*. Poor Leporello is forced to admit that he has been snitching. The whole scene bubbles along like champagne.

Donna Elvira breaks the mood as she rushes in and throws herself at Don Giovanni's feet. She begs her former lover to give up his immoral ways. Leporello is moved, but not Don Giovanni. He mocks Donna Elvira by proposing a toast to her ("Long live women and good wine!"). Angered and humiliated, she turns and runs out the door. As she is leaving, she screams as she sees the statue of the Commandant.

The music reflects the lines of the characters—the sternness of the Commandant, the cowardice of Leporello, and the cockiness of Don Giovanni. At several points in the music, Mozart has the singers repeat words or phrases. In this book, those repetitions appear only the first time they are sung, which makes the libretto less cluttered.

The fascination with Don Juan continued well into the nineteenth century with Richard Strauss's orchestral tone poem *Don Juan*.

It is claimed that Mozart composed the overture only one day before its performance.

Notice how the story and music build to a climactic moment.

Don Giovanni, excerpt from Act II, Scene 5 (1778)

GENRE: Opera   Soloists, chorus, and orchestra

CD 1 Tracks `46`–`49`

8 minutes 52 seconds

Donna Elvira screams.

0:00 `46` 0:00 **DON GIOVANNI:** Che grido è questo mai?

DON GIOVANNI: What's that scream about?

LEPORELLO: Che grido è questo mai?

LEPORELLO: What's that scream about?

DON GIOVANNI: Va a veder che cosa è stato.

DON GIOVANNI: (*to Leporello*) Go and see what's happened.

Leporello goes to the first door, looks out, screams, and returns.

LEPORELLO: Ah!

LEPORELLO: (*screaming*) Ah!

DON GIOVANNI: Che grido indiavolato! Leporello, che cos'è?

DON GIOVANNI: What a devilish scream! Leporello, what is it?

LEPORELLO: Ah! Signor! per carità! non andate fuor di quà! l'uom di sasso, l'uomo bianco, ah! padrone! io gelo, io manco. Se vedeste che figura, se sentiste come fa ta, ta, ta, ta!

LEPORELLO: Ah! Sir, for pete's sake don't go out there! The man of stone, the white man. Ah! Master! I'm cold; I'm shaking. If you had seen that form; if you had heard how it goes—ta, ta, ta, ta!

DON GIOVANNI: Non capisco niente affatto.

DON GIOVANNI: I don't understand this.

LEPORELLO: Ta, ta, ta, ta!

LEPORELLO: (*imitating the statue*) Ta, ta, ta, ta!

DON GIOVANNI: Tu sei matto in verità, in verità, in verità!

DON GIOVANNI: Really, you're crazy!

A knock is heard.

LEPORELLO: Ah! sentite!

LEPORELLO: Ah! Do you hear!

DON GIOVANNI: Qualcun batte! Apri!

DON GIOVANNI: (*impatiently*) Someone's knocking! Open it!

LEPORELLO: Io tremo!

LEPORELLO: I'm trembling!

DON GIOVANNI: Apri, dico!

DON GIOVANNI: Open it, I say!

LEPORELLO: Ah!

LEPORELLO: (*pleading and terrified*) Ah!

DON GIOVANNI: Apri!

DON GIOVANNI: Open it!

LEPORELLO: Ah!

LEPORELLO: Ah!

DON GIOVANNI: Matto! Per togliermi d'intrico ad aprir io stesso andrò.

DON GIOVANNI: Madman! In order to clear this up, I'll open the door myself!

Don Giovanni takes one of the candle stands from the table and goes to the door. Leporello crawls underneath the table.

LEPORELLO: Non vo' più veder l'amico, plan, pianin, m'asconderò!

LEPORELLO: I don't want to see my friend again. Quietly, very quietly, I'll hide!

With a rumbling of timpani, the marble statue of the Commandant enters the room.

1:30 `47` 0:00 **STATUE:** Don Giovanni! a cenar teco m'invitasti! e son venuto!

STATUE: Don Giovanni! You invited me to dine with you! And I have arrived!

Don Giovanni is somewhat startled but conceals his surprise under an air of cockiness.

DON GIOVANNI: No l'avrei giammai creduto; ma farò quel che potrò. Leporello! un'altra centa! fa che subito si porti!

DON GIOVANNI: I can hardly believe this. But I'll do what I can. Leporello, another dinner! Bring it immediately!

Leporello peers out from under the table with a bewildered look on his face.

LEPORELLO: Ah, padron! slam tutti morti!

LEPORELLO: Ah, master! We're as good as dead!

DON GIOVANNI: Vanne, dico!

DON GIOVANNI: Get to it, I say!

Leporello begins to crawl out.

STATUE: Ferma un po'! non si pasce di cibo mortale, chi si pasce di cibo seleste! Altre cure più gravi di queste, altra brama quaggiù mi guidò.

STATUE: Wait a minute! One who partakes of heavenly food does not partake of mortal food. Things more serious than these brought me down here.

Leporello crawls back under the table.

LEPORELLO: La terzana d'avere mi sembra, e le membra fermar più non sò.

LEPORELLO: I have the chills and I can't stop shaking.

DON GIOVANNI: Parla dunque! che chiedi? che vuoi?

DON GIOVANNI: (*to the Statue*) Speak, then! What do you want?

STATUE: Parlo: ascolta! più tempo non ho.

STATUE: I speak—listen! I don't have much time.

DON GIOVANNI: Parla, ascoltando ti sto.

DON GIOVANNI: Speak! I am listening.

LEPORELLO: Ah le membra fermar più non sò. la terzana d'avere mi sembra, le membra fermar più non sò!

LEPORELLO: Ah! I can't stop shaking. I have the chills.

STATUE: Parlo: ascolta! più tempo non ho.

STATUE: I speak—listen! I don't have much time!

Don Giovanni becomes more defiant.

DON GIOVANNI: Parla, ascoltando ti sto.

DON GIOVANNI: Speak! I am listening!

STATUE: Tu m'invitasti a cena, il tuo dover or sai, rispondimi, verrai tu a cenar meco?

STATUE: You invited me to dinner. Do you know your obligation? Answer me! Will you come to dine with me?

Leporello shakes with fear beneath the table.

LEPORELLO: Oibò, tempo no ha, scusate.

LEPORELLO: Oh! He doesn't have time, sorry.

DON GIOVANNI: A torto di viltate tacciato mai sarò.

DON GIOVANNI: (*coolly*) I will never be accused of being a coward.

STATUE: Risolvi!

STATUE: Decide!

DON GIOVANNI: Ho già risolto!

DON GIOVANNI: I have already decided!

STATUE: Verrai?

STATUE: You will come?

LEPORELLO: Dite di no! dite di no!

LEPORELLO: Say no. Just say no!

DON GIOVANNI: Ho fermo il core in petto, non ho timor, verrò!

DON GIOVANNI: My heartbeat is steady. I am not afraid! I will come!

The statue extends a hand toward Don Giovanni.

6:10 48 0:00 STATUE: Dammi la mano in pegno!

STATUE: Give me your hand as a pledge!

Still defiant, Don Giovanni gives the statue his hand.

DON GIOVANNI: Eccola! Ohime!

DON GIOVANNI: Here it is! Ah!

STATUE: Cos'hai!

STATUE: What's the matter?

DON GIOVANNI: Che gelo è questo mai?

DON GIOVANNI: It's freezing cold!

STATUE: Pentiti, cangia vita, è l'ultimo momento!

STATUE: Repent! Change your life! It's your last chance!

Don Giovanni tries to withdraw his hand.

DON GIOVANNI: No, no, ch'io non mi pento, vanne lontan da me!

DON GIOVANNI: No, no. I will not repent! Get away from me!

STATUE: Pentiti, scellerato!

STATUE: Repent, villain!

DON GIOVANNI: No, vecchio infatuato!

DON GIOVANNI: No, you stupid old man!

(continued)

STATUE: Pentiti!	**STATUE:** Repent!
DON GIOVANNI: No!	**DON GIOVANNI:** No!
STATUE: Pentiti!	**STATUE:** Repent!
DON GIOVANNI: No!	**DON GIOVANNI:** No!
STATUE: Sì!	**STATUE:** Yes!
DON GIOVANNI: No!	**DON GIOVANNI:** No!
STATUE: Sì!	**STATUE:** Yes!
DON GIOVANNI: No!	**DON GIOVANNI:** No!

With a desperate effort, he wrests his hand away from the statue.

STATUE: Sì! Sì!	**STATUE:** Yes! Yes!
DON GIOVANNI: No! No!	**DON GIOVANNI:** No! No!

The Commandant's statue begins to move toward the door.
Roaring flames begin to surround Don Giovanni.

STATUE: Ah! tempo più non v'è!	**STATUE:** Ah! There is no more time!
DON GIOVANNI: Da qual tremore insolito sentoassalir gli spiriti! dond'escono quei vortici di foco pien d'orror?	**DON GIOVANNI:** I feel my strength afflicted by really unusual trembling! Where are those horrible whirlpools of fire coming from?

A chorus of ghostly demon voices sounds from below.

7:42 **49** 0:00

DEMON VOICES: Tutto a tue colpe è poco! vieni! c'è un ma! peggior!	**DEMON VOICES:** This is nothing compared to your crimes! Worse things await you!
DON GIOVANNI: Chi l'anima mi lacera? Chi m'agita le viscere? Che strazio, ohimè, che smania! Che inferno, che terror!	**DON GIOVANNI:** Who rips my spirit? Who shakes my innards? What twisting, alas, what frenzy! What hell! What terror!
LEPORELLO: Che ceffo disperato! Che gesti da dannato! che gridi! che lamenti! come mi fa terror!	**LEPORELLO:** What a terrible look on his face! What gestures of a damned soul! What shouts! What wailing! It terrifies me!
DEMON VOICES: Tutto a tue colpe è poco!	**DEMON VOICES:** All this is nothing compared to your crimes!
DON GIOVANNI: Chi l'anima mi lacera?	**DON GIOVANNI:** Who rips my spirit?
LEPORELLO: Che ceffo disperato!	**LEPORELLO:** What a terrible look on his face!
DEMON VOICES: Vieni! c'è un mal peggior!	**DEMON VOICES:** Come! Worse things await you!
DON GIOVANNI: Chi m'agita le viscere? che strazio, ohimè, che smania! Ah! che inferno! che terror!	**DON GIOVANNI:** Who shakes my innards? What twisting, alas, what frenzy! Ah! What hell! What terror!
LEPORELLO: Che gesti da dannato! che gridi! che lamenti! Come mi fa terror!	**LEPORELLO:** What gestures of a damned soul! What shouts! What wailing! It terrifies me!
DEMON VOICES: Vieni! vieni! vieni! c'è un mal peggior!	**DEMON VOICES:** Come! Worse things await you!
DON GIOVANNI: Ah!	**DON GIOVANNI:** (*screaming*) Ah!

Don Giovanni utters his final sound, is enveloped by flames, and sinks to hell.
Leporello echoes the Don's shout.

LEPORELLO: Ah!	**LEPORELLO:** Ah!

1:12 Recording fades.

 An interactive Active Listening Guide can be downloaded from the online Resource Center for *Music Listening Today*, 4th Edition.

Beatriz Schiller/Time & Life Pictures/Getty Images

DON GIOVANNI ON STAGE IN LONDON Gerald Finley (as Don Giovanni) and Robert LLoyd (as Commendante) in the production *Don Giovanni* at the Royal Opera House in Covent Garden.

Following the immolation of Don Giovanni, the mood suddenly changes to something more lighthearted. Donna Anna, Donna Elvira, and Zerlina rush in, followed by Ottavio and Masetto. They find Leporello crawling about on the floor and demand to know what has happened. Leporello stammers out the story of what he just witnessed.

The music is again filled with wit and sparkle. Don Giovanni is already just a memory. In a brief duet, Donna Anna and Ottavio tell of their plans to marry after her year of mourning for her father is over. Donna Elvira pledges to end her days in a cloister. Zerlina and Masetto are anxious to be off so they can have dinner. And Leporello sets about finding himself a new master. As the six singers face the audience, they deliver the moral of the opera. The whole scene is so mischievous that one wonders whether Mozart was not really attempting to have the last laugh with the moralizing. The sextet sings:

> *Such is the end*
> *Of those who do evil.*
> *The death of the wicked*
> *Always matches their life.*

This last scene containing moralizing by the sextet has often been omitted from the opera. In the nineteenth century, it was thought out of place after the damnation of *Don Giovanni*. Mozart himself approved the deletion the second time it was staged.

MAIN POINTS OF THIS CHAPTER

1. Opera developed at the beginning of the Baroque period as an attempt to recreate the drama of the Ancient Greeks. Over the years, however, dramatic quality had given way to displays of virtuoso singing in operas with flimsy plots and little dramatic impact. Christoph Willibald Gluck began the reform of opera by integrating all of its components into a unified entity.

2. Two types of opera were important in the Classical period: opera seria and opera buffa. Opera seria are usually tragic and feature stories about ancient gods and heros. Opera buffa are filled with fun and frivolity, including the occasional use of popular tunes.

3. Mozart composed both opera seria and opera buffa. His seria operas were in Italian, and his buffa operas were in German. Many of his operas involved human rather than mythological characters. Many of his opera arias and overtures are often performed as concert works apart from the opera.

FEATURES TO LISTEN FOR

1. Notice how in the music of his opera *Don Giovanni* Mozart helps to portray the characters—the spinelessness of Leporello, the cockiness of Don Giovanni, and the sternness of the statue of the Commandant.

2. What is the role of the Demon Voices (CD 1 Track 49)? To whom are they singing their words?

3. Listen to two minutes of Mozart's *Don Giovanni* (CD 1 Tracks 46–49) and then to the duet from Monteverdi's *The Coronation of Poppea* (CD 3 Track 19). Notice two ways in which they are similar, and then two ways in which they are quite different.

Chamber Music

Until the Classical period, most instrumental music (except for keyboard) did not clearly indicate the size of the group for which it was written. As the orchestra became more standardized, composers began to specify the type of group for which they were writing. Apparently they felt that music for an orchestra was not as suitable for music created with a small group in mind, and vice versa. The music they created for small groups is known as **chamber music.**

Musicians to this day have continued to value chamber music, primarily because it permits a refinement and intimacy of expression that cannot be derived from a large musical organization. An orchestra has power and color; a string quartet provides a sense of involvement and clarity. One medium can be as musically satisfying as the other in the hands of skilled composers and performers.

THE NATURE OF CHAMBER MUSIC

The chief characteristic of chamber music is one player on each part. This definition refers to parts, not instruments. For instance, a string quartet consists of two violins, one viola, and one cello, but there are two *different* violin parts. So long as each has a different part, there could be three or more violins, and the work would still be considered chamber music.

Voices are not usually involved in chamber music, although early chamber works were influenced by vocal style. In fact, during the Renaissance, madrigals could be either sung or played on string instruments. In the twentieth century, Igor Stravinsky, Arnold Schoenberg, and others composed for voices in chamber compositions. Since the Renaissance, however, and particularly during the Classical period, chamber music has consisted of instrumental music.

The players perform chamber music while looking at their music notation; only soloists play from memory. In chamber music, the individual must be subordinate to the group, so memorizing is not called for. Furthermore, the undistinguished quality of the parts when providing harmony and the number of players involved make the memorized performance more susceptible to error.

The formal patterns found in chamber music in the Classical period are the same as those presented in earlier chapters in conjunction with the symphony and the concerto. Not only are the same forms used for individual movements, but the pattern of movements is also the same. The first movements of sonatas, string quartets, and other chamber works are in sonata form. The second movements have slow tempos and emphasize melody; often they are in a three-part form. The third movements of four-movement works are usually in the form of a minuet and trio. The fourth or last movements generally have a fast tempo and often are rondos. This arrangement of forms and movements tends to be true regardless of the particular combination of instruments used in a work.

LISTENING TO CHAMBER MUSIC

The methods for listening to chamber music are essentially the same as those for listening carefully and thoughtfully to music of any type. But because chamber music is performed by a small group, it lacks the tonal power and the lush, colorful sounds of a

The appeal of chamber music lies in its refined and intimate musical qualities, not its sensuous sounds.

full orchestra or chorus. Listeners must therefore concentrate on what is happening in the music itself. The composer's musical ideas and treatment of them in a composition are the heart of chamber music.

The fewer players there are, the easier it is to hear small errors in playing, so the performers must execute their parts with accuracy and unity. This feeling of oneness in musical performance is called *ensemble*. Chamber music is usually performed without a conductor, so the sensing of tempos, phrasing, and dynamics is the responsibility of each player.

Although one person is acknowledged to be the leader, the cues and nods that start and stop the group are so subtle that the audience sees only by watching carefully. This explains why the word *ensemble* refers both to the sense of unified performance by the players and to the chamber music group itself.

When a chamber music group is heard live in a home or small recital hall, something is added to the listeners' enjoyment. Perhaps the closeness of the performers provides a sense of involvement that makes listening to chamber music enjoyable. In any case, chamber music is best heard in a live performance in small recital halls or the living rooms of large homes.

Music for orchestra is generally far better known than chamber music, probably because more knowledge and attention are required for successful chamber music listening. Because there is a limited audience, few chamber groups can earn a living solely from performing. Today, chamber ensembles are found in residence at a number of universities.

CHAMBER MUSIC IN THE CLASSICAL PERIOD

Chamber music thrived in the Classical period, because the social setting encouraged its creation and performance. Most performances of music were still for private audiences. When hosts wished to provide after-dinner music for guests in their palatial homes, they often thought of a chamber group.

Haydn's experience with chamber music indicates its use during the Classical period. As mentioned in Chapter 17, his patron, Prince Nicholas Esterházy, happened to enjoy playing the baryton. The instrument looks something like a cello but has sloping shoulders and more strings that vibrate sympathetically. Haydn composed a great deal of music for his patron to play: 125 trios, 12 short divertimentos, and 2 duets. But he wrote many more chamber pieces than those involving the baryton.

In addition, musicians such as Mozart and Haydn and competent amateurs engaged in playing chamber music on an informal social basis. It was a fashionable thing to do during the Classical period.

THE SONATA

From the Classical period forward, the *sonata* became a sizable instrumental work in three or four movements. Classical sonatas are divided into two categories. The *ensemble sonata* is usually a composition for two instruments: piano and one other instrument. The *solo sonata* is for a single instrument.

The two parts are considered to be of equal importance in the ensemble sonata. In no sense is the piano accompanying the other instrument. As a matter of fact, some of the time the piano part contains a more important musical idea, while the other instrument plays accompanying material. Because the presence of the piano is assumed, the sonata is called by the name of the other instrument. So a violin sonata is for violin and piano.

Unlike other ensemble works, a solo sonata is usually played from memory. Although a few solo sonatas have been written for violin or other instruments, the solo sonata is most associated with the piano.

The word **ensemble** means "together" in French.

The person who plays the first violin part is usually considered the leader.

THE BARYTON is a very different instrument from the baritone horn. It is a member of the viol family.

A sonata frequently has one or more of its movements in sonata form. It's logical but confusing.

The piano sonata is presented in Chapter 20.

THE STRING QUARTET

With its instrumentation of two violins, a viola, and a cello, the **string quartet** is probably the most significant chamber ensemble. Early in the eighteenth century, compositions called **divertimentos** were common. As the name implies, they were diversionary, innocuous pieces. They could be played by either a quartet or a string orchestra. Haydn took the divertimento, deleted one of its two minuets, and gave it more musical substance. He called these new works *quartets* rather than divertimentos. The change did not occur quickly; it was stretched out over much of Haydn's adult life.

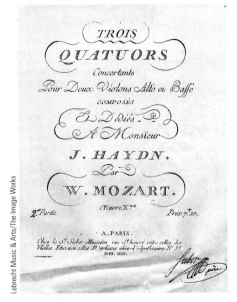

TITLE PAGE for the French publication of three of the six quartets that Mozart wrote and dedicated to Haydn. Mozart offered them "as children" to his friend.

Haydn's String Quartet, Op. 76, No. 3 ("Emperor")

Haydn's Op. 76, No. 3, is known as the "Emperor Quartet" because its second movement uses as its theme "The Emperor's Hymn," a melody based on a folk song that Haydn composed for Emperor Franz II a year before the quartet in 1796. This melody is the national anthems of Austria and Germany today and a hymn in several mainline Protestant churches.

The six quartets in Op. 76 were commissioned and dedicated to a Count Endödy for a fee of a hundred ducats. They were the exclusive property of the count "for a certain number of years" before being published in 1799 and selling well. They were composed late in Haydn's career, and he finished only two more quartets during the remainder of his life.

The first movement is in sonata form. The second movement features "The Emperor's Hymn," and the fourth is lively and in sonata form. The third movement is a minuet and trio, which is a stylized version of a popular dance of the time. Third movements of Classical symphonies and quartets usually follow a form more closely than other movements do. Essentially, the form is a large three-part *A B A* form, with each large part having subsections:

Minuet	Trio	Minuet
A	*B*	*A*
a a b a' b a'	*a a b a' b a'*	*a b a'*

The music is in a clear three-beat meter, with the first violin being responsible for most of the themes. The second violin, viola, and cello generally have accompanying parts that occasionally contain a melodic figure. The minuet is in major, whereas the trio begins in minor, but its *b* theme is in major. The term *trio* is the result of a tradition in which the contrasting part of a minuet was played by two instruments plus accompaniment.

OTHER TYPES OF CHAMBER MUSIC GROUPS

Almost every conceivable combination of instruments has had chamber music written for it, but certain types of chamber groups are more common, including the sonata and the string quartet. Another likely string group is the *string quintet* (two violins, two violas, and one cello). The *piano trio* (violin, cello, and piano) is another ensemble for which a lot of music has been composed. The *woodwind quintet* (flute, oboe, clarinet, French horn, and bassoon) was not common in Haydn's time, but it has become a standard chamber ensemble in the twentieth century. Brass ensembles have the least standardized instrumentation. Perhaps the *brass quintet* (two trumpets, a French horn, a trombone, and a tuba) has most frequently drawn the attention of composers.

It is not unusual to find one nonstring instrument added to a string quartet. For example, Mozart's work for clarinet and string quartet has the title Clarinet Quintet in A Major, although only one clarinet is present. If a piano plus a string quartet is called for, the work is a piano quintet. Apparently, the presence of strings is taken for granted in such ensembles, so the added instrument is cited in the name of the group.

String Quartet in C Major, Op. 76, No. 3, "Emperor" Third Movement (1797)

GENRE: Chamber Music   Moderate Tempo   String Quartet

CD 3 Tracks **38** – **39**

5 minutes

Form: Minuet and Trio

Minuet

0:00   **38**   0:00   First violin plays the *a* theme of the minuet in a major key and three-beat meter.

0:22   The *a* theme is repeated.

0:44   The *b* theme of the minuet begins.

0:57   The *a* theme is extended.

1:23   The *b* theme is repeated.

1:37   The extended *a* theme is repeated.

Trio

2:04   **39**   0:00   First violin plays the *a* theme of the trio in a minor key.

0:10   The *a* theme of the trio is repeated.

0:19   First violin plays a link to the next theme.

0:35   First violin plays the *b* theme of the trio in a major key.

0:44   The *b* theme is repeated as cello plays contrasting phrases.

0:54   The *a* theme of the trio is extended.

1:22   The *b* theme is repeated.

1:41   The *a* theme is extended.

Minuet

1:52   The *a* theme of the minuet returns.

2:14   The *b* theme of the minuet returns.

2:27   The extended *a* theme of the minuet returns.

2:56   The minuet concludes quietly.

 An interactive Active Listening Guide can be downloaded from the online Resource Center for *Music Listening Today,* **4th Edition.**

Quintet by Mozart is
n A, not B-flat, the key
inets today. There is a
ence in timbre between
inets, and this quintet is
or the A clarinet because
ey of A major. This means
inetist is looking at notes
ut, of course, sounding
rd lower.

MOZART'S CLARINET QUINTET

The Clarinet Quintet in A Major, K. 581, is a relatively late work by Mozart, written after his Symphony No. 40. It is in the best polished style of the eighteenth century. The form is clearly delineated, the instrumental parts are well balanced, and everything is neat and enjoyable.

FIRST MOVEMENT The first movement is in sonata form. Its first theme consists of a simple, songlike portion played by the four string instruments. The clarinet follows playing a florid passage containing many rapidly moving notes.

The development begins quietly with the first theme presented in a different key. Other figures from the exposition are also heard.

The recapitulation is very similar to the exposition, except for small changes.

The movement closes, as did the exposition, with a statement of the opening theme.

SECOND MOVEMENT In the second movement, the clarinet plays a beautiful melody that could easily be an aria in a Mozart opera. The *B* portion of the movement contains contrasting melodic material played by the violin, with the clarinet adding decorative melodic comments from time to time, which are later taken up by the violin. The opening melody returns, again played by the clarinet.

THIRD MOVEMENT The third movement is an elegant-sounding minuet and trio. This minuet is unusual because it has two trios, one for the strings and a second one giving the clarinet a chance to show off its capabilities at playing notes over a wide range along with its varied timbre.

Wide changes of pitch are quite easy on the clarinet because of its register key, which is operated by the player's left thumb.

FOURTH MOVEMENT The fourth movement is both a form and a musical process: *theme and variations*. The basic idea of theme and variations is simple: Take a melody and cast it in different settings. The process is something like taking a number of pictures of a house, but each time under different conditions and from different angles. One picture might be at daybreak, another during a rainstorm, another from ground level, and so on.

The meter signature indicates that the half note (♩) gets the beat. Therefore, the music moves more quickly than it appears to in the notation.

WOLFGANG AMADEUS MOZART
Clarinet Quintet in A Major, Fourth Movement (1789)

GENRE: Chamber Music   Moderately Fast Tempo   Clarinet and String Quartet

CD 4 Tracks 1 – 7

9 minutes 37 seconds

Form: Theme and Variations

Theme

0:00 1 0:00   Violins play *a* part of the theme and then repeat it.

(continued)

0:29   They continue with *b* part of the theme and then repeat it.

Variations

0:59 **2** 0:00   Variation 1. Clarinet plays a freewheeling melody as violins play the *a* half of the theme. Each half of each variation is repeated throughout the movement.

0:29   Clarinet and violins play *b* part of the theme.

1:57 **3** 0:00   Variation 2. Violin plays an ornamented version of the theme as second violin and viola play repeated notes.

0:32   Violins continue the *b* portion of the theme.

3:02 **4** 0:00   Variation 3. Viola "sobs" out its variation of the theme in a minor key.

0:38   Violin plays chromatic notes before viola returns with its variation.

4:16 **5** 0:00   Variation 4. Clarinet and violin play fast notes, and the key returns to major.

0:30   Clarinet plays wide leaps as violin plays rapidly moving notes.

1:00   Transition begins to next variation.

5:33 **6** 0:00   Variation 5. Violins play a slow-moving figure heard in the second variation. Clarinet joins in halfway through.

1:17   The *b* portion of the variation is played.

2:37   Soft, slow chords link to the coda.

8:38 **7** 0:00   Coda. Violins and clarinet energetically play the *a* portion of the theme.

0:55   The movement ends with two short, solid chords.

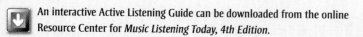

An interactive Active Listening Guide can be downloaded from the online
Resource Center for *Music Listening Today, 4th Edition.*

The idea of theme and variations is, of course, best understood by listening carefully to an example by a master composer such as Mozart.

The difference between varying and developing a theme can be made clearer by thinking about what Mozart did in developing themes in his Symphony No. 40 and contrasting that with what he did in varying the theme in his clarinet quintet. *Development* involves fragmenting and remolding a theme. **Variation** consists of placing the theme in a new setting or giving it a new harmonic, rhythmic, or melodic costume.

MAIN POINTS OF THIS CHAPTER

1. Chamber music is played by small groups of instrumentalists with only one player on each part.

2. Chamber music is an important feature of Classical music. Composers wrote enormous amounts of music for performances in large rooms, not concert halls.

3. Chamber works utilize the same forms as the other instrumental music of the time. Although chamber works with four movements were not uncommon, many chamber works omit the minuet and trio movement found in symphonies.

4. If a string ensemble includes a non-string instrument, then the ensemble is referred to by the name of that instrument. So an ensemble consisting of a violin, cello, and piano is called a "piano trio."

5. A sonata is a chamber work in three or four movements for solo piano or piano and another instrument. When another instrument is involved, the role of the piano is as important as that of the other instrument.

6. Theme and variations are an important type of music, both as movements in multi-movement works and stand-alone works. The concept of theme and variations is to treat a theme in a variety of settings.

7. A minuet and trio is a three part (ABA) form based on the minuet. It has a clear triple meter and is often used as a third movement of symphonies and string quartets.

FEATURES TO LISTEN FOR

1. To make sure you sense the beat and its metrical pattern in the Minuet and Trio from Haydn's "Emperor" Quartet, count the moderately fast beats to yourself as you listen to the music: 1–2–3 1–2–3, and so on (CD 3 Track 38).

2. Notice that the minuet in the "Emperor" Quartet is in major and that its trio is in minor.

3. Listen to how each variation in the fourth movement of Mozart's Clarinet Quintet has its own particular character. Which one seems to be the most cheerful sounding? Which one sounds a bit sad?

4. In the first variation (CD 4 Track 2) of Mozart's Clarinet Quintet, notice how easily the clarinet moves between high and low notes.

20 Piano Sonatas

The harpsichord was the keyboard instrument of choice during the Baroque period, except for music in churches. But in the latter half of the eighteenth century, the instrument fell out of favor and was replaced by the piano. Because of the piano's increasing popularity, composers wrote music for it using the same forms that were in vogue for orchestral and chamber groups. These works for solo piano, called *sonatas*, continue to be a vital part of the music played by pianists today.

THE SONATA

As was pointed out in Chapter 19, a sonata is for either solo piano or for piano plus one other instrument. In either case, sonatas are similar to the orchestral works by the particular composer. The first movement is in sonata form, with the same general use of keys and development of themes and motives. The second movement is slow and features melody. It is often in A B A form, but other forms are also used. The main difference between sonatas and symphonies is that the third movement of a sonata is not the usual minuet and trio. That movement is eliminated, and the third movement becomes the final movement. Usually it is in rondo form.

The sonatas of the Classical period are not just miniature versions of larger works. Indeed, sometimes they are longer and occasionally seem more serious. Composers during this time also composed many of them: Mozart wrote seventeen and Haydn, thirty-one. Beethoven composed thirty-two such works, and they represent a major contribution to the music that pianists play.

For example, the first movement of Beethoven's Fifth Symphony is less than eight minutes long, but the first movement of his "Waldstein" Sonata is more than eleven minutes long.

THE PIANO

In Mozart's time, the piano was essentially a drawing-room instrument. Its tone was light and delicate, and composers wrote for it accordingly. During Beethoven's lifetime many improvements were made in the piano, probably the most important of which was the addition of metal braces to the frame across which the strings were strung. These braces permitted heavier strings, because the frame could now withstand the greater tension required to bring such strings up to pitch. In turn, the greater tension and heavier strings gave the piano more power. The combination of Beethoven's forceful music and a more powerful instrument inevitably enabled the piano to gain a prominent place in the concert hall.

Later the entire frame was made of cast iron, which is an absolutely rigid material.

The piano of today has changed only slightly since the beginning of the nineteenth century. The key action has been made a bit more responsive, and a pedal has been added to permit certain sustaining effects, but these improvements are minor.

The type of piano construction affects the musical results. The grand piano is superior to the upright in structural design. In order to fit inside the case of an upright, the low strings have to be shortened and tuned with less tension. So the upright or spinet lacks the volume and consistency of tone found in the grand piano. The smaller the instrument, the more serious the loss of tone quality. Concert music such as a Beethoven sonata understandably is shown off to best advantage when performed on a high-quality grand piano.

MOZART'S PIANO SONATA NO. 11

Mozart composed his eleventh piano sonata (K. 331) in the summer of 1778 while in Paris with his mother. It is one of the four piano sonatas that he wrote that summer, probably as a way of publicizing his abilities as a composer and performer. It is likely that he had hopes for a high-paying position in a prominent court.

> Like Bach sixty years earlier, Mozart was not successful at finding a high-paying court position.

Sonata No. 11 is typical in that the first movement is in sonata form, but the second is different from most second movements in sonatas. In an effort to appeal to the lighter tastes of Paris audiences, he substituted a minuet and trio.

The third movement, "Rondo alla Turca," follows the usual practice by being in modified rondo form. But it is certainly not typical in terms of its appeal to audiences. It is one of Mozart's most frequently played piano works.

The movement opens with a slightly Middle Eastern–sounding theme in minor, which probably accounts for the "alla Turca" in the title. It consists of many rapidly moving notes and is repeated, as are almost all the sections in this movement.

> Mozart's music is hardly Turkish. It was a fad in Paris at the time to refer to any music that sounded even slightly Middle Eastern as "Turkish."

The B portion of the rondo switches to major and is the theme that is more easily remembered.

The music moves to the C section, then back to B, then A, and one more time for a somewhat more active-sounding B. The movement ends with a short coda.

WOLFGANG AMADEUS MOZART

Piano Sonata No. 11 in A Major, K. 331, Third Movement, "Rondo alla Turca" (1778)

GENRE: Solo sonata   Piano

CD 4 Tracks 8 – 12

3 minutes 15 seconds

Form: Rondo

0:00	8	0:00	First part of A section features a lively melody in minor; is repeated.
		0:14	Second half of A section, which concludes with opening music; is repeated.
0:41	9	0:00	B section is in major and presents an energetic melody; is repeated.
0:55	10	0:00	C section features moving, even notes in minor.
		0:13	Second half of the C section. Section is repeated.
		0:40	B section returns; is repeated.
1:50	11	0:00	First part of A section returns; is repeated.
		0:14	Second part of A section returns; is repeated.
		0:41	A vigorous version of B section returns; is repeated.
2:45	12	0:00	Coda begins. Contains repeated notes and chords.
		0:30	Movement concludes with three solid chords.

An interactive Active Listening Guide can be downloaded from the online Resource Center for *Music Listening Today, 4th Edition.*

LISTENING GUIDE

BEETHOVEN'S PIANO SONATA NO. 21 ("WALDSTEIN")

Beethoven's instrument was the piano, and his compositions for the instrument constitute some of his greatest contributions to music. His piano sonatas are known by their number as well as their key or nickname. In 1804 he wrote a piano sonata dedicated to Count Ferdinand von Waldstein, a friend and benefactor. This sonata, No. 21, reveals many elements of Beethoven's musical style, especially for the piano.

> The numbers of the thirty-two sonatas are in the order in which they were published.

First Movement

The first movement is typically in sonata form. But there is much more to the movement than its form. To begin with, the first theme is not like anyone's before him (and possibly since). It begins with a soft thumping chord that is repeated thirteen times before any note is changed! And when the pattern does end, it leads into two short, motivelike figures (circled in the example).

The same idea is repeated immediately, but this time the chords are "broken" so that pitches are sounded one after another instead of simultaneously.

Several points merit comment about the first theme:

- It is not melodious. Its musical value lies in its potential for development.

- It does not contain notes of much length. Rather, it relies on the sounding of many tones to maintain the intensity that Beethoven wanted here.

- It starts softly and works up to—or, rather, erupts into—the short melodic figures. This sense of eruption is typical of Beethoven's music.

- It is highly suitable for the piano but would fail as a vocal melody.

> A sense of drama is one of the characteristics of the Romantic style of the nineteenth century.

The transition to the second theme illustrates another of Beethoven's techniques when writing for piano: the use of broken chord patterns. He likes to have the patterns and scales come toward or move away from each other. The simultaneous contrast of pitch direction is called *contrary motion*:

The second theme is in the remote key of E major. The practice of Classical composers was to write the second theme in the key that centered five notes above the original key center. Beethoven is more harmonically daring and moves to the key *three* notes higher. The traditional adherence to key schemes was breaking down even by the early 1800s.

Piano Sonata No. 21, Op. 53, "Waldstein," First Movement (1804)

GENRE: Sonata   Piano

CD 4 Tracks 13 – 17

11 minutes 11 seconds

Form: Sonata

Exposition

0:00   13   0:00   First theme in major, with many repeated notes and two motives. (Repeats at 1:28)

Allegro con brio

       0:22   First theme repeated with a different accompaniment. (Repeats at 1:50)

0:56   14   0:00   Second theme in a different major key, then repeated with some changes. (Repeats at 2:24)

dolce e molto legato   cresc.   sf

       0:28   Transition begins with triplet figures. Then sixteenth notes take over. (Repeats at 2:52)

       1:05   Codetta with its own theme. (Repeats at 3:28)

Development

4:55   15   0:00   Motives from first theme modulate.

       0:38   More triplet figures.

       1:27   Music becomes quiet, then slowly builds.

Recapitulation

6:45   16   0:00   First theme returns.

       0:23   Short, quiet interlude.

       0:34   First theme repeated with a different accompaniment.

       1:10   Second theme returns.

       1:18   Second theme repeated in minor and then in major.

       1:38   Transition begins with triplet figures.

Coda

9:00   17   0:00   Coda theme in minor but soon repeated in major.

       0:29   Motives from first theme, with frequent changes of key.

       1:19   Long chords followed by pauses.

       1:26   Second theme returns quietly, followed by pauses.

       1:59   First theme returns vigorously.

       2:11   Movement ends with short, abrupt chords.

 An interactive Active Listening Guide can be downloaded from the online Resource Center for *Music Listening Today, 4th Edition.*

BEST-KNOWN WORKS

chamber music:
- String Quartets Nos. 7 and 14

choral:
- *Missa solemnis*

orchestra:
- Piano Concertos Nos. 3, 4, and 5 ("Emperor")
- Violin Concerto
- *Egmont Overture*
- *Overture to Leonore No. 3*
- Symphonies Nos. 3 ("Eroica"), 5, 6 ("Pastoral"), 7, 8, and 9 ("Choral")

opera:
- *Fidelio*

piano:
- Sonatas Nos. 8 ("Pathétique"), 14 ("Moonlight"), 21 ("Waldstein"), and 23 ("Appassionata")

Ludwig van Beethoven ("Bay-toe-ven," 1770–1827) was born in Bonn, Germany. His father was an alcoholic musician who hoped that young Ludwig would be a prodigy like Mozart and bring in lots of money. Although talented, young Beethoven never became the prodigy his father hoped for. At the age of twenty-two, he set off for Vienna, which was to be his home for the remainder of his life.

Beethoven had little formal schooling. He studied composition with several teachers, including a few lessons with Haydn, and made a name for himself as a pianist. He was able to win the support and admiration of the aristocracy and in ten years established himself as a composer and performer. Although he was trained in the formal style of the Classical period, other events left a lasting impression on Beethoven. One was the revolutionary spirit that was awakening in Europe, which erupted in the French Revolution in 1789.

Then there was Beethoven's own personality. Were he alive today, he would probably identify himself with humanitarian causes and social protest groups. For example, as early as 1792 he had thought of setting German dramatist-poet Friedrich von Schiller's "Ode to Joy" to music. The ethical ideals of the universal human race and its basis in the love of a heavenly Father expressed in the poem appealed to Beethoven, and he used it as the text for the last movement of his Ninth Symphony. He was probably the first composer in history to be considered a "personality." His mature works sound like no one else's music.

Beethoven's high ideals did not carry over to his dealings with publishers. He was sometimes unscrupulous with them.

Beethoven's personality was also affected by a gradual loss of hearing that eventually led to complete deafness. The condition was evident by the time he was twenty-eight, and it caused him to lose contact with others and to withdraw into himself. His final compositions were products of this time in his life, and they tend to be more personal, meditative, and abstract.

How was it possible for Beethoven to write entire symphonies when he was deaf? The process can be understood if you think about your own experience. You can recall melodies and the sounds of people's voices in your memory, even though you aren't actually hearing them. Trained musicians can think out a large amount of music in their minds. And Beethoven was clearly a well-trained musician with outstanding abilities!

There is a second reason for his ability to compose while deaf. It was his custom to write down themes in a sketchbook. Then he would work over these themes, revising and rewriting them, and trying them out to determine their suitability for the piece he had in mind. This process went on over a period of years, so the themes for many of his later compositions had actually been worked out when he was still able to hear fairly well.

Beethoven was not a "natural" composer as Mozart was. He poured much effort into each measure he wrote, as is evident from the manuscript on page 181. As someone once said, his manuscripts look "like a bloody record of a tremendous inner battle."

Beethoven was more successful in writing instrumental music than vocal music. He composed much excellent chamber music, with his string quartets representing a high point for that ensemble. His five piano concertos and one violin concerto are staples in the music performed in concert halls today. His overtures to dramas and his opera are also performed often. He was not as at ease with music for singers. He composed only one opera, *Fidelio*, and compared its writing to the process of childbirth. He

ONE OF BEETHOVEN'S EAR TRUMPETS, an early type of hearing aid. The mechanist J. N. Mälzel, inventor of the metronome, made a variety of ear trumpets for the increasingly deaf composer.

did compose two major religious works, however, and his Ninth Symphony features a chorus and soloists in the fourth movement.

Beethoven's death from jaundice and cholera occurred during a thunderstorm, a coincidence that seems appropriate to the man and his life.

Following the second theme, the *triplets* (three notes to the beat) take over and become the main thought leading to the codetta:

In a work such as this sonata, the pianist plays an enormous number of notes.

The coda is greatly expanded. Instead of stopping after the closing theme, the first theme starts up again. Soon its two motives are treated to another development. This second development is much like the first, with the addition of rapidly moving scale passages.

Second Movement

The second movement is hardly a movement at all. Instead, it is a short section that Beethoven labeled "Introduzione." It sounds like an introspective introduction to the third movement.

There is an unconfirmed story that Beethoven wrote a lengthy second movement but was persuaded by a friend to exchange it for the present short version.

Third Movement

The third movement is a rondo—but what a rondo! Unlike the rondo in Haydn's Concerto for Trumpet in E-flat, with its short, happy melodies and four-minute length, this rondo has those monumental qualities that we will observe in Beethoven's Fifth Symphony. As a result it is more than twice as long as Haydn's rondo. Its theme is presented several times, as happens in rondos, but several times it is treated like a theme in a symphony as it appears three times in a row, each time more magnificent than before.

MAIN POINTS OF THIS CHAPTER

1. By the beginning of the Classical period, the piano had replaced the harpsichord as the most common keyboard instrument. Composers wrote many sizable works for it, including many sonatas.

2. These sonatas followed the same forms as those used for symphonies, concertos, and chamber works, with the exception that often they had only three movements instead of four.

3. Mozart composed many piano sonatas. They have a light, tuneful character, which was very suitable for the piano available during his lifetime.

4. The nature of the piano changed greatly from the time of Mozart to Beethoven. The most important change was the addition of metal braces on the frame, which permitted greater tension on the strings, which in turn allowed the instrument to produce louder and more powerful sounds.

5. Beethoven's thirty-two piano sonatas are longer and more profound than Mozart's. They contain many repeated notes and sudden changes of dynamic level. His music is also technically more demanding, and it makes greater use of the high and low notes available on the piano.

6. In addition to piano sonatas and symphonies, Beethoven composed many outstanding overtures, chamber music works, concertos, and vocal compositions. Some of his greatest music was written after he become deaf.

FEATURES TO LISTEN FOR

1. Listen in Mozart's "Rondo alla Turca" for the contrast between the A section, which is in minor but has a lively character, and the B section, which is in major and has a hardy, optimistic quality.

2. Notice how many times Beethoven uses a series of repeated notes in the first movement of his "Waldstein" Sonata.

3. Listen to the two motives circled in the first theme in the Listening Guide enough times to remember them. Then, play the exposition of the "Waldstein" Sonata while you count the number of times you hear either of those two motives.

4. Listen to and compare the first theme of Beethoven's "Waldstein" Sonata with its second theme.

5. Listen to and compare the A section of Mozart's "Rondo alla Turca" (CD 4 Track 8) with the opening section of Beethoven's "Waldstein" Sonata (CD 4 Track 13).

The Symphony *and* Beethoven

Our discussion of the symphony is presented in conjunction with one of the biggest names in concert music: Ludwig van Beethoven. He did not develop the genre, but he certainly changed it in a massive way.

With Beethoven, the symphony became the most important and largest musical genre during his lifetime and for nearly a hundred years afterward. Beethoven composed just nine symphonies, and most of them take about forty minutes or more to perform. Haydn wrote more than a hundred symphonies and Mozart about fifty, some as short as fifteen minutes. But number and length were not the only differences.

THE SYMPHONY

A **symphony** is a large work composed for an orchestra that is divided into movements, usually four. The four movements present a contrast of tempo and mood.

BEETHOVEN'S SYMPHONY NO. 5

Beethoven composed his Symphony No. 5 in C Minor, Op. 67, between 1804 and 1808, when it received its premiere performance. Less than twenty years passed between when Mozart composed his Symphony No. 40 and Beethoven composed his Symphony No. 5. But what huge changes Beethoven wrought in his symphony!

The difference might best be described by the word *more*. Mozart and Haydn developed themes and had some contrast in their music, but Beethoven presents much more development and more contrast of mood and character. In some of Beethoven's music, including his Fifth Symphony, he seems to want to burst the limits of musical sound. Musical ideas are worked and reworked and reworked again. Some chords are almost hammered into the listeners' ears, and at other times a quiet interlude is suddenly interrupted with a burst of sound.

The result of the sudden contrasts, the many repeated notes, and the extensive development of themes is music infused with more emotion. "The whole is greater than the sum of its parts" applies to all music, but especially to Beethoven's music. He achieved in it an emotional quality that had never existed before. His music often has more—much more—emotional content than the typical symphony or sonata of composers just one generation before him.

Beethoven was fortunate—and so is anyone who listens to it—that his music tends to be a bridge from the Classical style to the approaching Romantic style; it contains the best of both worlds. His training was in the style of Mozart and Haydn, as reflected in his early works. But then he added that "more" quality to his music, expanded it, and gave it greater emotional impact. His Fifth Symphony demonstrates these qualities well. From the "Fate knocking at the door" motive in the first movement, to the beautiful and dramatic second movement, to the lively and playful third movement, to the dramatic bridge leading to the monumental fourth movement, this symphony can appropriately be thought of as an emotional musical journey of epic proportions.

Beethoven also increased the size of the orchestra, including the addition of trombones and the piccolo.

Resource Center
See "Hear It Now: Development in Music," in the *Music Listening Today, 4th Edition,* Resource Center.

First Movement

There have been several attempts to explain the origin of this motive. One is that it is Fate knocking at the door; another claims that the three dots and a dash stand for the letter *V* in Morse code. Neither of these theories has been substantiated. The latter is especially doubtful because Morse code was developed years after the writing of the symphony!

This movement is a prime example of how Beethoven took what appears to be an ordinary theme and built something monumental out of it. It begins with a four-note motive. These four notes are repeated again and again, and they become the basis for the main theme:

And what happens to that theme? It is treated as a germinal idea. For example, right after the first theme is presented, it is developed somewhat in the transition leading to the second theme:

Notice the extensive use of sequence in this example.

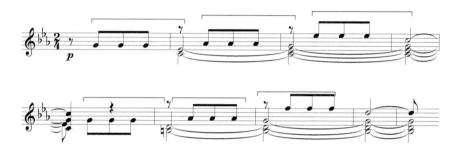

Most of the development section is an outgrowth of the original theme. Beethoven does such things as fill in the interval of the original motive:

Sometimes to the filled-in interval he adds the inversion—the upside-down version—of the motive:

He reiterates a few simple musical ideas based on the theme:

He also fragments themes. The notes circled in the second example in the Listening Guide are the two middle pitches from the transition played by the French horn. The two pitches are echoed between the woodwinds and the strings, and then the segment is fragmented further until just one note is echoed:

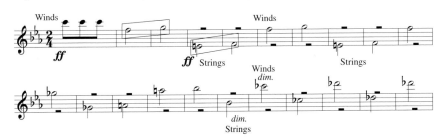

The first two-note fragments have boxes around them in the example.

There are also long, gradual crescendos and abrupt changes from loud to soft.

The recapitulation is followed by an extended coda. In fact, the coda in Beethoven's symphonies is almost as important as the other three sections of sonata form. He seemed to regard it as a second development section. A synthesis of the themes of the coda can be seen in this example:

The first theme is circled here.

The pitches of the first theme and the rhythm pattern of the transition are combined. The two-pitch fragment emphasized in the development appears again, this time in a downward sequence.

LUDWIG VAN BEETHOVEN

Symphony No. 5 in C Minor, First Movement (1808)

GENRE: Symphony   Allegro con brio (fast, with energy)   Symphony orchestra

CD 2 Tracks 1 – 5

7 minutes 32 seconds

Form: Sonata

Exposition

0:00 1 0:00 Orchestra vigorously plays the four-motive from the first theme in minor. (Repeated at 0:41)

0:07 First theme followed by motive in sequence. (Repeated at 0:48)

0:22 Transition built around repeated fragments of first theme. (Repeated at 1:03)

0:44 French horn expands on four-note motive and creates two-note motive. (Repeated at 1:25)

(continued)

LISTENING GUIDE

| 0:46 | 2 | 0:00 | Strings and woodwinds softly play second theme in a major key. Inverted version of four-note motive is soon heard on low strings. (Repeated at 1:28) |

p sweetly

| | | 0:21 | Codetta based on four-note motive. (Repeated at 1:49) |

Development

2:54	3	0:00	French horns, then strings play first theme. Four-note motive, sometimes inverted, is passed sequentially among sections.
		0:28	Winds and strings play full-sounding chords followed by silences.
		0:36	Strings play first theme.
		0:46	Winds and strings alternate playing the two-note motive derived from first theme. Soon reduced to one note.
		1:09	Orchestra plays portion of first theme loudly, followed by soft notes in the woodwinds.
		1:17	Motive repeated five times leading to . . .

Recapitulation

4:17	4	0:00	First theme.
		0:20	Short oboe cadenza.
		0:34	Transition.
		0:55	French horn plays expanded motive.
		0:58	Violins and woodwinds play second theme, again in major, followed by transition.
		1:24	Violins outline chords based on first theme.

Coda

5:59	5	0:00	Strings vigorously play many repeated notes.
		0:16	Expanded and extended treatment of four-note motive.
		0:42	Woodwinds and strings alternate four-note motive. It is then fragmented to two notes.
		1:08	Orchestra forcefully repeats first theme.
		1:32	The movement closes with brusque chords.

 An interactive Active Listening Guide can be downloaded from the online Resource Center for *Music Listening Today, 4th Edition.*

Second Movement

nsidered closely related if
natures are no more than
r flat different.

The second movements of almost all symphonies created in the eighteenth and nineteenth centuries are slow and melodic in character. In addition to the contrast in character, second movements also differ in their home key. If the symphony is in a major key, the tonic of the second movement is usually in the major key four notes higher. For example, a symphony in G major would have a second movement in C major, a key that has one less sharp than G. If the key is in minor, the second movement is in the major key three steps higher. In the case of Beethoven's Symphony No. 5 in C Minor, the second movement is in E-flat major. Its signature is the same as the signature of C minor. The main point to remember is that the second movement is in a *different* key from the rest of the symphony.

note (♪) receives the beat
. Therefore, the music
n more slowly than it
should.

Several forms can be found in second movements of symphonies. The most common is the large three-part form, A B A. Theme and variations are also encountered some of the time, and even sonata form with a shortened development section is used.

LUDWIG VAN BEETHOVEN
Symphony No. 5 in C Minor, Second Movement (1808)

GENRE: Symphony   Andante con moto (walking)   Symphony orchestra

CD 4 Tracks 18 – 22

10 minutes 1 second

Form: Theme and variations

Themes

0:00   18   0:00   Theme 1: major, in three-beat meter with three parts. **Part 1:** violas and cellos.

0:24   Part 2 of first theme: woodwinds.

0:36   Part 3 of first theme: violins.

0:53   Theme 2: violins and woodwinds.

1:14   Brasses play second theme in an expansive style.

1:30   Music becomes quiet and mysterious.

Variation 1

1:58   19   0:00   On theme 1: Strings play steadily moving notes.

0:33   On theme 1: Strings play third part.

0:51   On theme 2: Woodwinds and violins are featured.

1:12   On theme 2: Brasses play in an expansive manner.

1:29   Music becomes quiet and mysterious.

Variation 2

3:52   20   0:00   On theme 1: Lower, then upper strings play rapidly moving notes.

0:36   On theme 1: Lower strings play rapidly moving notes.

1:12   On theme 1: Woodwinds quietly play fragments.

1:58   On theme 2: Orchestra plays in a majestic style.

2:44   On theme 1: Woodwinds play short notes in minor.

Variation 3

7:18   21   0:00   On theme 1: Violins play first part.

0:25   On theme 1: Woodwinds play second part.

0:35   On theme 1: Strings play third part.

(continued)

Coda

8:09 0:00   Tempo increases as bassoons play beginning of first theme.

0:14   Violins play fragments of second theme.

0:29   Woodwinds and strings alternate parts of first theme.

1:18   Low strings begin a crescendo using fragments of first theme.

1:48   Movement concludes with abrupt chords.

An interactive Active Listening Guide can be downloaded from the online Resource Center for *Music Listening Today, 4th Edition*.

The second movement of Beethoven's Fifth Symphony reveals his ability to write beautiful melodies. He is so often thought of in terms of the brusque, forceful qualities in some of his music that it is easy to forget he could write lovely lyric melodies as well.

This movement of the Fifth Symphony is a theme and variations built on two melodic ideas. The first one contains three shorter melodic sections. During the course of the second movement, these ideas are varied by changing the melody and ornamenting it, and by altering the harmony, rhythm, dynamics, tempo, and type of accompaniment.

Third Movement

The third movement of the symphonies of Haydn and Mozart was a stylized dance — the minuet. With its graceful 3/4 meter, it provided a nice contrast to the lyric, melodious second movement. Even the three-part form of the minuet was followed, with the middle section being called the *trio*. This movement was in the home key of the symphony.

Beethoven made two important changes in the minuet of his predecessors:

- He called for a faster tempo, which gave the movement a more lively, energetic, jovial character. No longer was 3/4 felt in three beats per measure; rather, the music is felt in one strong beat per measure.

- He named the movement "Scherzo," a word that means "joke" in Italian. Accordingly, the movement did not just fulfill a formal pattern; it could — and often did — contain surprises for its listeners.

This was not the first time Beethoven had composed a scherzo for a symphony. The first one appears in his Third Symphony.

The main theme of the third movement is one that several other composers of the time had also used. In fact, the theme had acquired a name — the "Mannheim rocket." The *Mannheim* part of the name comes from the southern German city that figured prominently in the development of the symphony, and the *rocket* probably came from the fact that it is the ascending notes of a chord.

The trio of the movement is interesting in that it starts out sounding like a lively fugue, but Beethoven does not follow through with a full-blown fugue. In musical terms, he wrote a *fugato*—a fugue-like passage.

Another feature of the movement is its attachment to the fourth movement. A movement normally comes to an end, and a few moments of silence are observed before the next movement begins. Beethoven and composers who followed him sometimes connected two movements.

Fourth Movement

The fourth movements of Classical symphonies are lively and filled with happy melodies. Apparently, the hope was to have the listeners leave feeling good. Often fourth movements are rondos. They were almost always in the home key of the symphony.

LUDWIG VAN BEETHOVEN

Symphony No. 5 in C Minor,
Third Movement (1808)

GENRE: Symphony   Allegro (fast)   Symphony orchestra

CD 4 Tracks [23] – [26]

5 minutes 28 seconds

Form: Scherzo and trio

Scherzo

0:00 [23] 0:00   Low strings play "rocket" theme softly in minor; music has an "eerie" character.

0:19   French horns forcefully play second theme in major.

0:40   Low strings softly play the "rocket" theme.

1:03   Orchestra plays second theme loudly.

1:24   Strings softly play opening theme.

Trio

1:58 [24] 0:00   Cellos and basses play a dancelike theme in a major key. Other instruments soon follow in imitation.

0:16   Imitative section is repeated.

0:59   Low strings play a short link to opening theme.

Scherzo

3:28 [25] 0:00   Low strings quietly play opening theme. More strings enter playing pizzicato (plucking).

0:21   Woodwinds play second theme softly.

Bridge to Fourth Movement

4:46 [26] 0:00   Strings quietly sustain a long note as timpani quietly play a slow, steady stream of notes.

0:13   Three-note pattern begins in violins and is repeated many times as music grows louder, key changes to major, and music leads without a break to fourth movement.

 An interactive Active Listening Guide can be downloaded from the online Resource Center for *Music Listening Today, 4th Edition.*

But Beethoven seems to have been more interested in leaving a serious but positive impression on his audiences. His optimism had deeper roots than just pleasant, cheery music.

The fourth movement of Beethoven's Fifth Symphony is in sonata form. A rondo would not have accommodated the monumental concept of this movement. The themes, especially the first one, contribute to it.

An unusual feature of this fourth movement is the brief appearance of a theme from the third movement. The appearances of themes from other movements would become more common later in the nineteenth century, but it was very rare at the time the Fifth Symphony was composed.

LUDWIG VAN BEETHOVEN

Symphony No. 5 in C Minor, Fourth Movement (1808)

GENRE: Symphony   Allegro (fast)   Symphony orchestra

CD 4 Tracks 27 – 30

8 minutes 32 seconds

Form: Sonata

Exposition

0:00 27 0:00   Orchestra, especially brasses, plays first theme.

0:33   French horns begin transitional theme.

0:59   Strings play second theme.

1:25   Codetta; same phrase appears three times.

Development

2:00 28 0:00   Violins play a portion of second theme.

0:08   Fragment from second theme becomes more prominent as music progresses through different keys.

0:23   Low strings play four-note motive as fragments of second theme continue.

0:59   Climax reached as orchestra loudly plays four-note motive followed by a pause.

1:34   Portion of scherzo theme played softly by violins and woodwinds.

Recapitulation

4:09 29 0:00   First theme played vigorously by orchestra.

0:33   Transition featuring French horns.

1:04   Second theme played by violins.

1:30   Woodwinds play theme for the codetta.

Coda

6:09 30 0:00   Second theme in violins over four-note motive from development in low strings.

0:31   Transition features woodwinds and French horns.

1:14   Tempo suddenly becomes very fast.

1:38   First theme played twice as fast (diminution) by brasses.

2:19   Movement concludes with several V-I cadences and successive soundings of final chord.

 An interactive Active Listening Guide can be downloaded from the online Resource Center for *Music Listening Today, 4th Edition.*

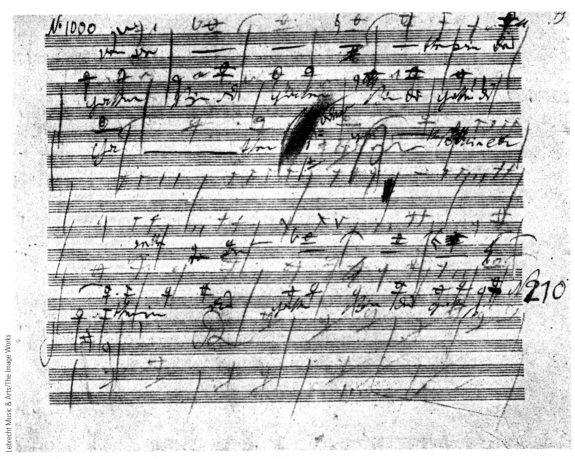

A PAGE FROM BEETHOVEN'S AUTOGRAPH MANUSCRIPT reveals his creative turmoil.

APPRECIATING BEETHOVEN'S MUSIC

The "Waldstein" sonata and the Fifth Symphony have provided a good idea of what Beethoven's music is like. What is it about his music that causes people to continue to listen to it today? What about it has contributed to continuing interest in the man himself? Among the many potential reasons, four stand out:

- *Contrast.* Beethoven's music is filled with dramatic contrasts. His themes often seem to be paired by opposites that can be thought of as male/female, rough/smooth, loud/soft, brusque/tender, and so on. A placid passage can be suddenly broken as a *sforzando* chord is sounded, or a raging section can abruptly cease and change to a gentle melody.

- *Motive development.* Beethoven's music is a showcase of developing musical ideas, especially short, simple ones. A theme becomes a seed that grows and takes many shapes, and it is fascinating to follow that musical process.

- *Sense of drive.* Beethoven's music contains a wonderful drive or what has been described as "inevitability." This quality is difficult to put into words, but his music seems always to be heading toward its final destination. Even though it has many changes and stops, the sense of inevitability is still there. Listeners sense that though the music is quiet at a particular moment, that situation will not last. The musical journey will resume and continue on to its inevitable conclusion.

- *Personality.* Beethoven's music has a personality all its own. His mature works don't sound like those of Mozart, Haydn, or any other composer. A person does not need to be familiar with a lot of concert music to sense that there is something unique about

Features of Classical Music

Melodies	Often consist of short, tuneful phrases strung together; usually have a light, elegant quality; statement–answer pattern
Rhythm	Metrical with a steady beat, except in recitatives
Texture	Mostly homophonic
Harmony	Tonal with modulations mostly to nearly related keys; continuo part no longer present
Dynamic levels	Gradual crescendo and decrescendo developed
Performance media	Orchestra; chamber music groups; piano replaces harpsichord; vocal music
Forms	Sonata, theme and variations, rondo, and minuet and trio; forms often contain balanced and symmetrical phrases
Genres	Symphony, solo concerto, sonata, chamber music, opera

Beethoven's music. It presents listeners with dramatic contrasts, a fiery spirit, huge amounts of thematic development, and an inner sense of musical logic.

MAIN POINTS OF THIS CHAPTER

1. The symphony is a large work for orchestra with four movements.
   - The first movement is in sonata form and has a moderately fast tempo.
   - The second movement is often in A B A form, but other forms such as theme and variation are also used. It tends to have a slow tempo and features melody.
   - The third movement was traditionally a minuet and trio, but Beethoven gave it a faster tempo and called it a scherzo.
   - The fourth movement often used rondo form and a lively tempo. Beethoven's fourth movements, however, are sometimes massive and exhilarating.
2. Beethoven was especially fond of developing themes. Some of his music is filled with repeated, inverted, and fragmented motives. He also lengthened the coda section so that it almost became a second development section.
3. Beethoven's music often contains surprising changes in dynamic level and the nature of themes. A forceful, powerful theme can be followed by a tender melody, and a loud chord can suddenly appear in a quiet passage.

FEATURES TO LISTEN FOR

1. In the first movement of Beethoven's Symphony No. 5, listen for the many appearances of the four-note motive and the different ways it is treated.
2. Also in the first movement, notice the great contrast between the first and second themes.
3. Listen for the three distinct parts of the first theme in the second movement of Beethoven's Symphony No. 5. There is also a second theme with a grandiose quality that appears in the first and second variations.

4. Notice the sudden changes in dynamic level in the scherzo portion of the third movement of Beethoven's Symphony No. 5. A theme that is played very softly is played again at a loud dynamic level, and vice versa.

5. Listen for the imitation in the trio section of the third movement.

6. Notice the long build-up in the bridge section leading to the powerful opening music of the fourth movement.

7. Listen for the manner in which Beethoven utilizes sonata form for the fourth movement of his Symphony No. 5. Also notice the brief return of a theme from the third movement.

PART V

Romantic Music

	1820	1850
Historical Events	● Monroe Doctrine (1823)	California gold rush ● (1848–1855) Revolutions in Europe (mid 1800s)
Visual Arts	● Delacroix, *The Bark of Dante* (1822)	
Literature and Theater	Keats (1795–1821) Byron (1788–1824) Poe (1809–1849)	Hawthorne (1804–1864) Tennyson's work (1829–1892 Dumas (1802–1870) Dickens's work (1836–1870) Hugo's work (1824–1885) Longfellow's work (1839–1882)
Philosophy and Science	Daguerre photography ● (1839)	Schopenhauer (1788–1860) ● Morse telegraph (1840s) Kierkegaard's work (1841–185
Music	Schubert (1797–1828) Liszt (1811–1886)	R. C. Schumann's work (1831–1856) Verdi's work (right) ▸ (1830–1901) Mendelssohn's work (1824–1847) Chopin's work (1830–1849) Berlioz's work (1830–1869)

Michael Dwyer/AP Photo

1875   **1900**

● Franco-Prussian War (1870–1871)   ● First automobiles (1885)

American Civil War (1861–1865)   ● Spanish-American War (1898)

                                                           Boer War in South Africa ●
                                                           (1889–1902)

Renoir's work (1862–1919)   ● Munch, *The Scream* (1893)

        ● Corot, *Villa*   Cezanne's work (1863–1906)
           d' Avray (c. 1867)
        Degas's work   ● Monet, *Rouen Cathedral*
        (1852–1912)   (1897)

Dostoevsky's work (1844–1881)   Wilde's work (1878–1900)

                                                           Kipling's work (1888–1936)

        Twain's work (1869–1910)

        Tolstoy's work (1852–1910)

T. H. Huxley's work (1845–1895)   ● Mill's death (1873)   Bergson's work (1877–1941)

  ● Darwin, *Origin of Species* (1859)   ● Bell telephone (1876)   Marconi radio ●
                                                                     (1901)
        Nietzsche's work (1870–1900) ● Edison light bulb and phonograph (1879, 1877)

        Smetana's work (1855–1884)   Debussy's work (1885–1918)

                                                           Puccini's operas (1893–1904)

                              ● Wagner,   Dvořák's work (1871–1904)
                                Bayreuth
        Brahms's work   (1872–1883)
        (1853–1897)

        Mussorgsky's work (1858–1881)   ▲ Tchaikovsky, *The Nutcracker* (top)
                                                             (1891–1892)

The Art Archive/Picture Desk

22 Romance and Romanticism

To most people, the word *romantic* refers to the emotion of love. To scholars, however, it means much more. It comes from *romance*, which originally referred to a medieval poem written in one of the Romance languages (those that developed from Latin) and dealing with a heroic person or event. Later, the word took on the connotation of something far away and strange or something imaginative and full of wonder. Yes, it also includes the idea of love—romantic love.

Romanticism came of age during the nineteenth century. It began in some of the music of Beethoven and Schubert, and it continued into the early years of the twentieth century, roughly from 1820 to 1900. In fact, elements of romanticism are still encountered in some music being written today. The Romantic outlook affected every type of music, and it brought several kinds of music to their high point of development.

CHARACTERISTICS OF ROMANTICISM

Romanticism was an artistic viewpoint that also predominated in dance, theater, the visual arts, and music throughout the nineteenth century. What were the features of this outlook?

The love of mystery and the unknown is evident in the song "The Erl King," discussed in Chapter 23.

- Romanticists were fascinated by the unknown and stood in awe of the world. They were impressed by the mystery, not the clarity, of the world and its inhabitants. At times, they were almost mystic. They seemed especially fascinated by the mystery and power of evil.

- Romanticists also tended to rely on emotion and imagination rather than rational intellect, which had been central to the Classical outlook. Feelings replaced reason. Truth became what a person *felt* to be true, so it was wrong to deny one's feelings. Poet John Keats wrote in one of his letters: "I am certain of nothing but the holiness of the heart's affections, and the truth of the imagination. What the imagination seizes as beauty must be truth." Inevitably, Romanticism grew to distrust reason and science. To quote Keats again, this time from his poem "Lamia":

During Keats's lifetime the word *philosophy* was a synonym for *science*.

  > *Do not all charms fly*
  > *At the mere touch of cold philosophy?*

- Romanticists were fascinated by the long ago and far away. During the Classical era, intellectuals had thought of medieval times as the "Dark Ages"; the Romanticists considered them heroic. Literature is filled with examples of this attitude, including Alfred Lord Tennyson's *Idylls of the King,* John Keats's "Eve of St. Agnes," Samuel Taylor Coleridge's "Christabel," and Sir Walter Scott's *Ivanhoe.*

- Not only were the Romanticists impressed by the unknown forces of the world; but they also reveled in the struggle against those forces. In Coleridge's poem *The Rime of the Ancient Mariner,* the sailor is "alone on a wide, wide sea."

- Romanticists were enthralled by nature. They had a rural outlook instead of the urban outlook of the Classical period. In Mozart's day the cities—London, Paris, Vienna—were the centers of artistic activity, so they attracted people with creative and artistic interests. To Romanticists, however, nature had more appeal because it represented a world untainted by humans. Sometimes nature was extolled to the

Photograph © 2010 Museum of Fine Arts, Boston Jean-François Millet, French, 1814–1875 Potato Planters, about 1861 Oil on canvas 82.5 × 101.3 cm (32 1/2 × 39 7/8 in.)/Gift of Quincy Adams Shaw through Quincy Adams Shaw, Jr., and Mrs. Marian Shaw Haughton, 17.1505

THE VIRTUES OF RURAL LIFE were celebrated by artists of the Romantic period, as shown in *Potato Planters* by Jean François Millet.

point of pantheism—the belief that God and nature are one. The rural interest of the time led to landscape painting, poems on natural phenomena, and works such as Beethoven's Symphony No. 6 ("Pastoral").

Beethoven intended the music of his Symphony No. 6 to convey the moods evoked during his visits to the countryside around Vienna.

- Many Romanticists resented rules and restraints. They regarded the Classical period as cold and formal and were unimpressed by its rational deductions and universal laws. They felt perfectly capable of making their own rules—and proceeded to do so in their artworks. They cherished freedom, limitless expression, passion, and the pursuit of the unattainable. After all, what more glorious struggle could there be than seeking the impossible? This search is perhaps best represented in the legend of the Holy Grail.

The Holy Grail was the cup that Jesus used at the Last Supper. It was believed to have special powers.

- Beginning with Jean-Jacques Rousseau and the Earl of Shaftesbury (A. A. Cooper) and continuing through the American Henry David Thoreau in the nineteenth century to the present time, a group of philosophers have expounded the idea of natural goodness. The "artificialities" of civilization are rejected because they corrupt people. William Wordsworth summed up the Romanticists' thinking on nature when he wrote in his poem "The Tables Turned":

> *One impulse from vernal wood*
> *May teach you more of man,*
> *Of moral evil and of good,*
> *Than all the sages can.*

Vernal means springtime, and *sages* refers to wise men.

- Because Romanticists were highly subjective and individualistic, it is not surprising that they tended to be self-centered. Works of art were no longer objective examples of a person's skill. Instead, they were considered a projection of the person who created them. Romantic artists felt that a bit of their psyche had been given to the world in their poems and preludes. Their works were now created for posterity, for an audience that someday, somewhere, would appreciate their true value.

Musée du Louvre, Paris/A.K.G, Berlin, Superstock

THE BARK OF DANTE, by Eugène Delacroix. Two features of Romantic art and music are evident in this work: love of drama and admiration of the Middle Ages.

National Gallery of Art, Washington, D.C./Superstock

VILLA D'AVRAY, by Jean-Baptiste-Camille Corot. Another characteristic of Romanticism was love of nature, which is evident in Beethoven's Symphony No. 6 and many other musical works of the nineteenth century.

- Some Romanticists were nonsocial, if not antisocial. They withdrew into a world of their own, surrounded by a close circle of friends and admirers. Yet the Romantic era saw the establishment of the concert hall with its large audiences, and some Romantic musicians thoroughly enjoyed the adulation of the public.
- Romantic musicians were often concerned with the other fine arts as well as with philosophy. They were familiar with the writings of Johann Wolfgang von Goethe and Alphonse Lamartine, and many times they knew the writers personally. Franz

Liszt wrote a number of literary works, including a book on gypsy music and another entitled *Life of Chopin*. Robert Schumann's literary interests led him to edit a music magazine. Richard Wagner wrote lengthy treatises on music, art, and philosophy. Romantic composers believed strongly in a unity of the arts. This attitude is epitomized in the music dramas of Wagner.

Unfortunately, Liszt's book contains many inaccuracies.

Wagner's music dramas are presented in Chapter 26.

ROMANTIC ART

Eugène Delacroix's *The Bark of Dante* (page 188) depicts the struggling souls of the wicked people of Florence, Italy, trying to escape from Hell by climbing into the boat with the ancient Roman poet Virgil and the fourteenth-century poet Dante Alighieri, whose best-known work was *The Inferno*. It demonstrates the interest of Romantic artists in subjects from the past and their fascination with evil and its consequences. In the painting the sea and clouds swirl around ominously. The twisted and pained bodies of the Florentines are very much involved in the scene as they struggle hopelessly. There is little symmetry; Dante (in the green cloak) stands about a third of the way from the left. Straight angles are absent, too, as the bodies of the sinners writhe throughout the picture.

The Romanticists' love of nature can be seen in Jean-Baptiste-Camille Corot's *Villa d'Avray* (page 188). The painting is of a peaceful rural scene filled with flowers, beautiful trees, and a lake. The two figures in the foreground blend in with the scene. The lake is calm and reflects the villa on the other side. The message of the picture could easily be *Nature is good and beautiful*.

A *Traveler Looking over a Sea of Fog* by Caspar David Friedrich shows another aspect of Romanticism: the individual-against-all-the-elements attitude, its self-absorbed outlook. Friedrich's belief was that the artist's feeling is his law. The erect, determined posture of the man viewing the fog and mountains is expressed well in the famous nineteenth-century poem "Invictus" by William Ernest Henley, which begins, "I am the master of my fate, the captain of my soul."

The Wanderer above the Sea of Fog, 1818 (oil on canvas), Friedrich, Caspar David (1774–1840)/ Hamburger Kunsthalle, Hamburg, Germany/The Bridgeman Art Library

A TRAVELER LOOKING OVER A SEA OF FOG, by Caspar David Friedrich. The heroic character was a part of Romantic art and music, culminating in Richard Strauss's tone poem *Ein Heldenleben* (*A Hero's Life*).

THE SPLIT PERSONALITY OF ROMANTICISM

Every era in history seems to carry its contradictions. In the case of the **Romantic period,** those contradictions are massive. On the one hand, it produced much extremely beautiful and tender music and works of art. On the other hand, it showed a fascination with evil and misery. Song after song and opera after opera end unhappily, often with the hero or heroine (or both) dying. For example, in Schubert's "Der Erlkönig" ("The Erl King") the son dies in his father's arms; in Wagner's *Götterdämmerung*, after Brünnhilde rides her horse into the funeral pyre of her beloved Siegfried, flames and then a flood engulf the home of the gods, Valhalla.

The fascination with evil led to the inclusion of the Dies irae chant in several musical works and compositions such as *Mephisto Waltz* (Mephisto being another name for the devil), *Danse Macabre*, and *Totentanz* (*Dance of Death*). The disasters of the nineteenth

THE DEATH OF SIEGFRIED, BY HENRI DE GROUX The Death of Siegfried is a scene from the Nibelungenlied, the epic poem made famous by Wagner's "Ring Cycle" operas.

Christie's Images/Corbis

century certainly did not reach the heights of mayhem that can be seen in films or described in books over the past few decades. They did, however, reveal a side of Romanticism that seemed to enjoy being miserable.

Romanticists also had their optimistic and happy side that loved beauty. The music of Brahms, Mendelssohn, Tchaikovsky, Grieg, Schumann, and many others contains rich harmonies and luscious melodies. Such music is difficult to top in terms of sheer beauty. Many paintings also reveal a love of beauty; Corot's *Villa d'Avray* is one example. Beauty of motion and movement was (and still is) one of the main goals of ballet. Often its stories are pure and lovely fantasy and present beauty that seems to exceed anything in ordinary life. The scene of the Snow Maidens dancing gracefully in *The Nutcracker* to Tchaikovsky's beautiful music as snow falls gently around them seems to be as total an experience of loveliness and beauty as can be conceived.

Michael Dwyer/AP Photo

THE SNOW MAIDENS of Tchaikovsky's *The Nutcracker.*

MAIN POINTS OF THIS CHAPTER

1. Romanticism refers to the style that prevailed from roughly 1820 to 1900. The term refers to more than romantic love. It is marked by these characteristics:

   • Fascination with mystery and the unknown, including the power of evil.

   • Reliance on emotion and imagination. Feelings replaced reason as a guide to actions.

   • Fondness for the long ago and far away. A new interest in medieval times emerged.

   • Attraction to the struggle with unknown forces. Many stories involved a struggle against overwhelming and magical forces.

   • Resentment of rules and restraints. Romanticists felt perfectly capable of making their own rules and loved freedom of expression.

   • Fascination with nature. Nature appealed to romanticists because it represented the world untainted by humans.

   • Individualistic view of life. Works of art and music became personal creations.

2. The Romantic period seemed to have a split personality. On the one hand, it loved beauty and passion. On the other, it was fascinated with suffering and the idea of evil.

3. Romantic music represents a significant change from the music of Mozart and Haydn. Its melodies are more warm and flowing, harmonies richer, dynamic levels more extensive, and rhythm more flexible. Many of these works are longer and have a more monumental character.

FEATURES TO LISTEN FOR

What makes music in the Romantic style of the nineteenth century different from the Classical style of Mozart and Haydn? Several things:

1. The melodies are more flowing and passionate. Whereas the melodies of Classical composers many times consisted of short fragments strung together, melodies in Romantic style are often sweeping and expansive.

2. The harmonies are much richer. Chords contain more notes. Also, many more chromatic notes are used. Changes of key occur more often and to keys that are harmonically more distant. Harmony became much more than the functional accompaniment encountered in many works of the Classical period.

3. Rhythm is treated more freely, especially in speeding up and slowing down the tempo. A rather steady beat and metrical rhythm are not abandoned, but they are less structured.

4. Changes in dynamic levels are more frequent, with many of the soft places softer and the loud places louder. Often, the dynamic levels have an almost undulating quality.

5. The tonal qualities are richer. The size of the orchestra increased significantly, and several new instruments, such as the piccolo and English horn, are added.

6. The works, especially those for large ensembles, are often quite a bit longer. Many Romantic composers admired and desired long works.

7. The element of contrast in music begun by Beethoven is a feature of nineteenth-century music. Tender portions are often contrasted with stormy sections, for example.

8. These features of Romantic music often coalesce to produce music of outstanding beauty. Many works remind one of eating an especially rich-tasting dessert.

23 Early Romantic Music

The Romantic attitude and outlook had a massive impact on music. Changes happened not so much in new forms or techniques of composing, although some changes occurred in those areas, but more in what composers tried to accomplish in their works. Their music tended to be much more personal and expressive. They reveled in the qualities of mystery, emotional release, love of nature, and inner feelings that were fashionable during the nineteenth century.

THE ART SONG

Lied ("leed") is the German word for "song"; Lieder is its plural.

The songs Schubert wrote are called art songs. An **art song,** or **Lied,** is a musical setting of a poem. The order is important here. Composers of art songs first select a suitable poem and *then* compose music that will best project the mood and thought of the text. The idea of preserving and building on the message of the words is fundamental to the art song.

Because the setting of the words was so vital, composers were not primarily concerned with writing a lovely melody. They wanted a good melody, of course, but more than that, they wanted the melody to express the words. The idea of expression also carried over to the piano part, which evokes a mood, paints a picture, or enriches ideas beyond what a singer can achieve. For example, through rapidly moving notes and changes of dynamic level, the piano can suggest wind blowing through the trees.

Singers of art songs must project the idea of the song. Sometimes they are called on to convey different roles in the same song. Any mood can prevail in an art song—anger, sadness, anxiety, joy, pity, contentment.

Stan Honda/AFP/Getty Images

THE ART SONG COMBINES poetry, melody, the expressiveness of the human voice, and the tonal power of the piano.

The demands on singers of art songs are, therefore, somewhat different from those required of opera singers. In fact, singers tend to specialize in one type of vocal music or another. The art song is less demanding in a technical sense; the vocal range is narrower and there are few virtuoso passages. But singers of art songs must be versatile and able to project the essence of a character or situation. Because art songs are sung in small recital halls, singers must establish a rapport with the audience while maintaining a balance between good taste and expressiveness. In some ways, art songs and chamber music have several musical similarities. Both are intended to produce a sense of intimacy, refinement, and listener involvement.

A sense of involvement is not achieved if the listener does not understand the words. Most art songs are in languages other than English. As was pointed out in Chapter 12, word placement in vocal music is crucial, so translations are difficult. In fact, strictly speaking, something is lost in translation, no matter how carefully it is done. Many words have shades of meaning that cannot be translated. For these reasons, art songs are usually sung in their original languages.

Translation difficulties are only part of the language problem. Many of the poems that Schubert and other composers set to music are not of high literary merit. Some of them seem overly sentimental to people today who have grown up with down-to-earth (if not downright earthy) popular songs.

Art songs are a type of music well worth knowing, however.

- They reveal much sensitivity and skill in combining words and music.
- They are very expressive of their texts. For example, when the singer of "Der Erlkönig" sings "My father, my father, can't you see . . . ," listeners can really sense the child's frustration and fear.
- The human voice can be a very expressive and beautiful musical instrument. When coupled with the tonal power of the piano in the infinite variety of the art song, the result can be very moving.

The different roles for the singer are crucial in "The Erl King."

SCHUBERT'S "DER ERLKÖNIG"

Schubert wrote "Der Erlkönig" ("The Erl King") when he was only eighteen. He chose a text from the great German writer Goethe. The overall mood of the song is one of fear and suspense because of the mythical king of the elves. According to legend, whoever is touched by him must die. The singer is required to represent the narrator, the father, the son, and the Erl King—quite an assignment. The piano sets the mood and helps delineate the characters in the song, as well as plays the role of the horse.

Before listening to the song, read over the text to determine which of the four roles the singer is presenting. As you listen, notice how Schubert, the singer, and the pianist treat the different roles. For example, be aware of how "My son, it's only a misty cloud" differs from "You lovely child, come . . ." and how "My father, my father, now don't you hear . . ." differs from "My son, my son, all I can see . . ." Notice not only the difference in the tone quality of the singer's voice for each role but also how the entire mood changes when the Erl King speaks.

None of the music is repeated in "Der Erlkönig." New lines of melody follow one another until the song ends. The term for this type of song is **through-composed,** meaning that no line repeats. The accompaniment adds to the mood with an agitated triplet figure and a foreboding bass pattern, which depicts the urgency of the scene.

"Der Erlkönig" (1815)

GENRE: Art song (Lied)   Fast tempo   Soloist and piano

CD 2 Tracks 6 – 8

4 minutes 5 seconds

Form: Through-composed

0:00	6	0:00	Piano sets an agitated mood.

	0:23	**NARRATOR:** Wer reitet so spät durch Nacht und Wind? Es ist der Vater mit seinem Kind; Er hat den Knaben wohl in dem Arm, Er fasst ihn sicher, er hält ihn warm.

Who rides so late through the night wind?
It is a father with his child.
He holds the boy within his arm,
He clasps him tightly, he keeps him warm.

FATHER: "Mein Sohn, was birgst du so bang dein Gesicht?"

"My son, why do you hide your face in fear?"

SON: "Siehst, Vater, du den Erlkönig nicht? Den Erlenkönig mit Kron' und Schweif?"

"See, father, isn't the Erl King near?
The Erl King with crown and shroud?"

FATHER: "Mein Sohn, es ist ein Nebelstreif."

"My son, it's only a misty cloud."

1:29	7	0:00	**ERL KING:** "Du liebes Kind, komm, geh' mit mir! Gar schöne Spiele spiel' ich mit dir; Manch' bunte Blumen sind an dem Strand, Meine Mutter hat manch' gülden Gewand."

"You lovely child, come, go with me!
Such pleasant games I'll play with thee!
The fields have flowers bright to behold,
My mother has many a robe of gold."

SON: "Mein Vater, mein Vater, und hörest du nicht, Was Erlenkönig mir leise verspricht?"

"My father, my father, now don't you hear

What the Erl King whispers in my ear?"

FATHER: "Sei ruhig, bleibe ruhig, mein Kind; In dürren Blättern säuselt der Wind."

"Be calm, be calm and still, my child;
The dry leaves rustle when wind
blows wild."

ERL KING: "Willst, feiner Knabe, du mit mir geh'n? Meine Töchter sollen dich warten schön; Meine Töchter führen den nächtlichen Reih'n Und wiegen und tanzen und singen dich ein."

"My lovely boy, won't you go with me?
My daughters all shall wait on thee,
My daughters nightly revels keep,
They'll sing and dance and rock thee
to sleep."

SON: "Mein Vater, mein Vater, und siehst du nicht dort Erlkönigs Töchter am düstern Ort?"

"My father, my father, can't you see the face
Of Erl King's daughters in that dark place?

FATHER: "Mein Sohn, mein Sohn, ich seh' es genau, Es scheinen die alten Weiden so grau."

"My son, my son, all I can see
Is just the old gray willow tree."

ERL KING: "Ich liebe dich, mich reizt deine schöne Gestalt, Und bist du nicht willig, so brauch' ich Gewalt."

"I love thee, thy form enflames my sense;
Since thou art not willing, I'll take
thee hence!"

3:15	8	0:00	**SON:** "Mein Vater, mein Vater, jetzt fasst er mich an! Erlkonig hat mir ein Leid's gethan!"

"My father, my father, he's grabbing my arm,
The Erl King wants to do me harm!"

NARRATOR: Dem Vater grauset's, er reitet geschwind, Er hält in Armen das ächzende Kind, Erreicht den Hof mit Müh' und Noth: In seinen Armen das Kind war tot!

The father shudders, he speeds through
the cold
His arms the moaning child enfold,
He reaches home with pain and dread:
In his arms the child was dead!

The song ends with two solid-sounding chords.

 An interactive Active Listening Guide can be downloaded from the online Resource Center for *Music Listening Today, 4th Edition.*

Austrian National Tourist Office/
Austrian National Travel Office

Franz Schubert

Franz Schubert (1797–1828) is often considered, along with Beethoven, to be a composer who marked the beginning of the Romantic style in music. And there is much about his life to justify his reputation as the prototype of the Romantic artist. Born into the family of a schoolteacher in a Vienna suburb, the young Schubert displayed creative talent while he was still a boy. After completing school, he tried to follow in his father's footsteps, but he could not accept the routine involved in teaching. He preferred to spend his time composing music.

Schubert did not adjust well to adult life. He never held a real job and made only halfhearted attempts to find one. He had a small circle of friends, who appreciated his talents. They housed and fed him when he was in need, which he often was. He was not good at dealing with publishers, who made hefty profits from his music.

As the years passed, Schubert became lonelier and more discouraged. He was even unlucky in love and once contracted venereal disease. He was not in good health the last five years of his short life, but his compositions kept on coming. He died from typhus at the age of thirty-one, leaving almost no worldly goods—except a vast store of beautiful music.

Schubert's Symphony No. 8 ("Unfinished") was not left incomplete because he was heartbroken over a failed romance, as is sometimes claimed. He simply never got around to finishing it.

Schubert was a versatile composer. He wrote piano works, chamber music, and symphonies. But it is his vocal music, especially his six hundred songs, that ensured his place in the world of music.

BEST-KNOWN WORKS

chamber music:
- Piano Quintet ("Trout")
- *Arpeggione* Sonata

orchestra:
- *Rosamunde* (incidental music)
- Symphonies Nos. 8 ("Unfinished") and 9 ("The Great")

songs (more than 600) including:
- "Der Erlkönig"
- "Gretchen am Spinnrade"

song cycles:
- *Die schöne Müllerin*
- *Winterreise*

Dissonance is heard as the child expresses fear, and the father's music has a reassuring quality. Notice how effectively Schubert ends the song. The piano stops, and the singer declaims, "In his arms, the child"—a pause to allow anticipation to build up—"was dead."

Art songs provide a kind of music that is not duplicated in arias or folk songs; those forms of vocal music have other qualities and functions.

Mendelssohn's *Elijah*

During his rather short life, Mendelssohn made many trips to England. He composed his oratorio *Elijah* for the Music Festival of Birmingham in that country, where it was first performed in August 1846. It follows the oratorio tradition begun by Handel about one hundred years earlier. That is, it features distinct recitatives, arias, and choruses, and follows a biblical text.

The references to Elijah are from the first Book of Kings. During those Old Testament times, the Israelites were divided into two kingdoms, the southern (Judah) and the northern (Israel). Israel had turned from Jehovah to the worship of Baal, a deity of storm and rain from Canaan. The prophet Elijah was one of the few persons in Israel to remain faithful to the "God of Abraham." He spoke out forcefully against Baal and challenged its followers to test whose deity was the true God.

A biblical prophet was not so much a person who predicted the future as a social critic who pointed out the wrongs of society.

Animal sacrifices at religious events were a common practice during Old Testament times.

Religious tolerance was not an Old Testament virtue!

The challenge consisted of slaying a young bull and putting it over a wood pile. No fire was to be started. Each god would be called on to ignite the offering. As you can tell from the Listening Guide, the followers of Baal were unsuccessful. Their calls went unanswered.

As the oratorio continues, Elijah's calm, confident prayer is promptly answered. The flames consume the offering, and the prophets of Baal are taken away and slain. The people's loyalty is changed from their former false god back to Jehovah. At the end of his life, Elijah is taken up to heaven in a fiery chariot.

SOLO AND CHAMBER MUSIC

This type of piece is often called a "character piece." It is discussed in Chapter 24.

Although the Romantic era is noted for large compositions, its composers continued to produce many excellent works for small groups and solo works other than concertos. Schubert composed an enormous amount of chamber music, as did Mendelssohn. Two other early Romantic composers merit mentioning: Carl Maria von Weber (1786–1826) and Robert Schumann. Weber is known for his operas. Schumann is an important name in the world of music and is presented in the next chapter.

LISTENING GUIDE

MENDELSSOHN

Elijah (excerpt)

GENRE: Oratorio for soloists, chorus, and orchestra

CD 4 Tracks 31 – 35

0:00 [31] 0:00 Elijah accepts the challenge of the Baalites to test whose god is the true God by igniting a fire under the slain young bull. He points out that there are many followers of Baal present, but he alone stands for the Lord Jehovah.

> *Call upon your God, your numbers are many;*
> *I, even I only remain one prophet of the Lord;*
> *Invoke your forest gods and mountain deities.*

Chorus of Baalites begins very confidently. The tenor and bass parts are divided. They are followed by the women, and then are combined.

[32] 0:00 Chorus continues with same words, but music becomes more leisurely.

33 0:00   Elijah begins to taunt the followers of Baal. The word "peradventure" means "possibly."

> *Call him louder! For he is a god.*
> *He talketh; or is he pursuing; or is he on a journey;*
> *or peradventure he sleepeth; so awaken him.*
> *Call him louder, call him louder!*

0:40   Baalites begin to sound worried as their voices enter one after another in imitation.

34 0:00   Elijah's words take on a harsh quality.

> *Call him louder! He heareth not.*
> *With knives and lancets cut yourselves after your manner.*
> *Leap upon the altar ye have made;*
> *Call him, and prophesy.*
> *Not a voice will answer you,*
> *None will listen; none will heed you.*

35 0:00   The chorus of Baalites begins to sound somewhat frantic. "Baal, look how he's making fun of us!" they cry. The chorus concludes with the words "Hear and answer!" sung twice. Each time, there is a deathly silence that drives home the futility of their pleading.

0:00   Elijah sings a calm recitative asking everyone to gather around him.

 An interactive Active Listening Guide can be downloaded from the online Resource Center for *Music Listening Today, 4th Edition.*

Best-Known Works of Mendelssohn

orchestra:

- Incidental Music for *A Midsummer Night's Dream*
- Symphonies Nos. 3 ("Italian") and 4 ("Scottish")
- Violin Concerto

oratorio:

- *Elijah*

Best-Known Works of Hensel

choral:

- *Gartenlieder*

songs:

- Op. 7

FELIX MENDELSSOHN

FANNY MENDELSSOHN HENSEL

It is appropriate to couple **Felix Mendelssohn** (1809–1847) and his older sister, **Fanny** (1805–1847), in the same biographical sketch. The two were very close during their childhood and remained so throughout their lives. They took music lessons and read Shakespeare's plays together, and their young lives were certainly idyllic ones. Their father was a wealthy banker who hired musicians to come to the Mendelssohn home in Berlin to give concerts and later to play music that one of his children had composed.

In his adult life, Felix became a very successful pianist, composer, conductor, and organizer of concerts. He was one of the first conductors to stand in front of the orchestra, and he was very influential in stimulating an interest in the music of Bach with his performance of the *St. Matthew Passion*. He made ten journeys to England to conduct and perform and was warmly received by Queen Victoria at Buckingham Palace.

And what about Fanny's musical career? She, too, was a gifted composer and pianist, but her father insisted that a lady of her social standing should not become a professional musician.

As caring a brother as Felix was, that did not keep him from discouraging Fanny's efforts at composing.

Eventually, she married the painter Wilhelm Hensel. She did not completely give up her interest in music, but she refrained from pursuing it as a career. She performed occasionally as a piano soloist and composed more than two hundred works, mostly songs, chamber music, and short piano pieces. Only a few of her compositions have been published.

In May 1847 Fanny died of a stroke during a rehearsal for one of the family concerts. Felix was crushed. Although his own health was failing, he composed a string quartet in her memory. He also journeyed to visit her grave, which was especially hard on him and hastened his death about six months later. He was buried near his sister.

You have probably noticed by now a distinct absence of women's names among composers. Shouldn't there be a nearly equal number of men and women? Why such a preponderance of males? Granted, a few women have been successful composers: Hildegard of Bingen and Péronne d'Armentières in early music, Fanny Mendelssohn Hensel and Clara Schumann in the nineteenth century, and others. But the number of women composers and their compositions is small.

As is true of most things in life, there is no single, simple explanation for the paucity of women composers. Several factors very likely contribute to the situation. A major one was the fact that it was a "man's world" until only the past couple of decades. Women usually could not own property, vote in the few democratic countries that had elections, engage in enterprises outside the home, or travel overnight without an escort. They were generally treated as the property of their husbands. They were often discouraged from composing by their fathers or husbands, which happened in the case of Fanny Mendelssohn. Such circumstances hardly encouraged women to have the fortitude to compose music and hope to have it published.

An additional impediment to women composers is that it has seldom been easy for *anyone* to have compositions published. Until a composer had achieved a certain degree of name recognition, which made a publisher more confident of sufficient sales, getting a work published was no easy matter, a situation that is still true today. There are a number of works now well regarded for which composers had difficulty finding a publisher. And yet a pub-lisher's cautious approach is understandable. After all, how many sales of a symphony could be anticipated at a time when there were few permanent orchestras and no residuals from the sale of recordings?

Another reason for the lack of women composers was the prejudice they faced in pursuing instruction in harmony, counterpoint, orchestration, and similar subjects. For example, the Paris Conservatory did not permit women in advanced theory classes until the late 1800s.

A few women authors, such as George Sand and George Eliot, were able to break the male dominance by writing under a male pseudonym. An undetermined number of Fanny Mendelssohn Hensel's songs were published under Felix's name! Are there other works by women published under a man's name? We don't know, but if it happened once with Fanny Mendelssohn, it probably happened with other women, too.

Has the situation changed for women in the world of musical composition? Fortunately, in at least two important ways it has. Much research has recently been conducted on locating compositions by women, and a considerable body of music has been uncovered. The other change is in the acceptance of women composers. Whether the playing field is level between men and women today in terms of recognition for their compositions is difficult to determine. However, Ellen Taafe Zwilich, Joan Tower, Libby Larsen, and others are rightfully being recognized for their works. Perhaps in another hundred years the question about the lack of women composers will no longer be a logical one to raise.

MAIN POINTS OF THIS CHAPTER

1. An art song is a musical setting of a poem for solo singer and piano. It developed in Germany and is often called a lied (song) or its plural, lieder. Its main purpose is the musical expression of the text, not necessarily a singable tune.

2. Art songs in foreign languages are seldom translated into English. It is very difficult to match the translated words with the music effectively.

3. In an art song the piano does more than accompany the singer. It plays an equal part in evoking a mood and reinforcing the effect of the words of the song.

4. Art songs are best heard in recital halls, not large concert halls.

5. Because their main purpose is to express the words, many art songs are through-composed. This gives the composer more freedom, since it is not necessary to repeat lines of music if they don't suit the text.

6. Mendelssohn's oratorio *Elijah* is typical in its use of a dramatic Old Testament story. It features the challenge that Elijah makes to the followers of Baal to see whose god will ignite a fire under the offering.

FEATURES TO LISTEN FOR

1. In Schubert's *Der Erlkönig:*
   - The mood of nervousness and foreboding the piano part creates in the introduction
   - In each of the last three sections sung by the son, the ascending pitch level and louder dynamic levels as the song progresses
   - The differences in the nature of the music for each of the four roles in the song

2. In Mendelssohn's *Elijah:*
   - The way the music expresses the increasing worries of the followers of Baal when the fire fails to ignite
   - How Elijah taunts the followers of Baal
   - The silences after the Baalites call out "Hear and answer!"

Romantic Piano Music

The Romantic period tended to exhibit two different viewpoints regarding piano music. One outlook exploited the power and brilliance of the instrument; the other treated the piano in a more intimate, sensitive way. These two approaches were by no means mutually exclusive, but they were distinctive enough to be noticeable. For example, Liszt composed much piano music that dazzled his audiences with technical display and forceful sounds. Chopin, on the other hand, often wrote piano pieces that sought to enchant listeners with their beauty.

One type of piano music might be thought of as extroverted and the other as introverted.

The Romantic period featured piano music. An enormous amount of music was composed for the instrument, not only at concert level but for amateur players as well. The piano was the most popular instrument in the home during the nineteenth century.

Piano recitals became important during this time. Many composers were also pianists themselves and introduced their own works to the public; Liszt, Beethoven, and Frédéric Chopin are among the composers who did this. But gradually a class of virtuoso performers emerged who were known for their interpretative abilities as well as their stunning technical virtuosity.

CHARACTER PIECES

Romantic composers did not want to be confined to the carefully balanced forms that Mozart and Haydn had used so well. To replace the rondo, sonata, and other forms, composers in the nineteenth century created many free, short forms that are often referred to as **character pieces,** such as the ballade, berceuse, étude, prelude, impromptu, fantasia, scherzo, and nocturne.

The **ballade** ("bah-*lahd*") and **berceuse** ("bair-*soos*") are songlike pieces. The ballade is the longer and more complex of the two and is supposed to hark back to the ballad poems of the Middle Ages. An **étude** ("*ay*-tood") is an instrumental piece that develops a particular technique. Études were written for all instruments but were especially popular for the piano. In the hands of Chopin, Liszt, or similarly gifted composers, an étude is transformed into an exciting concert work. A **prelude** is a short work for piano.

Étude comes from the French word for "study."

An **impromptu** is supposed to convey the spontaneity its name suggests. A **fantasia** or **fantasie** is a free and imaginative work. The **scherzos** by Chopin are not as playful as those by Beethoven. Instead, they are longer and more serious, although the typical triple meter and fast tempo of the scherzo are retained. **Nocturne** was the name given by the Irish composer John Field to his piano pieces with a songlike melody. Chopin adopted the title from Field and wrote many beautiful, lyrical nocturnes.

The word *nocturne* refers to night song.

Another type of character piece consisted of stylized dance forms such as the mazurka, polonaise, and waltz. What Romantic composers did was essentially the same as what Bach had done with his Baroque keyboard suites. The Romantic composers, however, used different dances and wrote in a very different style from their Baroque and Classical predecessors. They expanded the forms so that each dance became a separate piece rather than just one part of a larger suite.

These character pieces were often intended to convey an air of improvisation as if they were an inspiration—a momentary feeling that had been rendered in sound. The impression of improvisation is an illusion, however, because Chopin and his contemporaries labored carefully over each measure they wrote. They worked hard at sounding spontaneous.

There is a feature of Romantic music that cannot be seen in music notation but is used frequently in performing the music. It is known as **rubato** ("roo-*bah*-toh"). Rubato is a

Chopin was known to spend as much as six weeks on a single page of music, changing note after note, stomping around in frustration, and breaking pens. Sometimes he would return to exactly what he started with.

Rubato originally meant "robbed" in Italian.

style of performance in which the performer deviates slightly from the exact execution of the rhythm. A fraction of time is borrowed from one note to lengthen another. Chopin was occasionally criticized as a performer for his use of rubato. Some listeners charged that he could not keep a steady beat. Undoubtedly he could, but he sometimes chose not to. He wanted the music to have the free expression that the Romanticists admired.

CHOPIN'S NOCTURNE IN D-FLAT

Chopin composed about twenty nocturnes. Most of them have an introspective, delicate, lyric quality. The Nocturne in D-flat, Op. 27, No. 2, is one of the most voluptuous and passionate of these works. It contains rich harmonies and many musical "sighs"

LISTENING GUIDE

FRÉDÉRIC CHOPIN
Nocturne in D-flat Major, Op. 27, No. 2 (1835)

GENRE: Character piece   Piano

CD 4 Tracks 36 – 38

5 minutes 55 seconds

Form: Rondo (A B A C A B)

0:00   36   0:00   Accompaniment begins and is soon followed by a tender melody (A):

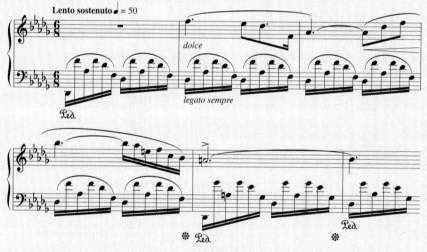

0:42   37   0:00   B melody begins and is repeated and varied several times.

1:14	A melody returns.
1:57	B melody line resumes and is extended, leading to a climactic moment.
3:24 38 0:00	A melody returns. Much use of decorative figures.
0:34	B portion returns and grows more passionate.
1:09	Coda begins with a descending, "sighing" interval.
1:30	Sighing figure repeated.
2:31	Nocturne closes with a simple cadence after an ascending, fading scale.

 An interactive Active Listening Guide can be downloaded from the online Resource Center for *Music Listening Today, 4th Edition.*

consisting of descending intervals and delayed resolutions of phrases and harmonic progressions. The left-hand part is made up of six continuously moving notes for each beat. The notes are actually chords that are sounded in a broken style. The right hand plays a songlike melody that is decorated with grace notes and other melodic figures. Although the music notation makes the rhythm look steady and regular, pianists almost always take liberties with the rhythm, as Chopin himself did in his own playing.

Pianists also use the pedals a great deal in playing Romantic music. The *Ped.* marking in the notation tells the pianist to depress the damper pedal, which lifts the dampers and allows the strings to resonate freely. Richness is added to the music when the dampers are raised. Proper pedaling also contributes to smooth, lyric phrasing. The composer and performer must plan carefully for the use of the pedals because unwanted notes that are allowed to sound create a blurring effect.

As you listen to the Nocturne, notice the effect of the long note in the melody and the accompanying notes in the fifth and sixth measures of the opening theme. You can sense that the long note is going to move up a half step, which it finally does. But Chopin makes listeners wait what seems like an extra long time for it to resolve. He is a master at such toying with listeners' expectations.

Broken style means that the notes of a chord are sounded neither together nor in succession.

Grace notes are printed half the size of other notes and have no prescribed rhythmic value.

Resource Center
Learn more about how Chopin works with listeners' expectations in "Hear It Now: A Composer's Dilemma," in the *Music Listening Today, 4th Edition,* Resource Center.

Frédéric Chopin

Frédéric Chopin ("*Show*-pan," 1810–1849) was the son of a French father and a Polish mother. He exhibited much talent at an early age and received his musical education at the Conservatory in Warsaw. Before he was twenty, he was on his own in the world. He left Poland and traveled awhile before settling in Paris. Shortly after his departure from Poland, the Poles revolted against the Russians and their czar. In time the Russians crushed the revolt, which caused Chopin much anguish.

Chopin's loyalty to Poland remained strong throughout his life.

His abilities as a composer and pianist made him a sought-after musician in Paris. Soon he acquired a circle of artistic friends—the painter Eugène Delacroix, musicians Franz Liszt and Hector Berlioz, writers Victor Hugo, Honoré de Balzac, Alphonse de Larmartine, Alexandre Dumas (père), and Heinrich Heine. Through this group of friends, Chopin met George Sand, and they lived together for nine years.

George Sand was the pen name of Amandine Aurore Lucie Dupin, Baroness Dudevant, who was one of the outstanding writers of the time with more than a hundred books to her credit. She favored novels in which love transcended the

obstacles of convention and social class. She had liaisons with a number of famous men, but her most lasting relationship was with Chopin.

When they first met, Chopin, who had always been drawn to beautiful women and loved the polished and elegant life, was repelled by her: She had adopted a number of masculine attitudes and habits, including wearing men's clothes and smoking cigars. And she was not physically attractive. Yet in time he was drawn to her. Her fame as a writer and her strong personality seemed to be a good balance for his not very forceful ways. When they separated, she did not seem to be affected. But Chopin lived only another two years before his death from tuberculosis.

Liszt wrote of the separation: "In the breaking of this long affection, this powerful bond, he had broken his life."

Most composers before Chopin wrote well in a variety of types of music. Chopin was different. He was one of the first major composers to limit his writing to one or two areas. He wrote almost exclusively for the piano, and it is this music that made a place for him in the world of music. He is often referred to as "the poet of the piano."

BEST-KNOWN WORKS
orchestra:
• Piano Concertos Nos. 1 and 2

piano—character pieces:
• Études (24), including "Black Key," "Winter Wind," and "Revolutionary"
• Fantasies, including *Fantasie-Impromptu,* Op. 66
• Nocturnes (21)
• Preludes (24, one in each major and minor key)
• Scherzos (4)

piano—stylized dances:
• Polonaises, including Op. 53
• Mazurkas
• Waltzes, including "Minute Waltz"

piano—sonatas (3)

VIRTUOSO MUSIC

Another type of piano music was for the virtuoso performer. Audiences during the nineteenth century were fond of dazzling, showy music and stunning performances by musical idols such as the pianist Franz Liszt and the violin virtuoso Niccolò Paganini.

LISZT'S *LA CAMPANELLA*

Liszt admired the virtuoso skills of Paganini on the violin. This admiration led to Liszt's transcribing six of Paganini's violin works for piano under the title *Transcendental Études after Paganini*. *La Campanella* (*The Little Bell*) is the third of these pieces. Liszt retains the bell effect by sounding a high D-sharp repeatedly throughout the piece.

Transcriptions were popular in the Romantic era. They offered the new public audience the opportunity of hearing technically stunning variations on operatic melodies and other works not originally written for piano. Because there were no recordings and few orchestras, a piano recital was often a listener's only contact with concert music.

La Campanella is a typically Romantic composition, for several reasons:

- It is virtuoso music; even a good professional pianist does not undertake it lightly.
- It demands of the player the full range of techniques developed in the Romantic period.
- It is an attempt to make the piano more orchestral in sound and concept. The very name of the piece suggests that the piano is to be descriptive of something more than itself.

Even though *La Campanella* is technically awesome, it is musically rather simple. It is a set of scintillating variations on a simple melody in which the opening two-measure phrase is stated and then repeated twice with a concluding phrase. After the main theme is presented again, there is a contrasting section. It, too, is composed of short, repeated phrases. The piece has a form of *a a b*.

The technical devices of piano playing are too numerous to cover fully here. A few examples provide an idea of what Liszt did in the way of virtuoso display. One involves rapidly repeated notes, which Liszt used often. It may seem that the pianist is simply rapping his or her finger repeatedly on the key with tremendous speed. Not so. It is much easier to play notes rapidly in succession if the key is struck with a different finger for each sound. Here is an example of where that technique is used:

Liszt also calls for very fast playing of the chromatic scale:

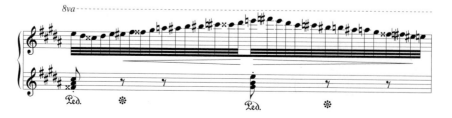

Liszt arranged many of the transcriptions in the form of duets for two persons playing at the same keyboard.

There were no orchestras that toured in those days.

The *8va* sign tells the performer to play the notes one octave higher than written.

A CONTEMPORARY CARICATURE of Liszt lampoons his extraordinary virtuosity.

Alternating hands gives the pianist more speed and power:

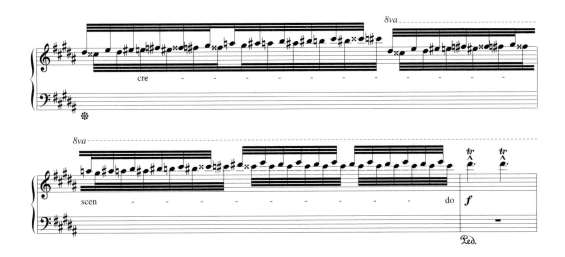

FRANZ LISZT
La Campanella (1851)

GENRE: Virtuoso piano work   Piano

CD 2 Tracks [9] – [10]

4 minutes 17 seconds

Form: Theme and Variations (*a a b*)

0:00	[9]	0:00	Introduction based on motive from the theme.
		0:09	The *a* theme with a few decorative notes.

		0:25	The *a* theme repeated with more decorative notes one octave higher.
0:40	[10]	0:00	The *b* portion of theme built on a sequential figure; leads to a fragment of *a* in sequence.
		0:36	The *a* theme played in high notes that alternate an octave apart; then repeated.
		1:04	The *b* theme with rapidly repeated notes; leads to sequence on *a* theme with trill on high notes.
		1:59	The *a* theme returns softly and is repeated with many fast, high notes.
		2:29	The *b* theme returns with a freer tempo and much contrast between high and low notes.
		3:06	Coda begins as *a* theme is repeated at a faster tempo.
		3:37	*La Campanella* closes with a soft but accented chord.

 An interactive Active Listening Guide can be downloaded from the online Resource Center for *Music Listening Today, 4th Edition.*

LISTENING GUIDE

NICCOLÒ PAGANINI

FRANZ LISZT

BEST-KNOWN WORKS OF LISZT

orchestra:

- *Hungarian Rhapsodies* Nos. 2 and 14
- *Les Préludes*
- Piano Concertos Nos. 1 and 2
- *Totentanz* for Piano and Orchestra

piano:

- *Harmonies poétiques et religieuses*
- Sonata in B Minor
- *Transcendental études* (6)

Niccolò Paganini (1782–1840) and **Franz Liszt** (1811–1886) had much in common. First, they were the supreme virtuoso performers of the nineteenth century on their respective instruments: Paganini on the violin and Liszt on the piano. Second, they both came from modest circumstances. Third, for what it's worth, both successfully pursued many women over the course of their lives.

Paganini had the more interesting reputation. Part of his fame was the result of his appearance and character. He had a pale, long face with hollow cheeks and thin lips that seemed to curl in an evil smile, and his eyes had a piercing quality. There were also popular suspicions that he was influenced by the devil.

Paganini was even forced to publish letters from his mother to prove that he had human parents!

His ability to play the violin was legendary, and he added a new dimension to the playing of the instrument. He developed a repertoire of violin tricks and technical maneuvers that he guarded jealously, refusing to have much of his music published for fear that others might find out exactly what he was doing.

One of Paganini's violin pieces is the basis for a work by Rachmaninoff that is presented in Chapter 29.

On the night of March 9, 1831, Liszt attended a recital by Paganini. The daz-zling virtuoso left an indelible impression on the nineteen-year-old Liszt, who became consumed with the idea that he could do for piano technique what Paganini had done for the violin. Liszt canceled all his concerts for two years and began to retrain himself. He spent hours practicing techniques such as octaves, trills, scales, and arpeggios (playing notes of a chord successively rather than simultaneously). He returned again and again to hear Paganini and take notes on what he did. He even imitated some of the visual effects of Paganini's appearance: his black, tight-fitting clothes, tossing hair, and facial expressions.

Traditionally, pianists had performed with their backs to the audience and played with the music in front of them. Liszt was one of the first to turn the piano to its familiar sideways position and to memorize his music. His chiseled profile fascinated the audience, especially the women, as he crouched over the keys, alternately caressing and pounding them.

Behind the image of the sensational artist, which Liszt did not discourage, there was a musician of depth and a man of generous heart who helped many young musicians. There was also a prolific composer. Although he is especially known for his piano music—and many more piano transcriptions—he also composed many works for orchestra as well as about sixty religious works.

Toward the end of his life, Liszt took minor religious vows and had the title Abbé Liszt.

Liszt's exploitation of the range of the piano can be heard in the long trill on the high D-sharp, only a few notes from the top of the keyboard.

Perhaps virtuoso compositions may not be as intellectually challenging as other types of musical works. But most of them—and *La Campanella* is certainly one—contain some really imaginative writing. The high notes of the piano are used in a way that is not found in Mozart or Beethoven sonatas or other piano music. And the variations are fresh and attractive. One must be a virtuoso pianist to play these works well. Technical virtuosity, or any artistic endeavor, whether achieved by an Olympic figure skater or a fine pianist, demands exceptional dedication and talent. It is a pleasure to observe such performances, especially if the observer has tried some skating or piano playing and therefore can appreciate better the skill demanded.

CLARA SCHUMANN'S SCHERZO, OP. 10

As seems true of many recognized composers in the eighteenth and nineteenth centuries, Clara Schumann wrote successful musical works before the age of twenty. Her Op. 10, a scherzo for piano, was written when she was nineteen. It reveals her inclination toward virtuoso music with its tempo marking: *Presto, Scherzo con passione* (Very fast, Scherzo with passion). Audiences at that time liked such music.

The form is clear: a scherzo and two trios that are not quite as passionate as the scherzo. Sudden accented chords and trills help make the music dramatic. In true virtuoso style, the notes come in rushes of sound, which build to a climactic point. The two trios are more melodic. It is a work worthy of her outstanding abilities as one of the finest pianists of her day.

Clara wrote to her husban
from Paris: "It is extraordi
that my Scherzo is so well
I always have to repeat it."

CLARA SCHUMANN
Scherzo, Op. 10 in D Minor (1838)

GENRE: Character piece   Presto (very fast)   Piano

CD 4 Tracks 39 – 41

4 minutes 59 seconds

Form: Scherzo with two trios

0:00   39   0:00   Introduction.

0:08   Scherzo begins; very rhythmic with accented chords.

0:36   Scherzo repeated.

1:04   Scherzo varied, growing softer leading to trio.

1:30   40   0:00   Trio 1; slower and smoother.

0:42   Scherzo returns forcefully.

2:41   41   0:00   Trio 2; melody in clearly marked style but gentler than scherzo.

1:32   Scherzo returns and builds to fiery ending.

 An interactive Active Listening Guide can be downloaded from the online Resource Center for *Music Listening Today, 4th Edition.*

Musée d'Orsay, Paris/Réunion des Musées,
Nationaux/Art Resource, NY

**BEST-KNOWN WORKS OF
ROBERT SCHUMANN**

chamber music:
- Piano Quintet

orchestra:
- Piano Concerto
- Cello Concerto

*piano, many character
pieces, plus:*
- *Carnaval*
- *Fantasia in C*
- *Kinderscenen*

song cycle:
- *Frauenliebe und Leben*

**BEST-KNOWN WORKS OF
CLARA WIECK SCHUMANN**

piano:
- Romances
- Soirées Musicale

violin and piano:
- Three Romances

Robert Alexander Schumann (1813–1856) and **Clara Wieck Schumann** (1819–1896) were husband and wife. Robert's father was a bookseller and writer, who encouraged his son's musical interests. Robert entered law school at the University of Leipzig in Germany but gave it up to pursue his ambitions to become a piano virtuoso. However, he permanently injured his hands in an attempt to develop finger strength with a mechanical device. His interests moved on to the founding of an important music magazine and to composing. Besides a great deal of piano music, he wrote chamber music, concertos, and symphonies. He composed about 150 songs, many of them written the year after he married Clara.

Clara Wieck was the daughter of Robert's piano teacher, and he fell in love with her when she was sixteen. At that time she was already well on her way to becoming an outstanding concert pianist. Her father strongly opposed their marriage, so the couple had to wait until she was twenty-one (minus one day) before getting married. Their marriage was a happy one, and they had eight children. In spite of Robert's bouts with mental illness, Clara continued her career as a concert pianist, although her family demanded more and more of her time.

In nineteenth-century Germany, children seldom could or would go against their father's wishes.

Two years before his death, tormented by hallucinations, Robert leaped into the Rhine River. He was saved, but he spent the remainder of his life in an asylum. Those were difficult years for Clara. At the age of thirty-seven, she lost her husband, to whom she was devoted. She later found herself attracted to the twenty-two-year-old protégé of her husband, Johannes Brahms. Brahms remained a bachelor and Clara never remarried, but they did remain close friends and admirers.

For the last forty years of her life, Clara continued to teach and give concerts. Although she was a promising composer, she was not able to devote much time to this aspect of her great talent. She did write a few works for piano and a piano trio, however. Throughout her adult life, she promoted Robert's music through her performances.

Clara went on tour again after Robert's death. She gave the last of her thirteen hundred public concerts at the age of seventy-two.

MAIN POINTS OF THIS CHAPTER

1. The Romantic period is sometimes called the "Golden Age of the Piano." The piano was easily the most popular keyboard instrument of the time. Not only were virtuoso performers drawn to the instrument, amateurs were also attracted to it.

2. There were no recordings in the nineteenth century, so piano transcriptions/arrangements of symphonies and opera arias were the only way most people heard those works.

3. Numerous short, solo works were composed for piano. They are often referred to as "character pieces." Some were intended to sound like the inspiration of the moment (fantasie and impromptu), whereas others were intended to project a mood (nocturne and ballad). Some consisted of stylized dance music (polonaise and waltz).

4. Pianists use the pedals to contribute to smooth, lyrical phrasing of the music and other artistic effects.

5. The word "rubato" is the term for taking small liberties with the tempo in order to achieve greater artistic expression.

6. Chopin wrote almost exclusively for the piano. He is sometimes referred to as the "poet of the piano."

7. Liszt was very likely the greatest pianist of his day in terms of playing and creating technically demanding music. He was greatly influenced by Niccolò Paganini's accomplishments in advancing techniques for playing the violin.

FEATURES TO LISTEN FOR

1. In Chopin's *Nocturne:*
   - The lyrical nature of the A melody with its wide range and many decorative notes
   - The places where Chopin delays for a moment the expected progression of the music
   - The many times that the pianist takes small liberties (rubato) in maintaining a steady beat

2. In Liszt's *La Campanella:*
   - The virtuoso techniques—the many rapidly repeated notes, the rapid chromatic scales, the alternations between high and low notes, and especially the effect of the trills on the high D-sharp

3. In Clara Schumann's Scherzo:
   - The smoother and more calm nature of the two trios, compared to the scherzo sections

25 Program *and* Ballet Music

Program music and ballet music have several things in common. The most significant similarity is their association with something not musical—a story, event, or place. The fact that the stimulus for the music was something non-musical meant that composers did not need to follow the forms that had prevailed in the Classical period. Although the result might be the general pattern of a form, composers of program and ballet music were more interested in writing imaginative music.

NATURE OF PROGRAM MUSIC

The term *program music* refers only to instrumental music. Vocal music usually has specific references through its words.

Publishers and others sometimes give a work a name, because names are easier to remember than numbers.

Instrumental works that composers consciously associate with non-musical ideas are called *program music*. The particular associations are often indicated in the title, or in some cases by an explanation included in the score—the "program." Works that have been named by a publisher or other person are not really program music.

Program music became especially important in the nineteenth century. It provided one type of "form" for a major work. Some program works, however, actually follow one of the traditional forms, even if the composer does not admit doing so. And the opposite may also be true: A composer may compose a work with a title such as Sonata No. 2 that was sparked by some non-musical association.

Musical sounds cannot really tell specifically about an event or a person. Only a song and its words can do that in music. Musical sounds can, however, convey an atmosphere, a general feeling. Listeners may hear some massive chords and assume that they signify something great or big—the coronation of a king or a large animal walking. The idea of largeness or importance is there, but not the specifics. It is possible to make up a story to go with a musical work, of course, but that story may not be what the composer had in mind. Furthermore, instrumental music that tries to tell a story in detail becomes almost comic. It loses its value as musical expression and becomes something closer to sound effects.

Identifying the non-musical association is not really all that important anyway. Good program music has substance in and of itself; it can stand without the story because of its musical qualities.

TYPES OF PROGRAM MUSIC

There are several types of program music: concert overtures, incidental music, tone poems (also called symphonic poems), and program symphonies.

Concert Overture

Tchaikovsky's overture celebrates the victory of the Russians over Napoleon in 1812. The score calls for six cannon, and some performances of it include fireworks.

An **overture** to an opera is an instrumental introduction that incorporates programmatic ideas from the story that follows. A **concert overture** is similar, but it is an independent one-movement work that is not associated with an opera. Sometimes it is in sonata form. Several overtures of this type were composed in the nineteenth century. Examples include Felix Mendelssohn's seascape *Hebrides* (*Fingal's Cave*) and Piotr Ilich Tchaikovsky's *Festival Overture "1812."*

Incidental Music

Early in the nineteenth century, composers were often asked to write **incidental music** for a drama or play. They would compose an overture and five or six other pieces to be performed during the play or between various acts. Although strictly instrumental music, these works are associated with a particular drama. Beethoven wrote a number of incidental works, including some of his better-known overtures, such as *Egmont* and *Coriolan*. Mendelssohn composed incidental music for Shakespeare's *A Midsummer Night's Dream*. Georges Bizet wrote *L'Arlésienne* for a drama, as did Edvard Grieg (1843–1907) for Ibsen's drama *Peer Gynt*.

Today the music composed as incidental music for plays is usually heard in suites extracted from the complete works.

Tone Poem

The most important type of program music is the **tone poem,** or **symphonic poem.** It is a rather long, complex orchestral work in one movement that develops a poetic idea, creates a mood, or suggests a scene. It differs from the concert overture in that it is much freer in its structure. The symphonic poem was developed by Liszt and Berlioz and expanded by Richard Strauss (1864–1949).

One of the best-known tone poems is *Les Préludes* by Liszt. Its programmatic association is a philosophical poem by Alphonse de Lamartine. The poem begins:

> *What else is life but a series of preludes to that unknown song*
> *whose first solemn note is intoned by Death?*
> *Love is the enchanted dawn of all existence;*
> *but what destiny is there whose first delights of love*
> *are not interrupted by some storm?*

In this work Liszt developed the technique of theme transformation, which Berlioz uses so well in his *Symphonie fantastique*.

Notice the fascination with the unknown and the heroic sentiments of these lines of Romantic poetry.

PROGRAM SYMPHONY

The main difference between a tone poem and **program symphony** is the presence of more than one movement in a program symphony. Some of the themes usually appear in more than one movement.

BERLIOZ'S *SYMPHONIE FANTASTIQUE*

Berlioz's *Symphonie fantastique* (*Fantastic Symphony*) is a program symphony. And what a program it has! Berlioz had become infatuated with the actress Harriet Smithson. To ease his pain and indulge his fantasies, he decided to compose a symphony. He wrote this about the music:

> *A young musician of morbid sensibility and ardent imagination in a fit of lovesick despair has poisoned himself with opium. The drug, too weak to kill, plunges him into a heavy sleep accompanied by strange visions. The sensations, feelings, and memories are translated in his sick brain into musical images and ideas. The beloved one herself becomes for him a melody, a recurrent theme that haunts him everywhere.*

This recurrent theme is a **fixed idea,** or in French **idée fixe,** that becomes a melodic fragment associated with a particular person or object. The fixed idea, then, is subject to changes in rhythm, harmony, tempo, meter, and elaboration with other tones, but its characteristic pattern of intervals is retained. This technique is called **theme transformation.**

Listeners may not be aware of the retained pattern of pitches, but they can usually sense its presence.

AUDIENCES OF BERLIOZ'S TIME were sometimes taken aback by the power of his musical vision. This cartoon satirizes Berlioz's willingness to expand the orchestra and experiment with new instruments, such as the English horn. The cannon is meant here as an outrageous joke.

Bettmann/Corbis

Resource Center
See "Hear It Now: What Is Transformation?" in the *Music Listening Today, 4th Edition,* Resource Center.

Theme transformation should not be confused with theme development or theme and variations. Variation involves keeping the theme intact to some extent and arranging the variations so that they contrast with one another. Development involves retaining the theme but manipulating it, often by breaking it into fragments.

Transformation is a looser concept in which a few characteristic intervals are preserved, sometimes with new material interspersed. The retained intervals give the music a sense of unity, and the transformations provide variety. Composers in addition to Liszt and Berlioz exploited this technique; Brahms was masterful in its use.

What are the strengths of Berlioz's music, especially his *Symphonie fantastique*? At least two features stand out:

- His fertile and vivid imagination. Not only is the program associated with the work a bit far out and exaggerated, but the music also builds on those sometimes bizarre scenes into a wonderfully imaginative "soundscape." No one can accuse Berlioz of composing run-of-the-mill music!

- His masterful use of instruments. Berlioz's expertise in orchestration shows in his ability to get the best out of each instrument and combine their sounds to get the effects he wants to achieve.

Symphonie fantastique contains five rather long movements. Berlioz provided descriptive commentary for each movement.

I. REVERIES, PASSIONS "He remembers the weariness of the soul, the indefinable yearning he knew before meeting his beloved. Then, the volcanic love with which she at once inspired him, his delirious suffering."

A slow introduction establishes a reverent atmosphere. Soon the *idée fixe* is heard:

The orchestra builds up to mighty climactic moments of sound, which is typical of Berlioz's Romantic style.

II. A BALL "Amid the tumult and excitement of a brilliant ball, he glimpses the loved one again."

This movement is a waltz. Its introduction features the harp playing in contrast to rapidly repeated notes in the strings. A waltz is marked to be played sweetly and tenderly. This movement is in a three-part form, with the middle section containing the fixed idea.

III. SCENE IN THE FIELDS "On a summer evening in the country, he hears two shepherds piping. The pastoral duet, the quiet surroundings . . . all unite to fill his heart with a long absent calm. But *she* appears again. His heart contracts. Painful forebodings fill his soul. The sun sets — solitude — silence."

The movement begins slowly. It features the English horn, which had only recently been included in the orchestra when Berlioz composed the work. The *idée fixe* appears in the middle section of the movement, which is in a three-part form. Before the movement concludes, a distant rumble of thunder can be heard played by the timpani as the English horn plays a melancholy melody.

IV. MARCH TO THE SCAFFOLD "He dreams that he has killed his beloved, that he has been condemned to die and is being led to the scaffold. The procession moves to the sound of a march somber and wild, now brilliant and solemn . . . at the very end the fixed idea appears for an instant like the last thought of love interrupted by the fall of the ax."

The movement is basically a march. Also, in spite of Berlioz's desire to write program music, this movement is essentially in sonata form.

V. DREAM OF A WITCHES' SABBATH "He sees himself at a witches' sabbath surrounded by a host of fearsome specters who have gathered at his funeral. Unearthly sounds, groans, shrieks of laughter . . . the melody of his beloved is heard, but it has lost its noble and reserved character. It has become a vulgar tune, trivial and grotesque. It is *she* who comes to the infernal orgy. A howl of joy greets her arrival. She joins the diabolical dance. Bells toll for the dead. A burlesque of the Dies irae. Dance of the witches. The dance and the Dies irae combined."

The movement opens in a slow tempo. There are flickering scales played softly on muted violins and violas to create an eerie, unearthly quality. In the allegro portion that follows, the theme of the beloved is transformed into a grotesque dance played by the clarinet. It is as if everyone is mocking him. Laughter can be heard in the bassoon part that accompanies the fixed idea. Soon bells toll for the dead (himself), followed by the

Brackets have been placed over the fixed idea in the music examples.

The themes from the first and second movements may look different in the examples because they are in different meters and keys, but the pattern of pitch intervals is the same in each.

One of the characteristics of nineteenth-century Romanticism was its interest in nature and rural scenes.

A *scaffold* is the platform on which criminals were hanged or beheaded.

The Dies irae appears in many Romantic works, including Rachmaninoff's *Rhapsody on a Theme of Paganini*, presented in Chapter 29. It was also discussed in Chapter 24.

Hector Berlioz

BEST-KNOWN WORKS

choral:
- *Requiem*

orchestra:
- *Harold in Italy*
- *Roman Carnival Overture*
- *Symphony fantastique*

Hector Berlioz (1803–1869) was born in a small town near Grenoble, France. His father was a well-to-do physician who expected his son to follow in his footsteps. Hector was even sent to Paris to attend medical school, but he was much more interested in the musical life of the city, so he gave up medicine for music.

Berlioz soon found himself part of a group of artists and writers, including the painter Delacroix and the writer Hugo. His parents cut off his funds, so he gave music lessons, sang in a theater chorus, and did other odd jobs of a musical nature. He became fascinated with the music of Beethoven and the dramas of Shakespeare. While attending one of these plays, he first saw the actress Harriet Smithson and became obsessed with her. He made no attempt to meet her but was content to visit rehearsals of her plays. He would take solitary midnight walks around Paris and write letters with lines such as, "Trust me, Smithson and Berlioz will be reunited in the oblivion of the tomb."

In 1830 Berlioz was awarded the coveted Prix de Rome, which provided an

During a rehearsal Berlioz saw Harriet in the arms of a stage lover. He emitted a loud shriek and ran from the theater.

allowance and an opportunity to work in Rome. During that year he composed *Symphonie fantastique.* When he returned to Paris, a hectic courtship of Harriet Smithson followed. Both families objected, but the two married anyway. It was a stormy marriage, and it lasted until Hector left about nine years later to live with an Italian opera singer.

Like several other composers of the nineteenth century, Berlioz also wrote reviews and articles. He was the author of an important book on orchestration. His literary efforts earned him income and allowed him to promote his ideas about music. He tried his hand at several operas and wrote a gigantic requiem, but he was at his best with programmatic works.

traditional religious Dies irae ("Day of Wrath") motive, taken from the medieval Mass for the dead, played by the bassoons and tuba.

In the "Ronde du sabbat" ("Witches' Dance") portion of the movement, a driving rhythm first heard in the cellos and basses is taken up by other instruments. The combination of the various lines creates an intricate fabric of sound.

WITCHES' SABBATH (detail) by Francisco Goya. In this painting Goya captured the same ghoulish quality that Berlioz was able to put into the "Witches' Dance" portion of his *Symphonie fantastique.*

HECTOR BERLIOZ

Symphonie fantastique, Op. 14, Fifth Movement (1830)

GENRE: Program music   Orchestra

CD 2 Tracks [11] – [15]

9 minutes 44 seconds

0:00	[11]	0:00	Muted strings and eerie music give impression of unearthly sounds.
		1:21	Clarinet shrilly plays distorted version of *idée fixe*.
1:38	[12]	0:00	Woodwinds, then orchestra, play loud, grotesque version of *idée fixe*.

	1:17	Funeral bells sound three times interspersed with a fragment of the music used for Witches' Dance.

Dies irae

3:22	[13]	0:00	Dies irae sounds in low brasses.

	0:22	French horns and trombones play Dies irae with note values cut in half (diminution). Funeral bells interspersed throughout this section.
	0:32	Woodwinds play fast, distorted version of Dies irae.
	0:38	Second phrase of Dies irae played by French horns. Then woodwinds play fragments of fixed idea while brasses play the chant.

Witches' Round Dance (Fugato)

5:15	[14]	0:00	Theme enters four times in low strings and woodwinds. A short episode follows.

	0:48	Theme enters three more times in woodwinds, low strings, then orchestra. Another episode containing the "laughing motive" follows.
	1:45	Low strings play fragments of Dies irae. Then portions of the Witches' Dance build slowly to a climactic moment with syncopated chords.
8:00	[15]	0:00	Violins play Witches' Dance as low brasses sound Dies irae.
	0:32	Woodwinds play Witches' Dance again.
	1:05	Dies irae returns in low brasses and percussion as music begins to build.
	1:44	Movement ends in a burst of sound.

 An interactive Active Listening Guide can be downloaded from the online Resource Center for *Music Listening Today, 4th Edition.*

RICHARD STRAUSS

Another major nineteenth-century composer of program music was Richard Strauss. His tone poems are monumental in size and sound. At least four or five are performed frequently: *Don Juan, Death and Transfiguration, Till Eulenspiegel's Merry Pranks, Don Quixote,* and *Also Sprach Zarathustra.*

A portion presenting majestic chords from *Also Sprach Zarathustra* achieved popularity from its use in the sound track of the film *2001: A Space Odyssey*.

Strauss also composed three successful operas, plus songs and two concertos for French horn and orchestra, but today he is best remembered for his programmatic works.

BALLET AND BALLET MUSIC

Ballet is an art form in which music and the visual aspects of body movement, costumes, and scenery are combined for the psychological and artistic satisfaction they provide. Ballet is to dance as concert music is to music—an intellectually and emotionally satisfying creation.

There is no clear distinction between concert music and ballet music. Composers originally wrote music specifically to be danced to. But in the past one hundred years, every style of music has also featured ballets. Some ballet music is heard more often today as concert music than in conjunction with a ballet.

Composers often arrange ballet scores as orchestral suites.

Traditionally, the music for a ballet was the result of a collaboration between a composer and a choreographer. Sometimes the choreographer is quite explicit about the type of music desired; at other times only a vague outline is provided for the composer. In a few instances in this century, the dance has been created first, and then the composer has written the music to fit the dance. But the opposite procedure has probably happened more often, when a ballet was created for an existing piece of music.

Like opera, early ballet stories were based on mythological subjects. During the nineteenth century, many plots of ballets had a fairy-tale quality, which is true of Tchaikovsky's *Swan Lake*, *Sleeping Beauty*, and *The Nutcracker*.

TCHAIKOVSKY'S *NUTCRACKER*

David Crossland/Germany Images/Alamy

THE NUTCRACKER looks like an old-fashioned soldier in dress uniform. A lever in its back caused the jaw to move up and down. It would crack a nut that had been placed in its mouth.

Tchaikovsky was already a famous composer by the time he composed the music for *The Nutcracker* in 1891, only two years before his death. It is the shortest and best-known of his three ballets, consisting of fifteen musical works and an overture. A suite of eight pieces from the ballet was organized and presented in 1892, the same year that the ballet itself was given its premiere performance at the Maryinski Theater before the czar and his court.

The story is filled with fancy and magic, as are many ballet stories. At a Christmas party, Clara receives a gift of a Nutcracker from the eccentric Drosselmeyer. Her brother, Fritz, breaks her new gift. Sadly, she cradles the broken Nutcracker and puts it to sleep in a toy cradle before she goes to bed.

After everyone has fallen asleep, she sneaks back into the room to look at the Nutcracker. Magically, the Christmas tree begins to grow to enormous size. Large mice appear from the corners of the room and challenge the toy soldiers, who are led by the Nutcracker. The soldiers are about to lose the fight when Clara throws a shoe at the Mouse King, and the invading mice flee. The Nutcracker is then transformed into a handsome Prince. The Prince invites her go with him to his kingdom. On the way, they stop in a snow-covered pine forest and then go to the Kingdom of the Sweets, where Clara is treated to a lavish banquet, complete with entertainment and dancers from several different lands—Arabia, China, Spain, Russia—as well as by the Reed Flutes.

The Nutcracker ends as Clara awakens to find that she has had only a vivid dream.

Classical ballet began in the courts of Europe, especially France, about three hundred years ago. Its main goal was to achieve grace and courtliness, not artistic expression. Deportment and etiquette were supreme virtues among the aristocracy. In the court of Louis XIV of France, for example, everyone took dancing lessons, and this dancing was not a type in which they just shuffled around. One feature of such dancing was proper ballet posture; another was a balance of footwork and elevation — the ability to rise on the toes and to leap gracefully. Ballet posture was based on a straight and quiet spine; a stiffened, straight knee; and a level hip line. The hips were not to lift, thrust out, or rotate; and the shoulders were not to ripple.

From such principles and practices there developed a systematic set of positions and steps that are basic in classical ballet. From these and other movements, which often carry French names, the **choreographer** (the designer of dances) plans routines and sequences for a complete scene. The choreography is carefully designed to fit with the music and its story, if there is one. (Not all ballets are developed around a story.)

The first truly Romantic ballet was *La Sylphide* (1832) by Jean Scheitzhöffer. Its story was one of love between a supernatural being and a human. If not remembered for its music, this ballet can make two claims to fame: (1) The female lead wore a tight-fitting costume with a short, flared skirt that became the standard for women in all Romantic ballets. (2) It was the first ballet in which the leading ballerina danced on the points of her slippers, which created the technique for dancing on the toes, referred to as *en pointe*.

Other ballets that followed in the Romantic tradition are *Giselle* by Adolphe Adam, *Coppélia* by Leo Délibes, and the three ballets by Tchaikovsky mentioned in this chapter.

The art of ballet remained relatively unchanged until the twentieth century. Ballet is a beautiful art form, but it is also artificial. The first reaction against these artificialities occurred near the turn of the twentieth century, when Isadora Duncan threw off her corset and shoes and danced barefoot throughout Europe. She believed that dancing should be harmonious and simple, with no ornaments. Although she devised no new techniques, she gave ballet a more natural look. Her ideas were adopted by Michel Fokine, Ruth St. Denis, Martha Graham, Agnes de Mille, and others. To some extent, the separation between classical ballet and modern dance still exists.

The music for ballet also changed greatly in the twentieth century. One of the most important landmarks in ballet is *The Rite of Spring*, with music by Stravinsky, which is presented in Chapter 32. Other well-known twentieth-century American ballets are *Rodeo*, *Appalachian Spring*, and *Billy the Kid*, all with music by Aaron Copland.

Kevin Fleming/Corbis

The music for the ballet is not heavy and serious; that would not be in the character of the story. All of it is beautiful and very listenable. The eight parts of the *Nutcracker Suite* are:

1. Miniature Overture
2. March
3. Dance of the Sugar Plum Fairy
4. Russian Dance, "Trepak"
5. Arab Dance
6. Chinese Dance
7. Dance of Reed Flutes
8. Waltz of the Flowers

The "Waltz of the Flowers" is danced in tribute to Clara by the Sugar Plum Fairy's attendants.

LISTENING GUIDE

PIOTR ILICH TCHAIKOVSKY
"Waltz of the Flowers" from *The Nutcracker* (1891)

GENRE: Ballet music   Waltz tempo (3/4)   Orchestra

CD 4 Tracks 37 – 39

6 minutes 52 seconds

Form: Rondo (*A B A B C A B*)

0:00	37	0:00	Woodwinds and harp open with fragment of A theme.
		0:21	Harp cadenza.
		1:08	A theme played by French horns with flowing notes in clarinet.

		1:24	A theme repeated.
		1:40	B theme enters in violins and then repeated.
		2:12	A theme played by French horns and clarinets.
		2:43	B theme played by violins and then repeated.
3:14	38	0:00	C theme enters in oboe, with contrasting line in violins.

		0:17	C theme repeated.
		0:31	C theme extended by cellos, then violins with contrasting line in woodwinds.
4:40	39	0:00	A theme returns played by the French horns as violins play flowing notes.
		0:30	B theme returns in violins and is repeated one octave higher.
		1:10	Coda begins softly but then starts to build as fragments of B are heard.
		1:41	Music suddenly becomes softer with a short passage in two-beat meter.
		2:12	"Waltz of the Flowers" concludes with full-sounding chords.

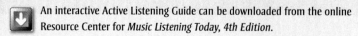

An interactive Active Listening Guide can be downloaded from the online Resource Center for *Music Listening Today, 4th Edition.*

Piotr Ilich Tchaikovsky

Until early adulthood **Piotr Tchaikovsky** ("Chy-*koff*-skee," 1840–1893) seemed destined to follow in his father's footsteps by working in a government position. At the age of twenty-three, however, he decided to become a musician, resigned his job, and entered the newly founded Conservatory of Music in St. Petersburg. He did well, and in three years he had finished his course of study. He was recommended for a teaching position in the new Conservatory in Moscow, where he taught harmony for twelve years.

Throughout his life Tchaikovsky was plagued by the fact that he was a homosexual. He once described his existence as "regretting the past, hoping for the future, without ever being satisfied with the present." He married a Conservatory student, a rather unstable girl who was madly in love with him. The marriage was a disaster. Finally, on the verge of a complete mental breakdown, he went to live with his brothers in St. Petersburg.

Tchaikovsky visited New York City in the early 1890s and conducted at Carnegie Hall.

Nadezhda von Meck entered his life at this point. She was a wealthy widow who, though a recluse, successfully ran her inherited business empire and the lives of her eleven children. She was impressed by the beauty of Tchaikovsky's music and decided to support him financially. There was, however, one unusual stipulation: So that she could be sure she was supporting a composer, not a personal friend, she required that they should never meet. And so it was. For thirteen years, they carried on an intense and devoted relationship— all by letters.

In 1893 while in St. Petersburg to conduct his Sixth Symphony, Tchaikovsky contracted cholera and died. Although he was born and lived in Russia, his music is not particularly nationalistic, especially in contrast to the music of some of his contemporaries, who are discussed in subsequent chapters.

BEST-KNOWN WORKS

ballet:
- *The Nutcracker*
- *Sleeping Beauty*
- *Swan Lake*

opera:
- *Eugene Onegin*

orchestra:
- Piano Concerto No. 1
- Violin Concerto
- *Romeo and Juliet*
- Festival Overture "1812"
- Symphonies Nos. 4, 5, and 6

MAIN POINTS OF THIS CHAPTER

1. Program music is instrumental music that the composer associates with a non-musical idea. Instrumental music cannot tell a specific story, but it can convey general impressions. The program for such a work is indicated in its title, which is sometimes accompanied by a poem or other descriptive material.

2. For Romantic composers, program music became a means of organizing a work without resorting to the forms developed during the Classical period. It was also a source of musical material that had hardly been tapped.

3. Four types of program music were composed:
   - Concert overture—an independent piece in one movement with programmatic associations
   - Incidental music—written to be performed in conjunction with a play or drama
   - Tone poem (or symphonic poem)—a large, one-movement work for orchestra that develops a poetic idea, suggests a scene, or creates a mood
   - Program symphony—a multimovement work that is built around an idea or story.

4. Berlioz's *Symphonie fantastique* represents his fantasies about his beloved in five different situations. The work is unified through a theme (fixed idea) that is transformed. The basic pitches of the fixed idea are retained while its rhythm, harmony, and timbre are changed.

5. Ballet is an art form that combines body movement, costumes, scenery, and music in an artistic way. It began in the courts of France about three hundred years ago, where its main goal was grace and courtliness.

6. Choreographers usually create the dance movement to go with a particular musical work. Composers sometimes arrange suites consisting of music from the complete ballet.

FEATURES TO LISTEN FOR

1. In Berlioz's *Symphonie fantastique:*
   • The places where phrases of the "Dies irae" chant appear
   • How effectively Berlioz writes for the various instruments, such as the woodwinds playing the grotesque witches' dance and the stern sound of the low brasses sounding the "Dies irae"
   • How the "Witches' Round Dance" theme enters in one section of the orchestra after another with increasing intensity
   • How the "Witches' Round Dance" theme is combined with the "Dies irae" theme.

2. In Tchaikovsky's "Waltz of the Flowers":
   • How the music falls into four-measure-long groups, which makes the work especially easy to listen to
   • The elegance and grace of the music

Romantic Opera

26

Italian opera dominated the opera world until the nineteenth century. But that situation was about to change. Several other distinct styles of opera developed during the Romantic period. One was the German style, followed later in the century by the French and Russian styles. Italian opera also changed, but less dramatically.

THE ITALIAN STYLE

At the beginning of the nineteenth century, Italian opera was still in the style of Mozart's *Don Giovanni*, discussed in Chapter 17. Gioacchino Rossini (1792–1868) even based his opera *The Barber of Seville* on the characters in Mozart's *The Marriage of Figaro*.

With Vincenzo Bellini (1801–1835) Italian opera reached a high point of interest in melody. The arias in his operas, such as *Norma*, emphasize beautiful singing through technically demanding melodic lines, cadenzas, and ornamentation. This style of opera is termed **bel canto,** which means "beautiful singing" in Italian. Gaetano Donizetti (1797–1848) also contributed to the bel canto style of opera. Although these early operas often lack convincing dramatic qualities, the brilliance of the soloists' lines and the beauty of the melodies make them highly enjoyable listening.

The two most important names in Italian opera in the nineteenth century were Giuseppe Verdi and Giacomo Puccini. Both wrote operas that contained the beauty of bel canto melodies, but they added much more to their music.

There are some differences in the two operas. Figaro is a valet in Mozart's opera, not a barber as he is in Rossini's.

In Europe, especially Italy, opera was very popular. Its appeal reached well beyond the upper classes.

VERDI'S *RIGOLETTO*

Rigoletto is hardly the typical hero—he is a hunchbacked court jester. And he isn't even a nice guy. His one redeeming virtue is his love for his daughter, Gilda. Rigoletto's master, the womanizing Duke of Mantua, has been able to get Gilda to fall in love with him while he pretended to be a poor student. He manages to seduce Gilda, which motivates Rigoletto to plot the Duke's murder. But Gilda really loves the Duke, even when she finds out that he is a liar and a cheat. In the end, she sacrifices her own life to save his. As often happens in Romantic opera, evil overcomes good.

The Duke's aria "La donna è mobile" ("Woman is fickle") expresses the Duke's pleasure-seeking personality. It also shows Verdi's ability to compose rousing music. He knew that the aria would be a hit, and he didn't want it to leak out of rehearsals and have everyone singing it before the opera opened. Therefore, he waited until as close as possible to the premiere to give the music to the tenor who had the Duke's role.

"La donna è mobile" achieved a popular status in the United States in the 1950s as recorded by a tenor named Mario Lanza.

PUCCINI'S *LA BOHÈME*

La bohème (*The Bohemian*) is a story of the artsy, hippie life on the Left Bank of the Seine in Paris. The curtain rises on the run-down garret where four young men live: the poet Rodolfo, the painter Marcello, the philosopher Colline, and the musician Schaunard. It's Christmas Eve, and they can't afford fuel for a decent fire. Colline and Schaunard come back and flourish some of that rare item—money. The landlord, who seems to have heard of their good fortune, soon comes to ask for the rent. By the use of a little

A *garret* is an unfurnished space just under the roof.

GIUSEPPE VERDI
"La donna è mobile" from *Rigoletto* (1851)

GENRE: Aria, opera   Soloist and orchestra

CD 5 Track 1

2 minutes 4 seconds

Form: Strophic

0:00   1   0:00   Orchestra plays short introduction.

0:13	La donna è mobile	Woman is fickle
	Qual piuma al vento,	Like a feather in the breeze,
	Muta d'accento	She changes her words
	E di pensiero.	And her thoughts.

La   don - na è   mo - bi - le   qual   piu - ma al   ven -   to.

mu - ta   d'ac - cen -   to   e   di   pen - sie -   ro.

0:22	Sempre un amabile	Always a lovable
	Leggiadro viso,	And beautiful face,
	In pianto o in riso,	Crying or laughing,
	é menzognero.	Is lying.

0:31	La donna è mobile, ecc.	Woman is fickle, etc.

1:08	é sempre misero	The man's always miserable
	Chi a lei s'affida,	Who believes in her,
	Chi le confida	Who carelessly trusts
	Mal cauto il core!	His heart to her!
	Pur mai non sentesi	And yet one who never
	Felice appieno	Enjoys love on that breast
	Chi su quel seno	Never feels
	Non libra amore!	Really in love!

1:27	La donna è mobile, ecc.	Woman is fickle, etc.

2:04   Aria concludes with tenor singing high note and decisive chords by the orchestra.

 An interactive Active Listening Guide can be downloaded from the online Resource Center for *Music Listening Today, 4th Edition.*

The young men's break comes when the landlord brags about his virility with women, and they threaten to tell his wife.

trickery, they are able to get rid of him. They decide to celebrate at the Café Momus, and everyone except Rodolfo leaves; he is finishing some writing and plans to join them shortly.

Soon there's a knock at the door. It is Mimi, who has not met Rodolfo before. Her candle has gone out, and she can't see to get up the stairs to her apartment. She is also weak and out of breath, so Rodolfo gives her a little wine and offers her a chair. As he helps her search for the key she has dropped on the floor, a draft of wind blows out their candles. They grope in the dark for her key. He finds it and, thinking quickly, slips it into his pocket without telling her. As they continue feeling along the floor, Rodolfo's hand meets hers and he exclaims, *"Che gelida manina!"* ("How cold your little hand is!") Then begins one of those glorious arias and a duet that show off Romantic opera at its best.

How fortunate for the plot that the wind just happened to come along at that moment!

In good operatic tradition, Mimi and Rodolfo fall in love very quickly. Musically, it all works very well, even if it isn't quite realistic. The scene would not be effective opera if their relationship were allowed to grow more naturally over several hours.

Giuseppe Verdi ("*Vair*-dee," 1813–1901) was born in a small town in northern Italy, the son of a poor innkeeper. He probably would not have had a musical education had it not been for the support of a prosperous merchant who paid for two years' study in Milan. When Verdi returned, he fell in love with the merchant's daughter. The marriage was a happy one, but misfortune struck. His two children and his young wife died within a three-year span.

Although Verdi's first opera had been moderately successful, the next one was not. That failure, coupled with the tragedies in his family, caused him to give up composing for a year. He was finally persuaded to write another opera on the story of Nebuchadnezzar, the biblical king of Babylon. It was an immediate success and it launched Verdi on a career that spanned more than fifty years. Part of his success lay in his selection of high-quality libretti. He was also an excellent dramatist and sensed what would be effective onstage.

Verdi's career was helped by the strong nationalistic feelings of the Italians, who were attempting to free themselves from the control of Austria. Cries of "Viva Verdi" rang out in Italian opera houses, both in admiration of Verdi and in allegiance to Italy. To many patriots, the letters of his name represented "Victor Emmanuel, *Rex d'Italia*."

The phrase means "Victor Emmanuel, king of Italy." He was Italy's first king.

In spite of his fame, Verdi remained a simple man who preferred the quiet of his farm to the pressures of society. His second wife was a sensitive and intelligent woman who encouraged him in his work. Verdi was able to produce one masterpiece after another. He wrote his last operas when he was nearly eighty years old.

Giacomo Puccini ("*Poo-chee*-nee," 1858–1924) was a generation younger than Verdi and perhaps not so sophisticated a composer. He possessed a wonderful gift of melody, however, and an instinct for successful theater. These attributes made his operas very popular.

Verismo operas have no mythological queens or gods.

Puccini belonged to a group of opera composers who stressed *verismo* (realism). Their characters came from everyday life, and they rejected heroic or exalted themes from mythology and history. In *La bohème*, for example, four young men occupy a shabby, cold apartment and have trouble meeting the rent and finding enough to eat.

Alfredo Dagli Orti/Galleria d'Arte Moderna Rome/The Art Archive/Picture Desk

BEST-KNOWN WORKS OF VERDI

opera:
- *Il trovatore*
- *La traviata*
- *Rigoletto*
- *A Masked Ball*
- *Aïda*
- *Otello*
- *Falstaff*

Lebrecht Music & Arts/The Image Works

BEST-KNOWN WORKS OF PUCCINI

opera:
- *La bohème*
- *Tosca*
- *Madame Butterfly*
- *Turandot*

The rest of *La bohème* is equally beautiful and not long, as least by the standards of nineteenth-century opera. Act II is a delightful scene at the Café Momus in which Musetta, Marcello's former love and a notorious flirt, sings a tantalizing waltz. In Act III, Mimi and Rodolfo have had a falling out. There is a hint of impending doom because of Mimi's deteriorating health from tuberculosis.

In Act IV the setting is again the garret, and there are several musical dramatic parallels to the first act. This time Musetta enters, saying that Mimi is downstairs, too weak to climb up them—an ironic parallel to the events of the earlier act. Mimi is helped into the room, and the friends leave quickly to get medicine and a doctor. Rodolfo and Mimi

GIACOMO PUCCINI

La Bohème, Act I (excerpt)

GENRE: Opera   Soloists and orchestra

CD 2 Tracks 16 – 19

13 minutes 38 seconds

0:00   16   0:00   (Rodolfo holds on to Mimi's hand.)

Rodolfo

Che ge-li-da ma-ni-na, se la la-sci ri-scal-dar. Cer-
How cold your lit-tle hand is! Let me warm it in my own. Your

-car che gio-va? Al bu-io non si tro-va.
key, don't mind it, it's far too dark to find it.

Ma per fortuna,	But soon the light
è una notte di luna	of the moon will help us,
e qui la luna	and in the moonlight
l'abbiamo vicina.	we'll look by the window.
Aspetti signorina,	So listen pretty maiden,
le dirò con	while I tell you
due parole chi son,	in a few words
chi son,	just who I am,
e she faccio, come vivo.	what I do and how I live.
Vuole?	Can I?
Chi son, chi son?	I am, I am?
Sono un poeta,	I am a poet,
Che cosa faccio?	What is my work?
Scrivo. E come vivo?	Writing. Is it a living?
Vivo.	Barely.
In povertà mia lieta	In poverty I gladly
scialo da gran signore	lavish on lonely ladies
rime ed inni d'amore.	rhymes and hymns of love.
Per sogni e per chimere	In dreams and flights of fancy
e per castelli in aria	and castles in the air
l'anima ho milionaria.	truly I am a millionaire.

Ta- lor dal mio for - zie - re ru-ban tut-ti i gio-
And now two eyes have stol - en ev-'ry price-less pos-

-iel - li due la - dri gli oc - chi bel - li.
-ses - sion of my es-teemed pro-fes - sion.

V'entrar con voi pur ora,	You've been here just a short time,
ed i miei sogmo usati	but all my usual day dreams
e i bei sogni miei	and all my other fancies
tosto si dileguar!	now they have disappeared!
Ma il furto non m'accora	But still the theft doesn't grieve me
poichè. poichè v'ha preso	because, because here at last
stanza la dolce speranza!	sweet hope has seized my heart and being!
Or che mi conoscete	Now that you know about me,
parlate voi,	tell about you.
deh! parlate, chi siete?	Won't you tell me who you are?
Vi placcia dir!	Please say you will!

Mimi

4:27 **17** 0:00 Si. Mi chiamano Mimi
ma il mio nome è Lucia.
La storia mia è breve,
A tela oa seta recamo
in casa e fuori.
Son tranquilla e lieta
ed è mio svago far gigli e rose.

Yes. They call me Mimi,
but my name is Lucia.
My story is a short one,
I do embroid'ry on silk
inside and outside.
I'm content and happy;
for leisure I make lilies and roses.

Che parlano di sogni
e di chimere,
quelle cose che han nome posesia.

Lei m'intende?

They speak to me of fancies
and illusions,
of such pleasures as only poets know.

Are you listening?

Rodolfo

Si.

Yes.

Mimi

Mi chiamano Mimi,
il perchè non so.
Solia, mi fo il pranzo
da me stesea,
Non vado sempre a messa
ma prego assai il Signor.
Vivo solla, soletta,
là in una bianca cameretta;
guardo sui tetti e in cielo.
Ma quando vien lo sgelo
il primo sole a mio,
il primo bacio dell'aprile è mio!
il primo sole è mio!
Germoglia in un vaso una rosa,
Foglia a foglia la spio!
Così gentil il profumo d'un flor
Ma i flor ch'io faccio, ahimè!
i flor ch'io faccio, ahimè,
non hanno odore!

They call me Mimi,
but I don't know why.
Living alone, I eat
a simple dinner.
I seldom go to Mass,
but often pray to God.
I'm alone and it's lonely,
up there in my one room apartment;
looking at the roof tops and sky.
But when the frost is over,
sunshine's first rays are mine,
then comes the first sweet kiss of April
The first bright sunshine is mine!
A rose starts to bud in its vase,
leaf by leaf it opens!
How tender then is the scent a flower
But the flowers I make,
the flowers I fashion, too bad,
they have no fragrance!

Altro di me non le saprei narrare:
sono la sua vicina che la vien
fuori d'ora a importunare.

Other than that, there's not much more
to tell you, I am merely a neighbor
who intruded and came at a bad time.

(Rodolfo's friends call from the courtyard to urge him to hurry to the Café Momus.)

Schaunard

9:06 **18** 0:00 Ehi! Rodolfo!

Hey! Rodolfo

Colline

Rodolfo!

Rodolfo!

Marcello

Olà! Non senti!

Hey! Can't you hear us?

(Rodolfo, though annoyed, goes to the window to answer.)

Marcello

Lumacia!

You big snail!

(continued)

Colline

Poetucolo!   Second-rate poet!

Schaunard

Accidenti al pigro?   Did you have an accident?

Rodolfo

Scrivo ancor tre righe a volo.   I have to rewrite three lines.

Mimi

Chi son?   Who are they?

Rodolfo

(turning to Mimi)
Amici.   Friends.

Schaunard

Sentirai le tue.   You'll be hearing from us.

Marcello

Che te ne fai lì solo?   How can you stay alone there?

Rodolfo

Non son solo. Siamo in due.   I'm not alone. Someone's with me.
Andante da Momus, tenete il posto.   Go on to Momus. Reserve a table.
ei saremo tosto.   We'll be there shortly.

(Rodolfo watches at the window to make sure his friends leave. They gradually disappear.)

Marcello, Schaunard, Colline

Momus, Momus, Momus   Momus, Momus, Momus
zitti e discreti andiamocene via.   Quiet and discrete, we're off to eat.
Momus, Momus!   Momus, Momus!

Marcello

Trovò la poesia!   He's found true poetry!

Schaunard, Colline

Momus, Momus, Momus!   Momus, Momus, Momus!

9:43 **19** 0:00 (Rodolfo turns to see Mimi looking so beautiful in the moonlight.)

Largo   Rodolfo
O so - a - ve fan - ciul - la_____ o dol - ce
What a beau-ti-ful maid - en_____ what a sweet

vi - so di mi - te cir - con - fu - so al-ba lu - nar,_____
vi - sion, sur - round-ed by the kind - ly moon-light's glow_____

in te, rav - vis - so_____ il so gno ch'io vor -
in you I see now_____ the fond - est dream that

re - i - sem - pre - so - gnar!
long a - go I al - ways dreamed!

(continued)

gnor! — Che m'a - mi di', — lo t'a — mo! —
sir! — Say you love me, — I love — you!

Strings, harp, flute
Rodolfo and Mimi A - mor, a - mor! —
(off stage) My love, my love

A - mor. —
My love. —
dying away (curtain)

The curtain falls, and the music for Act I ends as Mimi and Rodolfo leave the stage arm in arm.

An interactive Active Listening Guide can be downloaded from the online Resource Center for *Music Listening Today, 4th Edition.*

THE FINAL ACT OF *LA BOHÈME* ends with the death of Mimi in the arms of Rodolfo. Often the duet is staged so that it is sung with a soft spotlight shining on the couple.

Clive Barda/ArenaPal/Topham/The Image Works

recall their first meeting. The old themes are heard, but the music is no longer robust. It is weak and shattered. The friends return. They talk quietly among themselves, hoping Mimi can sleep. Suddenly, they realize that she has died. "Mimi! Mimi!" Rodolfo cries out. The orchestra strikes the same chords heard in the love music from Act I. This time, however, the music is heavy with grief. The curtain falls.

Romantic operas usually end tragically. It's more dramatic that way.

THE FRENCH STYLE

The French did not develop quite as distinct a style of opera as the Italians or the Germans did. Yet their operas do sound different. The more distinctive French quality would flourish at the turn of the century in the impressionistic music of Debussy and Ravel.

Three French opera composers merit attention. One is Charles Gounod ("Goo-*noh*," 1818–1893). His best-known work is *Faust*, in which a man named Faust sells his soul to the devil in exchange for eternal youth. Another composer of French opera was Jules Massenet ("Mass-en-*nay*," 1842–1912). His best-known operas are *Manon* and *Thaïs*; the "Meditation" from that opera is often heard as a solo for violin or singer.

The opera that nearly everyone has heard about, and most people find very attractive, is *Carmen* by Georges Bizet. Actually, *Carmen* was first presented at the opéra comique with spoken lines instead of sung recitatives. It is not as long and serious as the operas usually presented at the Opera House in Paris. Ironically, it was not initially very well received, which broke Bizet's spirit, and he did not live long after its premiere. Today *Carmen* is the most popular opera in the Western world.

Although *Carmen* takes place in Spain and contains much Spanish-sounding music, it is in French and was composed by a Frenchman.

The opéra comique was more a family theater, and probably the femme fatale role of Carmen was disturbing to its patrons.

THE GERMAN STYLE

German opera differs from Italian opera in a number of ways. To begin with, the languages are very different. Italian words end in one of the five vowel sounds of the language. German words often conclude with consonants, many of them with hard *t*'s and *k*'s. The subjects are no longer ancient Greek gods but rather the Nordic gods of northern Europe. And the music is different, too. German opera tends to sound heavier and less lighthearted than that of Italy or France.

In 1821, the German composer Carl Maria von Weber ("*Vay*-ber," 1786–1826) wrote *Der Freischütz* (*The Freeshooter*), an opera based on German folklore. The story involves a marksman who receives from the black huntsman seven magic bullets. Six of the seven do as he wills, but the seventh does as the devil wills. The devil also gets the soul of the one who is hit by the bullet. Besides mysticism, the opera features peasants, rustic scenes, and hunting horns.

The black huntsman is the devil.

Weber completed two more operas before his early death. Although they are seldom performed today, they exerted a significant influence on Richard Wagner, one of the musical giants of the nineteenth century.

WAGNER'S MUSIC DRAMAS

More than any previous opera composer, Richard Wagner consciously tackled the dilemma of balance between music and drama. In his lengthy philosophical discourses, he often indicated his belief that poetry and music should be one. To meet his artistic goals, he created a different kind of opera, one that he called **music drama.**

Music dramas required a new and different approach to the concept of libretto, so Wagner wrote his own texts. The topics were mythological because he felt that such stories appealed best to the emotions. Wagner's favorite libretto themes were also rich with philosophical overtones—the struggle between good and evil, the contest between the physical and the spiritual, and the idea of redemption through love. Because these overarching themes are present, the characters in the music dramas are not personalities but more like symbols or pawns being pushed about by uncontrollable forces. In this respect, Wagner approaches the drama of the ancient Greeks.

Wagner frequently associates a musical motive with a particular character, emotion, or idea. In his music such a motive is called a **leitmotiv,** or leading motive. As soon as various leitmotivs are established, Wagner weaves them in and out of the music at appropriate times to enhance the intrigue of the plot and to provide unity in the work. Such use of motives permits the orchestra to assume a much more vital role in the music drama, because it can expand on the people and ideas referred to in the text.

Each of his operas has a score the size of a large book.

Because the division of music into recitatives, arias, and choruses interrupts the forward motion of the drama, Wagner eliminated these forms as independent sections. Instead, he created a flowing, melodious line to serve as an unending melody. The vocal

THE TWILIGHT OF THE GODS ends with flaming death, flood, and utter destruction. But because of the power of love, a new world will emerge.

line emphasizes the expression of the words being sung. With its continuous interweaving of motives, the orchestra contributes to the impression of never-ending motion.

To increase the impression that a musical work is seamless, Wagner used much chromatic harmony. By making half-step alternations in the chords, he weakened the magnetic pull of the harmony toward the tonic. The absence of a strong tonic means that sometimes the music seldom arrives at a cadence point, so the feeling of key becomes nebulous.

Wagner did not treat the orchestra as mere accompaniment for the singers onstage. The importance of the orchestra in his works equals, or perhaps exceeds, that of the singers. In a real sense, his orchestra is symphonic, both in size and in its ability to stand almost without the vocal parts.

Wagner's most ambitious achievement was a cycle of four complete operas titled *Der Ring des Nibelungen* (*The Ring of the Nibelung*). The four operas in the cycle are *Das Rheingold* (*The Gold of the Rhine*), *Die Walküre* (*The Valkyries*), *Siegfried*, and *Götterdämmerung* (*The Twilight of the Gods*).

The story of the cycle revolves around gold that had been fashioned into a ring and is guarded by the Rhine maidens in the Rhine River. The gold is stolen and a curse put on it. The curse states that if the possessor will renounce love, he will rule the world. The result is a chain of misfortunes affecting all the characters in the drama.

WAGNER'S GÖTTERDÄMMERUNG

Portions of his music dramas are often performed as concert pieces without singers.

In Romantic operas, the course of events often hinges on curses or magic potions.

In an earlier opera in *The Ring* cycle, Wotan, king of the gods, made his favorite daughter, Brünnhilde, mortal because she disobeyed him. She falls into a deep sleep, surrounded by a wall of fire. Siegfried passes through the flames and awakens her. Siegfried and Brünnhilde fall in love and become husband and wife.

While on one of his adventures, Siegfried gains possession of the ring. Unfortunately for him, he does not know about the curse. He is subsequently murdered by the evil Hagen, who lusts after the gold.

The immolation scene occurs very late in *Götterdämmerung*. It takes place in front of a castle on the Rhine River. In this scene, Brünnhilde sings her farewell before joining Siegfried in death by riding her horse into his funeral pyre. Before ending her life, she takes the ring from Siegfried's finger and puts it on. She also bequeaths it to the Rhine maidens upon her death. After she disappears into the flames, a flood engulfs the stage. The flood is followed by a fire. Valhalla, the home of the gods, is destroyed, along with its inhabitants. *Götterdämmerung* ends in tragedy for all except the Rhine maidens.

The immolation scene is presented in the Listening Guide. The stage actions appear in parenthetical statements. The text is provided in the original German and in English.

As you listen to this scene, pay careful attention to Wagner's use of the leitmotivs. Notice how they not only enhance the text but continue the story, even after the characters have died.

Although *Götterdämmerung* ends tragically, the final leitmotiv is "Redemption by love." The philosophically minded Wagner was saying through this leitmotiv that the most powerful force of all is love and that, in spite of all that had happened, a new world will emerge through its power.

LISTENING GUIDE

RICHARD WAGNER
Immolation scene from *Götterdämmerung* (1874)

GENRE: Opera   Soloist and orchestra

CD 5 Tracks 2 – 10

7 minutes 54 seconds

0:00   2   0:00   The trumpets and trombones play the leitmotiv for "Law" at a loud dynamic level.

Lebhaft (Lively)

Brünnhilde, the ring on her finger, takes a torch from one of the men.
She then sings to a pair of ravens, which are Wotan's messengers.

0:13   Fliegt heim, ihr Raben! raunt eurem Herren,   Fly home, you ravens! Tell your master
was hier am Rhein ihr gehört!   what you have heard here on the Rhine!

0:27   3   0:00   The orchestra plays the "Magic fire" and "Loge, god of fire" leitmotivs.

Brünnhilde continues singing to the ravens.

An Brünnhildes Felsen fliegt vorbei: Fly past Brünnhilde's rock,
der dort noch lodert,   where Loge is still burning,
weiset Loge nach Walhall!   and tell him to go to Valhalla!
Denn der Götter Ende dämmert nun auf: Because the end of the gods now is dawning.

She throws the torch onto the pyre. The two ravens fly into the background.

so—werf' ich den Brand   See—I throw the torch
in Walhalls prangende Burg.   into Valhalla's glorious fortress!

0:52   Strings play many notes to represent fire.

The pyre bursts into flames. Brünnhilde turns to her horse.

1:34   4   0:00   Grane, mein Ross.   Grane, my steed,
sei mir gegrüsst!   Greetings to you!

0:20   The French horns and other instruments sound the "Ride of the Valkyries" leitmotiv.

Weisst du auch, mein Freund,   My friend, do you know
wohin ich dich führe?   where I am leading you?
Im Feuer leuchtend.   Into the blazing fire.

2:04   5   0:00   The flute and Brünnhilde sound the "Redemption by love" leitmotiv.

liegt dort dein Herr, Siegfried, mein   Your master lies in there, Siegfried, my
seliger Held.   blessed hero.
Dem Freunde zu folgen,   Are you eager to follow your friend?
wieherst du freudig?   Are you neighing?
Lockt dich zu ihm die lachende Lohe?   Are you attracted by the laughing flames?

(continued)

0:40	Fühl' mein Brust auch, wie sie entbrennt;	Notice my breast also, how it is burning;
	helles Feuer das Herz mir erfasst.	bright flames consume my heart.
	Ihn zu umschlingen, umschlossen, von ihm,	To hold him, to be held by him,
	in mächtigster Minne vermählt ihm zu sein!	to be united with him by the power of love!
1:12	Hei-a-ja-ho! Grane! Grüss deinen Herren!	Hei-a-yo-ho! Grane! Greet your master!
	Siegfried! Siegfried! Sieh!	Siegfried! Siegfried! See!
	selig grüsst dich dein Weib!	Joyfully your wife greets you!

1:30 The brasses play the "Ride of the Valkyries" leitmotiv.

Brünnhilde mounts her horse and rides it into the flaming pyre.

3:38 **6** 0:00 The orchestra plays the "Magic fire" leitmotiv at a loud dynamic level.

Flames engulf the area in front of the castle, which also soon catches fire.

The "Magic sleep" leitmotiv is heard.

When everything seems to be burning, the glow is extinguished. Soon only a cloud of smoke is seen. The Rhine begins to rise, and its waters pour over the fire. Three Rhine maidens ride the waves and appear by the funeral pyre. Hagen, Siegfried's murderer, panics when he sees them. He tosses down his spear and shield, and then plunges into the waters, crying:

Two Rhine maidens grab Hagen and drag him down under the water. Another Rhine maiden triumphantly holds up the recovered ring.

A descending pattern played by the strings suggests Hagen's drowning.

1:31 The oboes and clarinets play the "Rhine maidens" leitmotiv.

5:18 **7** 0:00 The brasses sound the solemn "Valhalla" leitmotiv.

The Rhine gradually returns to its banks, and the Rhine maidens play with the ring in its calm waters.

0:12 An interweaving of leitmotivs is heard. The oboes and clarinets play the "Rhine maidens"; the violins play "Redemption by love"; the brasses sound "Valhalla." That leitmotiv grows more prominent as the music progresses.

5:47 **8** 0:00 "Rhine maidens" motive and "Redemption by love" motive are played together. Brasses play "Valhalla" motive.

From the ruins of the burned castle, the men and women see the red glow in the heavens. In that glow appears Valhalla, with gods and heroes sitting together.

7:08 **9** 0:00 The music grows louder as the brasses sound the "Siegfried" leitmotiv.

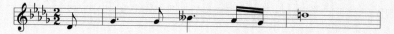

Flames overcome Valhalla. The gods disappear in the flames.

7:36 **10** 0:00 Strings sound "Redemption by love" leitmotiv.

1:13 The curtain falls with a long chord.

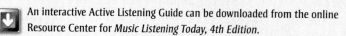

An interactive Active Listening Guide can be downloaded from the online
Resource Center for *Music Listening Today, 4th Edition.*

Richard Wagner ("*Ree*-card *Vahg*-ner," 1813–1883) was an artistic phenomenon. Born in Leipzig, Germany, he was the son of a minor police official who died when Richard was still an infant. His mother married an actor and playwright, who encouraged his stepson along similar lines. For most of his career, Wagner was largely self-taught. At the age of twenty, he became a chorus master in a small opera house in Leipzig and produced his first operas.

Success was slow in coming, and for the next ten years it seemed that Wagner would spend his life hovering on the edge of poverty. His first successful opera was *Rienzi*, which earned him a position as conductor for the king of Saxony. Other successful operas followed in the 1840s.

In 1848 Wagner became associated with the political uprisings that were taking place in Europe. He even published two articles in a magazine that advocated anarchy. A revolution broke out in Dresden in 1849, and the king and his court fled. Wagner was forced to escape to the home of his friend Franz Liszt in Weimar. Because there was a warrant out for his arrest, Wagner soon fled over the border into Switzerland. At that point, he seemed a ruined man. But he was helped by some willing patrons, and the years in Switzerland were some of his most productive. During this time he began work on *The Ring of the Nibelung*.

Bavaria, now part of Germany, was an independent state at that time.

Wagner became estranged from his wife, who had grown unsympathetic to his artistic aims and desires. He became involved with a succession of married women. In 1864 again all seemed lost. At that point, fate seemed to step in. A nineteen-year-old admirer of Wagner's music ascended to the throne in Bavaria. He was Ludwig II, known as "Mad Ludwig." He summoned Wagner to Munich, where he resumed work on *The Ring of the Nibelung*.

By 1876 Wagner had reached the top of the operatic world. That year he opened his first Bayreuth ("By-royt") festival. Later he built an opera house there, and the Bayreuth festivals continue today. It is the only theater in the world devoted exclusively to the music of one person. He is buried at Bayreuth, which in a sense is his monument.

Lebrecht Music & Arts/The Image Works

BEST-KNOWN WORKS

opera:
- *The Flying Dutchman*
- *Tannhäuser*
- *Lohengrin*
- *Tristan and Isolde*
- *The Meistersingers of Nuremberg*
- *The Ring of the Nibelung*

MAIN POINTS OF THIS CHAPTER

1. Romantic opera can be divided into three national groups: Italian, French, and German. Each has its own distinctive style.

2. Italian opera features beautiful singing (bel canto) and realism (verismo). Its best known composers are Giuseppe Verdi and Giacomo Puccini.

3. French opera was often more serious, like those of Charles Gounod. A lighter type of French opera was the opera comique. Bizet's *Carmen* is an example, although it ends tragically.

4. German opera tended to be longer and heavier than Italian and French operas. It was begun by Carl Maria von Weber, but the giant of German opera was Richard Wagner.

5. Wagner developed his plots around characters from Nordic mythology. He wrote his own librettos and directed his own staging. He called his operas "music dramas." His most ambitious achievement was a series of four operas titled "Der Ring Des Nibelungen."

6. Wagner no longer divided the music into recitatives, arias, and choruses, because he thought such divisions interrupted the flow of the drama. He created motives to represent characters and ideas. The orchestra then had an important role because it could play the leitmotiv even when the singer was not on stage.

FEATURES TO LISTEN FOR

1. In Verdi's "La donna è mobile":
   - The strophic form and not particularly emotional quality of the music
2. In Puccini's *La Bohème*:
   - The similar quality of the arias sung by Rodolfo and Mimi
   - How the singers hold on to certain high pitches for several seconds and the musical impact of these long, high notes
3. In Wagner's "Immolation Scene":
   - How the leitmotivs fit the nature of the character or idea—the energetic, forceful quality of Brünnhilde's leitmotiv contrasts with the swimming, happy nature of the leitmotiv for the Rhine maidens

Late Romantic Music

27

The composers of the Romantic period never completely abandoned the forms used by Mozart and Haydn in the Classical period. In fact, some composers, especially in the last half of the nineteenth century, used traditional forms extensively. Most of these compositions were for orchestra, although quite a few of them involved piano, chamber music, and choral groups.

The works created in the century after the Classical period do not sound at all like their predecessors. They are noticeably different, for the reasons mentioned in Chapter 22.

The music composed between about 1785 and 1910 constitutes the heart of the repertoire for the symphony orchestra.

BRAHMS'S SYMPHONY NO. 4

Brahms composed only four symphonies, but each has a prominent place in the repertoire of the symphony orchestra. By the second half of the nineteenth century, composers were treating symphonies as monumental efforts. Brahms was so awed by the symphonies of Beethoven that he waited to complete his first symphony until he was forty-three years old. An earlier aborted attempt at writing a symphony became his First Piano Concerto. He completed his Fourth Symphony nine years later in 1885.

Of all the Romantic composers, Brahms liked to use traditional forms the most. In fact, during his lifetime he was considered by many musicians to be an outmoded conservative. But conservative, Romantic, or whatever, he composed much music of extraordinary quality.

First Movement

The first movement is in sonata form. It begins with a theme that has the sweeping, Romantic quality of many of Brahms's melodies:

The theme is worked with and manipulated throughout much of the movement. For instance, in the next few measures the same idea appears at *twice* its original speed—**diminution**. The notes don't follow the theme exactly, but the general idea is present:

At the end of the development section, the same idea appears at *half* its original speed—**augmentation.** At this point in the movement, Brahms retains the melodic line but alters the rhythm:

At another place, the theme is varied and exchanged between the first and second violins:

Elsewhere it is exchanged between the strings and woodwinds:

Resource Center

See "Hear It Now: Development in Music," in the *Music Listening Today, 4th Edition,* Resource Center.

One could go on for pages showing the many ways Brahms fragments, varies, develops, and transforms the theme. Almost from the time the theme appears, he is developing it and blending it into the structure of the music in such a way that throughout the symphony he maintains the warm sounds of the Romantic style. From it he extracts two motives, circled in the Listening Guide, that appear often in the movement.

The second theme combines two melodic ideas. One is played by the horns and a few woodwinds. It sounds somewhat like introductory music—and perhaps it is, because soon a passionate melody starts in the cellos and horns. A portion of the theme, including the triplets, is also used as a unifying motive in the movement. Sometimes it is exchanged with the first motive.

A third theme appears later in the movement, but it is not developed extensively.

LISTENING GUIDE

Johannes Brahms

Symphony No. 4 in E Minor, First Movement (1884–1885)

Genre: Symphony   Orchestra

CD 5 Tracks 11 – 15

13 minutes 22 seconds

Form: Sonata

Exposition

0:00 11 0:00   First theme, which contains two motives (circled), played by violins.

0:37   First theme repeated.

1:03   Transition.

1:39 12 0:00   Second theme, also containing a motive, begins in woodwinds.

0:06 Second part of second theme sounded by cellos and French horns with a rhythmic accompaniment. Violins repeat theme in high notes.

0:44 Violins and woodwinds exchange fragments of first theme.

1:11 Third theme introduced by French horn and flute, then oboe.

1:19 Modified second theme returns in woodwinds.

2:23 Codetta begins in woodwinds with fragments of first theme.

Development

4:19 **13** 0:00 First theme played by violins; then motive from it modulates several times.

0:47 Three accented notes from first theme are exchanged among strings.

1:25 Motives from second and first themes played softly by woodwinds.

1:59 First part of second theme played forcefully by strings and French horn.

2:19 Second theme played by woodwinds as violins play fragments of first theme pizzicato.

2:34 Motive from first theme alternates between violins and woodwinds.

3:18 First theme returns in augmentation in woodwinds.

Recapitulation

8:05 **14** 0:00 First theme returns in violins at the original tempo.

0:30 First theme repeated accompanied by rippling notes in woodwinds.

1:13 Second theme returns in woodwinds and French horn, followed by cellos over rhythmic accompaniment.

1:32 Violins repeat second theme.

1:57 Motive from first theme exchanged between woodwinds and violins.

2:22 Third theme played by oboe and French horn.

2:49 Motive from second theme played softly by woodwinds, then loudly by strings.

11:58 **15** 0:00 Coda contains two-note fragment from first theme played in imitation between strings and French horns; intensity of music increases.

0:31 Violins continue playing two-note fragment from first theme as intensity of music increases.

1:22 Movement concludes after five abrupt chords and final cadence of two long chords.

 An interactive Active Listening Guide can be downloaded from the online Resource Center for *Music Listening Today, 4th Edition.*

Four qualities stand out about Brahms's music in general and his Fourth Symphony in particular:

- The sheer beauty of the music. Listening to the rich sounds of its melodies and harmonies could be compared to eating a piece of a perfectly baked German chocolate cake.
- The skill with which themes are organized and developed. This is much more than sensual pleasure in listening to this symphony. Brahms is masterful in working with themes and utilizing forms.

You can listen to Brahms's your heart, or your head, which is the best way.

A listener's score for the first movement of Brahms's Symphony No. 4 is available for downloading.

- The quality of optimism and good feeling. This is a subjective element, of course, but there is something about Brahms's music that gives the feeling that things are right and will continue to turn out right. There is no sense of hand-wringing or self-pity in the music.

- The noble quality of the music. The word *noble* doesn't do justice to the music of Brahms and many other composers, but it comes as close as any. It means "possessing outstanding or superior qualities." There is something extraordinary about the music of Brahms and many other composers, something that is beyond or better than what we usually encounter in everyday life.

Second, Third, and Fourth Movements

Brahms is especially gifted in writing melodious second movements, and his Fourth Symphony is no exception. It is built around two themes. The first consists of a short pattern that is immediately followed in inversion and repeated several times. The second theme is a warm, flowing melody first played by the cellos.

The third movement is filled with an optimistic, jovial spirit. Its theme appears in two versions at the same time, with one being the inversion of the other.

Johannes Brahms

BEST-KNOWN WORKS

chamber music:
- Clarinet Quintet
- Trio in E-flat for Horn, Violin, and Piano

choral:
- A German Requiem

orchestra:
- Concerto for Piano No. 2
- Concerto for Violin
- Symphonies Nos. 1, 2, 3, and 4

Johannes Brahms (1833–1897) was the son of a rather shiftless double bass player in Hamburg, Germany. Johannes started his musical career by playing piano in the notorious waterfront area of the city. He was highly talented and by the age of twenty-five became the accompanist for one of the finest violinists of the day. He studied composition with Robert Schumann, and the Schumanns took the shy young man into their home. Brahms grew fond of Clara, and he was much help to the family during Robert's illness.

Brahms was aware that he had extraordinary talent as a composer and, for this reason, never accepted a position that made heavy demands on his time. Unlike Beethoven, he left no rejected versions of his music for posterity to find. He wanted the world to know only his best work, so his rough sketches were deliberately destroyed.

It was said that Brahms burned as many of his works as he allowed to be published.

Brahms never composed an opera or a tone poem. His coolness toward opera may be due to the overblown competition between his admirers and those of Wagner. The division concerned artistic philosophy as much as it did personalities. The Wagnerites believed that music was a means for communication of emotions and ideas. The admirers of Brahms viewed music as an end in itself and therefore favored absolute music. Brahms ignored the controversy as best he could and went about his composing. Because there is some truth in both views, the dispute has never been resolved.

The slur marks (⌒) cause the rhythmic emphasis to occur off the beat in the first and third measures. Portions of the melody appear throughout the movement.

The fourth movement is one of the most unusual and musically interesting found in the symphonies of the nineteenth century. It is a massive **chaconne,** which is a set of variations on a short theme. The theme for this movement is only eight measures long with only one note per measure. It is very plain and solid.

Allegro energetico

f Woodwinds, Brasses

Thirty-five variations and a coda follow. At the beginning of the thirteenth variation, the speed of the notes of the theme is slowed to one half their original speed. During this middle section of the movement, the theme is only implied in the harmony. It is easy to tell when the theme returns, because it is played forcefully again, as it was at the opening of the movement. The return of the original theme gives the movement an overall three-part form in addition to the variations of the chaconne. The continually repeated pattern provides unity to the music, while the variations provide contrast.

DVOŘÁK'S AMERICAN STRING QUARTET IN F MAJOR

The quartet Op. 96 (No. 12) by Antonín Dvořák is often called the *American Quartet* because he wrote it in the town of Spillville, Iowa. For three years in the 1890s, Dvořák was director of the Conservatory of Music in New York City. He was home-

This was the twelfth quartet that Dvořák had published.

Antonín Dvořák

Antonín Dvořák (1841–1904) was born into the family of a Bohemian innkeeper and amateur musician. He grew up listening to the folk music of his native land. After several years of conflict between Dvořák's music teacher and his father, an uncle provided him with the funds needed for a year of music study in Prague. When the money ran out, he earned his living playing in café bands and the National Opera Orchestra.

When Dvořák was about forty, his fortunes changed. He submitted a composition to the Austrian Commission. Although the prize he won was small in monetary terms, it gained for him the devoted friendship and unsparing help of committee member Johannes Brahms. Brahms opened many doors to publishers and conductors for Dvořák, who was genuinely grateful.

By 1885 Dvořák was recognized throughout the world. A few years later, he accepted the directorship of the Con-

servatory of Music in New York at a salary twenty times what he was earning in Prague. While in America, he was introduced to African American music by his pupil Harry T. Burleigh. He also became acquainted with the music of the Native Americans. He was the first composer, native or foreign born, to recognize these musical treasures.

Dvořák once expressed his gratitude in a letter to Brahms: "All my life [I] owe you the deepest gratitude for your good and noble intentions toward me, which are worthy of a truly great artist and man."

After three years in the United States, Dvořák returned to Bohemia, where he became director of the Prague Conservatory. When he died, a national day of mourning was declared in his honor.

Peter Joslin/ArenaPal/Topham/ The Image Works

BEST-KNOWN WORKS
chamber music:
• String Quartets Nos. 10, 11, and 12

orchestra:
• Concerto for Cello
• Concerto for Violin
• *Slavonic Dances*
• Serenade for String Orchestra
• Symphonies Nos. 8 and 9

American Quartet, First Movement (1893)

GENRE: Chamber music   String quartet

CD 5 Tracks 16 – 20

7 minutes 12 seconds

Form: Sonata

Exposition

0:00   16   0:00   First theme played by viola, then repeated by first violin.

0:20   Transition based on measures 3 and 4 of first theme.

1:33   17   0:00   Second theme played softly by first violin.

0:27   Transition using first three notes of second theme.

0:55   Codetta based on measures 1 and 2 of first theme begins softly.

Development

2:37   18   0:00   Viola plays altered version of first theme.

3:48   19   0:00   New melodic idea played by second violin is imitated by first violin, viola, and cello.

Recapitulation

4:22   20   0:00   First theme played by viola and repeated by first violin.

0:19   Transition begins based on measure 4 of first theme.

0:22   Cello plays short countermelody.

0:35   Violins play fragments from first theme.

1:37   Second theme played by first violin, then repeated by cello as music begins to build.

2:33   Coda begins with first part of first theme.

2:48   Movement closes with loud chords.

 An interactive Active Listening Guide can be downloaded from the online Resource Center for *Music Listening Today, 4th Edition.*

n for the viola part in the
uide uses the alto clef,
clef for the viola. Middle
middle line of the clef. It
he extensive use of ledger

sick for his native Bohemia, so he spent his summers living among the Czech-Bohemian people of that town. But this quartet is largely Bohemian in character, not American.

The *American Quartet* contains the traditional four movements, with the same pattern of forms and tempos found in most symphonies, concertos, and chamber works of the Classical and Romantic periods. And because the Romantic period is noted for its large works, it is worth remembering that nineteenth-century composers also wrote much excellent chamber music. Dvořák's *American Quartet* is only one example of this fact.

First Movement

The first movement of this quartet is in the traditional sonata form. The first theme is built around four one-measure phrases. These one-measure phrases become the germinal ideas for much of the movement. Dvořák uses many dotted-note figures in his music.

Several features stand out about Dvořák's music, specifically the first movement of this string quartet:

- The energy and vitality of the music
- The good-natured quality of the music
- The skill with which Dvořák worked with the four melodic ideas that make up the first theme
- The songlike beauty of the second theme

Second, Third, and Fourth Movements

The second movement is in a three-part form. The main melody is flowing and sentimental. The middle section of the movement is also melodious, with the first and second violins playing three notes apart.

The third movement has a scherzolike quality. It contains five brief sections in an *A B A B A* pattern.

The fourth movement is a rondo, with the pattern of *A B A C A B A*, which is sometimes termed *sonata rondo*. It has a lively character. It also contains many dotted-note patterns, which Dvořák was fond of using.

The scherzo is discussed in conjunction with Beethoven's music in Chapter 21.

TCHAIKOVSKY'S SYMPHONY NO. 4

Much music of the Romantic period is luscious and beautiful, but some of it is vibrant and fiery. The fourth movement of Tchaikovsky's Fourth Symphony is such a work. It begins with a flurry of notes, which are then contrasted with a simple Russian folk song melody called "The Birch Tree." The folk melody contains only four lines in an *a a b b*

PIOTR ILICH TCHAIKOVSKY

Symphony No. 4 in F Minor, Op. 36, Fourth Movement (1871)

GENRE: Symphony   Orchestra

CD 5 Tracks 21 – 24

9 minutes 12 seconds

Form: Sonata

Exposition

0:00   21   0:00   First theme with its many fast notes is played forcefully by strings in a major key.

(continued)

	0:16	Second theme (Russian folk melody) introduced by oboe in a minor key.

	0:30	Woodwinds and violins exchange two-note figure.
	0:50	First theme in major repeated by violins.
	1:03	Transition played by brasses and woodwinds.
1:38	**22** 0:00	Second theme played softly by oboe in minor.
	0:16	Woodwinds repeat second theme.
	0:30	Second theme played vigorously by French horns.
	0:46	Second theme repeated by trombones as violins play swirling notes.
	1:01	First half of second theme played quietly by oboe.
	1:16	Sections of orchestra rapidly exchange melodic figures.
	1:49	First theme played by violins, followed by transition in basses and strings.

Development

4:13	**23** 0:00	Second theme played by violins in minor.
	0:17	Second theme repeated with flute adding contrasting line, then theme repeated in major.
	0:49	First part of second theme leads to several rapid exchanges between sections of orchestra.
	1:14	Fragments of second theme played by trombones and imitated by trumpets.
5:46	**24** 0:00	Portion of introduction to first movement played by brasses. French horns and then strings follow as music grows softer.
	1:39	Transition begins in French horns with rapid exchanges between woodwinds and violins as music gradually grows louder and higher.
	2:12	Rapidly moving notes exchanged between violins and woodwinds.

Recapitulation

	2:18	First theme returns in violins.
	2:29	Transition played energetically by brasses and strings.
	2:45	Second theme played loudly by brasses.
	2:58	Coda with many fast passages and tremolos in violins.
	3:26	Movement concludes with timpani and a long, solid chord.

 An interactive Active Listening Guide can be downloaded from the online Resource Center for *Music Listening Today, 4th Edition.*

form and has a range of only the first five notes of a minor scale. How different can two themes be? The movement also cycles back in the development section the stirring introductory music to the first movement. Other characteristics of Tchaikovsky's style can be heard, especially the rapid exchanges of notes among the sections of the orchestra and the gradual buildup to climactic points. It's a real attention-grabbing piece of music.

MAIN POINTS OF THIS CHAPTER

1. Romantic composers, especially in the last half of the nineteenth century, often used the same forms as Classical composers. The musical material they poured into those forms, however, was very different. Often what they included in a form was longer, larger in concept, and more emotional than what Mozart and Haydn composed.

2. Brahms was especially skilled at working with themes, which gives his music just the right blend of something old and something new.

3. Both diminution and augmentation are found in the first movement of Brahms's Symphony No. 4. In diminution the theme is presented faster (usually twice as fast) as the original. Augmentation is the opposite; the theme appears in much longer note values.

4. Although many fine symphonies and concertos were written in the Romantic period, composers during that time also wrote much chamber music. Dvořák's "American" String Quartet is but one example among many, many possibilities.

5. The fourth movement of Tchaikovsky's Symphony No. 4 contains a good example of the very contrasting nature of themes often found in Romantic music. It also demonstrates the fact that composers during that time brought back in one or more movements of a work a theme that had appeared in an earlier movement of that work (cyclical form).

FEATURES TO LISTEN FOR

1. In the first movement of Symphony No. 4 by Brahms:
   - How portions of the two motives from the first theme appear throughout the movement
   - The rich, passionate nature of the second theme
   - The repeat of the second theme by the violins at a higher pitch level
2. In the first movement of Dvořák's "American" Quartet:
   - The happy, energetic quality of the music
3. In the fourth movement of Tchaikovsky's Symphony No. 4:
   - The extremely different character of the two themes
   - The insertion of the theme from the introduction to the first movement into the fourth movement

28 Nationalism

It should be noted that almost no Romantic composers *lived* as peasants. They admired the simple life from a distance.

Romanticism exalted the inherent goodness of humankind in its natural condition. Eighteenth-century intellectuals had considered common folk to be untutored and rough; the Romantics admired them. They thought the life of the simple folk to be good and right because it was largely uncorrupted by society. Furthermore, the life of the common people was a source of subject matter that composers and artists had seldom tapped before.

CHARACTERISTICS OF NATIONALISM

Many nationalistic works are also programmatic.

When associated with the arts, **nationalism** refers to a deliberate, conscious attempt to develop artworks that are characteristic of a particular country or region. Often, nationalism involves specific subject matter, such as a painting of a national event or an opera about a historical character.

During the nineteenth century, this search for nationalistic expression was mainly an attempt to break away from the prevailing German-Austrian style. Bach, Mozart, Beethoven, Schubert, Liszt, Schumann, Brahms, and Wagner had long ruled the musical world. To men such as Modest Mussorgsky in Russia, Bedřich Smetana in Bohemia, and Edvard Grieg in Norway, it was time for something different. They knew that Russians and Bohemians and Norwegians were as capable of composing music as were the Germans! And they set about proving it.

There was an additional reason for nationalism in the arts during the nineteenth century: It was a time of rising patriotism. Italy and Germany were finally formed as nations. Unfortunately, wars were frequent. In such conflicts a nation's efforts involved the average citizen to a degree unknown in previous centuries. No longer were wars fought largely by professional soldiers for a king. Now the cause was one's country. In short, the times were a good incubator for nationalism in the arts.

The language of the directions does not affect the actual sounds, but it offers an idea of the composers' outlook toward their music.

In their efforts to assert their independence from foreign influences, some composers indicated the tempo markings and other musical directions in their native language rather than the more internationally accepted Italian. So Debussy wrote *Vif* instead of *Vivace*, Wagner wrote *Schnell*, and some American composers in this century wrote *Lively* or *Fast*, to cite a few examples.

THE RUSSIAN FIVE

Until well into the nineteenth century, Russia had little musical tradition of its own. The czars imported French and Italian opera as well as French ballet. Michael Glinka (1804–1857) was the first Russian composer to write an opera on a Russian theme. Today he is generally considered to be the father of Russian music.

More important was a group of five Russian composers, known as the Russian Five, who lived in the latter half of the Romantic period. The leader of the informal group was Mily Balakirev ("Bal-*lah*-kee-ref," 1837–1910). He himself was not a talented composer. Instead, he had a different but important role: to persuade other Russian composers that they didn't need to imitate the German style in order to compose good concert music. He urged them to draw on the musical resources in traditional Russian music. Four composers, especially, listened to Balakirev's advice: Modest Mussorgsky, César Cui (1835–1918), Aleksandr Borodin ("*Bor-o-deen*," 1833–1887), and Nikolay Rimsky-Korsakov (1844–1908).

Most of the Russian Five had little formal training in music. Balakirev was self-taught. Cui, an engineer, was not a particularly successful composer.

Borodin was a celebrated chemist and an excellent composer. Had he been able to devote more time to composing, his name would be far better known in the music world than it is today. His Second Symphony is performed often, as are *In the Steppes of Central Asia* and String Quartet No. 2. His greatest work was an opera, *Prince Igor,* which was completed after his death by Rimsky-Korsakov and Alexander Glazounov (1865–1936).

Rimsky-Korsakov represents a phase of Romanticism called **Exoticism.** Like many other Romantic composers, he felt drawn by the mystery and splendor of Eastern cultures. For example, his best-known work is *Scheherazade,* a tone poem based on the Persian legends in *A Thousand and One Nights.* His "Song of India" from the opera *Sadko* and "Hymn to the Sun" from *Le Coq d'Or* (*The Golden Cockerel*) are other works that reveal his keen interest in Asia. Rimsky-Korsakov also wrote nationalistic music and worked avidly to advance the cause of Russian music.

Steppes are the treeless tracts of land in southeastern Europe and Asia.

For awhile Rimsky-Korsakov was a sailor in the Russian navy, during which time he visited many foreign countries.

MUSSORGSKY'S *BORIS GODUNOV*

Of the Russian Five, the most original was Mussorgsky. He was also perhaps the least skilled technically of the five, but he is the one whose music best represents Russian character and culture. His most significant work, his opera *Boris Godunov,* is derived from a play by the great Russian writer Aleksandr Pushkin. It does not follow a sequential plot, as do most operas. Pushkin's play contained twenty-four scenes. Mussorgsky adapted the libretto himself, using only seven scenes and changing them extensively.

The story is about Czar Boris, who ruled from 1598 to 1605. The plot assumes that Boris had the young Prince Dimitri murdered in order to gain the throne, and the murder is presumed to have taken place before the opera begins. Boris's feelings of guilt are central to the plot, and they finally lead to his death. There is a scheming Polish

Later research has indicated that Boris was innocent of the crime.

A SCENE FROM *BORIS GODUNOV*

Coronation scene from *Boris Godunov* (1870–1872)

GENRE: Opera   Bass singer, chorus, and orchestra

CD 5 Tracks `25` – `28`

9 minutes 17 seconds

Form: *A B A*

0:00	`25` 0:00	Gong and tuba sound two long, low notes; brasses play long chords.
	0:16	Woodwinds and strings play pizzicato a steady series of notes.
	0:50	After a silence, gong and brasses repeat opening music.
	1:00	Woodwinds and strings repeat steady series of notes.
	1:36	Trumpets herald Prince Shuisky, who sings:

> *Long live and reign, Czar Boris Feodorovich!*
>
> ***Chorus***   *Long live our great and noble Czar!*
>
> ***Shuisky***   *Praise him!*

1:56	`26` 0:00	Chorus sings melody based on Russian folk song.

Allegro moderato

> *As the sun lights all heavens*
> *So reigns our great and noble Czar Boris!*
> *Hail to Boris, lord of Russia,*
> *Hail to our sovereign Boris!*
> *Long live our Czar!*
> *Czar, our father, hail.*
> *We hail thee, our father,*
> *Our gracious Czar, thou our gracious Czar!*
> *Great and glorious will thy reign be,*
> *Father of Russia!*

0:54	Music changes often between two- and three-beat meter to fit text.

> *Sing, rejoice ye, people!*
> *Sing, rejoice ye, Russian people!*
> *Sing, rejoice ye, faithful people!*
> *Sing, rejoice ye, people!*
> *Come, exalt our Czar!*

1:16	Trumpet heralds the words of the Boyars.

> ***Boyars***   *Hail to thee Czar Boris Feodorovich!*
> *Long life to thee!*
> *As the sun lights all heaven,*
> *So reigns our great Czar, glory!*

1:28	Pattern of steady notes from opening of scene is played as chorus continues, with some phrases in imitation.

> *Czar, our father beloved!*
> *Long life to thee!*

2:08	Russian folk song melody returns.

> *As the sun lights all heaven,*
> *So reigns our great Czar, glory!*
> *Sing the glory of the Czar of Russia, glory!*
> *Glory! Glory!*

4:43	`27` 0:00	Music becomes quiet as horns hold a long note. Boris sings of his torment:

> *My soul is sad!*
> *Against my will strange tremors and evil premonitions oppress my spirit.*
> *O saint long dead,*

> *O thou my royal father!*
> *Thou see'st in heaven the faithful servant's tears!*
> *Look down on me and send a blessing from on high upon my kingdom!*
> *May I be true and merciful, as thou,*
> *And justify my people's praise.*

1:58   Boris decides to proceed with his coronation.

> *Now let us go and kneel in prayer before the tombs of Russia's kings.*
> *And then the people all shall feast.*
> *Come, ev'ryone from nobleman to serf;*
> *All shall find room, all find an honored welcome!*

2:36   After a flurry of sound played by orchestra, sopranos sing.

> *Long live and reign our great and noble Czar!*

7:29 28 0:00   Church bells ring freely.

0:07   Opening music returns. Sections of chorus sing "Thou our gracious Czar!" in imitation.

> *Long life to thee, Czar Boris Feodorovich!*
> *Hail to thee!*
> *As the sun lights all heaven,*
> *So reigns our great Czar of Russia,*
> *Glory and long may he reign!*

1:00   Chorus vigorously sings in three-beat meter as low brasses play in two-beat meter.

> *Glory! Glory! Glory!*

1:46   "Coronation Scene" concludes after chorus sings a final "Glory" and two closing chords played by orchestra.

 An interactive Active Listening Guide can be downloaded from the online Resource Center for *Music Listening Today*, 4th Edition.

princess, who with an ambitious pretender to the throne seeks to capture the Kremlin, the huge Moscow fortress from which the czars ruled.

The scene of Boris's death is one of the most moving in opera. The original final scene has a simpleton beggar alone on the stage, having been tricked out of his most valued coin by a gang of ruffians. He seems to symbolize that the real losers are the Russian people, who suffer from the greed and ambition of those who want to be czar.

The music reveals Mussorgsky's innate musicianship and his flair for the dramatic. The prologue features the Russian people. Afraid for their future after the death of the czar, they pray for a ruler for their land. To encourage a public clamor for himself, Boris sends one of his lieutenants (Prince Shuisky) to tell the crowd that he still refuses to become czar. A chorus of religious pilgrims approaches and sings before the curtain falls.

The coronation scene, which follows the prologue, is one of the best-known scenes in the operatic repertoire. It takes place in a courtyard in the Kremlin; the Cathedrals of the Assumption, Annunciation, and the Archangel flank the stage.

In several ways Mussorgsky was ahead of his time, musically speaking. Twice in the coronation scene a scale containing only whole steps is implied. The scale (called the **whole-tone scale**) would be used quite often twenty-five years later in the music of Impressionistic composers. In addition, there are places in the coronation scene in which two-beat against three-beat meter is implied. Again, such combination of meters (called **polymeters**) would become much more common in the twentieth century. At several places in the orchestral portions of the coronation scene, Mussorgsky has adjacent chords harmonically as far apart as possible. For example, a C major chord is followed by one built on F-sharp. Again, this portends the breaking away from tonal harmony by twentieth-century composers.

A generation later, Debussy, who first heard Mussorgsky's music while in Russia, used whole-tone scales in his music.

Modest Mussorgsky

ArenaPal/Topham/The Image Works

BEST-KNOWN WORKS

opera:
- *Boris Godunov*
- *Khovanschina*

orchestra:
- *A Night on Bald Mountain*

piano:
- *Pictures at an Exhibition*

During his lifetime **Modest Mussorgsky** (1839–1881) was considered the least accomplished and important of the Russian Five. Today, because of his innovative style and the rugged Russian quality of his music, he is considered the greatest of the five.

He was born into a prosperous landowning family. He showed much talent at the piano at an early age, but he refused to practice and did not seem headed toward a musical career. Instead, he entered a military academy. Soon, he began drinking heavily, but his skill at the piano and good singing voice made him popular at parties. While still in the military, he met Borodin and Balakirev. They sparked his interest in composing, and he soon left the army.

Mussorgsky's musical genius was not recognized at the time, partly because of his own personality. First, there was the heavy drinking and occasional bizarre behavior in public. His drinking led to delirium tremens and his death at the age of forty-two. Second, he was undisciplined about his work and rarely finished anything he started. Much of his music was finished and revised by Rimsky-Korsakov, and the twentieth-century Russian composer Dmitri Shostakovich (1906–1975) revised his opera *Boris Godunov.*

The coronation scene from *Boris Godunov* has several notable features:

- The music has a virile, masculine quality. It exudes the rugged, hardy character that one associates with the peasantry of Russia at the beginning of the seventeenth century. Mussorgsky's admiration for the vigor of the Russian people has found its way into his music.

- The words, music, and drama fit together very effectively. Boris's solo is expressive and flexible. It suggests an aria and recitative in which the union of words and music fits perfectly. His prayer sounds somewhat like a chant, which is appropriate because chant is a feature of Russian Orthodox worship.

- The resonant sound of Boris's bass voice gives the impression of a mighty man, the leader of all Russia, a man who can bend steel with his bare hands.

- The scene is filled with color, both visually and musically. A coronation is an impressive event to see.

Mussorgsky's innovations and fresh, nationalistic approach were almost too much for the audience in 1872; even his friends and admirers had trouble understanding *Boris Godunov.* It was rejected twice for performance by the Imperial Opera. Only after two revisions and a performance of three of its scenes at a benefit concert was all of *Boris Godunov* performed.

A listener's score for the coronation scene from Mussorgsky's *Boris Godunov* is available for downloading.

BOHEMIA

There is no country of Bohemia today, although at one time it was a distinct area of central Europe with its own language and cultural identity. Today most of it lies in the Czech Republic. This rather small area produced two important composers who promoted its music: Antonín Dvořák and Bedřich Smetana. Throughout most of the nineteenth century, Bohemia was part of the Austrian empire, so the style of Dvořák and Smetana does not differ all that much from the prevailing Romantic style of the time. But its nationalism is expressed in the use of folk melodies and native subject matter.

SMETANA'S *MOLDAU*

The Moldau is the best known of Smetana's series of tone poems called *Má vlast*. The program that Smetana placed in the score reads:

> *Two springs pour forth in the shade of the Bohemian forest, one warm and gushing, the other cold and peaceful. Coursing through Bohemia's valleys, it grows into a mighty*

BEDŘICH SMETANA
The Moldau from *Má vlast* (1874)

GENRE: Tone poem   Orchestra

CD 5 Tracks 29 – 33

12 minutes 43 seconds

0:00	29	0:00	*Source of river, two springs:* Rippling sounds in flutes, then clarinets.
1:07	30	0:00	*River theme:* Strings play flowing melody.

1:53		*The hunt:* Brasses play fanfare figures.
4:06	31 0:00	*Wedding dance:* Strings and woodwinds play happy dance music.

6:00	32 0:00	*Nightfall and water nymphs in moonlight:* Slow, high notes in violins with rippling sounds in flutes.

2:39	*River theme:* Violins
3:30	*St. John's Rapids:* Brasses and timpani play turbulent music.
4:45	*River theme:* Orchestra plays theme faster and louder.
11:44 33 0:00	*Historic castles:* Brasses play choralelike melody.

0:19	*River fades away:* Long decrescendo depicts river fading into distance far beyond poet's gaze.
1:32	*The Moldau* concludes with two forceful chords.

 An interactive Active Listening Guide can be downloaded from the online
Resource Center for *Music Listening Today, 4th Edition.*

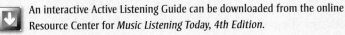

Mary Evans Picture Library/The Image Works

Bedřich Smetana

BEST-KNOWN WORKS

opera:
- *The Bartered Bride*

orchestra:
- *Má vlast (My Fatherland)*, which includes *The Moldau*

Bedřich Smetana (1824–1884) was born in a small town in Bohemia, the seventh child of a music-loving brewer. Family activities included playing string quartets at home. Smetana studied for a while in Prague, served as music master for a rich family, and later became pianist for Kaiser Ferdinand, who had abdicated the German throne and was living in Prague. After about ten years, Smetana moved to Gothenburg, Sweden. He earned a good living there, but the climate was bad for his wife's failing health, so he moved back to Prague several years later.

Like Beethoven, Smetana became deaf toward the end of his life. Some of his best compositions were written when he was deaf.

Smetana once said that he simply could not write absolute music. Perhaps his feelings of nationalism were too strong to allow him to think of music in absolute terms.

stream. Through thick woods it flows as the gay sounds of the hunt and the notes of the hunter's horn are heard ever closer. It flows through grass-grown pastures and lowlands where a wedding feast is being celebrated with song and dance. At night, wood and water nymphs revel in its sparkling waves. Reflected on its surface are fortresses and castles—witnesses of bygone days of knightly splendor and the vanished glory of martial times.

The stream races through the St. John's Rapids, "finally flowing on in majestic peace toward Prague and welcomed by historic Vyšehrad," the legendary castle of ancient Bohemian kings. "Then it vanishes far beyond the poet's gaze."

OTHER NATIONALISTIC COMPOSERS

Norway

Edvard Grieg (1843–1907) was the leading proponent of Scandinavian music. Among his well-known works are the *Peer Gynt Suites*, which were originally composed as incidental music for Henrik Ibsen's play. He also wrote a melodious piano concerto, as well as many shorter piano pieces and chamber works.

Finland

Jean Sibelius ("Yon Si-*bay*-lee-us," 1865–1957) was Finland's most famous composer. Most of his more nationalistic music was composed early in his career. One of the themes from his tone poem *Finlandia* became the national anthem of Finland. He also used native themes as the basis for program works such as *The Swan of Tuonela* and *Pohjola's Daughter*. The themes in many of his symphonies often have a folklike quality, even if they are not actually folk melodies.

England

The music of Edward Elgar (1857–1934) strikes a consonant note in the hearts of English audiences. Although his music is not very different from that of other Romantic composers, nor is it particularly nationalistic, it possesses a distinctively English quality. Elgar is the composer of *Pomp and Circumstance*, the stately march that is played at so many graduations. His best-known work is *Enigma Variations* for orchestra. Elgar wrote on the score the initials of the friend or family member who is associated with each particular variation. Guessing that person's identity becomes the puzzle or enigma. Fortunately, listeners today can enjoy the beauty of the music without the need to figure out who is being represented.

Several English composers in the early part of the twentieth century are also nationalistic. The most important of these is Ralph Vaughan Williams (1872–1958). He helped revive interest in English folk music and also contributed to the improvement in the music of the Church of England. He selected texts for his many vocal works from England's finest poets and used themes from earlier English composers in such works as Fantasia on a Theme by Tallis. Other important works of Vaughan Williams include Symphony No. 2 ("The London Symphony") and Fantasia on "Greensleeves."

His family name is *Vaughan Williams*, not just *Williams*.

Italy

Italian nationalism in the nineteenth century was largely confined to opera. Nationalism in instrumental works did not become evident until the twentieth century in the music of Ottorino Respighi ("Res-*pee*-gee," 1879–1936). His *Pines of Rome* and *Fountains of Rome* are definitely nationalistic. His style is strongly Romantic, even if the composition dates from the twentieth century.

Verdi's role in Italian nationalism is discussed in Chapter 26.

Spain

Spanish nationalism is found in the music of Isaac Albeniz (1860–1909), Enrique Granados (1867–1916), and Manuel de Falla ("*Fi*-ya," 1876–1946). Each of these composers exploited the rhythms of Spanish dance and the colorful sounds of its music. Although their careers extended into the twentieth century, their music is essentially Romantic in character.

France

As the Romantic era progressed, French composers began to develop a style that was different from the prevailing German style. A truly distinct French style did not appear, however, until the Impressionistic music of Debussy and Ravel, which is presented in Chapter 29.

United States

Nationalistic music was slow to develop in the United States. Very little existed prior to 1900, but from the 1930s through the 1950s such composers as Samuel Barber, Howard Hanson, William Schuman, and especially Aaron Copland had become associated with music's nationalistc movement.

MAIN POINTS OF THIS CHAPTER

1. Nationalism refers to the deliberate, conscious attempt by a composer to create a work that is characteristic of a particular country or region. It is achieved by the use of folk songs, dance rhythms, songs about a national hero or event, musical descriptions of a country, and so forth.

2. Part of the impetus for nationalism in the nineteenth century was the desire to break away from the prevailing German-Austrian style that had dominated music for so many years. To indicate their feelings, some composers wrote directions in their native language instead of the traditional Italian.

3. A group of largely self-taught composers emerged in Russia, which was to become known as "The Russian Five." The least technically skilled among them was Mussorgsky, whose opera *Boris Godunov* is still widely performed. He was ahead of his time in his use of whole tone scales and polymeters.

4. Nationalism did not appear in Spain, Italy, or the United States until the twentieth century.

5. A phase of nationalism known as exoticism was motivated by an attraction to cultures in India and the Middle East.

FEATURES TO LISTEN FOR

1. In Mussorgsky's "Coronation Scene":
   - How the opening chords alternate between tonal centers that are harmonically very far apart
   - How the opening section gradually twice builds from low, slow notes to higher, rapidly moving notes
   - The meter changes between two-beat and three-beat when the chorus sings "Sing, rejoice ye people"
   - The quality of the bass voice when Boris sings his solo
2. In Smetana's *Moldau*:
   - How well the opening section gives the impression of flowing water starting as a small stream and then becoming a mighty river
   - How well the music fits with the various scenes

Features of Romantic Music

Melodies	Often flowing and "warm"
Rhythm	Metrical but often with slight deviations in steadiness of beat
Texture	Homophonic texture predominates
Harmony	Rich and full sounding, with many chromatic alterations and frequent modulations
Dynamic levels	Very soft to very loud
	Often change, with an undulating quality
Performance media	Large orchestra "Golden Age of the Piano"
Forms	Most of the forms of the Classical period still used, but followed much more freely
Genres	Symphony Chamber music Art songs (*Lieder*) Character pieces for piano Program music Ballet music Nationalistic music Opera
Other features	Sometimes intensely personal and emotional Many virtuoso works Some Impressionistic works

PART VI

Twentieth-Century Music

	1900	1925
Historical Events	First airplane ● (1903)	Russian Revolution ● (1917)　　Great Depression (1929–c. 19[...] World War I (1914–18) ● Panama Canal finished (1914)
Visual Arts	● Munch, *The Scream* (1893) Kandinsky's work (1896–1944) Picasso, *Three Musicians* ● (1921) Rivera's work (1921–1957) Lipchitz's work (1912–1973)	Mondrian's Cubism (1919–1944) Braque's work (1891–196[...]
Literature and Theater		Kafka's work (1915–1924) Joyce's work (1882–1941)
Philosophy and Science	Freud, key works (1899–1939) B. Russell's work (1905–1970) Einstein's theories (1905–1940s)	
Music	Mahler (1860–1911) Berg's work (1907–1935) Sibelius's work (1899–1957) Stravinsky, *Rite of Spring* (top) ▲ (1913) Rachmaninoff (1873–1943) Webern's work (1904–1945) Schoenberg's work (1899–1951) Prokofiev's work (1891–1953) Bartok's work (1903–1945) Villa-Lobos's work (1920–1959) Shostakovich's work (1926–1975) ◆ Varèse's work (1883–1965) Hindemith's work (1895–196[...]	Rodrigo's work (1923–1999 Britten's work (1930–1976

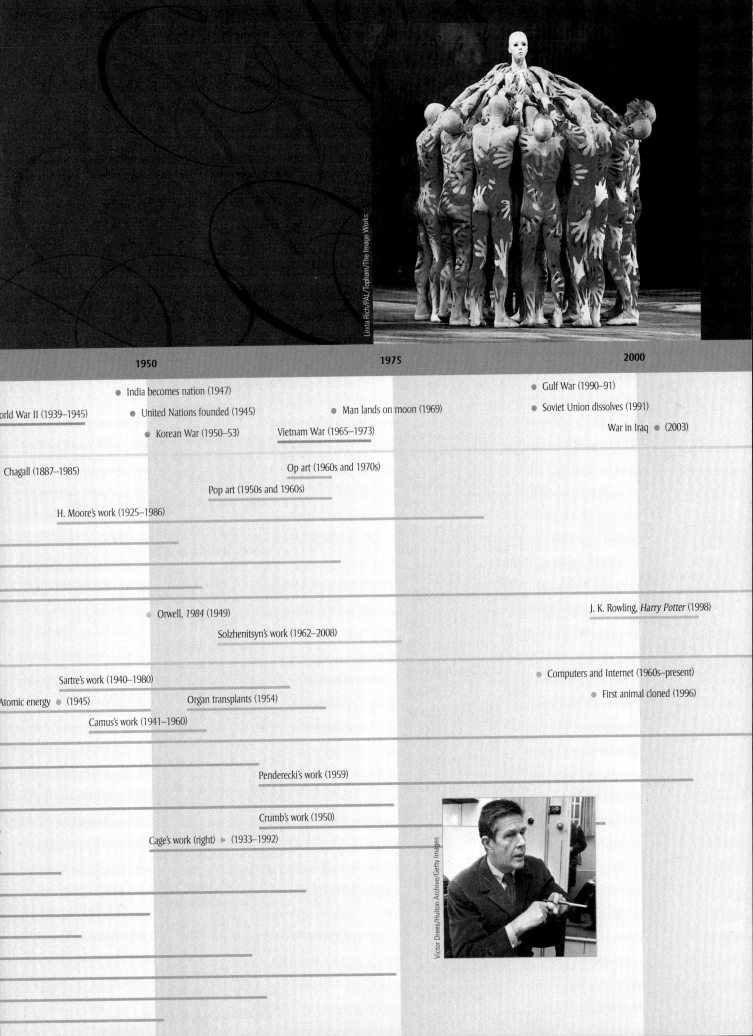

Linda Rich/PAL/Topham/The Image Works

1950　　　　　　　　　　1975　　　　　　　　　　2000

- India becomes nation (1947)　　　　　　　　　　● Gulf War (1990–91)
World War II (1939–1945)　● United Nations founded (1945)　● Man lands on moon (1969)　● Soviet Union dissolves (1991)
- Korean War (1950–53)　Vietnam War (1965–1973)　War in Iraq ● (2003)

Chagall (1887–1985)　　　　　　　Op art (1960s and 1970s)
　　　　　　　　Pop art (1950s and 1960s)
　H. Moore's work (1925–1986)

● Orwell, *1984* (1949)　　　　　　J. K. Rowling, *Harry Potter* (1998)
　　Solzhenitsyn's work (1962–2008)

Sartre's work (1940–1980)　　　　● Computers and Internet (1960s–present)
Atomic energy ● (1945)　Organ transplants (1954)　● First animal cloned (1996)
　Camus's work (1941–1960)

Penderecki's work (1959)

Crumb's work (1950)

Cage's work (right) ▶ (1933–1992)

Victor Drees/Hulton Archive/Getty Images

29 Impressionism *and* Post-Romanticism

The early years of the twentieth century witnessed two types of music that had their roots in the nineteenth century. Impressionism focused on the subtle and fleeting inner impressions of an outer world. It represented a substantial change from the prevailing German/Austrian style. On the other hand, Post-Romanticism was an attempt to pump life into Romanticism by doing more—making works longer and for larger groups. Both Impressionistic and Post-Romantic composers were successful in terms of producing a number of works that are well worth knowing.

CHARACTERISTICS OF IMPRESSIONISM

Impressionism was an artistic viewpoint in which poets, painters, and composers tried to capture something incomplete, of the moment, a sensation. It is based on the belief that experiences in life are largely impressions rather than detailed observations. To achieve this, Impressionists stressed informality and rarely carried a moral or message. They were also fond of nature and commonplace scenes—sunsets, people in casual poses, water lilies in a pond, and the like.

Several Impressionistic painters, for example, tried to catch the atmosphere of a particular time and place by making rough sketches at two or three different times during the day, because the impression of a scene changed with different lighting. The painting would often be finished in the studio. They also avoided hard outlines and used subtle blending of primary colors.

Some painters used a technique called *pointillism* in which dots of paint are placed close together. Seen up close, the picture looks like a newspaper photo when viewed through a magnifying glass; when viewed from a short distance, however, the dots appear to blend.

In his painting of the Rouen Cathedral, Monet (see next page) was not really trying to represent the cathedral. He did not try to show the entire front of the building or to represent the detail of its stonework. Rather, in a manner characteristic of Impressionistic painters, he used its lines and shapes as objects for the interplay of light, shadow, and color. From his vantage point in a window opposite the church, Monet painted at least thirty identical versions of this scene at different times of day and under varying weather conditions.

Impressionistic poetry and drama were highly symbolic. The writers tried to capture fleeting moments by presenting a sequence of images in words. They intentionally kept their poems in an inconclusive and fragmented condition, which left the meaning up to the reader. Impressionistic writer Maurice Maeterlinck wrote in one of his essays, "Beneath all human thoughts . . . there lies the vast ocean of the Unconscious. All that we know, think, feel, see, and will are but bubbles on the surface of this vast sea."

In one sense, Impressionism represented French nationalism, although it was more of a cultural nationalism than the usual political type. Many works by Impressionistic composers are programmatic. What makes Impressionistic music different from most other program music is that the non-musical associations are with impressions, not stories or characters.

The Impressionistic movement was unique in the extent to which writers, artists, and musicians knew one another and often worked together. And they held similar points of view about the arts. The painter wanted to capture a fleeting moment on canvas, the

Impressionism probably owes its name to painter Claude Monet, who in 1874 exhibited a picture called *Impression—Sunrise.* Critics took up the term to make fun of the new movement.

A picture that you see on a website is made up of thousands of tiny dots called *pixels.*

Rouen Cathedral in Full Sunlight: Harmony in Blue and Gold, 1894, Monet, Claude (1840–1926)/Musée d'Orsay, Paris, France, Lauros/Giraudon/The Bridgeman Art Library

MONET'S IMPRESSIONIST PAINTING of Rouen Cathedral

author in the printed and spoken word, and the composer in the transitory world of musical sounds. These artists shared a fondness for subtle nuances of light and shadow, vague contours, and veiled thoughts.

What to Listen For in Impressionistic Music

- A generally lighter timbre and tone than heard in the music of Brahms and Wagner. The size of the orchestra is somewhat smaller. The harp and flute are more prominent, and less use is made of brass instruments.

- Subtle tonal colors, including chords with notes added simply because the composer wanted that particular sonority. The C E G chord sometimes is a C E G A chord.

- Harmonies with a less functional role in favor of a more tonally colorful role. Sometimes chords move in parallel motion, something that was not allowed in traditional tonal harmony.

- More subtle and blurred rhythm. The metrical pattern is often not easily felt.

- A weaker tonal center, especially when a whole-tone scale is used.

- Limited use of the forms developed in the Classical period and little development of themes. Many works are rather short and programmatic.

- Sensual, somewhat subtle music that does not attempt to project any messages. Rather, expect sensitive, subtle musical works that are simply to be enjoyed.

All steps in a whole-tone scale are equidistant, so it has no single tonal center.

Debussy considered the development of themes to be "musical mathematics."

Impressionism partly bridged the change from the Romantic style of the nineteenth century to the music of the twentieth century. It did not leave all its Romantic tendencies behind. Rather, it exemplified the French love of nuance and color and, in so doing, pointed the way toward the future.

DEBUSSY'S "CLAIR DE LUNE"

"Clair de lune" ("Moonlight") is one of Debussy's best-known compositions. It is part of his *Suite bergamasque* for piano but is usually heard today as a separate piece. It has also been transcribed for orchestra.

CLAUDE DEBUSSY
"Clair de lune" (1890; rev. 1905)

GENRE: Character piece Piano

CD 2 Tracks [20] – [22]

5 minutes 1 second

Form: *A B A*

0:00   [20]   0:00   Opening section (A) begins softly with a gradually descending melody.

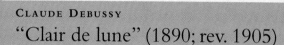

0:35   A melody repeated.

1:25   Music becomes somewhat louder and more animated.

2:02   [21]   0:00   Contrasting section (B) begins softly.

0:23   B melody repeated an octave higher as music grows more intense.

0:42   B melody repeated quietly.

3:13   [22]   0:00   Opening melody (A) returns very softly.

0:37   Phrases of A melody repeated several times.

1:14   Music gradually fades as chords are played in harplike manner.

1:49   "Clair de lune" concludes very quietly.

An interactive Active Listening Guide can be downloaded from the online Resource Center for *Music Listening Today*, 4th Edition.

The opening melody has several places in which the last note of one measure is tied to the first note of the next measure. (In music a **tie** is a curved line connecting two notes of the same pitch so that they sound as one long note.) The effect is to blur the meter of the music at those points. At other points he calls for two equal notes to the beat when the rest of the work uses three. At another place he even specifies *tempo rubato*, indicating rhythmic flexibility.

The skeleton of the melody—its basic notes—is quite simple. It is a descending major scale, to which Debussy merely adds a few alternating notes, almost as decoration. It certainly is not the solid kind of melody that Bach and Beethoven favored! Debussy adds other effects, such as rolling out the notes of some of the chords in a harplike manner instead of having them sounded together, which also tends to obscure the rhythm. At other places he doubles notes of the melody an octave higher, which gives the music a more open, almost haunting effect.

The overall effect is luscious and romantic.

RAVEL'S *DAPHNIS AND CHLOÉ*, SUITE NO. 2

About 1910 Maurice Ravel composed a ballet for the famous impresario of Ballet Russe, Sergei Diaghilev, about whom more will be said in Chapter 32. The story concerns a shepherd, Daphnis, and his love for the beautiful Chloé. Today the ballet's music is most often heard in the form of two suites. Suite No. 2 contains some of Ravel's most Impressionistic music, especially the opening section called "Lever du jour" ("Daybreak"). The woodwinds and then the strings provide a rich accompaniment of rippling notes. One can almost sense the glow of the sunrise in the melody. The recording includes a part for chorus in which the singers vocalize on a neutral syllable.

MAURICE RAVEL
Daphnis and Chloé, Suite No. 2,
"Lever du jour" ("Daybreak") (1910)

GENRE: Ballet music   Orchestra

CD 5 Tracks 34 – 36

5 minutes 39 seconds

0:00	34 0:00	Woodwinds and harps play rippling figures over slow notes in low strings.
	0:29	More instruments join in as music begins long crescendo.
	0:56	Music reaches climactic point, then begins gradual decrescendo.
1:15	35 0:00	Violas and clarinet play rich-sounding melody.

	0:25	Flute plays brief contrasting figure; then melody resumes in strings.
	0:45	Clarinet plays brief contrasting figure; then melody resumes.
	1:11	Violins continue melody at higher pitch level; harp and woodwinds take up rippling figures, and chorus enters.
	1:36	Chorus continues singing "Ah" as violins continue melody.
	1:55	Music reaches another climactic point and then begins to grow softer.
	2:06	The tempo becomes faster and more dancelike and soon reaches another climactic point.
4:03	36 0:00	Melody begins in lower strings as rippling figures return.
	0:33	Climactic point by orchestra and chorus; then music grows softer.
	1:04	Oboe quietly repeats the same melodic figure several times.
	1:28	Clarinet plays some of the figure in augmentation.
	1:36	The "Daybreak" part of Suite No. 2 concludes quietly.

An interactive Active Listening Guide can be downloaded from the online Resource Center for *Music Listening Today, 4th Edition.*

LISTENING GUIDE

Debussy, Ravel, & Rachmaninoff

CLAUDE DEBUSSY

MAURICE RAVEL

SERGEI RACHMANINOFF

Claude Debussy ("Deb-yew-*see*," 1862–1918) was born in a small town near Paris. At the age of eleven, he entered the Paris Conservatory, where he often revolted against the rules of composition his professors tried to teach him. When he was twenty-two, he won the Prix de Rome, which included study in Italy. Although he did go to Rome, he much preferred the bustle and gaiety of Paris. He also valued the company of painters and writers.

Debussy's early admiration for Wagner faded after a second visit to Bayreuth in 1889, and he developed a dislike for things Germanic. He wrote a number of articles about music, which offered him a chance to vent his feelings. Regarding Wagner, he wrote, "The French forget too easily the qualities of clarity and elegance peculiar to themselves and allow themselves to be influenced by the tedious and ponderous Teuton." He claimed that "beauty must appeal to the senses, must provide us with immediate enjoyment."

The fact that **Maurice Ravel** (1875–1937) followed Debussy both chronologically and stylistically has tended to place him in the background despite his many fine compositions. He was born into the family of a mining engineer who had once aspired to be a musician himself. Ravel studied at the Paris Conservatory and, though highly qualified for the award, was four times passed over for the Prix de Rome. The arbitrary nature of these decisions caused a public furor that eventually led to the resignation of the Conservatory's director.

A French patriot, Ravel drove an ambulance along the front lines during World War I. After the war he was recognized as France's greatest composer. He died at the age of sixty while undergoing surgery for a rare brain disease that had seriously affected his speech and motor coordination.

One of his best-known works, and certainly the most unusual, is the hypnotic *Bolero*, in which the same melody and rhythm pattern continue throughout the seventeen minutes of the work.

Sergei Rachmaninoff (1873–1943) was born in northwestern Russia. His parents were both amateur pianists, and his mother was his first teacher. Later he studied at the conservatory in St. Petersburg and then Moscow. In his younger days, he revealed much talent, but he tended to be lazy and spent too much time skating.

He was equally gifted as a composer and pianist, both of which he emphasized at various times in his life. He first toured the United States in 1909, which led to a contract with Edison Records and then RCA Victor. He emigrated to America after the Communist revolution in 1917, but remained homesick for his native land, and felt a loss of inspiration after that time. Nevertheless, he completed his *Rhapsody on a Theme of Paganini* and Symphony No. 3 while in America. He become ill on a concert tour in 1943, and was diagnosed with lung cancer. He died shortly thereafter.

BEST-KNOWN WORKS OF DEBUSSY

opera:
- *Pelléas et Mélisande*

orchestra:
- *La Mer*
- *Nocturnes*
- *Prelude to the Afternoon of a Faun*

piano:
- *Images*, Sets 1 and 2
- *Suite bergamasque*

BEST-KNOWN WORKS OF RAVEL

orchestra:
- *Bolero*
- *Daphnis et Chloé*, Suite No. 2
- *Ma Mère l'Oye* (Mother Goose)

piano:
- *Gaspard de la nuit*
- *Le tombeau de Couperin*

BEST-KNOWN WORKS OF RACHMANINOFF

piano:
- Preludes
- Concertos Nos. 2 and 3

orchestra:
- Symphonies Nos. 2 and 3
- *Vocalise* for Soprano
- *Isle of the Dead*

POST-ROMANTICISM

The Romantic outlook did not go quietly into the night. In fact, elements of it are still found in music being written today—and probably always will be. Some composers who lived near the end of the nineteenth century and into the twentieth continued the Romantic tradition by composing works that were more massive and extensive than those of their predecessors.

RACHMANINOFF'S *RHAPSODY ON A THEME OF PAGANINI*

Rhapsody on a Theme of Paganini is one of the best loved of Sergei Rachmaninoff's compositions. It is based on a theme written by the legendary nineteenth-century violin virtuoso Niccolò Paganini. The work opens with a short introduction and one variation before the theme is presented by the violins. It is essentially a simple melody: The same melodic and rhythm pattern is heard on the tonic or home chord, then the dominant chord, then a return to the tonic, and two concluding notes on the dominant. That portion of the theme is repeated before the second half of the theme appears. This half maintains nearly the same melodic pattern and the same rhythmic ideas presented in sequence.

At first, the variations are modest in scope. The piano plays decorative versions of the theme that little by little move farther from it. Variation 7 combines the theme played by the low strings and the Dies irae theme played slowly by the piano. Variation 10 again opens with the Dies irae played by the piano, which is then taken up by the orchestra.

The following Listening Guide and music on the ancillary CD begin with Variation 18 and go to the conclusion of the work.

For a number of reasons, this work represents post-Romanticism well. First, it was composed in 1934, well after the Romantic style had been predominant. Second, the theme is by Paganini, who in some ways was the quintessential Romantic musician. Third, the work includes a quotation of the Dies irae theme, which is associated with death and mystery—favorite topics of Romanticists. Fourth, it is basically a rhapsody containing a free expression of feelings, even though it is in the form of a theme and variations.

Gustav Mahler and Anton Bruckner (1824–1896), an earlier Romantic composer, both exhibit one of the traits of Romanticism: a tendency toward musical elephantiasis. Mahler's Third Symphony holds the dubious distinction of being the longest ever written. It takes about one hour and thirty-four minutes, with the first movement alone requiring nearly forty-five minutes to perform. His Eighth Symphony is sometimes called the "Symphony of a Thousand" because it requires so many people to perform it: a huge orchestra, additional brass, and male, female, and children's choirs. Mahler is nevertheless able to handle these musical resources with skill and discretion.

Rhapsody on a Theme of Paganini (1934)

GENRE: Rhapsody   Piano and orchestra

CD 5 Tracks 37 – 41

7 minutes 52 seconds

Form: Theme and Variations

0:00	37	0:00	Theme played by violins.
	38	0:00	*Variation 18:* Piano plays sensuous melody based on inversion of theme.

		0:44	Orchestra plays theme and then repeats it.
		2:15	Piano plays fragments of theme as variation winds down.
		2:40	*Variation 19:* Quick tempo, with fast notes in piano that outline theme.
3:12	39	0:00	*Variation 20:* Built around two-note figure taken from theme; violins accompany with fast, running notes.
		0:33	*Variation 21:* Features piano melody built around notes of chords.
4:11	40	0:00	*Variation 22:* Soft and marchlike.
		0:27	Music becomes smoother and louder.
		0:39	Piano plays many fast notes.
		0:54	*Variation 23:* Piano and orchestra exchange fragments of theme.
		1:17	Short piano cadenza.
		1:35	*Variation 24:* Piano softly plays fragments of theme. Tempo increases as theme is played by woodwinds and violins.
		1:46	Virtuoso passages in piano.
6:36	41	0:00	*Coda:* Piano plays fast notes based on theme.
		0:45	Dies irae played by brasses.
		1:08	Work concludes somewhat quietly with two short chords.

 An interactive Active Listening Guide can be downloaded from the online
Resource Center for *Music Listening Today, 4th Edition.*

MAIN POINTS OF THIS CHAPTER

1. The basic outlook of Impressionism (1890–1920) was that experiences in life are based more on impressions than on detailed observations. Impressionistic artists and composers, who were mostly French, believed that the arts should appeal more to the senses than the intellect. Subtle shadings of color and timbre were favored in both art and music.

2. Impressionistic music differed from the prevailing German/Austrian style in several ways:
   - Use of whole tone scales
   - Smaller orchestra; did not involve the brasses as much
   - Subtle, flexible rhythms
   - Chords that contain added notes
   - Limited development of themes
   - More subtle sound
3. Post-Romanticism expanded on the Romantic outlook of the nineteenth century. Many of its works are larger in scope and longer than those in the Romantic period.

FEATURES TO LISTEN FOR

1. Debussy's "Clair de lune":
   - The descending pitches of the A melody
   - The subtle nature of the rhythm, especially the blurring of the meter in the A melody
   - The delicate, sensitive nature of the music
2. Ravel's "Daybreak" ("Lever du jour") from *Daphnis and Chloé*:
   - How the idea of daybreak is established at the beginning
   - The long, extended crescendos and decrescendos
3. Rachmaninoff's *Variations on a Theme of Paganini*:
   - The changes in the theme in each of the seven variations in the excerpt
   - The appearance of the "Dies irae" near the end of the work

30 Music *in the* Twentieth Century

Twentieth-century music may at times be confusing and difficult to understand, but dull it is not. It's as fascinating and challenging as twentieth-century life was.

THE TREMENDOUS AND TUMULTUOUS CENTURY

The twentieth century was not for the faint of heart, either socially or artistically. It witnessed two world wars and numerous lesser conflicts, a great economic depression and general prosperity, and thousands of discoveries and inventions ranging from organ transplants to computers to exploration in space.

Most of these changes had both benefits and liabilities. For example, as the peoples of the world seemed to be drawing closer together, at the same time they seemed to be becoming more aware of their differences, and in many regions various groups of people worked to assert their particular identities.

Nor did the marvels of technological progress make people any happier. Information is passed along in milliseconds to almost any place in the world, but the quality of what is said often is no better than what hundreds of years ago was written with a quill pen and delivered by hand. Astronauts traveled into space, but they returned to Earth and its many problems.

As was pointed out in Chapter 1, there is a big difference between just hearing music and really listening to it.

As the twenty-first century begins, the pervasive influence of technology grows stronger in many areas of life. It has had a major impact on the amount and type of music people hear, as well as how they think about music. It has also played a very important role in the production and reproduction of music. But, again, it has had both positive and negative results. People today hear much more music than ever before, but they seem to listen to it less and less carefully.

Diverse and complex factors also existed in twentieth-century concert music. It seems to be divided into numerous camps. Two have already been covered in the previous chapter: Impressionism and Post-Romanticism. Others include: Neoclassicism, Serialism, Primitivism, Expressionism, and Minimalism. Other types are folkloric, experimental, avant garde, and what is considered mainstream. Each of these types represents a view about music and played a role in the development of twentieth-century music.

If twentieth-century music is marked by diversity, dramatic change, and expansion, those same qualities mean that it is also musically very rich. For instance, some twentieth-century music:

- Expanded musical elements in earlier music
- Was influenced by new sources of music, such as Africa and Asia
- Was the result of sophisticated intellectual efforts
- Was a revival of musical practices that were in fashion several centuries earlier
- Was a repudiation of nineteenth-century music
- Probed new and largely untested ways of creating musical works

TWENTIETH-CENTURY ART

For much of history, artists played the role that cameras do today. That is, they tried to create an accurate rendition of a person or a scene. But with the invention of photography in the nineteenth century, and especially with its widespread use in the twentieth, the goal of artists changed. Instead of producing images of what was seen, artists became more interested in interpreting what they saw and creating visual objects that are of interest solely for their visual properties. Their use of shape and color became somewhat like composers' use of sounds in music. This change led to a wide variety of types of artworks.

As the twentieth century saw the return to certain techniques used in musical compositions written in earlier centuries, painters also revisited techniques of artists centuries earlier. Pablo Picasso's *Three Musicians* is a type of Cubism called "collage Cubism," in which the impression is given that the portions of the painting are pasted up like pieces of paper (which is what the word *collage* means in French). The separate pieces are fitted together firmly as little architectural blocks. More than pattern concerned Picasso in *Three Musicians*, however. He tried to project the image of musicians as traditional figures of the comedy stage. Their humanness is sensed behind the screen of costumes and masks.

Picasso, Pablo, *Three Musicians*. Fontainebleau, summer 1921. Oil on canvas, 6'7" × 7'3 3/4" (200.7 × 222.9 cm). The Museum of Modern Art, New York. Mrs. Simon Guggenheim Fund. Photograph © 2002 The Museum of Modern Art, New York. Estate of Pablo Picasso/Artists Rights Society (ARS) New York/Art Resource, Inc.

THREE MUSICIANS by Pablo Picasso, 1921. The twentieth century no longer saw the grandiose works of art and music that marked the Romantic period. Instead, smaller and more playful works such as those of Picasso in art and Stravinsky in his Neoclassical compositions replaced them.

Piet Mondrian developed a completely nonrepresentational, abstract style. He restricted himself to horizontals and verticals and a few simple colors with no shading. In this way it would be virtually impossible to paint a picture of something. In spite of these limitations, Mondrian succeeded in creating lively, attractive paintings. At first glance it may look easy to imitate Mondrian's style successfully, but the limitations actually make it very difficult.

An important current in twentieth-century painting was fantasy. Many painters became interested in "the inner eye"—the introspective look at imagination and feeling. Such a view seems to be the artistic counterpart to Freudian psychology and its interest in dreams and the subconscious. Marc Chagall appeared never to lose the memories and dreams of his childhood in a Jewish community in Russia. His painting *Snowing* expresses some of that personal mystery and fantasy. Does it contain shades of the highly successful Broadway musical *Fiddler on the Roof?*

DESCRIBING TWENTIETH-CENTURY MUSIC

There is an old saying about "not being able to see the forest for the trees."

With the Baroque, Classical, and Romantic periods, it is possible to describe their main intellectual and artistic features. That is a much more difficult task with twentieth-century music. Perhaps part of the problem is the lack of perspective; we are simply too close to it.

Part of the reason for the lack of cohesion in twentieth-century music is probably due to the diversity and fragmentation in twentieth-century society itself. Core values and beliefs that prevailed in the Classical and Romantic eras no longer seemed to be in effect.

Equally important is the fact that there is so much music to consider. No longer can an understanding of music be confined to concert music of Europe and America. Music from every part of the globe became available, as well as all types of folk and popular music. Also, more universities and conservatories offered instruction in composition, so more people wrote and made music than ever before. What's more, ever since the Romantic period, composers consciously tried to avoid writing music that sounded too much like any other composer's style. Imitating someone else flew in the face of the idea of creativity as conceived over the past two centuries.

Stravinsky's *Rite of Spring* is presented in Chapter 32.

Another reason that it is hard to name one set of standard features for music in the twentieth century is its ever-changing character. For instance, Stravinsky's *Rite of Spring* was modern and novel when it premiered in 1913, but that certainly was not true for long. In fact, it was not even true for Stravinsky a decade later; he had moved on to another style. And Stravinsky was not alone among composers in changing styles.

Some labels are helpful in understanding twentieth-century music, just as period labels such as *Baroque* and *Romantic* are useful in learning about the music of earlier centuries. But such designations should be used with care when discussing twentieth-century music. Composers usually do not like being categorized. They consider their pieces unique works that should be evaluated on their own merits, which is only fair. Still, the use of classifications—the *isms,* for example—can aid in looking at and thinking about the concert music of the twentieth century.

WHAT TO LISTEN FOR IN TWENTIETH-CENTURY MUSIC

Rhythm

Rhythm is a much more important element in twentieth-century music than it was in previous centuries. Some (not all) of the music composed in the twentieth century broke away from the idea of regular metrical patterns. The "tyranny of the bar line" had long since gone. Composers felt free to mix meters, either by actually changing the signature or by displacing the accents. At one point in Stravinsky's *Rite of Spring,* the meter changes with each measure: 3/16, 5/16, 3/16, 4/16, 5/16, 3/16, and so on.

Measures traditionally contained two, three, or four regular beats. New asymmetrical patterns are found in some twentieth-century works. Measures with five or seven beats per measure are used, as well as measures in which the beat pattern is not regular, as in this 8/8 pattern:

♩. ♩. ♩ × 3 + 3 + 2

Furthermore, musicians felt free to have more than one rhythmic pattern sounding at the same time, what is termed *polyrhythm.*

Some composers consciously tried to return to rhythmic devices found in folk/ethnic music, such as rhythmic ostinatos—the persistent repetition of short rhythm patterns.

The increased attention given to rhythm had a corresponding increase in the importance of percussion instruments. More percussion instruments were used, and they were featured more prominently. In fact, some works were composed for percussion ensembles; others featured percussion instruments.

Melody

The concept of melody expanded far beyond potentially singable melodies in the traditional major and minor tonalities. Melodies were often no longer warm and flowing as in the preceding century. In fact, melody as such seemed less important in twentieth-century works. Melodies were often conceived nonvocally in their use of wide, awkward leaps and irregular phrases. Sometimes no actual melody can be found in a work. Yet some beautiful melodies exist in the music of the previous century.

Twentieth-century composers broke away from the balanced patterns of phrases found in Baroque and Classical music. No longer were four measures complemented by another four measures. The clearly defined structure of melodies was loosened considerably.

Harmony and Counterpoint

Romantic harmonies are rich and colorful, and chords were built around the traditional pattern of thirds. Twentieth-century composers frequently broke away from that pattern and wrote chords in fourths, fifths, and seconds. More often, however, they added notes to chords just because they wanted that particular sound at that particular place in the music.

Chord progressions in traditional harmony provide a syntax that helps organize the music. Twentieth-century composers did not completely abandon traditional tonal progressions, but they certainly were far less concerned about following them. In fact, not only were they much less interested in tonal centers but some composers also deliberately composed music with no tonal center whatsoever.

Some twentieth-century composers wrote music in two or more keys that sounded at the same time. The term for this technique is **polytonality.** For example, at one point in *Rite of Spring* Stravinsky has an F♭, A♭, C♭ chord in the lower pitches and an E♭, G♭, B♭, D♭ in the upper pitches, a sonority that includes all seven pitches of the C-flat major scale.

Some twentieth-century music was written not in the major/minor keys of the preceding three hundred years but in the modes that prevailed in the Renaissance and earlier periods. This was especially true of music that drew on folk sources.

As the attention given to harmony decreased in the twentieth century, the amount of counterpoint increased. At times, the counterpoint sounds like it was written by a resurrected J. S. Bach. Other twentieth-century counterpoint is very different, because it is filled with dissonance.

Examples of chords:
Seconds—C D E F
Thirds—C E G
Fourths—C F B♭
Fifths—C G D

The principle of dissonance resolving to consonance that has prevailed for more than two hundred years is sometimes not followed in twentieth-century music.

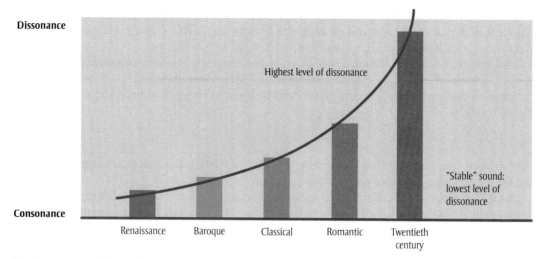

THE INCREASING USE OF DISSONANCE in music through history

Dissonance

The changes in harmony led to one of the things people notice first about twentieth-century music: dissonance. A few composers carried the idea of dissonance to its limit, for example, by asking the pianist to push an elbow down on the keyboard or by specifying a stick that is $14\frac{3}{8}$ inches long and pushing it down on the keys. Often dissonance is used to add a certain color to the music, not to create or resolve tension, as it had been traditionally employed. In any case, the amount of dissonance in twentieth-century music is much greater than at any other time in history.

Timbre

A synthesizer can produce almost any sound. It is not limited to the standard timbres of instruments.

Twentieth-century composers opened up a new world in terms of timbre with the synthesized sounds and effects available through technology. Even without technology, composers freely milked every possible sound from conventional instruments and the human voice—shrieks, babbling, tongue-clucking, banging, squeaking, buzzing, and sounds made with parts of the instrument removed. Some works for piano call for placing thumbtacks, rubber bands, coins, and other objects on the strings to create different timbres.

The technique is called **prepared piano.**

The idea of timbre became the central element in some works that consist of organized series of tone colors rather than themes and melodies.

Form

Tone rows are presented in Chapter 33, and chance and electronic music in Chapter 34.

A few composers wrote works in sonata and other forms. But formal patterns seemed not to be very important to most twentieth-century composers. Some attempted other approaches to organizing their music, and several of these are described in the following chapters.

Sources

The advent of tape recordings made possible a knowledge of many kinds of music that had not been known before. Also, the field of ethnomusicology has researched many types of music.

Musicians in the twentieth century knew more about music from every historical age and part of the globe than their predecessors did. Ease of communication and improved scholarship into the world's treasure trove of music made this possible. Twentieth-century music is pancultural and panhistorical as no other music has been before. A number of twentieth-century composers drew heavily on elements of music from non-Western cultures, as well as from past times.

MAIN POINTS OF THIS CHAPTER

1. The many changes and challenges in the twentieth century had a huge impact on music. They included expanded musical elements, new sources for music, sophisticated intellectual approaches to composing, a revival of some of the musical practices of earlier periods, and new ways of creating musical sounds.

2. The several "isms" in twentieth-century music help to organize its varied styles in one's mind.

3. The element of rhythm became much more important and complex with the use of mixed and asymmetrical meters and polyrhythms.

4. The concept of melody was expanded well beyond the idea of a beautiful theme. Many times melodies are impossible to sing because of their wide range and/or many altered notes.

5. The level of dissonance in harmony and counterpoint increased significantly. Notes were added to chords to achieve a desired sound, and they were sometimes arranged in patterns other than the traditional thirds. Some music was created without any tonal center, whereas other music was polytonal.

6. A wide variety of timbres are heard, both from voices and traditional instruments as well as from electronic instruments.

7. Twentieth-century music was pancultural and panhistorical as no music had ever been before.

31 The Mainstream

Much twentieth-century music was an expansion and evolution of previous musical styles. It is hard to know what to call this body of "conventional" music. Some writers have coined the word **folkloric,** because the music was partly derived from folk or ethnic sources, but that was not true of even a majority of this style. *Traditional* is not an accurate word, because most twentieth-century composers broke with nineteenth-century traditions to some extent. *Cosmopolitan* and *eclectic* are not accurate descriptions either, because many composers did not attempt to integrate a variety of musical styles in their compositions. **Mainstream** seems to say it best; it refers to music that is neither experimental nor committed to any one particular approach to writing music.

Three mainstream works are discussed in this chapter: Concerto for Orchestra by Béla Bartók, the Aria from *Bachianas Brasileiras No. 5* by Heitor Villa-Lobos, and the Dies irae from *War Requiem* by Benjamin Britten.

BARTÓK'S CONCERTO FOR ORCHESTRA

Bartók composed his Concerto for Orchestra in the summer of 1943 for a one-thousand-dollar commission from the Boston Symphony Orchestra. "The general mood of the work," he wrote, "represents, apart from the jesting second movement, a gradual transition from the sternness of the first movement and the lugubrious death-song of the third to the life-assertion of the last." The work is called a concerto because single instruments and sections are treated in a concerted way, as in Baroque music. There is also an element of virtuoso performing skill in the concerto. It is one of the masterpieces of twentieth-century music.

As pointed out in Chapter 4, *concerto* refers to the contrast between groups of instruments. Sometimes the difference is size, and sometimes it is the kinds of instruments.

First, Second, and Third Movements

Although the movements are independent and no themes are carried over from one movement to another, Bartók considered them as leading from one to another, as was just pointed out. The opening theme of the first movement is based on the interval of a fourth, with appearances of the theme separated by shimmering chords played by the strings. The main theme ascends and descends rapidly and contains a syncopated figure. The second half of this theme is nearly the exact inversion of the first half, with the interval of a fourth again being prominent.

The second movement is entitled "Games of Pairs," because the wind instruments are paired off at specific pitch intervals: the bassoons in sixths, the oboes in thirds, the clarinets in sevenths, the flutes in fifths, and the muted trumpets in seconds. This is the jesting movement that Bartók mentioned in his synopsis. After the five short sections featuring pairs of instruments, the brasses play a chorale accompanied by the snare drum with its snares not engaged. The opening music of the movement follows the chorale, which gives the movement a three-part form.

The third movement is the "lugubrious death-song." The melody is folklike and is played by the oboe. The music is rhapsodic and seems to rise to a peak moment of tragedy.

Fourth Movement

Bartók called the fourth movement "Interrupted Intermezzo." The opening melody has a Hungarian folk quality. The first six complete measures of the theme all begin on the same note—A-sharp—and the five-note pentatonic scale is used. The second melody sounds almost like a waltz, but not quite. Its meter changes often, usually by adding or subtracting half a beat. It gives the music a certain awkward charm. This melody also has a Hungarian folk character and is a reworking of a folk song.

The third theme is different. Bartók adapted a theme from the Seventh Symphony by the Russian composer Dmitri Shostakovitch. That symphony, often referred to as the "Leningrad Symphony," is a somewhat programmatic work that Shostakovitch composed in 1941 during the siege of Leningrad (St. Petersburg today) by the invading German Nazis. Bartók wanted to express his revulsion at Nazi Germany, which had taken over Hungary several years before and caused him to flee his native land. The theme is interrupted by rude noises, which seem to represent the "rough, booted men," as Bartók referred to the Nazi occupiers.

Hungarian folk music often uses the pentatonic scale.

Leningrad suffered terribly, and thousands of its citizens died in the long siege. Shostakovitch served as a fireman during those years.

LISTENING GUIDE

BÉLA BARTÓK
Concerto for Orchestra, Fourth Movement (1943)

GENRE: Concerto Orchestra

CD 2 Tracks 23 – 25

4 minutes 26 seconds

Form: Rondo

0:00 23 0:00 Short introduction; then oboe plays A theme.

0:15 Clarinet and flute repeat A theme, then extend it.

0:45 Oboe plays A theme again.

0:59 24 0:00 B theme begins in violas.

0:18 Violins play B theme as English horn plays contrasting part.

0:42 Oboe again plays A theme.

2:05 25 0:00 C theme begins in clarinet. Crude noises follow, played by trumpets and woodwinds.

0:23 Violins play a parody of C theme, followed by more blatant noises.

0:35 Inversion of C theme, followed by more rude noises.

0:48 Violins and violas play B theme.

1:23 English horn plays A theme fragment, followed by extended flute solo.

2:11 Movement concludes quietly with three quick notes.

 An interactive Active Listening Guide can be downloaded from the online Resource Center for *Music Listening Today, 4th Edition.*

Béla Bartók

BEST-KNOWN WORKS

chamber music:
- String Quartets Nos. 4, 5, and 6

orchestra:
- Concerto for Orchestra
- Music for Percussion, Strings, and Celesta
- Piano Concerto No. 3

piano:
- Mikrokosmos

Béla Bartók (1881–1945) was born in a small city in Hungary. His mother was his first music teacher. After Béla's father died, she became a schoolteacher. They moved quite often, but finally settled in Pressburg (today Bratislava), where Béla studied piano and composition. After finishing his studies at the Royal Conservatory, he concertized throughout Europe.

Bartók and another important Hungarian composer, Zoltán Kodály ("Koh-die-ee"), first became recognized outside Hungary as collectors of Hungarian folk music. They lugged their early recording equipment from one village in Transylvania to another, recording the music of the people. In 1907 Bartók became a professor of piano at the Royal Conservatory and spent most of the next thirty years in Budapest. His compositions received little attention outside Hungary until the late 1920s.

When he left Hungary, he could take almost nothing with him, so commissions for compositions were an economic necessity.

After the rise of Hitler and the subsequent collaboration of Hungary with Nazi Germany, Bartók felt impelled to leave his homeland. In 1940 he came to the United States to live. He was appointed to a position at Columbia University, primarily to continue his folk music research. He received a few commissions from ASCAP and from jazz clarinetist Benny Goodman.

ASCAP stands for American Society of Composers, Authors, and Publishers.

Bartók's earlier compositions were often barbaric, with many thick, dissonant chords. His most recognized works were composed between 1926 and 1937. One of the more interesting is his *Mikrokosmos*, a set of 153 piano pieces in six volumes that are arranged so that the music progresses from simple pieces to works of awesome difficulty.

During the latter part of his life, Bartók appeared to mellow. His music became less dissonant and more accessible. He died of leukemia, with his true stature as a composer still not fully appreciated.

Fifth Movement

The fifth movement is in a large three-part form. It features a theme of nearly continuous running notes and much contrapuntal writing, especially in the *B* section. The theme of that section is treated fugally, and it appears again at the conclusion of the movement.

HEITOR VILLA-LOBOS: *BACHIANAS BRASILEIRAS*

The Brazilian composer Heitor Villa-Lobos was a man of tremendous energy who adopted musical ideas from many sources. His greatest inspiration was the music of the Brazilian people. His *Bachianas Brasileiras* and *Chiros* are filled with rich sounds that alternate between being romantic and boldly dissonant.

Villa-Lobos composed nine *Bachianas Brasileiras,* in which he tried to combine the style of Bach with the indigenous music of Brazil. Villa-Lobos wrote: "This is a special kind of musical composition based on an intimate knowledge of J. S. Bach and also on the composer's affinity with the harmonic, contrapuntal, and melodic atmosphere of the folklore of the northern region of Brazil." The Aria of *Bachianas Brasileiras No. 5* was composed in 1938; in 1945 he added a second movement to it.

The Aria is for a soprano accompanied by eight cellos—hardly a typical instrumentation. The music is not typical either. During the first third of the work, the singer just vocalizes a luscious melody, first on "Ah" and then for the last third by humming.

The middle section is somewhat like a Brazilian popular song, with its syncopation and frequent changes of tempo. The soloist's melody has an improvised quality.

A wordless song is called a

To project the sound of hu
trained singers hum with t
apart and their lips barely

HEITOR VILLA-LOBOS
Aria from *Bachianas Brasileiras* No. 5 (1938)

GENRE: Aria   Soloist and cellos

CD 6 Tracks **1**–**3**

7 minutes 51 seconds

Form: *A B A*

0:00	**1** 0:00		Cellos play short introduction.
	0:13		Soprano, doubled by a cello, vocalizes melody on "Ah."

Aria from Bachianas Brasileiras No. 5 by Heitor Villa-Lobos. Copyright © 1947 (renewed) by Associated Music Publishers, Inc. (BMI). International Copyright Secured. All Rights Reserved. Reprinted by permission.

1:12		Soprano resumes singing melody.
2:01		One cello plays melody.
3:10	**2** 0:00	Soprano sings middle section.

> *Lo at midnight clouds are slowly passing, rosy and lustrous,*
> *O'er the spacious heav'n with loveliness laden,*
> *From the boundless deep the moon arises wondrous,*
> *Glorifying the evening like a beautiful maiden,*
> *Now she adorns herself in half-unconscious duty,*
> *Eager, anxious that we recognize her beauty,*
> *While sky and earth, yes all nature with applause salute her.*

1:31	

> *All the birds have ceased their sad and mournful complaining,*
> *Now appears on the sea in a silver reflection*
> *Moonlight softly waking the soul and constraining*
> *Hearts to cruel tears and bitter dejection.*
> *Lo at midnight clouds are slowly passing, rosy and lustrous,*
> *O'er the spacious heavens dreamily wondrous.*

6:32	**3** 0:00	Soprano hums the melody.
	0:52	Music begins to slow down gradually.
	1:20	Aria concludes quietly as soprano holds a long note and then moves up one octave.

An interactive Active Listening Guide can be downloaded from the online Resource Center for *Music Listening Today, 4th Edition.*

Heitor Villa-Lobos

BEST-KNOWN WORKS

instrumental:

- *Bachianas Brasileiras Nos. 1, 5, and 9*
- Concerto for Guitar and Orchestra
- Etudes for Guitar (12)

Heitor Villa-Lobos (1887–1959) was born in Rio de Janeiro, the son of a librarian who was an avid amateur musician. He taught his son cello and strongly encouraged him in music. When Heitor was twelve, his father died, and he composed a piece in his father's memory. Soon Villa-Lobos began playing cello professionally. As a young man, he traveled throughout Brazil and heard the music of its people. Although he never collected folk music in a systematic way, he seemed to absorb it, and it had a major impact on the more than eleven hundred works he composed during his lifetime.

In the 1920s he made two trips to Paris, where he met a number of the composers who were living there at the time. He studied their compositions and absorbed some of their techniques. In the 1930s he was director of music education for Brazil. He drafted a curriculum for its schools and organized several mass concerts, one of which involved forty thousand children! He made several journeys to the United States in the 1940s and founded the Brazilian Academy of Music.

His music is a blend of Brazilian folk music and Western concert music that seems to incorporate the best elements of each.

BRITTEN'S *WAR REQUIEM*

The entrance to the new cathedral is through the shell of the old one.

Saint Michael's Cathedral had stood in Coventry, England, since medieval times. During World War II, it was bombed and burned out. Only its walls remained with their mute, empty windows. Rather than rebuild using the former shell of Saint Michael's, it was decided to leave the ruined shell there as a reminder of war's devastation. The new cathedral was dedicated on May 30, 1962, and Benjamin Britten was commissioned to write a work for that occasion.

Britten decided to use the traditional Mass for the Dead, or Requiem, as it is more commonly known. But he wanted his *War Requiem* to convey the message of tragedy and despair over the horrors of war. Therefore, he interspersed the words of the Latin Requiem with the antiwar poems in English by Wilfred Owen. Owen was an English soldier who was killed just before the end of World War I. His poems were published posthumously, and they speak to the harshness and futility of war:

> My subject is War, and the pity of War.
> The Poetry is in the Pity . . .
> All a poet can do today is mourn.

Appropriately, Britten dedicated his *War Requiem* to four friends who died in World War II.

War Requiem is a monumental work in six sections, the same ones found in the traditional Requiem Mass. The work requires about eighty-three minutes to perform and calls for orchestra, chorus, boy choir, and three soloists. Its music is neither grand nor glorious, but rather is stark and often quite dissonant. It is highly effective in expressing its message.

Britten used the text of the Dies irae but not the same chant melody that Berlioz and Rachmaninoff used in their works, which were presented in Part V.

The Dies irae is the second section of the *War Requiem*, and only the first portion of it is included in the Listening Guide. Its music is not flowing; instead, each syllable seems chopped off from its adjacent one. The meter is an asymmetrical seven beats in each measure. The musical effect is one of a limping, twitching march that belies the "wondrous trumpet" phrase in the text and emphasizes "trembling," which is also contained in the text. The rhythmic pattern sounds before each new section for the chorus.

Dies irae from *War Requiem,*
excerpt from beginning (1962)

GENRE: Oratorio, requiem   Chorus and Orchestra

CD 2 Tracks 26 – 27

3 minutes 45 seconds

Form: Strophic with interludes

0:00   26   0:00   French horns and trumpet exchange short passages rather quietly.

0:27   Men sing first three lines of the text:

Dies irae, dies illa	*Day of wrath, day of anger*
Solvet saeclum in favilla,	*The world will dissolve into ashes,*
Teste David cum Sibylla	*As witness David and the Sibyl.*

0:49   Horns and trumpets exchange more passages. Music grows louder.

1:19   Women sing second three lines of the text:

Quantus tremor est futurus,	*What trembling there will be*
Quando Judex est venturus,	*When the Judge shall come;*
Cuncta stricte discussurus!	*All shall thoroughly be shattered!*

1:40   Brasses and percussion play a more extensive passage.

2:15   27   0:00   Chorus, with the brasses continuing to play figures, sings next three lines of the text:

Tuba mirum spargens sonum	*The wondrous trumpet, spreading its sound*
Per sepulchra regionem	*To the tombs of all regions,*
Coget omnes ante thronum.	*Will gather all before the throne.*

0:24   Brasses using mutes continue.

0:59   Chorus sings final three lines of the text somewhat softly:

Mors stupebit et natura,	*Death will be stupefied, also nature,*
Cum resurget creaturam,	*When all creation arises again*
Judicanti responsura.	*To answer to the Judge.*

1:30   After brasses play a few more figures, the section closes quietly.

 An interactive Active Listening Guide can be downloaded from the online
Resource Center for *Music Listening Today, 4th Edition.*

AP Photo

SOLDIERS ATTENDING A SERVICE in the ruins of Coventry Cathedral on May 13, 1945, a few days after World War II had ended in Europe.

Nigel Luckhurst/Lebrecht/The Image Works

Benjamin Britten

Benjamin Britten (1913–1976) was born in the seacoast town of Lowestoft, England, the son of a dental surgeon and a musical mother. He began putting patterns on paper before he was five, but by the age of six or seven the notes became associated with what he had in mind. By the age of fourteen, he had composed a number of works for piano and voice. He was given a scholarship to the Royal College of Music and by the age of twenty-one was earning his living largely as a composer.

He immigrated to the United States in 1939 but returned to England in 1942.

He toured America again several times, usually giving performances with his lifetime companion, tenor Peter Pears.

Britten wrote for every medium and for varied levels of musical difficulty. He was most successful in writing operas, three of which are frequently performed: *Peter Grimes, Albert Herring,* and *Billy Budd.* He once said of composing: "It is the easiest thing in the world to write a piece virtually or totally impossible to perform—but . . . that is not what I prefer to do; I prefer to study the conditions of performance and shape my music to them."

BEST-KNOWN WORKS

orchestra and voice:
- *War Requiem*
- *Serenade for Tenor, Horn, and Strings*

choral:
- *A Ceremony of Carols*

OTHER MAINSTREAM COMPOSERS

Russia

Dmitri Shostakovitch (1906–1975) was born in St. Petersburg and spent most of his life in Russia when it was under the control of the Communist regime. He entered the Conservatory at St. Petersburg when he was thirteen and composed his First Symphony when he was nineteen. Several times in his career he had problems with the Communist Party because his works were well liked in the West. Public apologies and some politically correct works were required from Shostakovitch to get himself back in good standing. Before he died, he completed his Fifteenth Symphony, making him the first major composer since Beethoven to write more than nine.

England

Ralph Vaughan Williams and Edward Elgar are mentioned in Chapter 28. In addition to these composers, England produced a number of others who contributed to its great tradition of choral music, including William Walton (1902–1983).

France

Following World War I, France went through a strong anti-Romantic reaction. The informal leaders of this movement away from Romanticism were a poet, Jean Cocteau (1889–1963), and an eccentric musician, Erik Satie ("Sah-*tee*," 1866–1925). Satie reacted to past music in his own inimitable way by writing little compositions entitled, for example, *Three Pieces in the Shape of a Pear, Three Flabby Preludes for a Dog,* and *Dried Embryos.* The purpose of such titles was to satirize the seriousness of Romantic composers.

On one occasion, Satie composed some music *not* to be listened to. When the audience listened to it, he became irritated and urged them not to.

Lili and Nadia Boulanger

The odds were against the Boulanger sisters. Both lived in France at a time when it was very difficult for a woman to make her mark as a composer or conductor.

Lili Boulanger (1893–1918) suffered from poor health for much of her short life, so the odds were even more difficult for her. She won the Prix de Rome at the age of nineteen, however, becoming the first woman to be awarded that coveted honor. She composed about twenty-one works, many of which are available on recordings. Her last composition, *Pie Jesu,* was dictated to her sister, Nadia, because she was no longer able to hold a pen. She died at the age of twenty-four from Crohn's disease.

Nadia Boulanger (1887–1979) had a greater impact on the world of music. Although she composed only a few works herself, she combined a dynamic personality and a photographic memory for music to become one of the most influential composition teachers of the twentieth century. She taught two generations of composers at the Paris Conservatory, the école Normale de Musique, and especially at the American Conservatory in Fontainebleau. It was there that she taught Aaron Copland and a long list of prominent American composers.

Nadia did not limit herself to just teaching composition. She was a highly successful conductor and was the first woman prior to World War II to conduct the Paris Philharmonic, the New York Philharmonic, the Royal Philharmonic in London, the Philadelphia Orchestra, and the Boston Symphony. She promoted a number of old and neglected works, such as music by Monteverdi. Fortunately, Nadia lived a rich and full life of ninety-two years.

LILI BOULANGER

NADIA BOULANGER

From this stream of irreverent thought came a group of French composers known as The Six. The most important of these were Darius Milhaud ("*Mee-yo*," 1892–1974), Arthur Honegger ("*Own*-eh-gair," 1892–1955), and Francis Poulenc ("Poo-*lahnk*," 1899–1963).

Milhaud lived for a while in Brazil, where he became acquainted with Latin American music. He also visited New York City and heard jazz, which made a lasting impression on him. He was a prolific composer, especially of small works.

Honegger was more conservative than Milhaud. One of his compositions is a tone poem, *Pacific 231*, which depicts a steam engine. By the time he composed it, tone poems had become passé. His most successful works were large in scope, with the oratorio *Le Roi David* (*King David*) being the best known.

Poulenc's music more clearly expresses the Cocteau–Satie outlook. It is charming and pleasant. Most of it was written for small groups, although he also composed two operas.

Latin America

> Chávez's Toccata for Six Percussionists is probably the best-known work for that type of ensemble.

Villa-Lobos is discussed earlier in this chapter. Carlos Chávez (1899–1978) was Mexico's leading composer. His *Symphonia India* is based on Mexican Indian music, and his Toccata for Percussion Instruments is an exciting, rhythmic work.

Alberto Ginastera ("Hee-nah-*stair*-ah," 1916–1983) was an Argentine composer who achieved fame for his instrumental and vocal works. His music sparkles with Latin American qualities.

MAIN POINTS OF THIS CHAPTER

1. Many twentieth-century compositions were not experimental, avant garde, or allied with any particular approach to composing music. They constitute the mainstream of twentieth-century concert music.

2. Some twentieth-century works were influenced by folk music, whereas others were influenced by musical practices that had existed in the Baroque and Classical periods.

3. Bartók's Concerto for Orchestra was titled as a concerto because individual instruments or small groups of instruments are contrasted with one another, somewhat similar to what was done in Baroque music.

4. The music of Villa-Lobos often combines elements of Brazilian folk music with traditional Western concert music. The "Aria" from his *Bachianas Brasilerias No. 5* is largely a vocalise, which is a song sung on a neutral syllable.

5. Britten's *War Requiem* was commissioned for the dedication of a new cathedral that replaced the one bombed out in World War II. It uses the words and sections of the traditional Requiem Mass, but none of its music.

FEATURES TO LISTEN FOR

1. Fourth movement of Bartók's Concerto for Orchestra:
   - The changing meters in both the A and B sections
   - The five-note pentatonic scale in the A theme
   - The satirical nature of the C section
2. "Aria" by Villa-Lobos:
   - The beauty of the wordless vocalise

- The subtle difference between the effect of the melody when it is sung and when it is hummed
- The unusual accompaniment of eight cellos

3. "Dies irae" from Britten's *War Requiem*:
   - The change in the dynamic levels among the four sections sung by the chorus
   - The use of brasses and percussion in playing their sections and when accompanying the singers
   - The effect of its asymmetrical 7/4 meter

Expressionism *and* Primitivism

People seem to have known it all along, but in the twentieth century it was brought out into the open and explored as never before: Human behavior is a complex matter that is influenced by competing, contradictory, and sometimes concealed forces. Are humans basically good or fundamentally bad? Is the glass half full or half empty? Is everything folly and meaningless, as the writer of Ecclesiastes says, or does the writer of Psalm 100 have it right with the words "For the Lord is good and his love endures forever"?

Events in Europe in the first twenty years of the twentieth century especially caused people to wonder about the nature of the human race. World War I raged from 1914 to 1918. It was a particularly horrible and senseless war, with the use of poison gas and a million casualties in the trenches of France and elsewhere. And for what purpose? No good seemed to have come from it; no Pax Romana resulted that provided political and economic stability. Instead, the ruling houses of Austria, Germany, and Russia were deposed, only to be replaced with confusion and turmoil that soon led to takeovers by repressive totalitarian regimes. It was a great time to be cynical and to see humans as weak and attracted by evil.

It was also a time of intellectual questioning of the established ways. In Germany, Friedrich Nietzsche's philosophy of "might makes right" was respected and believed. In Vienna, Sigmund Freud was developing his psychoanalytic theories of neuroses, which focused attention on the dark and shrouded aspects of the human mind. Charles Darwin's theories of evolution and the survival of the fittest had challenged the assumptions about the dignity and place of human beings in the scheme of things.

> Even a saint such as Paul had trouble doing what he should and not doing what he shouldn't. (See Romans 7:15.)

> *Pax Romana* refers to the peace that prevailed in Europe when the Roman Empire ruled it.

EXPRESSIONISM

Because one role of creative artists is to be commentators on and give expression to the attitudes and feelings of society, it is logical that art and music would reflect European society of that time. The chief artistic style for doing this was **Expressionism.** In a sense, Expressionism was the opposite of Impressionism: Where Impressionism had been essentially happy, bright, and outward looking, Expressionism was morose, dark, and inward looking.

Expressionist painters included Franz Marc, Wassily Kandinsky, Oskar Kokoschka, and Edvard Munch. They tried to shock their viewers with distortions and blatant colors.

Expressionist writers centered on the dark side of people. Elements of Expressionism found their way to the United States in the writings of Franz Kafka. This tradition continued with the American writers William Faulkner and Tennessee Williams and the introspective and profound Irish writer James Joyce.

The poem "The Sick Moon" by the Belgian Albert Giraud is typical of Expressionist poetry. This is its first stanza:

> Impressionism was very much associated with France; Expressionism was associated with Germanic thought.

You nocturnal deathly sick moon,
Up there in the heavens' dark pillow,
Your look too full with fever
Captivates me like a strange melody.

The poem attracted the Expressionist composer Arnold Schoenberg, who included it in his set of songs *Pierrot Lunaire (Moonstruck Pierrot)*, which he composed in 1912. The music calls for eight instruments and one singer, who uses a speech–song style called **sprechstimme.** The written pitches in the music for the singer are only approximate, and no sustained pitches are to be produced. Schoenberg's intent was to merge the spoken word and music as much as possible. The effect is eerie and nonvocal in the traditional sense.

Expressionism and Impressionism did have one point in common: Both had a natural affinity among writers, artists, and composers who knew each other. Some were talented in more than one art. The painter Kandinsky wrote plays and poetry, and the composer Schoenberg painted and even exhibited in several shows of Expressionist art.

It would be a mistake to dismiss Expressionism as just a passing fad. Because it touches on and explores a side of human nature, it merits a place in the world of the arts.

BERG'S *WOZZECK*

Alban Berg composed *Wozzeck* ("Vot-tzek") between 1917 and 1921. He adapted the libretto himself from a play by Georg Büchner, which he saw in 1914. The opera follows a carefully worked-out plan, one that is partly symphonic in nature:

Act I	Exposition
Act II	Development
Act III	Catastrophe

Each of the three acts contains five scenes that are organized around a specific musical form or compositional technique. For example, Act III—the one discussed here—is organized as a theme and variations.

Scene 1	Variations on a theme
Scene 2	Variations on a single tone
Scene 3	Variations on a rhythm pattern
Scene 4	Variations on a chord
Scene 5	Variations on continuous running notes

A short orchestral interlude is heard between the scenes. Berg did not intend for listeners to be conscious of these forms or techniques. Instead, he wanted the audience to be caught up in the drama and its emotional impact. The techniques used in each case, however, contribute to the dramatic and musical effect.

The story of the opera is about Franz Wozzeck, a poor and rather incompetent soldier. He is persecuted by his sadistic captain and used as a guinea pig by the company's somewhat demented doctor. He is betrayed by his mistress, Marie, who sleeps with another man. Driven to madness, Wozzeck stabs her and later drowns trying to wash the blood off the knife and his hands.

Prior to Act III, Wozzeck has been driven to desperation by Marie's unfaithfulness, a beating from the man who slept with her, and the actions of the captain and doctor.

The libretto with an English translation of the original German for Act III, Scene 2, appears in the Listening Guide. In it Marie and Wozzeck walk by a pond. She is anxious to get back home, but he wants to sit and talk. They comment on the blood-red color of the moon in the sky. After tenderly kissing her, he pulls a knife and plunges it into her throat. Throughout the scene one note is softly but persistently heard. As Marie is stabbed, it is sounded over and over by the timpani. In the orchestral interlude that follows, it becomes overpowering as it increases to two ear-splitting crescendos. The rhythm pattern of the interlude becomes the musical basis for the next scene.

Arnold Schoenberg is discussed in conjunction with his tone row music in Chapter 33.

Several twentieth-century works are based on the sad clown figure known variously as *Pierrot, Petrushka,* or *Pagliacci.*

These sections differ from the usual exposition/development/recapitulation of sonata form.

The story in no way resembles one that Mozart might have used for one of his operas!

WOZZECK AND MARIE shortly before he stabs her in a jealous rage.

LISTENING GUIDE

ALBAN BERG

Wozzeck, Act III, Scene 2 (1921)

GENRE: Opera   Soloists and orchestra

CD 6 Tracks 4 – 5

4 minutes 50 seconds

Forest path by a pool. Dusk is falling. Marie enters with Wozzeck, from the right.

0:00   4   0:00

MARIE: Dort links geht's in die Stadt. 's ist noch weit. Komm schneller!	**MARIE:** The town lies over there. It's still far. Let's hurry!
WOZZECK: Du sollst dableiben, Marie. Komm, setz' Dich.	**WOZZECK:** You must stay awhile, Marie. Come, sit here.
MARIE: Aber ich muss fort.	**MARIE:** But I must go.
They sit down.	
WOZZECK: Komm. Bist weit gegangen, Marie. Sollst Dir die Füsse nicht mehr wund laufen. 's ist still hier! Und so dunkel.—Weisst noch, Marie, wie lang' es jetzt ist, dass wir uns kennen?	**WOZZECK:** Come! So far you've wandered, Marie. You must not make your feet so sore, walking. It's still, here in the darkness.—Tell me, Marie how long has it been since our first meeting?
MARIE: Zu Pfingsten drei Jahre.	**MARIE:** At Whitsun, three years.
WOZZECK: Und was meinst, wie lang' es noch dauern wird?	**WOZZECK:** And how long, how long will it still go on?

She jumps up.

1:23 MARIE: Ich muss fort.

MARIE: I must go!

WOZZECK: Fürchst Dich, Marie?
Und bist doch fromm! Und gut! Und treu!

WOZZECK: Trembling, Marie? But you are good
(*laughing*) and kind and true!

He pulls her down again on the seat; he bends over her, in deadly earnest.

Was Du für süsse Lippen hast, Marie!

Ah! How your lips are sweet to touch, Marie!

He kisses her.

Den Himmel gäb' ich drum und die Seligkeit,
wenn ich Dich noch oft so küssen dürft!
Aber ich darf nicht! Was zitterst?

All heaven I would give, and eternal bliss,
if I still could sometimes kiss you so!
But yet I dare not! You shiver?

MARIE: Der Nachttau fällt.

MARIE: The night dew falls.

2:41 ⑤ 0:00 WOZZECK: Wer kalt ist,
den friert nicht mehr! Dich wird
beim Morgentau nicht frieren.

WOZZECK (*whispering to himself*): Whoever
is cold will shiver no more in the
cold morning dew.

MARIE: Was sagst Du da?

MARIE: What are you saying?

WOZZECK: Nix.

WOZZECK: Nothing.

A long silence. The moon rises.

MARIE: Wie der Mond rot aufgeht!

MARIE: How the moon rises red!

WOZZECK: Wie ein blutig Eisen!

WOZZECK: Like a bloodred iron!

He draws a knife.

MARIE: Was zitterst?

MARIE: You shiver?

She jumps up.

Was willst?

What now?

1:16 WOZZECK: Ich nicht, Marie! Und kein
Andrer auch nicht!

WOZZECK: No one, Marie! If not me,
then no one!

He seizes her and plunges the knife into her throat.

MARIE: Hilfe!

MARIE: Help!

She sinks down. Wozzeck bends over her. She dies.

WOZZECK: Tot!

WOZZECK: Dead!

He rises to his feet anxiously and then rushes silently away.

2:09 Scene change — orchestral interlude.

An interactive Active Listening Guide can be downloaded from the online
Resource Center for *Music Listening Today, 4th Edition.*

Scene 3 takes place in a tavern. Wozzeck is almost out of his mind and tries to forget
his crime. The music is a dissonant and distorted version of barroom dance music and is
played on an out-of-tune piano onstage. Marie's friend Margret sings a weird-sounding
folk tune. After a while she notices blood on Wozzeck's hands and sleeve, and she thinks
it smells like human blood. He flees in terror as people in the tavern close in on him.
The mood of the scene is increased throughout by the twitching, persistent rhythm pattern first heard in the previous interlude. Only the tempos at which it is performed are
altered to suit the needs of the drama.

The rhythm pattern has a hypnotic
effect and contributes to the sense
of horror.

In Scene 4 Wozzeck returns to the site of the murder to get rid of the knife. The
orchestra adds a macabre, almost surreal tonal backdrop of sounds for his shrieks and
shouts. The moon and pond seem to turn to blood as he loses his sanity. He wades into
the water to wash the knife and himself.

Popperfoto/Getty Images

Best-Known Works

chamber music:
- Lyric Suite

opera:
- *Lulu*
- *Wozzeck*

orchestra:
- Concerto for Violin

Alban Berg (1885–1935), the son of a factory worker, was born in Vienna. At the age of fourteen, he took up composing, an interest that occupied his time when he was confined by asthma and poor health. His father died the next year, leaving the family in difficult financial straits; only the help of a well-to-do aunt allowed Alban to remain in school. After graduation from high school, he took a position as an accountant for the government.

He was largely self-taught until the age of nineteen, when he answered a newspaper ad placed by Schoenberg for composition students. Schoenberg accepted the young man and, because Berg was poor, did not charge him for more than a year. From then on the lives of the two men seemed woven together. They were mutually supportive of each other when most of their works were received coolly by audiences.

Actually, audiences were sometimes extremely hostile to their works.

Berg's place in history is largely the result of his opera *Wozzeck*. Never in good health, Berg died as a result of complications following a bee sting.

The captain and the doctor—his two tormentors—happen to walk by and hear someone drowning. They offer no help, commenting that the sound of someone drowning "is not good to hear." As Wozzeck drowns, the sounds of the orchestra seem to engulf him. The orchestral interlude that follows is much longer than the other interludes. It presents musical motives associated with Wozzeck's life, and it seems to sob to a close.

Scene 5 is an epilogue that takes place the next morning outside Marie's house. A group of children sing ring-around-the-rosy. The child of Marie and Wozzeck rides a hobby horse. One of the children cruelly taunts the boy: "Hey! Your mother's dead!" At first the child does not understand and continues to ride the horse. The children decide to go see the body. They run off. The child continues to ride for a few more moments, and then he also runs after the other children. The opera does not end with a clear-cut conclusion. The music simply stops.

What is so moving and compelling about *Wozzeck*?

- It is gripping drama. Its unvarnished realism has a hard-hitting impact that grabs and keeps one's attention.
- The music is excellently crafted to add to the impact of the drama. What the music lacks in traditional beauty is more than made up for in its dramatic power. The audience usually feels emotionally wrung out when *Wozzeck* concludes.
- The music is ingenious in terms of its use of forms and compositional techniques.

Many twentieth-century works of music do not have clearly developed endings.

PRIMITIVISM

Primitivism was not so much a point of view about art and life as it was a fascination with the art and music of non-Western and nonliterate societies. African sculpture and masks began to interest the artistic world, as did Paul Gauguin's paintings of Polynesian culture. Nineteenth-century writers, artists, and composers had been attracted by the beauty and mystery of the "long ago and far away"; twentieth-century artists admired the power and vitality of the arts of these societies.

PAUL GAUGUIN, 1843–1903, *Where do we come from? What are we? Where are we going? (D'ou venons nous . . . ?)*, Oil on canvas, 1897. Gauguin believed that the renewal of Western art and civilization must come from "the Primitives" such as the Polynesian natives he painted in the South Pacific.

STRAVINSKY'S *THE RITE OF SPRING*

The high point of Primitivism in music was probably reached in 1913 with the premiere of Igor Stravinsky's ballet *La Sacre du Printemps (The Rite of Spring)*. The music was written for a production by Sergei Diaghilev, impresario of the Ballet Russe. Each year he brought a new and stunning ballet production to Paris. With keen artistic judgment and calculated showmanship, he decided in 1913 to capitalize on the Parisians' interest in primitive art. He chose to produce a ballet about prehistoric ceremonies that culminated in the sacrifice of a human being—a real change from the usual lovely stories found in ballet prior to that time.

The work opens with a bassoon solo in its upper range, giving the music a haunting quality. The pitches of the melody keep returning to the opening note, and the rhythm pattern is irregular, with frequent stops and starts. The introduction contains dissonant, strange sounds with coloristic effects.

In the "Dance of the Adolescents" that follows, Stravinsky unleashes the force of rhythm. The effect is like the wild beating of savage drums. Much of the music is quite dissonant, and the rhythm patterns are irregular. A steady series of eighth notes begins with this irregular pattern:

1-2-3-4   1-2-3-4-5   1-2   1-2-3-4-5-6   1-2-3   1-2-3-4   1-2-3-4-5

The "Dance of Abduction" is even wilder. A scampering tune is played by the woodwinds and answered by a French horn call. The meter signatures change often. Polyrhythms are also part of the rhythmic interest of the music.

"Round Dances of Spring" brings some relief from the frenzied music that precedes it. The tempo is slow, and the flutes and other woodwinds play a melody that resembles an American Indian tune.

The music becomes energetic again in "Games of Rival Tribes." The idea of competition is expressed by pitting one section of the orchestra against another, each with its own distinctive music. The music is bitonal in a number of places.

The "Entrance of the Sage" brings back the main thematic material with a thick orchestration. The music becomes slower and more majestic at this point.

Act I ends with "Dance of the Earth." It also suggests violence and upheaval.

The second and final act of *The Rite of Spring* depicts the sacrifice of a young maiden so that the God of Spring will be satisfied. It is similar in style to the first act but is rarely played apart from the ballet. Just the opposite is true of the music for Act I.

Resource Center
See "Hear It Now: Primitive Qualities in Music," in the *Music Listening Today, 4th Edition*, Resource Center.

Bitonal refers to music that is in two different keys at the same time.

The ballet must be seen with this part of the music to appreciate the full impact of the work.

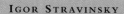

IGOR STRAVINSKY

The Rite of Spring, excerpts from Act I (1913)

GENRE: Ballet music   Orchestra

CD 2 Tracks 28 – 30

4 minutes 57 seconds

"Dance of the Adolescents"

0:00 28 0:00 Orchestra plays persistent, driving chords with an irregular pattern of accents.

0:20 Muted trumpet plays short melodic figure that descends by half steps.

0:49 Bassoon plays simple melody derived from previous rhythm pattern.

1:19 Brasses break persistent rhythm with sustained notes; then rhythmic pattern returns.

1:43 29 0:00 French horn sounds short melodic figure that is gradually taken up by other instruments.

0:21 Flute repeats French horn melody.

0:37 Trumpets play a third short melody as music grows more active.

1:01 Piccolo plays earlier French horn melody; other instruments follow.

"Dance of Abduction"

3:20 30 0:00 Brasses hold long notes that soon give way to music with a rapid tempo and irregular meter.

0:15 French horns play primitive-sounding motive.

0:59 Timpani leads, and other instruments respond in irregular metrical patterns.

1:27 Flute plays long trilled note as "Dance of Abduction" ends.

An interactive Active Listening Guide can be downloaded from the online
Resource Center for *Music Listening Today, 4th Edition.*

To listeners hearing it for the first time, *The Rite of Spring* may sound like a jumble
of random notes. It may even seem that the players can play anything they want and
no one would notice the difference. Such an idea is of course incorrect. Stravinsky
carefully planned everything in the score and wrote detailed instructions for playing
each part. He tells the timpanist when to change from hard to soft sticks, the French

horn players when to tilt the bells of their instruments upward, and the cellists when to retune a string so that a chord can be played on open strings to achieve a more raucous effect.

Musicians generally consider Stravinsky's *The Rite of Spring* to be one of the masterpieces of twentieth-century music. Why?

- Its exploitation of rhythm is exceptional. Stravinsky had an uncanny sense of when to accent notes or change the metrical pattern.

- The themes are used in an imaginative and interesting way. What Stravinsky often did was create a short tune and then repeat it many times, but each time with slight changes. Like every composer whose music has lasted over the centuries, Stravinsky was able to manage the tension between the needs for unity and variety in his music.

- Although a traditional symphony orchestra plays the work, Stravinsky demonstrates great ability to find new timbres and create new sounds.

- Dissonance is also handled in a masterful way. Some chords are very dissonant, but many are not. It's not just that Stravinsky employs dissonant sounds; rather, it is that he knew *when* to use dissonance—and when not to.

Igor Stravinsky

Igor Stravinsky (1882–1971) was born in St. Petersburg, Russia, where his father was a singer with the Imperial Opera. Although he studied music, his parents hoped that he would become a lawyer. He studied law at the University of St. Petersburg and composition with Rimsky-Korsakov at the same time.

Stravinsky soon became associated with Sergei Diaghilev, manager of the famous Ballet Russe, who signed the twenty-eight-year-old composer in 1910 after hearing only one of his works. The ballet he composed for the Ballet Russe was *The Firebird*. It was so successful that he was commissioned to write another, *Petrouchka*. Both ballets are based on Russian folk tales. He was then given a third commission for a ballet, *The Rite of Spring*.

When he was eighty, Stravinsky was the honored guest of President John F. Kennedy at the White House. He was also the subject of a special one-hour program on national television.

Just before World War I, Stravinsky moved to Switzerland. The revolution in Russia cut off his income, and the Ballet Russe disbanded for a while. He lived in Switzerland for eight years while recovering from a serious illness.

After the war ended, Stravinsky settled in Paris. He became a French citizen and traveled widely as a conductor and pianist. He continued to compose, but he abandoned the style he had used for the three ballets with the Ballet Russe. In 1939 he came to the United States to lecture. World War II prevented his return to Europe, so he settled in Hollywood and became an American citizen. He retained his esteemed position as one of the greatest composers of this century.

Despite superficial changes of style, Stravinsky remained true to his objective concept of music: Because a musical work is something a composer creates, it is essentially an object, not a manifestation of his psyche. Therefore, a composer's works do not need to be consistent personal creations. Skill at composition is what matters; the composer's personality is irrelevant.

BEST-KNOWN WORKS

ballet:
- *The Firebird*
- *Petrouchka*
- *The Rite of Spring*

chamber music:
- Octet
- *L'Histoire du soldat*

choral:
- *Symphony of Psalms*

opera:
- *Oedipus the King*
- *The Rake's Progress*

Stravinsky's *Rite of Spring* premiered at the Théâtre des Champs Elysées in Paris on May 29, 1913. Stravinsky had written two previous ballets for the great impresario Sergei Diaghilev and the Ballet Russe, and both had been successfully performed in Paris, so both men were already well known there. The premiere was an event of importance among Parisian society; the theater was filled with dignitaries, royalty, and renowned musicians.

None of them could have anticipated what would happen that May evening. Instead of the expected lovely music, beautiful costumes, and toe dancing, the audience was subjected to some harsh-sounding chords and dancers in not-so-pretty costumes making angular, rough motions. No one knows what set off the audience more, the dancing or the music, but the audience reacted—to an extreme. One writer reported:

> A certain part of the audience, thrilled by what it considered to be a blasphemous attempt to destroy music as an art, and swept away with wrath, began very soon after the rise of the curtain to whistle, to make catcalls, and to offer audible suggestions as to how the performance should proceed. . . . The orchestra played on unheard. . . . The figures on the stage danced in time to music they had to imagine they heard.

Linda Rich/PAL/Topham/The Image Works

A MODERN PERFORMANCE of Igor Stravinsky's *Rite of Spring*

One critic yelled as loudly as he could, "The music is a colossal fraud!" The ambassador from Austria laughed derisively. One lady reached out into the adjoining box to slap the face of a man who was hissing. Another lady rose majestically in her seat and spat in the face of one of the noisemakers. The eminent French composer Maurice Ravel alone shouted, "Genius!" Backstage, Stravinsky held on to the choreographer, Waslaw Nijinsky, to keep him from going into the audience and fighting with those who disapproved.

Probably no one that evening thought about it in this way, but they were violently disagreeing about the nature of art. Must it always be beautiful? Can't art sometimes stir the emotions and affect people deeply? Can art be *of* life, or must it always be *better than* life?

If nothing else, Expressionism demonstrated that art goes much deeper than beauty in the sense of being pretty. There is nothing pretty about Berg's *Wozzeck* and many sections of Stravinsky's *Rite of Spring,* but they continue to attract listeners again and again. The poet Keats was right when he wrote, "A thing of beauty is a joy forever," but were he writing today, he might have revised that line to read, "A thing of human feeling is a fascination forever."

Sergei Prokofiev is discussed in Chapter 33.

Primitivism also appealed to other composers in the years just before World War I. Béla Bartók composed *Allegro Barbaro* for piano in 1911, and several of his other works are wild and rhapsodic. Some of Sergei Prokofiev's early works have driving rhythms and blatant harmonies. Ernest Bloch's Violin Sonata, written in the 1920s, has a hard-driving character.

MAIN POINTS OF THIS CHAPTER

1. Expressionism was an artistic point of view that had an inward, dark, and pessimistic outlook on human nature. It was centered in Germany following World War I, and in many ways it was the opposite of French Impressionism.

2. Its music is often dissonant, and it sometimes uses a style of singing called sprechstimme, in which the singer combines singing and speaking.

3. Primitivism refers to works of art, dance, and music that were influenced by non-Western and nonliterate societies. The music often features strong and irregular rhythms and simple short melodies.

4. Stravinsky's music for the ballet *The Rite of Spring* caused a riot to break out at its premiere in Paris in 1913. In addition to its subject matter and unusual costumes, the music is quite dissonant and sometimes bitonal. The rhythm patterns are irregular and contain many polyrhythms.

FEATURES TO LISTEN FOR

1. Berg's *Wozzeck:*
   - The foreboding, dissonant quality of the accompanying orchestra
   - The steady beats played by the timpani before, during, and after Wozzeck stabs Marie
   - The way the vocal lines indicate Marie's unease and wanting to leave and Wozzeck's stalling

2. Stravinsky's *Rite of Spring:*
   - The powerful irregular rhythm in the "Dance of the Adolescents"
   - The short melodic ideas interspersed by the bassoon, French horn, and trumpets
   - The mixed meters and dissonant chords in the "Dance of Abduction"

33 Neoclassicism *and* Tone Row Music

Styles of music seem to move toward being either products of emotion and feelings or the result of thoughtful intellectual effort. The Baroque style was more emotional than that of the Renaissance. The pendulum then swung back toward intellectual control in the Classical period, but after a few generations it swung back again toward the highly subjective music of the Romantic period.

The twentieth century saw the dichotomy between thought and feeling continue in its music, but with a definite swing toward more intellectually oriented music. One approach was **Neoclassicism,** which seeks to capture the spirit and attitude of the Classical writers, artists, and musicians of the eighteenth century. The other was tone row music and serial compositions, which are discussed later in this chapter.

The prefix *neo* means "new."

Picasso, Pablo Les amoureux—Lovers, 1923. Canvas, 130.2 × 97.2 cm. Chester Dale Collection/ National Gallery of Art, Washington, D.C., USA/© ARS/Erich Lessing/Art Resource, NY.

THE LOVERS by Pablo Picasso recalls the cool, quiet, classic quality of ancient Greek and Roman art. The figures seem as delicately posed as statuary in an art museum.

NEOCLASSICAL STYLE

The Neoclassical style is evident in Pablo Picasso's painting *The Lovers*. If you were to imagine what a picture with such a title would look like, it probably would *not* depict a man and a woman in the cool, detached attitude seen in Picasso's painting. Emotional and passionate it is not. Delicate, sensitive, balanced, and thoughtful it is.

Notice that a minimum of lines and shadings is used, but they achieve the desired effect. Notice also that the figures are dressed not in modern clothing but in garments that seem more like those of the ancient Greeks or Romans. The painting projects an attitude of tender love yet in a restrained way.

NEOCLASSICISM IN MUSIC

After *The Rite of Spring,* Stravinsky changed to shorter, more concise music written for a limited number of instruments. Why did he do this? Because of his beliefs about what a composer should do with sound. He wrote: "What is important for the clear ordering of the work, for its crystallization, is that all the . . . elements . . . should be properly subjugated to the rule of law before they intoxicate us." In Stravinsky's eyes, writing a musical composition is like solving a problem; it is a task to be done by applying the brain. Therefore, music is intended to do nothing except demonstrate the composer's ability to contrive interesting tonal and rhythmic combinations of sounds.

Sometimes Neoclassicism in music has been given the euphonious name "Back to Bach." Several Baroque forms, such as the concerto grosso, were revived during this time, and there was a renewed emphasis on counterpoint; the harpsichord has also enjoyed a rebirth of interest, so the allusion to Bach is reasonable.

PROKOFIEV'S *CLASSICAL SYMPHONY*

The *Classical Symphony* is Op. 25 in Prokofiev's list of works, so it is an early work. To have this symphony follow the style of Mozart and Haydn, he made a number of musical decisions:

Prokofiev composed his *Classical Symphony* in 1916–1917.

- It would not be long. The first movement, for example, is just over three and a half minutes—a fraction of the length of most nineteenth-century symphonies.

- It would be for small orchestra. The score does not call for trombones or for percussion other than timpani, and only two instruments are featured on each of the other brasses and the woodwind parts.

- It would contain the types of themes typically found in the Classical style. And, sure enough, the themes are collections of short melodic ideas that are connected. The harmonies are less rich and complex than those found in music of the nineteenth century.

One of the themes in the first movement is marked to be played *con Eleganza*—"with elegance."

Sergei Prokofiev

Courtesy of Malcolm Brown

Sergei Prokofiev (1891–1953) was born in a village in southern Russia. His mother taught him to play the piano and encouraged him to compose music. By the time he was nine, he had written a three-act opera. After his family moved to Moscow, Prokofiev studied with outstanding teachers of composition, including Rimsky-Korsakov.

His early compositions were rather dissonant, and his teachers thought him something of a musical revolutionary.

After the Communist revolution, he left his homeland and lived in Paris, where he continued to compose and give concerts. In 1933 he decided to return to

the Soviet Union, where he was greeted warmly by the public and initially by the government. As he grew older, his music became more mellow.

Following World War II, Prokofiev and Shostakovich were accused of being "formalistic," a charge meaning that their music was considered too sophisticated by government officials. He did not allow governmental pressure to interfere with his work, however.

His style could vary from Neoclassical in the *Classical Symphony* to Neo-Romantic in his ballet *Romeo and Juliet*. He clearly was able, in Stravinsky's words, to subject his compositions "to the rule of law." That fact allowed him to be as Classical or Romantic as he wished at any moment in each musical work. Sergei Prokofiev was one of the giants of twentieth-century music.

BEST-KNOWN WORKS

ballet:
- *Cinderella*
- *The Love of Three Oranges*
- *Romeo and Juliet*

orchestra:
- *Classical Symphony*
- *Lt. Kijé Suite*
- Piano Concertos Nos. 1 and 3
- Violin Concerto No. 2

piano:
- Sonatas (10)

- It would call for a style of playing that is neat and precise.
- It would follow traditional forms. The first movement is in sonata form, the second movement follows a large three-part form, the third is a stylized dance, and the fourth returns to sonata form.

First Movement

The first movement is presented in the Listening Guide.

SERGEI PROKOFIEV

Classical Symphony, Op. 25, First Movement (1917)

GENRE: Symphony   Orchestra

CD 2 Tracks 31 – 34

3 minutes 43 seconds

Form: Sonata

Exposition

0:00 31 0:00 Orchestra plays opening chord loud, followed by violins playing first theme.

0:21 Transition consisting of short melodic fragments begins in woodwinds.

0:48 32 0:00 Second theme played lightly by violins as bassoon plays steady, short notes.

0:22 Violins repeat second theme.

0:31 Short codetta.

Development

1:32 33 0:00 Silent measure; then violins play part of first theme as music modulates often.

0:19 Transition played by woodwinds and violins.

0:25 Second theme played forcefully by violins followed by other sections of orchestra.

Recapitulation

2:33 34 0:00 First theme played by violins.

0:09 Transition begins in woodwinds; other sections follow.

0:31 Second theme played very quietly by violins at a high pitch level.

0:56 Coda begins as woodwinds and violins outline chords.

1:12 Movement closes in a rush of sound.

 An interactive Active Listening Guide can be downloaded from the online Resource Center for *Music Listening Today,* **4th Edition.**

Second Movement

This movement is quiet and songlike. The main melody seems to be the epitome of delicate, refined beauty.

Third Movement

The third movement is a gavotte—sort of. It does have all the features of the **gavotte** of earlier times, but is actually quite twentieth century in its free use of keys. The form is interesting. The movement opens and closes with the same music. Between the two appearances of that music, there are two sections of contrasting music, each repeated. When the second of these sections is repeated, the oboes add a line of counterpoint.

The stylized dance form used in the symphonies of Haydn and Mozart was the minuet. Prokofiev parted from the Classical tradition a bit in this movement.

Fourth Movement

The movement is marked *Allegro vivace* with a metronome marking of 152 beats per minute. In other words, the notes fly by, especially for the violins. Prokofiev reveals his twentieth-century harmonic thinking with a number of interesting key changes. The codetta presents a third theme, which is used prominently in the development section.

It is hard *not* to like Prokofiev's *Classical Symphony*. It has all the attributes of the music of Mozart and his contemporaries—the tuneful themes, the well-thought-out forms, the neatly balanced phrases, and generous amounts of charm and beauty. But Prokofiev has taken those characteristics and added a richer palette of harmonies and treatment of melodies.

HINDEMITH'S *KLEINE KAMMERMUSIK*

The full title of Hindemith's work is *Kleine Kammermusik für Fünf Bläser*, Op. 24, No. 2, which translated is *Little Chamber Music for Five Winds*. The five instruments are flute, oboe, clarinet, bassoon, and French horn, which constitute the usual woodwind quintet.

Paul Hindemith

Paul Hindemith (1895–1963) was born in Hanau, Germany, and his Neoclassical works have a certain Germanic, "academic" quality. As a teenager he played in dance bands and then became a member of the Frankfurt Opera Orchestra. For awhile he played viola in the Amar-Hindemith Quartet. He became professor of composition in Berlin, but his modernistic music was banned by Hitler in 1934. He left Germany, lived in Turkey for a few years, and then came to the United States and taught composition at Yale University until 1953. He returned to Europe and taught at the University of Zürich until his death.

Hindemith composed sonatas for virtually every instrument. He also wrote a large amount of chamber music and a number of motets and choral works. A few of his works were large in scope, including his program symphony *Mathis der Mahler* (*Matthias the Painter*), inspired by three paintings by Mathis Grünewald on the altar at Isenheim, Germany. He also wrote two books on music theory in which he promoted his views about consonance and dissonance.

The work demonstrates Hindemith's Neoclassical tendencies in its sparse use of instruments and in the short, concise format of its movements.

The first movement is cheerful in quality and follows a loose sonata form. The second movement is a subdued and graceful waltz consisting of rather short sections. The third is an elegant slow movement with long melodic lines. The fourth movement is short and fast. It is built around a short, pounding theme that alternates periodically with free-sounding solos for each instrument.

The fifth movement is very fast, with a symmetrical form: A B C B A. The differences among the themes are as much rhythmic as melodic. The first theme has accents falling

PAUL HINDEMITH

Kleine Kammermusik für Fünf Bläser, Op. 24, No. 2, Fifth Movement (1922)

GENRE: Chamber music   Woodwind quintet

CD 6 Tracks 6 – 7

2 minutes 52 seconds

Form: Rondo (*A B C B A*)

0:00   6   0:00   Lively A theme played by flute, oboe, and clarinet.

0:13   B theme has oboe playing off the beat as bassoon plays a line in contrary motion.

0:24   French horn enters with contrasting part.

0:37   All except French horn play figure based on B theme.

0:49   Transition introduced by oboe.

1:03   7   0:00   Wide-ranging C theme begins in flute, then repeated with rhythmic accompaniment.

0:36   B theme played quietly by oboe, then repeated with flute as music grows more intense.

0:47   Music becomes more dissonant as French horn enters.

0:55   A theme returns in flute, oboe, and clarinet, then French horn.

1:18   Coda begins with clarinet and bassoon playing softly.

1:25   B theme returns forcefully with much dissonance.

1:46   Movement closes with three solid chords.

 An interactive Active Listening Guide can be downloaded from the online Resource Center for *Music Listening Today, 4th Edition.*

logically on the beat. In the second theme the accents occur off the beat, while a bass line sounds on the beat. Also, when the pitches of the second theme ascend, the bass line descends in contrary motion, and vice versa. The melodies are not flowing ones but, rather, are cohesive fragments more in the style of the Classical period. Irregular meter can be seen in the first two themes. In fact, Hindemith changes it so often that he doesn't bother with meter signatures. And he uses chromatic notes so freely that he doesn't bother with a key signature either.

OTHER NEOCLASSICAL WORKS

Prokofiev was by no means the only composer attracted to Neoclassicism. Stravinsky has already been discussed; the milestone Neoclassical work by him was his Octet for Wind Instruments, which he composed in 1923. Other works by Stravinsky that reveal strong Neoclassical tendencies include the ballet *Apollo* (*Apollon Musaagète*), *Jeu de cartes* (*Game of Cards*), *Oedipus Rex*, *Pulcinella*, Suites Nos. 1 and 2 for Small Orchestra, and *Symphony of Psalms*.

Although known first for his compositions on Jewish themes, Ernest Bloch (1880–1959) composed two concerti grossi and a number of suites. Several twentieth-century French composers adopted the Neoclassical approach as well. Among them were Jacques Ibert (1890–1962), Francis Poulenc, and Darius Milhaud. A number of American composers also took a Neoclassical approach. They are discussed in Part VII.

TONE ROW MUSIC

It had worked for almost three hundred years. Music from popular songs to symphonies had a tonal center around which it functioned. The key of a work may have strayed and for a time become lost, but inevitably it was there and the music returned to it. This principle of a tonal center and the movement of chords in relation to that tonal center seemed as necessary to music as the law of gravity seems to us.

But was it? Arnold Schoenberg did not think so. He and other composers initially wrote works (mostly Expressionistic ones) that centered around no particular key. In short, that music was **atonal.** But Schoenberg was not satisfied. He felt the need to develop a new system for composing. About 1923 he devised a means of "composing with twelve tones," as he termed it.

The heart of Schoenberg's system is its **tone row.** The basic row, which the composer determines before writing the composition, includes the twelve different pitches of the chromatic scale, with no pitch being repeated before the row is complete. In this way no tonal center can be implied, because all the notes in the chromatic scale are treated equally.

Tone row music is linear, although it does contain some chords. The predetermined row is treated in four ways: (1) the *original*, (2) the **retrograde** (backward, in reverse order), (3) the **inversion** (all intervals reversed from their original direction), and (4) the **retrograde-inversion** (reverse pitch direction and reverse order). Any of the forms of the row can be transposed.

Although at first glance the idea may seem limited, it has been calculated that there are more than 479,001,600 rows available!

SCHOENBERG'S VARIATIONS FOR ORCHESTRA

As its title implies, the work is a set of variations on a theme. There certainly was nothing new about that. What was new was the use of the tone row theme and the ways in which it is varied.

Flutter tonguing is actually created by a fluttering motion of the tongue.

In Germany the musical note H is B-natural, and B is B-flat. Therefore, the four notes of Bach's name in music are B-flat A C B-natural. Several composers have since written works based on his name as a tribute to him.

The overall plan for Variations for Orchestra consists of an introduction, the theme, nine variations, and a finale. The introduction contains a series of sounds including tremolos in the violins and *flutter tonguing* by the flute. It also includes a time-honored motive built around the notes B-flat, A, C, and B-natural, which in German spells *B A C H*. Bach himself used this pattern of notes to spell his name as a fugue subject in his last composition, *The Art of the Fugue*.

The variations are short, sometimes only twenty-three measures long. They often feature small groups of instruments, not the entire orchestra. The finale is longer than any of the variations. The work closes after a final statement of the B A C H motive.

Here is the basic tone row for Variations for Orchestra:

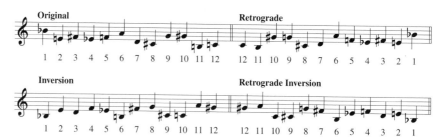

The structure of the music is very carefully planned. For example, the chords are derived from one version of the row, and the number of notes in the melodic phrases corresponds to the number of notes in the chord.

Tone row compositions present problems for listeners not familiar with this type of music. The concept of the row is not hard to understand, but the row itself can seldom be heard in the composition. Furthermore, its chromatic nature makes it difficult to remember. Actually, the row is mainly a compositional technique or approach for composers; hearing the row as such is not necessary for listeners.

The idea of manipulating timbre also fascinated Schoenberg and other Expressionist composers. He devised a technique for doing that, which he gave the German name

Lebrecht/The Image Works

Arnold Schoenberg

BEST-KNOWN WORKS

chamber music:
- *Pierrot Lunaire*
- *Trio for Strings*

orchestra:
- *Chamber Symphony No. 1*
- *Variations for Orchestra*
- *Verklärte Nacht*

Arnold Schoenberg ("*Sh(r)n*-bairg," 1874–1951) was born in Vienna. He began studying violin when he was eight and became an avid participant in amateur chamber music performances. After his father's early death, he went to work as a bank clerk. He had little formal training at an advanced level.

For many years he had shown an interest in composing, and that interest increased until he decided to make it his life's work. He spent two years in Berlin as music director for a cabaret and then returned to Vienna. He served in the Austrian army for two years during World War I. In 1925 he was appointed professor of composition at the Berlin Academy of Arts, where he remained until Hitler came to power. Because of the anti-Semitic actions of the new regime, he decided to leave Germany for the United

States, where he taught at the University of California at Los Angeles (UCLA) until his death.

Schoenberg is important in the world of music as much for his leadership and innovative ideas as for his compositions. Prior to 1908 he stood in the tradition of Wagner and composed large Romantic works. About 1908, however, he started turning to music for smaller groups. His music became more contrapuntal and much more chromatic. Over a period of time, he began to write music that had no tonal center. He also moved even further toward Expressionism.

About 1923 he devised the tone row system, which he followed for most of the remainder of his life. This was a system that was to leave its mark on the world of music.

ARNOLD SCHOENBERG
Variations for Orchestra excerpt (1928)

GENRE: Tone row   Orchestra

CD 6 Tracks [8] – [9]

1 minute 2 seconds

Form: Theme and variations

0:00 [8] 0:00   Cellos begin with original version of the row.

0:13   Retrograde-inversion of the row begins on a different note from original.

0:31 [9] 0:00   Retrograde of the row begins on same note as original.

0:11   Inversion of row begins on same note as retrograde-inversion.

0:30   Theme concludes quietly.

 An interactive Active Listening Guide can be downloaded from the online Resource Center for *Music Listening Today, 4th Edition.*

Klangfarbenmelodie. It involves changing the timbre along with the pitch changes. This is accomplished by giving different instruments various notes of the melody so that even though the melody is present, it is not heard in its complete form played on just one instrument.

Schoenberg vigorously denied that his music was cold and intellectual. When the requirements of tone row composition are considered, that denial may seem inaccurate. His music does contain much activity crammed into most of its measures. It seems as if he compressed the dimension of time, causing what happens to the sounds to be much more concentrated than in previous music. Schoenberg obviously did not conceive of music in the rambling dimensions of the Romantic period.

The German word *Klangfarbenmelodie* literally means "manufactured tone color melody."

SERIALISM: BEYOND TONE ROWS

Anton Webern (1882–1945) was a student of Schoenberg. Like his teacher, Webern began writing atonal works. Although he composed in the same style as Schoenberg, Webern's music is more austere and economical. Of his thirty-one compositions, the longest is just ten minutes, and all his music can be performed in less than three hours! His dynamic levels are often very soft, and his frail tone row melodies are subtly passed from one instrument to another. If he had written more sparsely, it seems that the music would disappear completely.

Webern's Five Pieces for Orchestra

One of Webern's atonal works was his *Five Pieces for Orchestra,* Op. 10. Actually, the use of the word "orchestra" in the title is misleading, because it is not for the usual symphony orchestra. The eighteen instruments include cow bells, guitar, mandolin, and a small reed organ called a harmonium. The fourth piece has the distinction of probably being the shortest work ever written: 6⅓ measures that take less than thirty seconds to perform. The Klangfarbenmelodie technique largely replaces traditional melodies in these pieces.

Webern expanded the concept of tone row music with the introduction of **Serialism.** In it, the principles of tone row music are carried further with the development of one or more series of pitches within the row. The idea was subsequently extended to rows or series of articulations, dynamic levels, and rhythmic values. Serialism represented additional intellectual control over musical sounds.

Consider the basic row for Webern's Concerto for Nine Instruments:

Articulation refers to tonguing, slurring, and the style with which notes are played.

Brackets have been placed over the four subrows.

The row can be divided into four subrows. In turn, each of these subrows can be divided into three segments, each consisting of two adjacent notes and one that is either a line or a space farther away. The first three notes can be thought of as a miniature row, followed by its transposed retrograde-inversion, retrograde, and inversion.

The Concerto for Nine Instruments begins:

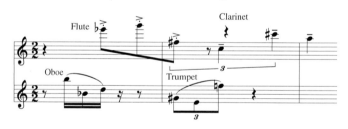

Anton Webern (1883–1945) grew up and lived most of his life in Austria. He attended Vienna University, eventually earning a doctorate in musicology. In 1904 he became one of Schoenberg's first students, and they became lasting friends and admirers. During most of his career, he held conducting positions, but he changed jobs quite often, sometimes holding a position for less than a year. Following World War I, he helped Schoenberg run the Society for Private Musical Performances. Later he conducted the "Vienna Workers Symphony Orchestra."

World War II was a difficult time for him. He found it hard to make a living and took a job as an editor and proofreader for Universal Edition. In addition, one of his sons was killed in the war.

Webern was accidently shot just after the war ended by an American soldier as he stepped outside his house to enjoy a cigar during a strict curfew, which was in force because of his son-in-law's black market activities.

Although his compositions found limited acceptance by audiences, he had a great influence on other composers, including Stravinsky.

"Doomed to total failure in a deaf world of ignorance and indifference, he inexorably kept on cutting out his diamonds, his dazzling diamonds, of whose mines he had a perfect knowledge."—Igor Stravinsky

In this example, the groups of three notes are retained, although with **octave displacement,** which is the technique of sounding a pitch in an octave higher or lower from most of the others in the row. The first group is played by the oboe, the second by the flute, the third by the trumpet, and the fourth by the clarinet. In addition, a different rhythm is associated with each three-note group, and different articulations are specified.

Malevich, Kazimir (1878–1935) *Suprematist Composition: White on White.* 1918. Oil on canvas, 31 1/4 × 31 1/4". Acquisition confirmed in 1999 by agreement with the Estate of Kazimir Malevich and made possible with funds from the Mrs. John Hay Whitney Bequest (by exchange). /The Museum of Modern Art, New York, NY, USA/Scala/ Art Resource, NY

A STYLE OF PAINTING that features total intellectual control can be seen in Kasimir Malevich's *Suprematist Composition: White on White.* Painted in 1918, the work is devoid of anything except what is absolutely necessary.

A number of composers, including Stravinsky, were attracted to the principles of tone row and serial music and used them in some of their compositions. Other composers made tone row or serial music their dominant style.

MAIN POINTS OF THIS CHAPTER

1. Neoclassicism was an attempt by composers and artists to capture the spirit of the Classical period.

2. Neoclassical works feature smaller groups, shorter compositions, classical forms, restrained quality, and melodies consisting of short melodic ideas connected together.

3. Tone row music is based on the twelve pitches of the chromatic scale, which means that the music can have no tonal center; it's atonal. The row is not the actual melody, but rather the framework of pitches around which the composition is built.

4. A tone row can appear in four different versions: the original row, retrograde (backwards), inversion (upside down), and retrograde-inversion (backwards and upside down).

5. Serialism is the application of the principle of tone row music to other aspects such as dynamic levels, rhythm values, timbres, and articulations.

6. Klangfarbenmelodie is somewhat like pointillism in painting. The various pitches of a melodic line are distributed among several different instruments. Many times the notes are also placed in different octaves.

FEATURES TO LISTEN FOR

1. First movement of Prokofiev's *Classical Symphony:*
   - The nature of both the first and second themes with their short melodic ideas connected together
   - How the second theme is played so delicately in the exposition and then sounded so forcefully in the development

2. Fifth movement of Hindemith's *Kleine Kammermusik:*
   - The contrary pitch motion and contrasting rhythm between the oboe and bassoon in the first appearance of the *B* theme
   - The *ABCBA–Coda* form of the movement

3. Theme of Schoenberg's *Variations for Orchestra:*
   - The musical logic of the four versions of the tone-row theme

4. Third piece of Webern's *Five Pieces for Orchestra:*
   - The subtle manipulation of timbres

New Sounds *and* New Techniques

34

With the end of World War II in 1945, the world moved into a new era. In a faltering manner, the nations and peoples of the world started to rebuild in both a physical and an emotional sense. Most people realized that whatever might happen in the future, things would never be the same again.

Along with the monumental changes that have come about in the more than six decades since that time, new generations of composers have been active. New ways of making music have become available through technological advances, and different attitudes about music and music listening have evolved.

From about 1945 to 1960, the competition for leadership in the world of concert music was between those who favored strict control of musical sounds through Serialism and those who favored only a few specifications through chance music and improvisation.

EXTENSIONS OF SERIALISM

Although Schoenberg devised the tone row system in the 1920s, until about 1950 only a few of the major composers were attracted to it. The tone row approach began to find more favor after 1945, partly because of the influence of Webern.

As mentioned previously, Webern extended the idea of a row beyond pitches to include series of articulations, dynamic levels, and rhythmic values. The leading proponents of what is described as **total Serialism** were the French composers Pierre Boulez (b. 1925) and Olivier Messiaen (1908–1992). In one of his works, Messiaen uses one series for the melody, another for the dynamics, and another for the rhythm; each of the series is a different length.

Other composers who favored highly controlled works in the 1950s were Luciano Berio (1925–2003) in Italy, Milton Babbitt (b. 1916) in the United States, and Karlheinz Stockhausen (1928–2007) in Germany. The music they created during those years is very complex, so it is difficult for listeners to perceive and performers to render accurately. Over the years some of these composers have changed their approaches to composing.

Tone row music may have been originally rejected because of its association with Expressionism.

CHANCE MUSIC

The American John Cage (1912–1992) was a major promoter of **chance** or **aleatory music.** In such music the sounds are partly the result of chance, so they are unpredictable. A player might be instructed to play anything that comes to mind or just rest. Or the notes can be the result of throwing dice or dropping pages of music on the floor.

At first glance, such musical practices may seem like a put-on, but they are not. They are the application in music of an existential outlook on life. For centuries Western civilization believed in progress, the idea of moving toward a goal. Through increased knowledge — which in turn led to such practical outcomes as improved medical care, more food, and increased leisure — it was thought that the human race was progressing. However, the idea of progress came under attack in the twentieth century from proponents of existential philosophy and from advocates of Asian religious beliefs. The idea of progress is false, they maintained. There is only change, not progress.

COMPOSER JOHN CAGE said of his music, "I have nothing to say and I am saying it."

ROY LICHTENSTEIN'S WHAAM! has no message. According to Lichtenstein, "Stylistically, my work is devoid of emotional content. And it's what I want." He and his musical counterpart, John Cage, created works that were so obvious that they invite no interpretation. They represent a complete rejection of the nineteenth-century belief in art as the conveyor of great ideas that need to be studied and pondered.

The term *aleatory* comes from a Latin word meaning "dice" or "gambler," which in the ancient world signified chance.

The implications of the only-change, no-goal-toward-which-to-progress philosophy are enormous. It is like removing the goal lines and uprights on a football field and ceasing to keep score or time: The game just happens. About the only assumption that can be made is that the players will eventually tire and stop playing.

This philosophical position rejects the idea that works of art must have meaning. As Cage said, "My purpose is to eliminate purpose." Depicting a can of Campbell's soup or creating a painting that looks as if it came from a comic book is not, as some people believe, a comment on the vulgarity of contemporary civilization. The content of such works is so obvious that it no longer encourages interpretation by the viewer, which is the way the artist wants it. A picture is a picture—and that's all.

The epitome of Cage's views was his work *4′ 33″*, which premiered in 1955. The pianist simply sits at the piano that long but never plays a note!

In his book *Silence*, Cage urges the composer to "give up the desire to control sound, clear his mind of music [in the usual sense] and set about discovering means to let sounds be themselves rather than vehicles for man-made theories or expressions of human sentiments." Using chance devices to determine sounds is one way in which Cage and others try to get listeners to just consider the sounds and not attempt to read meaning into them.

These ideas have been attempted by a number of composers, including Karlheinz Stockhausen. In a complete change from his electronic works of the 1950s, Stockhausen's *Originale* (1961) is based on a series of simultaneous, incoherent "happenings." In one scene the directions are "Pianist and percussionist put on clothes brought in by cloakroom attendant. The pianist takes off his cultic robes and puts on Oriental female costume. . . . When he is ready, he begins to brew up tea at the piano."

ELECTRONIC MUSIC

As music moved into the 1960s, both serial and chance music faded and electronic music began to receive much more attention. Prior to that time, technologically created and produced music had been confined to a few expensively equipped studios. When the cost of such equipment dropped enough in price, many more composers started to work with computers and synthesizers.

The term *musique concrète* means "concrete music" in French.

There are two general types of electronic music. One is **musique concrète.** Recordings are made of actual sounds—parts of human speech, the buzzing of an insect, the soothing sound of water running, the shrill sound of a whistle, and so on. Then the recording, which in the 1960s was on magnetic tape, is manipulated by the composer:

• It can be speeded up or slowed down.

• It can have other sounds added by splicing.

• Some of the partials of a sound can be filtered out.

• The order in which sounds appear can be arranged and altered.

An American advocate of *musique concrète* was Vladimir Ussachevsky (1911–1990), who was one of the founders of the Columbia–Princeton Electronic Music Laboratory in New York City. *Musique concrète* has been used successfully as background music for movies, plays, and ballets, especially when eerie music is appropriate.

Another type of electronic music consists of sounds produced on electronic equipment such as synthesizers and computers. Such music had its beginning in the Studio for Electronic Music of the West German Radio in the 1950s but today is actively pursued throughout the world.

Technology offers a composer total control over the music, for several reasons:

The structural model of the pavilion that Le Corbusier designed for the Philips Radio Corporation at the World's Fair in Brussels, 1958. Scale 1:6 on dark gray platform.

• There are no performers to alter the music, either intentionally or unintentionally by making mistakes. Once the right button is pushed, the equipment plays exactly what the composer entered into it. Therefore, there is no longer any need for music notation.

• Any pitch is possible, including ones so high that most humans cannot hear them, as well as **microtones,** which are intervals closer than the half steps found on keyboards and many instruments.

• Any combination of pitches is possible.

• Any rhythm is possible, no matter how complex, including multiple rhythms occurring at the same time.

• Any timbre is possible. Electronic devices can filter out or increase partials in a sound to achieve any tone quality the composer wishes.

• Any dynamic level is possible. The sounds can be almost inaudibly soft or so loud that they cause physical damage to the loudspeakers (and listeners' eardrums!). Crescendos and decrescendos can be regulated exactly.

The line between *musique concrète* and electronic music is by no means clear-cut.

• Any electronically created sound can be combined with any recorded sound in any way the composer desires. Actual sounds of instruments can be *sampled* (recorded) and incorporated into electronic compositions.

• The computer can be programmed in conjunction with other electronic equipment to make some of the decisions in the creation of music. When this happens, the creator of the program becomes to some extent the "composer of the composer."

The world of electronic music has changed rapidly, and it has been around only a few decades in anywhere near the form in which it is found today. No solid repertoire of such music exists. Each new work is to some degree an experiment.

VARÈSE'S *POÈME ÉLECTRONIQUE*

Poème électronique by Edgard Varèse comes as close as any work to being a masterpiece of this type of music. It was created in 1958 for the Brussels World Fair and was a part of the pavilion designed by the Swiss architect Le Corbusier (Charles Edouard Jeanneret-Gris, 1887–1965) for the Philips Radio Corporation (page 303). Not only did Le Corbusier design the exterior, but he also used a planned sequence of colored lights and images to be projected on the interior walls while Varèse's three-track tape was played through 425 loudspeakers.

LISTENING GUIDE

EDGARD VARÈSE
Poème électronique, beginning (1958)

GENRE: Electronic music   Synthesizer

CD 2 Track 35

2 minutes 50 seconds

Form: Rondo

0:00	35	0:00	Sounds of a large bell, wiggling sounds, and sirens.
		0:43	Driplike sounds, followed by something sounding like squawks.
		0:56	Three-note pattern ascends three times.
		1:11	Low sound sustained along with rattling sound, then siren, and more squawks.
		1:28	Siren sounds are played again and followed by more squawks. Soon more chirping sounds are heard.
		2:04	Sound of percussion instruments, as well as siren.
		2:35	Large bell sound, along with sustained tones.
		2:50	Recording fades.

 An interactive Active Listening Guide can be downloaded from the online Resource Center for *Music Listening Today, 4th Edition.*

There was a consensus that it was really very different!

The interior of the pavilion contained many different shapes and angles. When visitors walked through the building, they were greeted with different colors, images, and musical sounds. Varèse realized that people would not go through the pavilion according to an established path; they were free to move about as they wished, which meant that there was an element of chance in what they encountered. The reactions of the visitors in 1958 to what they saw and heard ranged from anger and fear to curiosity and awe.

Varèse's work certainly represents a break with traditional music. It has no melody, harmony, beat, or meter. Instead, it is a series of organized sounds, mostly of a *musique concrète* nature. They pop in and out of a soundscape that is either interesting or confusing, depending on one's individual inclinations.

The use of electronic music in conjunction with visual images has fascinated both concert and popular composers. The potential of electronic music has barely been tapped. It offers vast possibilities for working with sounds and images, and many composers today are exploring this new medium.

Although he was born in France, **Edgard Varèse** (1883–1965) lived most of his life in America. Appropriately, his first composition after he moved to his new country was entitled *Amériques*. It called for an orchestra plus an unusual combination of percussion instruments: drums of different types and sizes, siren, rattle, sleigh bells, castanets, glockenspiel, and xylophone. Ten years later he composed a work that is better known today—*Ionization*—which uses thirty-seven different percussion instruments played by thirteen musicians.

Varèse came to music via a different route than most composers. He was trained in engineering and mathematics.

His scientific leanings led to his contact in 1927 with engineers at the Bell Telephone Company laboratories to urge them to create machines that would synthesize musical sounds.

Notice the year that he made his request to Bell Telephone and how far ahead of his time Varèse was.

When magnetic tape recorders became available in the 1950s, he was the first to explore their potential for music making. Those efforts led to *Poème électronique* in 1958.

BEST-KNOWN WORKS

electronic:
- *Poème électronique*

flute:
- *Density 21.5*

instrumental:
- *Ionization*

ECLECTICISM

Although contemporary music is very pluralistic, with composers writing in widely divergent styles, some composers use what they think is the best of each style. They take various elements from different styles and synthesize music that is uniquely their own, a practice known as **Eclecticism.** They owe allegiance to no musical system or viewpoint, and their compositions are not easily classified. Whether or not Eclecticism is successful depends on the abilities of the particular composer.

CRUMB'S *NIGHT OF THE FOUR MOONS*

George Crumb's series of four songs, entitled *Night of the Four Moons*, contains elements of a number of styles and demonstrates aspects of several types of twentieth-century music. It was composed during the *Apollo 11* moon flight, July 16–24, 1969. Crumb writes of the work:

> *I suppose that* Night of the Four Moons *is really an "occasional" work, since its inception was an artistic response to an external event. The texts — extracts drawn from the poems of Federico García Lorca — symbolize my own rather ambivalent feelings vis-à-vis* Apollo 11.

It was commissioned by the Philadelphia Chamber Players and uses a chamber ensemble consisting of an alto singer, alto flute (doubling on piccolo), banjo, "electric" cello (that is, a cello amplified through a speaker), and one percussionist playing a number of instruments: large drum, crotales (metal shells strung together), cymbals, tambourine, Japanese Kabuki blocks, bongo drums, Chinese gong, Tibetan prayer stones, vibraphone, and African thumb piano (mbira). The singer's part requires *sprechstimme* and whispering, in addition to singing.

George Crumb

George Crumb (b. 1929) is a truly eclectic composer. He grew up in Charleston, West Virginia. His music studies include a bachelor's degree from Mason College, a master's degree from the University of Illinois, advanced study in Berlin, and a doctorate from the University of Michigan. He recently retired after teaching composition for thirty years at the University of Pennsylvania.

His compositions are almost entirely for soloists or chamber groups, and many of them involve the use of electric or amplified instruments. His music juxtaposes contrasting styles, ranging from the Western concert music tradition to folk/ethnic music and hymns. Much of his music contains mystical, symbolic, and theatrical elements. He has been the recipient of many awards and grants, including a Pulitzer Prize, a Grammy, and six honorary degrees.

BEST-KNOWN WORKS
- *Ancient Voices of Children*
- *Black Angels*
- *Music for a Summer Evening*

LISTENING GUIDE

GEORGE CRUMB

"The moon is dead, dead . . ." from *Night of the Four Moons* (1969)

GENRE: Chamber music   Mixed chamber ensemble

CD 6 Tracks 11 – 12

2 minutes 37 seconds

Form: Free

0:00	11	0:00	Flute with plucked sounds.	
		0:17	Repeated notes on drums.	
		0:23	Singer: La luna está muerta, muerta	The moon is dead, dead
		0:43	Flute with plucked sounds.	
1:05	12	0:00	Singer sings same line again.	
		0:17	Extended flute solo.	
		0:47	Singer sings opening line again.	
		1:05	Flute with plucked sounds.	
		1:18	Whispered over flute mouthpiece: Pero resucita en la primavera.	But it is reborn in the springtime.

An interactive Active Listening Guide can be downloaded from the online Resource Center for *Music Listening Today, 4th Edition.*

The score is preceded by two pages of instructions to the performers. These directions include specifications about their placement on the stage, stage lighting, the dress of the singer (a Spanish cabaret costume), and stage entrance and exit style ("should be solemn and suggest a somnambulistic, trancelike quality").

The text of the work consists of fragments of García Lorca's poems, which are in Spanish. The text for the first song, "La luna está muerta, muerta . . ." ("The moon is dead, dead . . .") is included in the Listening Guide. The music has some of the sparse quality developed by Webern, some elements of theater, some aleatory techniques promoted by Cage, and much interest in timbres. The unifying element is a chirping figure played by the flute.

Crumb writes of this song:

"The moon is dead, dead . . ." is primarily an instrumental piece in a primitive rhythmical style, with the Spanish words stated almost parenthetically by the singer. The conclusion of the text is whispered by the flutist over the mouthpiece of his instrument.

Features of Twentieth-Century Music

Melodies	Many nontraditional scales and melodies Often not vocal in character, with an angular contour
Rhythm	Prominent, with much use of irregular meters and complex patterns Polyrhythms Increased role for percussion instruments
Texture	Renewed interest in counterpoint, but homophony still present
Harmony	Often dissonant Some polytonality Some works with *no* tonal center
Dynamic levels	From very soft to extremely loud
Timbre	Conventional instruments and vocal sounds retained, but many new sounds developed from them Wide variety of timbres produced by electronic instruments
Performance media	Much music for small groups, often containing both voices and instruments Synthesizers and electronically amplified instruments
Forms	Return to some of the forms used in Baroque and Classical periods
Genres	Opera Ballet music Chamber music Tone row music, serialism Some chance music Electronic music
Other features	Music often intellectually oriented Some techniques adapted from non-Western cultures

CODA: THE TWENTY-FIRST CENTURY

In *A Tale of Two Cities* Dickens was writing about the time of the French Revolution in 1789.

Charles Dickens began *A Tale of Two Cities* with the well-known phrase, "It was the best of times, it was the worst of times . . ." This observation seems especially appropriate for the world of concert music today.

It is the best of times in terms of the number of persons composing music, the number of orchestras, public and private financial support, freedom to compose what one wishes, and availability of music of all types at almost all times and in all places. More people are involved with music than at any other time in history. The level of performers is far better (with a few exceptions such as Paganini and Liszt) than in preceding centuries.

But it also seems like the worst of times in terms of the communication and understanding between composers and audiences. As a result, composers sometimes appear to be increasingly elitist and aloof, and the public responds with apathy toward new music.

Nevertheless, musicians in the twenty-first century can build on a rich heritage of music, and technology has made its creation and dissemination far easier and faster than ever before. So what is the future of music? No one knows, of course. But two predictions seem safe:

• There will always be music. Humanity has found sound and its manipulation too intellectually fascinating and too emotionally satisfying to abandon it. In fact, the indications are that music and the other arts will be valued still more in the years to come. They offer people a counterbalance to a world that often seems impersonal and unfeeling.

• Music in the future will differ from what it was in the past and is today. Creative minds are restless and forever unsatisfied with previous accomplishments. They want to experiment, to try new ways. Truly creative people are simply unable to accept imitations or be content with the efforts of others.

By definition, creativity involves bringing forth something new and unique. And so in the world of music, as with any creative undertaking, there will always be something fresh, new, and different.

MAIN POINTS OF THIS CHAPTER

1. Several composers extended Webern's serialism to cover nearly all aspects of a musical work to achieve total serialism.
2. Chance or aleatory music is partly or wholly the product of some chance event, such as rolling dice, dropping pages of music, or allowing performers to play whatever they wish.
3. *Musique concrète* is the recording of sounds and then the manipulation of those sounds by various means.
4. Electronic music is also produced through computers and synthesizers. Over the years this process has progressed from analog recording (continuous but varying power) to recording in digital form (use of digits, usually numbers).
5. Eclecticism is the practice of combining aspects of two or more different styles in the same work.
6. If human experience is a valid guide, it is clear that there will always be music, and that the music of the future will be different from what it is today.

FEATURES TO LISTEN FOR

1. Varèse's *Poème électronique*:
   - The great variety in the timbres of sounds and their arrangement
   - What is *not* there — metrical rhythm, melody, and harmony
2. Crumb's "The moon is dead, dead":
   - The similarities among the banjo, flute, and percussion instruments that each time precede the singer
   - The final words being whispered by the flutist over the mouthpiece of the instrument

PART VII

Music *in* *the* United States

	1700	
Historical Events		Revolutionary Wa (1775–1783)
Visual Arts		Copley (1738–1815)
Literature and Theater		
Philosophy and Science		
Music		▲ Billings, "Chester" (1770, 1778)

CHESTER : L.M.

And Slavry clank her galling chains.   New-englands God for ever reigns.

Let tyrants shake their iron rod.   We fear them not we trust in God.

Howe and Burgoyne and Clinton too.
With Proscot and Cornwallis join'd.
Together plot our Overthrow.
In one Infernal league combin'd.

When God inspir'd us for the fight.
Their ranks were broke their lines were forc'd.
Their Ships were Shatter'd in our sight.
Or swiftly driven from our Coast.

The Foe comes on with haughty Stride
Our troops advance with martial noise.
Their Vet'rans flee before our Youth.
And Gen'rals yield to beardless Boys.

What grateful Off'ring shall we bring.
What shall we render to the Lord?
Loud Hallelujahs let us Sing.
And praise his name on ev'ry Chord.

Fotos International/Hulton Archive/Getty Images

1900

2000

0

Louisiana Purchase (1803)

War of 1812 (1812–1815)

Westward expansion (1840s–1860s)

Civil War (1861–1865)

Transcontinental railroad (1869)

World War I (1914–1918)

Great Depression (1929–1940)

World War II (1941–1945)

Korean War (1950–1953)

Vietnam War (1965–1975)

Terrorist attacks (1993; 2001)

Iraq Wars (1991; 2003)

Eakins's work (1870–1916)   Wood, *American Gothic* (1930)

...art's work (1777–1828)

Homer, *Breezing Up* (1876)

Cassatt's work (1888–1926)

F. L. Wright's work (1893–1959)

Saarinen's work (1946–1961)

Lichtenstein, *Wham!* (1923–1997)

Pei's work (1917–)

Poe's work (1827–1849)

Cooper's work (1820–1851)   Longfellow's work (1839–1882)

Hawthorne, *The House of Seven Gables* (1851)

Whitman, *Leaves of Grass* (1855)

Twain's work (1869–1910)

Sandburg's work (1919–1967)   T. Williams's work (1935–1983)

O'Neill's work (1888–1953)   Mailer's work (1948–2007)

M. Graham's work (1894–1991)

Lewis's work (1912–1951)

Frost's work (1913–1963)   A. Miller, *Death of a Salesman* (1949)

Hemingway's work (1925–1961)   Baldwin's work (1958–)

First steamboats (1787)

Reaper invented (1831)

Lightbulb, phonograph (1879, 1877)

James's work (1863–1916)

Dewey's work (1903–1952)   TV (1945)

Automobiles (Early 1900s)

Airplanes (1903)

Radio (1906)

Atomic energy (1945)

DNA discovered (1953)

Satellites (1957–present)

Internet (1985)

Gottschalk's work (1845–1869)

Foster's work (1848–1864)

Jazz (Early 1900s to present)

Sousa's work (1886–1932)   Gershwin's work (1898–1937)

Copland's work (1917–1990)

Country (1920s–present)

A. C. Beach's work (1883–1944)

MacDowell's work (1896–1908)

Hanson (1896–1981)

Swing (1930–1945)

Soul (1950s & 1960s)

Bernstein's work (1943–1990)

W. Schuman's work (1935–1992)

Barber's work (1928–1981)

Ives (1874–1954)   Cage's work (1933–1992)

Rock (bottom left) (1960s–present)

Glass's work (1937–)

Zwilich, *Concerto Grosso* (1985)

J. Williams's work (1932–)

Adams's work (1971)

35

American Music before 1920

The United States of America has a unique history. North America was only thinly populated by Native Americans until the arrival of Europeans in the early part of the seventeenth century. When Europeans did arrive, they came to stay, not just to take the gold and other treasures and head back home, as happened in Central and South America. For the first century and a half after the first settlements, the question was not whether America would be a colony, but whose colony it would be. The English, Dutch, Spanish, and French all laid claims to it at one time or another.

America represented a fresh start, a chance to develop a new country that was largely unfettered by ties to the past. It was a circumstance that has rarely happened in history. This situation led to the fruition of ideas that today we take for granted—ideas such as all people are created equal and government should function democratically.

Even though the American experience was good for democratic government and the common good of its citizens, it was not so helpful in the development of the arts. They had a slow start in America and did not really flourish until the twentieth century.

Why were the arts slow to develop in America? There are several reasons:

- For much of the first three hundred years of its history, its people were occupied with practical matters related to settling a new land. Except for a tiny number of prosperous families on the eastern seaboard, they had little time for the arts.

- Rightly or wrongly, the Puritans, who were among the earliest settlers, thought that art and theater were undesirable. At best, they considered them worthless diversions; at worst, they were products of the devil. The only music permitted in church was the unaccompanied singing of psalms and hymns. Not surprisingly, the first book published in America was the *Bay Psalm Book*.

- America had almost no titled families to patronize the arts. This fact contributed much to the development of a democratic society, but it removed an important source of patrons for composers and artists.

- Initially, Americans brought their language and arts with them from their former lands. They thought that European art and music were superior to whatever might be developed in the colonies or in the young nation. For hundreds of years, the attitude was one of transplanting the superior culture from Europe, not of developing a culture that was distinct and indigenous. In short, Americans suffered from a cultural inferiority complex, a condition that has not entirely disappeared even today.

ART IN AMERICA

American artists were affected by the factors just mentioned. As a result, they developed a simpler, more down-to-earth style than that of European artists. Instead of painting members of the nobility, they painted common people doing common activities. And until the twentieth century their works were not noticeably influenced by intellectual theories about art.

Winslow Homer's *Breezing Up*, painted in 1876, suggests mood, feeling, and atmosphere in a vivid way. The picture of three small boys and a fisherman in a sailboat evokes the pleasure of sailing in a nice breeze. It's a simple, straightforward work of art.

Grant Wood's *American Gothic* is one of the most famous American paintings (page 314). It has graced doormats and T-shirts and has been seen in cereal commercials on

New York was once called New Amsterdam; Louisiana was named for King Louis of France; and *Florida* comes from a Spanish word referring to "the land of flowers."

There were no democratic nations in the seventeenth century. The belief in the equality of all people was a revolutionary idea that developed in America.

The first edition of the *Bay Psalm Book* published in 1640 had no music. Music was not included until the ninth edition in 1698.

Until well into the twentieth century, it was believed that an aspiring artist, composer, or performer should spend some years studying in Europe.

Breezing Up (A Fair Wind) 1873–76 (oil on canvas) Homer, Winslow (1836–1910)/National Gallery of Art, Washington, D.C., USA/Bridgeman Art Library

Breezing Up (A Fair Wind), 1873–76, by Winslow Homer (1816–1910), oil on canvas

television. It depicts something very American in its matter-of-fact representation of life. It celebrates the homely, simple virtues of rural life, of America as it once was. The use of the term *Gothic* is intended as an ironic comparison with the massive and complex structures found in the European Gothic tradition. The pointed-arch window of the dwelling in the background is an example of what is sometimes called "carpenter Gothic," which is the American version of a European style carved ornately in stone.

In spite of its slow start, American music is a rich and rewarding type of music to know and understand, especially, of course, for Americans. It is an essential part of a course that covers music listening today.

American music can be divided into three broad categories: folk, popular, and art. American folk music is discussed in Chapter 40. The latter two types are presented in the following chapters.

THE EIGHTEENTH CENTURY

The most sophisticated music written in the American colonies before the Revolutionary War was the product of the Moravian communities around Bethlehem, Pennsylvania, and Winston-Salem, North Carolina. These people had come from what is today part of the Czech Republic, bringing with them a rich musical heritage. Besides music for church services, they also wrote chamber works. There were several active composers among the Moravians, but John Frederick Peter (1746–1813) was the most skilled. He immigrated to America in 1770.

Probably the first native-born American composer was a musical amateur, Francis Hopkinson (1737–1791), a friend of George Washington and a signer of the Declaration of Independence. In 1788 he published some songs, for which he also wrote the words. He dedicated the book to Washington. Hopkinson's most famous song was "My Days Have Been So Wondrous Free."

William Billings (1746–1800) was a tanner by trade and later one of a talented number of singing-school masters. He had an insatiable drive to write music and was a firm believer in American music for Americans. He explained in his first collection, *The New England Psalm Singer* (1770), that he would follow his own rules for composition. One of the techniques he used in his hymns was "fuguing," which was an impressive name for simple imitation.

Washington was humble in his response to Hopkinson:

I can neither sing one of the songs, nor raise a single note on any instrument to convince the unbelieving, but I have, however, one argument which will prevail with persons of true estate (at least in America)—I can tell them that it is the production of Mr. Hopkinson.

Billings was not modest in making claims about fuguing:

[Fuguing] is twenty times as powerful as the old slow tunes. Each part striving for mastery and victory. The audience entertained and delighted. Now the solemn bass demands their attention; next the manly tenor. Now here, now there, now here again! O ecstatic! Rush on, you sons of harmony.

The model for the man was Wood's dentist.

AMERICAN GOTHIC by Grant Wood, 1930. This portrait of an Iowa farm couple contains some of the simple but strong elements found in American music.

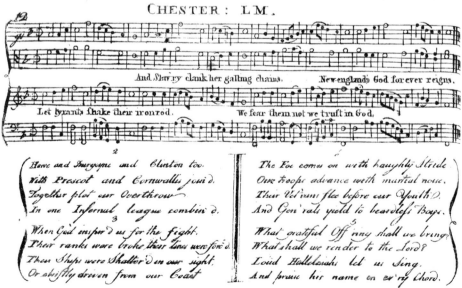

CHESTER: LM.

And Slav'ry clank her galling chains.　　New-england's God for ever reigns.

Let tyrants shake their iron rod.　　We fear them not we trust in God.

2
Howe and Burgoyne and Clinton too.
With Prescot and Cornwallis join'd.
Together plot our Overthrow
In one Infernal league combin'd.

3
When God inspir'd us for the fight,
Their ranks were broke their lines were forc'd.
Their Ships were Shatter'd in our sight.
Or swiftly driven from our Coast

4
The Foe comes on with haughty Stride
Our troops advance with martial noise.
Their Vet'rans flee before our Youth.
And Gen'rals yield to beardless Boys.

5
What grateful Off'ring shall we bring?
What shall we render to the Lord?
Loud Hallelujahs let us Sing,
And praise his name on ev'ry Chord.

As is true of a great deal of American culture, much of its patriotic music consists of songs with European roots. The origin of "Yankee Doodle" is unknown, but it was introduced in the colonies by a British doctor named Shackburg about twenty years before the Revolutionary War began. It was first sung by the British to ridicule the New Englanders, who promptly took it over as their own song by adding new verses.

The melody of "The Star-Spangled Banner" was adapted from a popular English drinking song, "To Anacreon in Heaven." This song to an ancient Greek poet was probably composed by John Stafford Smith (1750–1836). The words were written by an American lawyer, Francis Scott Key. During the War of 1812 between the Americans and the British, Key went aboard a British ship in Chesapeake Bay to negotiate the release of a Dr. William Beames, who was being held prisoner by the British. On September 13, 1814, the British fleet sailed up the bay to bombard Fort McHenry, which guarded Baltimore harbor. Before the battle began, Key, Beames, and a companion were transferred to a small boat behind the fleet.

All night Key paced the deck, wondering if the American flag would still be there in the morning. If it were, it would mean that the fort had withstood the challenge and that Baltimore had been saved. "By the dawn's early light" Key could see the Stars and Stripes still flying, and he was moved to begin the poem that is sung today. By that afternoon he had finished it, and a week later it appeared in the *Baltimore American*. The words were sung for the first time by an actor in Baltimore. It was not officially made the national anthem until 1931.

"My Country 'Tis of Thee" ("America") is sung to the same melody as the British national anthem, "God Save the King (or Queen)," which was written by the English composer Henry Carey (1685–1743). The words sung in this country were written in 1832 by the American Samuel Francis Smith (1808–1895), somewhat by accident. Lowell Mason was searching for music to arrange for children to sing in church. He had been given a collection of songs used in German schools. Not knowing German, Mason had asked Smith, a student at Andover Theological Seminary, to set English words to them in his spare time. It took Smith only half an hour one February day to write his words to the tune, which he did not realize at the time was "God Save the King."

"America, the Beautiful" is sung to a hymn tune, "Materna" ("O Mother, Dear Jerusalem"), by Samuel A. Ward, an obscure organist from Newark, New Jersey. The words were the creation of Katherine Lee Bates (1859–1929), a professor of English at Wellesley College and author of a number of books and poems. She was so impressed by her first visit to the summit of Pike's Peak in Colorado that the opening lines of the poem seemed just to come to her. They were printed in a magazine called *The Congregationalist* on July 4, 1895, and were subsequently set to several different tunes, but the "Materna" melody is the only one heard with the poem today.

John Philip Sousa's "The Star and Stripes Forever" is discussed later in this chapter. "Hail Columbia!" is another patriotic march. Feeling the need for a song to help unify the young nation, in 1798 Joseph Hopkinson wrote the words and set them to a melody that had been written as an inaugural march for George Washington nine years earlier. The composer of the march is generally believed to be Philip Phile. In those days, America was often referred to as Columbia (the feminine form of Columbus), as can be seen in the designation *District of Columbia* for the national capital area.

"God Bless America" was composed by Irving Berlin (1888–1989), an emigrant from Siberia who came to America at the age of five. He was a prolific composer of musicals but today is best remembered for his songs. The original version of "God Bless America" was composed for a musical in 1918, but Berlin decided that its solemn quality didn't fit the comedic elements of the show. In 1938 he decided to write a "peace" song, and he recalled his song from twenty years earlier. Singer Kate Smith introduced the slightly revised version in a radio broadcast that December. It was an immediate sensation and has become the unofficial national anthem.

Whatever Billings lacked in training was offset by his natural musical ability. Despite some rough places, his music possesses a vigor that continues to fascinate many musicians and listeners. A number of Billings's tunes are still performed today. The tune "Chester" is one of his best known. A version of it from Billings's *Singing Master's Assistant* is shown on page 314. The melody is in the tenor part, which is the third line from the top. The music has a plain and direct quality.

During the eighteenth century, music in America was not confined to religious situations; a folk music tradition was also developing. Much of this music, as is pointed out in Chapter 40, consisted of adaptations of music from England and much of it was not published.

"Chester" was the theme for one of the movements in William Schuman's *New England Triptych*, which was written in 1956.

THE NINETEENTH CENTURY

When the nineteenth century began, the former colonies had been the United States of America for little more than a decade. Its population was just over five million people, who lived almost entirely east of the Appalachian Mountains. Most of its goods were still imported from Europe, and there were serious doubts that the young nation would survive. The arts were still in a largely embryonic state. Over the next hundred years, these conditions would change dramatically.

The name *Mason* is an important one in American music. Lowell Mason (1792–1872) wrote many hymns, including "Nearer, My God to Thee," and conducted the Handel and Haydn Society in Boston. Two of his sons founded the piano-manufacturing company of Mason and Hamlin, and a third son became a famous music teacher. Mason led a campaign against some of the religious music of his day, which came into being after the decline of Billings's "fuguing tunes." As part of this effort, Mason published a large number of music collections.

Not only did America import much of its music, it also imported musicians. European virtuosos found it profitable to tour the United States. The most sensational of these was the singer Jenny Lind, who was advertised by her brilliant promoter, P. T. Barnum, as "the Swedish Nightingale."

An early American piano virtuoso was Louis Moreau Gottschalk (1829–1869). He was a handsome man who cultivated some of the mannerisms of Liszt. He often left his white gloves on the piano for his female admirers to fight over. He wrote sentimental pieces with such tear-jerking titles as "The Last Hope" and "The Dying Poet." "The Banjo," which is based on American rhythms and melodies, became very popular in Europe in the 1850s.

Louis A. Jullian (1812–1860) chose a different approach. He kept his white gloves on as he conducted with his jeweled baton. He played some high-quality music, including some by American composers. But his biggest success was a number titled *Fireman's Quadrille*, during which, as flames burst from the ceiling, the local fire department would rush into the hall to dramatically quench the blaze.

For sheer spectacle no one equaled Patrick Gilmore (1829–1892), a bandmaster who organized supercolossal extravaganzas. One was the Great National Peace Jubilee in Boston in 1869. The performers included a chorus of ten thousand and an orchestra of a thousand, with cannons and a hundred firemen pounding anvils in the "Anvil Chorus" from Verdi's *Il Trovatore*! The only way for Gilmore to top that was to organize a World Peace Jubilee, which he did. For this event he brought Johann Strauss from Vienna to lead his *Blue Danube Waltz*. Although the orchestra was restricted to one thousand players, the chorus was increased to twenty thousand singers!

From Jullian's orchestra came a young German violinist named Theodore Thomas (1835–1905), who organized his own orchestra in 1862. Thomas maintained high standards of performance and tried to educate his audiences. In so doing he laid the foundation for the symphony orchestras of today. He traveled widely throughout the United States and for a time was the conductor of the New York Philharmonic. Later, he organized the Chicago Symphony and was its conductor for many years.

The political upheavals in Europe, and especially Germany, in the mid-1800s brought thousands of immigrants to the United States. Some were musicians who soon became affiliated with orchestras and opera companies throughout the country. The European immigrants constituted an audience for the German symphonic music that Thomas's orchestras performed for them.

Late in the nineteenth century, several American composers began to write longer and more sophisticated works. Most of these composers lived around Boston, and almost all of them had studied in Germany at one time or another. For this reason most of their music sounded similar to works of European composers. The "Boston" or "New England" group included George W. Chadwick (1854–1931), Horatio Parker (1863–1919), Arthur Foote (1853–1937), John Knowles Paine (1839–1906), and Amy Cheney Beach (1867–1944), who was the first American woman to write a symphony. She is probably the best known of these composers today.

Edward MacDowell (1861–1908) had excellent musical training. He studied at the Paris Conservatory when he was eleven years old. After his return to America, he became a professor of music at Columbia University. Most of his works are for piano, including the often played "To a Wild Rose" from *Woodland Sketches*. He also wrote four piano sonatas and two piano concertos. His Suite No. 2 ("Indian Suite") is a landmark because of its early use of Native American music.

MacDowell was a classmate of Debussy's at the Paris Conservatory. Later he played for Liszt at Weimar.

THE EARLY TWENTIETH CENTURY

Soon after the turn of the century, the popularity of German Romanticism began to recede in America, only to be replaced by attempts to imitate French Impressionism. The best-known American who wrote in this style was Charles Tomlinson Griffes (1884–1920). He started out composing in the German tradition but later switched to the Impressionistic style of Debussy and Ravel. "The White Peacock" from his *Roman Sketches* is frequently performed. Charles Martin Loeffler (1861–1935) also wrote Impressionistic-sounding music.

Sousa and Wind Band Music

Not all music at the turn of the century in America was heard inside concert halls. Some of it was band music that was enjoyed while relaxing on the grass in a park or town square on a warm summer's evening. In the early 1900s, most Americans lived on farms or small towns. Most small towns had a bandstand from which local bands performed, often with more enthusiasm than skill.

The popularity of the band as a concert ensemble—very much an American musical institution—encouraged the development of a number of virtuoso performers, such as Arthur Pryor on trombone and Herbert Clarke on trumpet. It also resulted in a number of composers who wrote marches and overtures for wind bands.

Sousa thought out "The Stars and Stripes Forever" on a ship while returning from Europe. He then wrote it down verbatim when he reached shore. The march follows the traditional march form, except for the addition of a **break,** or **dogfight,** before returning to the main melody of the trio. This march is also famous for the decorative countermelody played by the piccolo when the melody of the trio reappears after the dogfight.

Although the melody of the trio may seem simple, it is not. It consists of two sections that are each sixteen measures long. These are further divided into four smaller phrases. The rhythm of two notes on the upbeat leading to one longer note pervades the melody. Other than one instance of syncopation, the melody is rhythmically quite straightforward.

Sousa's bands were not large, ranging between forty-eight and fifty-two players. They consisted of about twenty-five clarinet and saxophone players, sixteen brasses, six percussion, and one string bass. Sousa did not perform his marches at as fast a tempo as some directors take them today. He gave them a dignified, not a harried, sound.

Dogfight is a term band directors often use to describe a part of a march in which there is a rapid exchange of musical material among sections of the band.

JOHN PHILIP SOUSA on the cover of his most famous work. Sousa wrote more than ninety marches, which are still widely performed today. Much of his music was patriotic.

AP Photo

JOHN PHILIP SOUSA
"The Stars and Stripes Forever" (1896)

GENRE: March   Wind band

CD 6 Tracks 13 – 15

3 minutes 6 seconds

Form: *a a b b c d c d*

0:00	13	0:00	March opens with a few introductory measures.

First Strain

	0:04	Melody for first strain contains syncopation and features brasses followed by a drum roll.
	0:17	First strain repeated.

Second Strain

0:30	14	0:00	Melody for second strain is more energetic.
		0:14	Second strain repeated.

Trio

0:58	15	0:00	Music changes key and becomes softer and more songlike.

0:27	"Dogfight" featuring low brasses playing repeated notes in sequence.
0:48	Trio repeated with lively countermelody played by the piccolo.
1:17	"Dogfight" repeated.
1:38	Trio repeated with brasses playing melody loudly as piccolo plays countermelody.
2:09	"The Star and Stripes Forever" ends with a short, abrupt chord.

> An interactive Active Listening Guide can be downloaded from the online Resource Center for *Music Listening Today, 4th Edition.*

Roger Viollet/The Image Works

John Philip Sousa

The person most recognized for his contributions to band music is **John Philip Sousa** (1854–1932). Sousa was born in Washington, D.C., of a Portuguese father and a Bavarian mother. The first ten years of his career were spent as a violinist in a theater orchestra. In 1880 he became leader of the U.S. Marine Corps Band. After twelve years he left that position to form his own band. It was very popular (and financially successful) and toured extensively until his death forty years later. He helped develop the sousaphone, a version of the tuba that can be carried over the shoulder while marching. Despite his busy schedule, Sousa found time to compose operettas and marches, as well as write novels and an autobiography. He is remembered today only for his marches and is often referred to as the March King.

IVES'S SYMPHONY NO. 2

Ives composed his Second Symphony between 1897 and 1901. It is a rather early work and is somewhat conservative for Ives. Except for having five movements, it is a relatively standard symphony.

FIRST MOVEMENT The movement has a moderate tempo and consists mostly of music for strings. In several respects it is a long introduction, including the fact that it is attached to the second movement without a break.

SECOND MOVEMENT This is a lively movement that features quotations from two old American hymns: "Bringing in the Sheaves" and "When I Survey the Wondrous Cross." The latter of these tunes is played in long note values (augmentation), sometimes with portions of the other themes serving as counterpoint. The hymn tunes are two of the four themes used in the movement.

Sheaves are bundles of grain stalks; but in the song, bringing them in is a metaphor for saving souls.

THIRD MOVEMENT The third movement is slow and melodious.

FOURTH MOVEMENT This movement is slow and majestic.

FIFTH MOVEMENT In this movement Ives quotes from American folk and patriotic songs, in contrast to the second movement and its quotations from hymns. One of the songs is Stephen Foster's "Camptown Races," and another is "Columbia, the Gem of the Ocean." Another song sounds a bit like Stephen Foster's "Old Black Joe," but it is not. Instead, it is from a work titled *The American Woods* by Brookfield. A fragment of the bugle call "Reveille" is also used. The use of segments of other pieces is often referred to as **quotation music.**

Stephen Foster is discussed in Chapter 37.

Charles Ives

Lebrecht/The Image Works

Charles Ives (1874–1954) was born in Danbury, Connecticut, the son of a bandmaster. His father was no ordinary town bandleader. He encouraged his son to listen carefully and to experiment with different tonal effects. "Stretch your ears" was his advice. So Charles tried such things as retuning the piano and writing for two bands playing different pieces of music while marching toward each other.

Ives attended Yale University as a music student. After graduation he went to New York City, where he made a fortune in the insurance business. He composed his music alone and had little contact with other musicians. Because he had no need to make money, he did not try to have his compositions published and sold. For this reason, for many years almost no one knew about them. Many of them sat in the barn at his country home in Connecticut. Partly because of health problems, he stopped composing around 1915, almost forty years before his death.

Shortly after the turn of the century, Ives was writing novel harmonies and

rhythms that did not appear in Europe for another decade. He experimented with such techniques as polytonality, dissonant counterpoint, atonality, polyrhythms, chords with added notes, unusual melodic intervals, and *sprechstimme*. Ives was also fond of weaving fragments of familiar tunes into his works. He seemed to thrive on the element of surprise and what was novel.

Ives studied composition with Horatio Parker at Yale, but the conservative Parker and the experimental Ives had quite different ideas about what music should be!

Ives's Symphony No. 3, composed between 1901 and 1904, was awarded the Pulitzer Prize in 1947. The insurance man Ives took the seed of American music planted by the tanner Billings a century before and made it flourish. But until the 1940s, no one knew it.

BEST-KNOWN WORKS

orchestra:
- Symphonies Nos. 2 and 3
- *Three Places in New England*
- *The Unanswered Question*

organ:
- Variations on "America"

piano:
- Sonata No. 2 ("Concord")

songs:
- "The Cage"
- "Lincoln, the Great Commoner"

Symphony No. 2, Fifth Movement (1897–1901)

GENRE: Symphony Orchestra

CD 6 Tracks **16** – **20**

9 minutes 7 seconds

Form: *A B A B C*

0:00	**16**	0:00	Opens with violins scurrying through notes rapidly.

	0:23	French horns play fragment of Stephen Foster's "Camptown Races."

	0:45	Snare drum and piccolo take up short segment of "fife and drum" music.
	0:57	Trombone plays fragment of "Camptown Races."
	1:14	Strings play opening theme as French horns play fragments of "Camptown Races."
1:47 **17**	0:00	French horn plays a quiet, tender melody that sounds like a Stephen Foster song.

	0:48	French horn repeats songlike melody.
	1:17	Woodwinds and violins play a transitional figure that begins somewhat like "Joy to the World." Then trombones play fragments from slow melody.
	2:04	Violins play scurrying theme again.
	2:22	French horns loudly play fragment of "Camptown Races."
4:31 **18**	0:00	Snare drum and piccolo play short section of "fife and drum" music.
	0:12	Trombones and bassoons play fragment of "Camptown Races."
	0:29	Violins play opening scurrying music and are soon followed by woodwinds and low strings playing fragments of "Camptown Races."
	0:54	Trombones begin portion of "Columbia, the Gem of the Ocean." Other instruments follow.
5:52 **19**	0:00	Cello plays songlike melody as flute plays contrasting figures.
	0:49	Cello repeats songlike melody.
	1:17	Orchestra plays transition.
	1:30	French horns forcefully play part of songlike melody.
	2:13	Trombones and then trumpets play phrase of "Columbia, the Gem of the Ocean."
	2:26	Trumpet plays part of the bugle call "Reveille."
8:22 **20**	0:00	Trombones play very loudly "Columbia, the Gem of the Ocean" while orchestra provides vigorous accompaniment.
	0:26	Series of closing chords.
	0:48	Movement ends after "Reveille," followed by portion of "Columbia, the Gem of the Ocean" and dissonant chord.

 An interactive Active Listening Guide can be downloaded from the online Resource Center for *Music Listening Today*, **4th Edition.**

MAIN POINTS OF THIS CHAPTER

1. The arts developed slowly in America because:
   - people were occupied with settling the new land
   - the Puritans were suspicious of worldly pleasures, including the arts
   - almost no wealthy families were available to patronize the arts
   - Americans thought that European music and art were superior
2. The most sophisticated music before the Revolutionary War was the product of the Moravians. During those years William Billings composed vocal music that is still admired and performed today.
3. The words to most of America's patriotic songs were written and then added to pre-existing melodies.
4. America produced few composers of art music during much of the nineteenth century. The "New England" or "Boston" group emerged toward the end of the century, along with Edward MacDowell, the first composer to use Native American themes in a work.
5. Band concerts were an important part of the American musical scene in the early years of the twentieth century. Known as the "March King," John Philip Sousa was the most successful composer of wind band music.
6. The most innovative American composer in the early years of the twentieth century was Charles Ives. Some of his techniques predated their use by European composers. He often quoted from American songs in his music.

FEATURES TO LISTEN FOR

1. Sousa's "The Star and Stripes Forever":
   - The high countermelody played by the piccolo in the Trio
2. The fifth movement of Symphony No. 2 by Ives:
   - Use of quotations from the songs "Camptown Races" and "Columbia, the Gem of the Ocean"
   - The contrasting melodic figures played by the violins when the slow melody first appears and by the flute the second time it's heard
   - The very energetic nature of the beginning, including the "fife and drum" quotation

36 Concert Music since 1920

What changes took place in American concert music in the decades following World War I? In a word, *plenty*! To begin with, American composers and American performers came of age. Over the years, they shed their feelings of musical inferiority and gradually assumed a leadership role in the world as performers and as composers.

Part of the reason for the rise of American music was the nation's good fortune in coming out of both world wars with its land virtually unscathed. True, in both wars thousands of American young men died in combat, but their numbers were nowhere near those of Europe and Japan, and the battles took place thousands of miles away from the shores of the then forty-eight states. America did not become exhausted in a struggle for survival or have its cities decimated, as was true of England, Germany, Japan, Russia, and a host of smaller countries.

In addition, a number of outstanding musicians fled to the safety and freedom of the United States prior to and during World War II. These musicians and composers provided America with an enormous musical infusion.

Over the years, America's training of musicians also became better, until it reached a point where it was no longer necessary to study in Europe to achieve success. Of the three composers featured in this chapter—Aaron Copland, Ellen Taaffe Zwilich, and John Adams—only Copland studied overseas for any length of time, and he was almost two generations ahead of Zwilich and Adams. In fact, today thousands of students from Asia and Central and South America, plus some from Europe, come to the United States to study music at American universities and music schools.

The quality and quantity of concert music in the United States have also been advanced by the National Endowment for the Arts (NEA), which was established in 1965. The NEA represents the first promotion of the arts by the federal government. A sizable portion of the NEA's funds are passed on to state arts councils, which in turn cooperate with and support arts efforts in large and small communities throughout the nation. A number of major foundations have also continued or increased their support of music.

The United States and Japan have led the world in the development and use of technology for music making and listening. Starting with the phonograph invented by Thomas Edison in 1877 through radio, television, tape, long-playing records, compact-disc players, CD-ROM and DVD, and now iPods, with their music and images, the procession of technological advancement has significantly affected, and continues to affect, the music that people hear and how they listen to it.

Although it is impossible for any three works to give the total picture of the rich and diverse conglomeration of American concert music since 1920, Copland, Zwilich, and Adams each represent important aspects of concert musical fabric.

Stravinsky, Hindemith, and Schoenberg were but three important composers who came to America.

NATIONALISM

Although Nationalism was one of the features of nineteenth-century Romanticism in Europe, it did not appear in American music until well into the twentieth century. Besides, until then only a small amount of concert music was being composed in America, and those few composers were attempting to emulate European models. The greatest interest in nationalistic music occurred from the 1930s through the 1950s. Composers most associated with this movement were Samuel Barber (1910–1981), Howard Han-

THE NATIONAL SYMPHONY ORCHESTRA with Principal Conductor Iván Fischer in the Kennedy Center Concert Hall, Washington, D.C. Along with the Public Broadcasting System (PBS), the Kennedy Center has contributed to the growth of American music at the national level.

son (1896–1981), Roy Harris (1898–1979), William Schuman (1910–1992), and especially Aaron Copland (1900–1990).

Barber composed *Knoxville: Summer of 1915* and Adagio for Strings. Hanson wrote an opera, *Merry Mount,* and promoted American music as director of the Eastman School of Music for forty years. Harris composed Symphony No. 4 ("Folksong Symphony"). Schuman wrote *New England Triptych* and an opera, *The Mighty Casey.*

> Although Charles Ives revealed strong nationalistic tendencies in Symphony No. 2, his music was almost unknown until the 1940s.

COPLAND'S *APPALACHIAN SPRING*

Copland composed *Appalachian Spring* in 1943–1944 for the outstanding choreographer and teacher Martha Graham. It is about the courtship and wedding of a couple in rural Pennsylvania in the 1800s. Copland writes some very American-sounding melodies for it, in addition to using the Shaker song "Simple Gifts." The overall spirit of the ballet is calm and its music often hymnlike, which suits the character of the people being portrayed.

Copland provides this synopsis of the score:

> Today *Appalachian Spring* is heard in an orchestral suite that Copland himself arranged.

1. Very slowly. Introduction of the characters, one by one, in a suffused light.

   The bride enters, then the groom, a neighbor, and a revivalist and his flock. The music is built around a motive derived from a major chord. Soon a hymnlike melody emerges.

> The interval between the notes of the theme is often four or five steps, which adds to the open, simple sound of the music.

Moving forward

mf *cantabile*

A Scene from Copland's ballet *Appalachian Spring,* with Martha Graham dancing the bride's role

2. Fast. A sudden burst of unison strings in A major arpeggios starts the action. A sentiment both elated and religious gives the keynote of this scene.

The theme is a lively one that sounds like it could have come from no other country than the United States.

Copland soon combines the high, rapidly moving part with the long notes in the trombones and basses as the flute plays a contrasting line.

3. Duo for bride and her intended—scene of tenderness and passion.

4. Quite fast. The Revivalist and his flock. Folksy feeling—suggestions of square dance and country fiddlers.

5. Still faster. Solo dance of the bride—presentiment of motherhood. Extremes of joy and fear and wonder.

The music of this section is particularly sensitive and tender.

6. Very slowly (as at first). Transition scene to music reminiscent of the introduction.

Some of the music of this section is derived from the second section.

7. Calm and flowing. Scenes of daily activity for the bride and her farmer husband. There are variations on a Shaker tune.

   This section of *Appalachian Spring* is presented in the Listening Guide.

   Variation 5 of the preceding section was for many years the theme music for CBS News.

8. The bride takes her place among her neighbors.

   This section is a quiet coda that balances the introduction. The neighbors depart, and the newlyweds remain "quiet and strong in their new house." The music closes with a serene passage for strings, which sounds, in Copland's words, "like a prayer."

Copland succeeded in writing music that sounds very American. In it he captures the simplicity and strength of a part of American life from its past.

LISTENING GUIDE

AARON COPLAND
Appalachian Spring, Section 7 (1943–1944)

GENRE: Ballet music   Orchestra

CD 2 Tracks 36 – 38

3 minutes 11 seconds

Form: Theme and variations

0:00   36   0:00   "Simple Gifts" melody played by clarinet.

p simply expressive

        0:33   Variation 1: Oboe and bassoon.

1:02   37   0:00   Variation 2: Violas play melody in augmentation. Strings follow in imitation.

        0:49   Variation 3: Trumpets and trombones play melody.

2:16   38   0:00   Variation 4: Woodwinds, slowly and softly.

        0:18   Variation 5: Full orchestra in a majestic style.

        0:56   Section 7: Concludes with a full-sounding chord, followed by sustained note by French horn leading to next section.

NEOCLASSICISM

In the decades following World War II, a number of composers in America moved toward a more intellectual, Neoclassical style of music. Most of them composed absolute music. The major composers in this group include Roger Sessions (1896–1985), Elliott Carter (b. 1908), and Ellen Taaffe Zwilich (b. 1939).

ZWILICH'S *CONCERTO GROSSO 1985*

Ellen Taaffe Zwilich's *Concerto Grosso 1985* was commissioned by the Washington Friends of Music to commemorate Handel's three hundredth birthday. Accordingly, she composed a work expressly with Neoclassical elements, including the use of a

Ellen Taaffe Zwilich

Ellen Taaffe Zwilich was born in 1939 in Miami, Florida, the daughter of an airline pilot. She studied music at Florida State University and the Juilliard School before playing violin for several years in the American Symphony Orchestra under Leopold Stokowski. She also studied composition with Roger Sessions and Elliott Carter. In 1969 she married Joseph Zwilich, who died ten years later.

Since 1975 her career has been a series of commissions, awards, and performances by major symphonies under highly esteemed conductors. In addition to the Pulitzer Prize for Symphony No. 1, she has been awarded the Elizabeth Sprague Coolidge Chamber Music Prize and the Arturo Toscanini Music Critics Award and has received two Grammy Award nominations. She has received a Guggenheim Fellowship as well as grants from the New York State Council on the Arts, the Martha Baird Rockefeller Fund for Music, and the National Endowment for the Arts.

BEST-KNOWN WORKS

chamber music:
- String Quartet

orchestra:
- *Concerto Grosso 1985*
- Concerto for Trombone
- Symphonies Nos. 1 and 2

LISTENING GUIDE

ELLEN TAAFFE ZWILICH

Concerto Grosso 1985, First Movement (1985)

GENRE: Concerto grosso   Orchestra

CD 2 Tracks 39 – 40

2 minutes 43 seconds

Form: *A B A B A B*

0:00	39	0:00	Orchestra sounds three sustained notes in unison.
		0:18	Violins play several angular short-short-long figures as opening note continues.

0:35	40	0:00	Violins play Handel's theme while low strings and harpsichord play the continuo part.

0:21	Violins interrupt Handel's theme and play short – short – long figure over a long, low note.
0:40	Oboe continues Handel's melody accompanied by continuo part.
0:57	Short – short – long figure returns in violins and alternates with woodwinds.
1:16	Violins play Handel's melody.
1:29	Short – short – long figure returns in violins over a sustained low note.
1:39	Dissonant chord is held while fragments of short – short – long theme appear.
2:06	Chord grows louder as the movement concludes.

 An interactive Active Listening Guide can be downloaded from the online Resource Center for *Music Listening Today, 4th Edition.*

theme from Handel's Sonata for Violin and Continuo in D Major. Her admiration for the work is clear from what she has said about it. "I performed [it] many years ago, and I especially love the opening theme of the first movement. . . .Throughout [*Concerto Grosso 1985*] I found myself using compositional techniques typical of the Baroque period, including terraced dynamics, repeated phrases . . . techniques I would not normally use, but I felt inspired to do so because of the fact that this piece was based on Handel." Adhering to Neoclassical practice, Zwilich wrote for a small orchestra and includes a harpsichord. She also gives solo instruments, especially the violin and oboe, prominent roles.

The five movements of *Concerto Grosso 1985* follow a symmetrical pattern, with the last one similar to the first, and the fourth matching the second. The first and fifth use passages from Handel's sonata, with the other movements using shorter quotations.

The first movement contrasts majestic-sounding music in twentieth-century style and its angular melody with Handel's theme. Both the old and new lines have one aspect in common: a repeated rhythmic pattern of short–short–long and a similar melodic outline. Zwilich also adds a long pedal tone in the bass that contrasts with the more dissonant lines above it.

MINIMALISM

At times, twentieth-century composers seemed intent on seeing how *much* they could work into their compositions in terms of techniques and musical ideas. **Minimalism** is a reaction against the technical complexities and highly charged emotional content in much of the concert music of the previous centuries. Minimalist composers are intent on seeing how *little* they can do in their music and yet create something interesting and satisfying to listen to. They take a small amount of musical material and repeat it again and again, usually with small modifications.

The effect on listeners of the continual repetition of Minimalist patterns is almost hypnotic. And with good reason. Minimalist music changes very little and does so at a slow rate. These conditions also contribute to the considerable length of most Minimalist music. Minimalist musicians do not think of their musical works as finished products, but rather as processes. What happens during the music is considered more important than the final result.

Minimalism in music has been largely confined to America. Composers associated with this type of music include Philip Glass (b. 1937), Steve Reich (b. 1936), and John Adams (b. 1947). Glass, who attended the Juilliard School, worked in New York for two years before moving to Paris. While there he was employed copying music for Ravi Shankar, the well-known sitar player. Shankar's Indian music gave Glass an appreciation of the idea of "change within repetition."

Minimalism didn't exactly take off with audiences and critics. Glass had to drive a taxi in the daytime and rehearse his group of six players at night. But success did come over time, including music for the award-winning movie *The Thin Blue Line* (1988) and a song collection, *Songs from Liquid Days* (1986) with Paul Simon and Linda Ronstadt. Rock star David Bowie also made a Minimalist pop album called *Low* in 1977.

Minimalism is sometimes referred to as "trance music," a name that is rejected by Minimalist composers.

Although both Javanese and African music contain much repetition of musical material, Minimalism has been almost exclusively developed by American composers.

ADAMS'S *SHORT RIDE IN A FAST MACHINE*

Short Ride in a Fast Machine exudes energy and fun. It is a short work for orchestra and two synthesizers. When asked about the title, Adams responded, "You know how it is when someone asks you to ride in a terrific sports car, and then you wish you hadn't." Appropriately, he uses the descriptive term *delirando*, meaning "frenzied," for the work.

The work was composed in 1986 for the Great Woods Festival in Mansfield, Massachusetts.

Adams shows his Minimalist approach to music by having the brasses play a very rhythmic pattern that evolves as the music flies along:

changes to

changes to

changes to

changes to

The repetition of rhythmic motives, which mutate as the music moves along, are the basis for the work. Then there are the insistent sounds of the wood block. The music tends to propel itself to its frenzied conclusion.

JOHN ADAMS
Short Ride in a Fast Machine (1986)

GENRE: Program music   Orchestra

CD 6 Tracks 21 – 22

4 minutes 2 seconds

0:00	21	0:00	Wood block begins insistent pattern; synthesizers and woodwinds soon join in with faster pattern. Brasses enter with irregular pattern that evolves through several different versions.
		0:33	Brasses play even notes; music grows more uneven and dissonant.
		1:02	French horns enter with uneven rhythm pattern punctuated by bass drum.

| | | 1:43 | Brasses play even-note pattern as music gradually grows louder and more dissonant. |
| 2:53 | 22 | 0:00 | Solo trumpet enters. Lower brasses play slow notes in contrast to orchestra. |

		0:29	Brasses continue long notes as music sounds more majestic; horns play persistently repeated notes.
		0:57	Earlier portion of music returns.
		1:05	Music grows more frenzied until it abruptly concludes.

 An interactive Active Listening Guide can be downloaded from the online Resource Center for *Music Listening Today, 4th Edition.*

John Adams

John Adams was born in 1947 in Worcester, Massachusetts, and grew up in Vermont and New Hampshire. He majored in composition at Harvard, earning both his bachelor's and master's degrees there. In 1971 he accepted a position at the San Francisco Conservatory of Music. From 1978 through 1985, he was composer-in-residence for the San Francisco Symphony. Adams has spoken of himself as "a minimalist who is bored with minimalism."

He has written for a wide range of media: orchestra, opera, video, film, and dance. His most widely seen stage events are his two operas, *Nixon in China* (1987, which was telecast on PBS) and *The Death of Klinghoffer* (1991). The former is about President Richard Nixon's historic visit to China after nearly a quarter century of no formal contact between the two nations. In 2002, he wrote *On the Transmigration of Souls* to commemorate the victims of September 11.

Adams may feel bored with Minimalism, but he gives his music tremendous vitality.

BEST-KNOWN WORKS

opera:
- *The Death of Klinghoffer*
- *Nixon in China*

orchestra:
- *Harmonielehre*
- *Harmonium*

piano:
- *China Gates*
- *Phrygian Gates*

MAIN POINTS OF THIS CHAPTER

1. A sizable amount of nationalistic American music was composed between 1930 and 1950. Composers Aaron Copland, Samuel Barber, and Howard Hanson promoted American music by using folk songs and writing music about American places and events.

2. Copland was able to retain the interest and respect of trained musicians while writing music that pleased concert-going audiences.

3. As the century progressed, a number of American composers turned to Neoclassicism. Ellen Taafe Zwilich combined elements of Handel's music and its Baroque style with twentieth-century composition techniques in her *Concerto Grosso 1985*.

4. Minimalism is a type of music in which composers make the minimum number of changes, yet still create interesting music. Mimimalist composers include Philip Glass, Steve Reich, and John Adams.

FEATURES TO LISTEN FOR

1. Copland's *Appalachian Spring:*
   - Augmentation of the "Simple Gifts" melody in the second variation, and the imitation near the end of it
   - Change of melodic character in the variation played by the trumpets and trombones
   - Augmentation of the melody when played in a majestic manner by the full orchestra

2. Zwilich's *Concerto Grosso 1985*, first movement:
   - The contrast between Handel's smooth melody and the jagged character of the twentieth-century melody
   - The effect of the long dissonant chord as fragments of the twentieth-century melody are played near the end of the movement
3. Adams's *Short Ride in a Fast Machine:*
   - The gradual mutation of the rhythmic patterns, especially during the beginning minute and a half
   - The wide intervals between the pitches in the melody played by the trumpet

Popular Music *and* Jazz *to* 1950

Music critic Sigmund Spaeth has asserted that the history of popular music "is an index to the life and history of a nation." All music is an index to some extent, of course, but the popular and folk types seem more closely attuned to experiences of a majority of the people of a nation than music created for the concert hall. In any case, popular music merits investigation.

The term **popular music** implies music that is widely known, usually through commercial enterprises such as sheet music publishers, record companies, and radio and television. In contrast, folk music is passed among the people on an informal basis, with little or no commercial involvement. Furthermore, popular music is much more closely involved with business and economics than is concert music. Although money certainly plays a role in concert music, that role is not nearly as important as it is in popular music.

The popular music discussed here is mostly secular. Large amounts of religious music existed as well, but in white churches the traditional music inherited from Europe prevailed. A rich musical tradition also developed in black churches, but only recently have scholarly investigations been conducted in this area. A definite relationship existed between religious and secular music in both black and white churches, which is what one would expect, but there were also noticeable differences.

The terms *popular music* and *folk music* are general. There are always exceptions to these generalizations.

POPULAR MUSIC BEFORE 1850

The popular music of colonial America and the early days of the new nation was heavily European in character. Its dances were originally the same ones found in Paris and London. After the Revolutionary War, these dances fell out of favor because of their association with European monarchies, and country dances largely replaced them. For example, a dance imported from France, the cotillion, became the quadrille. It eventually developed into the square dance, which became very popular in nineteenth-century America and is still danced today.

Not much is known about the popular music in the early days of America. Secular songs were not published with words and music together until nearly 1700. Prior to that time, song sheets contained only words. The people then must have been guided by an oral tradition regarding which tunes to sing with which set of words, because often the sheets did not indicate a tune. Even if a tune was indicated, that information is of limited usefulness to researchers today, because sometimes the same tune was known by different names.

As will be discussed in Chapter 41, the words to popular songs were printed on sheets of paper called *broadsides*.

The **parlor song** was an important type of popular music in early nineteenth-century America. These songs were purchased in sheet music form and sung in the homes of the rapidly expanding middle class. They generally required only modest music-making skill. All of them were in major keys—even the sad songs. The accompaniments, which were usually played on the piano or small pump organ, were rather easy. Many of them were based on Irish folk melodies, which can partly be explained by the large number of Irish immigrants who came to the United States during those years.

The texts and moods of parlor songs were usually sentimental and filled with nostalgia, and they often dealt with death. One well-known song of this type was "The Ocean Burial," which began with the words "O! Bury me not in the deep, deep sea." Later this song was transformed into "O! Bury Me Not on the Lone Prairie," and it became one of the more popular cowboy songs.

It is hard for us today to understand the appeal of sentimental music, just as it would be difficult for people who lived in the nineteenth century to understand why songs today often have so little sentimental quality.

A few popular soloists or groups toured America prior to the Civil War. One was the Englishman Henry Russell (1812–1900). Although he spent only about seven years in the United States, he greatly influenced Stephen Foster and the Hutchinson Family Singers.

The Hutchinson family consisted of three brothers and their sister, and they reached the height of their popularity in the 1840s. Many songs sung by Russell and the Hutchinsons promoted social causes. One song, "The Maniac," drew attention to the terrible conditions in mental asylums at the time. Other songs dealt with women's rights, the abolition of slavery, and the evils of alcohol. Sometimes the music of the Hutchinsons and similar performers was presented in melodramatic scenes that included acting.

People today would find such melodramatics comical, but audiences at the time were impressed.

FOSTER'S "BEAUTIFUL DREAMER"

"Beautiful Dreamer" is a good example of the sentimental parlor song that was popular in the nineteenth century. Its gentle, quaint text seems to us to come from another age, which in fact is the case. The song nevertheless has a tender charm and beauty that is still appealing.

Stephen Foster

Foster Hall Collection, Center for American Music, University of Pittsburgh Library System

BEST-KNOWN WORKS

songs:
- "Beautiful Dreamer"
- "Camptown Races"
- "Hard Times"
- "Jeannie with the Light Brown Hair"
- "My Old Kentucky Home"
- "Oh! Susanna"

The most popular composer of his time was **Stephen Collins Foster** (1826–1864). He was the ninth child in a prosperous family that lived near Pittsburgh, Pennsylvania. He revealed his sensitive, artistic nature as a boy, but his interest in music was discouraged by his family, who simply could not understand it. In 1846 he went to Cincinnati to work as a bookkeeper for his brother. In his spare time, he wrote songs. About half of them were for the popular minstrel shows, and the other half were the more sentimental parlor songs. In 1848 Foster sold "Oh! Susanna" for one hundred dollars. It quickly became a hit with the forty-niners on their way to the goldfields of California.

"Oh! Susanna" was so popular that soon twenty editions of it appeared, nineteen of them pirated!

Foster's music is generally associated with the South, even though he lived for only a few months in Bardstown, Kentucky, about forty miles south of Louisville, and made only one boat trip to New Orleans. But something about the African American songs he heard along the Ohio River and around Bardstown must have made a great impression on him. Some of his songs idealized life in the South, but his attempts at black dialect in some of them can at times obscure their melodic charm.

Foster never saw the Suwannee River in northern Florida. He liked the sound of its name, which he changed slightly to "Swannee."

By 1860 Foster seemed to lose his ability to compose attractive songs. He moved to New York to give his career a boost, but the move did not help. He began drinking heavily, and his wife left him. He died in 1864 at the age of thirty-eight after an accident in a Bowery flophouse. A piece of paper with the words "Dear friends and gentle people" was found in his pocket. Perhaps it was an idea for another song by the composer of some of America's favorite music.

Hoping to cash in on Foster's death, his publisher claimed that this song was his last, which it was not. The publisher had bought the song from Foster and had the plates engraved a year or so before he died, but for some unknown reason had not yet released it.

By the time of the Civil War (1861–1865), a popular music–publishing industry was in place. Sheet music was to popular composers at that time what recordings are to popular music today. Without sheet music, it would have been impossible for most people to know the music of Foster or other songwriters.

The Civil War spawned quite a few new songs, or old songs with new words. A few of these, especially Julia Ward Howe's "The Battle Hymn of the Republic" and Dan Emmett's "Dixie," are still sung today.

Some Civil War songs had of words, one for the Unic the other for the Confede the melody of "The Star-S Banner" had different wo

STEPHEN FOSTER
"Beautiful Dreamer" (1863)

GENRE: Parlor Song   Soloist and piano

CD 6 Track 23

3 minutes 28 seconds

Form: Strophic

0:00   23   0:00   Short introduction played by piano with a cello.

0:16   Singer begins:

> *Beautiful dreamer, wake unto me,*
> *Starlight and dew drops are waiting for thee;*
> *Sounds of the rude world heard in the day,*
> *Lull'd by the moonlight have all pass'd away!*

0:49   Contrasting section:

> *Beautiful dreamer, queen of my song,*
> *List while I woo thee with soft melody;*

1:06   Opening melody returns:

> *Gone are the cares of life's busy throng*
> *Beautiful dreamer, awake unto me!*
> *(last phrase repeated)*

1:32   Introduction played again.

1:47   Second verse:

> *Beautiful dreamer, out on the sea*
> *Mermaids are haunting the wild lorelie;*
> *Over the streamlet vapors are borne,*
> *Waiting to fade at the bright coming morn.*
> *Beautiful dreamer, beam on my heart,*
> *E'en as the morn on the streamlet and sea;*
> *Then will all clouds of sorrow depart,*
> *Beautiful dreamer awake unto me!*
> *(last phrase repeated)*

3:28   Song closes with a few measures played by piano and cello.

An interactive Active Listening Guide can be downloaded from the online Resource Center for *Music Listening Today, 4th Edition.*

TOWARD TIN PAN ALLEY AND RAGTIME

The transcontinental railroad linking the east and west was completed only four years after the end of the Civil War.

Following the Civil War, America witnessed rapid territorial and economic expansion. It was also a time of social unrest and of social causes such as the antisaloon movement. During these years, there was much victimization of Native Americans, and the robber barons who built the railroads amassed their fortunes. For the first twenty-five years following the Civil War, popular songs looked to the past more than to the future.

Tin Pan Alley

Tin Pan Alley started at 28th Street, then moved to 42nd Street, and finally to the Brill Building on 47th Street.

Beginning about twenty years before the end of the nineteenth century, popular music changed with the emergence of a nationwide music industry for the promotion and publication of songs. The center of this industry was New York City, which dominated both musical theater and popular music. The origin of the term **Tin Pan Alley** has never been clearly determined, and neither has its location. Essentially, it referred to the popular music industry, much as the word *Hollywood* refers to the motion picture industry today.

It was (and still is) the nature of the commercial music industry to issue a huge number of songs, most of which had very short lives. Most of the songs barely paid their printing costs. But every so often, a song came along that made its composer and publisher wealthy. The first to reach into the millions in sales was the early 1890s song "After the Ball" by Charles K. Harris.

"After the Ball" sold ten million copies at about fifty cents a copy.

The payment to performers was an early version of a now illegal practice later known as *payola*.

To amass large numbers of sales, publishers hired "pluggers" to go into music and department stores to play and sing the publisher's music for the customers. A number of well-known songwriters began as pluggers—Irving Berlin, Jerome Kern, George Gershwin, and others. In addition, publishers made outright payments to performers, who were then mostly in vaudeville, to perform particular songs.

The decade of the 1890s was termed the *Gay Nineties* because it was relatively prosperous and trouble-free.

Tin Pan Alley songs of the 1890s were remarkably similar to one another. They were set in 3/4 waltzlike meter, had a form that consisted of a lead-in verse and a chorus in thirty-two-measure form (*a a b a,* each with eight measures), and simple harmony. Some of these Gay Nineties songs include "Meet Me in St. Louis" (a song promoting

Scott Joplin

Scott Joplin (1868–1917) was born near Texarkana, Texas. He showed much musical talent, learning to play the banjo, and to some extent the piano, on his own. He then studied with a local classically trained teacher and began a career as an itinerant pianist. He settled for a number of years in Sedalia, Missouri, where he played at the Maple Leaf Club, which provided the name for his most successful ragtime piece. In 1899 "Maple Leaf Rag" sold one million copies.

In 1900 Joplin moved to St. Louis to work more closely with his publisher, John Stark. Two years later, his first major composition was a ballet suite that included ragtime music. An opera, *Guest of Honor,* followed, but the music for it

has since been lost. In 1907 Joplin moved to New York and wrote an instruction book on ragtime music, which over time earned him the informal title "King of Ragtime." After his contract with Stark ran out in 1909, he made many piano rolls. Joplin also devoted much of his attention to an opera, *Treemonisha,* for which he wrote both the libretto and the music and planned the choreography. It was not successful and was performed only once during his lifetime in 1915. The opera's failure contributed to his failing health. By 1916 he had to be institutionalized, and he lived less than two more years. *Treemonisha* was published and staged in 1972 and awarded the Pulitzer Prize in 1976.

the World's Fair there in 1904), "In My Merry Oldsmobile," and "The Bowery." There were some songs about women betrayed ("Only a Bird in a Gilded Cage") and some Irish American songs ("My Wild Irish Rose" and "Who Threw the Overalls in Mistress Murphy's Chowder?").

The lyrics of "The Bowery" tell of the naughty things people say and do there. It is said that the song reduced property values in that part of lower Manhattan for a while.

Ragtime

Ragtime existed in two related forms. One form consisted of popular songs; it was popular between 1890 and 1920. The other form was for piano and was a forerunner of jazz. Ragtime songs were usually peppy tunes in 2/4 meter with a lot of syncopation. Some of the better-known titles include "Hot Time in the Old Town," Irving Berlin's "Alexander's Ragtime Band," which is basically a march instead of a rag, and "Way Down Yonder in New Orleans."

"Hot Time in the Old Town" is reported to have been based on a song heard in a famous St. Louis bordello.

Rags have balanced phrasing and key centers, two beats to the measure, and catchy melodies with lots of syncopation accompanied by steady, even chords in the bass. They are sectional in form.

Although many ragtime songs were written, today rags are known almost exclusively as solo piano music. The most recognized composers of piano rags were Ben Harney (1871–1938), Tom Turpin (1873–1922), and, most notable of all, Scott Joplin.

The rise of piano rags paralleled the rapid increase in the sales of pianos in America between 1890 and 1920, after which a decline began. Piano rags also benefited from the development of the mechanical player piano, which was operated by small holes punched in rolls of paper that were pulled across pneumatic tubes connected to the keys. In fact, some rags existed only on piano rolls and not on sheet music. The performance of "Maple Leaf Rag" on the ancillary CD was originally a piano roll made by Joplin himself.

Piano rags, as many a pianist has discovered, are not easy to play well. Both Harney and Joplin wrote instruction books for playing them.

SCOTT JOPLIN
"Maple Leaf Rag" (1899)

GENRE: Ragtime music   Piano

LISTENING GUIDE

CD 6 Tracks 24 – 27

2 minutes 38 seconds

Form: *a a b b a c c d d*

0:00	24	0:00	The section (or *strain*) begins in major with steady chords and syncopated melody.

		0:19	The strain repeated.
0:36	25	0:00	The strain begins higher and descends.
		0:18	The strain repeated.
		0:36	The strain returns.
1:29	26	0:00	The strain begins in a new major key.
		0:17	The strain repeated.
2:03	27	0:00	The strain returns in original major key.
		0:17	The strain repeated.
		0:35	"Maple Leaf Rag" ends with two solid chords.

An interactive Active Listening Guide can be downloaded from the online Resource Center for *Music Listening Today, 4th Edition.*

Ragtime did not follow the path through Tin Pan Alley to the public, as did most popular music. Instead, its home was the large and small cities of the Midwest—St. Louis, Sedalia, and Kansas City, Missouri; Moline, Illinois; New Albany, Indiana; Oskaloosa, Iowa; as well as Memphis and Indianapolis.

Three major developments in the 1920s brought an end to ragtime and major changes in the popular music industry:

1. The rapid demise of sheet music and piano roll sales and a corresponding rise in the sale of recordings.
2. The advent and development of commercial broadcasting. In January 1922 there were twenty-eight broadcasting stations; by December of that year, there were 570.
3. The introduction of sound motion pictures in 1927. Within two years of that date, 320 songwriters and composers were working in Hollywood.

Another musical phenomenon affected American popular music in a profound way in the 1920s and 1930s: the popularization of jazz.

BLUES

The **blues** began as folk music (their musical characteristics are discussed in Chapter 41), but a few words listing musical features can't provide the true flavor of the blues. Beyond their lowered notes in the scale and *a a b* pattern of lines covering twelve measures, there is something about a singer's tone quality, small shadings of intonation, and basic melancholy feeling that makes the blues sound "blue." The vocalist always sings alone of his or her personal and usually unhappy feelings; blues songs are not for a vocal ensemble.

The first publication of blues dates back to 1912, but the high point of their popularity came in the 1920s and early 1930s with performances by vaudeville singers. The best-known blues singers were Ma Rainey (Gertrude Pridgett, 1886–1939) and Bessie Smith.

Bessie Smith is often referred to as the "Empress of the Blues."

SMITH'S "LOST YOUR HEAD BLUES"

Bessie Smith recorded "Lost Your Head Blues" in 1926. She is joined on the recording by two other jazz greats: Fletcher Henderson on piano and Joe Smith on trumpet. Although each *a* line is repeated, Smith varies it slightly.

Bessie Smith

Bessie Smith (1894–1937) was born in Tennessee but was "discovered" singing in Selma, Alabama. She was contracted by Columbia Records in New York. Between 1924 and 1927 her recordings of the blues sold more than two million discs, making her the highest-paid black performer of the time. She died as the result of an automobile accident in 1937.

In popular music, and certainly in the blues, the performer is far more important than the writer of the music; often he or she is hardly mentioned. Smith was successful because she projected a magnetism that comes through, even though the recordings of the 1920s lack the fidelity of recordings today. But her success can be attributed even more to her expressive singing voice and style. She adjusted her tone quality and added subtle nuances in pitches to make her singing memorable.

BESSIE SMITH
"Lost Your Head Blues" (1926)

GENRE: Blues   Soloist, piano, trumpet

CD 6 Track **28**

2 minutes 52 seconds

Form: Strophic, *a a b*

| 0:00 | **28** | 0:00 | Short introduction. |

0:11   The *a* line is based entirely on tonic, or I, chord. Short trumpet break follows Bessie's singing.

    I was with you baby when you did not have a dime.

0:22   Repeat of *a* line is mostly based on subdominant, or IV, chord, but returns to tonic at the end. Another trumpet break follows.

    I was with you baby when you did not have a dime.

0:32   The *b* line is mostly based on dominant, or V, chord, but concludes on tonic, followed by a trumpet break.

    Now since you got plenty money you have throw'd you good gal down.

    The rest of the verses follow the same pattern, except for the final verse, when the breaks also occur in the middle of lines.

0:43   *Once ain't for always, two ain't for twice. (Repeat)*
    When you get a good gal, you better treat her nice.

1:16   *When you were lonesome, I tried to treat you kind. (Repeat)*
    But since you've got money, it's done changed your mind.

1:48   *I'm gonna leave, baby, ain't gonna say goodbye. (Repeat)*
    But I'll write you and tell you the reason why.

2:19   *Days are lonesome, nights are long. (Repeat)*
    I'm a good old gal, but I've just been treated wrong.

2:52   Song concludes quietly.

 An interactive Active Listening Guide can be downloaded from the online Resource Center for *Music Listening Today, 4th Edition.*

JAZZ

The roots of **jazz** are complex, but certainly some of them reach back to the African heritage of African Americans. Other influences include minstrel show music, work songs, blues, French-Creole and Latin American music, and especially ragtime.

These bands were small by today's standards.

The traditional beginning of jazz lies with the brass bands that played for funerals in New Orleans. As a part of the procession to the grave site, the band played solemn versions of hymns like "Nearer My God to Thee." After the burial, the band would assemble a couple of blocks away from the cemetery and break into a ragtime version of a hymn or tune like "Didn't He Ramble." The bands were competitive in their ability in *cutting* or *bucking*, the terms for such playing. The style eventually moved to the red-light district and the bordellos of New Orleans.

The "jazz funeral" is still practiced in New Orleans today.

Like folk music, jazz was created by generally untrained musicians who could not have written down what they played or sang, even had they wanted to. But it differs in two ways: (1) It sprang up in the cities, so its roots are urban; and (2) only a few people perform jazz, while many listen.

Some of the early jazz musicians didn't want to learn to read music because they claimed it might hinder their creative abilities.

Elements of Jazz

MELODY   The most notable feature of jazz melodies is the **blue notes.** These notes are created by altering the major scale by lowering the third, fifth, or seventh steps. The chords that accompany these notes are not altered, however, so there is a dissonance between the lowered melody note and the note in the chord. The result, however, is not so much dissonance as it is a particular tonal effect.

HARMONY Traditional jazz harmony is as conservative as a church hymn. Most chords consist of the three primary triads used for harmonizing most simple songs: tonic (I), dominant (V), and subdominant (IV). As jazz matured, however, its harmonic palette became much richer and more sophisticated.

RHYTHM Jazz assumed many of the rhythmic characteristics of ragtime—a meter of two beats per measure combined with a countless variety of syncopated melodic figures. Jazz rhythms cannot be written precisely in traditional notation. Jazz musicians make small deviations in timing and emphasis, which most trained musicians cannot execute without guidance and practice.

TIMBRE Jazz has its own tonal colors. Certain instruments and certain styles of playing have become associated with jazz. The saxophone was intended to be a concert instrument, but jazz players took it up and produced a different timbre. Brass instruments in jazz often use mutes. Some of these mutes have distinctive names, such as *cup*, *wah-wah*, and *plunger*.

The style of singing jazz is quite different from that used for singing an art song or a folk song. Jazz singers employ more colors and "bend" the pitch for expressive effect.

FORM Jazz has no overall form that applies to all its styles. The form generally consists of a series of variations on a simple harmonic pattern. As mentioned previously, the blues have a traditional pattern of three lines set in an *a a b* pattern. Sometimes the singer does not sing all the way through a section, and an instrumentalist fills in with a short solo called a *break*.

IMPROVISATION Making up music on the spot is fundamental to jazz. Traditionally, jazz was not written down, but, as it developed, it was often arranged with at least some of the music notated. The extemporaneous creation of music gives jazz an ever-fresh quality. Improvising in jazz is based on the chords of the tune. Players are not confined to just the notes of the chords, especially as jazz has evolved, but they are aware of them and make up their music accordingly.

The plunger mute was originally a rubber sink plunger.

The idea of "note bending" was a vocal technique derived from field hollers. It was picked up by instrumentalists and used in jazz.

JOE "KING" OLIVER'S CREOLE JAZZ BAND

Michael Ochs Archives/Getty Images

Typically, the players in a jazz performance agree that they will play a certain piece in a particular key. They also agree on an order in which each player is featured, although it can be changed during the performance by a nod of the head. Each player in turn improvises a chorus while keeping in mind the harmony of the song. Often for the final time through the piece, everyone joins in simultaneous improvised counterpoint. Only the musical instincts and good ears of the players, as well as the basic chord patterns of the piece, keep the music together.

Often during jazz improvisation, the melody can no longer be detected in the mosaic of sound. This happens because players sound many notes in addition to the former melody, and the tune becomes pretty well obscured.

The key can be decided in a few seconds. Jazz musicians are usually "easy" about such things.

Types of Jazz

Until the end of World War I, jazz had been mostly confined to the South, especially New Orleans. A number of factors led to the movement "up the river" to St. Louis, Chicago, and other cities in the North. One was the closing of Storyville, the red-light district in New Orleans. Many jazz musicians who worked in the bordellos lost their jobs and had to seek work elsewhere.

The U.S. Navy had Storyville shut down because it was concerned about its impact on the physical and moral health of the servicemen.

In addition, during World War I many young men, who had previously never thought they would see much more than the area where they grew up, were assigned to military camps and bases all over the United States. Furthermore, travel between cities by train was easy and not too expensive, if one was willing to ride coach class. If a jazz piano player lost his job in New Orleans, he could buy a ticket and head for St. Louis or Chicago. One of the best-known bands to make such a move was Joe "King" Oliver's Creole Jazz Band.

DIXIELAND The predominant type of jazz in the 1920s was **Dixieland.** It consisted of music in two beats to the measure with a strong upbeat and a "busy" quality when several players were improvising at the same time. The bands were small, usually four to seven players. Originally, they did not include drums; keeping the beat was the piano player's job. Drums were added in later years. Dixieland bands loved to describe their music as being "hot," which meant that it was somewhat faster and louder than people were accustomed to at the time.

What was "hot" in the 1920s seems rather tame to most listeners today.

LOUIS ARMSTRONG
"Come Back, Sweet Papa" (1926)

GENRE: Dixieland jazz   Trumpet, trombone, sax/clarinet, bass

CD 6 Track 29

2 minutes 32 seconds

Form: Variations on tune

0:00 29	0:00	Short introduction played by trumpet and saxophone.
	0:08	Sax plays chorus.
	0:28	Sax repeats chorus.
	0:48	Trumpet takes up chorus as trombone adds melodic figures.
	1:08	Trumpet repeats chorus.
	1:27	Trombone plays sliding notes (glissando), and trumpet continues as clarinet improvises contrasting part.
	1:49	Piano plays chorus.
	2:08	Clarinet, trumpet, and trombone play chorus together.
	2:32	Piece concludes with characteristic rhythm figure.

 An interactive Active Listening Guide can be downloaded from the online Resource Center for *Music Listening Today, 4th Edition.*

LISTENING GUIDE

LOUIS ARMSTRONG

Louis Armstrong (1900–1971) was born on the Fourth of July into a poor and unstable New Orleans family. As a boy he became involved with street life and at the age of twelve was sentenced by the juvenile court to the Colored Waifs' Home. It was there that he learned to play the cornet. After two years in the home, he was released; he did odd jobs and played whenever the opportunity presented itself.

Armstrong's first name is pronounced "Loo-ie," which indicates the French tradition in his native New Orleans. He also acquired the nickname "Satchmo" for "satchel mouth."

Good fortune struck when Joe "King" Oliver took an interest in Armstrong, including sending him jobs that he couldn't accept himself. In 1919 Oliver moved to Chicago, and Armstrong was recognized as the best trumpet player in New Orleans. Two years later Oliver telegraphed Armstrong to join him in Chicago. Two years after that, Fletcher Henderson offered him a job with his outstanding band in New York.

After leaving Henderson's band some years later, Armstrong led several groups of his own, including the Hot Five. By the 1940s he was featured on many radio shows and appeared in a number of films. His last movie was *Hello, Dolly!* In his later years, he sang as much as he played. He served as a goodwill emissary for the U.S. State Department on a number of worldwide tours.

Armstrong was once asked to define jazz. He replied to the effect that "If you don't know, I can't explain it."

Armstrong is considered the first great improvising soloist. He established a high standard of performance that has lasted for generations. In so many ways, he caught the elusive quality and joy of jazz.

The song "Come Back, Sweet Papa" is a good example of Dixieland style. The tune was written by Paul Barbarin and Bob Russell, but in jazz what the players do with a tune is much more important than the original tune. If a recording had been made of "Come Back, Sweet Papa" a day or even a few minutes after the version on the ancillary CDs, it would be similar but not exactly the same, because the players make up some of what they play as they go along.

Notice that there are no drums in the Hot Five.

"Come Back, Sweet Papa" was recorded by Louis Armstrong and his Hot Five in Chicago on February 22, 1926. On the recording Armstrong plays cornet. Other instruments heard on the recording are trombone, sax/clarinet (the same player doubling), piano, and banjo. The recording has a twangy quality, due largely to the inadequacies of recording equipment in 1926. It could be remastered today to sound "warmer," but why? Part of its charm lies in its original timbre.

The most famous scat singer was Ella Fitzgerald.

Scat singing was an instrumental style of singing introduced by Armstrong in a recording of a song called "Heebie Jeebie." It sets syllable sounds without meaning to an improvised vocal line. The sounds are usually sung quite quickly.

Octave tremolos are the rapid alternation between two notes an octave apart.

BOOGIE-WOOGIE After the Great Depression hit in 1929, for economic reasons people often hired only a piano player rather than a six- or seven-piece band. This situation encouraged the development of a type of jazz piano playing called **boogie-woogie.** It features a persistently repeated bass figure over which the player improvises trills, octave

Edward Kennedy "Duke" Ellington (1899–1975) lived a very different life from that of Louis Armstrong. Ellington was born in Washington, D.C., into the middle-class family of a butler. He studied both art and music when he was young, and his piano lessons included instruction in the popular ragtime style of the day. Although he was successful in his art studies, he decided on music and formed a band that played at social events in the Washington, D.C., area.

Ellington's interest in art is reflected in a number of his song titles that mention colors, including "Mood Indigo" and "Black, Brown, and Beige."

In 1923 he joined a five-piece combo called The Washingtonians and went to New York. Success didn't come easily, but three years later he was playing at the Cotton Club, which at that time was the most expensive nightclub in Harlem. It catered to white audiences who wanted to hear good jazz.

Over the years, Ellington's band was responsible for many musical innovations, including echo chambers in recordings to increase reverberation (which became standard practice later), the flatted fifth, the amplified bass, and the baritone saxophone. By the 1950s his group seemed to be declining after twenty years, but a stunning performance at the Newport Jazz Festival in 1956 revived it. He composed a number of sacred works in his later years and made goodwill tours for the U.S. State Department.

Ellington's compositions were partially group efforts. He would begin playing a musical idea on the piano, and other members of the band would join in and add ideas. He would then massage these ideas into a final composition. Duke Ellington and his band left a legacy of elegant jazz.

Jazz bands were noted for a high turnover rate. Not so with Ellington. For example, Harry Carney, his baritone sax player, was with him for forty-seven years!

Michael Ochs Archives/ Getty Images

DUKE ELLINGTON

tremolos, and other melodic figures. Boogie-woogie was often called "eight to the bar," because the repeated bass part has eight notes per measure.

8va- -

SWING By 1935 jazz had progressed from small groups improvising in Dixieland style to intricate arrangements for bands of twelve to nineteen players. Much of their music was written down. Many pieces were played in four rather fast beats per measure, and the chords were far more complex than they had been in earlier jazz. The term **swing** may well have come from the bouncy quality of the music.

The Swing Era was a time when audiences danced. Its concert halls were such places as the Roseland Ballroom in New York and the Palladium in Hollywood. It was also a time when the more successful bands had regular broadcasts over national radio networks.

Improvisation was still an important part of swing. Arrangers marked places for a soloist to *ad lib*—to improvise at liberty or at will. And there were many outstanding soloists: Gene Krupa on drums, Harry James on trumpet, Coleman Hawkins on saxophone, Artie Shaw and Benny Goodman on clarinet, and others. It was also the era of outstanding bands: Glenn Miller, Paul Whiteman, Les Brown, Count Basie, Woody Herman, and especially Duke Ellington. These bands had outstanding arrangers who had as much to do with the musical results as the composers of the tunes. Ellington's "Take the 'A' Train" is typical of swing music.

The Swing Era was also known as the Big Band Era.

DUKE ELLINGTON

"Take the 'A' Train" (1941)

GENRE: Big band jazz   Large jazz band

CD 2 Tracks 41 – 42

2 minutes 26 seconds

Form: *a a b a*

41	0:00	Short introduction, then saxes play first part (*a*) of the tune.

	0:17	Saxes repeat first part of the tune.
0:29 42	0:00	Saxes play a contrasting section (*b*).
	0:11	Saxes play *a* part again.
	0:22	Saxes play *a* variant of the tune as a muted trumpet improvises contrasting part.
	0:33	Variant of *a* section is repeated.
	0:46	Muted trumpet continues with *b*.
	0:57	Trumpet and saxes repeat variant of *a*.
	1:08	Modulation to new key.
	1:14	Saxes embellish variant of *a* as trumpet improvises. Then variant is repeated.
	1:37	Trumpet and saxes play variant of *b*, concluding with a cascading chord sounded by trumpets and trombones.
	1:48	Saxes play original *a* tune against lively rhythmic pattern in trumpets.
	1:59	Saxes quietly repeat part of *a* several times as music slowly fades.
	2:26	"Take the 'A' Train" concludes quietly with a long chord.

An interactive Active Listening Guide can be downloaded from the online Resource Center for *Music Listening Today, 4th Edition.*

MAIN POINTS OF THIS CHAPTER

1. The parlor song was a common type of popular music in the nineteenth century. It was intended for amateur performers in the home.

2. Tin Pan Alley became the name for the popular music industry around 1880. At that time, popular songs existed in sheet music form and were promoted by song pluggers in stores.

3. Two important forerunners of jazz were blues and ragtime. Blues included blue notes (lowered thirds, fifths, and sevenths in the melody) and followed a twelve-bar form. Ragtime was primarily for piano and contained much syncopation in a lively two-beat meter.

4. America's greatest contribution to the world of music, jazz, developed early in the twentieth century in New Orleans. It has a variety of roots, but its African American heritage is clearly the most important one.

5. Jazz consists largely of improvisations on popular songs. It contains much syncopation, lively rhythms, blue notes, and distinctive tone colors, and features such instruments as the saxophone and trumpet played with a jazz quality.

6. Dixieland has a lively, "busy" quality when the small group of players improvise at the same time.

7. Boogie-woogie, composed for piano, featured an ostinato bass figure played by the pianist's left hand while the right hand played many decorative notes and melodic figures.

8. The swing era (1935–1950) featured bands of fifteen or more players playing music for dancing. Arrangements consisted of popular tunes that had a bouncy quality.

FEATURES TO LISTEN FOR

1. Foster's "Beautiful Dreamer":
   - The tenderness and beauty of the melody
2. Joplin's "Maple Leaf Rag":
   - Frequent use of syncopation in the upper notes in contrast to the more steady lower notes
3. Smith's "Lost Your Head Blues":
   - The *aab* form of the stanzas and the chord changes
   - The added melodic figures played by the muted trumpet at the end of the singer's lines
4. Armstrong's "Come Back, Sweet Papa":
   - Improvised counterpoint between trumpet and the trombone
   - Improvised counterpoint near the end of the piece when the clarinet, trumpet, and trombone play at the same time
5. Ellington's "Take the 'A' Train":
   - Complex nature of the *a* theme
   - The way the piece builds, especially toward its conclusion

38 Popular Music since 1950

In many ways America today is not all that different from America in 1950. Its governmental structure and economic system are virtually unchanged, and most of its core beliefs and values are still somewhat intact. But in other ways, America has moved far from what it was in 1950.

A number of these changes have had a major impact on music, and especially on popular music.

- The population of the United States has nearly tripled since 1950. Therefore, several segments of it easily became large enough to draw the attention of the media and make the marketing of specially oriented products, including music, well worthwhile.

- The decade of roughly 1947–1956 saw a huge increase in the number of children born, partly because veterans of World War II had to delay having families until after the war.

- The general economic level of the United States reached new heights. Most teenagers are able to buy recordings, movie tickets, and clothes and other products especially created for them as never before.

- Television replaced radio as the prime form of mass-media entertainment. Network radio, which in the 1930s and 1940s had been an extremely important cultural force, almost disappeared except for its news function. Instead, hundreds of local radio stations sprang up, many of which catered to audiences of a particular age level or ethnic group. Most of these stations survived (and often thrived) by playing recordings of popular music interspersed with spot commercials.

- Recordings could be produced and marketed by small companies, which greatly reduced the influence of the few large record companies that had controlled the industry in the previous decades. These small companies were much more innovative and responsive to changes in audience tastes than the established companies. Without these new companies, many of the developments in popular music would have happened much more slowly, if indeed at all.

- America's minority populations became much more conscious and proud of their particular identities. For quite a few years, most whites could not understand the feelings that the "Black is beautiful" slogan evoked or the feelings of so many African Americans. The awareness of ethnic and racial identity greatly influenced people's choices in popular music.

THE POPULAR MUSIC INDUSTRY

The years since 1950 have witnessed a major expansion of the mass marketing of commercial popular music. The industry continued to produce a large number of songs, very few of which would be successful. But the few that became "hits" made huge amounts of money for the recording company, publisher, and performer.

One of the causes for the expansion was increased economic prosperity, which meant that more money was available for the products that the under-twenty-one market wanted, including music. Another factor was the sizable increase in population of the United States. By the turn of this century, there were more than 30 million teenagers, and it is estimated that they were able to spend more than 150 *billion* dollars.

The sales of popular music are mostly to young people under the age of twenty-one, and the industry focuses almost all its efforts on them.

ROCK BAND **KISS** PERFORMING IN COSTUME From left, bass player Gene Simmons, guitarist Ace Frehley, and guitarist/singer Paul Stanley.

The years since 1950 have also been a time of rapidly increased means of hearing music. From the long-playing records in the 1950s to CDs to the downloading of songs from the Internet on handheld devices, music became far more available. In addition, it has became even more pervasive in society, as music is heard nearly everywhere one goes, a fact that was pointed out in Chapter 1.

Only a few recording companies exerted control of much of the popular music industry prior to 1950. That situation ended, and soon many different record labels and types of popular music became available. Over the years the industry and performers learned that bad publicity is better than good publicity, and certainly better than no publicity. For example, to keep her name before the public, the performer Madonna (Madonna Louise Ciccone) tried to alter her "bad-girl" image to a "good-girl" image in a matter of just a couple of years. Others wore bizarre clothing or makeup when performing. Some performers resorted to sensationalism or repulsive acts such as biting off the head of a bat during a concert.

What matters to Madonna and other performers is that people are aware of them, even if it's not in a positive way.

Although popular music is as much a sociological and economic phenomenon as it is musical, a small number of popular performers and musicians have created some truly imaginative pieces of music. Some of the time these works represent crossovers between popular and concert music. In other cases, popular performers have demonstrated much creativity and originality. Whatever the case, popular music is a fascinating mix of many kinds of music that have been influenced by a number of factors. No discussion of it, even one the size of an entire book, can do it justice.

BLUES AND SOUL

Two of the main types of American popular music were born in the rural South. And just as the South was segregated on the basis of race until a few decades ago, its popular music also had strong racial associations. The *blues* is the music of the blacks, and *country* is the music of the whites.

Blues began as a type of folk music, as described in Chapter 41. As many African Americans migrated over the years from the South to the cities of the North, the blues moved with them. It spoke of the harsh life that they encountered in the northern cities. The acoustic guitar was replaced by the electric guitar, and piano, drums, and other instruments were added to accompany the singers. The music became louder than before, and blues singers often adopted a shouting style, even though they usually used a microphone. The style of piano playing was similar to what was used in boogie-woogie, with its heavy left-hand repeated patterns. Drums were eventually added as well.

Rhythm and Blues

By the 1950s saxophones and backup vocal ensembles had completed the migration of the blues from the country to the city. And it had acquired a new commercial name: **rhythm and blues.** Entertainers such as Chuck Berry (b. 1926) and Bo Diddley (Elias McDaniel, b. 1928–2008) created a music that became the basis of rock and roll, which began to appear in the mid-1950s.

The name *Motown* is a contraction of "Motor Town," a nickname sometimes given Detroit. Gordy once described the Motown sound as "rats, roaches, struggle, talent, guts, love."

Motown Records was a major force in promoting rhythm and blues. It was founded in Detroit in 1958 by then–auto worker and part-time songwriter Barry Gordy, with seven hundred dollars he borrowed from his credit union. At first, success was limited. The real breakthrough happened in 1964 with a recording of "Where Did Our Love Go?" by the Supremes.

That's 87,142 times the value of Gordy's initial investment!

Motown Records carefully developed its stars and their recordings, including choreography and arrangements slicked up for white audiences. In addition to the Supremes, its major stars were Smokey Robinson, The Temptations, Stevie Wonder, and Michael Jackson, who began as a boy singing with his brothers but later moved to solo appearances during his long career. In 1988 Motown Record Corporation was sold to MCA, Inc., for $61 million.

CHUCK BERRY, THE SUPREMES, STEVIE WONDER, AND MICHAEL JACKSON

Soul

Rhythm and blues gradually gave way to a more general concept of African American music: **soul.** This term is somewhat nebulous, but it is strongly associated with the racial and cultural identity of African Americans and is created primarily for them. Musically, it is a synthesis of blues, jazz, and gospel. On the surface its prominent musical characteristics are not all that different from those of rock. But underneath there lies a wealth of subtle tonal and rhythmic nuances that make soul distinctive and highly expressive.

RAP

Rap became the popular music phenomenon of the 1990s. It is half spoken, not sung in the usual sense of the word, with strong, persistent rhythm. The most notable feature of rap is its messages, which contain simple rhymes. They often talk about violence, resentment, and aggression in harsh and unvarnished terms. Favored topics include guns, drugs, murder, sex, and hatred of authority, as can be seen in these lines referring to what some police believe:

> *They have the authority*
> *To kill the minority*

Some rap is plain ugly, with displays of racism and homophobia, and it demeans women, who are often referred to as "bitches" or "ho's" (whores). The result: The sales of rap CDs boomed. By 2003 rap had more than a thirteen percent share of the recording market, which is nearly double its share only eight years earlier.

In its rather short history, rap has tended to divide into two categories. One is "gangsta rap" with its angry, violent messages, heavy rhythm, and little melody or harmony. The other, sometimes called "pop rap," speaks about unity and has more melodic interest. Queen Latifah's (Dana Elaine Owens) "Unity," for example, talks about respect and community.

In *"Cop Killer,"* rapper Ice-T bragged about slitting a policeman's throat and watching his family mourn. A few years later, he was playing a detective in the TV series *Law and Order: Special Victims Unit.*

COUNTRY MUSIC

Country music was (and still is) the "people's music" among the whites in the South. It began as folk music but evolved into a national phenomenon and a huge commercial enterprise.

Characteristics of Country Music

SINGING STYLE The style of singing is a direct carryover from the style used for folk songs. It has a lonesome quality and is sung with a clear tone and no vibrato. It tends to be nasal and slightly tense or strained. Often singers let their voice "break" to add emotion to a moment in a song. Yodels are sometimes added, especially in the West. Above all, the singing projects sincerity, or it is just not country music.

INSTRUMENTS Country music is traditionally played on stringed instruments—the fiddle, dulcimer, guitar, banjo, and mandolin. The *fiddle* is a violin played in a distinctive way with a straight, penetrating tone, short and rapid bow strokes, and much sliding from one note to another. Some country music festivals have fiddling contests. The *mandolin* is associated with Italy but became widely used in some types of country music.

Often fiddlers perform tricks, such as playing the instrument behind their backs, holding the bow between their legs while moving the fiddle with their hands and arms, and similar antics.

MELODY AND HARMONY Country music is simple and direct. As it became more popular, major and minor scales replaced the extensive use of the older modal scales. Its songs are mostly harmonized with the three primary chords found in so much music in the Western world: tonic, dominant, and subdominant.

RHYTHM The rhythm is simple, with only a little syncopation. Most of the songs are two beats to the measure.

TEXTS The texts of country songs are an interesting blend of realism and sentimentality. Topics include death, drinking, nostalgia, loneliness, and, the perennial favorite, broken love.

Development of Country Music

The move of country music away from its folk status to the world of popular music coincides with the widespread use of recordings and radio in the 1920s. Record companies realized the commercial potential of what was then called *hillbilly* music. They recorded singers such as Uncle Dave Macon from Tennessee, the Carter Family from Virginia, Gid Tanner and his Skillet Lickers from Georgia, and especially Jimmie Rodgers from Mississippi.

Radio broadcasts were vital to the growth of country music because a large part of its audience lived in remote, rural, mountainous areas. The radio show that eventually became the Grand Ole Opry started in 1925 on WSM in Nashville with two unpaid performers and no commercial sponsor!

The lack of a sponsor seems unbelievable today.

A brakeman was one of the crew on a locomotive.

COUNTRY GREATS HANK WILLIAMS AND LORETTA LYNN

The first major country music star was Jimmie Rodgers (1897–1933) from Meridian, Mississippi, who was known as the "Singing Brakeman." His career was short—only six years. But during those years, he recorded 111 songs and sold twenty million records, an amazing feat for that time. He was quite eclectic in the music he performed, which included work songs, white blues, love songs, and melancholy ballads.

Country music had a close cousin in country-western music. Part of the commercial success of this music was due to the popularity of movies about cowboys and the music performed in them. Some performers became well known in these films: Gene Autry, Ernest Tubb, Maurice "Tex" Ritter, and the Sons of the Pioneers, which at that time included Roy Rogers (Leonard Slye).

"Your Cheatin' Heart" was No. 1 on *Billboard* magazine's country chart in 1953 and was No. 7 in 1962 with Ray Charles's recording.

Country music grew rapidly after World War II. The most important name in country music from the early 1950s was Hank Williams (1923–1953), who, like Jimmie Rodgers, had a short career. He and his band, the Drifting Cowboys, recorded such perennial favorites as "Your Cheatin' Heart," "I'm So Lonesome I Could Cry," and "Hey, Good Lookin'." Other important names include Johnny Cash, Tennessee Ernie Ford, Merle Haggard, Patsy Cline, and Loretta Lynn, whose life story was made well known in her autobiography and subsequent movie, *Coal Miner's Daughter*.

Types of Country Music

Hank Williams died at the age of twenty-nine from a combination of alcoholism and barbiturates prescribed by a con-man doctor.

The success of country music led to several variants in its style. *Rockabilly*, as its name suggests, was strongly influenced by rock. It was mostly the product of Sun Records and was represented by Carl Perkins (1932–1998), Elvis Presley (1935–1977), and Jerry Lee Lewis (b. 1935).

Another variant is sometimes referred to as *honky-tonk*. It centered around Austin, Texas, and its most recognized performer is Willie Nelson (b. 1933).

Bluegrass has no songs about truck drivers or urban situations.

A third variant, **bluegrass,** attempted to return country music to its traditional roots. Only acoustic (nonelectric) instruments are used, and its song topics return to the less commercial ones of early years. Bluegrass music can largely be credited to one man, Bill Monroe (1911–1996), who grew up in Kentucky. Monroe was a virtuoso performer on the mandolin.

Country music's growth has made Nashville "Music City, USA," complete with a new Grand Ole Opry House in 1975, television and recording studios, publishing houses, agents, and amusement parks. Names such as Dolly Parton, Faith Hill, Barbara Mandrell, Tim McGraw, Kenny Rogers, and a host of others are familiar to the many millions of people who enjoy country music today.

ROCK

It would be easy to say that **rock** is the musical progeny of a union between blues and country music, because it contains important elements of both. But it is much more than that.

Rock often vents strong feelings of revolt. As one writer has said, rock "expressed a visceral impatience with sociopolitical norms." Although rock first appeared in the mid-1950s, it did not begin to dominate the popular music scene until the mid-1960s. The fact that these years also witnessed the emergence of the baby-boomer generation as college-age young people at the same time as the turmoil over the Vietnam War can hardly be a coincidence.

Rock had its start with a Cleveland disc jockey named Alan Freed, who played rhythm and blues. He probably coined the term **rock and roll,** as it is used today, as he called his radio program "Moondog's Rock and Roll Party." Later Freed moved to New York City as a disc jockey for WINS, which soon became that city's leading popular music station.

At about the same time, white groups began recording their own versions of rhythm and blues. The first such hit was Bill Haley's (1925–1981) "Rock around the Clock." Elvis Presley was soon to follow with songs such as "Heartbreak Hotel," which in 1956 succeeded in both the black and white segments of the market—something that rarely happens.

Presley is easily the most remembered country-rock star. His dynamic singing and personal magnetism greatly enlarged the audiences for both country and rock music. His recordings have sold an astounding one *billion* worldwide, with 111 albums or singles going gold, platinum, or multiplatinum. In addition, he appeared in thirty-three films and sang hundreds of concerts. The public's fascination with Presley continues. His home, Graceland, in Memphis is the second most visited home in the United States; only the White House exceeds it.

Characteristics of Rock

RHYTHM The heart of rock is its strong beat. Often the beat is incorporated in a simple melodic figure played in the bass parts. Another feature of rock rhythm is its prominent *backbeat*. The backbeat is what audiences clap along with: 1-**2**-3-**4,** 1-**2**-3-**4.** In some types of rock, this backbeat is incorporated with other rhythm patterns to create a complex combination of rhythms.

MELODY AND HARMONY The melodies and harmonies of rock are strongly influenced by folk music. It has an elemental simplicity. Rock has more songs written in the modes than other types of music, which again reveals some of its folk heritage.

"Rock around the Clock" was the theme song for the 1955 motion picture *Blackboard Jungle,* in which rebellious students smashed the teacher's valuable collection of jazz records. Later it was the theme for the popular television show *Happy Days.*

As described in Chapter 41, modes are scale patterns other than major or minor.

ELVIS PRESLEY, THE KING In the years since his death, he is reported to have been seen in hundreds of different places.

Fotos International/Hulton Archive/Getty Images

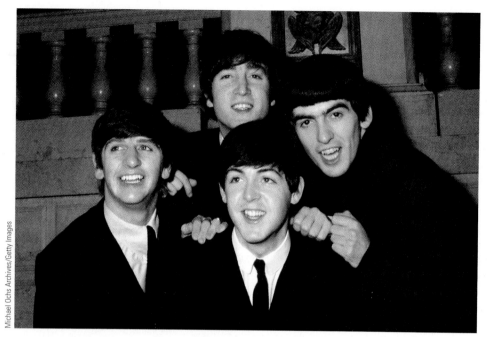

THE BEATLES: GEORGE, JOHN, PAUL, AND RINGO

FOLK-ROCK POET AND
PERFORMER BOB DYLAN

TIMBRE The tonal qualities of rock depend on the particular style. "Hard" rock is very loud with distorted sounds, which is not true of "soft" or "pop" rock. Rock's sounds are almost always amplified electronically, which affects the timbre of the music. The style of singing can vary from raucous, almost shouted sounds of undetermined pitch to energetic but tuneful. Singers work hard at developing individual styles that listeners can easily identify.

LYRICS The form of a rock song is usually built around its lyrics. Songs are often strophic and have more verses than traditional Tin Pan Alley songs. Often lines of text are freer in phrase lengths than the usual thirty-two measures in *a a b a* form. Some rock music uses sophisticated lyrics in terms of rhyme schemes and frame of reference, and sometimes the lyrics do not follow metrical patterns.

PERFORMANCES Most rock musicians are very conscious of visual effects. Some have experimented with subjective mental states in concerts and on videos, or what has often been termed "psychedelic" rock. Some of these images have been fantasy, some subliminal, and some probably influenced by drugs. Because of the enormous amount of money that top rock stars earn, they can afford the best in terms of lighting and other visual and sound effects. Rock concerts are usually more than just music. They include stunning lighting and dramatic effects to captivate their audiences.

Developments in Rock since 1965

BRITISH INFLUENCE The close relationship between British and American popular music has a long history. Therefore, it was not surprising when two British groups, The Beatles and the Rolling Stones, became very influential in the American rock music scene. In fact, after the mid-1960s the rock music styles of the two countries became almost indistinguishable from each other.

FOLK ROCK Rock had its urban folk form in the music of Bob Dylan (Robert Zimmerman, b. 1941), who was associated with Greenwich Village in New York City. He infused his music with both folk qualities and social protest lyrics. Other singers of folk rock included Judy Collins and Joni Mitchell.

FUSION The combination of two or more different musical styles is called **fusion.** The fusion of rock with other styles was inevitable, given its enormous popularity. One fusion occurred between rock and jazz. Several groups successfully blended these two types of music. Blood, Sweat and Tears and Chicago perform a variety of types of rock music. The combination of styles is heard particularly in the treatment of rhythm. Some of these works were considerably longer than the usual rock song.

Another fusion involved the influence of classical music in rock. Three British musicians or groups achieved recognition for this type of music: Keith Emerson, the Bee Gees, and Deep Purple. Emerson, with Greg Lake and Carl Palmer, also produced popular versions of music by such composers as Copland and Mussorgsky.

George Harrison and The Beatles were among the first, if not *the* first, to include elements of Asian music in their rock works. Indian music especially attracted Harrison.

SATIRE AND PUNK One piece of evidence regarding the maturing of rock was its increasing use of satire. Frank Zappa (b. 1940) and the Mothers of Invention engaged in theatrics and put-ons that caused audiences to wonder about the seriousness of it all. Zappa himself kept interviewers guessing about the nature of his artistic intentions with his rambling and unclear statements.

While Zappa may have been having fun with audiences, *punk* rock was deliberately being rebellious. The feelings of rebellion were directed at both the norms of society and the rock establishment, which these performers thought had sold out to commercial interests. The musical impact of these groups was probably less than their social impact, as they sometimes engaged in repulsive behavior in their performances.

MUSIC VIDEOS

The present generation of young people is sometimes described as "the Video Generation." It has grown up with visual images provided by television and other technology. And these images are not just pictures or designs, but frequent, often rapid-fire moving images that flash across a screen.

It was only a matter of time before popular music began to combine music and visual images. This effort led to the establishment of MTV (Music Television) in the early 1980s. Initially, the purpose of the videos was the promotion of recordings. One of the early and most widely recognized music videos was Michael Jackson's "Thriller," which was taken from his 1983 album of the same name.

Music videos can be divided into four main types:

- Videos that present a performer in a concert format
- Videos that present music in a dance format
- Videos that present a story, which may or may not relate directly to the lyrics of the song
- Videos that present fantasy images, often on the premise of a dream

Music videos rely heavily on the manipulation of images, using computers and other technological equipment.

Any survey of a musical style is limited in the amount of information it can provide and in the conclusions it can draw. This seems especially true of rock, because it changes so rapidly and because it is a complex social-psychological-musical phenomenon. Whatever else may be said of rock, it is truly a fascinating topic and a creative type of music.

OTHER TYPES OF POPULAR MUSIC

Although soul, country, and rock cover much of the popular music scene since 1950, they certainly do not account for all of it. Several other types of popular music were influential as well.

Some rock groups vary their style quite a bit, which blurs their classification.

An art form has evolved to a more mature state when it can poke fun at itself.

Punk rock groups did not lack for interesting names, including Weirdos, Sex Pistols, the Lewd, the Mutants, the Ghouls, Flesheaters, Slash, Search and Destroy, Circle Jerks, Crime, Damage, and Destroy All Music.

Even on network television, one shot is almost never maintained for more than four seconds. The time span is shorter yet in music videos.

TITO PUENTE

Latin American

Latin American music has influenced the popular music of the United States since at least the 1920s, when the husband-and-wife team of Vernon and Irene Castle popularized the tango. By the 1930s the *rumba* had become a popular dance. Cuban music soared in popularity as "The Peanut Vendor" recorded by Don Azpiazú became the first Cuban hit record. Also, Xavier Cugat, who was born in Spain but lived most of his life in Cuba, and his band were appearing in a number of motion pictures.

A *rumba* is a dance in a rapid two-beat meter with an intricate contrasting part played by the percussion. It is Afro-Cuban in origin.

Interest in Latin American music reached a high point in the 1950s and 1960s with the popularization of the *mambo*. The person most responsible for the interest in this dance music was Tito Puente (1923–2000), who was born in New York City of Puerto Rican parents. His most successful recording from this period was "Dance Mania."

The 1970s saw the advent of a "hot" style of Latin American music called *salsa*. It originated in the Cuban nightclubs in the 1940s, from where it spread to the rest of the Caribbean and then on to the United States. Three cities became known as the "salsa triangle": San Juan in Puerto Rico, Miami, and New York.

Salsa means "sauce" or "spice."

Another type of Latin American music is associated with the American West. Austin, Texas, became the center for an amalgamation of Mexican and country music called *Tex-Mex*. The best-known singer of Latin American music in the 1970s was Linda Ronstadt. She grew up in Tucson, Arizona, the daughter of a part-Chicano father.

Although *reggae* originated in Jamaica in the 1960s, it did not become widely known in the United States until fifteen or so years later. Reggae features accents on the backbeat with simple melodies and few chord changes. Bob Marley (1945–1981) and the Wailers presented colorful sounds that became popular with the 1976 song "Roots, Rock, Reggae."

The interest in Latin American music is very strong. In 1992 Puente recorded "Numero 100," his one hundredth recording. The Miami Sound Machine with Gloria Estefan is another example of Latin American music that appeals to a wide audience.

Modern Jazz

The share of the radio and record market occupied by jazz slipped to about 2 percent.

Jazz reached a turning point in the 1950s: It became more sophisticated—gone was the strong beat that people could dance to. In its place was a music that began for the first time to be considered seriously as concert music by its audiences and many of its performers. No longer was it music for the players; instead it became music for listeners. In the process, jazz lost its appeal to the young people, who moved to rock and rhythm and blues.

The change began with a style of jazz called **bebop** or, more common, **bop.** It was the product mainly of Charlie "Bird" Parker (1920–1955) and Dizzy Gillespie (John Birks, 1917–1993). Bop contains nearly continuous syncopation, dissonant chords, and freely developed melodies. Bop groups were usually small combos, not the big bands of the 1940s. The string bass was often responsible for maintaining the beat. Some of its musical passages were played in unison, often with lots of notes.

Miles Davis (1926–1991), Dave Brubeck (b. 1920), and the Modern Jazz Quartet turned toward a "cool" style of jazz. Their music was more intellectual and well ordered, and it was also performed by small groups.

Dizzy Gillespie defined bop by saying that in bop you go Ba-oo Ba-oo Ba-oo instead of Oo-ba Oo-ba Oo-ba.

BRUBECK'S "BLUE RONDO A LA TURK"

Dave Brubeck's "Blue Rondo a la Turk" reveals its more sophisticated nature in its title. First, it alludes to rondo form in which the same music returns several times with other music interspersed between its appearances. Second, it refers to Turkish music and its frequent use of asymmetrical rhythm patterns. Appropriately, the first section of the piece opens with nine rapid beats per measure arranged in a 1 2, 1 2, 1 2, 1 2 3 pattern. "Blue Rondo a la Turk" also has a "cool," intellectual quality, especially in its long sax and piano solos.

A less well-understood type of jazz is called **free jazz.** It was first developed by Ornette Coleman (1926–1967) about 1960. Other practitioners of this style include John Coltrane (1926–1967) and Cecil Taylor (b. 1933). Free jazz usually involves collective improvising, no predetermined chord progressions or tonality, playing deliberately out of tune, and expanded forms that are longer than those usually encountered in jazz.

Markus Stuecklin/Keystone/AP Photo

DAVE BRUBECK

DAVE BRUBECK

"Blue Rondo a la Turk" (1959)

GENRE: Modern jazz   Drums, bass, saxophone, piano

CD 6 Tracks [30]–[31]

3 minute 53 seconds

Form: Rondo

0:00	[30] 0:00	Piano, bass, and drums play nine fast notes in a 2 + 2 + 2 + 3 pattern, with every fourth measure in a 3 + 3 + 3 pattern.
	0:11	Saxophone joins in.
	0:22	Piano, bass, and drums continue without saxophone.
	0:45	Saxophone enters as piano drops out.
	1:08	Saxophone plays main thematic idea again.
	1:19	Piano begins transition based on main theme.
	1:53	Music suddenly changes to four-beat meter with a more leisurely character. This is briefly interrupted three times by the opening music.
2:14	[31] 0:00	Saxophone begins lengthy improvised solo accompanied by bass and drums.
	1:39	Recording fades.

 An interactive Active Listening Guide can be downloaded from the online Resource Center for *Music Listening Today, 4th Edition.*

Marilyn Kingwell/ArenaPal/Topham/The Image Works

WYNTON MARSALIS at Lincoln Center in New York City

Some jazz composers, notably Miles Davis, moved to electronic sounds and changes that made their works jazz-based compositions. Davis's "Bitches Brew," created in 1969, uses a number of electric instruments and an almost rocklike rhythm pattern that is ornamented with Latin American figures. In 1995 Wynton Marsalis (b. 1961) and his Septet followed in Davis's footsteps with "Citi Movement," a thirty–seven–minute–long ballet. These compositions represent high artistic aspirations. Jazz has indeed moved far from what its founding fathers back in New Orleans had started early in the twentieth century.

MAIN POINTS OF THIS CHAPTER

1. Blues, rhythm-and-blues, and soul were developed by African Americans. Their most important offspring is jazz.

2. Country music and variants of it were developed by whites in the south. Nashville is the home of country music and has become very successful commercially.

3. Country music features simple melodies and harmonies, a "lonesome" slightly nasal singing style, and realistic and often sentimental lyrics.

4. Variants of country music include bluegrass (no electric instruments or commercial lyrics), rockabilly (a combination of country and rock), and country-western (cowboy songs on western topics).

5. Rock music developed in the 1960s and became very popular. Its characteristics include a strong beat and especially a strong backbeat, many melodies that reveal the influence of folk music, sometimes very loud singing and playing, forms that follow the lyrics instead of a traditional pattern, and generally today stunning visual and dramatic effects at its concerts.

6. Originally rock was known as rock 'n roll. Later variants include soft rock, acid rock, punk rock, fusion, and satirical rock.

7. Jazz became much more sophisticated as it made the transition from a type of performers' music to a style intended for listeners. Several of its variants include bop with its small group playing music containing much syncopation, cool jazz with its much more intellectual qualities, and free-form jazz that has no predetermined chords.

8. Additional types of popular music include Latin American with its salsa, Reggae from the Caribbean, Rap, and Hip-Hop.

FEATURES TO LISTEN FOR

1. Brubeck's "Blue Rondo a la Turk":
   - 2 + 2 + 2 + 3 pattern of rapid beats for three measures, which are followed by one measure in a 3 + 3 + 3 pattern
   - The cool style of the long sax solo

39 Music *for* Stage *and* Film

Music for stage performances and films is somewhat different from concert music. Such music does not stand alone. It always involves a visual element and usually drama. Composers therefore face somewhat different requirements when writing for stage or film. They need to create music that is effective in tandem with the action and story with which they are working. In spite of this apparent limitation, this requirement has produced a body of beautiful and interesting music.

EARLY CONCERTS

Public performances of music in the 1700s were mostly confined to four cities: Philadelphia, New York, Boston, and Charleston. These performances were hardly concerts in the current sense of the word. They included songs, dances, recitations, card tricks, and even balancing acts. Audiences were noisy, and performers often had to request them to be quiet. In fact, for many years some of the audience was allowed to sit onstage.

On bad nights the audience threw nuts, fruit, and even bottles at the performers!

No clear division existed between popular and concert music in stage productions, a situation that lasted until about 1830. Songs were almost always included in early public performances, but few of those songs have survived.

A few types of musicals existed. Most of these had skeletal plots around which composers created some songs, but most of the music for these stage productions has been lost.

MINSTREL SHOWS

An indigenous American type of stage show is the **minstrel show,** which developed in the decades before the Civil War. These shows enjoyed enormous popularity and existed well into the twentieth century.

After the Civil War, blacks became the main performers in minstrel shows.

Minstrel shows featured the exaggerated portrayal of black people by white performers wearing blackface. The shows consisted of songs, dances, jokes, skits, and satirical speeches. Originally, there were only four performers seated in a semicircle. They didn't sit still for long, however; they were almost constantly in motion, even when sitting. Banjo and fiddle players occupied the middle two seats. The other two performers were logically called "end men." They played the bones and tambourine and engaged in entertaining horseplay. The music for minstrel shows was generally in a major key, had a lively tempo, and contained much repetition of short motives.

The bones were two small clappers played with the fingers. They were originally animal bones but were later made of hardwood.

The well-known song "Dixie" has each of these characteristics.

Two names are especially associated with minstrel shows: Stephen Foster, who was discussed in Chapter 37, and Dan Emmett (1815–1904). Emmett composed "Dixie" while working with a minstrel show company.

VAUDEVILLE

Late in the 1800s, a new and important form of stage entertainment appeared: **vaudeville.** It descended from minstrel shows, the English music hall, and the "burlesque" type of entertainment offered in saloons. Vaudeville usually consisted of a succession of individual acts—singers, dancers, jugglers, magicians, and animal acts. They were typically headed by a well-known comedian or singer.

By the turn of the century, vaudeville was playing in thousands of theaters across the United States. It thrived into the days of silent movies, with which it often shared the stage. Many performers who later became famous through the movies, radio, or television got their start in vaudeville: Sophie Tucker, George M. Cohan, Jimmy Durante, Jack Benny, and Ed Wynn, to name a few. Interestingly, vaudeville left no discernible body of music.

The origin of the word *vaudeville* is French. It refers to light or satirical texts sung to already-existing tunes. Later the term was applied to a comedy with music.

MUSICAL COMEDY AND BROADWAY MUSICALS

The Black Crook, first produced in 1866, is often credited with being the first American musical. Actually, it was quite European in character; the more-American musical comedies were at least a generation in the future. Along the way, three European-born and -trained composers contributed much to the development of this genre of music: Victor Herbert (1859–1924), Rudolf Friml (1879–1972), and Sigmund Romberg (1887–1951). Their stage works, called *operettas*, were filled with beautiful melodies, and their stories were pure escapism. Many of them were placed in exotic locations and times.

Probably the richest time period for **musical comedy** was the thirty years between Jerome Kern's *Show Boat* (1927) and Leonard Bernstein's *West Side Story* (1957). Other notable composers of musical comedies during this time include Richard Rodgers and Oscar Hammerstein II, Frederick Lowe and Alan Jay Lerner, Cole Porter, and Irving Berlin. The stories became more real, and the music was integrated more logically into the story line. No longer were songs just strung together around a flimsy plot. These musicals consisted of one good tune after another. Some of the songs were not only quite expressive but also rather sophisticated. Artistic dance scenes were often incorporated as well.

Some of the musical comedies during these years had quite serious stories, along with some comedy—*South Pacific, Show Boat, Lady in the Dark, Carousel, The King and I,* and others.

BERNSTEIN'S *WEST SIDE STORY*

West Side Story (music by Leonard Bernstein and lyrics by Stephen Sondheim) is an updated version of Shakespeare's *Romeo and Juliet*. Instead of rival families, however, there are rival gangs; one is Puerto Rican (Sharks) and the other native New Yorkers (Jets). Maria is Puerto Rican, and Tony is of Polish descent. They meet and fall in love at a dance, but the obstacles to their happiness cannot be overcome. Tony unintentionally kills Maria's brother in a gang fight. Then Tony is told falsely that Maria has turned against him, so he allows himself to be stabbed. He dies in Maria's arms.

The song "Tonight" (Quintet) appears before the gang fight (rumble). The two gangs, the Jets and the Sharks, each claim that the other started the feud and that they will whip the other. Anita (girlfriend of Maria's brother) looks forward to a time of lovemaking after the fight. Maria and Tony are consumed with thoughts about their newfound love. Each of the two gangs and three individuals is positioned apart, both in staged versions and in the film. The music provides wonderful counterpoint of the different moods and music expressing those moods.

Since *West Side Story*, musical comedies have moved away from the emphasis on the composer and the songs. The librettist, director, and choreographer have assumed new importance. Some musicals are built around a concept rather than a story. *Chorus Line* and *Cats* are two such "concept" musicals.

The movie version of *West Side Story* won the Academy Award for Best Picture in 1961.

In Shakespeare's play, Romeo comes from the Montagues and Juliet from the Capulets. The two families hated each other.

"Tonight" (Quintet) from *West Side Story* (1957)

GENRE: Musical comedy   Vocal ensemble

CD 2 Tracks [43] – [45]

3 minutes 36 seconds

| 0:00 | [43] | 0:00 | Orchestra plays fast, rhythmic music over steady notes in low instruments. |

0:07   The members of the rival gangs sing:

SHARKS	**JETS**
	The Jets are gonna have their day, tonight!

0:12   *The Sharks are gonna have their way, tonight!*

0:17

The Puerto Ricans grumble: "Fair fight."

But if they start a rumble,
   we'll rumble 'em right.

0:25   *We're gonna hand 'em a surprise,*
   tonight.

We're gonna cut 'em down to size, tonight.

We said, "O.K., no rumpus,
No tricks."
But just in case they jump us,
We're ready to mix, tonight!

0:44	*We're gonna rock it tonight,*
	  we're gonna jazz it up and
	  have us a ball!
		We're gonna rock it tonight,
		  we're gonna jazz it up and
		  have us a ball!

	They're gonna get it tonight;
	  the more they turn it on,
	  the harder they'll fall!
		They're gonna get it tonight;
		  the more they turn it on,
		  the harder they'll fall!

0:57		*Well, they began it!*

	Well, they began it!
	And we're the ones to stop 'em
	  once and for all, tonight!
		And we're the ones to stop 'em
		  once and for all, tonight!

1:07   Anita sings in a sexy manner:

Anita's gonna get her kicks, tonight.
We'll have our private little mix, tonight.
He'll walk in hot and tired,
   so what?
Don't matter if he's tired,
   as long as he's hot, tonight!

| 1:26 | [44] | 0:00 | Tony sings the song "Tonight" that he and Maria sang together earlier. |

Tonight, tonight!
Won't be just any night,
   tonight there will be no morning star.
Tonight, tonight,
   I'll see my love tonight and for us,
   stars will stop where they are.

Today the minutes seem like hours,
   the hours go so slowly,
   and still the sky is light.
Oh moon, grow bright,
   and make this endless day
   endless night!

0:50   Orchestra takes up the "rumble" music again.

0:57   The Jets urge Tony to be present for the anticipated fight.

> We're counting on you to be there,
>   tonight.
> When Diesel wins it fair and square,
>   tonight.
> That Puerto Rican punk'll
>   go down,
> And when he's hollered "Uncle,"
> We'll tear up the town!

1:14   Maria sings "Tonight," and the Sharks keep urging Tony to be there.

Tonight, tonight	So I can count on you, boy?
	(Tony) All right.
won't be just any night	We're gonna have us a ball!
	(Tony) All right.
tonight there will be no morning star.	Womb to tomb!
	(Tony) Sperm to worm!
	I'll see you there about eight.
	(Tony) Tonight.

1:27   The Jets sing about the anticipated fight as Maria continues.

Tonight, tonight	
(Anita) Tonight,	We're gonna rock it tonight!
I'll see my love tonight	

1:33   Anita enters singing about her date with Bernardo.

(Anita) Tonight, late tonight,	
we're gonna mix it tonight.	
(Maria) and for us,	
stars will stop where they are.	
	They're gonna get it tonight.

3:06   45   0:00   Tony joins Maria in singing "Tonight" as Anita, the Jets, and the Sharks sing in anticipation of events to come.

> (Tony and Maria) Today the minutes seem like hours,

Anita's gonna have her day	
	They began it
	They began it,
Anita's gonna have her day	
Anita's gonna have her day	
(Sharks) They began it	They began it,
the hours go so slowly	
(Anita) Bernardo's gonna have his way	
tonight, tonight!	
(Sharks) They began it!	and we're the ones
and still the sky is light.	to stop 'em once and for all
We'll stop 'em once	
and for all	
Oh moon, grow bright!	
The Sharks are gonna have	The Jets are gonna have
their way,	their way,
and make this endless day	
The Sharks are gonna have	The Jets are gonna have
their day,	their day,
(Anita) Tonight, this very night,	
endless night,	
We're gonna rock it tonight,	We're gonna rock it tonight,
tonight! tonight!	tonight!

0:31   Singers and orchestra end on a long, brilliant chord.

An interactive Active Listening Guide can be downloaded from the online
Resource Center for *Music Listening Today, 4th Edition.*

Leonard Bernstein

BEST-KNOWN WORKS
ballet:
- *Fancy Free*
- *On the Town*

musical:
- *West Side Story*

orchestra:
- *Candide: Overture*

Leonard Bernstein (1918–1990) was born in Lawrence, Massachusetts, of Russian-Jewish parents. His businessman father moved the family to Boston shortly after Leonard's birth, and he graduated from the Boston Latin School and Harvard University. Later, he studied at the Curtis Institute in Philadelphia.

During his career he developed a number of successful television programs on musical topics, appeared as a piano soloist, and composed a variety of types of music. For a decade he was conductor of the New York Philharmonic Orchestra.

OPERATIC MUSICALS

Claude-Michel Schonberg and Arnold Schoenberg are not related genetically or musically.

Les Misérables used a rotating stage. It made sixty-three turns in each performance.

A noteworthy trend in music for the stage in recent years is a growing number of the successful musicals that are virtually operas—every word in them is sung. Three examples of this trend are *Phantom of the Opera* by Andrew Lloyd Webber and *Les Misérables* and *Miss Saigon* by Claude-Michel Schonberg. There are, however, several differences between them and the operas of Mozart, Verdi, and other composers as performed by the major opera houses of Europe and the Americas.

- The style of singing is more like what is heard in musicals.
- The singing is amplified, although no microphones are visible and the sound levels are not particularly loud.
- The vocal parts are technically less demanding; no virtuoso singing ability is required.
- The accompanying orchestra is rather small.
- They are sung in English in English-speaking countries.
- They contain one or more humorous sections and characters.
- The action onstage moves at a faster pace.

These musicals have international roots; they are no longer just Broadway musicals. Lloyd Webber is British and Schonberg is French. Furthermore, these musicals opened in London and Paris, respectively, and came to New York after having enjoyed much success overseas.

Phantom of the Opera is based on a story about a phantom (who is actually a man with a terribly scarred face) who haunts the Paris Opera House. It has been made into at least two movies and a stage play. The plot revolves around the love of the phantom for a beautiful young soprano. He sabotages the efforts of the opera managers to promote her place in the company. He also tries to win her affection and keep her from her fiancé. Fortunately, he fails. *Phantom* is quite theatrical, and at times it contains elements of old-style film music, with its sinister theme and crashing chandelier.

Schonberg's *Les Misérables* and *Miss Saigon* were both originally written in French with the text by Alain Boubil. English translations were carefully prepared later.

PHANTOM OF THE OPERA Actors Emmy Rossum as Christine Daae and Gerard Butler in *The Phantom of the Opera*

Les Misérables is based on the great novel by the French writer Victor Hugo. It tells of a man, Jean Valjean, who while young committed a petty crime for which he spent several years in jail. Although initially bitter after his release, his feelings change after being befriended by a kindly priest. He eventually adopts a new name and becomes a factory owner and mayor of his town but is still pursued by an unrelenting police inspector. One of his good deeds is to raise as his own an illegitimate girl, Cosette. Her mother had worked for a while in Valjean's factory, but she had fallen on hard times and died while Cosette was quite young.

Times are hard in France in the 1830s, and Valjean joins a band of students who hope to bring about another revolution to better the lives of the poor. The revolution fails because the people do not rise up as they did in 1789. Valjean saves Cosette's fiancé, who was one of the revolutionaries, by carrying him unconscious through the sewers of Paris to safety. The young man recovers, and the couple marry. Finally, they learn the truth about all that Valjean has done for them. *Les Misérables* closes with Valjean being escorted into heaven by Cosette's mother and the stirring marching song of the revolutionaries.

Miss Saigon is a much more contemporary story about Chris, a U.S. Marine in the war in Vietnam, who falls in love with a Vietnamese girl named Kim. Despite his best efforts, he is forced to leave her behind when the Americans withdraw. Two years later, now married to an American woman, Chris learns that Kim is alive and that he has a young son in Vietnam. He returns to see her and the child. Kim, realizing that the best hope for her son's future is with his father in America, decides to give him up to Chris. In her grief-stricken state, she commits suicide, dying as Chris bends over her in anguish as the curtain falls.

Each of the three musicals mentioned here is filled with memorable music. All are well worth knowing.

AMERICAN OPERA

Opera has never been as popular in America as it has in many European countries. Some of the reasons for this are mentioned in Chapter 12, but certainly the lack of operas in English is significant. Another probable reason is the lack of an American aristocracy to fund and support opera.

It is not that American composers have failed to write several first-rate operas. Rather, it is that only a few of them seem to have achieved a permanent place in operatic repertoire. One candidate for this permanent status is Howard Hanson's *Merry Mount*, which is based on a story by Nathaniel Hawthorne set in New England.

Another candidate is *The Medium* by Gian-Carlo Menotti, who was born in Italy but immigrated to the United States when he was seventeen. *The Medium* is based on a grisly story of a devious old lady who claims to communicate with the dead in fake séances. Eventually, her conscience begins to bother her, and she imagines that something clutched her throat during a séance. Disaster follows. Menotti's *Amahl and the Night Visitors* was one of the first operas composed for television. After its premiere on the *Hallmark Hall of Fame* in 1951, it became an annual Christmas telecast for nearly two decades.

GERSHWIN'S *PORGY AND BESS*

The opera that has secured for itself a solid place in American operatic repertoire is not a true opera but rather, in the composer's words, a "folk opera." *Porgy and Bess* by George Gershwin is based on a story by DuBose Heyward set in Charleston, South Carolina. It is about a beggar named Porgy, who cannot walk and must get around in a goat cart. Gershwin could see the dramatic possibilities in the story and decided to compose an opera based on it.

Les Misærables is probably the world's most popular musical, with an audience approaching forty million. It has been translated into fourteen languages and has won thirty-one awards.

A Listening Guide for the finale of *Les Misérables* is included in the *Study Guide.*

Miss Saigon contains many parallels to Puccini's opera *Madame Butterfly*, the story of an American naval officer who fathers a child with a young Japanese woman while on tour in Japan and then abandons her.

A Listening Guide for the duet "I Still Believe" from *Miss Saigon* is included in the *Study Guide.*

In the late 1800s and early 1900s, many American cities had "opera houses," but they were used mostly for concerts and other events, not operas.

The Medium uses only five singers and an actor who plays the role of a person who is deaf and cannot speak. Its orchestra is very small; there is no chorus, and it lasts for less than an hour.

The U.S. Department of State has on several occasions supported overseas tours of *Porgy and Bess.*

George Gershwin

Best-Known Works

orchestra:
- *American in Paris*

orchestra and piano:
- Concerto in F
- *Rhapsody in Blue*

opera:
- *Porgy and Bess*

musicals:
- *Of Thee I Sing*
- *Girl Crazy*
- *Strike Up the Band*

George Gershwin (1898–1937) was born and educated in Brooklyn, New York. His family was poor but was able to afford piano lessons for him. At the age of sixteen, he was employed as a song-plugger by a Tin Pan Alley publisher, and his career in music began. He often collaborated with his brother, Ira, who wrote the lyrics for many of George's songs.

Although successful and now financially well off, Gershwin was ambitious about composing concert music. His first big success came with *Rhapsody in Blue* in 1924. He originally composed it for piano and jazz orchestra; later he asked Ferde Grofé to arrange the orchestral parts. Whatever he lacked in developing musical ideas he more than made up for in his sparkling tunes and moving melodies.

George Gershwin died in Hollywood of a brain tumor after unsuccessful surgery to save his life.

OPERA SINGERS IN PERFORMANCE Opera singers Donnie Ray Albert and Clamma Dale in a Kennedy Center production of *Porgy and Bess*.

To make the story as real as possible, Gershwin has the characters speak many of their lines instead of singing recitatives. He also incorporates the music of the black people of Charleston — the blues and features of jazz — into the opera. Although he does not include actual folk songs, the music has a folklike quality. Its jazz elements are written down rather than made up on the spot.

The story of *Porgy and Bess* is filled with tragedy. Porgy leads a lonely life; Bess, a loose-living woman, comes to town with her lover, Crown. Neither Bess nor Crown is accepted by the people of Catfish Row. Crown kills a local man in a fight, and Bess takes refuge from the police in Porgy's shanty. Their relationship grows into genuine love.

When Crown learns of Bess's love for Porgy, he sets out to kill him. In the fight between the two men, Crown is stabbed and dies. Porgy is taken off to jail on suspicion of murder.

Now is the moment the character Sportin' Life has been waiting for. He represents the easy, evil life that Bess left behind when she moved in with Porgy. Because Porgy may never be freed from jail, Sportin' Life is able to persuade Bess to go back to New York with him. But Porgy is released, and when he returns home, he finds Bess gone. "Where is she?" he asks. "New York," answer his neighbors. *Porgy and Bess* closes with the pathetic scene of Porgy climbing into his goat cart to go to New York to find Bess.

GEORGE GERSHWIN
"Summertime" from *Porgy and Bess* (1934–1935)

GENRE: Opera   Soprano and orchestra

CD 6 Track 32

2 minutes 28 seconds

0:00 32 0:00 Introduction soon falls into a gentle rocking sound between two notes.

0:25 Soprano begins:

Summertime an' the livin' is easy,
Fish are jumpin',
an' the cotton is high.
Oh yo' daddy's rich,
an' yo' ma is good-lookin',
So hush, little baby,
don't yo' cry.

1:21 Song continues with much the same melody as singers join in accompanying part.

One of these mornin's
You goin' to rise up singin',
Then you'll spread yo' wings
an' you'll take the sky.
But till that mornin'
there's a nothin' can harm you
With Daddy an' Mammy standin' by.

2:28 After a long note on the word *by*, during which the accompaniment plays some chromatic harmony, the song ends quietly.

 An interactive Active Listening Guide can be downloaded from the online Resource Center for *Music Listening Today, 4th Edition.*

The song "Summertime" appears near the beginning of the opera and helps establish the opera's setting. The mood is lazy and relaxed as the mother sings her baby to sleep. The accompaniment suggests a gentle rocking motion. The song includes some vocal devices such as a slide, or glissando, and a little catch on the word *cry*.

MUSIC FOR FILMS

In a sense, commercial movies have almost never been silent. In the small, low-priced theaters a pianist pounded out music at appropriate places as the film flickered by on the screen. In upscale theaters small- to medium-sized orchestras played music especially composed for the film. This body of theater music has now been largely forgotten.

Role

Today, of course, music is an integral part of almost every commercial film, even showings of old silent movies. Why? Because music contributes to a film in a number of ways.

- It creates a more convincing atmosphere of a particular time and place. A scene with a ship sailing through the seas calls for one kind of music, and a scene in a crowded western saloon requires another.

In many ways, music can express such feelings better than words.

- It gives the viewers cues about the unspoken thoughts of the characters or the yet unseen implications of a situation. If a man is looking at a woman and he is filled with feelings of love and desire, the music can project his feelings.

- It provides neutral filler or background sound. Although such music is of little interest in itself, it does fill the empty places in a film.

- It helps build a sense of continuity in a motion picture. This is done by associating certain music with a particular character or situation.

Almost no movie ends in silence, even if it lacked much of a musical score.

- It supports and contributes to the buildup of a scene, including giving the film a solid ending.

Development

It wasn't much of a beginning back on October 6, 1927, with *The Jazz Singer,* the first motion picture with music. The sound portion consisted of just five songs, including Irving Berlin's "Blue Skies." Its sound quality was vastly inferior to what we are used to today. To help the picture succeed, Warner Brothers picked a well-known vaudeville performer, Al Jolson. Impressive by today's standards or not, *The Jazz Singer* opened the door, and soon "all-talking, all-singing, all-dancing" films would follow.

It was as though a great divide had been reached that separated silent movies from films with sound. Within a few years of *The Jazz Singer,* Hollywood was attracting top musical talent for its productions. Many of the best Broadway composers and arrangers worked there—George Gershwin, Jerome Kern, Irving Berlin, Cole Porter, and Harold Arlen.

Both Miklos Rozsa and John Williams have pointed out that music for a film has to be immediate in its effectiveness. Musical ideas cannot be introduced gradually.

At first glance, composing some music to serve the five purposes described earlier would seem to stifle creative quality. After all, the music must match the film to the second, so little development of musical ideas is possible. Either because or in spite of these limitations, a number of excellent composers established their professional reputations through their film music—Miklos Rozsa, Erich Korngold, Henry Mancini, Alfred Newman, Dimitri Tiomkin, James Horner, Max Steiner, Jerry Goldsmith, Maurice Jarre, Bernard Herrmann, and John Williams, among others. Some of their music has found a life apart from the movie for which it was made in terms of commercial recordings. Some of it has almost assumed a folklore status, such as the shrieking sounds from the violins that Herrmann wrote for the soundtrack for Alfred Hitchcock's *Psycho* and Williams's ominous throbbing sounds for the shark in *Jaws.*

STAR WARS EPISODE III: REVENGE OF THE SITH Actors Natalie Portman as Senator Padme Amidala with C-3PO (Anthony Daniels) and Hayden Christensen as Anakin Skywalker in *Star Wars: Episode III Revenge of the Sith.*

LucasFilm/20th Century Fox/The Kobal Collection/Picture Desk

WILLIAMS'S MAIN TITLE FROM *STAR WARS*

Although John Williams composed the music for *Star Wars* to enhance the scenes in the films, he also succeeded in writing music that people find interesting to listen to apart from the film. Musical passages in the work associated with the characters and

JOHN WILLIAMS
Main Title from *Star Wars* (1977)

Orchestra

CD 6 Tracks 33 – 35

5 minutes 47 seconds

0:00	33	0:00	Opening fanfare.
		0:08	Main theme played by trumpets and brasses, strings, then entire orchestra.
2:04	34	0:00	Battle music begins.
		0:19	Main theme returns in French horns, followed by strings, then entire orchestra.
3:20	35	0:00	Princess Leia's theme played by low strings.
		0:48	Main theme returns.
		1:20	Battle music begins in brasses; then music grows slower and softer.
		1:58	Closing section (*coda*) begins in brasses. Music becomes slow and powerful.
		2:33	After drum roll, music concludes decisively.

 An interactive Active Listening Guide can be downloaded from the online Resource Center for *Music Listening Today, 4th Edition.*

LISTENING GUIDE

John Williams

Bachrach/Hulton Archive/Getty Images

John Williams was born in 1932 in New York City, but at the age of sixteen moved with his family to Los Angeles. His father was a musician, so music was a logical career choice for John. He studied at UCLA, intending to become a concert pianist. After three years in the U.S. Air Force, he spent a year at the Juilliard School of Music in New York, still concentrating on piano, and then returned to Los Angeles, where he studied composition with the noted Mario Castelnuovo-Tedesco.

Soon Williams was in demand as a pianist-arranger, starting in television in 1958. He composed music for nearly every kind of TV program, ranging from *Wagon Train* to *Gilligan's Island* to *Mod*

Squad. By the 1970s he had become a major composer in American films. His efforts have continued, reaching a total of eighty-one film scores plus twenty-nine television shows and special events such as the Olympic Games.

During his long career Williams has been widely recognized for his composing: five Oscars (forty-five nominations), four Golden Globes, twenty Grammies, and fourteen honorary degrees.

Williams's attention has not been confined to music for television and films, however. From 1980 to 1993, he was conductor of the Boston Pops Orchestra. In addition, he has composed a number of concert works and adapted some of his film music for orchestra.

BEST-KNOWN WORKS

film scores:
- *Star Wars* and its sequels
- *Superman*
- *Close Encounters of the Third Kind*
- *Jaws*
- *The Towering Inferno*
- *Indiana Jones and the Temple of Doom*
- *Dracula*

situations. For example, the music for the beautiful Princess Leia sounds very different from the music for the spaceship!

Like opera, motion pictures like *Star Wars* have a bigger-than-life quality. In fact, the roots of a great deal of film music go back to nineteenth-century Romanticism. The heritage of a space epic with Romantic music may seem to be a bit of a contradiction. But love and conflict exist, whether the actors are wearing jeans and riding a horse or wearing spacesuits and floating through space.

MUSIC AND VISUAL IMAGES

Technology has opened up an easy union of music with visual images. One attempt at doing this is MTV, which was discussed in Chapter 38. Sometimes the role of movies in the promotion of music, especially popular music, has been overlooked. The film versions of Broadway musicals did much to further that type of music, which is also true of Latin American music and some of the big-band music of the Swing Era. But videotape and DVD now offer even more intriguing possibilities.

MAIN POINTS OF THIS CHAPTER

1. Music for stage and film is created to contribute to a dramatic situation. Some of it is of a quality that is beautiful and interesting to listen to, apart from what is seen in the film or on stage.

2. Minstrel shows were an early form of stage entertainment. They consisted of songs, dances, jokes, and skits by whites portraying blacks. Vaudeville was another type of variety show with music. It was supplanted by sound motion pictures.

3. Operetta and many of the earlier musical comedies consisted of fanciful stories with pretty songs. Later, some musicals were quite serious. A few recently popular musicals are virtually operas in that every word in them is sung.

4. Opera has not achieved the popularity in American that it enjoys in Europe, although several excellent operas have been composed by Americans.

5. Music contributes to the impact of a film in several ways. It provides an atmosphere, gives clues about unspoken thoughts, provides continuity, and creates a background.

FEATURES TO LISTEN FOR

1. Bernstein's "Quintet" from *West Side Story:*
   - Change in meter when the singers sing the words "We said, O.K., no rumpus, no tricks."
   - Difference between the singing style of the gang members and the style of Tony and Maria.
   - Counterpoint among the gang members, Anita, and Tony and Maria in the final 30 seconds

2. Gershwin's "Summertime" from *Porgy and Bess*:
   - Blues elements, especially in the orchestral accompaniment
   - The singer's treatment of the words "hush" and "cry"
3. "Main Title" from *Star Wars* by John Williams:
   - Differences between the main theme and the theme for Princess Leia
   - The Romantic, heroic quality of the work

PART VIII

Music
around
the World

NORTH AMERICA

Atlantic Ocean

SOUTH AMERICA

Pacific Ocean

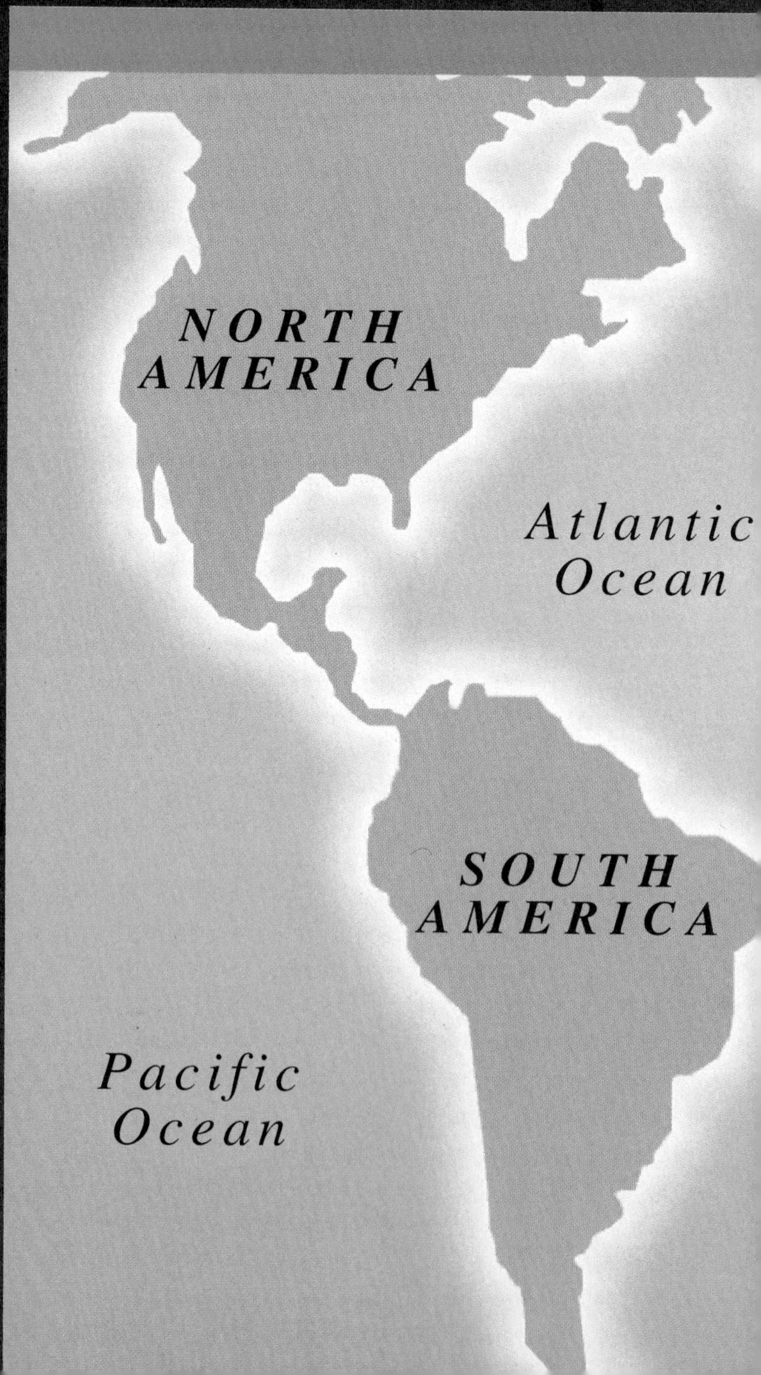

EUROPE

ASIA

Japan

Middle
East

China

India

Pacific
Ocean

AFRICA

Indian
Ocean

Indonesia
Bali

AUSTRALIA

40

Folk *and* Ethnic Music

What's different about a song of the Huron in America, the music of the Bantu in Africa, the chantey of English sailors, and the Hindu religious music of India? It's a good question, and a topic that merits attention.

WHAT IS FOLK AND ETHNIC MUSIC?

Folk music is different from concert music because it is the music of the common people of a particular nation or ethnic group. And because it is the music of a sizable group of people, it has qualities that cause the people of a particular culture to like and remember it. It is music that has been tested by a large segment of people or a nation. If it had not met with their approval, it would have been forgotten and passed into oblivion.

Music also exists that can be identified with a particular group of people but is not the product of those people. Such music is often referred to as **ethnic.** It is also representative of its particular culture, but not of the music of the common people of that culture.

Western concert music is a type of ethnic music because it is a product of a particular civilization. As used in this book, however, *ethnic* refers to non-Western music.

All folk music is ethnic music because it is the product of a particular culture. But the opposite is not true: Not all ethnic music is folk music because usually ethnic represents the efforts of a small, elite group of musicians.

KNOWING FOLK AND ETHNIC MUSIC

Why learn about folk and ethnic music? Such music does not appear on programs in the concert halls of Europe and America, nor is it played on radio stations other than educational ones, and even there only rarely. Recordings of most such music are limited, and they are sold only in a few specialized music stores.

In spite of this situation, there are at least three good reasons for learning about folk and ethnic music: (1) Elements of such music often find their way into concert music. (2) Folk and ethnic music reflect the attitudes and values of a culture. (3) Today we encounter other cultures and their music more and more.

INFLUENCE OF FOLK AND ETHNIC MUSIC

Melodies from concert music have also appeared occasionally in popular music.

Composers and musicians have often been influenced by folk and ethnic music, sometimes more than they like to admit. Occasionally over the past two hundred years, actual folk tunes have been used in symphonies and other concert music. In other cases, even if no actual folk melodies are used, composers have written folklike tunes.

Popular music has also been very much influenced by folk music, both in America and around the world. Often the popular music in an African or Asian country is a blend of its traditional folk/ethnic music idioms and Western popular music. The balance between indigenous folk music and popular music can vary considerably. Some contains a lot of folk or ethnic qualities, whereas other popular music has only a little.

The author has heard the original recordings of American popular songs being played in rather out-of-the-way places in Japan and Thailand.

But more than melodies are involved here. Composers sometimes appropriate and adapt ideas they hear in folk and ethnic music. They take a rhythmic or melodic pattern and alter it for use in a composition. For example, Aaron Copland drew heavily on elements of square dance music in his "Hoe-Down" from *Rodeo*.

Reflecting Culture

Music and the other arts are windows to the culture in which they exist. They represent the attitudes and values of a people. The sensitivity and subtlety of Japanese *koto* music, for example, says more about Japanese character and beliefs than can a thousand words.

Knowing the politics, history, and economy of a nation is certainly worthwhile. It is also valuable to have a sense of its character, its cultural "soul." The former provides basic factual information; the latter provides insight into a society's character.

The Global Village

A hundred years ago, people were born, lived, and died in the same small geographic area. The customs and way of life of that area were all they ever experienced or knew about. How different it is today! The journey across the Atlantic from England to America used to require months on a sailing ship, but now it is covered in a little over six hours on a jet. Mail and news, once transported by ship, are now instantaneous via satellite and other technology. A famine or war in some far-off place such as Somalia used to be scarcely noticed, if it was known at all. Today such tragedies are seen live on television in vivid color.

It is a fact: People have contact with and are affected by other peoples around the world to a degree that no one could have imagined a hundred years ago. Each year since 1900, the people of the world have been drawn closer and closer together. Today we live in a "global village." Provincialism is now as out-of-date as the hoopskirt and the high Prince Albert shirt collar!

Not only have travel and communication been made vastly quicker and easier but peoples from many diverse cultures are becoming U.S. citizens in ever-increasing numbers. Even small towns in the heartland of America have recent emigrants from Southeast Asia and Latin America; no longer are immigrants confined to large cities such as Los Angeles, Miami, or New York. Ethnic radio stations and newspapers in languages other than English are commonplace. The yellow pages of telephone books list a wide array of restaurants featuring ethnic foods, and mosques and temples now stand beside Christian churches and Jewish synagogues.

It is important, therefore, to know about and understand the other residents of our global village, including their cultures and their arts. Learning about the music of other peoples is no longer an academic exercise. It has become an essential aspect of being an educated person. Not only is it useful to know something about folk/ethnic music, but it is important to respect and honor the music of other cultures. Their music and way of life are as logical and right for them as ours are for us.

A CULTURAL HERITAGE is kept alive by this North American Indian taking part in a dancing contest during a powwow in northern Utah.

Estimates vary, but around the middle of the twenty-first century the traditional majority of Americans of European descent will become a minority.

HOW ARE FOLK AND ETHNIC MUSIC DIFFERENT?

What is different about most folk and ethnic music? What features do most such music have in common?

Lack of Uniformity

A symphony by Mozart is published in notation. Therefore, when it is performed by competent musicians, it sounds similar from one performance to another. As for musical instruments, a modern B-flat clarinet is very much like thousands of other B-flat clarinets.

The different performances of the symphony would not be identical, of course.

The lack of uniformity makes it difficult to determine which version of a song is the most authentic one.

It's different with most folk music. A song may be performed in a particular way by an individual, and another person in the same culture living only a few miles away may perform it quite differently. A homemade musical instrument is truly one of a kind, although it may be similar to other instruments.

Creation

Folk and ethnic music are usually created by an individual, which is also true of concert music. But there the similarity ends. In concert music, the composer is closely identified with his or her composition—Beethoven's Fifth Symphony, Prokofiev's Third Piano Concerto, and so on. On the other hand, the originator of a folk melody is rarely known. In fact, he or she might not even admit to such an accomplishment, because in some cultures songs are supposed to be gifts from the gods. Besides, in folk music no one seems to care who created a song.

Individual Changes

There is another reason that the creator of a song is seldom recognized. Once the song is created, it begins a process of modification. Performers usually feel free to make changes, generally small ones. Over the years a song can evolve to become quite different from how it started out. A folk song is a living organism; it is ever changing. That is one of the virtues of folk music.

Importance of the Performers

Because folk music is seldom set in notation, and because modifications are accepted and even encouraged, performers of folk and ethnic music have a much more important role than they do in Western concert music. No longer are they confined to the role of being a re-creator of a work from notation. They become at least co-creators of the music.

Improvisation

One of the reasons that performers have such an important role is that often they are expected to *improvise*—to make up music on the spot. However, they do not usually improvise out of thin air—that is, without any guidelines at all. Each type of music (African, Hindu religious, jazz, and so on) has performance traditions and practices that musicians are expected to follow. It's a bit like a basketball team: The players have some plays or plans for scoring and defense, but usually they have to adjust them on the spot, depending on what the other team does. They operate within a system yet have the freedom to try their own ideas when it seems desirable.

Audience

Today we are used to having music performed for an audience, either in person or by listening to a recording. In the case of folk and ethnic music, the audience, if there is one at all, is much less important. In many parts of the world, music is performed at events in which everyone participates; there are few listeners as such. Some of the time, the music is performed as part of a ceremony to appease or thank gods, which makes a human audience irrelevant.

When an audience becomes unimportant, performers no longer need to worry about people *liking* their music. It also removes any commercial considerations, because no tickets or royalties are possible. Therefore, folk and most ethnic music is created for reasons other than to make money.

Subtleties, Shadings, and Sophistication

Each type of music contains a number of small things that add much to its character and are an integral part of the music. For example, in some styles of music the performers "bend" or "shade" certain tones in a melody to make the music more expressive. Such sophisticated subtleties are easily overlooked by listeners not familiar with the particular musical style, because the music sounds so different to them.

In general, when a musical style is strong in one element, it is relatively undeveloped in some others. African music, for example, is noted for its rhythms, but its other aspects are less notable. Balinese music contains a kaleidoscope of timbres, but it does not have the harmonic or melodic interest of many other types.

Most folk and ethnic music consists of short works, often songs. True, some African rituals last for hours, but the same music tends to be repeated over and over with only slight variations. Without a system of notation, works of music are usually rather short-winded. This short length allows for little development of themes, something that is important in Western concert music.

Shading is an integral part of traditional Japanese music. In Japanese culture it is believed that a melody sung without such inflections lacks expression.

Oral Tradition

Much of the world's music is never rendered in notation. Yet some of the music that has existed for hundreds of years has not been forgotten or changed in a noticeable way. How is this possible? By passing it from one person or generation to another by word of mouth, what is known as **oral tradition.** It is difficult for those of us who are used to preserving thoughts in writing or through recordings to understand the ability that people can acquire to remember what they hear. When they want or need to, people can recall quite accurately, especially if the song or story is not too long.

Preservation

Until about a hundred years ago, almost no one seemed to care about preserving folk or ethnic music. Western intellectuals did not seem to consider it worth saving, and the musicians who created and performed it seemed happy with what oral tradition had given them. Over the years, interest in preserving and studying folk and ethnic music increased. Today a number of ethnomusicologists with recorders and notepads are working and living in many parts of the globe in an attempt to preserve this vast musical treasure.

One type of flute found among the natives of Oceania and Hawaii is blown through the nose.

Actually, the music is wasted on the snakes, which have no hearing. The snakes respond to the swaying body of the charmer.

Folk/Ethnic Instuments

A vast number of musical instruments have been created throughout the world. Although each has unique characteristics, folk/ethnic instruments have been classified by scholars into four broad groups according to the way they produce sounds.

Aerophones

This category comprises instruments that are played by blowing. The most common of these are flutes. Some are played sideways, as we are accustomed to seeing today, but many are played straight in front of the player's mouth.

Some reed **aerophones** are also found. Some of these use a double reed like that of an oboe; others have a single reed and mouthpiece like that of a clarinet. The *pungi* played by snake charmers in India is an example of a reed instrument.

Animal horns are simple instruments that approach the buzzing of the lip membranes on brass instruments. They are hollowed out and blown from the small end. The Jewish *shofar* is one such instrument.

Paul Springett/Alamy

AEROPHONE A snake charmer plays for a cobra.

IDEOPHONES Bunaq tribesmen of Borneo play gongs.

A **CHORDOPHONE**, in this case a folk fiddle, played by a traditional Moroccan player and singer near Marrakesh, Morocco.

The term *membranophones* is easy to remember because it contains the word *membrane*.

An ethnomusicologist studying Mexican music wanted to hear a certain song that was sung for a particular festival. He located the performer, who didn't want to sing it. "We're not having the festival now," he explained. Finally, the man was coaxed into singing it but broke into laughter before finishing because singing the song apart from the festival seemed ridiculous to him.

Ideophones

These are the percussion instruments other than drums. Bells, chimes, xylophones, and rattles are all examples of **ideophones.**

Membranophones

Membranophones are all the types of drums encountered throughout the world. Drums are constructed from wood, metal, coconut shells, and clay. Some are struck with sticks, others are hit with the hand or fingers, and friction drums are rubbed with a piece of animal hide. Some have straight sides, others taper in, and a few have the shape of an hourglass.

Chordophones

This fourth group includes all string instruments. Most of these are plucked—harps, lyres, and zithers. The strings on some **chordophones** are struck with mallets, and a few are bowed as the violin's.

Unlike orchestral instruments, which are quite standardized, folk instruments lack uniformity. They may be similar to one another, but no two are alike. And they are traditionally taught individually, usually by rote. Because there are few instruction books for learning to play them, the way they are played varies widely.

MUSIC AND CULTURE

All the many types of music in the world are products of particular societies and cultures. Although all societies have some type of music, many do not even have a word for music. In some instances, it's the same as the word for "work." In one Native American tribe the word means "song," and it includes dancing and ritual.

As has been pointed out, music and the other arts provide much insight into the character and customs of a people. The cultural difference between a piano concerto by Prokofiev, for example, and a song of the Aleuts in Alaska lies in the relative importance of the cultural elements. In the case of the Aleut music (and almost all other folk and ethnic music), a knowledge of language, customs, thought forms, and other aspects of culture is necessary for a full understanding of the music. The Prokofiev piano concerto is much more able to stand alone; it is not as embedded in everyday culture.

It is, of course, possible to analyze a folk or ethnic work apart from its cultural setting, but the music loses much of its meaning when this is done. In fact, some Indian scholars object to putting Hindu ragas in notation and to discussing only the features of the music. They are correct in their concern for the cultural relevance of the music, but the amount of time one can devote to learning about any given type of music is limited. Therefore, we have no choice but to consider mainly the musical aspects in college-level music courses.

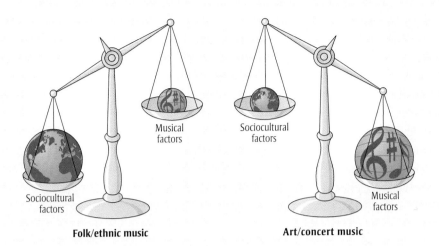

Musical
factors

Sociocultural
factors

Sociocultural
factors

Musical
factors

Folk/ethnic music

Art/concert music

In *folk* and *ethnic* music, sociocultural considerations outweigh musical factors, whereas in art/concert music, the opposite is true.

LISTENING TO FOLK AND ETHNIC MUSIC

Listening to folk or most ethnic music requires a somewhat different approach from what is needed for listening to concert music. Listening to what happens in a melody and the rhythm of a work is still necessary, but the listener must also consider the cultural factors.

One way to think about and listen to folk and ethnic music is to imagine two columns. One column is under the heading *Musical* and the other is under the heading *Sociocultural*. Here is an example that could easily be true of much of the music from Africa.

Musical	*Sociocultural*
Drums in several sizes	From Africa
Polyrhythms	Highly trained drummers
Very steady tempo	Everyone participates
Call-and-response	Male drummers and soloist
Some improvisation	Aspects of a tonal language
Simple melody	Simple dances to music
Phrases often repeated	Performed "by ear"—no notation
African singing style	Instruments of skins and gourds

As with most types of music, several hearings of the same piece are recommended so that you become somewhat accustomed to the style. Keep in mind, too, that the music was not created as concert music, but it is very effective in relating its message and in representing African culture.

Listen to "Mitamba Yalagala Kumchuzi" (CD 6) again. As you listen this time, keep in mind the sociocultural setting of the music.

MAIN POINTS OF THIS CHAPTER

1. Folk music is the music of the common people of a particular nation or ethnic group. Ethnic music is identified with a particular culture and is usually performed by trained musicians.

2. It is important to know something about folk/ethnic music because elements of it are sometimes found in concert music; it reveals the attitudes and values of a culture; and the peoples of the world today are interconnected as never before.

3. Performers of ethnic music are often expected to improvise. Each type of music, however, has performance traditions and practices that the musicians are expected to follow.

4. Folk/ethnic music differs from concert music in several ways:
   - Creators of such music are usually unknown.
   - Performers feel usually free to make small changes in it.
   - Some of it is largely improvised within the guidelines of the type of music.
   - The response of an audience, if there is one, is not important.
   - It contains subtleties that are easily missed by persons who are unfamiliar with that type of music.
   - Much of it does not exist in notation, but is preserved by oral tradition.

5. Folk/ethnic instruments can be divided into four groups according to how they produce sounds.
   - Aerophones produce sound when air is blown into them.
   - Ideophones are percussion instruments other than drums such as rattles and xylophones.
   - Membranophones include the wide variety of drums with heads made from animal skin.
   - Chordophones include all types of string instruments.

6. Cultural elements are more important in folk/ethnic music than they are in concert music.

Folk Music *of* Europe *and the* Americas

41

Europe stretches from the Ural Mountains in Russia several thousand miles west to England and Ireland. With the settling of North and South America by the various nations of Europe, the culture of western European civilization was transported across the Atlantic Ocean and later halfway around the world to Australia and New Zealand. The emigrants from Europe came upon lands already occupied by Native Americans in the north and Incas, Aztecs, and other peoples to the south. Later, slaves were brought to the Western Hemisphere from Africa.

The resulting combination of music from multiple countries and sources is a wealth of music styles, with each influencing and enriching the others.

EUROPEAN FOLK MUSIC

European folk music is built around the features presented in Part I. These include melody, harmony, timbre, accompaniment, form, subject matter, and rhythm.

Melody

Melodies are built on the seven-note major and minor scales. In addition, many folk melodies use seven-note scales other than major or minor, or what are termed *modes*. A few pentatonic scales are encountered, particularly in eastern Europe. A **pentatonic scale** has five notes in the pattern of the black keys on a piano. Generally, the range of the melodies is about one octave, and they do not contain many repeated notes.

Harmony

Accompanying chords are built in thirds, with the three primary chords predominating. The presence of harmony is an important difference between Western music and much of the music of other parts of the world.

Timbre

The style of singing found in Western folk music is natural and relaxed, at least to Western ears. Many folk singers use little vibrato, and no attempt is made to impress listeners with the singer's vocal prowess. The instruments used in folk music are equally unpretentious. The guitar, accordion, harmonica (mouth organ), dulcimer, and other easily transported instruments are generally used.

The dulcimer looks like a long, flat violin with three strings. It is placed on the player's lap and plucked with a quill. Two of its strings produce a drone.

Although most Western folk music consists of songs, there is a body of instrumental music associated with dances. The fiddle tunes found in western Europe and America are part of this tradition.

Accompaniment

Originally, folk music was often performed without any accompaniment. Most of it is now accompanied by an instrument, however, which is often played by the singer.

Form

A characteristic of Western folk music is the singing of different sets of words to the same melody. The musical term for the repeating of a song with different verses, or *stanzas*, is **strophic.** Although some European folk songs have twenty or more stanzas, four or five is typical.

Subject Matter

European folk songs include a larger percentage of epic tales and love sentiments than is found in other cultures. One important type of song is the **ballad.** Its words tell a story, often a sad one, in five or more stanzas. Traditionally, ballads are sung by one singer. In English ballads the singer usually relates a tale about someone else, which gives the song a sense of detachment. In American ballads the singer often sings about himself or herself, but an attitude of detachment is nevertheless retained.

Rhythm

The rhythm of Western folk music is regular and metrical. Traditionally, ballads have a common iambic meter and stanzas of four lines in which a four-foot line alternates with a three-foot line.

   "Barbara Allen" is a good example of a ballad as well as of many characteristics of Western folk music. It is the most popular ballad of the Western world and is found in hundreds of versions.

Samuel Pepys wrote of singing "Barbara Allen" on January 2, 1666, in London. Both the English and the Scots claim the song, and some ninety-eight versions of it were found in Virginia alone!

LISTENING GUIDE

ENGLISH BALLAD

"Barbara Allen" (late 1600s)

GENRE: Ethnic music   Vocalist, guitar

CD 6 Track 36

4 minutes 28 seconds

Form: Strophic, ballad

The first verse begins after a short guitar introduction.

1. *In Scarlet town where I was born,*
   there was a fair maid dwellin',
   made many a youth cry well a-day,
   and her name was Barb'ry Allen.

2. *'Twas in the merry month of May,*
   when green buds they were swellin',
   Sweet William came from the west country,
   and he courted Barb'ry Allen.

3. *He sent his servant unto her,*
   to the place where she was dwellin',
   "My master's sick, bids me call for you,
   if your name be Barb'ry Allen."

4. *Well, slowly, slowly she got up,*
   and slowly went she nigh him,
   but all she said as she passed his bed,
   "Young man, I think you're dying."

5. *He turned his pale face to the wall,*
   and busted out a cryin',
   "Adieu, adieu, my dear friends all,
   Be kind to Barb'ry Allen."

6. *Well, lightly tripped she down the stairs.*
   she heard those church bells tollin',
   and each bell seemd to say as it tolled,
   "Hard-hearted Barb'ry Allen."

7. *And she looked east, and she looked west.*
   She seen his pale corpse a-comin',
   "Lay down, lay down that corpse of clay,
   that I may look upon him."

8. *"Oh, mother, mother go make my bed,*
   go make it long and narrow.
   Sweet William died for me today.
   I'll die for him tomorrow."

9. *They buried Sweet William in the old churchyard.*
   They buried Barbara beside him.
   Out of his grave grew a red, red rose,
   and out of hers a brier.

10. *They grew and grew up the old church wall,*
   'till they could grow no higher.
   And at the top, twined in a lovers' knot,
   the red rose and the brier.

 An interactive Active Listening Guide can be downloaded from the online Resource Center for *Music Listening Today, 4th Edition.*

In addition to its metrical rhythm, "Barbara Allen" has a simple melody that is largely built out of the notes of its main chord. The singer on the recording, Pete Seeger, uses a plain, unemotional style as he accompanies his singing on a guitar.

AMERICAN FOLK MUSIC

Just as English is the predominant language in the United States, the British Isles are the main source of its folk music. Many songs were imported from England, and many others are patterned after British types. The style of performance is also closely related to its English heritage.

One adaptation of the English ballad is the **broadside.** The name comes from the old English practice of printing ballads on large sheets of paper called broadsides, which were sold on the streets. Broadsides were often about current events or famous personalities. About two hundred such songs were circulated in the United States. The poetry of broadsides is not always of high quality, but it reflects the interests of the people of the time.

The ballad style is found in many American folk songs associated with occupations — sailors, cowboys, lumberjacks, miners, farmers, and so on.

Non-British music came to America with various immigrant groups. In a few cases, such music was incorporated into the culture. For example, "Du, du liegst mir im Herzen" is a German song that has been adopted into the culture; "Alouette" is a French-Canadian example; "Chiapanecas" ("Mexican Clapping Song") is a Latin American contribution that is clapped and stomped at many major-league ballparks.

Some non-British songs have had new words set to their melodies. The Pennsylvania Dutch song "Marjets wann ich uffschteh" became "Go Tell Aunt Rhody." Unfortunately, much non-British music was lost in America. Still, there are various types of American folk music.

> Folk music scholars in the early twentieth century found Elizabethan English folk songs better preserved in remote Appalachian hamlets than in England itself.

> The word *Dutch* as used in *Pennsylvania Dutch* is a perversion of *Deutsch*, which is the German word for "German."

Work Songs

Songs that accompany labor are not characteristic of American folk music, except for sea chanteys and African American music. "Blow the Man Down" is an example of a sea chantey. Its words hardly convey a deep message:

> Come all ye young fellows that follow the sea,
>   to the way haye, blow the man down,
> And pray, pay attention and listen to me,
>   give me some time to blow the man down.

> *Chantey* is pronounced "shantey."

Occupational Songs

Although few songs accompanied work, many of them were about work. Cowboy ballads, which were modeled after the English ballad, often had a melancholy tone. In "The Cowboy's Lament," the dying young man says:

> Get sixteen gamblers to carry my coffin
> Six purty maidens to sing me a song,
> Take me to the valley and lay the sod o'er me,
> For I'm a young cowboy an' know I done wrong.

The development of the railroads provided another source for occupational songs. Some of them are about men who built the railroads ("Drill, Ye Tarriers, Drill"), some describe famous personalities ("John Henry" and "Casey Jones"), and others tell about particular trains ("Wabash Cannonball").

Mark Humphrey/AP Photo

FOLK ARTIST SHAWN COLVIN

FIDDLER EVERETT BUGG at the Great River Road Opry, Hillview, Illinois

"The Ox-Driving Song" tells about the troubles of the teamsters who drove their wagons over muddy roads and washouts:

When I got there, the hills were steep,
'twould make any tenderhearted person weep
to hear me cuss and pop my whip
and see my oxen pull and slip.

Dance Music

The most important type of folk dancing was square dancing. If no instruments were available, the dancers sang the music as they danced. Usually, the words had little significance; sometimes words were added simply to complete a line of music. A good example of dance music is "Skip to My Lou":

Flies in the buttermilk, two by two,
flies in the buttermilk, two by two,
flies in the buttermilk, two by two,
skip to my Lou, my darling!

CHORUS:
She's gone again, skip to my Lou,
she's gone again, skip to my Lou,
she's gone again, skip to my Lou,
skip to my Lou, my darling.

My girl wears a number nine shoe,
my girl wears a number nine shoe,
my girl wears a number nine shoe,
skip to my Lou, my darling.

CHORUS

Dance music was often played on fiddles. Most of the tunes, called **hoedowns** or **breakdowns,** were in a fast tempo with two beats to the measure. Their heritage is the reels and hornpipes from the British Isles. Jigs were also popular fiddle music for dancing. Fiddle tunes had some imaginative titles: "Devil's Dream," "Lost Indian," "Orange Blossom Special," "Leather Britches," and others.

The fiddle and the violin are the same—sort of. The difference comes in the way they are played. Fiddlers handle the bow somewhat differently and hold the instrument lower in front of the chest. No vibrato is used. They sometimes tune strings to nonstandard pitches. The instrument itself may be an inexpensive mail-order model or a handmade version.

One old catalog lists a "Special Stradivarius Model" for $9.95, including bow, case, extra strings, instruction book, and fingering chart!

Self-Expression

Many songs, in both folk and concert music, serve to express deep feelings. The white spiritual "The Wayfaring Stranger" is one example:

I'm just a poor, wayfaring stranger,
A-trav'ling through this world of woe,
Yet there's no sickness, no toil, no danger,
In that fair land to which I go.

I'm goin' there to see my mother,
I'm goin' there no more to roam,
I'm just a-goin' over Jordan,
I'm just a-goin' over home.

"A-goin' over Jordan" refers to dying.

"Simple Gifts" was discussed in Chapter 3.

Arrangements

Sometimes composers find songs that they consider worth arranging for concert or recital hall performance. They leave the original melody largely intact and devise an accompaniment for piano or orchestra. Aaron Copland did this with the Shaker song "Simple Gifts." The song comes from the period between 1837 and 1847.

The accompaniment for "Simple Gifts" is in keeping with the text and melody by being open and uncluttered. There are only very brief introductory measures based on the melody for each section of the song. Sometimes the chords are sounded off the beat in a subtle way, but generally everything is plain and understated.

NATIVE AMERICAN MUSIC

Native Americans came to the Americas during the Ice Age thousands of years ago, when an ice bridge existed across the Bering Strait between Siberia and Alaska. Their music differs very much from that of the English tradition.

The functional nature of Native American music is apparent in the names given to the rituals. A sun dance or a rabbit dance was created for a specific purpose. Sometimes that purpose was to appease or influence spirits, and at other times it was to sing about events in life.

Native American instruments traditionally consisted of a variety of drums, usually played with sticks. Many types of rattles were also developed. Several kinds of flutes were played, especially by the men, who performed love music on them to impress their chosen young women.

Mark Booth/Alamy

A NATIVE AMERICAN DANCER

The Native American population was never large, and it was spread over a vast land area. Its music differs according to the particular tribe and geographic location.

- The Eskimos and the tribes of the Pacific Northwest developed music characterized by nonstrophic forms, complex rhythms, and small melodic intervals.
- The tribes of California and the extreme Southwest sing with a harsh vocal sound. Their songs consist of two or more separate sections that are repeated, alternated, and interwoven.
- A third broad area includes Utah, Nevada, and the interior of northern California. In this region the singing is more relaxed in style, and the songs are made up of paired phrases, with each phrase repeated.
- A fourth type of Native American culture is distinguished more by language than geography. It consists of the Navajo, Apache, and some western Canadian tribes. Their melodies have a wide range, and male singers freely perform in high, falsetto voices.
- The Pueblo and Plains tribes display more tension in singing and favor a two-part song form.
- Native Americans in the eastern and southern parts of the United States feature singing responsively, with shouts tossed back and forth between leader and group.

Native American music has not had much effect on the other types of American music for two reasons. First, most Native Americans did not live close to non–Native Americans. They have often lived apart on reservations, and their music has tended to be confined to the tribe.

Second, Native American music is quite different from Western music. In some respects, it is more Asian than Western. When one culture incorporates music from another, the two styles are likely to be similar. Some change—but not too much—is accepted in a musical style. In the few instances in which Native American music has been incorporated into compositions, it has been changed quite a bit.

Margin: The Native American population was no more than one to two million in all of the United States and Canada.

Margin: No Native American music was found in concerts before about 1890, and even today there are very few works that show the influence of this music.

AFRICAN AMERICAN MUSIC

In a complex and pluralistic society such as the United States, the sources of the cultural mixture are hard to determine, so it is difficult to know which aspects of African American music were transplanted from Africa and which were developed in America. In any case, some of the African rhythmic ideas, call-and-response patterns, love of instruments, and improvisation are now part of American music. Africans brought something perhaps more important than any technical features: a strong interest in music and a desire to involve listeners in the music.

Calls and Hollers

Margin: Sometimes hollers were used to warn other slaves of impending danger.

One early and important feature of African American folk music was the spontaneous individual **calls and hollers** heard in the fields and other workplaces. Their purpose was to relieve loneliness and stress, as well as to express feelings. Musically, they were short melodic fragments that were highly decorated. They were mostly improvised. Few calls and hollers were recorded before they largely disappeared, but they played a role in the development of the blues, which led directly to jazz.

Spirituals

An important form of African American religious folk music was the **spiritual.** Until after the Civil War, these songs existed by oral tradition among blacks. The first book of spirituals containing both words and music was not published until 1867.

Michael Ochs Archives/Getty Images

THE FISK JUBILEE SINGERS
In seven years, they raised $150,000, a large amount of money at that time.

During Reconstruction, several colleges for the recently freed slaves were established in the South by various church groups. To help raise money by giving concerts, singing groups were formed at these colleges, most notably the Fisk Jubilee Singers at Fisk University in Nashville. Initially, the group sang a variety of songs, but no spirituals. They soon found, however, that spirituals were enthusiastically received by audiences. The Fisk Jubilee Singers were both a musical and a financial success as they toured New York City, Washington, D.C., and Europe.

Spirituals drew heavily on biblical texts. Some of these texts use Bible stories as thinly veiled parallels to the plight of the African Americans as slaves. The spiritual "Go Down, Moses" is a good example:

> *When Israel was in Egypt's land,*
> *Let my people go.*
> *Oppressed so hard they could not stand,*
> *Let my people go.*

Spirituals were sung with much inflection and subtlety. What is seen in the notation of a spiritual is only the skeletal outline for what was actually sung. In fact, quite a bit of improvising took place during the singing. Spirituals were originally sung by a group, not a solo singer.

Folk Blues

Blues songs were the most important type of secular folk music among African Americans. In contrast to spirituals, blues songs were for individual singers to cry out against life's problems. The topics of the blues ranged from problems with work (too much or not enough), crime, infidelity, loneliness, and rejection. These sentiments were generally sung in a three-line form (*a a b*).

> *My mama told me before I left home,*
> *My mama told me before I left home,*
> *You better let them Jacksonville women alone.*

Furthermore, lines of the blues are harmonized in a rudimentary way. The musical interest was in the way the melody was sung. Blues singers tend to slide between pitches to put more emotion in the music. Many embellishments are also added. Usually, singing blues is accompanied by the guitar. Sometimes it is played in "bottleneck" style by running a knife blade on the strings, which creates a timbre something like that of a Hawaiian guitar.

Work Songs

Songs created to accompany work are definitely a contribution of African Americans. The song text is not always related to the job at hand; often the words are only to supply a pleasant accompaniment to labor.

Instruments

The *gutbucket* is an inverted washtub with a rope pulled through it, which is connected to a stick. The pitch is varied according to the tension the player exerts on the stick and thereby the rope.

Particular instruments are prominent in African American folk music, just as they are in Africa. Some instruments are conventional; others are intended to provide sound effects. Included in the latter category are washboards, pans, cowbells, bottles, various clappers, and the gutbucket.

LATIN AMERICAN MUSIC

Latin American music includes a wide variety of types, partly because the music of Spain, the parent culture of Central and South America, is so varied. Spanish music includes the music of the gypsies and the Basque people of northern Spain, Arabian influences resulting from six hundred years of occupation by the Moors, and French influence from Provence. With the Spanish conquests in the New World, elements of its music were transported to the Americas.

In addition to the influences of Spanish and Portuguese colonialism, the music of Central and South America was heavily influenced by African music brought by black slaves. This influence is especially strong in Haiti and the other Caribbean nations of Cuba, Jamaica, and Trinidad, the Guianas on the northern coast of South America, and northern Brazil. Central and South America also have large Indian populations, which in some areas have retained their native languages. Recent emigrations from Asia have also played a role in the music of Latin America.

Joe Sohm/Visions of America, LLC/Alamy

MARIACHI BAND ON RIVER WALK A mariachi band performs on a footbridge in San Antonio, Texas.

What has resulted from the contacts among these four groups is a varied and wonderfully mixed heritage. Many countries have terms for these mixed cultures, such as *mestizo* (Native American and Spanish), *mulato* (African and Spanish), and *zambo* (African and Native American).

Since the Spanish came to the New World, the various types of music have been adapted so much that it is often impossible to tell the origins of a particular style of music. For example, the *bolero* was originally Spanish, but in Cuba its rhythm became more complex. Among other features that carried over from Spanish music are the frequent use of rhythms having three notes to the beat, the presence of a line of harmony moving parallel to the melody but three notes below, and melodies with a narrow range.

The **bolero** is a dance in four beats to the measure containing complex rhythmic patterns.

Mexican music is largely Spanish in character, more so than most Latin American music. Although some Mexican Indians have retained their musical heritage, Indian influence is not significant in Mexican music. The Mexicans have a narrative type of song called a **corrido.** Like the English ballad, it relates a happening or tells a story.

Instruments play an important role in Mexican music and are sometimes featured in interludes of songs. The often-heard *mariachi band* consists of from three to twelve performers playing violins, guitars, trumpets, and other instruments.

Another type of Latin American music is the **son,** which appeared during the early part of the twentieth century and became a popular urban type of music played by groups consisting of strings and percussion. In the Mexican "Sones de Hausteca," the violin player shows the influence of the virtuoso style of concert violinists in the United States. Two of the male singers sing in parallel thirds, which is typical of Mexican music. At times, the harmony and melody don't fit together all that well.

MEXICAN FOLK SONG
"Sones de Hausteca"

GENRE: Ethnic music   Vocalists, violin, guitar

CD 6 Track 37

1 minute 48 seconds
Form: *Son*

0:00 37	0:00	Violinist begins and is soon accompanied by guitar.
	0:30	Male singer enters, sometimes sliding his voice up into falsetto (high false voice).
	0:40	Two other men join in, singing in thirds.
	0:49	Soloist sings the melody.
	0:57	Violinist solos with many fast notes.
	1:38	Rhythmic pattern with short repeated notes is heard in violin and guitar.
	1:48	Recording fades.

An interactive Active Listening Guide can be downloaded from the online Resource Center for *Music Listening Today, 4th Edition.*

LISTENING GUIDE

MAIN POINTS OF THIS CHAPTER

1. European folk music is similar to American folk music in most respects. Melodies in the five-note pentatonic scale are encountered more often, especially in the music of Eastern Europe.

2. Many European folk songs are strophic, with different verses sung to the same melody. Ballads are songs in which the singer relates a story, often a sad one, in five or more verses.

3. American folk music is a mixture of music from many different sources, especially the British Isles. Broadsides consisting of words printed on a single sheet of paper were an early example of American folk music.

4. Several types of American folk music can be identified. They include work and occupational songs, dance music, and songs in which singers express their feelings.

5. Dance music was often played on violins (fiddles). Square dancing with its quick tempo and duple meter was the most prevalent type of dance music.

6. Native American music varied a great deal according to tribe and region. Most of it is functional music. It is quite different from most Western music and therefore not easily assimilated into it.

7. Many features of African American music have been incorporated into American music. These include spontaneous calls and hollers, spirituals, work songs, and folk melodies in which individual singers cry out against life's problems.

8. Latin American music is a mixture from a variety of sources, especially Spanish, Indian, and African. Mexican music includes a ballad-like *corrido* and small instrumental groups called *mariachi*.

FEATURES TO LISTEN FOR

1. "Barbara Allen":
   • The detached style of the singer as he relates a sad story

2. "Sones de Hausteca":
   • Occasional use of the falsetto voice by the singer
   • The melody in parallel thirds when more than one singer sings

Music *of* Africa *and* *the* Middle East

42

The continent of Africa is a huge landmass about a fourth larger than all of North America. The Sahara extends for thousands of miles across its upper half. To the south of the Sahara are the black peoples whom we usually associate with that continent. For the remainder of this book, the word *African* refers to the music from the southern two-thirds of the continent.

To the north of the Sahara, and especially to the east extending from Egypt in the northeastern corner to Iran and Pakistan north of India, lies what is often referred to as the Middle East. These peoples are largely Muslim, with Turks and Arabs being the largest ethnic groups. Sitting in the middle among these countries is Israel, with its unique heritage.

The music of sub-Saharan Africa and that of the Middle East contain many differences within them, and this discussion can offer only a small sample of each overall type of music.

AFRICAN MUSIC

What are the main characteristics of the music of the peoples who live south of the Sahara? Many of the features of folk music mentioned in Chapter 41 are found in African music, but several are particularly important.

Relationship with Language

African languages are tonal in character. As pointed out earlier, in such languages the meaning of sound varies depending on the pitch and manner in which it is said. Because they are tonal, African languages have a musical quality about them. There is a strong similarity between the singsong speech of a language and the music of the people who speak it. Even the drums used in some African music attempt to imitate the pitches and inflections of the language. These "talking drums" are capable of sending messages that are clearly understood by the people who speak that particular language.

Actually, the drums do not "talk" so much as they signal. The process is similar to how bugle calls functioned at one time in an army.

Here is an example of how the pitches of a language influence the rhythm and pitches found in the music:

Text:	"Wo ho te sen?" ("How do you do?")
Tone levels:	Low high, low high
Rhythm:	Short long, short long
Melody:	

At best, rendering non-Western music in notation can only approximate the actual sounds.

Association with Dance

Just as language is closely related to African music, so is dance. Dance is used in rituals, worship, celebrations, and for recreation. It is also considered a natural accompaniment to the music. Some dances are for just the men, and women participate in others. Much of the time, anyone can join in the dancing, often to be observed and rewarded with coins if the dancer was judged to be good by the onlookers. Few people are passive when African music is being performed.

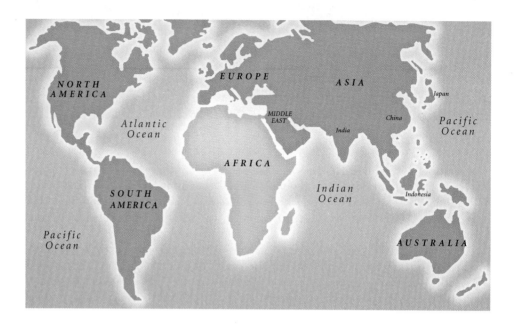

AFRICA AND THE WORLD

SWAZI DRUMMERS IN SOUTH AFRICA

Rhythm

The music played by groups of percussion instruments best illustrates the complexity of rhythm in African music. The music starts out simply with a basic rhythm, or "time line," which might be compared with the role of the bass drum in a marching band in keeping the group together. Soon other percussion instruments are added over the time line part until as many as five distinct rhythm patterns are sounding at the same time—polyrhythm. Then enters the master drummer, who plays the rhythm of a particular piece of music. After a while he gives a rhythmic signal to change to another piece. This process continues until the performance is completed.

Several other points should be mentioned about African instrumental ensembles, especially as found in Ghana and other West African countries.

- Rarely do African drummers tap their feet; they do not think of following a beat as do Western musicians.

- Not only do the rhythm patterns of the various instruments differ, but they also do not begin at exactly the same moment, as is usually true in Western music. In fact, they would lose some of their rhythmic flavor if they did.

- Often the meter is unclear as to whether it is in two or three beats. At one moment the pattern seems to be clearly two beats to the measure, but a little while later a three-beat pattern may be perceived. This metric ambiguity makes the music more fascinating.

Improvisation

There is less improvising in African percussion ensembles than is generally supposed; the musicians are often playing preexisting music that has been passed on by oral tradition. Performers, especially master drummers, are allowed to make small changes and alterations in the music, partly to relieve tedium. African musicians do not, however, play whatever they happen to feel like playing; they perform within certain clearly understood guidelines.

Functional Music

Music is very much a part of the daily lives of Africans. For example, it is called on to cure illnesses, appease gods, and celebrate the births of babies. There are songs for praising cattle, telling about animal hunts, and paddling a canoe. There is also some music that is simply for entertainment, and a small amount that is played for ceremonies involving a king or chief.

A few African men earn their livelihood from their music making, especially drummers. These musicians learn their trade from infancy. They are carefully taught, often by their fathers, and they do not perform publicly until they become truly competent as young adults.

Because most African music is functional, it does not take place in a performer/audience situation. Musical performances are truly participatory events in which there is little distinction between performer and audience. Because African music is functional, its musicians want their work to have an impact. They do not care whether it is considered "beautiful" in the sense that Western musicians often think about music.

Lack of Uniformity

It has been estimated that sub-Saharan Africa contains between five hundred and seven hundred languages or dialects. Such diversity of languages is significant in that continent's music because its music and languages are virtually inseparable. Therefore, the music of one tribe may differ a lot from that of another only a short distance away. And the music that is so vital to one tribe often makes little sense to other tribes, even though they both sound like African music to us.

Four major languages exist just in the small nation of Zambia. These languages are so different that commerce and government are conducted in English, which was used when Zambia was Northern Rhodesia and under British control.

Form

African music features what is termed *call-and-response* form. In this form a leader sings or plays a phrase, and then the group responds with its rendition of the phrase. The pattern is something like a game of musical tennis. Sometimes the response is not identical because members of the group will make small alterations in what they have heard. At other times, the response begins before the original phrase is completed, and the result is a brief period of simple counterpoint or harmony.

Some African songs follow a pattern in which the original melody returns or is set in a two-part form.

Melodic Characteristics

African melodies are often altered and ornamented with slight changes of pitch, trills, slides, and other decorative notes. Some of the scales on which the music is based are not very different from those found in Western music, but the style in which they are used is quite different.

Beliefs about Music and Instruments

Africans have strong beliefs about the spirit of an instrument. For example, a drum is not just a drum; instead, it has an almost human quality. The maker of a drum wants to make sure the drum "speaks" as it should. So he may unobtrusively pick up pebbles to put in the drum from the yard of a woman known to be a gossip. In addition, he may add a piece of lion skin so that the drum will roar, a piece of frog skin to help the drum remain supple, and pieces of metal so that it will rattle. Other musical instruments are similarly "doctored" to achieve a more interesting sound.

The practice of attributing human qualities to inanimate objects is termed *animism*.

Instruments

Drums hold the dominant position among African musical instruments. They are constructed of various materials and are made in a variety of sizes. Some are played with the hands; others are played with sticks. An especially interesting drum has an hourglass shape with strings connecting its two heads. The player holds it under the arm and squeezes the strings against his body to change the tension of the heads, which affects the pitch of the drum. In this way, the drum can "talk."

The *mbira,* or thumb piano, is a feature of African music. It usually has about eighteen short strips of metal or cane that sound against a resonating box. Simple flutes are also found in African music, as is a single-string instrument called a *gonje,* which is played with a bow.

Other African instruments include a gourd with beads strung around it. It is shaken in performance, often by a woman. A double bell that looks like a cowbell is also heard, as are various rattles, hand claps, and whistles.

Most of these features of African music — the polyrhythms, instruments, drumming, call-and-response patterns, and so on — can be heard in "Mitamba Yalagala Kumchuzi" (CD 6), which was presented in Chapter 2.

MBIRA

MIDDLE EASTERN MUSIC

The Medes (the people who live in present-day Iraq) and the Persians have a history of conflict that goes back almost two thousand years.

As mentioned earlier, the term *Middle East* usually refers to the Arab world that extends thousands of miles from the northwest coast of Africa from Casablanca on the Atlantic Ocean to the eastern borders of Pakistan north of India. The people who inhabit this vast stretch of land are more united in their religious faith — Islam — than by their culture or language. The people of Iran, for example, consider themselves Persian and speak Farsi, not Arabic. The Turks constitute another major segment of the Middle East, whereas another large segment is centered in Egypt and yet another stretches across North Africa.

Although the land encompassed by the Middle East is large, the population is not, at least in comparison with that of Africa, Europe, or the Far East. The people tend to be spread along the shores of the Mediterranean Sea and the Indian Ocean. They are no more homogeneous than are the peoples of sub-Saharan Africa.

Music of the Middle East is in a difficult situation because most musicians, especially those who perform popular music, are considered low class. Also, in Islam only restrained chanting is allowed of verses from the Koran. The situation is not helped by the fact that in the Middle East music is based on complex and confusing theories that vary from one area to another. Some of these theories maintain that the best music encourages a trancelike higher level of life.

Most Middle Eastern music is monophonic. Singers, who are usually men, produce a tense, nasal tone quality. They also improvise many ornaments to the basic melodic line. Rhythm is treated very freely, which permits singers and instrumentalists to add their own decorative notes to the music. The ornamental figures are very prominent in "Segah," which is from Iran.

A number of instruments are associated with music from the Middle East. One is the *ud,* which is a plucked string instrument with a pear-shaped body. Another string instrument is the *rebab,* which is generally considered the direct ancestor of the violin. The *tombak* is a drum in the shape of an hourglass that is played with the fingers.

THE MIDDLE EAST

IRAN
"Segah"

GENRE: Ethnic music   Vocalist, violin

CD 6 Track **39**

2 minutes 2 seconds

0:00	**39**	0:00	Violin plays an ornamented melody.
		0:31	Singer begins a free-sounding melody with many vocal trills.
		0:55	Violin plays a more elaborate melody.
		1:10	Singer adds many vocal trills to the melody.
		1:47	Violin again plays highly decorated melody.
		2:02	Recording fades.

 An interactive Active Listening Guide can be downloaded from the online Resource Center for *Music Listening Today, 4th Edition.*

There are few concerts in the Middle East. Most performances are informal, many times in cafés. In that setting one may sip a drink while listening. As an added attraction, some pieces featuring gyrating female dancers for which the Arab world is noted may be interspersed among the more thoughtful works.

Jewish Music

Israel is situated in the middle of the Arab world, which over the centuries has created many political tensions and wars. Modern Israel is very different from its neighbors. Not only is it the only well-established democracy in the region; it is also much more Western and up-to-date. It is a nation with a fascinating history.

Over the centuries Jewish religious music has remained rather well unified, in spite of the Diaspora in the Middle Ages and subsequent centuries. Judaism was much less evangelistic than Christianity. It tended to keep its faith within the group, and it seldom incorporated regional music into its worship.

The traditional religious music of Judaism consisted of prayers and invocations, not anthems and other ensemble music. Today its religious music varies according to the degree of orthodoxy. The more-orthodox congregations permit only unaccompanied chanting by cantors; the more-liberal congregations (at least in the United States) often employ Gentile instrumentalists and singers and allow them to perform adaptations of music written for Christian worship. The orthodox chants are similar to some of the chants adopted by the early Christian Church (see Chapter 7). A few Jewish melodies have been adapted for use as hymn tunes in Christian churches.

The modern nation of Israel was founded in 1948, and most of its population emigrated there from other countries—Poland, Ethiopia, and many other nations, and in recent years, especially Russia. These immigrants have retained some of the musical influences of their former lands, so it is not unusual, for example, for German Jews to sing German or Yiddish songs or for Armenian Russian Jews to sing songs of their former homeland. In addition, the influence of the Middle East and its Arab culture has also been felt. When Israelis sing Arab songs, however, they sing them in a Jewish style.

David Taylor Photography/Alamy

EGYPTIAN MUSICIAN playing a rebab

The Diaspora was the scattering of the Jewish people from Palestine to many different parts of the world.

Jewish music and worship practices were very influential in the early Christian Church.

A CANTOR CHANTING

Because the common bond among the people of Israel is religious, not ethnic, attempts have been made to create a new and unifying folk music tradition. New popular songs have been composed with texts on economic and political topics. Folk songs in Israel today are accompanied by tambourines, accordions, and guitars — instruments that represent Israel's diverse musical heritage.

MAIN POINTS OF THIS CHAPTER

1. African music features complex rhythms, some improvisation according to traditional guidelines, and call-and-response form. It also varies a great deal from tribe to tribe and is usually associated with dancing.

2. African instruments include a wide variety of drums, rattles, and the thumb piano. Africans ascribe almost human qualities to their instruments. "Talking drums" imitate the pitches of a particular language and are used for signaling purposes.

3. Middle Eastern music is largely monophonic, with its melodic line highly ornamented in a rhythmically free manner. It is inhibited somewhat by the fact that most musicians have a low social status and complex theories about music.

4. Several instruments are used in Middle Eastern music, including the plucked string *ud* and a drum with an hourglass shape.

5. The music of Israel is very cosmopolitan, except for its religious music, which varies according to the degree of orthodoxy of the particular congregation.

FEATURES TO LISTEN FOR

1. "Mitamba Yalagala Kumchuzi":
   • The presence of several rhythm patterns at the same time
   • The call-and-response pattern between the leader and the group
2. "Segah":
   • The highly ornamented melodic line performed by the violin and the singer
   • The quality of the singer's voice

Music *of* Asia

43

What do the three-note songs of the Aborigines of Australia, the ragas of India, and the gamelan music of Bali have in common? In many ways they are different, but each comes from that vast portion of the world called Asia and its related countries along the Indian and Pacific oceans.

INDIAN MUSIC

India is overwhelming. About thirteen percent of the world's people live there. Somewhat protected from outside influences by the giant Himalayan Mountains to the north and the vast Indian Ocean to the south, India developed a unique and fascinating civilization. Where else does one encounter snake charmers, wandering holy men (some of whom wear no clothes), the ritual bathing in the Ganges River, opulent wealth alongside unbelievable poverty, and the superb Taj Mahal?

And where else does one find music like Indian classical music? Its roots reach back at least two thousand years, and it has existed largely unchanged since then. Today Indian classical music still thrives, but along with it is heard popular music from movies, some rock music from England and America, traditional hymns as well as other Christian music, and even some wind band music that is a carryover from the more than 250 years of English rule.

In a country as large as India, it is not surprising to find sizable differences and diversity. So, its classical music tends to divide into two major types: the *karnataka* music of southern India and the *Hindustani* music of northern India. The music of the north was influenced by Persia and the culture of the Middle East as the result of invasions from those countries over the centuries. It contains more improvisation and showy music. The music of the south is more traditional and is based on composed songs. It also sounds busy and contains more ornamented melodic lines.

What makes Indian music, from both the south and the north, special?

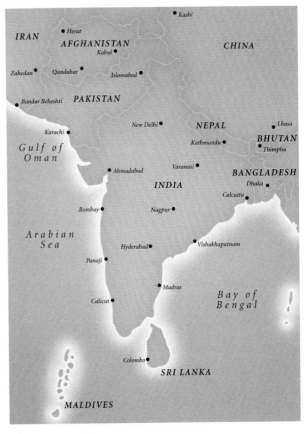

INDIA AND ITS NEIGHBORS

Ragas

It would be easy to describe a raga as a scale or melodic formula, but that would neglect its important affective and philosophical overtones. **Ragas** are intended to express and generate feelings — "colors of the mind." Each raga is thought to have a personality of its own with its own rules. Usually, ragas are associated with particular human emotions, Hindu deities, seasons of the year, and so on.

Theoretically, thousands of ragas exist, but only about fifty are performed today. They vary in length, but the average is about twenty to twenty-five notes. Two tones tend to stand out in each raga, one being four or five notes higher than the other. The basic raga is treated to many alterations, including slides, pitch bending, and other figures.

The word *raga* comes from a Sanskrit word meaning "coloring."

393

The following is a raga from northern India. The small noteheads indicate slides or zigzag figures, and the brackets mark off the phrases.

Talas

Instead of using the metrical rhythms found in Western music, both concert and popular, Indian musicians use rhythmic cycles of anywhere from 5 to 128 beats, called **talas.** Most talas are 5 to 8 beats long. Below is an example of a 14-beat tala. The / marks in this example indicate how the beats are organized into subgroups.

/ • • • • • / • • / • • • / • • • • /   (5 + 2 + 3 + 4)

Musical Instruments

Indian scholars have grouped musical instruments into three classes, based on how the sound is produced.

STRING INSTRUMENTS The first category includes instruments that produce sound by plucked or bowed strings. The instrument that is most associated with Indian classical music is the *sitar*. It is a large, complicated instrument with five strings for playing the melody and thirteen more strings that ring in sympathy with the melodic strings. It has a bowl-shaped body made from wood and a row of pegs along the neck. A similar instrument found in southern India is the *veena*, which has fewer strings and a gourd or papier-mâché jug-shaped resonator attached to the neck.

WIND INSTRUMENTS These include bamboo flutes and the clarinet-like *pungi*, which is the instrument of choice among snake charmers.

PERCUSSION INSTRUMENTS These are instruments on which the sound is produced by striking. These consist mostly of a wide variety of drums. The most important of these is the double-headed *tabla*, which consists of two small drums played with the hands and fingers. There are also percussion instruments that produce sound by striking a solid object such as a gong.

MAN PLAYING A SITAR NEXT
TO A MAN PLAYING A TABLA

John Henry Claude Wilson/Robert Harding World Imagery/Getty Images

Performances

Concerts of Indian music are informal. Although people in the audience sometimes sit on chairs, traditionally they sit on mats. They may count time with their hands, converse with one another, or offer comments and encouragement to the players. There is no printed program because the entire performance is not planned out. In fact, Indian musicians do not rehearse together before a concert. A concert consists partly of existing songs and partly of improvised music. Performances may last as long as three to four hours without an intermission. They are often held at cultural clubs that offer a series of programs that include music, dance, drama, and movies.

The performers sit on the floor and do not play from notation. The group is usually small, consisting of one singer and several instrumentalists. There is little or no applause at the conclusion of the concert; the audience simply leaves, except for a few persons who hang around to chat with the performers.

Western musicians would find the lack of applause very unnerving, to say the least.

Texture

Indian music has a layered texture. The top layer consists of the singer or solo instrument. The second layer is the drone that is a part of most Indian classical music. It is played by one or more tambouras or a simple reed organ. The lowest layer consists of percussion. This layer is performed by the tabla player and sometimes other instruments like the tambourine. Ten musicians constitute a large ensemble by Indian standards; the number is usually fewer than that.

The tamboura *is a large string instrument that sounds a few pitches almost continuously throughout the music.*

The three layers—the flute, the drone, and the tablas—can easily be heard in "Raga Hansa-Dhwani." The flute player improvises on a type of five-note pentatonic scale over the drone part. The rhythmic structure consists of a cycle of sixteen beats sounded by the tabla player. The "Hansa-Dhwani" is an evening raga that conveys the joyful mood of a bird flying.

Only the first portion of its nearly thirteen minutes is included on the ancillary CD.

LISTENING GUIDE

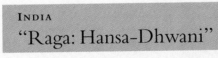

INDIA
"Raga: Hansa-Dhwani"

GENRE: **Ethnic music**   Drone, flute, tablas

CD 6 Track 40

2 minutes 13 seconds

Form: Raga

0:00	40	0:00	Drone begins.
		0.02	Flute enters playing a melody with many decorative notes.
		0:14	Tabla starts its rhythmic cycle.
		0:25	The three instruments continue. Flute improvises short phrases based on a pentatonic scale.
		1:13	The tempo quickens slightly.
		1:39	Flute "bends" the pitch of several notes.
		2:13	The recording fades.

 An interactive Active Listening Guide can be downloaded from the online Resource Center for *Music Listening Today, 4th Edition.*

Form

Indian music is balanced between composed music and music that is improvised by the performers. Performances normally contain four types of improvisation.

- The performance begins with an opening—a free-sounding improvised section based on the raga. It is performed without the tala.
- The next portion is quite rhythmic and works through variations and combinations of groups of notes.
- A third section consists of improvisation on one melodic line. The music of this section gradually becomes more elaborate and showy.
- The fourth section fits both the raga and the tala of the composition. If it is sung, no words are used. Instead, the performer sings the Indian note names—*sa, ri, ga,* and so on. The section grows more complex as it moves along.

Today in India a prospective musician studies either Western or Indian music; few musicians know both types. Indian music is usually learned from a religious teacher, a *guru*, who traditionally receives no pay for his lessons. The guru's purpose is to guide his disciple spiritually and musically.

Cultural Outlook

All music is interwoven with its cultural setting. In the case of India, that setting is highly otherworldly and laced with religious belief. Indian musicians see music as the mystical transfer of human emotion into sound. They even have a special word for it—*bhava*. They believe that without *bhava* the music lacks feeling and "soul."

Traditions and beliefs seem unchangeable in India. One of these beliefs involves the obligation of a musician to preserve the music and pass on to the next generation what the guru taught. There is also the belief, at least among some musicians, that performing a raga apart from its nonmusical association violates cosmic laws and may cause some calamity.

One Indian musician told a European musicologist, "You in the West play love music when there is no love and winter music in the summer. No wonder you have had several large wars in this century."

CHINESE MUSIC

SOUTHEAST ASIA

China and India have a number of things in common. Both possess very large populations; one out of every five human beings is Chinese. Both also have music traditions that reach back thousands of years. And in both countries, music is very much interwoven with philosophy. In fact, one early Chinese emperor ordered musicians and astrologers to work together in calculating the length of pipe to be the standard pitch for music during his reign because he wanted it to be in harmony with the universe.

Much Chinese music is built on the five-note pentatonic scale. It consists mostly of melody; harmony is largely absent. The most distinctive feature of Chinese music is the instruments used to play it and the resulting timbres. String instruments are especially important. One such instrument is the *pipa*, which is like a four-string lute with its pear-shaped body. Another is the *erhu*, which is a two-string fiddle with strings made of silk. An instrument that is strummed like an autoharp is also used. In addition, several types of flutes are played, as are double-reed instruments. The percussion section includes cymbals and, of course, a gong. No brasses are found in traditional Chinese music. A few large orchestras existed in China, which was rare outside the West.

The Chinese developed a unique type of opera. Heroic roles are sung with a rasping sound; heroines sing with a high, thin, "little girl" sound. The lines of opera consist of short phrases separated by instrumental interludes. A drum maintains a steady rhythm, and the sections of the music are concluded with a cymbal crash. It requires years of training to perform Chinese opera correctly.

Chinese music has a spotty history. At times it thrived; at other times it barely survived. After the fall of the last dynasty in 1911, China was declared a republic and the old music of the court went out of fashion. Since 1949 the Communist Party has ruled the mainland, and the traditional, sophisticated music was definitely discouraged. Some of the Chinese musical tradition is being preserved on Taiwan, but that country has rushed to adopt Western culture, including its music.

JAPANESE MUSIC

Much of the classical music of Japan was transported there by Chinese and Korean musicians around the eighth century. For many years it was performed mainly by court musicians, Buddhist priests, and scholars. It reached its peak in the seventeenth and eighteenth centuries, when by orders of its emperors Japan isolated itself from contact with foreign nations. Today Western-style music, both concert and popular, dominate the musical scene in Japan.

One of the features of Japanese music is the *koto*, which is a large instrument with thirteen strings. The strings are stretched over a soundboard about six feet long and are plucked and manipulated by the player. The bridges that hold the strings up off the body can be moved for different tunings.

Much music has been composed for the koto, both solo and in combination with voices or other instruments, such as the *shakuhachi* (a simple bamboo flute) and the *shamisen* (a three-string instrument). Even though a small group of musicians may perform koto music, they play the same basic melody but with different ornamentation and little or no harmony. Generally, Japanese music uses the five-note pentatonic scale. It is subtle and refined, and much attention is devoted to the tone color, pitch, ornamentation, and nuance of the sounds.

"Hakusen no" ("A White Fan") contains many features of traditional Japanese music. It consists of a single line without an accompaniment consisting of chords or contrasting line, as is found in almost all Western music. The singer's tone is more nasal than Westerners are accustomed to. In addition, both the singer and bamboo flute (shakuhachi)

The koto produces gentle, soft sounds.

Japanese girls playing the flute, "koto," and samisen, c. 1880 (hand coloured albumen print on card), Japanese Photographer, (19th century)/Private Collection, The Stapleton Collection/Bridgeman Art Library

SHAMISEN, KOTO, AND SHAKUHACHI

It is difficult to imagine an American song with the title "A White Fan."

shade tones so that the sounds sometimes slide from one to another. The percussion instruments offer only a minimum of rhythmic pattern. The topic of the song is also different from what one would normally encounter in Western music.

LISTENING GUIDE

JAPAN
"Hakusen no"

GENRE: Ethnic music   Singer, bamboo flute, percussion

CD 6, Track **41**

1 minute 45 seconds

0:00	**41**	0:00	Guitarlike instrument plays introductory notes.
		0:18	Singer begins; song contains some sliding notes.
		0:34	Simple percussion sounds begin.
		0:48	Flute plays long sliding notes.
		1:38	Singer sings low notes as guitarlike instrument continues.

An interactive Active Listening Guide can be downloaded from the online Resource Center for *Music Listening Today, 4th Edition.*

BALINESE MUSIC

Bali is one of the islands in the large series that make up the country of Indonesia. The cultural level of this island of less than three million people, who live in an area about the size of Delaware, has rightfully earned it a special place in the world of music and dance. Each village on Bali—and there are about fifteen hundred of them—has at least one instrumental group called a **gamelan.** Its music is strictly ensemble music, with little attention to individual parts or players. Traditionally, gamelan was played in courts, but more recently many are heard in concerts and in conjunction with shadow plays, in which shadows of puppets are projected on a screen. These performances present musical dramas on life and death, good and evil, justice and injustice, and other philosophical topics.

Gamelans can range from four to thirty players, with instruments in pairs, one using the pentatonic scale and the other a version of a seven-note scale. The tuning of these

Peter Horree/Alamy

AN INDONESIAN GAMELAN

scales is not precisely the same. These small pitch differences between them and the other instruments give the music a more shimmering quality.

The main instrument in many gamelans is the xylophone with metal keys. Other instruments include bamboo flutes, which are played in front of the player, not sideways. Drums, gongs, and cymbals of various sizes are also used. The larger drum is considered the male; the smaller one the female. Drummers direct the ensemble by setting the tempo and signaling changes in dynamic levels and transitions between sections. There are also gamelan consisting of other instruments, especially the *angklung*. It is made of hollow bamboo pieces of different lengths that are rattled back and forth to produce sound.

Gamelan music consists of large rhythmic cycles that are subdivided into smaller cycles. The melodies take place within this rhythmic framework. There are distinct melodic modes within the division of the scale. The main melodic line is often available in a type of notation, which uses the numbers 1 2 3 5 6 in recognition of the pentatonic scale. The parts for most of the other players are memorized.

To people unaccustomed to Balinese music, it may sound like a rain of pretty sounds. Those sounds, however, are sophisticated and subtle, and the result of careful planning. "Gender wajang" is typical of gamelan music with its pentatonic scale and shimmering timbres.

Only a small amount of "Gender wajang" is included on the recording.

BALI (INDONESIA)

"Gender Wajang"

GENRE: Ethnic music   Gamelan

CD 6, Track 42

1 minute 45 seconds

0:00	42	0:00	Melody figure alternates between two pitches that gradually grow softer and lower.
		0:35	Music becomes louder.
		0:42	New melody appears built on a five-note pentatonic scale.
		0:48	Music seems to pause several times after repeated notes.
		1:09	The tempo speeds up and then slows down.
		1:37	Another pause and repeated notes.
		1:45	Recording fades.

 An interactive Active Listening Guide can be downloaded from the online Resource Center for *Music Listening Today, 4th Edition.*

MAIN POINTS OF THIS CHAPTER

1. Melodies in Indian classical music are developed around ragas, which are melodic patterns that express "colors of the mind." Rhythm in Indian music is based on talas, which are rhythmic cycles usually consisting of five to eight beats.

2. Instruments associated with Indian music include the sitar (a string instrument), pungi (a wind instrument), and tabla (small drums that are played with the fingers).

3. Indian music is very intertwined with religious beliefs. Indian musicians believe music is the mystical transfer of human emotion into sound.

4. Chinese music is based on the five-note pentatonic scale. It features instruments such as the pipa, erhu, flutes, and percussion.

5. Japanese music features the koto, which is a large plucked string instrument. The music uses the five-note pentatonic scale and is refined and subtle in character.

6. The island of Bali in Indonesia is famous for its gamelan, which are instrumental ensembles. Its main instruments are xylophones with metal bars, flutes, and percussion. It uses both the five-note pentatonic scale and a version of a seven-note scale. The tuning of the scales adds to the color of the music.

FEATURES TO LISTEN FOR

1. "Raga: Hansa-Dhwani":
   - The rhythmic cycle played by the tabla
   - The many ornaments the flute adds to the melodic line

2. "Hakusen no":
   - The timbre of the singer's voice
   - The "bending" of notes played by the flute

3. "Gender Wajang":
   - Extensive use of the pentatonic scale
   - Changes in dynamic levels and tempos

Glossary

absolute music Music that is free of extramusical associations.

a cappella Unaccompanied choral music.

accent The emphasis placed on a note, usually by playing it louder.

accidental A sharp, flat, or natural sign that alters a pitch by one half step.

aerophone Any instrument that generates sound by vibrating a column of air.

aleatory music Music in which the sounds are partly or entirely the result of chance.

allemande A Baroque dance in moderate tempo and two-beat meter.

alto (contralto) The lower, heavier female voice.

aria An accompanied solo song, usually of some length and complexity, in an opera, oratorio, or cantata.

art music Music intended for careful attention to its sounds and expressive qualities.

art song A musical setting of a text by a composer for solo singer and piano.

atonality Music that is not in any key or tonality.

augmentation A compositional technique in which the note values of a theme are all lengthened proportionally.

backbeat The second beat in a measure.

ballad An English narrative song told in simple verses.

ballade A short, melodic piano piece.

ballet Music and bodily movements combined for artistic purposes.

bar See *measure*.

Baroque The style of music the prevailed from 1600 to 1750.

bass The lower, heavier male voice.

basso continuo See *continuo*.

basso ostinato A phrase in the bass line that is played again and again.

beat The pulse or throb that recurs regularly in music.

bebop See *bop*.

bel canto Literally, "beautiful singing" in Italian. Often it refers to a style of opera in the first part of the nineteenth century that featured much vocal technique and beautiful singing.

berceuse Instrumental pieces in a moderate tempo and accompaniment reminiscent of rocking a cradle.

binary form A balanced two-part form, *ab*.

bitonality Two keys occurring simultaneously.

bluegrass A type of country music in which acoustic instruments are used in an attempt to better capture the original qualities of country music.

blue note A note in major scale — usually the third, fifth, or seventh — that in jazz is lowered one half step while the harmony remains in major.

blues A type of song associated with African Americans in which a solo singer sings about some hardship; the usual form of the blues is *a a b*.

bolero A Spanish dance adapted by the Cubans, who made its rhythm more complex.

boogie-woogie A jazz piano style featuring a repeated figure in the bass part and a highly decorated melody line.

bop (bebop) An advanced jazz style for a small group, involving nearly continuous syncopation and a flowing melodic line.

break Contrasting section in the trio of a march; sometimes called "dogfight."

broadside A ballad printed on one sheet of paper, with a text often discussing political matters.

broken chord The notes of a chord sounded one after another rather than simultaneously.

broken style Notes of a chord played sequentially, not simultaneously.

cadence A melodic or harmonic formula that gives a sense of phrase ending. In poetic usage it sometimes refers to beat or tempo.

cadenza A section in which a soloist plays a free paraphrase on the themes of the work.

call-and-response The form found in African music in which phrases of music are exchanged between soloist and group.

calls Melodic phrases sung by the African American slaves while working in the fields.

canon Music in which one or more lines imitate one another for almost the entire work.

cantata A vocal composition in several movements for solo voices, instruments, and usually a chorus; it is usually based on a religious text.

cantus firmus A preexisting melody that is used as the basis for a polyphonic vocal work.

chaconne A work featuring variations on a pattern of chords repeated throughout the work.

chamber music Instrumental music in which each part is performed by only one player.

chance music Music in which some or all events are the product of chance.

chanson (1) A French polyphonic song of the seventeenth century. (2) The French word for "song."

chantey An English or American sailors' song.

character piece A short keyboard work expressing a mood or idea, composed during the Romantic period.

chorale A stately hymn tune used in the German Lutheran Church.

chord The simultaneous sounding of three or more pitches.

chordophone Any instrument that produces sound by vibrating strings.

choreographer The person who designs the movement of dancers.

chorus (1) A sizable group of singers that sings choral music. (2) A section of an opera, oratorio, or cantata sung by a chorus.

chromatic Melodic or harmonic movement by half steps.

classical music The popular term for concert music.

Classical period The prevailing style of music from 1750 to 1820.

clavier The general term for keyboard instruments during the Baroque.

coda (codetta) The concluding portion of a section or movement, usually giving the impression of an ending.

concert music Music created for the intellectual and psychological satisfaction it provides.

concert overture An overture not associated with an opera or drama.

concerted style Music in which one section of a performing group contrasts with another section or a soloist.

concerto A multimovement work consisting of music that contrasts a soloist with an orchestra or band.

concerto grosso A multimovement work contrasting a small instrumental group with a large group.

consonance A group of simultaneous sounds that seems agreeable or restful.

continuo (basso continuo) A bass line for keyboard and other instruments in which the player is given only a succession of single notes and other symbols from which to fill out the remainder of the harmony. Also, the instruments that play the continuo part.

corrido A Mexican narrative song.

counterpoint Two or more independent lines with melodic character occurring at the same time.

countersubject The secondary theme in a fugue.

country music A type of music containing folklike qualities that is especially popular with the white culture of the American South.

crescendo (cresc.) The music should gradually become louder.

cyclical form The appearance of a theme from one movement in another movement of a multimovement work.

decrescendo (decresc.) The music should gradually become softer.

development (1) The manipulation of themes in a musical work. (2) The section in sonata form devoted to the development of themes.

Dies irae The traditional Gregorian chant sung at funerals.

diminution The proportional reduction of all note values in a theme.

dissonance A group of simultaneous sounds that seems disagreeable or harsh.

divertimento A pleasant but not very complex instrumental work, usually consisting of stylized dances.

Dixieland A jazz style for a small group of players, consisting of two beats per measure and a rather lively tempo.

doctrine of affections (doctrine of affects) The Baroque practice of attempting to project states of feeling and ideas in music.

dodecaphonic music See *tone row music.*

double exposition The use of two expositions in a concerto, one for the orchestra and the other featuring the soloist.

downbeat The first beat of a measure, which usually receives the greater emphasis.

drone A low, continuous sound that lasts throughout a piece of music.

dynamics The amount of loudness in music.

Eclecticism The practice of combining what the composer believes to be the best features of several different styles.

electronic music Music produced through synthesizers and electroacoustic instruments.

encore A short work played at the end of a concert in response to an audience's applause.

ensemble An instrumental or vocal performing group.

episode Sections of a fugue in which the subject is not present.

equal temperament A system of tuning, in which the intervals are adjusted to divide the octave into twelve equal parts.

estampie An instrumental dance during the Middle Ages.

ethnic music Music that is characteristic of a particular culture or group of people.

étude A short instrumental work stressing some technical aspect of playing the instrument.

Exoticism A phase of Romanticism that draws on scenes from Asia and the Middle East.

exposition (1) The opening section of a fugue. (2) The opening section in sonata form.

Expressionism An early twentieth-century style that emphasized subjective and often disturbing emotions.

falsetto voice The "false" high voice that can be produced by males.

fanfare Short, brilliant-sounding music, usually featuring brass instruments.

fantasia A free-sounding instrumental work.

fantasie A short, free-sounding instrumental work.

figured bass A shorthand system of numbers and accidentals used by keyboard players in Baroque music for indicating chords.

finale The final movement of a multimovement work.

fine arts Type of art in which objects are created only for the psychological satisfaction that people find in them.

folk music The music of the common people of a society or geographic area.

folkloric A type of twentieth-century music that contains folklike qualities.

form The pattern or plan of a musical work.

free jazz A sophisticated type of jazz containing few stylistic guidelines.

frets Metal strips on the fingerboard of a guitar and similar instruments that help the player in finger placement.

fugato A short section of a work containing phrases of music in imitation.

fugue A composition in which the main theme (subject) is presented in imitation in several parts.

fusion The combination of two or more musical styles.

galant style The light, decorative style generally associated with the eighteenth-century French court.

gamelan A Balinese instrumental ensemble.

genre The term referring to a type or classification of music.

glissando A very rapid sliding of notes up or down a scale.

grace note A short decorative note that has no assigned rhythmic value.

Gregorian chant The monophonic chant originally sung unaccompanied in Latin by monks and priests in the Roman Catholic Church.

harmonic series (overtone series) The order in which overtones of a pitch occur.

harmony The simultaneous sounds of several pitches, usually in accompanying a melody.

hoedown A portion of a square dance.

homophony The texture consisting of a line of melody with accompaniment.

idée fixe **(fixed idea)** A theme that is transformed at various places in a composition.

ideophone A percussion instrument other than drums.

imitation The repetition of a theme in another part or line or a few beats later.

Impressionism An artistic viewpoint that emphasizes overall impressions rather than detailed or intellectual observations.

impromptu A short piano composition in a style that sounds improvised.

improvisation Music that is made up on the spot, usually according to stylistic guidelines.

incidental music Music composed to be performed in conjunction with a drama.

interval The distance between two pitches.

inversion (1) Turning a melody upside down so that an ascending interval descends, and vice versa. (2) Rearranging the notes in a chord so that its basic note is no longer the lowest one.

jazz An African American style of music developed in twentieth-century America that is characterized by improvised playing and syncopated rhythms.

key center See *tonic*.

key signature The pattern of sharps or flats at the beginning of a line of music that indicates which notes are to be altered by one half step.

Klangfarbenmelodie "Manufactured tone color melody"; melodies made up of different timbres.

leitmotiv A motive or theme that is associated with a particular character or idea in the music dramas of Richard Wagner.

libretto The text of an opera or oratorio.

Lied The German word for "art song." The plural of *Lied* is *Lieder*.

liturgy A ritual for public worship.

madrigal A free, secular, imitative work for voices.

mainstream Twentieth-century music that is neither experimental nor committed to a particular compositional viewpoint.

major scale A series of seven different pitches within an octave, with half steps between the third and fourth steps and the seventh and eighth steps.

Mass (1) The celebration of Holy Communion (Eucharist) in the Roman Catholic Church. (2) The musical setting of the Ordinary of the Mass.

measure A group of beats marked as a separate unit in music notation.

medieval motet An unaccompanied work composed during the medieval period for voices, using a cantus firmus from Gregorian chant, with other parts in vernacular languages added, and often containing complex rhythmic and melodic relationships.

medieval period The style of music that prevailed from approximately 1100 to 1450.

melody A series of consecutive pitches that form a cohesive musical entity.

membranophone Any instrument that produces sounds from a skin or other membrane.

meter The regular pattern of stressed and unstressed beats.

meter signature The two numbers, one above the other, at the beginning of a piece or section of a longer work that indicate the metrical pattern and how it is notated.

microtone An interval of less than a half step.

minimalism Music in which the composer makes as few changes as possible but still seeks to create an interesting work.

minor scale A series of seven pitches within an octave, with a half step between the second and third steps.

minstrel show A popular form of entertainment in the latter part of the nineteenth century and early twentieth century consisting of four actor/performers and a variety of lighthearted acts.

minuet and trio A three-part form in three-beat meter and the style of a minuet.

modes As used today, scale patterns containing seven pitches other than major or minor.

modulation Changing the tonal center as the music progresses, usually without a break.

monody A texture used in the early Baroque consisting of one melody with simple accompaniment.

monophony One melodic line without any accompaniment.

motet A sacred composition for voices.

motive A short musical idea that is a unifying element in a musical work.

movement A large independent section of an instrumental composition.

musical (musical comedy) A type of theater that features music as well as actions, scenery, and costumes.

music drama The term Richard Wagner used for his operas in which he tried to strike a balance between the music and the dramatic action.

musique concrète Natural sounds that are recorded and then modified and organized by a composer into a musical composition.

mute A device for muffling or dampening the sound of an instrument.

nationalism A deliberate, conscious attempt to develop artworks that are characteristic of a particular country or region.

Neoclassicism "New classicism;" music created according the rational outlook of the Classical period.

nocturne A type of nineteenth-century character piece for piano; originally, the word meant "night music."

octave A pitch that has twice or half the frequency of vibrations of another; usually the two pitches have the same letter designation.

octave displacement Using a note with the same letter name as a previous note but in another octave.

Op. (opus) Meaning "work" in Latin, it usually appears with a number to indicate the order in which the composer's works were written.

opera A drama set to music in which the lines of text are sung with orchestral accompaniment.

opera buffa Comic opera of the eighteenth and nineteenth centuries.

opera seria Dramatic opera, usually dealing with serious subject matter.

opus Latin for "work;" used to identify a composer's compositions.

oral tradition The process in which music is preserved by people through hearing the music, remembering it, and then performing it.

oratorio A sizable work for chorus, soloists, and orchestra, usually on a religious topic, that is performed without scenery, costumes, or acting.

Ordinary The parts of the Mass that are ordinarily included, regardless of church season: Kyrie, Gloria, Credo, Sanctus, and Agnus Dei.

organum The name for the early polyphonic music of medieval times.

ostinato A short, persistently repeated melodic, rhythmic, or harmonic pattern.

overture An instrumental introduction to a vocal work or an orchestral suite.

parlor song A sentimental type of song popular in the nineteenth century.

passacaglia A repeated set of variations based on a melodic ostinato in the lowest-pitched part.

passion An oratorio based on the suffering of Jesus on Good Friday, according to one of the four Gospels.

pedal (pedal point) A long note or notes that persist over an extended period of time while harmonies change.

pentatonic scale A five-note scale, usually with the pattern of whole steps and half steps encountered on the black keys of the piano.

phrase A rather short, logical segment of music; it is comparable to a clause or phrase in language.

pitch The perceived highness or lowness of a musical sound.

pizzicato Notes on a string instrument that are played by the player's fingers plucking the string instead of using the bow.

plainchant The traditional chant of the Roman Catholic Church.

plainsong See *Gregorian chant*.

polymeter The presence of two or more meters at the same time.

polyphony Music in which two or more melodic lines of approximately equal importance are sounded at the same time.

polyrhythm Two or more rhythm patterns occurring simultaneously.

polytonality Two or more tonal centers sounding at the same time.

popular music Music created primarily for commercial purposes.

post-Romanticism Works in the Romantic style composed after it was the prevailing style.

prelude (1) A short instrumental work. (2) A piece to be played as an introduction.

prepared piano A practice sometimes used in twentieth-century music in which tacks, chewing gum, paper, and other objects are placed in the mechanism of the piano so that it sounds different timbres.

Primitivism Music that seeks to contain rhythmic power and blatant expression.

program music Instrumental works associated by the composer with an extramusical idea or object.

program symphony A multimovement programmatic work for orchestra.

Proper The portion of the Mass that is "proper" for a designated day in the church year.

quotation music Music that makes extensive use of quotations from other music.

raga A melodic formula used in the music of India.

ragtime A forerunner of jazz, usually for piano in a marchlike style.

rap A type of African American music that consists of rapid delivery of words in a singsong style.

realization A keyboard player performing the music indicated by the figured bass.

recapitulation The section of sonata form in which the themes from the exposition are repeated.

recitative A style of singing that covers its text expressively, usually in an economical and direct way.

relative major (or minor) Major and minor scales that have the same key signature.

Renaissance motet A sacred vocal composition developed during the Renaissance.

Requiem The funeral Mass of the Roman Catholic Church.

retrograde The reverse version of a melody or tone row, in which the first note becomes the last, and so on.

retrograde-inversion The upside-down and backward version of the tone row.

rhythm The flow of music in terms of time.

rhythm and blues A term for African American popular music.

rhythmic modes The constant repetition of certain rhythm patterns, much like poetic meters.

ritornello form The orchestral form in which themes at the beginning of a concerto grosso return later in the movement.

rock (rock and roll) A popular style of music that contains features of both rhythm and blues and country music.

Rococo The decorative, light style prevalent in the eighteenth-century courts, especially France.

Romantic period The style of music that was prevalent from about 1820 to 1910.

rondo A form in which the theme appears three or more times with contrasting sections between its appearances.

rubato A performer's slight deviations from a strict tempo.

run A series of rapidly moving, scalewise notes.

saltarello A lively type of folk dance.

sampling The recording of a short segment of an instrument for inclusion in electronic music.

scale A series of pitches that proceeds upward or downward according to a prescribed pattern.

scherzo (1) The third movement of some symphonies and other works, usually in a playful style. (2) An independent work for piano composed during the Romantic period.

secular music Music that is worldly or nonsacred.

sequence The immediate repeating of a phrase or figure at a different pitch level from the original.

Serialism The application of the principles of tone row music to elements such as dynamic levels and articulations.

sforzando A loud, accented note or chord; it is indicated by the letters *Sfz*.

son A Mexican balladlike song.

sonata (1) A Baroque multimovement work for solo instrument. (2) A multimovement work for piano and another instrument, or for piano alone.

sonata form A form consisting of an exposition section, followed by a development section, and then a recapitulation of the themes from the exposition.

soprano The higher, lighter female voice.

soul A general term for several types of African American music.

spiritual A religious song unaccompanied by a choir, usually associated with African American churches.

sprechstimme A vocal style that is a combination of speaking and singing.

strophic form A song in which several verses of words are sung to the same melody.

subject The main theme of a fugue.

suite (1) A collection or group of stylized pieces of dance music. (2) A collection of parts of a larger work such as a ballet or opera.

swing A type of popular music containing many jazz influences that was arranged for big bands.

symphonic poem See *tone poem*.

symphony A large multimovement work for orchestra.

syncopation The displacement of an accent so that it occurs where it is not normally expected or does not occur where it is expected.

tala A rhythmic cycle of beats found in the music of India.

tempo The speed of the beats in a piece of music.

tenor (1) The higher, lighter male voice. (2) The line in a medieval motet that contains the phrases from Gregorian chant.

ternary form A three-part form, *aba*, in which the opening music returns.

terraced dynamics Abrupt changes in levels of loudness.

text painting (word painting) The compositional technique of having the musical sounds reinforce the words being sung.

texture The basic setting of the music: monophonic, homophonic, or polyphonic.

theme A central melody in a musical work.

theme and variations A work consisting of a theme and altered versions of that theme.

theme transformation The alteration of a theme that retains its characteristic intervals of melody or rhythm pattern.

through-composed song A song that contains no repetition of lines of music.

timbre Tone quality or tone color in music.

time signature See *meter signature*.

Tin Pan Alley The name associated with the popular music industry.

toccata A showy work, usually for a keyboard instrument.

tone poem A sizable orchestral work of program music.

tone row (twelve-tone or dodecaphonic music) A composition based on a row of pitches that uses each of the twelve tones in an octave.

tonic (tonal center) The specific pitch around which a piece of music is centered.

tonic chord A chord built on the first degree of a major or minor scale.

transcription An adaptation of a musical work for an instrument or voice for another instrument or voice, or for a group of either.

tremolo The very rapid alternation between or repeating of pitches.

trill The rapid alternation between a pitch and the adjacent higher pitch.

triplet Three equal notes on one beat.

trio sonata A Baroque sonata written for three players on melody accompanied by the continuo line.

troubadour French noblemen who created love poems and songs in the thirteenth century.

twelve-tone music See *tone row music*.

variation A section of music in which the melody, harmony, or rhythm of a theme is repeated with some changes.

vaudeville A popular type of stage entertainment in the early twentieth century consisting of music and other variety acts.

vibrato Slight, rapid fluctuations of pitch.

virtuoso A very technically skilled performer.

vocalise A song sung without words, usually sung on a single vowel sound.

voice (1) The human voice. (2) A part in an instrumental composition, especially a fugue.

Western music Music of Europe and the Americas.

whole-tone scale A scale in which the octave is divided into six whole steps.

wind band (wind ensemble) An ensemble comprising wind and percussion instruments.

Listening Guides INDEXED BY COMPOSER

Index of Composer Biographies

Index

Performers List CDS 1 AND 2

CD ①

1 Copland: "Hoe-Down" from *Rodeo*
London Symphony Orchestra; Aaron Copland, conductor
Originally released 1970. All rights reserved by Sony Music
Entertainment

4 Bizet: "Farandole" from *L'Arlesienne Suite No. 2*
Toronto Symphony; Andrew Davis, conductor
℗ 1981 Sony Music Entertainment

7 Copland: "Simple Gifts" from *Old American Songs*
William Warfield, baritone; Columbia Symphony Orchestra;
Aaron Copland, conductor
Originally Released 1963. All rights reserved by Sony Music
Entertainment

9 Rodrigo: *Concierto de Aranjuez*, II
John Williams, guitar soloist; Philadelphia Orchestra; Eugene
Ormandy, conductor
℗ 1974 Sony Music Entertainment

13 John Rutter/Lancelot Andrewes: "Open Thou Mine
Eyes"
The Cambridge Singers
℗ 1984 Collegium Records
Courtesy of Collegium Records

15 Gregorian chant: "Dies irae"
Schola Cantorum Amsterdam; Vim Van Gerven, director
℗ 1973 Sony Music Entertainment

16 Palestrina: "Sicut cervus"
Westminster Cathedral Choir; James O'Donnell, conductor
℗ 1991 Hyperion Records Ltd.
Courtesy of Hyperion Records Ltd.

19 Weelkes: "As Vesta Was from Latmos Hill Descending"
Consort of Musicke; Anthony Rooley, director
℗ 1988 Hyperion Records Ltd.
Courtesy of Hyperion Records Ltd.

Handel: *Messiah*

21 "The Voice of Him"

22 "Every Valley Shall Be Exalted"

24 "Hallelujah"
Le Grand Ecurie et la Chambre du Roy; Jean-Claude Malgoire,
director
℗ 1980 Sony Music Entertainment

27 Bach: "Zion Hears the Watchmen" (Section 4)
from Cantata No. 140
The American Bach Soloists; Jeffrey Thomas, conductor
℗ 1996 Koch International L.P.
Courtesy of The American Bach Soloists

29 Vivaldi: "Spring" Concerto from *The Four Seasons*, I
Pinchas Zukerman, violin and conductor; St. Paul Chamber
Orchestra
℗ 1981 Sony Music Entertainment

34 Bach: Toccata and Fugue in D Minor
Gustav Leonhardt, organ
℗ 1974 Sony Music Entertainment

38 Mozart: Symphony No. 40 in G minor, K. 550, I
Cleveland Orchestra; George Szell, conductor
Originally Released 1970. All rights reserved by Sony Music
Entertainment

43 Haydn: Concerto for Trumpet and Orchestra in E-Flat
Major, III
Y Chamber Symphony of New York; Gerard Schwarz, trumpet
soloist and conductor
℗ 1983 Delos
Courtesy of Delos

46 Mozart: Excerpt from Act III of *Don Giovanni*,
Kiri Te Kanawa, soprano; Ruggero Raimondi, bass; Chorus and
Orchestra of the Paris National Opera Theater; Lorin Maazel,
conductor
℗ 1979 Sony Music Entertainment

CD ②

1 Beethoven: Symphony No. 5 in C minor, Op. 67, I
Cleveland Orchestra; George Szell, conductor
Originally Released 1964. All rights reserved by Sony Music
Entertainment

6 Schubert: Der Erlkönig
Dietrich-Fischer Dieskau, baritone; Karl Engel, piano
℗ 1995 ORFEO International Music GmbH
Courtesy of Qualiton Imports Ltd.

9 Liszt: Grandes Etudes de Paganini, No. 3 in G-Sharp
minor "La Campanella"
Andre Watts, piano
Originally Released 1971. All rights reserved by Sony Music
Entertainment

11 Berlioz: "Dream of the Witches Sabbath" from
Symphonie Fantastique
New York Philharmonic; Leonard Bernstein, conductor
Originally Released 1969. All rights reserved by Sony Music
Entertainment

16 Puccini: Act I Duet from *La Bohème*
Placido Domingo (Rodolfo); Montserrat Caballe, (Mimi); London
Philharmonic Orchestra; Georg Solti, conductor
℗ 1974 BMG Music

20 Debussy: *Clair de Lune*
Philippe Entremont, piano
Originally Released 1961. All rights reserved by Sony Music
Entertainment

23 Bartok: Concerto for Orchestra, IV
New York Philharmonic; Pierre Boulez, conductor
℗ 1973 Sony Music Entertainment

26 Britten: "Dies Irae" from *War Requiem*
Atlanta Symphony Orchestra and Chorus; Robert Shaw, conductor
℗ 1989 Telarc International Corp.
Courtesy of Telarc International Corp.

28 Stravinsky: *The Rite of Spring*, Opening
Cleveland Orchestra; Pierre Boulez, conductor
Originally Released 1969. All rights reserved by Sony Music
Entertainment

31 Prokofiev: Symphony No. 1 in D Major "Classical," I
New York Philharmonic; Leonard Bernstein, conductor
Originally Released 1968. All rights reserved by Sony Music
Entertainment

35 Varèse: *Poème Électronique* (excerpt)
Realized by the composer on Electronic Tape
Originally Released 1960. All rights reserved by Sony Music
Entertainment

36 Copland: *Appalachain Spring* (excerpt)
London Symphony Orchestra; Aaron Copland, conductor
Originally Released 1971. All rights reserved by Sony Music
Entertainment

39 Zwilich: *Concerto Grosso 1985*, I
New York Philharmonic; Zubin Mehta, conductor
℗ 1989 Recorded Anthology of American Music, Inc.
Courtesy of New World Records

41 Ellington: "Take the 'A' Train"
Duke Ellington and His Famous Orchestra
Originally Released 1941. All rights reserved by Sony Music
Entertainment

43 Bernstein: "Tonight" from *West Side Story*
Original Cast Recording
Originally Released 1957. All rights reserved by Sony Music
Entertainment